MELVIN I. UROFSKY

DISSENT AND THE SUPREME COURT

Melvin I. Urofsky is a professor emeritus of history at Virginia
Commonwealth University and was the chair of its history depart-
ment. He is the editor (with David W. Levy) of the five-volume
collection of Louis Brandeis's letters, as well as the author of
American Zionism from Herzl to the Holocaust and *Louis D. Brandeis*.
He lives in Gaithersburg, Maryland.

DISSENT
AND THE
SUPREME
COURT

U.S. Supreme Court, 2014.
SEATED FROM LEFT, *Clarence Thomas, Antonin Scalia,*
Chief Justice John Roberts, Anthony Kennedy, and Ruth Bader Ginsburg;
STANDING, *Sonia Sotomayor, Stephen Breyer, Samuel Alito, and Elena Kagan*

DISSENT
AND THE
SUPREME
COURT

*Its Role in the Court's History
and the Nation's Constitutional Dialogue*

MELVIN I. UROFSKY

VINTAGE BOOKS
A Division of Penguin Random House LLC
New York

FIRST VINTAGE BOOKS EDITION, JANUARY 2017

Copyright ©2015 by Melvin I. Urofsky

The Library of Congress has cataloged the Pantheon edition as follows:
Urofsky, Melvin I.
Dissent and the Supreme Court / Melvin I. Urofsky
pages cm
Includes index.
I. Dissenting opinions—United States.   2. Dissenters—Legal status, laws, Etc.—United
States.   3. Judicial opinion—United States.   4. Supreme Court—United States.
5. Constitutional law—United States.
6. Government, Resistance to—United States.   I. Title.
KF8748.U76 2015   342.7302'9—DC23   2014048245

Vintage Books Trade Paperback ISBN: 978-0-307-74132-5
eBook ISBN: 978-1-101-87063-1

Book design by Iris Weinstein

www.vintagebooks.com

Printed in the United States of America
10 9 8 7 6 5 4 3 2 1

For my grandchildren,
Emma, Chloe, and Beck,
in the hope they will always hear the dissenting voice

CONTENTS

INTRODUCTION

In addition, the time may come when the minority opinion becomes the majority opinion. According to Rabbi Yehuda, "An individual opinion is cited along with the majority opinion as it may be needed at some time in the future."

—TALMUD, MISHNA EDUYOT I.5

When John G. Roberts Jr. testified before the Senate Judiciary Committee at his confirmation hearings in 2005, he indicated that he hoped the Court would return to its older practice of speaking with one voice—unanimous opinions founded on narrow grounds. Nearly everyone familiar with the Court and its history—scholars and practitioners alike—surely smiled at Roberts's seeming naïveté, and his dream evaporated almost as soon as he took the oath as chief justice. While there have been a few terms in which the Court spoke in one voice almost half the time, there have been others when the nonunanimous rate has exceeded 70 percent.

The role of dissent is a long and honored one not only in the history of the Court but in that of the United States as well. Many of the early settlers were either religious or political dissenters, and the colonies soon filled with immigrants holding a wide diversity of views on almost everything. The American Revolution came about because of popular dissension from the policies of His Majesty's Government, and once the colonies had achieved independence, they fell to squabbling among themselves. The Constitution imposed an order on the country that has worked remarkably well for more than 225 years, yet the Framers never intended to quash dissenting views. The First Amendment to the Constitution holds that "Congress shall make no law respecting an establishment of religion, or prohibiting the free exercise thereof; or abridging the freedom of speech, or of the press; or the right of the people peaceably to assemble, and to petition the Government for a redress of grievances." And the Framers included a process to amend the document when necessary.

The English statesman William Gladstone described the American Constitution as "the most wonderful work ever struck off at a given time by the brain and purpose of man." The Framers—those "demigods," as Thomas Jefferson hailed them—intended their work to serve the needs not only of a small nation of thirteen states clinging to the Atlantic Seaboard but of whatever that country might become. While there are some very specific clauses—members of the House of Representatives must be twenty-five years old, the term of a senator is six years—the great enabling clauses are far more general. What exactly do the following mean?

> —Congress shall have the power to lay and collect taxes, or to regulate interstate and foreign commerce, or
> —the executive power shall be vested in a president, or the judicial power in one supreme court, and such other courts as Congress shall establish, or
> —no state shall deny its citizens "due process of law" or "equal protection of the laws" or impose "cruel and unusual" punishment.

Contrary to the arguments of the so-called originalists that the meaning of the Constitution is and always will be the same, the historical evidence is clear that the Framers envisioned the meaning of certain phrases to change as the country grew and evolved, or, as James Madison put it, the meaning of the constitutional text should be "liquidated and ascertained" over time in the light of the emerging needs of a changing nation. Madison and Alexander Hamilton might not have used the phrase "living Constitution," but their essays in *The Federalist* show that they never intended the document to be static and frozen in the year 1787.

Ever since John Marshall handed down the Court's opinion in *Marbury v. Madison* (1803), it has been "emphatically the province and duty of the judicial department to say what the law is." Or, as another chief justice said over a century later, "the Constitution is what the Supreme Court says it is."

Because the powers of the Supreme Court—and indeed of the government itself—were still plastic in those days, Marshall sought to have the Court speak in one, authoritative voice and abandoned the English practice of all the judges delivering individual opinions seriatim. This did not sit well with some people, but it did help to build up the type of national government that the Framers had envisioned. Even in Marshall's day, however, there were dissents from the opinion of the Court. Nearly all of them are forgotten today, because they had no lasting jurisprudential value, they did not convince future courts, and, to use the terminology of this book, they did not contribute to the constitutional dialogue.

The constitutional dialogue is the device by which our nation has adapted its foundational document to meet the needs of a country that has expanded across the continent, and indeed across oceans, now counts more than 300 million souls, and has become both urbanized and industrialized. It has allowed us to take into account developments that the founding generation could never have envisioned—railroads, automobiles, airplanes, telephones, computers, and international relations involving not a few powers in Europe but nearly two hundred nation-states around the world. The United States began as a country in which slavery existed in nearly all of the former colonies; it took a civil war to end that bondage and what some have termed a "second reconstruction" to erode the legacy of racial segregation. Women and other minorities have won a rightful place in society, and the federal system of shared sovereignty between the states and the federal government is still alive and well.

Questions about these developments have come before Congress, the executive branch, and the courts. The answers have never been simple, because political, social, economic, cultural, and legal questions have been involved. All three branches of the federal government, as well as those of the fifty states and the American people, have been involved in debates ranging from the rights enjoyed by corporations to campaign finance laws to same-sex marriage. Starting almost from the founding, this debate has been continuous, lively, and, as I hope to show, essential to our nation's well-being.

Each generation of Americans has debated public policy in a variety of ways, and a majority of the questions asked have had no simple answers. If we look back at American history, hardly any major policy decision since the founding has not had advocates on two or more sides of the issue. That has made ours a vibrant democracy, but the debate has also taken place within the parameters of constitutional provisions—both those that empower certain options and others that limit them. While I refer to this debate among other branches of the government and the people, my main focus is on the debate within the Supreme Court.

In 1835, a French visitor to the United States, Alexis de Tocqueville, noted that "scarcely any political question arises in the United States that is not resolved, sooner or later, into a judicial question." Where other societies have sometimes taken to the streets to resolve important questions of government, in the United States we go to court both for private law matters, such as contract or tort issues, and for public law. It is one of the great strengths of our system, and it places a great deal of power in the hands of the nine men and women who sit in the Marble Palace in Washington.

I have always told my students that only the hardest cases get to the Supreme Court; if the issue is easy, it is resolved in the lower courts. Because the questions are hard, and because they cause disagreement among the people, it is not surprising that the justices of the high court will also disagree. But all of them understand that just because a majority decided that "A" is right in a particular case, it does not mean it will always be the law. The dissenter will point out what he or she perceives to be the weakness of the majority opinion, the faulty constitutional reasoning, or a failure to understand the actual facts of the case. If the dissent is strong enough, if it is well reasoned, it may persuade other judges in the future to overturn the majority decision and accept the minority view.

This does not happen often. Many cases, even if not unanimous, are decided correctly, and the dissent will be little noted nor long remembered. That is as it should be. While we expect the high court to take into account differing views, we also want it to resolve the case at hand correctly. But some issues are not easily determined, and that is where the dissent comes in. The dissenter is telling the majority, "Wait. I think you have this wrong. You need to look at that constitutional clause and its history again. You need to ask other questions."

Sometimes the separate opinion has an immediate impact. A draft dissent may win over sufficient votes to become the majority view. At other times, it may lead the majority to accept some of its points, and thus modify the holding. More important, the dissent tells lower courts and future justices that this rule needs to be examined carefully, and it should eventually be revised or overturned.

Louis Brandeis often said that his faith in time was great. He believed—rightly as it turned out—that many of the dissents he wrote in his twenty-three years on the bench would eventually prevail. His separate opinion in *Whitney v. California* (1927)—a concurrence that is in fact a dissent—is considered by many scholars to be the greatest dissent ever written, ultimately shaping our modern jurisprudence of free speech. It did that because in cases in the four decades following *Whitney* the Court had to take into account Brandeis's views. Even though Brandeis died in 1941, his opinion kept speaking to the Court, his ideas an essential part of the constitutional dialogue over the meaning and purpose of free expression in a democratic society.

This book traces dissenting opinion across American constitutional history. It is not, however, a history of dissent, and given the thousands of dissents that have been written, it would be impossible to deal with all of them. My concern has been those dissents that have played a critical role in the dialogue, and even there I am sure people will say, "What about this dissent? Isn't it important?" It may well be, but it would be impractical to deal with the entire dialogue. My purpose is to illustrate the dialogue, show how and why it is important, and look at representative justices and cases.

The dialogue that shaped constitutional understanding has also formed us as a nation. The constitutional dialogue does not take place in a vacuum, and in developing our understanding of the Constitution, it also molds us as a people. When the justices talk about the limits of free speech, for example, their decisions and the dissenting opinions create and most often expand how "We the People" can discuss and make our policy decisions. When the Court deals with difficult cases involving discrimination, it reflects the fissures in the broader society over how minorities will be treated and often not only serves to increase the rights of those groups but affects the public dialogue on those matters.

The dialogue that takes place among the justices is a reflection of a far larger dialogue taking place among the citizenry. We are still trying to answer the question asked many years ago by the Framers, "What kind of country shall we be?" So when the discussion in the chapters that follow talks about economic or civil liberties, or the contours of criminal justice procedure, or how enemy combatants should be treated, that discussion always, even if not at all times overtly, is tracking not only the constitutional dialogue taking place within the Court but the broader conversation between the Court and the other branches of government and between the justices and the people. These are not one-way monologues, and even if not every decision of the Court and its accompanying dissents lead to an overwhelming public reaction, the process is there. That is, I would suggest, the most important feature of the constitutional dialogue—the way it shapes not only the Constitution but our society.

DISSENT
AND THE
SUPREME
COURT

CHAPTER I

DISSENT AND THE CONSTITUTIONAL DIALOGUE

I am unable to agree with the judgment of the majority of the Court, and although I think it useless and undesirable, as a rule, to express dissent, I feel bound to do so in this case and to give my reasons for it.

— OLIVER WENDELL HOLMES JR.

Judicial dissent {is} wholly necessary. Dissent is no less a requirement in our legal system than it is in our political system. Historically, dissent is the way the voice of prophecy is first heard.

— IRVING DILLIARD

Dissents, like homicide, fall into three categories — excusable, justifiable, and reprehensible.

— WILLIAM HIRT

I don't approve of dissents generally, for I think in many cases where I differ from the majority, it is more important to stand by the Court and give its judgment weight than merely to record my individual dissent where it is better to have the law certain than to have it settled either way.

— WILLIAM HOWARD TAFT

Dissents augment rather than diminish the prestige of the Court. When history demonstrates that one of the Court's decisions has been a truly horrendous mistake, it is comforting—and conducive of respect for the Court—to look back and realize that at least some of the Justices saw the danger clearly, and gave voice, often eloquent voice, to their concern.

—ANTONIN SCALIA

Great Supreme Court dissents lie like buried ammunition for future generations to unearth when the time comes.

—KATHLEEN SULLIVAN

I shall in silence acquiesce. Dissents seldom aid in the right development or statement of the law. They often do harm. For myself I say: "Lead us not into temptation."

—PIERCE BUTLER

The right to dissent is the only thing that makes life tolerable for a judge on an appellate court.

—WILLIAM O. DOUGLAS

This sampling of opinion on the value of dissent—or lack of it—could have been multiplied tenfold. Even today, when four out of every five Supreme Court decisions include one or more dissenting opinions, there is still a debate over the merit of a judge's declaring that he thinks the majority of his colleagues misinterpreted the law. As will be clear from what follows, I strongly believe in dissent and that it has an important role to play in our constitutional dialogue, which is part of our greater national colloquy on public policy.

That phrase—"constitutional dialogue"—includes not just debates justices on the high court have with one another in specific cases or over particular jurisprudential ideas but also discussions between and among jurists, members of Congress, the executive branch, administrative agencies, state and lower federal courts, the legal academy, and last, but certainly not least, the public.

Clearly, when one looks at the dialogue, it is the majority opinion that has the louder voice. How five or more members of the high court

Potter Stewart, associate justice, 1958–1981

decide a case will be the law for the foreseeable future, and it is to this opinion that other parties in the conversation will pay heed. They will also note concurring opinions, which serve a variety of important purposes. Two of the most highly regarded opinions in the twentieth century—Justice Brandeis in *Whitney v. California* (1927) and Justice Jackson in *Youngstown Sheet & Tube Co. v. Sawyer* (1952)—were concurrences and in the long run proved far more influential than the majority view. Potter Stewart's famous comment on obscenity, "I know it when I see it," came from a concurrence. Concurrences also serve to limit the majority decision and help explain it. As a result, lower court judges often use the concurring opinion to escape what they may see as the overly broad or overly narrow strictures of the majority.

It is, however, the dissenting opinion with which we are here concerned, the voice that says, "Listen to me. I think those guys have got it wrong. This is why, and this is what the law should be." The acceptance of dissent as a legitimate part of judicial behavior is not universal. As William O. Douglas pointed out, "Certainty and unanimity in the law are possible only under a fascist or communist system, where, indeed, they are indispensable." For him, the dissent was an essential safeguard of democracy. But there are many democratic countries whose courts operate under the assumption—often written into law—that courts should speak with one and only one voice and that differences of opinion within the court should never be made public.

American courts initially followed the British precedent of seriatim, in which each judge wrote a separate opinion on the case. Most of the time, it proved fairly easy to pick out which party had won and why. In many cases, however, the judges varied so greatly in their reasoning and conclusions that it was difficult to see who had "won" or "why." Starting with Chief Justice Oliver Ellsworth, the Supreme Court began issuing an "opinion of the Court," a single judgment with straightforward reasoning and conclusions, a practice institutionalized when John Marshall became chief justice in 1801.

Not everyone welcomed this approach, but its benefits quickly won support from lawyers. If, as Holmes would later say, the law is a prediction of what the courts will do, one could now have a clearer idea of what judges had actually decided and rely on that judgment in future cases. Well into the twentieth century, the high court in more than nine out of ten cases issued a single "opinion of the Court." Because Congress gave the Court jurisdiction over an extremely wide range of cases, most of the issues that the justices heard involved neither constitutional nor statutory interpretation. Looking through *U.S. Reports* for these years, one is struck by the large number of garden-variety contract and tort suits that today would be resolved in a local municipal or state court. This is not to say that all of this work was inconsequential; some cases involved the powers of the states or the meaning of important constitutional clauses. The Supreme Court might have been the highest tribunal in the country, but it was far from the constitutional court it became after the 1925 Judges' Bill.

Because many of these cases had little importance to anyone besides the litigants, the justices believed, as Louis Brandeis would later say, that it was more important to decide the question than to decide it right. Even if some justices did not agree with the result, they would go along or, if they felt they could not, would merely note a dissenting vote, but they did not write an opinion explaining their disagreement. After 1925, when Congress gave the Court greater control over its docket, the bulk of the cases involved constitutional matters or questions of statutory interpretation. It became more important not only to decide but to decide rightly. As judges heard more constitutional questions, they found themselves developing jurisprudential theories that carried over from one case to another. Not only did they stop acquiescing, but they also felt it important to explain why they disagreed.

The Court, of course, had always heard constitutional issues, and in many of them dissenting judges had written opinions. Soon after Roger Taney became chief justice in 1836, he noted that it had "been the uniform practice in this court, for the justices who differed from the court on constitutional questions, to express their dissent."

By the time of the constitutional crisis of the 1930s, written dissents had become more common, and they proliferated in the 1940s. The constitutional dialogue often appeared to be a cacophony of voices, each with a different view of what a particular statute or clause of the Constitution meant. Not only has that dissonance continued to this day, but the frequency and intensity have if anything intensified.

Just as not all majority opinions are equal, neither are all dissents. Justice Robert Jackson noted that the vast preponderance of dissents are soon forgotten (the same might be said for many of the majority opinions as well); they play little part in the constitutional dialogue and rarely become accepted by the Court at a later date. But some dissents are important, and these are the ones we are concerned with, the so-called canonical or prophetic ones that become part of and influence the constitutional dialogue.

CASES INVOLVING FEDERAL constitutional questions may begin in either state or federal courts; if the former, the trial court's decision may be appealed through the state's appellate process until it is heard by the state's highest court and from there may be appealed to the U.S. Supreme Court. In federal court, the case will normally be heard in a district court and then go on to the court of appeals for the circuit in which the district court is located and from there to the Supreme Court. Questions of interpretation of acts of Congress are heard in federal courts. State statutes are interpreted in state courts, unless the law implicates some federal constitutional right.

With certain exceptions mandated either by the Constitution or by Congress, the Court has full control over which cases it will take on appeal through a writ of certiorari (known commonly as cert). Literally thousands of petitions for cert reach the high court every term, and the vast majority are deemed unworthy of review. For the most part, they do not raise the type of case or controversy that the justices believe requires their examination; in other instances, the question has been settled by prior decisions, and as far as the justices are concerned, the lower courts, following those precedents, resolved the suit correctly.

For the Court to accept a case, the rule of four governs. Meeting in their weekly conferences, four members of the Court must vote to grant cert. These cases may present a new issue that the Court has not previously ruled upon but that implicates a constitutionally protected right, or there is a question whether Congress or the president has exceeded authority or violated some specific constitutional prohibitions. Because the high court also oversees the federal court system, occasions arise when two or more of the circuit courts of appeals decide the same issue in different ways, and then the matter is resolved in the Supreme Court. And at times, because of changing social or economic conditions or perhaps personnel changes on the bench, the Court will choose to review an issue once thought settled. In these cases, the force of an earlier dissent may now prove decisive.

It would be a mistake to think that the nine members of the Court are automatons whose choice of which cases to review is determined by some precise, objective standard of mathematical certainty. The seventy to eighty cases that the Court accepts for full review each year are rarely easy and would not have gotten so far in the appellate process unless good arguments had been made by both parties. Aside from differences in judicial philosophy, the justices all have their own worldviews as to what values should be uppermost in their decision making. In the seven decades after the end of the Civil War, a majority of the justices believed in the supremacy of property rights over state attempts to ameliorate the worst aspects of industrialization. Then came a period when the justices placed individual rights, especially civil rights, at the heart of their concerns, and this raised a different set of difficult questions. As the well-respected judge Learned Hand wrote regarding constitutional interpretation, "fundamental canons [such as freedom of speech and due process] are not jural concepts at all, in the ordinary sense; and in application they turn out to be no more than admonitions of moderation, as appears from the varying and contradictory interpretations that the judges themselves find it necessary to put upon them."

The Constitution is the foundation point from which all decisions flow; in fact, according to the Textualist School, nothing else should matter except the words of that document, interpreted, as some would argue, only with the aid of contemporaneous materials such as *The Federalist* and the minutes of the state ratifying conventions. But of course many other factors come into play, such as precedents, long-established legal rules, changing social and economic conditions, and shifting public attitudes over the meaning and importance of individual liberties. "The meaning of today is not the meaning of tomorrow," Justice Benjamin N. Cardozo noted, so that "new times and new manners may call for new standards and new rules." The rise of the women's movement in the 1970s or the current drive for gay rights and same-sex marriage—and consequent changes in the legal rules—would not have been imaginable as coming to the high court just a generation earlier.

While we are more familiar with the legal ramifications of the civil rights, women's, and gay rights crusades, the difficulties facing the justices have been there for most of our history. "In the excitement produced by ardent controversy," declared Chief Justice John Marshall, "gentlemen view the same object through such different media that minds not unfrequently receive therefrom precisely opposite impressions." One of his contemporaries, Justice William Johnson, wrote, "We pretend not to more infallibility than other courts composed of the same frail materials which compose this."

Given that only the hardest cases reach the high court, and that in each question there are a multitude of precedents, rules, facts, and subjective considerations, it is little wonder that the nine justices would disagree. In matters involving affirmative action, flag burning, a right to die, physician-assisted suicide, same-sex marriage, and many others, the surprise would be not division but unity. Chief Justice Charles Evans Hughes expressed astonishment that "in the midst of controversies on every conceivable subject, one should expect unanimity of opinion upon difficult legal questions." But for nearly 150 years, the members of the Court did stress institutional harmony and often denigrated dissent. Even the great dissenters like Stephen Field, John Marshall Harlan, Holmes, and Brandeis believed that dissents should be rare and unanimity the rule.

Without doubt, the most frequent objection to a dissent is that it weakens the force of the decision and detracts from the court's institutional prestige. Judge Learned Hand summed up this argument when he wrote that the failure to secure unanimity "is disastrous because disunity cancels the impact of monolithic solidarity on which the authority of a bench of judges so largely depends." If people come to believe that the law is uncertain, that even learned judges cannot agree on what it means, they will lose respect for both the court and the law and feel free to disregard both.

In 1928, Charles Evans Hughes, who had been an associate justice and in two years would be named chief justice, found this argument unconvincing:

> When unanimity can be obtained without sacrifice of conviction, it strongly commends the decision to public confidence. But unanimity, which is merely formal, which is recorded at the expense of strong, conflicting views, is not desirable in a court of last resort,

whatever may be the effect upon public opinion at the time. That is so because what must ultimately sustain the court in public confidence is the character and independence of the judges. They are not there simply to decide cases, but to decide them as they think they should be decided, and while it may be regrettable that they cannot always agree, it is better that their independence should be maintained and recognized than that unanimity should be secured through its sacrifice.

Justice Henry Billings Brown, who served on the Court from 1890 to 1906, wrote that "if the authority of the Court is weakened by a dissent, it is probably because it ought to be weakened."

Even though experience shows that complete unanimity is a chimera, most judges acknowledge that there is pressure to achieve, as often as possible, an opinion of the Court, one that reflects the agreement of a majority of the members on a single rationale. This, of course, is what lawyers want, a certainty that the rule expressed in case A will apply to all similar and subsequent cases. The rationale of *stare decisis,* the doctrine of abiding by and adhering to previously decided cases, also plays a role. Courts over the years have applied this doctrine inconsistently; in one of his dissents, Justice Brandeis listed well over a hundred cases in which the Court had abandoned or reversed a prior decision. Nonetheless, most judges—especially those in lower courts—feel bound to at least start with reliance on past decisions. Again, remembering what Holmes said about the law, attorneys need and often demand consistency by the courts, a confidence that once a rule is established, it will not be quickly or easily abandoned. When the Court abruptly alters course, it taxes the public faith that is essential to its authority. Thus in a case in which he disagreed with the Court's decision, Justice John Paul Stevens nonetheless felt compelled to concur in the result. "I am firmly convinced that we have a profound obligation to give recently decided cases the strongest presumption of validity. . . . For me, the adverse consequences of adhering to an arguably erroneous precedent in this case are far less serious than the consequences of further unraveling the doctrine of *stare decisis.*" Lawyers and most judges do not want to open for future litigation questions that a decision of a court of last resort should have settled. Conversely, some judges do not believe that *stare decisis* should govern in constitutional cases, as opposed to questions of statutory interpretation.

Much of the criticism of dissent has, in fact, come from lawyers. In the wake of the split decision and then the reversal of the original holding in the *Income Tax Cases,* the Kansas lawyer Henry Wollman declared, "There never should be a dissenting opinion in a case decided by a court of last resort. No judge, lawyer or layman should be permitted to weaken the force of the court's decision, which all must accept as an unappealable finality." Wollman went on to admit that while there might be disagreement among the justices, "the curtain should not be raised to present the disagreeable picture of family discord and want of harmony." The interest of the public demands that in all cases—but especially in important ones—there be an end to litigation. The only beneficiary of a dissent is the losing party, who may feel somewhat assuaged. A few years earlier, a Philadelphia lawyer, Hampton Carson, confidently asserted the general uselessness of dissents. "The active practitioner is chiefly concerned with the law as it is declared, and pays little heed to a shrill or feeble shriek as to what it might or ought to be."

The Wollman and Carson articles were part of a larger raft of pieces appearing in law journals decrying dissent in both federal and state courts, but especially in the U.S. Supreme Court. In 1886, *The American Law Review* noted that "some of our contemporaries are earnestly discussing the question whether the practice of writing dissenting opinions ought not to be abolished by law." This criticism continued well into the twentieth century. In 1923, a lawyer compared a dissenting opinion to "the small boy making faces at the big boy across the street, which he cannot whip." Another wrote, "When a judge has fully combated his brethren in conference, it is, in our view, something like judicial treason for him . . . to show why the judgment of his fellows is worthy only of disrespect." Justice Robert H. Jackson reflected the practicing lawyer's view when he wrote that dissenting opinions rarely clarify the issues and in fact do just the opposite. "The technique of the dissenter often is to exaggerate the holding of the Court beyond the meaning of the majority and then to blast away at the excess. So the poor lawyer with a similar case does not know whether the majority opinion meant what it seemed to say or what the minority said it meant." As late as 1983, a lawyer could write that notwithstanding the great dissents in American constitutional history, "there remains a bias in the legal community against dissent."

Some critics believe that publishing a dissent may be harmful to the law itself. This belief is far more widespread in Europe than in the United States, and some countries have actually made it a crime for a judge to either publish a dissent or even make it known, publicly or privately, that disagreement existed on the court. The reason is that a written dissent will give some people, particularly those who agree with the losing side, cause to continue holding on to their belief about what the law is, and perhaps even act upon it.

While there still remain people who think dissents useless or worse, today for the most part we accept that dissent is legitimate and often helpful and plays an important role in the dialogue inside the Court as well as with other participants in the making of the law.

IF DISSENSION ON A COURT of last resort leads to uncertainty in the law, why, then, do members of that tribunal file opinions accusing the majority of having decided wrongly? First of all, for all practical purposes—and this is what lawyers are most concerned with—the majority opinion is the law, at least for the foreseeable future. While there are times, especially if a case has been decided by a 5–4 vote, when lawyers rightly worry that a change in personnel or some other factor might lead to a reversal, they also know that in the vast number of cases, the majority opinion will stand, if not forever, at least for the time frame that interests their clients. After all, for all of the dissents filed, only a few rise to the level of influencing the constitutional dialogue. Judges know this as well, yet they continue to file dissents for a number of reasons.

Chief Justice Charles Evans Hughes said it best: "A dissent in a court of last resort is an appeal to the brooding spirit of the law, to the intelligence of a future day, when a later decision may possibly correct the error into which the dissenting judge believes the court to have been betrayed. Nor is this appeal always in vain."

Benjamin Cardozo, whom many considered the greatest common-law judge of the twentieth century, believed this as well: "The voice of the majority may be that of force triumphant, content with the plaudits of the hour and recking little of the morrow. The dissenter speaks to the future, and his voice is pitched to a key that will carry through the years. Read some of the great dissents . . . and feel after the cooling time of the better part of a century, the glow and fire of a faith that was content to bide its hour. The prophet and martyr do not see the hooting throng. Their eyes are fixed on the eternities."

Time is important, because one never knows which dissents will eventually be vindicated and which consigned to the dustbin of history.

A more prosaic reason is that the cases that come to a court of last resort are for the most part difficult. Justice Tom Clark opined that "differences of opinion must be expected on legal questions as on other subjects. . . . Clergymen differ on theology. Professors argue over philosophy. The history of progress is filled with many pages of disagreement." Chief Justice William H. Rehnquist believed that it "may well be that the nature of constitutional adjudication invites, if it does not require, more separate opinions than does adjudication in other areas."

Why do judges dissent? The reasons are many, and they vary from case to case, term to term, and justice to justice. Clearly, the jurists disagree with either the results or the reasoning in a specific case. Justice Stephen Breyer believed that the reasoning, and the results, in a whole line of sovereign immunity cases were wrong and wrote that "today's decision reaffirms the need for continued dissent." Justice Antonin Scalia has written that he will dissent primarily if he considers the reasoning wrong, implying that it is possible to get a result he disagrees with yet he will concede that the majority reasoning is not wholly wrong.

Some dissents are more matters of pique than anything else, anger that the Court is not listening to the speaker, who "knows" that his is the right constitutional interpretation. One can point to any number of examples, but to mention only two, there is Justice James Clark McReynolds's opinion in the Gold Clause Cases. He dissented in such vitriolic terms that part of his comments did not appear in the decision. At one point, he bitterly declared, "This is Nero at his worst. The Constitution as we know it is gone!" Another such dissent is that of Justice Felix Frankfurter, resentful that the Court had ignored his insistence that it not get involved in the question of legislative apportionment.

Neither of these dissents has played a role in the dialogue, in part because of their strident tone. We may admire and be moved by eloquence, as in the Holmes opinions on free speech or Brandeis on the right of privacy, but do not respond well to petulance. Roscoe Pound, longtime dean of the Harvard Law School, warned against what he called the "heated dissent," one in which the emotions of the writer cloud the intellectual argument and offend the other members of the Court. Justice Lewis F. Powell Jr., the epitome of a southern gentleman, talked about the dispassionate nature of dissents, and said that news stories about "bitter" opinions and "deep-seated personal animosities" were wide of the mark. "Judges, like lawyers," he explained, "may disagree strongly without personal rancor or ill will. The fact is that genuine cordiality exists among the justices."

Sharply worded dissents by themselves do not cause rifts. Justice Antonin Scalia wrote, "I doubt whether any two justices have dissented from one another's opinions any more regularly, or any more sharply, than did my former colleague Justice William Brennan and I. I always considered him, however, one of my best friends on the Court, and I think that feeling was reciprocated." According to Chief Justice John

Roberts, all the members of the Court are quite sensitive to the need to avoid comments that could be taken as personal aspersions. One justice may say to another, "Do you really want to be that harsh?" And the writer may well be surprised—"I didn't realize that was going to be viewed that way"—and will change it. A justice is well aware that the person who wrote the opinion she is dissenting from today may be the same justice who will provide her with the fifth vote in another case tomorrow.

Choosing to dissent involves a number of factors to consider. How strongly does the justice feel about the issue? Are the facts in the case appropriate to the argument he wants to make? How "wrong" is the majority opinion? If it is a fairly narrow opinion, limited to the facts of the case in hand, it may not be worth the effort to write a dissent. "I think this case is wrongly decided," Louis Brandeis told Holmes. "But you have restricted the opinion so closely to the facts of the case, that I am inclined to think it will do less harm to let it pass unnoticed by dissent." Is the justice alone in disagreement, or are there one, two, or three others also voting in the minority? Does another dissenter's opinion accurately reflect the views of all those in the minority? If so, then not all need to write. But if not, then a separate dissent may be in order to clarify the differences. What do prior cases say about the doctrinal matters involved? Do they strongly support the majority view, or are they diffused across the jurisprudential spectrum? How far is one willing to go against the doctrine of *stare decisis*? Who is writing the majority opinion may also be a factor. Does she tend to make strong statements that could affect future cases well beyond the facts of this one, or does she write narrow and focused opinions? How has the justice voted in prior cases involving this issue? Some jurists feel bound by *stare decisis* even if they were in a minority, while others feel that if the prior decision was wrong, then it should not be followed. Whether another branch of government is involved may also be a consideration. Is the constitutionality of a congressional statute challenged, implicating the deference that one branch of government should pay to the judgments of another? Has the president done something beyond the powers granted in Article II? Is the issue so volatile that it could arouse the public, much as *Dred Scott* did in the nineteenth century or *Roe v. Wade* in the twentieth, and if so, what are the political considerations to be taken into account? How will a dissent affect people who are disadvantaged by the majority ruling? Will it provoke them into taking the law into their hands or give them hope that someday this "right" view will prevail?

ALL OF THESE CONSIDERATIONS are present in greater or lesser degree, but at the forefront of consciousness are questions involving the solution of the case at hand. Lawyers for the parties have submitted their briefs and then argued the case in court, at which time they were more likely than not to have been subject to intense questioning by the justices. Within a few days after oral argument, the justices will meet in conference—just the nine of them, no clerks or secretaries—and vote on the cases heard that week. A vote will be taken, and the chief justice, if he is in the majority, will assign the case either to himself or to one of the other justices voting with him. If the chief is in the minority, then the senior justice in the majority will assign the case. Depending upon the number of dissenters and the issues involved, they may have one of their number write the opinion, and all will sign on to it, or there may be multiple dissents, each person stressing a different argument, that may or may not draw a "join" from the other dissenters. It is during this stage of a case where we can see the constitutional dialogue in full view, in the interaction among the justices.

Nearly all justices have at one time or another said that when writing a majority opinion, they have little leeway, because they have to present an argument that will hold the other justices in the majority. "The spokesman of the court," said Robert Jackson, "is cautious, timid, fearful of the vivid word, the heightened phrase." "You have to make adjustments," Clarence Thomas has said, "to reflect the views of the majority. And if you can't do that, then you shouldn't write the opinion." William J. Brennan used to tell his clerks that the most important number in the Court was five, the number needed for a majority. When writing the Court's opinion, the justice has to be very careful not to make broad, sweeping generalizations lest she lose some of her votes. That is why majority opinions in most cases tend to be careful and precise, limited to the specific facts and not venturing into broad jurisprudential assertions. So part of the dialogue is between the justice assigned to write the majority opinion and the other members of the majority.

Sometimes, even without a dissent at hand, it is impossible to keep five votes on board. One example is a gender discrimination case, *Califano v. Goldfarb* (1977). Leon Goldfarb sued after a federal statute denied him Social Security benefits because he had not been receiving half of his support from his spouse before she died; similarly situated widows, however, received the payments. With Chief Justice Rehnquist in the 5–4 minority, William Brennan, as the senior justice, assigned the case to himself. In his draft circulations, Brennan tried to place gender in an equal category to race so that any governmental discrimination would be tried under a strict scrutiny standard. He and three other members of the majority were agreeable but not John Paul Stevens, who had been on the Court only a few months and was unwilling to go that far. As a result, Stevens filed an opinion concurring in the judgment but not in the rationale. Gender discrimination would henceforth be reviewed under an "intermediate" level of scrutiny but not under the same criteria that applied to racial categories. (Stevens had replaced William O. Douglas, who would have voted for strict scrutiny, and Stevens, who grew more sympathetic to gender discrimination claims over the years, would eventually have agreed. By that time, however, more conservative members had been appointed who would not go beyond intermediate scrutiny.)

In the wings, of course, is a waiting dissent, or at least the threat of one. "Dissents keep the boys on their toes," Hugo Black used to say.

Clearly, from the dissenter's point of view, the best result is that members of the majority will change their minds before the decision is handed down, even if there is no written dissent. It is not a common occurrence, but it does happen. Justice Robert Jackson once commented, "I myself have changed my opinion after reading the opinions of the other members of this Court. And I am as stubborn as most." In *Martin v. Struthers* (1943), a Jehovah's Witnesses case, Harlan Fiske Stone could not muster a majority in conference. He then wrote a powerful dissent in which he said, "This ordinance is a bald and unqualified suppression of the communication of ideas." In the face of that dissent, and another by Frank Murphy, Hugo Black, who had been assigned the opinion, changed his mind and wrote to sustain the opposite result. Justice Brennan said that "it is a common experience that dissents change votes, even enough votes to become the majority." How "common" that is, however, remains open to question. Certainly justices do change their minds; a study of votes in the Burger years shows that of justices who voted with the majority at conference, in 396 cases (17.3 percent) they circulated or joined a dissent. Chief Justice Stone said that while dissents sometimes changed votes on a case, for the most part they had "no discernible influence" at the time. The real influence of a dissent, "if it has any, comes later, often in shaping and sometimes in altering the course of the law."

In the Brandeis papers, there are a number of dissents written but never delivered. In some instances, he decided to quash his opinion for strategic purposes, in that the issue did not rank as high in his priorities as did other matters. But in some, the draft dissent led the Court to change its mind, not necessarily coming over fully to Brandeis's position, but modifying its ruling to meet some of his objections.

A draft dissent, or even the threat of one, will only rarely lead to a reversal of the Court's initial vote. The unpublished opinions of John Marshall Harlan II during his service on the Court (1955–1971) show that of some sixty-one undelivered opinions only nine were abandoned because the majority reversed itself. Typically, Harlan withdrew a draft of a concurrence or a dissent for the same reason as had Brandeis, because the author of the Court's opinion accommodated his views. Judge William A. Fletcher of the Ninth Circuit states it this way: "Somewhat paradoxically, a judge or justice may write a dissent in order not to have to write one." Sooner or later, he goes on, "all appellate judges have the experience of writing a draft dissent that ends up persuading the majority to his or her point of view."

An essential part of the constitutional dialogue is the response of the justice writing the opinion for the Court to arguments made by a dissenter. Once the conference has voted, the justice writing for the majority strains under multiple burdens. On the one hand, he or she cannot stray too far from what might have been a narrow agreement as to what should be said. On the other hand, the arguments of the dissent have to be taken into account, if for no other reason to prevent one or more members of the majority from changing their minds. From a strategic point of view, this may lead to the assignment of the case to the "justice whose views are closest to the dissenters, on the ground that his opinion would take a middle approach upon which both majority and minority could agree."

Justice Ruth Bader Ginsburg has written about what she calls the "in-house impact":

> My experience teaches that there is nothing better than an impressive dissent to lead the author of the majority opinion to refine and clarify her initial circulation. An illustration: The Virginia Military Institute Case, decided by the Court in 1996, held that VMI's denial of admission to women violated the Fourteenth Amendment's Equal Protection Clause. I was assigned to write the Court's opinion. The final draft, released to the public, was ever so much better than my first, second, and at least a dozen more drafts, thanks to Justice Scalia's attention-grabbing dissent.

Her good friend, fellow opera aficionado, and occasional nemesis, Antonin Scalia, wrote in a similar vein:

> Though the fact never comes to public light, the first draft of a dissent often causes the majority to refine its opinion, eliminating the more vulnerable assertions and narrowing the announced legal rule. When I have been assigned the opinion for the Court in a divided case, nothing gives me as much assurance that I have written it well as the fact that I am able to respond satisfactorily (in my judgment) to all the onslaughts of the dissents or separate concurrences. . . . Ironic as it may seem, I think a higher percentage of the worst opinions of my Court—not in result but in reasoning—are unanimous ones.

(Although we are concerned here primarily with the high court, this same dynamic is at work on state supreme courts as well as lower federal courts. Judge Frank M. Coffin, who served for many years on the federal Court of Appeals for the First Circuit, noted that when there are good arguments on both sides and the court is divided, "all the judges will welcome dissent." Not only does this improve reasoned analysis, but it may "even stimulate the Supreme Court to accept the case for review. On such occasions, it happens that even judges on the majority side do not hesitate to make suggestions that help strengthen the dissent.")

In the fall of 2009, C-SPAN aired a unique program, a series of interviews with all nine sitting justices as well as two retired members of the Court. In each of the segments, the interviewers asked about dissent, and what is remarkable is how nearly all the justices saw dissent as an essential component of the decisional process:

> *Chief Justice John Roberts:* Dissent is a very valuable part of our process. It shows the thinking of different parts of the Court. It shows that arguments have been fully considered, and it's valuable for the writer of the majority, because we have a healthy degree of skepticism about what we're saying up to the very end.

> *Justice Stephen Breyer:* I write an opinion and you write a dissent. I read what you say and I think, "Did I really say that? Oh dear. He has a good point. I better rewrite what I did. I better be certain that my argument is as good as I thought it was the first time." The impact of your dissent will be, at the least, to make me write a better opinion.

Justice Samuel Alito: You have to be ready to respond to the dissent, and the dissents here are very vigorous. They don't pull punches. So I think it ultimately improves the quality of the majority opinion.

Part of an intra-court dialogue is the threat of or the actual writing of a dissent or a concurring opinion that will not fully endorse the majority's conclusions or reasoning. The mechanics of the back-and-forth are far more complex and sophisticated than a note saying, "I am going to dissent." Sometimes the opposing justice does not disagree with all of the majority opinion. He or she may be satisfied with alterations that will not affect the major holding but restrict the jurisprudential rationale. Nearly all judicial opinions will undergo at least minor revision as a result of comments upon the initial draft.

The majority writer also has to take into account what might be called the dissent of "horrible possibilities." Because the dissenter need not trim her views to keep others happy, she can argue that the majority opinion will lead to a long list of terrible consequences. In *Stone v. Powell* (1976), the majority, by a 6–3 vote, ruled that a federal court cannot review on habeas corpus grounds a state court's determination regarding the admissibility of evidence obtained through an allegedly unlawful search and seizure. Justice Brennan dissented and charged that the decision would lead to a complete gutting of federal habeas proceedings for state prisoners on nearly all constitutional claims. "The groundwork is being laid today for a drastic withdrawal of federal habeas jurisdiction, if not for all grounds of alleged unconstitutional detention." There is a danger here, however, that law enforcement officials will seize upon the dissenter's exaggerated predictions and assume that is really what the majority decision means. To avoid this problem, some judges, such as Potter Stewart, would concur in the result, leave the dire consequences unstated, and then emphasize the narrowness of the majority opinion. Either way, the majority writer has to be more specific to ensure that the opinion does not open a floodgate of terrible practices, or to say that it actually is not quite as narrow as the concurrence argues.

Political scientists have studied what they term "judicial strategy" over a wide range of issues, such as which cases to accept for cert, assignment of opinions, and, of course, dissent. Holmes and Brandeis chose when to dissent, and because they did so infrequently, their opinions received great attention. Other judges, such as Felix Frankfurter, compulsively dissented or wrote separate opinions so often that few people took interest in them. As Walter Murphy noted, "A justice must learn not only how to put pressure on his colleagues but how to gauge what amounts of pressure are sufficient to be 'effective' and what amounts will overshoot the mark and alienate another judge." Frankfurter, as is clear from the record, managed to alienate most of his colleagues by both his abrasive personality and his endless and pedantic separate opinions.

After the conference has taken a vote, the majority opinion is assigned. When the author has a draft that she believes is in fairly good shape, it will be circulated to the other chambers. The most common response is "Please join me," meaning that a justice agrees with the opinion as to both result and reasoning. There may be some minor suggestions, but a joinder indicates that the responding justice is willing to go along with the opinion as written. Sometimes a justice will indicate that he or she is willing to join but wants more substantive changes. When writing for the majority, all justices would prefer that the margin be more than 5–4, and if they can pick up an additional vote—without, of course, losing one of the current supporters, and without sacrificing the core principle of their reasoning—they are happy to do it. Sometimes this can be done, and sometimes it cannot. In one case, Justice William Brennan went through five iterations of an opinion hoping to have Sandra Day O'Connor join fully so that he would have a 6–3 majority rather than 5–4, but in the end she wrote a separate opinion concurring in the result but not in the reasoning. (Brennan claimed that in some cases he circulated ten printed drafts before one was approved as the opinion of the Court.)

According to Chief Justice Rehnquist, justices who vote with the majority at conference usually join the majority opinion without waiting for the circulation of a dissent. If a justice does want substantive changes, he or she will usually spell them out. Justice Rehnquist wrote to Harry Blackmun, "I think you have written an excellent opinion in this case, but I am troubled by a couple of points which I want to call to your attention." Blackmun apparently made some changes, for Rehnquist joined the opinion and did not write separately.

Chief Justice Warren Burger told Thurgood Marshall, "I am unable to join an opinion in this case unless it reflects that a 'car stop' does not involve Miranda." The final opinion in fact upheld *Miranda* warnings for a car stop in which there was custodial interrogation, but Burger nonetheless joined the opinion.

Sandra Day O'Connor sent Byron White a list of changes with the following statement: "If you could see your way to incorporating this modification in your circulating draft I would be pleased to join." Apparently, White's changes did not fully satisfy O'Connor, so she filed a separate opinion concurring in part and concurring in the judgment.

Sandra Day O'Connor, associate justice,
1981–2006

Both Burger and O'Connor indicated that they planned to join, but Rehnquist did not, and there was no indication that he would do so if Blackmun did not accommodate him. Professor Murphy sees this as a "threat" to change a vote or to write separately, perhaps in dissent. According to Justice Scalia, members of the Court take these threats seriously, and "nothing causes the writer to be as solicitous of objections on major points as the knowledge that, if he does not accommodate them, he will not have a unanimous court, and will have to confront a separate concurrence." The mere prospect of a separate opinion, according to Scalia, "renders the majority opinion more receptive to reasonable suggestions on major points."

Given this "threat," the majority writer will have to consider several things. One is how many votes she has. If it is close, 5–4, or some members are wavering, she will be more amenable to change. If on the other hand she has seven or eight votes, she will be less willing to make anything other than minor changes. What the dissident justice asks is also important. If the requests deal with marginal matters that do not affect either the result or the reasoning, an accommodation can easily be made. But if the request strikes at the heart of the legal rationale, that will not be accepted. Chief Justice Rehnquist explained that if the result at conference had been reached by a unanimous or a lopsided vote, "a critic who wishes substantial changes in the opinion has less leverage."

In one case, Chief Justice Burger responded to a draft opinion by Justice O'Connor with a seemingly innocuous note that read, "I could happily join your opinion if you could add something along these lines." But "these lines" involved more than minor changes, and O'Connor responded, "Your remaining substantive comments would require a major alteration in the present draft. . . . I will circulate some revisions before long in hopes of resolving some of the questions. The revisions may not meet all your concerns." After seeing the revised draft, Burger declared, "I fear we are not on the same 'wave length' on this case, and I will have something around as soon as possible." O'Connor saw no reason to make any further accommodation because she had a solid majority for her opinion. In the end, Burger did write a concurrence, but it had little impact on the deliberations; no one else joined him.

(One might add here that who is making the threats is also a consideration. A Ginsburg, a Kennedy, or a Scalia presents the possibility of a strong and well-reasoned separate opinion, a possibility that no writer of a majority opinion would take lightly. Warren Burger, on the other hand, has never been considered a jurisprudential heavyweight, and a threat by him, as in this case, could be dismissed with a polite "Sorry, but no.")

All of these actions are part of the dialogue that takes place among the justices in fashioning an opinion. Chief Justice Rehnquist acknowledged that such give-and-take is inevitable, "and doctrinal purity may be muddied in the process." Another justice told an interviewer, "We don't negotiate, we accommodate." Whatever phraseology is used, justices are aware that while they may hold strong views on a particular issue, if they speak for the Court, they will more often than not have to tone it down somewhat in order to satisfy the other members of the majority. The dissenter, of course, does not labor under this restraint.

THREATENING TO WRITE SEPARATELY is one thing; actually doing so is another. Of course the minority justice or justices will write, and as noted above, a well-crafted dissent will have an impact not only on the majority opinion but possibly in the ongoing constitutional dialogue. A concurrence may also have those effects, but concurrences, like dissents, have costs involved, even if one has the help of capable clerks. They take time and energy and may well disrupt the institutional schedule by holding up decisions. In a 5–4 case, a concurrence in the result but not the reasoning means that there is no rule with precedential value that will govern future cases or guide lower courts in this area.

A concurrence may also go beyond the majority opinion, a clear signal that the issue might not have been resolved. A good example can be found in the physician-assisted suicide cases. In 1990, the Court had held that there was an individual right to refuse life-sustaining medical treatment. Advocates of physician-assisted suicide then stepped up their campaign and claimed that terminally ill patients had not only a constitutional right to die on their own but also a right to have a doctor's help in doing so. The Ninth Circuit in California agreed with this position on Fourteenth Amendment due process grounds, while the Second Circuit in New York reached a similar conclusion based on equal protection. The Supreme Court, as expected, took the two cases on appeal and also, as expected, ruled that there was no constitutional right to physician-assisted suicide. Chief Justice Rehnquist, whose wife had died in 1991 after a long battle with ovarian cancer, took note of the "profound and earnest" debate in the states over whether to permit such activity. He concluded, "Our holding permits the debate to continue, as it should in a democratic society"—a clear invitation to the public that in this area the popular will could create a right not found in the Constitution.

Although all nine justices agreed with the result—that no constitutional right existed—five members of the Court wanted to go further. Justice O'Connor qualified her support by saying that the ruling would not prevent a physician from prescribing a painkilling medication even if it hastened death—an acknowledgment of a practice that doctors, understandably, did not talk about very much. Four other justices—Stevens, Souter, Ginsburg, and Breyer—indicated that future individual cases involving terminally ill patients might be decided differently. Justice Souter wrote what I consider one of the best opinions of his career, in which he explained, following John Marshall Harlan II's dissent in *Poe v. Ullman* (1961), how a new constitutional right resulting from changing social conditions might be discovered.

If some critics view the dissent as undermining the authority of the Court or making the result less clear, others dislike the concurrence and see it as little more than an ego trip. This would be true, I think, for many of Felix Frankfurter's 132 concurrences, some of which do little more than claim that Frankfurter understood the law better than his colleagues.

Concurrences, however, like dissents, may be a useful tool in the judicial dialogue. Sometimes a concurrence in the result but not the reasoning will serve as the basis for future changes in the reasoning. In *Rochin v. California* (1952), Justice Frankfurter spoke for a unanimous Court in holding that the state had engaged in brutal, and thus illegal, conduct in catching and convicting a drug dealer. Frankfurter's opinion strongly condemned California's actions, but he based the reversal of the conviction on Fourteenth Amendment due process grounds. Hugo Black and William O. Douglas agreed with the result but entered concurrences stating that the reversal should have been on specific provisions of the Fourth and Fifth Amendments, a position that would ultimately be adopted by the Warren Court.

Most often, a separate opinion is, as Walter Murphy notes, "essentially an effort to resolve conflict within the Court by persuading, in one fashion or another, other Justices." If well written, according to Ruth Bader Ginsburg, it "may provoke clarifications, refinements, [and] modifications in the court's opinion." Given this limited objective, if the majority author makes changes that are acceptable both to other members of the majority and to the writer of the separate opinion, then the goal has been achieved and the separate opinion is withdrawn. This seems like a high price to pay, given the time and energy involved in the writing of the separate opinion and the revisions and circulations necessary to achieve consensus by the majority author, but it will seem well worth the effort if the final result has the support of a clear majority or, better yet, a fuller majority. It not only will resolve questions about the case under consideration but will provide clear guidance for lower courts in future litigation on this issue.

Concurring opinions are not dissents, in that they set out conclusions and rationales far different from the majority, but they play a role in the dialogue that is in many ways similar to a dissent. As Justices Scalia, Arthur Goldberg, and others have acknowledged, the threat of a separate opinion—concurrence or dissent—will cause the majority writer, as well as the other members of the majority, to rethink certain matters. Some may be minor, toning down some assertions, clarifying what is meant by others, or deleting sections that the dissident believes unnecessary or irrelevant. But some may go beyond what the majority can accept, and in close cases the concurrence will act like a dissent and, while upholding the result, can deprive the opinion of precedential value.

More attention is paid to dissent. While lawyers and judges may understand the distinctions made in a concurrence, the general public usually does not. After all, the result is still the same. A dissent, however, says to everyone, "This case is wrongly decided, reaching the wrong result through faulty reasoning." The vast majority of dissents are soon forgotten, but some, the ones we are interested in, live on in the dialogue. "The dissenting opinion," according to Judge Jesse Carter of California, is "a forecast of things to come. The writers of dissents are usually men who look forward . . . to the future." These are the great dissents, the "prophetic ones," those that foretell and are eventually on the "right" side of history.

One should note that some of the prophetic opinions took years before the Court adopted their views. Stephen Field's interpretation of the Fourteenth Amendment's Due Process Clause took a quarter century before it became majority opinion. The first justice Harlan's dissents in the *Civil Rights Cases* (1883) and *Plessy v. Ferguson* (1896) were not validated until the 1950s and 1960s. The free speech arguments of Holmes and Brandeis in the 1920s did not see full acceptance until 1969.

Justice Scalia has suggested that the decisions most likely to be overruled are those decided by a 5–4 vote. One might think that in closely divided cases the force of the dissent is nearly as great as that of the majority, and in some instances this may be true. But another reason is that ever since the 1930s the Court for much of the time has been closely divided, and in these instances the death or retirement of one or two justices can reverse the Court's direction.

In the Great Depression of the 1930s, the conservative bloc known as the Four Horsemen—Willis Van Devanter, James Clark McReynolds, George Sutherland, and Pierce Butler—could often pick up the necessary fifth vote to block state and federal measures designed to ameliorate the terrible economic conditions. The impasse led to the great constitutional crisis of 1937; although Roosevelt's Court-packing plan failed, later that year Van Devanter retired, and the following year Sutherland. With the appointments of Hugo Black and Stanley Reed, the New Deal now had a solid majority in favor of its measures.

Although we tend to think of the Warren Court as monolithically liberal, in fact from the time Earl Warren became chief justice in 1953 until Frankfurter's stroke and retirement in the summer of 1962, the Court was evenly divided between a conservative bloc led by Frankfurter and a liberal group who looked to Hugo Black for guidance. With Frankfurter's replacement by Arthur Goldberg, the "real" Warren Court began, and many of its most liberal decisions came in the next seven years.

Ever since the 1970s, there has been a conservative bloc of three to four justices, and a liberal or moderate bloc of the same number, with one or two justices such as Lewis Powell, Sandra Day O'Connor, and

Anthony Kennedy serving as the swing votes in the middle. How the replacement of any one justice can affect this balance and suddenly convert a previous dissent into a majority can be seen in the *Citizens United* case.

A conservative advocacy group, Citizens United, made a movie attacking Hillary Clinton, then in the running for the Democratic presidential nomination, wanted to make it available as a video on demand within thirty days of the primary elections, and produced advertisements promoting the film. The Federal Election Commission declared that showing the film would violate a ban that Congress had enacted in the McCain-Feingold Bipartisan Campaign Reform Act of 2002 (BCRA) and that the Court, by a 5–4 vote, had sustained the following year. Citizens United sued, claiming this provision violated its free speech rights. When the Court accepted the case for review, it also declared that it would revisit the ban on independent corporate political expenditures, which it had upheld in a 1990 case, even though that case had not played a role in the lower court litigation.

The major events that transpired between the Court's approval of BCRA in 2003 and its decision in *Citizens United* in 2010 were the death of Chief Justice Rehnquist and his replacement by John Roberts and the retirement of Sandra Day O'Connor and her replacement by Samuel Alito. Court watchers generally see Roberts as jurisprudentially similar to the man he replaced (and for whom he once clerked), but they view Alito as far more conservative than O'Connor, who for nearly two decades was the swing vote in 5–4 decisions and the fifth vote in the *McConnell* case upholding BCRA.

Justice Anthony Kennedy's opinion for the five-member majority (Roberts, Scalia, Kennedy, Thomas, and Alito) not only struck down the BCRA's thirty-day rule but also reversed *Austin*'s holding that prohibited independent political contributions by corporations, a rule that had been in existence for over a century. In it, Kennedy seemed to rely primarily on dissents in prior cases upholding limits on campaign donations, including the dissents he and Justice Scalia had filed in *Austin*. Of the six jurists who had formed the majority in *Austin* — Marshall, Rehnquist, Brennan, White, Blackmun, and Stevens — only Stevens was still on the bench in 2010. Of the three dissenters — O'Connor, Scalia, and Kennedy — the last two were still there, augmented by Roberts, Thomas, and Alito, all of whom had previously expressed their opposition to campaign finance restrictions. This bloc pushed its agenda even further in *McCutcheon v. Federal Election Commission* (2014), striking down the limits on what any individual could give during an election cycle.

The question, then, is whether the repeated dissents by Scalia, Kennedy, and Thomas over a twenty-year period finally convinced a majority of the Court, or whether the two newest members—ideologically aligned with them—made the difference. Certainly there has been not only an ongoing constitutional dialogue over campaign finance reform but a political one as well. The two decisions had Republicans cheering for what they considered a victory for free speech, while Democrats lambasted the Court for abandoning a century of precedent that had attempted to control the corrosive and corrupting effects of money in campaigns. The division on the Court may well reflect the political divisions outside, in this case over questions such as free speech and whether corporations have First Amendment rights. But as Justice Jackson once noted, "Conflicts which have divided the Justices always mirror a conflict which pervades society."

These conflicts are part of the larger dialogue, and while not all divisions within the Court echo questions of public policy being debated by the public, it is rare that a measure that splits the public—affirmative action, campaign finance, and the like—will not show up in the Marble Palace.

WE WILL BE LOOKING primarily at the dialogue that takes place within the Court and how dissent has affected that dialogue. The justices, however, speak not only with each other but with other participants in our constitutional government. For now, we can briefly mention these other members of the dialogue.

Aside from constitutional interpretation, a major task of the Court is statutory interpretation of the laws passed by Congress and signed by the president. Clearly, not every law requires a court hearing, and even those that may wind up in the district courts or the courts of appeals may not raise questions that require the Supreme Court's review. When the Court passes on legislation, two primary questions arise. The first is whether Congress had power under the Constitution to enact this statute in the first place. If Congress has exceeded this power, then the law is held unconstitutional, and the only way to override that type of decision is by the amendment process. The clearest example of this is the passage of the Sixteenth Amendment, authorizing Congress to tax incomes, a direct response to the Court ruling the income tax unconstitutional in 1895.

More often, the complicated process of drafting a bill has resulted in language that is far from clear as to either meaning or application, and the courts are asked to determine exactly what Congress meant. Some justices are willing to look at the statements made in the House or Senate to help derive congressional intent; others believe that such documents are irrelevant and that the only thing that matters is the wording of the statute itself.

Statutory interpretation that does not involve constitutionality can be remedied by Congress, in essence, saying to the Court, "That is not what we meant," and reenacting the statute with more precise wording. It should be noted that both a majority opinion and a dissent can lead to congressional revision. Two examples may suffice where a dissenter successfully called upon Congress to reverse a majority opinion.

In 1845, the Court ruled on a statute changing the way that customs officers reported and submitted collected money. The majority held that the wording of the new law abolished the importers' traditional common-law remedy to sue if a mistake had been made. In his dissent, Justice Joseph Story declared that he believed the majority had misinterpreted the statute, and he suggested that Congress correct this mistake. Congress responded with alacrity, making it plain that it had never been its intention to do away with the remedy.

More recently, the Court ruled that the Equal Pay Act required an employee who believed she was being discriminated against because of gender to file a complaint within 180 days of the violation. The Equal Employment Opportunity Commission had interpreted this provision to mean within 180 days of learning about the discrimination. Lilly Ledbetter had worked for many years at Goodyear before learning about the discrepancy in pay that affected her and other women employees. The majority decision, which said that the wording of the statute had to be taken literally, held that the law required filing within 180 days of the discrimination and effectively barred nearly all women from suing, because few if any would have known within six months that their pay was less than that of a man in a similar job. Justice Ruth Bader Ginsburg dissented for herself and three other justices, not only attacking the majority for its crabbed holding, but also calling on Congress to modify the law and to make it clear that the 180-day limit ran from the time one learned about the inequity.

Before the day was over, Senator Hillary Clinton of New York announced she would submit such a bill, and it soon became obvious that a majority in both houses of Congress would support it. Business lobbies inundated the White House with protests, and George W. Bush declared that if Congress passed such a bill, he would veto it. When Barack Obama became president, he immediately invited Congress to pass what he termed the "Lilly Ledbetter Fair Pay Law" and promised he

President Barack Obama signs the Lilly Ledbetter Fair Pay Act into law on 29 January 2009. Lilly Ledbetter is standing directly behind the president.

would sign it. Congress acted with alacrity, and Obama signed the bill as one of his first acts as president on 29 January 2009.

Recently, the Court found the wording of a statute to be so flawed that all nine justices called on Congress to remedy that statute's defects. The law, allowing restitution to victims of child pornography, left it uncertain how much a victim could collect and, if numerous people viewed the pictures on the Internet, whether the victim had to go after each one. A woman—"Amy Unknown"—had as a child been raped by her uncle, who took pictures and posted them on the Net. The woman had won a judgment of \$3.4 million against a man who had viewed the pictures. Five members of the Court said she could collect, but only in an amount commensurate to proximate damages. Three members dissented, saying their reading of the statute was that she could collect nothing, while one justice thought she could collect the full amount. All three opinions called on Congress to remedy the defects of the law.

The Court also interacts with the chief executive. In some cases, it is really more a question of whether the law he is executing is in fact constitutional. Although the president might have proposed the measure in the first place, the constitutional question will be whether Congress has the power, and the statutory query will be whether Congress meant for the president to act as he did. When the president or one of his cabinet members purports to act under the powers granted in Article II, questions deal solely with presidential power and authority. In any case involving the president or Congress, the Court nearly always repeats the mantra that deference is due to the judgments of the coordinate branches of government. Despite that, the Court has had no problem telling the president that he cannot do certain things.

One of the most famous cases involved Harry S. Truman and the steel seizure case of 1952. The threat of a strike by the United Steelworkers led President Truman to conclude that a strike would jeopardize steel production in the middle of the Korean War. Truman believed that he had the same power as Franklin Roosevelt had exercised during World War II, and in April he issued Executive Order 10340 directing Secretary of Commerce Charles Sawyer to seize and operate most of the nation's steel mills. Truman had no statutory authority to do this and claimed he was acting under the executive authority of the president.

Congress, however, had enacted the Taft-Hartley Act of 1947 that included procedures by which the government could secure an eighty-day cooling-off period to postpone any strike that might adversely affect the public interest. Truman, however, had no desire to utilize that law, which he had vetoed and which Congress had then passed over his veto. In the ensuing case, the Supreme Court voted 6–3 that Truman had exceeded his authority and that he had a congressionally sanctioned method that provided him a tool with which to handle the matter.

More recently, one can see a dialogue between the Court and President George W. Bush over the legal process due to detainees held at the Guantánamo Naval Base in Cuba. After the beginnings of the wars in Afghanistan and Iraq, the army captured prisoners, some of whom the Bush administration labeled "enemy combatants." It decided that these men would not be treated as prisoners of war but be held incommunicado and without redress to American courts. Cases attacking this policy began almost immediately, with a majority of the lower courts ruling that the administration had exceeded its authority under the Article II war powers. The first of these cases reached the Supreme Court in 2004, despite strong efforts by the Justice Department to prevent any courts from hearing these cases. In the series of cases that followed, the Court consistently told the president that he did not have the authority claimed and that it would be the Court, not the executive branch, that determined the jurisdiction of the high court.

In this case, we can see the justices—both the majority and the dissenters—reaching out beyond the courtroom to talk to the president, to Congress, and to the people. Around this time, Justice Kennedy spoke to a group at the Court and said that he considered education to be one of the most important tasks of a justice. Decisions and the reasons behind them had to be made clear not just to lawyers but to the public as well. When the decision in the last of these cases came down on 12 June 2008, Kennedy took the unusual step of orally delivering much of his opinion, which included a lengthy history of habeas corpus.

The treatment of detainees at Guantánamo, and the various Court opinions, became part of a very public dialogue in the 2008 presidential campaign between John McCain and Barack Obama. McCain, a former prisoner of war during the Vietnam conflict, did not support torture but argued that the government needed to be able to deal with terrorists outside the confines of the American criminal justice system. Obama, on the other hand, lashed out at the Bush administration for its flagrant disregard not only of human rights but of the Constitution as well and promised to close Guantánamo, a promise that Congress thwarted him from fulfilling.

The detainee issue was not the first issue debated on the Court that became part of the political dialogue on the campaign trail, nor will it be the last. Perhaps in no other way can the people signal their views on the Court decisions than by casting their ballot for or against a candidate who agrees with the majority or with the dissent. The justices' dialogue shapes the constitutional framework of an issue, but many if not most of these questions play out in a larger context. Many voters in 2008 had strong views regarding how the country should deal with the detainees, views that mirrored the various opinions expressed by the justices.

IN A DEMOCRACY, there are—or should be—many participants in a conversation on public policy. The Court, the president, and Congress all have voices that are clearly heard. But there are others for whom the constitutional dialogue is also important. One group consists of judges on state and lower federal courts. For them, the Supreme Court's constitutional rulings are supposed to provide guidance, and in most cases they do. When, however, there is a convincing dissent, these jurists may try to distinguish the facts of a case so that they can follow the dissent rather than the majority.

The dialogue with the legal academy may not generate much public attention, but it is of concern to jurists and to law professors, especially because many judges are former law professors. Louis Brandeis became the first justice to cite a law review article in a Supreme Court opinion. Acting through Felix Frankfurter, he also encouraged law reviews to analyze and criticize Supreme Court decisions, because through such examination mistakes could be made clear. Today, of course, citing law articles is a common practice, and in some cases one has what might be seen as "dueling sources" between the majority and the dissenting opinions. Chief Justice William Howard Taft (who taught at the Yale Law School prior to his appointment) accused Harlan Fiske Stone (the former dean of the Columbia Law School) of "hungering for the applause of the law-school professors."

Supreme Court cases, of course, are at the heart of most law school courses, and in the Socratic method employed in most schools, students and teachers engage in a rigorous analysis of cases—both the majority and the dissenting opinions. A dissenter may hope, even if she will never know, that her argument won over a young law student who will later utilize that reasoning, perhaps as a judge.

TRYING TO GAUGE the impact of Court decisions and of dissenting opinions on the public is difficult to do in any quantitative manner, but as historians we can see that certain cases at particular times in our history have had an impact far beyond the litigants involved. While the 1857 *Dred Scott* decision did not trigger the Civil War, it certainly aroused a storm of public criticism that helped inflame passions over the next few years. The dissenting opinion of Justice Benjamin Curtis was reprinted and received wide circulation, and its arguments can be found in the Lincoln-Douglas debates and in the 1860 presidential campaign.

Another dissent that found resonance with the public came in the 1972 case of *Sierra Club v. Morton,* in which the environmental group challenged the Interior Department's proposal to allow the development of a Walt Disney resort in Sequoia National Forest. The club claimed that the proposed resort, ski trails, and access roads would hurt the ecology of the forest. A 4–3 majority of the Court held that the club did not have standing to sue, because the development would not specifically harm any members of the organization.

William O. Douglas wrote an impassioned and wide-ranging dissent that took the unusual step of suggesting to Congress that a federal rule should exist to allow environmental issues to be litigated before federal agencies or courts "in the name of the inanimate object about to be despoiled, defaced, or invaded by roads and bulldozers and where injury is the subject of public outrage." He waxed poetic about nature: "The river is the living symbol of all the life it sustains or nourishes . . . including man, who are dependent on it or who enjoy it for its sight, its sound, or its life. The river as plaintiff speaks for the ecological unit of life that is part of it."

William O. Douglas on 189-mile hike to save the C&O Canal

As Professor Adam Sowards has shown, Douglas's dissent in this case, as well as his nonjudicial writings on the environment, helped create the modern American environmental movement. The Sierra Club reprinted Douglas's dissent many times, and other groups rallied to the cause. While Douglas cannot be given sole credit for awakening Americans to the need to protect trees and lakes, his eloquent dissents clearly spoke not to his brethren on the Court but to the American public.

In a recent term, two dissents spoke as much to the public as to the majority, if not more. In the first, the Court heard a challenge to Proposal 2, which amended the Michigan constitution to prohibit the use of race-based preferences for admission to state colleges and universities, thus negating a Court's earlier decision permitting such policies. A 6–3 majority held that nothing in their previous cases barred the people of a state from amending their constitution so long as there was no overt discrimination against a particular group. Justice Sonia Sotomayor filed a blistering opinion defending affirmative action, arguing that Proposal 2 did, in fact, discriminate against minorities, and practically accused the majority of racism.

In the second case, a 5–4 majority held that the town council of Greece, a small village in upstate New York, could begin its meetings with an overtly Christian prayer. Justice Elena Kagan sharply dissented, arguing that the majority ignored six decades of Establishment Clause jurisprudence as well as the intent behind the First Amendment's ban

Sonia Sotomayor, associate justice, 2009–

on an establishment of religion. Like Sotomayor, Kagan read her dissent from the bench. Both dissents gave rise to a number of newspaper editorials, letters to the editors, and in the age of the Internet, intense discussions on Internet chat rooms.

The appeal to the public is certainly behind the death penalty dissents of Thurgood Marshall, William Brennan, and Harry Blackmun. Marshall and Brennan dissented in almost every capital punishment case during their tenures, reiterating their belief that the death penalty violated the Eighth Amendment ban on cruel or unusual punishment. The two men also began the unusual practice of dissenting every time their fellow justices declined to hear an appeal brought by a death row inmate. Eventually, Harry Blackmun came to this position as well. In doing so, they went against two centuries of precedent as well as against the support of capital punishment by a majority of Americans. During the long time that these three justices served on the Court, they knew they would be in a minority; they hoped their dissents would convince the public and appeal "to the intelligence of a future day."

The Court's dialogue with the public takes many forms. The justices, even if they do not admit to it, are tuned in to public opinion. There have been very few instances in the past 225 years when the Court has pursued a jurisprudential path that runs contrary to public opinion. Textualists like Antonin Scalia will proclaim that what the public thinks should have no bearing on the work of the Court, which is to interpret the constant meaning of the Constitution. But Scalia is an outlier on this issue, and more moderate conservatives, such as Anthony Kennedy, Sandra Day O'Connor, and Lewis Powell have been sensitive to changing mores. In some instances, it will be the majority that invokes these changes; in others, it may be the minority. One cannot imagine a dialogue on the Court, no matter what the constitutional question, that ignored the political and social debate on the same question in the country at large.

Moreover, in recent years several of the justices have taken their views directly to the public in the forms of books, speeches, law review articles, and interviews. William O. Douglas started the trend, interspersing thoughts on jurisprudence among his various books and then writing a volume of memoirs on his Court years. More recently, William Rehnquist, John Paul Stevens, Sandra Day O'Connor, Antonin Scalia, Anthony Kennedy, Clarence Thomas, and Stephen Breyer have all published books on constitutional topics. Thomas has been a frequent speaker at conservative gatherings, while Scalia and Breyer have on several occasions debated each other over constitutional interpretation. Justice Kennedy has said this very explicitly: "I like to think of us as teachers that first teach ourselves and then teach others, and we're teaching what the law means."

Barry Friedman has convincingly argued that much of the Supreme Court's prestige and influence has resulted because it does pay attention to public sentiment. There is no question that the justices, who are for the most part politically quite sophisticated, are aware of the limits of public tolerance. When the Court has gone too far, as in *Dred Scott* or in opposing New Deal measures, there has been a public reaction. One can see the Court taking a firm stand in the case establishing an individual's right to die but treading carefully in the assisted-suicide cases, preferring to leave the matter to the political process.

In 1986, when the Court ruled that homosexuals had no right to engage in consensual sex, the gay community and some civil liberties groups praised the dissenters, but for the most part the public did not find the decision unwelcome. Over the next quarter century, however, public acceptance of gays and lesbians increased markedly, especially among younger adults. So when a split court in 2000 upheld the Boy Scouts of America policy to exclude gays, the general reaction was far more critical, and the dissent found fairly wide support. In 2003, the Court reversed itself and held that gays did have a right of privacy that the state could not impair. This time, the opinion stirred little controversy, and the dissent was seen as reactionary. Then, in 2013, with public opinion polls showing a majority of Americans supporting the right of gays to marry, the Court struck down DOMA, the Defense of Marriage Act, upholding the legitimacy of state laws permitting same-sex marriage. Commentators viewed Justice Scalia's bitter dissent less as an accusation that the majority was wrong than as a futile cry against changes with which he did not agree.

I am not implying that the Court was the most important player in all of these debates. Rather, policy making in a democracy involves multiple voices, and it is the dialogue between and among the participants that is critical. The dialogue on the Court is important, but it must be seen as part of a larger conversation that goes on in a democracy. The decisions of the Court have consequences that often go far beyond the questions raised by the immediate case, and the other participants in the conversation understand that well.

As we shall see, dissent has been an important element within the Court from its beginnings in the late eighteenth century. At the same time, the important dissents have involved the Court with other political actors, such as Congress, the president, and the public. Not all dissents have such an impact, and the vast majority of them are soon—and rightly—forgotten. The majority decided correctly, public opinion supported the results, Congress or the president accepted the results, or the cases themselves proved not to have lasting importance. But some dissents mattered greatly; they shaped the constitutional dialogue and in doing so shaped the type of government we now enjoy.

CHAPTER 2

FROM SERIATIM TO THE OPINION OF THE COURT

If any part of the reasoning be disapproved, it must be so modified as to receive the approbation of all, before it can be delivered as the opinion of all.

— JOHN MARSHALL

An opinion is huddled up in conclave, perhaps by a majority of one, delivered as if unanimous, and with the silent acquiescence of lazy or timid associates.

— THOMAS JEFFERSON

On 1 February 1790, the Supreme Court of the United States convened for the first time at the Water Street exchange in New York. With only three justices present, the Court adjourned until the next day, when it had a quorum. Nonetheless, the Court again recessed, for it had no cases on appeal, no subpoenas to issue, and no clerk to issue them. In fact, the only business of the Court that first term consisted of securing a clerk, adopting a seal, and swearing in some two dozen lawyers for practice before it, of whom eleven were members of Congress. On 10 February, the first term of the Court ended. At its second session on 2 and 3 August 1790, the Court conducted no business other than admitting additional lawyers to practice.

Over the next decade, the business of the Supreme Court grew slowly; the six justices decided a few important cases and also agreed on necessary procedures. Yet for many people at the time, the Court seemed not only the weakest branch of the new government under the Constitution but at times an almost superfluous one. Alexander Hamilton in *Federalist* 78 had termed the new federal court system "beyond comparison the weakest of the three departments of power." It was "the least dangerous branch" of the government, he explained, because it lacked the power of either purse or sword. When the new Capitol was being built, the architect made no provision for the Court because he forgot it existed. John Jay, whom President Washington named as the first chief justice, left in 1795 to serve as governor of New York. Four other members also resigned, and two nominees declined appointment even after the Senate had confirmed them.

For the most part, scholars have not considered the 1790s Court very highly, and the common wisdom is that it only became an influential institution after the arrival of Chief Justice John Marshall in 1801. One historian declared that "the outstanding aspect of the Court's work during its first decade was its relative unimportance."

Recent scholarship has helped us to understand that the Supreme Court did decide some consequential cases in its first decade and also set some important precedents. Even acknowledging the Court's accomplishments, however, does not weaken the argument that as an institution—as a branch of government coequal to the president and Congress—the Court did not come into its own until sometime during John Marshall's tenure.

ANGLO-AMERICAN LAW dates back to the Norman Conquest of England in the eleventh century. William the Conqueror and his successors sought to unify the country under the monarchy and as part of the plan established royal courts. Prior to the Norman Conquest, disputes had been resolved by local chieftains utilizing area customs and traditions, which varied widely across England. The new courts would establish uniform rules across the country—the "common law," which derived not from acts of Parliament (which did not meet until the middle of the thirteenth century) but from decisions of the courts.

The King's Court, or King's Bench, dates to the reign of King Alfred. At first, it was not specifically a law court but a forum consisting of the king and various advisers. In 1178, Henry II ordered that five judges of his household serve as Curia Regis, the King's Court, and refer only the most difficult cases to him. In 1215, Magna Carta provided for a court that would meet in a fixed place, and eventually this developed into the King's Bench meeting in Westminster, but with its judges also traveling on circuit in the countryside.

For almost a thousand years, decisions in these multi-judge courts were delivered orally by each member without prior consultation. From 1268 to 1535, scribes and lawyers recorded as best they could the opinions of the judges, and the unedited and unabridged compilations of these notes served as sources of legal precedent. Needless to say, these collections did not portray any consistent view of the law, because different lawyers hearing the same opinions might well reach contradictory interpretations of what had been said. Even when judges agreed on an outcome, they often differed on the legal rules supporting that conclusion. After official reports of judicial opinions began appearing in 1609, judges continued to use the seriatim, or separate method of delivering opinions, and there was strong support for the practice. Judgments made in the open and without prior consultation would be less likely—or would certainly appear less likely—to be infected by bribery or collusion with the Crown. Whatever the value of each judge speaking or writing separately, the problem of discerning a specific rule persisted.

Early American lawyers were essentially transplanted Englishmen schooled in the English common law. This excursion into English law is relevant not only for its antecedents for American law but also because of the reform efforts of William Murray, Lord Mansfield, who became lord chief justice of the King's Court in 1756.

Although American history often paints the English government at the time of the American Revolution as strong and autocratic, it was in fact fairly fragile. Parliament's legislative power had grown as a check on the monarch's power, and no unified or independent judicial authority existed. The Privy Council and the House of Lords constituted England's courts of last resort, but most appeals never got further than the three common-law courts—the Court of Common Pleas, the King's Bench, and the Exchequer. The growth of the empire and the prosperity it brought also increased the need of the commercial classes for more reliable law, and Mansfield sought to impose consistency on merchant law. He believed legal rules should be understood by those who had to obey them and that when two parties went to court to resolve a dispute, the result should be clear and certain.

To achieve this certainty, he needed to have his court speak authoritatively, and to accomplish this, he sought to abolish the practice of seriatim. He wanted the justices of the King's Bench to discuss a case in private and reach consensus not only on the result but on the reason-

*William Murray, 1st Earl of Mansfield, lord
chief justice of the King's Bench, 1756–1788*

ing to sustain the decision. There would then issue an anonymous and
unanimous "opinion of the court." Mansfield's reforms proved successful
in harmonizing merchant customs and the common law and, according
to his leading biographer, "established the basic principles that continue to govern the mercantile energies of England and America down
to the present day." His effort to do away with seriatim opinions proved
less enduring. Upon Mansfield's retirement in 1788, his successor, Lord
Kenyon, ended single opinions, and judges returned to the practice of
seriatim opinions.

American colonial and early state courts for the most part followed
English practices, and on multi-judge courts this meant delivering opinions seriatim. When word of Mansfield's efforts reached these shores, at
least some American jurists experimented with them. Edmund Pendleton became chief judge of the Virginia Court of Appeals (later the
Supreme Court of Virginia) in 1778, and he persuaded his colleagues
to adopt the Mansfield model. After the judges had reviewed a case in
private, they would issue a unanimous "opinion of the court." Thomas
Jefferson and his followers strongly condemned the practice, and when
Spencer Roane succeeded Pendleton in 1794, the judges returned to

issuing opinions seriatim. Jefferson feared giving courts too much power, and his dispute with Pendleton foreshadowed his later and more famous quarrel with John Marshall.

In Connecticut, the judges of the Superior Court also chose to follow Mansfield's way. In 1786, Oliver Ellsworth, later to be chief justice of the United States, joined the state court, and that same year the legislature passed a law requiring that in cases turning upon an interpretation of law, each judge of the Superior Court "give his opinion seriatim with the Reasons thereof, and the same reduce to Writing." The purpose of the statute was to facilitate appeals and to lay "a foundation . . . for a more perfect and permanent System of Common Law in this State." Even though the legislature had demanded written seriatim opinions, the judges ignored the mandate and adopted the practice of majority opinions for the court with an occasional dissent.

IT IS NO SURPRISE, therefore, that when the Supreme Court began to decide cases, it followed the English tradition of seriatim. We are not, however, dealing with an established court in this first decade, but rather one in flux with little leadership. When John Jay resigned as chief justice in 1795, Washington named as his successor John Rutledge of South Carolina in a recess appointment; the Senate, however, refused to confirm him because Rutledge had publicly attacked the Jay Treaty with Great Britain. Washington then offered the seat to Patrick Henry, who declined, and then nominated the associate justice William Cushing, whom the Senate immediately confirmed. Cushing, however, declined the promotion because of ill health and never took the oath of office. Finally, Washington nominated Oliver Ellsworth of Connecticut, who served for four years and tried to strengthen the institutional vitality of the Court.

During this period, the Court heard at least sixty-three cases; that is the number Alexander Dallas reported in the official reports, but it is generally agreed that he omitted many cases, possibly because he was not in court to hear them. Because the Judiciary Act of 1789 provided a broad jurisdiction for the high court, many of these cases involved neither great constitutional issues nor compelling problems of statutory interpretation. Today such suits would never get beyond a local state tribunal or possibly a federal district court. Forty-five of the decisions (71 percent) appeared as issued "by the Court"—what we now call a *per curiam* order—with no attribution to an individual justice. These very brief opinions contained practically no legal analysis and often carried a

Oliver Ellsworth, chief justice, 1796–1800

notation that the decision had been unanimous. In many cases, however, the Court gave no indication of the vote and on at least one occasion indicated that a *per curiam* order had been issued by a divided Court.

Seriatim proved the next most common method, accounting for one out of four cases in the Court's first decade. Of the sixty-three reported cases in the pre-Marshall era, only fourteen presented constitutional issues, and of these the Court decided seven seriatim. Why it chose to do this is unclear. Justice Samuel Chase indicated that the justices employed the method when in disagreement, but Justice James Wilson, in another seriatim opinion, indicated that all of the members of the Court agreed on the decision. In fact, we have evidence that the members of the Court felt no compunction about disagreeing, not only in the opinions, but in debating the issues. The official report of *Hayburn's Case* declared that "the discussion was full and the Bench divided on the question. Judges Iredell, Johnson, and Blair declaring in favor of the attorney general and Judges Wilson, Cushing, and the chief justice entertaining the contrary opinion."

Chief Justice Oliver Ellsworth tried to reduce the number of seriatim opinions, following the practice of the Connecticut court on which he had served. When he could get agreement, he delivered the opinion "for the Court," whether he had written it or not, and this innovation would take on greater significance during the Marshall era. A second innovation is that even when a majority of the justices agreed and issued an opinion "for the Court," individual members might differ and enter a separate opinion. In a case titled *Sims v. Irvine* (1799), Ellsworth delivered an opinion for a majority of the Court. Justice James Iredell, unable to attend the reading of the opinion because of an "indisposition," later delivered an opinion in which he wrote, "Though I concur with the other Judges of the Court in affirming the judgment of the Circuit Court, yet as I differ from them in the reasons for affirmance, I think it proper to state my opinion particularly."

Despite Ellsworth's efforts, the Court continued to issue seriatim opinions. Just as in the King's Bench before and after Lord Mansfield, seriatim opinions created substantial uncertainty and instability in the law. *Georgia v. Brailsford* (1793) is the first case in which the Court issued a complete opinion and dealt with competing claims over money paid to the marshal of the state. Four of the justices, including Chief Justice Jay, supported an injunction staying payment by Georgia until the conflicting legal claims could be worked out. Two other justices wrote opinions against an injunction. The justices delivered their opinions beginning with the most junior justice, Thomas Johnson, who is credited with the first dissent on the high court, and then proceeding in order of reverse seniority.

These early seriatim opinions indicate several things. One, of course, is the inability of the justices to agree on and articulate clear legal rationales for their decisions. Second, the justices did not explicitly acknowledge their disagreement with one another and concluded their opinions with a procedural statement on whether the injunction should issue. In this way, the justices could openly disagree with each other without explicitly dissenting.

In another case, *Calder v. Bull* (1798), the Court considered whether a statute passed by the Connecticut legislature overturning a state court probate decision violated the Constitution's Ex Post Facto Clause. Four justices wrote opinions, not only differing among themselves, but also confusing lawyers and legislators over what the clause actually meant. As the noted scholar David Currie wrote, "*Calder* illustrates the uncertainty that can arise when each justice writes separately." The practice of seriatim opinions, he concluded, "weakened the force of the Court's decisions."

The few important decisions of the Court elicited either a negative response or in some cases outright hostility. When the Court held in *Chisholm v. Georgia* (1793) that a citizen could sue a state in federal

John Marshall, chief justice, 1801–1835

court, Congress proposed and the states quickly adopted the Eleventh Amendment shoring up state sovereign immunity from suit. Although the vote in the case was 4–1, Justice James Iredell's strong dissent might well have fueled the drive of the amendment. After Ellsworth resigned because of ill health, President John Adams asked the former chief justice John Jay to take his old seat, and Jay refused. The Court in its first ten years, Jay believed, "lacked energy, weight, and dignity" and would be unable to earn "public confidence and respect." Jay would live to see that judgment proved wrong.

ON 20 JANUARY 1801, John Adams nominated his secretary of state, John Marshall of Virginia, to succeed Ellsworth as chief justice, despite much grumbling from within his own party. Opposition came from those who wanted someone with closer political ties to Adams's chief rival in the Federalist Party, Alexander Hamilton. The Senate delayed its vote for a week, hoping the president would change his mind, but Adams held firm, and the upper chamber confirmed Marshall's nomination on 27 January. "My gift of John Marshall to the people of the United States was the proudest act of my life," Adams later declared. "I have given to my country a Judge, equal to a Hale, a Holt or a Mansfield."

That Marshall would transform the Court, and by his vision forge it into an instrument of national unity as well as a coequal branch of government, did not appear so clearly to his contemporaries. Born in

Virginia in 1755, he joined the Continental army at age nineteen and served first as a lieutenant and then as a captain in the Virginia contingent. He saw action at Brandywine, Germantown, and Stony Point and endured the harsh winter encampment at Valley Forge. After the war, he studied law briefly with George Wythe at the College of William and Mary and began a successful practice in Richmond in 1783. In addition to service in the House of Delegates, he spent three years as the recorder of the Richmond City Hustings Court, the only judicial position he held before Adams named him to the high court, and played a significant role in the debates in Virginia over ratification of the Constitution. During the Adams administration he served first as a special envoy to France and then as secretary of state.

The appointment evoked little enthusiasm among either Federalists or Republicans. Oliver Wolcott, who served as Treasury secretary under Adams, feared Marshall would "read and expound the Constitution as if it were a penal statute, and [would] sometimes be embarrassed by doubts." The Jeffersonian paper the *Aurora* characterized him as "more distinguished as a rhetorician and sophist than as a lawyer and statesman." Jefferson spoke of the "lax, lounging manner," "profound hypocrisy," and devotion to "English principles" of his distant cousin.

We are less concerned with the great decisions that helped to shape the government and expanded its power under the Constitution than with the way Marshall forged the Court into a strong institution. Marshall strengthened the judiciary by establishing its authority as the final arbiter of what the Constitution means. "It is emphatically the province and duty of the judicial department to say what the law is," he declared in *Marbury v. Madison* (1803). He achieved his goals not only by the strength of his reasoning but by the way the Court delivered its opinions.

Like Pendleton in Virginia and Mansfield in England, Marshall believed that the Court should speak through one voice. In his first reported opinion as chief justice, a case involving marine salvage rights in time of war, Marshall found a middle ground on which to decide the suit. He then encouraged his colleagues, used to writing individual opinions, to work through the complex issues involved and agree on a unanimous opinion, which they consented should be delivered by the chief. Marshall strongly believed, as have many others, that the ruling in a case should be seen by the public as the decision of a collective court rather than of the author. The unanimity of a court added to its prestige and influence. In this institutional approach, dissents can be viewed as undermining the legitimacy of the Court's voice. Dissents are the products of one or more justices who openly disagree with the majority and shatter the illusion of a unanimous tribunal speaking in one voice.

Marshall disliked dissents and worked hard to avoid them, even to the point of modifying his own opinion in order to gain approval for his opinions for the Court. In an early case, he said, "I have been convinced that I was mistaken, and I have receded from this first opinion. I acquiesce in that of my brethren." In a pseudonymous letter to a Philadelphia newspaper, he defended the practice by explaining, "The course of every tribunal must necessarily be, that the opinion which is to be delivered as the opinion of the court, is previously submitted to the consideration of all the judges; and, if any part of the reasoning be disapproved, it must be so modified as to receive the approbation of all, before it can be delivered as the opinion of all." Certainly the power and authority of the great cases during the Marshall years—*Marbury v. Madison* (1803), *Fletcher v. Peck* (1810), *McCulloch v. Maryland* (1819), and *Gibbons v. Ogden* (1824), to name but a few—are all the greater because they came from a unanimous Court.

Separate opinions were indeed rare in the early years of the Marshall Court. Between 1801 and 1806, the Court decided sixty-seven cases with opinions. The chief justice delivered sixty of these opinions, with only two opinions of the Court delivered by other justices, and in one or both of these cases Marshall did not participate. (That Marshall delivered the opinion does not prove that he wrote it, and there is evidence that in some cases he did not even agree with the results. To him, however, institutional solidarity was more important than individual expression; in his thirty-four years on the bench, Marshall dissented only seven times.) The Court decided only five cases with seriatim opinions, and in each instance the reporter of the Court noted that Marshall had either been absent or recused himself. By 1808, the justices practically abandoned seriatim opinions, even in Marshall's absence. By 1814, the practice of one justice—be it the chief or an associate justice—delivering an opinion for the entire Court had been established.

Marshall must be given great credit for this development but not, as some have suggested, because he imposed his will on the other justices in an "act of audacity" and "assumption of power." Looking at the statistics, one might well assume that he achieved his goals through a *force majeure*. In the thirty-four years he occupied the center chair, he delivered 519 of the 1,100 majority opinions, including 36 of the 62 opinions in cases involving constitutional questions. Then as now, the people who go onto the Supreme Court are with few exceptions strong-willed and intelligent and not easily cowed by a chief with a strong personality.

Rather, Marshall convinced his brethren that the prestige of the Court would be enhanced if it spoke in one voice, and he worked cooperatively with them to achieve this goal. At the time, the justices only came to Washington for the terms, and they all lived together in the same rooming house and took their meals together. This not only forged collegial relations but gave them extensive time to discuss cases and to absorb Marshall's rationale as to why the Court needed to speak in one voice.

But while initially rare, there were some dissents and concurrences. Samuel Chase, who had written many opinions in the 1790s, issued a one-sentence concurrence in an 1804 insurance case. Justice Bushrod Washington, who almost always voted with Marshall, issued the Marshall Court's first recorded dissent the following year and felt compelled to explain that "in any instance where I am so unfortunate as to differ with this court, I cannot fail to doubt the correctness of my own opinion. But if I cannot feel convinced of the error, I owe it in some measure to myself and to those who may be injured by the expense and delay to which they have been exposed to shew at least that the opinion was not hastily or inconsiderately given." When Justice William Johnson dissented in an 1807 case, he began by declaring, "I have the misfortune to dissent from the majority of my brethren."

During Marshall's tenure as chief justice from 1801 to 1835, of 1,187 opinions, only 87 had either dissenting or concurring opinions (around 7 percent, the lowest rate of any period in the Court's history). From 1808 to 1816, the number of separate opinions increased slightly, although the rate of unanimity remained high. Why this flurry occurred is difficult to know. While occasionally a justice might explain why he felt it necessary to write separately, most times he did not. The appointment of three justices by Thomas Jefferson and two by James Madison brought new and supposedly Republican jurists onto the Court, and William Johnson alone accounted for half of the dissenting opinions. But most of the time, the Jeffersonian appointees, including Johnson himself, signed on to Marshall's philosophy of unanimity, and one of them, Joseph Story, became Marshall's jurisprudential right hand.

THOMAS JEFFERSON had not liked the idea of a single "opinion of the court" when Edmund Pendleton had advocated it on the Virginia high court in the 1770s, and he liked it even less when John Marshall managed to get his brethren to adopt the model during Jefferson's presidency. Jefferson loathed his distant cousin, and Marshall reciprocated these views. But the differences between the two went much further and have been part of the ongoing debate over the future of the United

Thomas Jefferson, third president of the United States

States and how it would be governed under the Constitution. Jefferson, the great apostle of revolution and civil liberties, never overcame his dread of centralized government. Marshall, on the other hand, never overcame the revulsion that he and others, such as his idol, George Washington, felt at what they considered the near breakdown of government in the mid-1780s. The debate, at its core, asked what kind of nation we should be.

Central in their debate was the role of the judiciary in a constitutional government. Jefferson openly declared, "The great object of my fear is the federal judiciary. . . . Let the eye of vigilance never be closed [against it]." Marshall, in decrying what he perceived as Jefferson's demagoguery, noted that the president "looks, of course, with ill will at an independent judiciary." The election of 1800 had placed the presidency and Congress in the control of the Jeffersonian Republicans, and only the court system remained under the control of the Federalists. In *Marbury v. Madison* (1803), the Court announced that it not only had the power to declare acts of Congress unconstitutional but that it stood as the chief interpreter of what the Constitution meant. Jefferson strongly disagreed, and as he later said, "To consider the judges as the ultimate arbiters of all constitutional questions [is] a very dangerous doctrine indeed, and one which would place us under the despotism of an oligarchy." As president, he feared that the Marshall Court would disembowel his program and thus thwart the will of the people's elected representatives. Because, as he put it, "few died and none retired," he set out on an ill-conceived plan to remove some of the Federalist justices by impeachment, but this proved too much for some of the moderate members of his own party who valued the ideal of an independent judiciary.

Nothing irked Jefferson more, however, than Marshall's success in forging the Court into a powerful instrument through the practice of speaking in one voice. "An opinion is huddled up in conclave," Jefferson charged, "perhaps by a majority of one, delivered as if unanimous, and with the silent acquiescence of lazy or timid associates, by a crafty chief judge, who sophisticates the law to his own mind, by the turn of his own reasoning."

Other associates of Jefferson's also shared this view. After Marshall's opinion in *McCulloch v. Maryland* (1819), with its expansive view of federal power, James Madison wrote to a friend, "I could have wished that the Judges had delivered their opinions seriatim. The case was of such magnitude, in the scope given to it, as to call, if any case could do so, for the views of the subject separately taken by them. This might either by the harmony of their reasoning have produced a greater conviction in the Public mind; or by its discordance have impaired the force of the precedent now ostensibly supported by a unanimous & perfect concurrence in every argument & dictum in the judgment pronounced."

The sage of Monticello showed even greater annoyance at the fact that Marshall had seemingly won over the Jeffersonians whom he and Madison had named to the bench. This annoyance burst out in a series of letters he exchanged in 1822 and 1823 with his first appointment to the high court, William Johnson. It is also an important dialogue on the value of seriatim as opposed to a single opinion.

Johnson has been described as the "first dissenter," but he was far more than a habitual contrarian. Louis Brandeis spoke of Johnson as one of the outstanding minds of the early Court, and Jefferson and his cohorts hoped Johnson would begin a process of changing the Court from a "subtle corps of sappers and miners constantly working under ground to undermine the foundations of our federated fabric" to one composed of Republicans "of sufficient talent to be useful." Johnson seemed a perfect nominee, a southerner who had been a state judge, a respected lawyer of irreproachable character, and a reliable member of Jefferson's party.

Once on the bench, however, Johnson had little impact on the Court's delivery practices. He induced the Court to abandon having the chief justice speak alone for the Court and instead rotate among the justices the delivery of the Court's opinions. He wrote an occasional important opinion, such as the one holding that there is no federal common-law criminal jurisdiction. Johnson earned his title as a dissenter primarily because he would on occasion disagree with his colleagues and enter a separate opinion. He is little remembered today because none of his separate opinions—with one exception—had any lasting influence, but historians who have examined his career have come away with an overwhelmingly favorable opinion and praise his industry, his learning, and his integrity.

The one exception came not in a dissent but in a concurring opinion in the otherwise unanimous decision in the "Steamboat Case"—*Gibbons v. Ogden* (1824). In that case, Chief Justice Marshall ruled that New York could not grant a monopoly to a steamboat line plying the waters of the bay between New York City and New Jersey. In one of his most popular opinions, Marshall set down a broad interpretation of the Commerce Clause, holding that where Congress had acted, as it had in this case to regulate some aspect of interstate commerce, the states could not enact their own regulations. Marshall left silent the question of whether states could regulate those features of interstate commerce touching upon their interests when Congress had not spoken. Implicit in his opinion is the idea of concurrent powers; that is, the states and the federal government shared sovereignty in certain areas, an idea that would have important ramifications later in the debate over states' rights.

Historians believe Marshall remained quiet on this point in order to assure slave states they could regulate free blacks and slaves within their borders. There had been a recent controversy in South Carolina, which had incarcerated a free black sailor when his ship docked in Charleston. Johnson, however, had just written a bitter circuit court opinion denouncing South Carolina's action, and in *Gibbons* he took a stronger position than Marshall about the supremacy of the federal commerce power. In his concurrence, he also accepted a broad interpretation of commerce and believed that congressional power was plenary, so that even when Congress had not spoken, states could not act. This argument is the first seed of what would later be called the "dormant commerce clause," a doctrine that has fascinated and befuddled students, law teachers, and judges ever since.

By and large, however, Johnson aligned himself with Chief Justice Marshall on the major constitutional decisions that laid the basis for a strong national government. As Mark Killenbeck has written, the most striking thing about Johnson's tenure is not what he wrote, either for the Court or in dissent, but what he did not say as the Court issued one opinion after another that Jefferson claimed made "the constitution . . . a mere thing of wax in the hands of the judiciary, which they may twist, and shape in any form they please." He joined with Marshall in *McCulloch v. Maryland* (1819) and *Cohens v. Virginia* (1821), both of which Jefferson and his states' rights allies condemned as repudiating the principles of the revolution of 1800, the election in which the Republicans had turned the Federalists out of office. Even when Johnson wrote, he often expressed himself at odds with the man who had appointed him. In an 1821 case, he took the notion of constitutionally implied powers even further than John Marshall had done in *McCulloch*. This was certainly not the voice of sound Republicanism that Jefferson had hoped would restrain John Marshall.

Jefferson had enough respect for the separation of powers that he would not have just written to Johnson castigating him for his "failures." The chance came, however, in the spring of 1822 when Johnson sent the retired president a copy of his two-volume *Sketches of the Life and Correspondence of Nathanael Greene.* A native of Rhode Island, Greene had been an early volunteer in the Revolutionary War and had risen through the ranks, eventually becoming one of George Washington's most trusted advisers. Jefferson clearly perused it and came across sentiments he found most welcome. The historical record, Johnson maintained, proved that the Federalists, while in power, had tried to exercise power not delegated by the Constitution. The distinguishing characteristics of the Republican Party were more popular and general than to be merely labeled protection of states' rights against national power, because "State rights, or United States' rights are nothing, except as they contribute to the safety and happiness of the people." Both parties had their faults, but between the Federalist Scylla and the Republican Charybdis, he would choose the latter.

Finally, Jefferson thought, Johnson was saying what he should have been arguing in the Court for the past eighteen years. After complimenting Johnson on the book, Jefferson got down to his real business—another attack on John Marshall. The subject of his uneasiness, he declared, "is the habitual mode of making up and delivering the opinions of the supreme court of the US." It would be far better if each member of the Court delivered his views seriatim, an approach, the ex-president declared, that "shewed whether the judges were unanimous or divided, and gave accordingly more or less weight to the judgment as precedent." That had been the practice before Marshall became chief justice, and it made the only possible controls on the Court—impeachment and individual reputation—meaningful, because a system in which all the justices spoke would force them to "reveal the reasons and authorities which governed their decisions" and would expose "the lazy, the modest & the incompetent." Jefferson concluded the letter with an attack on Federalists who now called themselves Republicans but took the name without the principles. While they might have abandoned the goal of a monarchy, they still sought a consolidated national government, and they did this through a judiciary that interpreted the Constitution in a way to elevate national over state authority.

Johnson responded that he had been surprised when he had arrived at the Court to "find our Chief Justice delivering all the Opinions in cases in which he sat, even in some instances when contrary to his own Judgment and vote." His experience on the South Carolina court had been just the opposite, but when he spoke to Marshall, "I remonstrated in vain; the Answer was, he is willing to take the Trouble, & it is a Mark of Respect to him. I soon however found the real cause. Cushing was incompetent, Chase could not be got to think or write—Patterson was a slow man & willingly declined the trouble, & the other two judges [Marshall and Bushrod Washington] you know are commonly estimated as one judge."

While there are some grains of truth in this statement—Cushing was old and in failing health—as the first Jeffersonian on the bench, the irascible Johnson might not have felt comfortable, especially when he complained about the Court speaking in one voice.

Some cases soon occurred in which I differed from my Brethren, & I thought it a thing of course to deliver my own Opinion. But during the rest of the Session I heard nothing but lectures on the Indecency of Judges cutting at each other, and the loss of Reputation which the Virginia appellate court had sustained by pursuing such a course etc. At length I found that I must either submit to circumstances or become such a cipher in our Consultations as to effect no good at all. I therefore bent to the current, and persevered until I got them to adopt the course they now pursue, which is to appoint someone to deliver the Opinion of the Majority, but leave it to the discretion of the rest of the Judges to record their opinions or not ad libitum.

There is a break in the correspondence, and Jefferson does not pick it up again until March 1823, when he once again urges Johnson to work at restoring seriatim opinions, "for in truth there is no danger I apprehend so much as the consolidation of our government by the noiseless, and therefore unalarming, instrumentality of the supreme court." Marshall had to be stopped from "cooking up opinions in conclave." Let every man speak up and "use his own judgment independently. . . . Throw himself in every case on God and his country, both will excuse him for error and value him for honesty."

When Johnson replied, he promised to work to reinstate seriatim opinions by the Court "on all subjects of general Interest, particularly constitutional questions. On minor subjects it is of little public Importance." He then defended himself and his votes on the Court; moreover, because he had always been with Marshall in all of the important constitutional cases, he challenged the former president to tell him in which cases the Court had erred.

Jefferson initially said that he could not undertake Johnson's request— "I am unable"—and then proceeded to do so, lambasting every major Marshall Court opinion from *Marbury* in 1803 to *Cohens v. Virginia* in 1821. The doctrines in all of these cases—and Johnson had not dissented in any of these decisions after he went on the bench—"betray the genuine monarchism of their principles." Jefferson continued his rant, claiming that the remedy for Marshall's alleged tyrannical leanings would be a return to the first principles, seriatim opinions where each judge would speak his own piece.

Jefferson's hatred of John Marshall, and his fear of the courts dominating the entire government, make his side of the exchange appear foolish, perhaps even paranoid. By 1823, the Jeffersonian Republicans had controlled the White House and Congress for more than two decades, and after a brief resurgence during the War of 1812 the Federalist Party disappeared. Of the appointments made by the two Federalist presidents, George Washington and John Adams, only Bushrod Washington and John Marshall still sat on the high court. If there had truly been a conflict between monarchists and republicans, the latter had been in the majority since 1811 and could easily have outvoted Marshall.

The fact is that the men named by Jefferson and Madison did not see John Marshall as the devil, nor did they disagree with his views on constitutional interpretation. They all believed, some more than others, that the Framers had intended the national government to be strong enough to overcome the difficulties that had plagued the Confederacy, and while states' rights had to be respected, they could not undermine the clear grants of powers that the Constitution had given to Congress.

They also understood that given the tripartite nature of the federal government, the courts—the "least dangerous branch"—had to exert their authority in order to carry out the obligations of Article III. Marshall's strategy—that a court that spoke with one voice carried greater influence than one that spoke with many—proved correct for the times. Nearly all of the great cases that are still studied in law schools today, and, even more important, still cited by courts, were handed down without dissent—*Marbury v. Madison, McCulloch v. Maryland, Cohens v. Virginia,* and *Gibbons v. Ogden,* to name a few.

Johnson did have an influence in that he got the chief justice to agree that voices other than his could deliver the Court's opinion, and while his separate opinions with the exception of the Steamboat Case did not instruct his successors, Johnson did make dissenting acceptable. After Marshall died in 1835, the Court would never again speak in as unified a fashion as it had during his tenure, but none of the chiefs who followed him would need to confront the question of the Court's proper role in American government.

CHAPTER 3

FROM MARSHALL TO *DRED SCOTT*

It has, I find, been the uniform practice in this Court, for the justices who
differed from the Court on constitutional questions, to express their dissent. In
conformity to this usage, I proceed to state briefly the principle on which I differ.

— ROGER BROOKE TANEY (1838)

T he edifice that John Marshall built, in which the Supreme
Court stood as an equal branch of government, has remained
solid until this day. The tool of a unanimous opinion of the
Court, however, began to weaken in his last years. Every chief justice
since has aspired to have the Court speak in a single voice, but no Court
since Marshall's has been as unified. The Marshall Court had a nonunanimous rate of just over 7 percent; the rate doubled during the tenure
of his successor, Roger B. Taney, to more than 15 percent.

There are a number of reasons for this. The political evolution of the
country, from Federalist to Jeffersonian Republican to Democratic, put
men on the bench who had views far different not only from Marshall
but from each other as well. The economic growth of the nation brought
Commerce Clause issues to the high court that did not fit easily into
the assumptions of the founding generation and that had no clearly discernible solutions. The malignancy of slavery, which grew slowly but

steadily in these years, burst out into public debate, and the Court split over it as did the country. By the time Andrew Jackson nominated Taney to succeed Marshall, the idea of separate opinions had gained legitimacy.

WHILE THE FEDERALISTS were nowhere near as monarchical as Jefferson charged, they as well as the Jeffersonians believed in government of the well-to-do. Jefferson often spoke of the aristocracy of talent, but he and his handpicked successors, James Madison and James Monroe, came from landed Virginia gentry. All three believed, as did the Federalists, that government should be staffed and managed by the upper classes. In the 1820s, however, a groundswell of reforms swept the country, including the abolition of property qualifications for voting. Andrew Jackson capitalized on this movement, and his Democratic Party, while nominally a successor to the Jeffersonians, had a much different view on the nature of government and who should be part of it. The business of government, Jackson believed, was so simple that any man could do it.

At the same time, the United States began shifting from an agrarian to a more mercantile society, and as historians have often said, Jackson stood for the "man on the make," the new entrepreneur who would seek his fortune through business endeavors rather than from the land. Government should do nothing that would impose restrictions on one group or give benefits to another. These developments led to a major shift not only in American politics but in law and constitutional thought as well.

Congress expanded the high court from seven to nine justices in 1837, and before he left office, Andrew Jackson had appointed five men to the Supreme Court. Roger Brooke Taney is today remembered primarily for his decision in the *Dred Scott* case, for which, as Senator Charles Sumner declared, "the name of Taney is to be hooted down the page of history." Legal historians, however, have in recent years rejected this view. While Taney is still condemned for his pro-slavery opinions and his opposition to Lincoln during the Civil War, in other areas he is acknowledged for finding creative legal solutions to questions about banking, commerce, and transportation. In some cases, he spoke as forcefully as his predecessor to uphold the power of the Court.

Taney came from a well-connected Maryland family that made its fortune in land, slaves, and tobacco. Initially a Federalist, Taney broke with the party when it failed to support the War of 1812 with England. After serving in the state legislature, he moved his law practice to Baltimore but continued to be politically active and was elected Maryland attorney general in 1827. He became a staunch supporter of Andrew

Roger Brooke Taney, chief justice, 1836–1864

Jackson; in 1831, the president named him attorney general and then in 1833 acting secretary of the Treasury. Taney became one of Jackson's closest advisers, helping map the strategy to kill off the Bank of the United States and backing Jackson in the nullification crisis with South Carolina. In that confrontation, Taney showed himself as strong a proponent of federal power as had John Marshall, but in matters of slavery and the rights of free blacks he deferred to state authorities. He argued that under neither the Commerce Clause nor the treaty power could the national government regulate slavery and race relations in the states.

Because of his role in the bank controversy, the Senate refused to confirm Taney when Jackson nominated him in early 1835 to replace the retiring justice Gabriel Duvall. When John Marshall died in July 1835, Jackson nominated Taney to succeed him. By the following spring, Jackson's supporters controlled the Senate and in March 1836 confirmed both Taney as chief justice and Philip P. Barbour to take Duvall's seat.

Taney took his oath on 28 March 1836, and by then the idea of a dissenting or concurring opinion had gained full legitimacy. The Taney-era justices also accepted their predecessors' reasoning on what types of cases justified dissent. As would be expected, these would be the important cases, the ones involving constitutional questions. Justice Story noted that "upon constitutional questions I ever thought it my duty to give a public expression of my opinions, when they differed from that of the Court." During the twenty-eight years that Taney headed the Court, it heard a little over one hundred cases involving constitutional questions, and there were separate opinions in 44 percent of them, two and a half times as high as in nonconstitutional cases. At that time, the Court had to take many minor cases; in most of those, the justices merely noted their disagreement but did not enter an opinion explaining why.

WHEN MARSHALL DIED IN 1835, he was the last officeholder appointed by the Federalists. Of his colleagues on the bench, only Joseph Story—who would serve until 1845—shared his nationalistic view of the Constitution and the protections it provided for property. A good example of how alienated Story felt from the new regime can be seen in three cases decided in the Taney Court's first full term in 1837. All three had been held over from Marshall's day, and in each of them the Taney Court distanced itself dramatically from what Story believed to be correct doctrine. Story partook in what can be termed a dialogue with the past, an appeal to precedent—prior decisions—which he believed had been correctly decided, and in essence asked the sages of the earlier Court to correct his misguided colleagues.

In *Mayor of New York v. Miln,* the Court upheld the constitutionality of a state law requiring the masters of ships arriving in the port of New York from outside the state to register all passengers and post bond that none would become a ward of the city. This was the first Commerce Clause case to come to the Taney Court, and if the justices had followed the Marshall Court precedents, the decision would have been relatively simple. In *Gibbons v. Ogden* (1824), one of Marshall's most popular opinions, the Court had held that the transportation of people was a form of commerce that came under the jurisdiction of Congress. By that ruling, the New York statute clearly burdened interstate commerce.

Miln, however, was not really about the New York law at all. By 1837, most of the slave states had prohibited the in-migration of free blacks. Starting in 1822, South Carolina and other southern coastal states had enacted laws requiring the temporary incarceration of free black sailors who entered their ports as crew members of visiting ships. If the Court found the New York statute unconstitutional, it would have to address the issue of southern regulation of free blacks entering the slave states.

The majority opinion by Philip Barbour ignored Marshall Court opinions on the scope of the commerce power and instead treated the New York law as a police regulation. Barbour, a Virginia native, declared that the states' police powers over "safety, happiness, and prosperity" were "complete, unqualified, and exclusive." Dissenting by himself, Story argued that the law interfered with congressional power over interstate commerce and concluded by remarking that he had the consolation of knowing that it had been Marshall's "deliberate opinion" that the law was unconstitutional.

In the second case of this trilogy, *Briscoe v. Bank of the Commonwealth of Kentucky,* the Court dealt with the question of whether a state could establish a bank and authorize it to issue notes that would be circulated as legal tender. When Marshall and Story had first heard the case in 1834, they had concluded that under the 1830 decision of *Craig v. Missouri* the notes were clearly unconstitutional. But between *Craig* and *Briscoe,* Andrew Jackson (with the help of his attorney general, Roger Taney) had attacked and destroyed the Bank of the United States, leaving the country without any congressionally approved form of legal tender.

The Jacksonian justices brushed *Craig* aside, and Justice John McLean's opinion described the states' power to charter banks and to define their powers as subject to "no limitation in the federal constitution." Both McLean and Story—again the lone dissenter—saw the central issue as the future of banking and currency policy in the country. After the Jacksonians had killed the Bank of the United States, and with it the nation's currency system, state banks such as the one in Kentucky offered a local, state-centered solution. Had Story, who in a long dissent argued against the constitutionality of the state currency, prevailed, state banks would have been barred from issuing notes that passed for currency, and the administration might have been forced to recharter a national bank. Jackson's appointees on the Court, however, shared his aversion to national banks. Once again Story ended his dissent by appealing to the spirit of his former chief. "Mr. Chief Justice Marshall is not here to speak for himself," but if he were, he would also find the Kentucky scheme unconstitutional.

Chief Justice Taney wrote his first major opinion in *Charles River Bridge v. Warren Bridge,* the third important case of that term. It is considered by many scholars a demarcation point between the older notion of vested property rights and the inviolability of charters and the new demands upon states to respond to the technological and economic realities of the early nineteenth century.

In 1785, Massachusetts had issued a charter to the Charles River Bridge Company to build a bridge linking Boston and Charlestown and to collect tolls as compensation for the erection and maintenance of the structure. In 1828, while the first charter was still in effect, the state authorized a second bridge only a few hundred feet away. The Warren Bridge Company would also collect tolls, but the new construction would be turned over to the state as a free bridge after the company had recovered its costs plus interest on its investment. Consumers clearly preferred a free passage, and revenues declined for the Charles River Bridge Company, which sued, claiming that the new charter violated the Constitution's Contract Clause.

Taney asserted that the older charter had to be read strictly, and it did not give the owners a monopoly. The interests of society outweighed the implied rights of the investors, and any other reading of the charter would be a disaster for new technologies. An implied monopoly would jeopardize the "millions of property, which have been invested in railroads and canals. . . . We shall be thrown back to the improvements of the last century." The older private road and turnpike companies would claim an implied monopoly in their charters and demand compensation from the railroads and canals that paralleled their routes.

While Story recognized the desirability of encouraging economic development, he thought Taney's opinion not only bad law but bad economics as well. In a fifty-seven-page dissent joined by Smith Thompson (a Monroe appointee) and approved in substance by John McLean, Story summoned case law running back to the Middle Ages to bolster his argument that the new charter was an unconscionable invasion of a recognized property right. Contrary to Taney's view, Story held that new investment would be impeded by unsettling what had been reasonable investor expectations.

Story's opinion in the bridge case might, in other circumstances, be seen as an early effort to write the type of dissent that fosters future constitutional dialogue. It pointed out why he thought the majority opinion wrong in terms of both law and public policy implications and then constructed the legal and economic arguments that would persuade future justices to undo Taney's damage. Although Story's friend the great New York jurist James Kent wrote to him that Taney's opinion "over-throws a great Principle of constitutional Morality," in fact the majority understood that changing times demanded a reconsideration of older ideas. The legal historian Morton Horwitz has argued that judges in the early part of the nineteenth century used the law to advance the commercial interests of the country. In doing so, they abandoned the

older Blackstonian concept of a common law derived from immutable principles of natural law and in its place adopted what Horwitz
terms an "instrumental" conception of law. Where eighteenth-century
judges—and John Marshall and Joseph Story surely belong in this
category—saw their task as discovering essentially changeless general
rules, American judges now sought to pragmatically determine what
best served the public interest in a society characterized by ceaseless
change.

The bridge case spoke not just to the situation in Boston but to similar and potential conflicts in other areas as well. Fulton's demonstration
of steam power had ushered in a new era for water transportation, and in
1826 George Stephenson's development of the steam locomotive opened
new vistas for land travel. In 1828, a group of Baltimore businessmen,
angry at the high rates charged by the canal monopolies, petitioned
the legislature for a charter to build the Baltimore & Ohio Railroad.
Investors who had sunk millions into canals did not view kindly the
implication that a new technology—the railroad—would render their
enterprises obsolete and worthless. Had the Court decided the bridge
case differently, it would have had far-reaching and negative implications for the development of American transportation.

Although Story found himself more and more out of tune with
the Jacksonian appointees, he wrote one dissent that is worth noting,
because it illustrates another part of the dialogue—that between the
Court and Congress.

At the time, when a collector of customs imposed a duty on imports,
if the importer believed that the tax had been erroneous, he could seek
court review of the matter by suing the collector at common law. When
this happened, the collector withheld the amount of the duties that the
court might compel him to repay instead of forwarding it to the Treasury. Some collectors, however, defaulted and did not account for the
money they accumulated to repay importers. To prevent this, Congress
passed a rider to an appropriation bill compelling the collectors to pass
on the money to the Treasury as soon as collected.

In *Cary v. Curtis* (1845), the majority opinion by Justice Peter V.
Daniel held that because the rider required the collectors to pass on the
money immediately, Congress had essentially abolished the importers'
common-law remedy to sue if a mistake had been made. Story and John
McLean dissented, and Story began with the usual apologia—"I regret
exceedingly being compelled by a sense of duty to express openly my
dissent from the opinion of the majority"—and then went on to argue
that it could not have been the intention of Congress to do away with the

common-law remedy for importers. The purpose of the rider had been to prevent misappropriations of money, not to change a long-established practice. In effect, Story believed the Court had misinterpreted the statute. Because this was not a constitutional question in which the Court had the last word but a matter of statutory interpretation, Congress could correct the Court's error by passing further legislation that would clarify its intent.

The decision came down on 21 January 1845. Thirty-six days later, Congress passed and President John Tyler signed the Declaratory Act of 1845, which made plain that it had never been the congressional intention to "take away, or be construed to take away, or impair, the right of any person or persons . . . to maintain an action at law against a collector." The case is not widely studied anymore, but it played an important role in later decisions involving the collection of customs duties. Story not only explained why he thought the majority mistaken ("Congress never had contemplated . . . ") but went on to invite Congress to either verify that in fact it had been its intention, by doing nothing, or correct the majority's error by enacting a clearly written expression of what it did mean.

Over the course of more than two centuries, legislative meaning has not always been expressed well, and there have been a number of cases where the justices have asked Congress to clarify its intent.

SHORTLY AFTER TANEY took his seat, a new rationale began to appear in the dissenting opinions. Prior to about 1839, dissenting justices who chose to write separately almost always explained their motivation in terms of the issue involved. For example, Justice Story in an 1830 case wrote, "I trust that the deep interest of the questions, and the novelty of the aspect under which some of them are presented, will furnish an apology for my occupying so much time." But around 1841, justices started expressing another set of justifications, frequently noting that even if they did not disagree with the results, they did not wish to be individually associated with the majority's opinion. Quite often we see this in cases involving slavery, such as *Groves v. Slaughter* (1841) and *Prigg v. Pennsylvania* (1842).

The Mississippi Constitution of 1832 prohibited the importation of slaves into the state "as merchandise, or for sale." The purpose was not to limit slavery in the state but to prevent an outflow of capital to other states. Migrants to Mississippi could bring in slaves with them, but slave traders could not bring human chattels in for the purpose of selling them. In 1836, Moses Groves, a Mississippi planter, purchased slaves from Robert Slaughter of Louisiana, giving him a note for $7,000. When the note came due, Groves refused to honor it, claiming that the sale of the slaves in Mississippi violated the state constitution. Slaughter sued and won in Louisiana federal court, and Groves appealed to the Supreme Court. The case involved far more than the single note; some $3 million was at stake because of the numerous slaves sold to planters in Mississippi.

In a straightforward opinion for the majority, Justice Smith Thompson ruled that the Mississippi constitutional provision did not go into force until 1837, when the state passed enabling legislation. The contract for the sale of slaves in 1836 was therefore valid and obligated Groves to pay Slaughter. Three justices entered concurring opinions because in their view Thompson had avoided the central constitutional question: Did Mississippi's ban on slaves as merchandise violate the federal Commerce Clause?

Justice McLean, while concurring in part in the result, nonetheless insisted on addressing this question. Congress, he declared, could regulate all interstate commerce, but slaves were not "merchandise" but "persons," and as such the states were free to prohibit the introduction of slaves into their domains. The antislavery McLean noted that his home state of Ohio could ban neither the cotton of the South nor the manufactured articles of the North, but it could keep out slaves. McLean went on to note that "the right to [exclude slavery] by a state is higher and deeper than the Constitution." Although here McLean's arguments about state powers dovetailed with those of the slave states, his argument implicitly indicated that Congress might have the power to regulate or even ban the interstate slave trade.

This Chief Justice Taney could not accept. In his concurrence, he noted that he had originally not intended to write separately, but now that Justice McLean had stated his opinion, he was "not willing, by remaining silent, to leave any doubt as to [his own beliefs]." Congress, he declared, had absolutely no power over slavery, a matter reserved solely to the discretion of the states. Justice Henry Baldwin expressed regret that McLean had raised an unnecessary matter, but now that he had, "I am not willing to remain silent, lest it may be inferred that my opinion coincides with that of the judges who have now expressed theirs." He then went on to push the envelope even further, claiming that the free states could not exclude owners traveling with their slaves, an issue totally irrelevant to the case. Congress, Baldwin implied, might be able to regulate the interstate movement of slaves, but only to protect slavery.

The following year saw another slavery case with seven of the nine justices writing separately. Although the Court decided *Prigg v. Pennsylvania* by an 8–1 majority, Justice Story's opinion for the Court seemed to imply that state officials could not be required to aid in the capture and return of runaway slaves, and this brought a concurrence from Chief Justice Taney arguing that all state officials had to help enforce the Fugitive Slave Law. Justices Thompson, Baldwin, James Wayne, and Daniel also chimed in with concurrences, each trying to explain what Story's argument meant or did not mean. Justice McLean, in dissent, explicitly argued that states had a right and a duty to protect their free black citizens from kidnapping and declared that the majority opinion threatened the liberty of all free blacks in the United States.

This rationale for writing separately appeared more and more frequently during the next two decades, and not just in the slavery cases. In 1853, Justice John Catron noted that he did not wish to express an opinion "further than to guard myself against being committed in any degree to the [majority] doctrine." In an admiralty case, Justice Daniel even declined to adumbrate his reasons for dissenting; he had made these clear earlier, and "my purpose is simply to maintain my own consistency." "I cannot consent by my silence," declared Justice Robert Grier in 1861, "that an inference should be drawn that I concur in the opinion just delivered."

Marshall-era justices explained their dissents only by reference to the issue involved in the specific case. Taney-era justices discussed the issues, of course, but, according to one scholar, seemed to be far more concerned about their individual judicial reputations. Supporting this contention is the increase in the number of dissents and concurrences without opinion; in Marshall's thirty-four years, there were only 41 such occurrences, while in the twenty-eight years of Taney's tenure there were 389. The dissent or concurrence without opinion served no purpose other than to indicate that the justice did not wish to be identified with the majority ruling. There was no effort to prove the majority in error or to appeal to future courts to take a different road. The institutional unity that Marshall had fostered was changing into an emphasis on the individual justices and their views.

There also appears to have been a breakdown in civility. When justices in the Marshall era dissented, they almost always "apologized" for not being able to go with the majority, and while pointing out errors in legal reasoning, they never showed disdain for their colleagues. Observe, however, how Justice Grier began his separate opinion in an 1860 case: "I wholly dissent from the opinion of the majority of the court in this

LIBRARY OF CONGRESS

Dred Scott

case, both as to the law and the facts. But I do not think it necessary to vindicate my opinion by again presenting to the public view a history of the scandalous gossip which has been buried under the dust of half a century, and which a proper feeling of delicacy should have suffered to remain so."

Justice Daniel dissented, as he put it, "chiefly to free myself on any future occasion from the trammels of an assent, either expressed or implied, to what are deemed by me the untenable, and, in this case, the irrelevant positions [of the majority]."

This notion of the Court as a collection of individuals rather than as a cohesive unit would have important implications later. Strong chief justices managed to impose some coherence on the vote, and until the early 1940s the number of cases with separate opinions never rose above one in six. What happened starting in the 1940s will be examined later.

THE FACTS OF *Dred Scott v. Sandford* (1857) are well-known and need only a brief review. Scott, a slave in Missouri, had spent some time with his former master in the Wisconsin Territory, where slavery was forbidden. Under the law at the time, a slave taken into free territory became free, and "once free, always free." Scott, for some reason, chose not to pursue his freedom until much later, and by then the agitation over slavery and the ill feeling it generated led the Missouri Supreme Court to abandon its own precedent upholding the "once free, always free" doctrine and hold that Scott was still a slave.

The basic question confronting the Supreme Court was fairly simple: Could a slave sue in federal court? A majority of the justices agreed that a slave was not a citizen of the United States and therefore did not have the requisite status to be part of a suit in federal court. Had the Court issued just that ruling alone, it would have upset abolitionists in the North, but it would not have made more than a tiny ripple in American law and politics.

In fact, the Court records indicate that a majority of the justices had agreed to a compromise. Samuel Nelson would write a short opinion rejecting Scott's claim on the very narrow ground that the Court, as a matter of comity, would follow the decision of the state court. Two justices, McLean and Curtis, disagreed and declared they would write dissents, and the compromise fell apart.

Chief Justice Taney was not unhappy about this, because he believed it possible to impose a judicial solution on a political problem, a course that was urged upon him by the recently elected president of the United States, James Buchanan. The new president hoped that a ruling from the high court would put an end to all the turmoil over slavery and spare his administration the need to deal with the issue. Taney tried to oblige, and no other case, with the possible exception of *Roe v. Wade* (1973), has ever called down such opprobrium upon the Court.

Since 1857, many commentators have argued that if ever a case required judicial restraint and a carefully crafted narrow opinion, this one cried out for it. Although the Court tried to frame the questions in legal and constitutional form, the antagonism between North and South, between the abolitionists and the advocates of slavery, and the question of who would decide whether there would be slavery in the new states carved out of the western territories made it impossible for any but the most limited of decisions to avoid causing a political ruckus.

On 6 March 1857—two days after Buchanan had taken the oath of office—Taney handed down the decision of the Court, although it was in fact seriatim, with each of his colleagues writing separately. Justice James Wayne, noting all of the opinions, opined that it would be a cause of regret that not all the members of the Court supported the decision, "if I did not know from its history and my own experience how rarely it has happened that the judges have been unanimous upon constitutional questions of moment." Of course, nearly all of the constitutional decisions in the Marshall era had been unanimous, but none of them had dealt with such a contentious issue.

Newspaper sheet with Dred Scott and his family

Although Taney's opinion is usually considered that of the Court—mainly because the chief justice said it was—as in all seriatim decisions, one has to count heads on each of the major issues. From this cacophony, we can conclude that seven of the justices agreed that Scott was still a slave, six that blacks could not be citizens of the United States, and either five or six held the Missouri Compromise—which had made all territories north of Missouri free—unconstitutional. Taney's opinion is one of the worst he ever wrote. He ignored precedent, distorted history, imposed a static construction on the Constitution, disregarded specific grants of power to the federal government in the

Newspaper article, "Dred Scott Decision"

document, repeated himself, and tortured meanings out of some of the more obscure constitutional clauses. As the legal scholar David Currie has noted, the decision has been widely lamented as bad policy and bad judicial politics, but it was also very bad law.

Taney's logic on the citizenship issues can only be described as convoluted. He admitted that blacks could be citizens of a particular state, and they might even be able to vote, as they did in some northern states. State citizenship, however, had nothing to do with national citizenship, and because black people could never be citizens of the United States, they could not sue in federal court. He therefore dismissed Scott's suit for lack of federal jurisdiction. Had he stopped there, much of the public outcry would have been muted, and Taney could have been accused of no more than faulty reasoning.

But Taney believed the Court should settle the political questions surrounding slavery once and for all and, in doing so, cement the South's claim that the Constitution protected slavery everywhere in the Union. Congress would have no power to limit the "peculiar institution," even in territories under federal control. He therefore went on to declare the Missouri Compromise of 1820 unconstitutional, the first time the Court had struck down a federal law since *Marbury v. Madison* more than a half century earlier. The decision not only destroyed the keystone of the constitutional settlement that had lasted nearly four decades but also cut the ground out from Stephen Douglas's proposal for "popular sovereignty," by which the people in a new state would determine whether it would be free or slave. The decision by itself did not cause the Civil War, but it surely hastened the breakup of the Union.

To try to make his opinion seem stronger, Taney ordered the clerk of the Court to have the opinions printed not in the usual order of seniority but according to who supported him most fully. Of those who wrote the six concurring opinions, only James Wayne of Georgia fully endorsed Taney's opinion, and he wrote only to note the Court's right to review all aspects of the case. Next came Samuel Nelson of New York, whose opinion, probably what had been the draft of the earlier compromise, dealt primarily with Scott's residence in free territory and concluded that in the area of slavery, states' rights trumped any federal power. Nelson relied solely on the ground that Missouri law governed the status of an alleged slave resident in the state, and under that law Scott remained a slave. After that, Robert Grier of Pennsylvania entered a short opinion seconding Taney's ruling on the unconstitutionality of the Missouri Compromise. Taney put these opinions close to his in an effort to make the Court's decision appear bisectional, but it did not work.

There were two dissents, one by John McLean and the other by Benjamin Curtis, and they were unquestionably the most important dissents handed down in the Supreme Court up to that time. They are important not just because of the case's significance but because their logic is the stuff of constitutional dialogue, pointing out the error of the majority and appealing to the future to set things right. In terms of jurisprudence, scholars have always considered the opinion of Curtis to be the more professional, both scholarly and polished, and as a result have paid less attention to McLean. Nonetheless, McLean, who for most of his career on the Court tried to secure a presidential nomination from one party or another, did make some important points. McLean was the strongest opponent of slavery on the Court, and his thirty-five-page dissent tore Taney's reasoning to pieces.

To begin with, he denied Taney's claim that Scott, as a slave, could not sue in federal court. The chief justice could not cite a single case in the Court's nearly seven decades of existence to support that assertion. In fact, McLean argued, his status as a slave did not mean that he was not a citizen of Missouri, and nothing in the acts of Congress establishing the jurisdiction of federal courts had ever held that slaves could not sue. True, slaves could not vote, but then neither could women or children, and no one questioned their right to sue in federal court.

John McLean, associate justice, 1830–1861

What status did Negroes hold? Taney had argued that a colored person, even a free one, could never be a citizen of the United States. McLean disagreed: "Being born under our Constitution and laws, no naturalization is required, as one of foreign birth, to make him a citizen. The most general and appropriate definition of the term citizen is 'a freeman.' . . . [As such] he is a citizen within the act of Congress, and the courts of the Union are open to him." Here McLean argued for what would become the basis for defining citizenship in the Fourteenth Amendment: the fact of birth in the United States made a person a citizen of the United States and of the state in which he resided.

Where Taney had tried to nationalize the protection of slavery and make it an affirmative duty both of Congress and of the state governments to do so, McLean held that Congress had no role to play at all. "Slavery is emphatically a State institution," and care was taken at the Philadelphia convention "to confer no power on the federal Government to interfere with this institution in the States." Moreover, in all of the clauses dealing with slavery—the slave trade, the ratio for representation, and the reclamation of fugitives—slaves were referred to as "persons, and in no other respect are they considered in the Constitution."

McLean did concede an important argument to the South, namely, that Congress had no power to interfere with the institution of slavery in the states. At the same time, he denied Taney's contention that Congress had to protect the property rights of slaveholders everywhere, including in the free states and the western territories. "Slavery is emphatically a State institution," which meant that individual states could choose not to tolerate slavery within their borders and that absent positive legislation to legitimize slavery and protect the interests of the slaveholders, the old rule of "once free, always free" remained in force. A slave entering a free state or territory automatically became free.

McLean also gave short shrift to Taney's argument that Congress did not have the power to ban slavery in the territories and therefore the Missouri Compromise was unconstitutional. Of course Congress had and still retained all of the power necessary to legislate for the territories. Taney's assertion that the word "territory" meant only "land" could not be sustained for a second, because the Constitution clearly referred to land in clauses unrelated to territories. One of the most significant legislative achievements of the Confederation Congress had been the Northwest Ordinance, the basic law for governing areas that would become future states, and the Framers knew quite clearly what made a territory.

Moreover, Taney had ignored the Court's own precedents. In the important case of *American Insurance Co. v. Canter* (1828), a unanimous Court, speaking through Chief Justice Marshall, had held that the people of Florida would not participate in political power until it became a state in the Union. Until then, "Florida continues to be a Territory of the United States, governed by virtue of that clause in the Constitution which empowers Congress to make all needful rules and regulations respecting the territory or other property belonging to the United States." Marshall went on to deal with the question of slavery in the territories and how that too fell under the power of the federal government over the territories. Taney had made no effort to rebut this ruling, nor would he have been able to, so the chief justice had ignored it in the hope that no one would notice. McLean made sure that did not happen.

Finally, McLean castigated the Missouri state court for ignoring its own precedent of "once free, always free" and went on to show how the courts of several of the slave states had previously upheld this rule. In fact, he quoted from some of these southern courts that free people of color are quasi-citizens and may enjoy all the rights that a state confers

Benjamin Robbins Curtis, associate justice, 1851–1857

on them, including, as was true in some northern states, the right to vote.

Taney fared even worse at the hands of the other dissenter, Benjamin Robbins Curtis of Massachusetts, who had been a student of Joseph Story's at Harvard. What is surprising is that the conservative Curtis had never been sympathetic to the abolitionists and had supported the Fugitive Slave Law of 1850. He was not pro-slavery but a staunch nationalist willing to placate the South to preserve the Union. Indeed, his endorsement of the 1850 statute led Millard Fillmore to appoint him to the high court the following year. His seventy-page dissent, sixteen pages longer than Taney's opinion and twice as long as that of McLean, therefore surprised many people. It remains, as one scholar declares, "one of the great masterpieces of constitutional opinion-writing."

Both Curtis and McLean had obviously read an early draft of Taney's opinion—he ordered the clerk of the Court not to deliver his final draft to anyone prior to 6 March—before writing their dissenting responses, but it is not clear whether they had read each other's. There is some overlap, especially in the major points that Curtis wanted to make: that free blacks enjoyed political rights in 1787; that in Anglo-American law birth has always been tied to citizenship; and that allowing slaves into a territory required allowing all of the laws of a slave society in as well, because slavery could not exist without the support of the necessary statutory law.

Taney had argued that blacks had not been citizens at the time of the adoption of the Constitution and that neither then nor later did free blacks have any rights under that document. Indeed, the Framers had considered them an inferior group, and little had changed since then. (Although Taney had early in his life freed his own slaves, he shared the disdain of blacks—free or slave—widespread throughout the South.)

Curtis refuted Taney's assertion by pointing out that in 1787 free blacks enjoyed all the rights of citizenship in several northern states. In Massachusetts, people of color who could meet the property requirements could vote. New Hampshire had conferred the suffrage on every male meeting the requirements of residency and property without any mention of color or descent, as had New Jersey. New York gave the right to vote to every male inhabitant, again without regard to color. Since then, he conceded, New Jersey had restricted the suffrage to white males, while New York, which still allowed blacks to vote, had added some qualifications. At the time of the ratification, however, there could be no question that in several states free blacks enjoyed the name and the privileges of citizenship. As citizens of their states, they were also citizens of the United States. Moreover, Curtis cited, among other authorities, an 1838 North Carolina case that explicitly declared liberated slaves to be "citizens of North Carolina."

No rights were lost by the adoption of the Constitution, which was ordained and established by the people of the United States, and the "people" included those men of color who enjoyed the franchise at the time. There is nothing in the Constitution, he declared, that "deprives of their citizenship any class of persons who were citizens of the United States at the time of its adoption, or who should be native-born citizens of any State after its adoption." Birth on a country's soil "creates the duties and confers the rights of citizenship." Curtis used prior Supreme Court cases, *The Federalist,* the actual wording of the Constitution, the history of citizenship under the Articles of Confederation, and other sources not to prove that Scott was in fact a citizen but to show that there was nothing in the history or the record of the case to prove that he was not.

Curtis, however, raised another question that had agitated southerners for several decades. If a free colored person could be recognized as a citizen of one state, did that mean he enjoyed all the privileges and immunities of citizens in other states? If a free black from Massachusetts, for example, journeyed to Virginia or Mississippi, could he claim all of the rights that a white man had in those states? Southern states recognized that white travelers from the North enjoyed privileges and immunities that their native white citizens had but feared the idea that they would have to extend this recognition to blacks.

Such fears had no foundation in fact, Curtis asserted, because even under the Constitution not all citizens were treated alike. A naturalized citizen, for example, could never be president. Citizens of the District of Columbia had no representation in Congress, and neither did the inhabitants of territories, who were clearly citizens of the United States. Citizenship included women, yet they did not enjoy the suffrage and had other restrictions upon them. The privileges and immunities available in a state depended upon the laws of each state. Curtis dismissed as nonsense the southern argument that somehow slavery was an exception to all of the rules regarding territory.

One other point Curtis made is worth noting. Southern slave owners and their judicial supporters had argued that slavery constituted an "exception" in terms of the broad grants of power to Congress. While the Commerce Clause gave Congress great authority, it did not apply to slavery, even though nothing in the Constitution said that. No exceptions, Curtis maintained, should be carved out "upon reasons purely political," and he went on to make a classic statement on how the Constitution should be interpreted: "When a strict interpretation of the Constitution, according to the fixed rule which governs the interpretation of the laws, is abandoned, and the theoretical opinions of individuals are allowed to control its meaning, we have no longer a Constitution; we are under the government of individual men, who for the time being have power to declare what the Constitution is, according to their own views of what it ought to mean."

As the historian Don Fehrenbacher has noted, the two dissents are more convincing than the majority opinions and not merely because, by modern standards, they were on the right side of history. Despite differences in writing style and professional ability, they agreed on the major issues as opposed to their colleagues, who, while each agreeing with one or more of Taney's assertions, did not provide sustained analysis and support for most of his conclusions. In some ways, McLean and Curtis were the true conservatives, following precedent and history to reach their deductions. Taney and his pro-slavery colleagues were, according

to Fehrenbacher, radicals, invalidating a major piece of federal legislation, denying to Congress a power it had exercised since the founding, and sustaining the abrupt reversal from precedent by the Missouri
court. While there is no lack of passion in the dissents, the overwhelming impression is that they are grounded in reason, while those of the
pro-southern justices are for the most part polemical.

Curtis, aware that Taney had ordered that none of the opinions be
made available before 6 March, sent a copy of his dissent to a Boston
newspaper so that it appeared on the same day he delivered it, perhaps
the earliest example we have of a deliberate effort by a dissenting justice
to engage in a constitutional dialogue with the public. The New York
publisher Horace Greeley soon after printed Curtis's dissent as a pamphlet, and it was used widely by candidates of the new Republican Party
in the 1858 and 1860 elections. Perhaps because Curtis had earlier been
denounced as a tool of the slave power, his ardent dissent carried even
greater power than did that of McLean, who had long been recognized
as a foe of slavery.

One might surmise that because of the intensity of the national debate
over slavery key questions would ultimately come to the high court. In
fact, President-elect Buchanan wanted the justices to decide these questions in the rather naive hope that if the Court spoke, people would listen and the tensions between the free North and the slave South would
evaporate. The bitterness apparent in the divisions within the Court
reflected that in the larger dialogue in the country. The Court's decision
greatly affected that dialogue, but not in the ways that Taney had hoped.

PREDICTABLY, southerners and their northern supporters cheered
the decision, while a majority of northerners attacked it or outrightly
rejected it. "Southern opinion upon the subject of southern slavery,"
exulted the Augusta, Georgia, *Constitutionalist,* "is now the supreme law
of the land, and opposition to southern opinion upon this subject is
now opposition to the Constitution, and morally treason against the
Government." "There is such a thing as The Slave Power," screamed the
Cincinnati *Commercial.* "It has marched over and annihilated the boundaries of the states. We are now one great homogeneous slaveholding
community."

Maine's high court ruled that blacks could vote in both state and
federal elections. The Ohio Supreme Court ruled that any slave coming into the state with his master's consent, even as a sojourner, became
free and could not be re-enslaved upon returning to a slave state, and
the New York Court of Appeals handed down a similar ruling. Several

states resolved to prohibit slavery, in any form, from coming onto their soil and enacted legislation automatically freeing slaves coming within their borders. But the case also raised fears in the North that the decision, if enforced, would impose slavery on the free states. Indeed, some extreme southerners argued that the Constitution would protect them taking their slaves anywhere in the Union, and Senator Robert Toombs of Georgia supposedly declared that one day he would call the roll of his slaves at Boston's Bunker Hill. In his famous House Divided speech in 1858, Abraham Lincoln predicted that if there should be another such Supreme Court decision, "We shall lie down pleasantly dreaming that the people of Missouri are on the verge of making their State free, and we shall awake to the reality instead, that the Supreme Court has made Illinois a slave State."

Lincoln also provides us with a good example of the constitutional dialogue at work. While many in the North rejected Taney's conclusion as well as his opinion of the black race, the fact remained that since John Marshall the nation had accepted the idea that the Supreme Court stood as the ultimate arbiter of what the Constitution meant. Taney certainly relied on that in his belief that the people would accept a court ruling on the slavery issue as final and binding. Lincoln worried about the impact Taney's reasoning would have on the public, especially regarding the meaning of self-government and how it operated. How could popular government succeed when the Court said that southerners who owned slaves trumped the rights of other citizens to keep slavery out of their states or that the federal government could not legislate for the territories? Lincoln believed self-government relied on "the individual rights of man," and he thought this included "black as well as white."

Lincoln had clearly read the dissents and in one speech declared he would not discuss Taney's opinion, because he could not "improve on McLean and Curtis." He then wanted to know how a judicial opinion affected democracy, especially the people who disagreed with it. Under what circumstances does a decision become a binding precedent on the future? Lincoln went on to list several factors, the presence of which would strengthen a decision's claim to precedential value and the absence of which would mitigate against it—unanimity of the justices, lack of partisan bias, the expectations of the legal community (local and state lawyers and judges), rigor of historical analysis, and acceptance in future cases. Clearly, the majority opinions in *Dred Scott* lacked all of these characteristics, but even beyond that Lincoln questioned how much deference popular democracy owed to precedent and quoted Andrew Jack-

Abraham Lincoln, sixteenth president of the United States

son's 1832 veto of the bill rechartering the Bank of the United States: "Mere precedent is a dangerous source of authority."

Lincoln then took on the chief justice's "assumed historical facts," especially Taney's reading of black Americans out of the Declaration of Independence and the Constitution. He enlisted Curtis's dissent to refute Taney's bad history and concluded that free blacks had indeed been included as part of the "people of the United States" who ordained and established the Constitution. Lincoln continued to use the dissents, especially that of Curtis, in his speeches attacking both the decision and

Stephen Douglas, who became the chief northern defender of Taney. He based his famous Cooper Union speech in February 1860 on Curtis's dissent, and there and in his other speeches before the election continued the dialogue, elaborating on issues that McLean and Curtis had raised. But where the two justices had looked backward into history to buttress their arguments, Lincoln looked to the future. It was not only could a house divided over slavery survive, but what effect would a decision like *Dred Scott* have not only on the nation but on the whole idea of democratic polity?

We should remember the dissents by John McLean and Benjamin Curtis more than we do. In many textbooks, in both college and law school, Taney's opinion is cited or read as a worst-case example of judges' interfering in the political process, but other than noting that the two men dissented, the textbooks make little of what they wrote. Yet what they said is important. They not only refuted what they believed to be Taney's bad law and even worse history; they pointed the way to what should be.

McLean died a month after Abraham Lincoln took the oath of office as president but before southern hotheads opened fire on Fort Sumter and plunged the nation into a civil war. Curtis resigned from the Court six months after the opinion, in part because the intense hostility displayed by Taney made life on the Court intolerable. The chief justice never forgave Curtis for his dissent, which he intuitively knew to have been the better argument. After he left the bench, Curtis, who lived to 1874, resumed his private law practice and argued some fifty-four cases before the Supreme Court. In 1868, he successfully defended Andrew Johnson in his Senate impeachment trial.

The Taney decision by itself did not cause the Civil War, and even had Curtis's opinion been the majority ruling, the war would still have come. No Supreme Court decision could resolve the slavery question. But the opinions certainly played a significant role in the politics of the day, and politics, we should always recall, is perhaps the most effective form of public dialogue. The decision effectively held unconstitutional the central plank of the new Republican Party—opposition to the extension of slavery into the territories—and energized northern antislavery politicians. This in turn made the South even more fearful that should Lincoln win, a Republican Congress and the justices he would appoint to the high court would destroy its "peculiar institution." The war, not future courts, undid the damage of the Taney opinion and made it irrelevant by abolishing slavery.

ALTHOUGH REPUBLICANS DAMNED the Taney opinion in *Dred Scott* and the Civil War made his comments on the status of slaves irrelevant, problems persisted. Taney not only had written about enslaved African Americans but had said that no person of color could ever be a citizen. The members of the Congresses that met during and after the war had to deal with this issue, and it is clear from the debates in the Senate and the House of Representatives that all of them believed that Taney's ruling remained the law. As Congress debated the civil rights bills and the proposed amendments to the Constitution, the arguments in both the majority and the dissenting opinions were rehearsed over and over again. What could Congress do to protect the freedmen, people who, under the majority opinion, essentially had no legal status at all? And what of the privileges and immunities that Curtis and McLean had written about? What did they mean, and how could the former slaves be ensured of those benefits? In looking through the debates in the *Congressional Globe,* we see the dialogue working out: the Court had spoken, the dissenters had proposed an alternative constitutional argument, and now Congress had to develop a workable solution to the problems created by the freeing of millions of slaves.

Beginning shortly after *Dred Scott* came down, the question of "what sort of nation shall we be" would be at the center of the national debate. It continued throughout the war and became the central feature of Reconstruction policy. The Curtis and McLean dissents played a key role in the political discourse of the 1858 and 1860 elections, but even after the secession had been crushed, lawmakers and the public did not know what force—if any—the Taney opinion still held. One can see in the congressional debates over status, citizenship, and Reconstruction policy an effort to rid the country of Taney's views and to adopt those put forward by McLean and Curtis.

The issue first arose in the debate over the admission of Oregon as a state in 1858 and 1859. The legislature of the Oregon Territory, as required by the laws governing the admission of territories as states, had submitted a draft constitution. Not only did the document prohibit slavery, but it also forbade any blacks—free or enslaved—to enter the state. Southerners had no problem with the latter provision, because states' rights advocates had long argued that states had the power to exclude whomever they wanted from within their borders, and they looked to Taney's opinion to argue that blacks had no rights that Oregon had to respect. Republicans in Congress, however, decried the Taney opinion and echoed the dissenting opinions' arguments that blacks—free or slave—had rights and that if a free black could claim citizenship in any state, which he could, then under the Privileges or Immunities Clause he could travel anywhere.

The Republican representative Charles B. Hoard of New York, for example, protested against "the right of any State to deny any free-born American, who is guilty of no crime, the right to be, that is the right to exist, in the land of his birth." The notion of birthright citizenship that McLean and Curtis had argued was becoming part of the evolving Republican ideology.

In 1866, Senator Reverdy Johnson, a Democrat from Maryland, took the floor to discuss the question of citizenship. His colleagues listened closely because Johnson had been one of Sandford's lawyers in the *Dred Scott* case. He was a unionist, however, and President Lincoln had turned to him for assistance on several occasions, including rewriting a legal code for Louisiana after it had been captured by Union forces. He had served in the Senate from 1845 to 1849, had then become attorney general, and had been returned to the Senate in 1863. He rose to comment on the proposed 1866 Civil Rights Act, which included an amendment defining citizenship through birth.

"Nobody is more willing," said Johnson, "to admit that it is very desirable that such a definition should be given." Ever since *Dred Scott,* the rule had been people of African descent, freeborn or slave, could not be citizens under the terms of the Constitution. Johnson did not defend Taney's opinion, but the decision in the case had never been overruled and therefore remained the law. He did not think that an act of Congress could overturn a constitutional decision of the high court and had come to the conclusion that a redefinition of citizenship "can only be safely and surely attained by an amendment of the Constitution." Legislation by itself, he warned, would never settle the controversy.

Others in Congress were not so sure and believed that citizenship could in fact be defined through legislation. Representative James F. Wilson, Republican of Iowa, took up the notion of birthright citizenship and thought it a very simple thing. Every person born in the United States is a citizen, and that "must include negroes, for they are persons and are born in the United States; and I submit that, under the rule thus laid down, all such persons must be considered citizens of the United States."

On 13 March 1866, after extensive debate and testimony revealing the horrors of how southerners were treating the freed slaves, Congress passed the Civil Rights Act of 1866. The bill indicated a massive shift in constitutional thought. Until then, the protection of individual rights had been considered a state responsibility; afterward, it was increasingly seen as part of the national government's role. The rights it listed directly reflected the Curtis and McLean dissents and included the whole gamut of a person's legal rights and responsibilities. It made all people ("excluding Indians not taxed") born in the United States citizens of the United States without regard to race or previous status as slaves, thus directly overruling *Dred Scott.*

Congress did not pass the bill without considerable doubts, for it ran counter to a long tradition of state supremacy in this area. President Andrew Johnson immediately vetoed it on the grounds that Congress had no power to legislate for the former Confederate states that had not been readmitted to the Union. Congress easily overrode the veto, but doubts persisted in the minds of many congressmen, even the Radical Republicans, that perhaps Congress really did not have the authority and that Reverdy Johnson had been right. In addition, it remained unclear how the Supreme Court would view the bill and whether it would uphold its constitutionality. So Congress took the basic provisions of the Civil Rights Act and incorporated them into a new constitutional amendment that would make explicit the power of Congress to legislate on behalf of the former bondsmen.

CHAPTER 4

FIELD, *SLAUGHTERHOUSE,* AND *MUNN*

All persons born or naturalized in the United States and subject to the jurisdiction thereof, are citizens of the United States and of the State wherein they reside. No State shall make or enforce any law which shall abridge the privileges or immunities of citizens of the United States; nor shall any State deprive any person of life, liberty, or property, without due process of law; nor deny to any person within its jurisdiction the equal protection of the laws.

— FOURTEENTH AMENDMENT, SECTION I

After the war, many Americans believed that the end of slavery would automatically give the freedmen all the rights and privileges enjoyed by white citizens in the South. But after Lincoln's assassination, Andrew Johnson became president, and he believed—and said—that the southern states could treat the former slaves as they wished. Congress had no power to interfere with what he deemed to be the internal affairs of sovereign states. The South responded with Black Codes that so restricted what the freedmen could do as to essentially re-enslave them. The resulting fight between the Republican Congress and Johnson led to the president's impeachment and near conviction, the establishment of congressional Reconstruction that placed southern states under military control, and the Fourteenth

Amendment, which the former rebel states had to ratify as a condition for reentry into the Union.

The amendment, ratified in 1868, includes revisions of how seats would be apportioned in the House (doing away with the old three-fifths compromise of 1787), the voiding of the Confederate debt and the validation of the Union debt, prohibitions on certain Confederate officials holding office, and definition of citizenship. The key clauses involved the guarantee of individual rights and limits on state powers to restrict those rights. Many assumed that this would be the end of both the rebellion and Reconstruction, but southern states continued to discriminate against the freedmen, and so Congress imposed the Fifteenth Amendment, declaring that the right to vote could not be abridged on account of "race, color, or previous condition of servitude." Both amendments, as well as the Thirteenth abolishing slavery, included innovative clauses giving Congress the power to enforce the articles by appropriate legislation, although Congress failed to use them for decades.

Nominally, the amendments applied only to the former slaves and to limits on how states could treat them. But did they mean more than that? Did phrases like "due process," "equal protection," and "privileges or immunities" apply to all Americans or just those who had been freed from bondage? If they did mean more, just what did they mean, and to whom did they apply?

The Civil War amendments, and especially the Fourteenth, have been at the heart of much constitutional litigation ever since. In the late nineteenth and early twentieth centuries, the Due Process Clause became the basis for the protection of property rights and for imposing barriers against government interference in the marketplace. Since the middle of the twentieth century, the Equal Protection Clause has been utilized in fights for the equal treatment of people of color, women, homosexuals, and other minorities. The Congress that drafted the amendments clearly meant them to remedy the ills of slavery and the civil war that it had caused. Unfortunately, no one at the time could have foreseen the constitutional problems that would arise out of the war and Reconstruction, or the interpretations future generations of justices would impose on the amendments.

The litigation began almost immediately. Some of the cases involved military trials of civilians, the validity of state and federal test oaths, federal jurisdiction, and the legitimacy of secession. Needless to say, the difficulty of the issues confronting the Court, most of them new because of the conditions created by the war and its aftermath, led to very few unanimous decisions. Although all nine justices agreed that civilians could not be tried in military courts when the civil courts remained open, four justices joined in a concurring opinion that verged on a dissent. Both of the major test oath cases were decided by 5–4 votes. While a unanimous bench upheld the power of Congress to enact Reconstruction legislation, the question of the legitimacy of secession brought a 5–3 vote.

When the Court upheld a Kentucky law excluding the testimony of black witnesses against a white defendant—in clear opposition to the 1866 Civil Rights Act—Justice Joseph P. Bradley entered a strong dissent, declaring that the 1866 law was a "legitimate consequence" of the Thirteenth Amendment. He continued, "Merely striking off the fetters of the slave, without removing the incidents and consequences of slavery, would hardly have been a boon to the colored race. Hence, also, the amendment abolishing slavery was supplemented by a clause giving Congress the power to enforce it by appropriate legislation." The enforcement section included the power to protect the lives and safety of former slaves and the "power to do away with the incidents and consequences of slavery, and to instate the freedmen in the full enjoyment of that civil liberty and equality which the abolition of slavery meant." In this case and others, it appears that the justices, all of whom had lived through the war and some of whom had firsthand experience in the drafting and adoption of the amendments, took it for granted that they had been framed in order to protect the rights of the former slaves and to resolve constitutional irregularities caused by the war and emancipation. In fact, in 1873 a majority of the justices agreed that the amendments had no other purposes. The dissents in the *Slaughterhouse Cases,* however, completely changed both the intent and the meaning of the Fourteenth Amendment.

THIS COMPLEX CASE gave the Court its first opportunity to interpret section 1 of the Fourteenth Amendment. The issue involved none of the Reconstruction-era civil rights laws but a rather mundane Louisiana public health statute—regulating where animals could be slaughtered in the city of New Orleans. The circumstances surrounding the litigation, however, reflected the political and racial turmoil of Reconstruction.

In 1869, the Louisiana legislature enacted a law requiring that all slaughtering in New Orleans be done in one central place—the Crescent City Slaughterhouse. This was primarily a sanitary regulation, and nearly every city in the country had put similar restrictions in place. As urban areas grew, the old practice of local butchers slaughtering in back of their shops and dumping the offal in the nearest stream had created myriad health problems. To have all of the slaughtering done in one area made a great deal of sense, and most of the city's population welcomed the law, which had been discussed for years. All butchers could use the slaughterhouse—in fact, the law required that it be open to all on an equal basis and imposed substantial penalties if any butcher was turned away—and then could do the actual butchering of the carcass back in their shops. The only economic burden on the butchers—and it was the same for every butcher in the city—was a small fee to rent space in the Crescent City Slaughterhouse.

Building a centralized facility was a fairly common approach to solving the health problems associated with butchering, and the idea of regulating trade in a centralized property was not confined to slaughtering animals. The central public market remained a part of the American economic scene well into the late nineteenth century. In fact, nothing about the Louisiana law violated the then accepted legal precedents regarding state and municipal police powers, nor did the state's decision to utilize a private company with an exclusive franchise. The New Orleans central slaughterhouse reflected mid-nineteenth-century trends for regulating businesses that could be hazardous to public health. There could be no question that slaughtering animals and dumping offal into municipal water supplies fit that category.

Although foes of the law cried out about corrupt government and monopoly, the opposition really stemmed from two other sources. The butchers had long been unregulated and had defeated earlier efforts to create a central slaughterhouse because of their organization and political clout—even though medical officials had been warning for decades that local slaughtering undermined the city's water supply and threatened public health. More important, the legislation had been adopted by a racially integrated legislature dominated by Republicans. White New Orleans after the war could not accept the idea of a biracial state government, even when it passed laws benefiting everyone. Hostility to the legislature helped the city's butchers gain public support in their opposition to the central slaughterhouse, even though the new regime would make New Orleans a healthier and cleaner city. The antagonism to the health regulations also fed upon hostility to the establishment of integrated public schools, the resentment the defeated South felt against continued military occupation, and the prominent role played by former slaves in the Reconstruction-era governments.

The butchers challenged the constitutionality of the law and in a brilliant move hired former justice John A. Campbell, whose tenure on the bench had not been particularly distinguished. He concurred in

John Archibald Campbell, associate justice,
1853–1861, and lead counsel in the
Slaughterhouse Cases

Dred Scott, but his concurrence was far more circumspect than Taney's opinion. After Lincoln's election, he worked for a peaceable solution to the growing crisis, but once Lincoln took office and declared that an insurrection existed, he resigned to join the Confederate government and eventually became assistant secretary of war. At the end of the conflict, having secured a pardon from President Andrew Johnson, he reestablished himself as one of the South's leading lawyers and argued forty-three cases before the Supreme Court, beginning with his representation of the New Orleans butchers.

Campbell took on the case, at least in part, because he was a bitter and hate-filled man. His impressive library and property in Alabama had been destroyed by Union troops, he had been imprisoned, and when released, he had gone to his new home in New Orleans and found the old familiar world he had known turned upside down. "We have," he complained, "Africans in place all about us. They serve as jurors, post office clerks, custom house officers and day by day they barter away their obligations and duties." While willing to accept a South without slavery, he could not see black people as anything but field hands and house servants. He hated Reconstruction, and starting in 1868 he and his law partner Henry Spofford launched a series of lawsuits designed to obstruct the Republican state governments of the South, of which the *Slaughterhouse Cases* are the best known. But he also attacked development projects sponsored by the Reconstruction Louisiana government, its powers to tax, and its plans to establish integrated public schools. At the same time he trumpeted the rights of butchers to ignore sanitary measures, he also defended the right of a New Orleans theater to segregate Negro patrons, even though a state statute forbade such discrimination.

We need to examine Campbell's strategy because not only is the case the first opportunity the Court had to interpret the Fourteenth Amendment but the former jurist's creative—indeed radical—proposals, while failing to win a majority, strongly influenced the four dissenting members, and their dissents led to a constitutional revolution.

Campbell chose to employ not only the Thirteenth and Fourteenth Amendments but also the Civil Rights Act of 1866. First, he claimed, compelling the butchers to slaughter only in a certain place and only upon payment to a favored group represented an illegal case of discrimination against the inherent rights of a citizen. He no doubt knew that in a recent test oath case Justice Stephen Field had written that as part of an American's inalienable rights, one finds "all honors, all positions are alike open to every one, and that in protection of these rights, all are equal before the law." In 1867, Field had relied on "inalienable rights"; now with the Fourteenth Amendment ratified, Campbell believed a stronger argument existed.

Although he despised the increase in federal authority that the Civil War amendments created, Campbell claimed that section 1 of the Fourteenth Amendment protected his clients from Louisiana's attempt to interfere with their God-given privilege to pursue a chosen calling. He had been, while on the Court, a strong supporter of states' rights; he now declared that federal authority limited the power of state legislatures as never before. Section 1 of the Fourteenth Amendment meant that the Constitution now "creates a national government and is not a federal compact," an idea that had been anathema not only to himself but to John C. Calhoun and other prewar champions of states' rights. The vehicle through which this authority would be exercised to curb the illegal actions of state legislatures would be the federal courts. Campbell argued that the Fourteenth Amendment, taken as a whole, gave the federal courts the authority to protect individual liberty, individual property, and individual honor and security from arbitrary and unjust state legislation. "Woe!, woe!, woe!" he declared in his brief, "to this country if these tribunals falter in the performance of their duties."

Campbell ignored the fact that the Thirteenth, Fourteenth, and Fifteenth Amendments had all been adopted to protect the former slaves and that nothing in the congressional debates even hinted that the framers had other interests—such as those of butchers—in mind. As long as southern state legislatures stayed under the thumb of Reconstruction governments (which they would do until 1877), the new federal authority could and should be used to curb them. He made no reference in his brief to slavery, its extinction during the war, or the plight of the freedmen after the war.

Campbell's opponents in the high court did not ignore these issues and emphasized the conditions that had led Congress to propose the amendments as well as the radical impact that Campbell's interpretation—if successful—would have on traditional ideas of federalism. In these early years after the Civil War, both North and South still viewed the Constitution as establishing a federal union in which power and sovereignty were shared between the national government and the states. The congressional framers of those amendments could not have intended what Campbell proposed.

The Court agreed. Justice Samuel Miller, who had once been a physician and thus very familiar with both slaughterhouse practices and urban sanitation needs in Iowa, spoke for the five-man majority. Miller first went over the history of the Civil War amendments. "In the light of this recapitulation, almost too recent to be called history, which are familiar to us all," he declared, "no one can fail to be impressed with the pervading purpose found in them all, lying at the foundation of each, and without which none of them would have been even suggested; we mean the freedom of the slave race . . . and the protection of the newly made freeman and citizen from the oppressions of those who had formerly exercised unlimited dominion over him."

Miller did, however, concede that others besides former slaves might fall within the amendments' protections, but that would be a secondary matter which could be raised at another time. He expressly reserved the question of nonracial discrimination until "some case of State oppression, by denial of equal justice in its courts," was presented.

Campbell had called for, and five members of the Court had rejected, the nationalization of all rights and their enforcement by the federal courts. Miller asked whether it was "intended to bring within the power of Congress the entire domain of civil rights heretofore belonging exclusively to the States." Did the framers expect the Court to become "a perpetual censor upon all legislation of the States, on the civil rights of their own citizens"? This was more than Miller could contemplate, and

Samuel Freeman Miller, associate justice,
1862–1890

he concluded that "no such results were intended by the Congress which proposed these amendments, or by the States which ratified them." Nothing in the Fourteenth Amendment barred the State of Louisiana from enacting a simple and much-needed health measure under the traditional police powers of a state.

Miller's opinion is simple and straightforward. The postwar amendments had a primary purpose, and this had nothing to do with a state's enacting health regulations. In fact, had he simply stopped and held the measure legitimate under the police power, it would have been sufficient. He made the mistake, however, of trying to answer some of Campbell's points and, in doing so, opened a can of constitutional worms. While one can say that the amendments had originated in the desire to free and then protect the former slaves, what exactly did the phrases mean? Did "involuntary servitude" mean nothing more than outright slavery? One could trace the origins of "due process of law" back to Magna Carta, but its meaning had evolved over time. Miller conceded that "equal protection of the laws" might apply to discrimination other than racial but carefully avoided saying what that might entail. As for "privileges and immunities," he noted that the Fourteenth Amendment spoke of both national and state citizenship, and therefore the "privileges and immunities" clause referred only to those rights "belonging to a citizen of the United States as such" and not those enjoyed by virtue of state citizenship. The right to slaughter animals did not "owe [its] existence to the Federal government, its National character, its Constitution, or its laws," and thus was not a privilege of national citizenship.

The problem is that Miller's history was incomplete. He argued that the framers of the Civil War amendments had never meant to disturb the relations of the states to the national government, when in fact that is exactly what they intended to do. The Bill of Rights had been adopted because in the latter eighteenth century the founding generation had believed that the greatest threat to individual liberties would come from a too powerful central government and that the states would be the champions of their citizens' rights. Slavery, the Civil War, and the ensuing treatment of freedmen after Appomattox had convinced the postwar Congresses that states posed the greater threat to civil liberties and rights. There is conflicting evidence as to whether the amendments had in fact been intended to apply the Bill of Rights to the states. The existence of the Enforcement Clauses in each of the amendments indicated that Congress had power regarding the protection of individual rights that had not been present before.

If, as the historian Jonathan Lurie has suggested, Miller's was a nostalgic opinion, looking back at what had once been, the dissenting opinions clearly pointed to the future. Those of Field and Bradley are, I believe, the first important dissents in that they not only pointed out the alleged errors of the majority but also laid out the map by which future justices could get it right. (Bradley, Noah Swayne, and Chief Justice Salmon P. Chase signed on to Field's dissent; Bradley also dissented alone, as did Swayne, although the latter merely emphasized his agreement with Field and Bradley.)

It should be noted that *Slaughterhouse* has never been reversed, and even after the dissenters' interpretation had been adopted, public health measures still received approval as being within the police power of the state. But in the dialogue over the meaning of the Fourteenth Amendment protections, the dissenting opinions, and not that of the majority, won out. Field's is by far the most important.

BY THE TIME of the *Slaughterhouse Cases*, Stephen Field had been on the Court ten years, and he had made explicit his views on a number of subjects. A Jacksonian Democrat, he opposed any efforts by the government to interfere in private business (with very limited exceptions for valid health and safety regulations) or to give any man or group an advantage over others. Field had a very clear view of what the Constitu-

Stephen Johnson Field, associate justice,
1863–1897

tion meant to him and never hesitated to dissent if he could not win over his colleagues by persuasion. In his thirty-four and a half years on the bench—the second-longest tenure in the Court's history—he wrote dissenting opinions in 86 cases and dissented a total of 220 times, 64 of them alone. As he explained in one dissent, "The only loyalty which I can admit consists in obedience to the Constitution and the laws made in pursuance of it."

Although Chief Justice Salmon P. Chase was the senior justice among the four dissenters, he was in poor health and would die less than a month after the decision came down. Field wrote the lead dissent, and if there had been hesitation in Miller's opinion, none could be found here. The opinion is as good a statement as any he made during his tenure of both his Jacksonian heritage and his political conservatism. It is also one of the great dissents in American constitutional history, in that it not only argued against the majority interpretation (as all dissents do) but set up an alternative reading of the Fourteenth Amendment that would ultimately win the approval of the Court.

Using language that Andrew Jackson would have applauded, Field attacked what he deemed the slaughterhouse monopoly: "The Act of Louisiana presents the naked case, unaccompanied by any public considerations, where a right to pursue a lawful and necessary calling, previously enjoyed by every citizen, and in connection with which a thousand persons were daily employed, is taken away and vested exclusively for twenty-five years . . . in a single corporation."

Field ignored the fact that the butchers had not been barred from their calling but had only been required to pursue one part of it at a specific location and to pay a small user's fee for the facility. One should note, however, that Field's attachment to the "right to pursue one of the ordinary trades" did not suddenly appear full-blown; it had been a personal crusade in his early career and a constant throughout his life.

Where Miller had reviewed the charges Campbell made against the Slaughterhouse Act on behalf of the butchers and dismissed them, Field took just the opposite approach and declared, "No one will deny the abstract justice which lies in the position of the plaintiffs." To do this, and before he could proffer what he thought the Fourteenth Amendment meant, he had to rebut the majority ruling that the statute reflected a valid exercise of the police power. The state, of course, could make rules for the health, safety, and well-being of the community—the traditional definition of the police power—and this Field fully admitted. But the police power had to be exercised in a way consistent with the constitutionally protected rights of the citizens; the state could not use the pretense of acting for the public good to impinge on these rights. This assertion that the state could only use the police power when it could prove a direct relation between the statute and the health, safety, and welfare of the community would have an important bearing during the Progressive Era, when conservative jurists used this argument to strike down protective legislation, claiming no relation existed between the laws and workers' health.

Field found that the act's provisions requiring inspection, landing, and slaughtering of the animals below the city of New Orleans to be a valid exercise of the police power. He well understood the health dangers of slaughtering within city limits and dumping refuse into the water supply. The problem involved granting one company exclusive control over all stock landing, yarding, and slaughtering in an area that encompassed three Louisiana parishes (the equivalents of counties) and covering 1,154 square miles. The health of the city might require removing the slaughterhouses from within the city, "but no such object could possibly justify legislation removing such buildings from a large part of the State for the benefit of a single corporation."

Miller had dismissed the antimonopoly argument because many times in the past states had awarded charters to companies granting them the sole right to conduct a certain business. Field, however, drew a distinction between the Louisiana slaughterhouse and these older grants, which had often been for the construction and maintenance of a road, ferry, or bridge, activities that normally fell within the purview of government. If the state chose not to construct a bridge itself, it could then charter a private company to do so. Slaughtering animals, however, did not fall in this category, which he characterized as "a right to pursue one of the ordinary trades or callings of life, which is a right appertaining solely to the individual." Here Field reflected the Jacksonian animus against monopoly and special privilege, and then he allowed himself to exaggerate to make his point. If Louisiana could give exclusive privileges to a seventeen-person corporation, they could:

> be equally granted to a single individual. If they may be granted for twenty-five years, they may be equally granted for a century, and in perpetuity. If they may be granted for the landing and keeping of animals . . . they may be equally granted for the landing and storing of grain . . . or for any article of commerce. . . . Indeed, upon the theory on which the exclusive privileges granted by the act in question are sustained, there is no monopoly, in the most odious form, which may not be upheld.

Field used this excursion into the realm of the horrid possibility to make a point: Do the recent amendments "protect the citizens of the United States against the deprivation of their common rights by State legislation"? He answered his question affirmatively, declaring that he believed the Fourteenth Amendment did provide this protection and that in fact it had been the intention of Congress in drafting the amendment, and the states in ratifying it, to do just that.

Relying on the wording of the Fourteenth Amendment, he directly contradicted Miller's claim that citizenship in the nation and in the state remained separate, with different rights adhering to each. Field certainly was correct in his argument that "a citizen of a State is now only a citizen of the United States residing in that State. The fundamental rights, privileges, and immunities which belong to him as a free man and a free citizen of the United States are not dependent upon his citizenship of any state." But what constituted these rights, privileges, and immunities? Were they, as Miller had claimed, no more than had existed before the adoption of the Fourteenth Amendment, such as the right of a citizen to seek the protection of the federal government while abroad or to use the nation's navigable waterways? If so, then the amendment had been "a vain and idle enactment, which accomplished nothing."

So far Field had rebutted the majority's assertions regarding the nature of the police power and its narrow view of the meaning of the Fourteenth Amendment. But if section 1 expanded the rights now tied to national citizenship, what did it mean? What rights should the courts be protecting against the incursions of the state legislatures? Here Field was less concerned about enumerating particular rights than in establishing broad categories, most notably "those privileges and immunities which were in their nature fundamental and which belong of right to the citizens of all free governments, and which have at all times been enjoyed by the citizens of several states." Clearly, one must include "the right to pursue a lawful employment in a lawful manner, without other restraint than such as equally affects all persons."

In other words, the states could not interfere with the equal enjoyment by all citizens of the United States of their privileges and immunities. Article IV had required that states treat each other's citizens equally; now the Fourteenth Amendment expanded the rights inherent in citizenship and forbade the states to restrict them. This concept the Louisiana statute had violated by allowing some citizens to pursue a lawful occupation while denying it to others. While the states retained their police powers, these had to be exercised in such a manner as to not interfere with basic rights.

He finished by declaring that "this equality of right, with exemption from all disparaging and partial enactments, in the lawful pursuit of life . . . is the distinguishing privilege of citizens of the United States. To them, everywhere, all pursuits, all professions, all avocations are open without other restrictions than such as are imposed equally upon all others of the same age, sex, and condition." This is, he maintained, "the fundamental idea upon which our institutions rest, and, unless adhered to in the legislation of the country, our government will be a republic only in name." Thus, from simply freeing the slaves and protecting their rights after emancipation, the Thirteenth and Fourteenth Amendments now also protected the rights of Americans to pursue their occupations with little or no interference from state governments. By occupations, Field, of course, meant not just tradesmen or craftsmen working in their shops but also the barons of big business who were then building great railroads, steel mills, and factories. While none of the Civil War amendments mentioned business and occupational liberty, Field's dissent now placed them firmly within the rights, privileges, and immunities of national citizenship.

One can question whether the framers of the Fourteenth Amendment had all of these ideas in mind when they added the phrase "privileges

Joseph P. Bradley, associate justice,
1870–1892

or immunities," but a credible case can be made that Field's opinion developed from traditions that predated the Civil War, specifically the Jacksonian animus against monopoly and special privilege and the Republican concept of "free labor" from the 1850s. The latter served as an important tool to distinguish the free North from the slave South, namely, that workers in the North had the freedom to choose their jobs and to leave them if they found the work repugnant. These two strains came together when Field declared, "There is a recognition of the equality of right among citizens in the pursuit of the ordinary avocations of life, and a declaration that all grants of exclusive privileges, in contravention of this equality, are against common right, and void."

Justice Joseph Bradley added a "few observations." Bradley had been appointed to the Court in 1870 by President Grant, and while he had been a Republican prior to the war, his main interest had been the preservation of the Union rather than the abolition of slavery. Unlike Field, Bradley showed more awareness of slavery and the racial discrimination that had led to the adoption of the Civil War amendments. In a case where a white man had murdered a black woman, Bradley had dissented when the Court denied federal jurisdiction under the 1866 Civil Rights Act. In his dissent, Bradley warned of the consequences if the former slaves had no access to federal courts for racially motivated wrongs.

Bradley had had earlier experience with the *Slaughterhouse Cases,* because he had heard them while on circuit in 1871. At that time, he had held the Louisiana law unconstitutional and had declared "there is no more sacred right of citizenship than the right to pursue unmolested a lawful employment in a lawful manner. It is nothing more nor less than the sacred right of labor"—sentences Field quoted approvingly in his dissent.

Where Miller had taken a narrow view of what national citizenship entailed, Bradley proposed a far broader understanding, and this is important because prior to the Fourteenth Amendment there had been little thought given to what it meant to enjoy national citizenship. The Fourteenth Amendment made people born or naturalized in the United States "citizens of the United States and of the State wherein they reside." The original Constitution does not define who is or is not a citizen. Prior to 1868, most people saw themselves as citizens of the state where they lived, and while they might have proudly claimed to be American citizens, the rights they enjoyed, their privileges and immunities, grew out of state rather than national law. Bradley now argued that the Fourteenth Amendment had reversed that.

Miller had resisted the idea that the Fourteenth Amendment had empowered the federal courts to become "a perpetual censor upon all legislation of the States, on the civil rights of their own citizens." Both Field and Bradley argued that that is exactly what had happened, and they clearly welcomed this development. In their view, anytime a state attacked the rights of a citizen of the United States, whether by an alleged police regulation or the granting of a monopoly, that citizen should be able to find redress in the federal courts, and they welcomed this role of the Supreme Court as a "censor." Moreover, in their view the courts had not only the responsibility but the authority to pass on the wisdom of the legislative policy, if in fact the constitutional power to act existed.

FIELD'S IDEAS of the inalienable rights included in the Privileges or Immunities Clause did not, however, extend beyond economic rights. The day after the Court announced the results in the *Slaughterhouse Cases,* it handed down an 8–1 decision in *Bradwell v. Illinois.* Myra Bradwell had been refused admission to the Illinois bar on the sole grounds of gender. Field not only joined the majority opinion by Justice Miller, which held that the right to practice law was not a privilege or immunity of American citizenship, but also the concurring and highly paternalistic opinion of Justice Bradley, who declared that women were unfit by reason of their natural "timidity and delicacy" to be lawyers. A couple of years later, he joined a unanimous Court in rejecting Virginia Minor's claim that the Privileges or Immunities Clause prevented Missouri from denying her the right to vote. Nor did Field take an expansive view of the Privileges or Immunities Clause, or even of the prime purpose of the Civil War amendments, in cases dealing with the protection of black rights, particularly voting.

Field continued, however, to defend liberty—as he saw it—and to attack economic privilege, as he understood it. The problem is that as the post–Civil War economy developed, and pushed the United States into its industrial revolution, Field's understanding of liberty and privilege moved away significantly from its Jacksonian origins. The right to choose a profession or trade transmuted into "liberty of contract," a doctrine that actually hobbled free labor. Where Jacksonians had opposed governmental intervention in the economy, reformers such as the Grangers in the 1870s, Populists in the 1890s, and Progressives in the first two decades of the twentieth century saw governmental regulation as the only means to rein in the arbitrary power of big industries and the railroads. Field got his chance to further the arguments he had made in *Slaughterhouse* just a few years later in *Munn v. Illinois* (1877). In his dissent in the latter case, Field expanded on his notion of freedom to choose an avocation and helped move the Court toward the subsequent adoption of substantive due process.

BETWEEN *SLAUGHTERHOUSE* AND *MUNN*, the Court unanimously upheld state authority to prohibit the sale of liquor in *Bartemeyer v. Iowa* (1874). *Slaughterhouse* made any privileges or immunities claim frivolous, yet Justice Miller spent much of his short opinion in the Iowa case on that clause and never really dealt with whether a prohibition statute offended due process. The dissenters in *Slaughterhouse,* without any objection from the majority, had declared that the right to pursue a calling constituted a "liberty" or "property" protected by the Due Process Clause. Clearly Bartemeyer, the liquor dealer in Iowa, had been "deprived" of his right to sell alcohol, but Miller chose for the most part to just ignore this claim.

Field and Bradley, however, concurred separately, and both needed to explain why they opposed the Louisiana law and not this one. Both men saw the Iowa law as a legitimate health measure, and as Field explained, "No one has ever pretended, that I am aware of, that the fourteenth amendment interferes in any respect with the police power of the State. . . . The judges who dissented from the opinion of the majority of the court in the Slaughter-House Cases never contended for any such position."

Field had "discovered" the Due Process Clause only after losing the fight in *Slaughterhouse* to expand the meaning of privileges and immunities. In the Iowa case, neither he nor Bradley defined what he saw as a legitimate exercise of the police power or how it related to the Due Process Clause of the Fourteenth Amendment. Nonetheless, both men had managed to enunciate what would become known as substantive due process, that is, that the ownership and use of property (and by this they meant more than just tangible property, but intellectual property and the property of employment) carried certain rights that are subsumed within the phrase "due process of law" and are thus protected against state regulation except in cases of the legitimate use of the police power.

Because of the 5–4 vote in *Slaughterhouse,* lawyers kept coming back to ask the Supreme Court to intervene against state regulation of business. A somewhat vexed Justice Miller would eventually complain that the Court's docket had become crowded with cases "in which we are asked to hold that state courts and state legislatures have deprived their own citizens of life, liberty, or property without due process of law. There is . . . some strange misconception of the scope of this provision in the Fourteenth Amendment."

The reason businessmen and their lawyers kept coming to the courts grew out of increasing efforts by state legislatures to place some controls over the rapidly expanding power of large railroads and other industries. For example, the Granger movement, which lobbied to protect the interests of farmers, managed to get several midwestern states to enact laws regulating grain elevator charges. The elevators provided storage facilities for farmers shipping their produce to urban markets, and in many rural areas with only one elevator the owner company took advantage of its monopoly to exact what farmers considered exorbitant rates. In 1875, the Illinois legislature set maximum rates that grain elevator operators could charge. The statute, however, only applied to elevators in Chicago, where farmers complained not only of the high rates but also that the various elevator owners conspired to fix prices.

The Court heard *Munn v. Illinois* in early 1877 along with four companion cases challenging state laws that regulated the prices railroads could charge to move goods and people. Known collectively as the *Granger Cases,* they gave the Court its first opportunity to explore just what the Due Process Clause meant in terms of state regulation of business.

Chief Justice Morrison R. Waite, whom President Grant had named to replace Chase, wrote the majority opinion upholding the law. He confirmed that the state police power extended to include the regulation of private property when "such regulation becomes necessary for the public good." He referred back to earlier English precedents to the effect that private property "affected with a public interest" could be controlled by the government and that property becomes "clothed with a public interest when used in a manner to make it of public consequence, and affect the community at large." Certainly, owners of property could do with it as they pleased, but if they elected to use it within the scope of "public interest," then they had to accept public regulation as one of the conditions for doing business. The Court majority refused to even consider the fairness or unfairness of the rate schedule. If the power to regulate existed, then the legislature had the discretion to set maximum rates. Acknowledging that this power could be abused, Waite declared that courts did not provide the proper remedy. "For protection against abuses," he wrote, "the people must revert to the polls."

The majority opinion did talk about property rights in businesses but held that so long as the businesses had a connection to the public interest, they were subject to regulation—even if the businesses predated the regulation. But attorneys for the elevator owners wanted to emphasize property rights, and they put forward an argument that had been building in legal and judicial circles since before the Civil War, one we now call "substantive due process." The concept of due process, occasionally called "the law of the land," dated back to Magna Carta and could be found in the Fifth Amendment to the Constitution, in many state constitutions, and most recently in section 1 of the Fourteenth Amendment. Traditionally, it had meant that a person could not be deprived of life, liberty, or property without a judicial hearing following accepted legal procedures. In *Munn,* the company's attorneys argued that due process meant more than simple procedural fairness in trials. They claimed that the guarantee of due process also protected private rights from arbitrary government interference.

This theory looked to the substance of legislation rather than at the procedure by which the law would be enforced. Substantive due process gave the judiciary the authority to overrule legislation that allegedly interfered with individual rights. While the American political and constitutional traditions opposed arbitrary use of government power that threatened individual liberty, this did not necessarily mean that the Due Process Clauses had been intended to protect business interests from state regulation—the argument that Munn's attorneys put forward. There was precious little they could suggest as precedent, and the Supreme Court had toyed with the idea only once—when Taney had applied the Fifth Amendment to hold that government could not interfere with the property rights of slaveholders in *Dred Scott*. Justice Bradley had put forward the idea tentatively in his *Slaughterhouse* dissent, but Justice Miller's majority opinion had dismissed it out of hand. In *Munn*, not only did Bradley vote with the majority, but he had developed the notion of "affected with a public interest" on which Waite rested his case.

Waite took a rather broad view of what business could be characterized as "affected with a public interest." Field would have none of this and believed that regulation was only appropriate for government-created monopolies. He pointed out that many of the cases cited in the majority opinion involved government regulation of companies that operated an exclusive franchise, through either the king's prerogative or a charter from a state. Munn's elevators were neither, but a private company with no exclusive franchise. He argued with some force that "all that is beneficial in property arises from its use, and the fruits of that use," and that any deprivation of the right to use property was in essence a loss of the property itself.

"Property does not become clothed with a public interest when used in a manner to make it of public consequence," because such a definition would cover just about every business enterprise. The majority had not really defined just what the phrase meant but seemed to imply that property could be regulated if the public, acting through the legislature, had an interest. "If this be sound law," Field declared, "if there be no protection, either in the principles upon which our republican government is founded, or in the prohibitions of the Constitution against such invasions of private rights, all property and all business in the State are held at the mercy of a majority of its legislature."

Field here and elsewhere showed how much he distrusted the democratic process and looked to the courts to protect individual rights—especially property rights—from popular hostility. "Government can scarcely be deemed to be free where the rights of property are left solely dependent upon the will of a legislative body without restraint." The Due Process Clause gave courts the power to review legislative acts and to determine if their substance deprived property owners of their rights. Due process, however, did not adversely affect the police power. Where Field differed from the majority is that it took a much broader view of what the police power entailed, and he took a very narrow version, one restricted to the peace, good order, morals, and health of the community. When it came to property, the state could do no more than provide rules governing disputes, protecting community morality, and abating nuisance. Other than that, the government had no business interfering in business. Field strongly believed, as he said in *Munn,* that the Fourteenth Amendment "places property under the same protection as life and liberty."

Even though Field—perhaps deliberately—failed to define the exact definition of substantive due process or its parameters, the idea soon found other adherents, especially in the state courts. Judge Robert Earl, speaking for a unanimous New York court, struck down a statute prohibiting cigar making in tenements. The law bore no relation to health or safety but interfered "with the profitable and free use of his property by the owner . . . and trammels him in the application of his industry and the disposition of his labor, and thus, in a strictly legitimate sense, it arbitrarily deprives him of his property and of some portion of his personal liberty." The following year, the Supreme Court held corporations to be "persons" within the meaning of the Fourteenth Amendment and said they could therefore enjoy the same rights, privileges, and judicial protection as did natural people.

By 1887, only Justice Miller remained from the *Slaughterhouse* majority, while Bradley and Field had been joined by men who shared their concern about the increasing role of government in the economy. Although upholding a state prohibition law in *Mugler v. Kansas* (1887), Justice John Marshall Harlan announced that the Court would no longer accept every statute "ostensibly" passed for the public welfare as a legitimate exercise of the police power. "If, therefore, a statute purporting to have been enacted to protect the public health, the public morals, or the public safety, has no real or substantial relation to those objects, or is a palpable invasion of rights secured by the fundamental law, it is the duty of the courts to so adjudge, and thereby give effect to the Constitution." In other words, it would be the courts, not the legislatures, that would determine whether a statute met the criteria necessary for the exercise of the police power or whether it violated those rights protected by the Due Process Clause.

In *Powell v. Pennsylvania* (1888), Justice Harlan exhibited classic deference to legislative policy making in upholding a state statute that regulated the manufacture and sale "of what is commonly called oleomargarine butter" and was clearly designed to protect the interests of dairymen. According to Harlan, the sale of this artificial product fell squarely within the police powers of the state and did not in any way violate the Fourteenth Amendment. Justice Field, however, entered a strenuous dissent, arguing that there was no real health or safety issue present, the kind that would justify the state's use of its police power. It was simply an out-and-out effort to privilege one group of entrepreneurs (the dairymen) and disadvantage another (the margarine makers). As such, it violated the Due Process Clause, and the Court should strenuously oppose any such policy.

Field in essence argued against the courts allowing the political branches to control policy making, and deference to legislative rate making fell next. In *Munn,* Waite had considered the reasonableness of rates to be outside the province of courts. Now, according to Justice Samuel Blatchford, the fairness of rates became "eminently a question for judicial investigation." If legislatures set unreasonable rates, it would be "in substance and effect" a deprivation of property without due process of law. Bradley objected strenuously and declared that rate making should be a legislative, not a judicial, prerogative.

Field was still on the Court to witness the triumph of substantive due process and what the Court called "freedom of contract" in *Allgeyer v. Louisiana* (1897). A Louisiana law banned the sale of property insurance within the state by any company not licensed to do business there. E. Allgeyer & Company of Louisiana had purchased marine insurance from the Atlantic Mutual Insurance Company, which was based in New York and not licensed in Louisiana. The state fined Allgeyer $1,000 for violating the law, and the company appealed. Justice Rufus Peckham spoke for a unanimous Court in striking down the law as a deprivation of property without due process of law:

> In the privilege of pursuing an ordinary calling or trade and of acquiring, holding and selling property must be embraced the right to make all proper contracts in relation thereto, and although it may be conceded that this right to contract in relation to persons or property or to do business within the jurisdiction of the State may be regulated and sometimes prohibited when the contracts or business conflict with the policy of the State as contained in its statutes, yet the power does not and cannot extend to prohibiting a citizen from making contracts of the nature involved in this case.

FIELD'S NOTION of substantive due process derived at least in part from an older theory of vested rights, and there is some support for the notion that the right to contract, to conduct a business, or to follow a particular profession might have been among the unenumerated rights referred to in the Ninth Amendment. There is little evidence, however, that the framers of the Fourteenth Amendment had meant to elevate commercial relations to such a point that they would be enshrined with constitutional protection.

The strength of Field's view of substantive due process derived, first of all, from its lodging in two specific portions of the Constitution—the Due Process Clauses of the Fifth and Fourteenth Amendments. By appealing directly to the words of the Constitution, defenders of liberty and property could claim that they wanted nothing more than to carry out the intentions of the Framers. There is no question that Field and others believed in a Jacksonian version of liberty—the freedom to compete and succeed in the marketplace without either the help or the hindrance of the state. Moreover, property at that time bore a far more central relationship to liberty than it does in our day. Field and his colleagues on the high court believed in the protection of private property as a means to uphold liberty against governmental overreaching. This belief did not arise with Field but could be found throughout English and American history. "Liberty and property are not only join'd in common discourse," a correspondent for *The Boston Gazette* observed in 1768, "but are in their own natures so nearly ally'd, that we cannot be said to possess the one without the enjoyment of the other."

Field also understood, as did other lawyers and judges in his time, that the basis of the Due Process Clauses lay in the venerable tradition of "the law of the land" that dated back to Magna Carta and had been sanctified by generations of scholars and jurists. The vagueness of the phrase also made it a powerful tool, because in essence it meant whatever judges said it did. It could thus absorb the vested rights tradition and, as Field showed, could be used to protect property from unwarranted efforts of state regulation.

Field, of course, did not erect the framework of substantive due process and freedom of contract by himself, but his dissents, especially in *Slaughterhouse,* played a critical role in persuading other judges who shared his views on liberty and property how the two could be protected. The problems of the two constructs are not the theories themselves but how justices used them and carried the protection of property rights to such an extreme as to cause a major constitutional crisis in the 1930s. Field, of course, cannot be blamed for the excesses of those who followed him. He should, however, be given credit for the intellectual vigor of his dissents that created an entire jurisprudence out of the Due Process Clause.

Field led the way, starting with his *Slaughterhouse* dissent, in creating what became the core principle of the Court in the Gilded Age: the protection of private property as a means to uphold liberty against governmental overreaching. Tied to this was a strong belief that only by ensuring security in property rights could economic growth occur. He summarized this view in an 1890 speech. "It should never be forgotten," Field told his listeners, "that protection of property and person cannot be separated. Where property is insecure, the rights of persons are unsafe. Protection to one goes with protection to the other; and there can be neither prosperity nor progress when either is uncertain."

Later courts did not overturn the majority rulings in either *Slaughterhouse* or *Munn,* and in fact both would be cited to support the notion of state police powers and the parameters in which they could operate. In the next 140 years, however, the sympathy or hostility of the Court toward such legislation waxed and waned depending on the Court's personnel and the political climate of the times. Substantive due process became a shibboleth by which conservative jurists could interpose their views to protect property rights against legislative regulation, a development Stephen Field no doubt would have applauded. Then, in the 1930s, the conservatives went too far in their war against the New Deal, and for a number of years the justices ignored substantive due process until it became evident that the theory could be utilized to protect rights of personal autonomy, a development that Field would surely have understood.

Justice Miller's narrow interpretation of the Privileges or Immunities Clause has not, however, fared as well, nor has his interpretation of what section 1 of the Fourteenth Amendment meant and to whom it applied. Justice William O. Douglas cited Field's *Slaughterhouse* dissent approvingly for the proposition that it stood as a barrier against the states infringing on individual liberties. Justice John Marshall Harlan II also endorsed Field's expansive view of what rights belonged to the "citizens of any free government." And in both 2010 and 2011, Justices Samuel Alito and Antonin Scalia declared that it is Field's interpretation, not Miller's, that governs what the Privileges or Immunities Clause means.

CHAPTER 5

JOHN MARSHALL HARLAN:
THE FIRST GREAT DISSENTER

*Mr. Justice Harlan has a hobby — a judicial hobby —
and that is the Constitution of the United States.*

— JUSTICE DAVID J. BREWER

John Marshall Harlan served on the U.S. Supreme Court from 1877 to 1911, the third-longest tenure in the Court's history, and during that time he heard 7,649 cases, wrote 703 opinions for the Court, and 316 dissents. In 107 of these dissents, he was joined by at least three colleagues. He became known in his time as the Great Dissenter, not for the sheer number of his separate opinions, but for their importance in helping to shape the country's constitutional development. Yet within a few years of his death on 14 October 1911, he became virtually forgotten until the Court began to undo the legacy of apartheid created in the latter nineteenth century against which Harlan had protested. Justice Felix Frankfurter dismissed Harlan as merely "an eccentric exception" in his views on the Fourteenth Amendment, and in 1949 not a single one of Harlan's dissents in the race cases appeared in the three most widely used constitutional casebooks for law schools, a situation that changed greatly over the next half century. While his views on the meaning of the Equal Protection Clause would, by themselves, have

John Marshall Harlan, associate justice,
1877–1911

guaranteed him a key place in the nation's constitutional history, Harlan also spoke to important questions of economic regulation and national expansion. Many of those views, like his opinions on racial segregation, would eventually be adopted by the Court.

HARLAN, originally a slaveholder and a Democrat, converted to the Republican Party and abandoned slavery after the war; like many in the border states, he opposed emancipation even as he fought for the Union. He believed that for slavery to end, it would have to occur gradually, and he condemned the Thirteenth Amendment as an unwarranted assault on the property rights of slaveholders. The Harlans had always opposed physical abuse of slaves, but they, like most white people of the time, did not see blacks as social or intellectual equals. The Republican Party's emphasis on legal equality attracted him far more than the Ku Klux Klan and the racial terrorism fostered by the Democrats in the defeated Confederate states. "These Ku Klux are enemies of all order," he declared, and anyone who opposed civil rights for the freedmen "is no friend of the law, [and] is an enemy of our free institutions." He would, as a justice, offer eloquent testimony to the need for legal equality, but Harlan never outgrew the paternalism of his class and its views

John Marshall Harlan in uniform as officer of the Union army

of racial hierarchy and separatism, views clearly expressed in his *Plessy* dissent.

In 1876, Harlan led the Kentucky delegation to the Republican presidential convention and helped secure the nomination for Rutherford B. Hayes of Ohio. After his election, Hayes appointed Harlan to the Louisiana Commission, sent to decide the disputed 1876 state election. As a reward for his service, Hayes nominated Harlan to the Supreme Court in October 1877, much to the dismay of some Republicans who did not believe that the former slave owner held true party principles. They need not have worried. More than any other justice in the late nine-

Ku Klux Klan cartoon by Thomas Nast:
"The Lost Cause, Worse Than Slavery" (1874)

teenth century, Harlan adhered to the principles that had led to the adoption of the postwar amendments.

HARLAN TOOK HIS SEAT soon after Field and Bradley had started their campaign of interpreting the Fourteenth Amendment to protect the property rights of individuals and corporations. He agreed that the Due Process Clause included substantive as well as procedural rights and voted with the majority in *Allgeyer v. Louisiana* (1897) to make "freedom of contract" a constitutional right. He wrote the opinion for a near-unanimous Court when it finally accepted Field's view that the Due Process Clause incorporated specific protections against state action regarding property. But where his fellow justices had little interest in protecting the freedmen or in interpreting the Fourteenth Amendment to allow Congress to safeguard them, Harlan did. In the race cases as elsewhere, he had no compunction about writing separately. As he put it, "Believing the doctrine announced by the Court to be unsound upon principle and authority, we do not feel at liberty to withhold an expression of our dissent from the opinion." The firmness of his convictions led Justice David Brewer, his colleague on the Court for many years, to remark that Harlan "retires at night with one hand on the Constitution and the other on the Bible, safe and happy in a perfect faith in justice and righteousness."

How to protect the freedmen had been a matter of high priority for the Republican-dominated Congress in the decade after Appomattox. In

1866, Congress passed two measures, one establishing the Freedmen's Bureau, and the other a civil rights act. The former placed protection of black civil rights directly under the control of the army, and its chief sponsor, Senator Lyman Trumbull of Illinois, declared that Congress had implied powers to protect the former slaves under the Thirteenth Amendment.

The Civil Rights Act of 1866, more than any other measure of the Reconstruction era, dramatically represented the shift in constitutional perception that individual rights would henceforth be protected by the national government rather than the states. Civil rights, as whites had long understood, included the whole gamut of a person's legal responsibilities, rights, and remedies, such as the ability to sue or be sued, to engage in a lawful trade, to own and convey property, and to be secure in one's life and property; in short, they touched on all the various activities in which free people engaged. This did not mean, however, that all people—even all free people—enjoyed equal rights. Every state had some restrictions on particular groups, such as women, minors, the mentally impaired, and convicted felons. Most states also limited the rights of aliens or members of racial minorities. While much of New England granted equal political rights to blacks at the time, Indiana, Illinois, and Oregon barred their settlement. In some northern states, they could not give testimony against whites. Prior to 1865, no one presumed that the federal government had any role whatsoever in these matters; afterward, the national government had new but untested powers to protect rights.

In the last of the great Reconstruction statutes, the Civil Rights Act of 1875, the Republican Congress tried to secure by law some semblance of racial equality that could be protected by the federal government and the courts. The law was not a general ban on discrimination but applied to those businesses traditionally associated with a public interest, such as inns and common carriers. By then, however, the North had grown weary of the struggle and had come around to the idea that the problem of racial relations should best be left to the states where blacks lived—the South. Most Americans, in all parts of the country, believed in white supremacy, and no one expected any statute to change these attitudes. Rather, the law aimed to protect the freedmen from deprivation of the minimal rights of citizenship.

When Harlan took his seat on 10 December 1877, he was the youngest member of the Court and its only southerner, and in three 1880 cases he joined the majority when it struck down southern state laws that clearly discriminated against blacks. The following year, he wrote for the Court reversing the conviction of an African American man for allegedly raping a white woman, on the grounds that even though Delaware no longer legally barred blacks from juries, in practice African Americans would not be seated on either grand or petit juries. Harlan was part of a unanimous Court that upheld an Alabama antimiscegenation law on the grounds that it applied equally to both blacks and whites.

Up to this point, the Court had not really dealt with how far the Fourteenth Amendment could reach to protect blacks. The jury cases had proved relatively simple because the state laws in question clearly prohibited blacks from serving, while the antimiscegenation laws dealt with an area—marriage—that had traditionally been within the purview of the states. The *Civil Rights Cases,* however, brought before the Court for the first time a major federal law, passed under the Fourteenth Amendment, that clearly tried to protect a particular class of people.

A crucial feature of the 1875 law prohibited racial discrimination in public places, what would later be called "public accommodations," and rested on the Enforcement Clause of the Fourteenth Amendment. Five cases testing the application of this section arose in both the North and the South, and the Court combined them for a single hearing in 1883 as the *Civil Rights Cases.* The government argued that the Thirteenth Amendment had not only abolished slavery but also conferred all the rights of free citizens on former slaves, while the Fourteenth Amendment gave Congress the power to legislate to protect those rights. The defendants maintained that the act went beyond the powers the Fourteenth Amendment gave to Congress, because it regulated social rather than political or legal rights.

Eight members of the Court agreed. Justice Joseph Bradley's opinion denied both of the government's contentions and, in doing so, robbed the amendments of much of their meaning for the next eighty years. Bradley argued that not every example of discrimination against Negroes could be interpreted as a badge of slavery. Therefore, the Thirteenth Amendment could not be invoked as a ban on all forms of racial prejudice.

The Fourteenth Amendment, however, had been drafted specifically to ensure freedmen's rights, but Bradley rejected the idea that Congress had any affirmative powers under the amendment. According to him, Congress could act only in a remedial manner. That is, if a state enacted a law that restricted the rights of black citizens, then and only then could Congress legislate to correct the injustice. Without prior state action, Congress could do nothing. Bradley then went even further to declare that the federal government had no power to legislate against acts of private discrimination, such as the exclusion of blacks from hotels, restaurants, or theaters. With this decision, the Court severely restricted congressional power to protect the freedmen, essentially leaving their fates to the states.

Bradley was undoubtedly correct in his assertion that not every act of discrimination constituted a mark of slavery, and the Fourteenth Amendment did say that "No State" could deprive a person of due process or equal protection. Purely private discrimination then as now remained beyond the reach of the Constitution. But there had also been a long tradition in Anglo-American law that the owners of private property used by the public could not discriminate to bar a class of customers. In England, for example, the owners of ferries and stagecoaches had been forbidden to deny service to any peaceful person willing to pay the fare. In many ways, Congress did no more in 1875 than include the freedmen in this long-standing practice. Bradley was horribly wrong—but very typical of his times—in his assertion that the former slaves had now reached a stage of equal citizenship where they no longer needed governmental protection.

John Marshall Harlan was the lone dissenter, and according to some his opinion is as impassioned about slavery and freedom as any in the Supreme Court's history. Roscoe Conkling, the former New York senator who had helped draft the postwar amendments, wrote to Harlan and told him his dissent was "the noblest opinion in the history of our country." Harlan began by accusing the majority of sacrificing

> the substance and spirit of the recent amendments . . . by a subtle and ingenious verbal criticism. . . . Constitutional provisions, adopted in the interest of liberty, and for the purpose of securing, through national legislation, if need be, rights inhering in a state of freedom, and belonging to American citizenship, have been so construed as to defeat the ends the people desired to accomplish, which they attempted to accomplish, and which they supposed they had accomplished by changes in their fundamental law.

The Court, he charged, had abandoned the long-standing rule requiring that in interpretation of constitutional provisions "full effect be given to the intent with which they were adopted."

Bradley had argued for a relatively narrow reading of the Thirteenth Amendment, and Harlan—who had originally opposed that amendment—answered with what remains one of its most far-ranging interpretations:

The Thirteenth Amendment, it is conceded, did something more than to prohibit slavery as an institution, resting upon distinctions of race, and upheld by positive law. My brethren admit that it established and decreed universal civil freedom throughout the United States. But did the freedom thus established involve nothing more than exemption from actual slavery? Was nothing more intended than to forbid one man from owning another as property? Was it the purpose of the nation simply to destroy the institution, and then remit the race, theretofore held in bondage, to the several States for such protection, in their civil rights, necessarily growing out of freedom, as those States, in their discretion, might choose to provide? Were the States against whose protest the institution was destroyed to be left free, so far as national interference was concerned, to make or allow discriminations against that race, as such, in the enjoyment of those fundamental rights which, by universal concession, inhere in a state of freedom? Had the Thirteenth Amendment stopped with the sweeping declaration, in its first section, against the existence of slavery and involuntary servitude, except for crime, Congress would have had the power, by implication . . . to protect the freedom established, and consequently, to secure the enjoyment of such civil rights as were fundamental in freedom. That it can exert its authority to that extent is made clear, and was intended to be made clear, by the express grant of power contained in the second section of the Amendment.

Interestingly, Harlan's theme about the "badges and incidents" of slavery would not cover much of what we today think of as civil rights, such as discrimination against women, gays, people with disabilities, and other minorities. But his point, and a very important one, acknowledged that Congress had the *power* to act to protect the freedmen. This authority, he believed, had been augmented and reinforced by the Fourteenth Amendment:

The citizenship thus acquired, by that race, in virtue of an affirmative grant from the nation, may be protected, not alone by the judicial branch of the government, but by congressional legislation of a primary direct character; this, because the power of Congress is not restricted to the enforcement of prohibitions upon State laws or State action. It is, in terms distinct and positive, to enforce "the provisions of this article" of amendment; not simply those of a prohibitive character, but the provisions—all of the provisions—affirmative and prohibitive, of the amendment. It is, therefore, a grave misconception to suppose that the fifth section of the amendment has reference exclusively to express prohibitions upon State laws or State action. If any right was created by that amendment, the grant of power, through appropriate legislation, to enforce its provisions, authorizes Congress, by means of legislation, operating throughout the entire Union, to guard, secure, and protect that right.

Harlan, in addition to rebutting what he saw as the wrong interpretation of the majority—that Congress could only act when states did something harmful to the freedmen—then argued that Congress had authority to act in an affirmative and proactive manner and that this power resided not only in the Enforcement Clauses but in the wording of the amendments themselves. Once it had been determined that the freedmen enjoyed certain rights as citizens, Congress could legitimately act to ensure those rights, and it did not have to wait until states actually subverted them.

Harlan laid out two important themes. One dealt with what we now call public accommodations, that is, private property and businesses that served the public. These included the right to equal treatment on public conveyances, such as stagecoaches, railroads, and steamships. Another would be inns, and a third would be places of public amusement. "I am of the opinion," he wrote, "that such discrimination practiced by corporations and individuals in the exercise of their public or quasi-public functions is a badge of servitude the imposition of which Congress may prevent."

Inns, public conveyances, and houses of entertainment not only secured their trade from the public but operated under a license from the state. This made any discrimination they practiced a form of state action, because, by allowing the innkeeper or railroad or theater owner to discriminate, the state was in effect endorsing that discrimination. The doctrine of state action would, like Harlan's theory of public accommodations, lie dormant for eight decades, until rediscovered by a Court intent on granting full civil rights to African Americans.

The *Civil Rights Cases* had enormous impact. The decision essentially did away with the powers that the Reconstruction amendments gave Congress and limited Congress's ability to act only in the face of overt discrimination by the states. The great tragedy is that Bradley's decision came at a time when the North was rapidly losing interest in protecting the rights of former slaves. Aside from that of aging abolitionists, there was little hostile criticism of the majority opinion. The Compromise of 1877, which had ended Reconstruction and permitted the former Confederate states to rejoin the Union, also implicitly confirmed that henceforth matters of race relations would be left to the states in which people of color lived. There would be a few cases where the discrimination proved too great and the Court intervened, such as the southern peonage laws that practically re-enslaved some blacks. The justices, like most of the country, had little interest in the former slaves.

Because of the near unanimity of the Court and the increasing indifference of the country to the fate of the former slaves, Bradley's interpretation eventually became accepted as the proper one. Not until the 1960s did the Court begin to dismantle Bradley's opinion. In 1961, it used Harlan's notion of state action to hold that a privately owned restaurant that rented space in a municipal parking garage could not deny service to a black customer. According to Justice Tom Clark, it would be a grave injustice for African Americans to be allowed to use the parking spaces in the public garage but be treated as second-class citizens without any rights in another part of the same publicly owned building.

Two years later, in one of the early sit-in cases, Justice William O. Douglas looked to Harlan's opinion in his concurrence. Although there was no specific restaurant segregation ordinance in New Orleans, local officials encouraged owners to maintain segregated facilities. Four students had been arrested and convicted for trespass when they refused to leave a lunch counter in a privately owned five-and-dime store after being refused service. The majority opinion, by Chief Justice Earl Warren, overturned the convictions on equal protection grounds.

Although Douglas agreed with the outcome and the reasoning, he would have gone further. He found the claim that the restaurant was private property to be ill-founded, because "access by the public is the very reason for its existence." There was too great a nexus between a restaurant and the state in the form of licenses, permits, health regulations, and the like for the owner to claim it as a purely private undertaking. To bolster his point, Douglas cited Harlan's assertion that insofar as the Fourteenth Amendment was concerned, "railroad corporations, keepers of inns, and managers of places of public amusement are agents or instrumentalities of the State, because they are charged with duties to the public." When another sit-in case reached the high court a year later, Justice Arthur Goldberg also looked to Harlan's argument that the civil rights enjoyed by the former slaves must mean nothing less than the same treatment that would be received by a white person.

When activists beseeched Congress to enact comprehensive civil rights protection, Congress framed its justification of the 1964 Civil Rights Act in terms of its power over interstate commerce. The *Civil Rights Cases* had never been overruled—they had never even been challenged—and neither the president nor congressional leaders thought they could act under the Enforcement Clause of the Fourteenth Amendment. In the lead case challenging the 1964 act, Justice Clark declared the *Civil Rights Cases* "without precedential value" and affirmed that Congress had the necessary power not only under the Commerce Clause but also under the Enforcement Clauses of the Thirteenth and Fourteenth Amendments. Although not referring to Harlan's dissent directly, the majority and concurring opinions used his analyses of both public accommodations and state action in upholding the law.

A few years later, the Court once again showed that it no longer believed the *Civil Rights Cases* controlling and adopted Justice Harlan's reasoning. An African American had tried to buy a house in St. Louis and had been refused solely on the grounds of his race. He sued in federal court under the 1866 Civil Rights Act (section 1982), which guaranteed all citizens would have the right to "inherit, purchase, lease, sell, hold, and convey real and personal property." The district court dismissed the suit on the grounds that section 1982 applied only to state action, not to private refusals to sell.

RA F020204-2/2/60-GREENSBORO,N.C: A group of Negro students from North Carolina A&T College, who were refused service at a luncheon counter reserved for white customers, staged a sit-down strike at the F.W.Woolworth store in Greensboro 2/2. Ronald Martin, Robert Patterson and Mark Martin are shown as they stayed seated throughout the day. The white woman at left came to the counter for lunch but decided not to sit down.   UPI TELEPHOTO fwb

Ronald Martin, Robert Patterson, and Mark Martin stage a sit-down strike after being refused service at Woolworth's in Greensboro, North Carolina.

The Supreme Court reversed and declared that the legislative history of the 1866 statute made clear that Congress had intended to ban private as well as state-sponsored discrimination. As for the source of congressional authority, Justice Potter Stewart looked not to the Equal Protection Clause of the Fourteenth Amendment, because that had not yet been ratified in 1866. Instead, he turned to the Enforcement Clause of the Thirteenth Amendment and, using the same logic as Harlan, held that the Thirteenth Amendment had been adopted to remove the "badges of slavery" from the nation's black people. It gave Congress sufficient authority to determine what constituted a badge of slavery and do away with it.

Harlan was very much a man of his time in his patrician and indeed racist outlook regarding blacks, but his constitutional views on many matters went well beyond those of his colleagues and even of some of his successors. The liberal icons William Brennan, William O. Douglas, and Thurgood Marshall at times found the brethren taking what they saw as too limited an interpretation of the Fourteenth Amendment and the powers it gave to Congress. Brennan cited Harlan to criticize what he deemed a much too limited construction given by the majority to the intentions of the amendment's framers regarding congressional authority. Douglas echoed Harlan's claim that the majority had taken "too narrow and artificial" a view of section 1983 in determining what constituted a violation of a person's civil rights and a couple of years later cited Harlan again to support his dissent that the majority misread the extent of governmental power. Thurgood Marshall, in the first case in which the Court spoke on the constitutionality of affirmative action, referred to Harlan's views on the type of equality that the Fourteenth Amendment had been enacted to secure.

Although Harlan's opinion is a good example of the efficacy of dissent in convincing future courts, and although his remained practically the sole voice on the Court at that time seeking equal rights for people of color, at least in terms of modern civil rights his viewpoint is somewhat restricted. Like most of his generation, he drew a distinction between civil rights and social rights. Civil rights were fundamental but narrow, and perhaps the most important component was the right to enter into a contract—the basis of economic activity and clearly a prerequisite if former slaves ever hoped to get ahead in the market. A business invited patrons to enter; the patrons had a right either to enter or not and, if they chose to do so, to make a contract to buy whatever the business sold. If Congress chose to do so, he believed, it could require all businesses to allow African Americans to patronize them on the same terms as white customers did.

Congress did not, however, have the power to enforce social rights, the most important of which involved the right to choose one's associates. Where did the boundary exist between a civil right and a social right? For example, suppose a theater owner put on a play and sold tickets to the public. It would be a civil right to buy a ticket, but could the owner then require that all blacks sit in a separate section? Today, of course, we would condemn such segregation as a violation of civil rights, but in the 1880s a powerful argument would be made that only the social rights of African Americans—to sit where they chose—had been violated, and neither the Thirteenth nor the Fourteenth Amendment protected social rights.

Even acknowledging that John Marshall Harlan's views on racial equality were not those of a modern civil rights proponent, one has to note the moral tone—the concern for the future of the freedmen—that is totally missing in Bradley's majority opinion, with its cavalier dismissal of the freedmen's claims. With all its limitations, Harlan's dissent would have allowed—but not guaranteed—outcomes that the framers of the Reconstruction amendments clearly had in mind and that the majority opinion foreclosed.

Harlan's dissent certainly fits Dean Kathleen Sullivan's description of "buried ammunition for future generations to unearth when the time comes." But how does it fit into the notion of dialogue, both within the Court and with the larger societal discussion of these issues? Harlan was literally a lone voice at the time, and neither his colleagues on the Court nor the great majority of white citizens—North and South—wanted to hear his message. The debate over what to do about the former slaves had been heated and active in the ten years following Appomattox and then had died down as the country looked to a new agenda. But his message remained, forgotten for a while but ready to be heard again when the nation began to grapple with the problems of racism after World War II. That message could also be found in the most famous case on race relations in the late nineteenth century, *Plessy v. Ferguson* (1896), and John Marshall Harlan's dissent there is still cited.

THE LOUISIANA LEGISLATURE passed the Separate Car Law in 1890 mandating the segregation of passenger trains within the state by prohibiting passengers, whether black or white, from occupying railcars not assigned to their race. In a clearly designed test case, Homer

Plessy, who was one-eighth black, bought a ticket and sat in a white car. The conductor asked Plessy if he was a "colored man" and, on receiving an affirmative reply, ordered Plessy to move to the colored car. Plessy refused, the conductor stopped the train, and a railroad detective arrested Plessy and took him to jail.

With the end of Reconstruction, blacks living in northern states for the most part enjoyed legal equality, and a number of states enacted laws protecting civil rights at the local level. The South, on the other hand, soon hit upon a means of keeping the former slaves in an inferior position—the legal separation of the races in all aspects of public life. In 1878, the Court ruled that states could not prohibit voluntary segregation by interstate common carriers, such as railroads or riverboats. A dozen years later, it approved a Mississippi statute requiring segregation on intrastate carriers. Only Justices Harlan and Bradley dissented, not on equal protection grounds, but because such laws interfered with interstate commerce.

Plessy's attorney argued that segregation on the basis of race violated both the Thirteenth and the Fourteenth Amendments, the former because it constituted a "badge of slavery" and the latter because it deprived people of color of equal protection. For a 7–1 Court, Justice Henry Billings Brown dismissed the Thirteenth Amendment claim out of hand. That the Louisiana law "does not conflict with the Thirteenth Amendment," declared Brown, "is too clear for argument. . . . A statute which implies merely a legal distinction between the white and colored races—a distinction which is founded in the color of the two races, and which must always exist so long as white men are distinguished from the other race by color—has no tendency to destroy the legal equality of the two races, or reestablish a state of involuntary servitude."

The Fourteenth Amendment had indeed been intended to establish an absolute equality of the races before the law, but "in the nature of things it could not have been intended to abolish distinctions based upon color, or to enforce social, as distinguished from political, equality, or a commingling of the two races unsatisfactory to either." Nowhere in the majority opinion can the phrase "separate but equal" be found, but the Court's ruling approved legally enforced segregation so long as the law did not make facilities for blacks "inferior" to those of whites.

Justice Harlan dissented and castigated the legislature for an act that penalized a citizen because he or she wanted to use public highways or common carriers. Such legislation was "inconsistent not only with equality of rights which pertain to citizenship, National and State, but with the personal liberty enjoyed by everyone in the United States." As for the majority's disingenuous contention that segregation did not in itself constitute discrimination, the Kentucky-born Harlan, the only member of the Court with firsthand knowledge of slavery, condemned segregation statutes as "conceived in hostility to, and enacted for the purpose of humiliating, citizens of the United States of a particular race." Such laws defeated the purpose of the Reconstruction amendments and made any real peace between the races impossible. He continued in what has been one of the most quoted dissents in our constitutional history:

> The white race deems itself to be the dominant race in this country. And so it is, in prestige, in achievements, in education, in wealth and in power. So, I doubt not, it will continue to be for all time, if it remains true to its great heritage and holds fast to the principles of constitutional liberty. But in view of the Constitution, in the eye of the law, there is in this country no superior, dominant, ruling class of citizens. There is no caste here. Our Constitution is color-blind, and neither knows nor tolerates classes among citizens. In respect of civil rights, all citizens are equal before the law. The humblest is the peer of the most powerful. The law regards man as man, and takes no account of his surroundings or of his color when his civil rights as guaranteed by the supreme law of the land are involved. It is, therefore, to be regretted that this high tribunal, the final expositor of the fundamental law of the land, has reached the conclusion that it is competent for a State to regulate the enjoyment by citizens of their civil rights solely upon the basis of race.

Some scholars charge that Harlan was not a true believer in civil rights as we now know them, and that he did not consider African Americans equal to whites. He was a man of his background and of his times, but perhaps, as one of his biographers suggests, Harlan was actually asking the white race, because of its dominant position, to help lift the black race to equality. He appealed to whites to uphold the achievements of the Civil War and to fulfill the American mission. Anglo-Saxons had long told themselves that their race had a special ability to establish free, democratic governments under the rule of law. In effect, Harlan appealed to white racial pride as he demanded a legal system that was blind to race.

Harlan, who during these years taught at the Columbian School of Law (now part of George Washington University), urged his students to see the Reconstruction amendments as opening doors from which the enslaved black race could take its rightful place as citizens of the nation. Moreover, they should do all they could to help. "I am ready to say that if there is a black man who can get ahead of me, I will help him along, and rejoice, and his progress in life does not excite my envy." He believed that "it is the desire of the white people in this country that [blacks] shall push themselves forward in the race of life." Harlan might have been a bit naive, but to his lasting credit he, alone among all of the members of the Supreme Court, saw the moral as well as the constitutional evil in Jim Crow, although even he could not guess at its full horrors.

Legal commentators at the time did not think very highly of Harlan's dissent. William Bowen, for example, who did not care for dissents at all, condemned Harlan's in particular: "Among the forms which Dissent has taken the most harmful is that which may be called the 'Dissent of Warning.' The office of this is to criticize the opinion of the court, and to warn an innocent public against the ills which will surely befall it if the court persists in its erroneous course. . . . The most drastic treatment of this kind to which the Court has ever had to submit at the hands of one of its members, is, perhaps, that furnished by Mr. Justice Harlan in Plessy v. Ferguson."

Nearly fifty years later, immediately after the Supreme Court handed down the landmark ruling in *Brown v. Board of Education,* the editors of *The New York Times* declared,

> It is eighty-six years since the Fourteenth Amendment was proclaimed a part of the United States Constitution. It is fifty-eight years since the Supreme Court, with Justice Harlan dissenting, established the doctrine of "separate but equal" provision for white and Negro races on interstate carriers. It is forty-three years since John Marshall Harlan passed from this earth. Now the words he used in his lonely dissent in an 8-to-1 decision in the case of Plessy v. Ferguson in 1896 have become in effect by last Monday's unanimous decision of the Supreme Court a part of the law of the land. . . .
>
> This is an instance of which the voice crying in the wilderness finally becomes an expression of a people's will and in which justice overtakes and thrusts aside a timorous expediency.

Ironically, Justice Brown—the author of *Plessy*—in an article written shortly after Justice Harlan's death, expressed doubt about the majority opinion he had written and suggested that Harlan might have been right in both that case and the earlier *Civil Rights Cases.** Harlan "thought that the arbitrary separation of citizens on the basis of race . . . was a badge of servitude wholly inconsistent with the civil freedom and equality before the law established by the Constitution."

ONE FINDS LITTLE MENTION of Harlan's dissent in *Plessy* until the 1960s, in part because of the strategy employed in the early cases mounted by the National Association for the Advancement of Colored People's Legal Defense Fund. Believing they would be unsuccessful in a head-on attack against segregation, Thurgood Marshall and his team—who certainly knew and appreciated the dissent—decided to emphasize the inferiority of facilities for African Americans and the lower salaries paid to black teachers. Not until the Texas law school case did the Supreme Court indicate that it would entertain a challenge to *Plessy,* and then the Legal Defense Fund launched the cases that would be consolidated in *Brown v. Board of Education* in 1954. Once that decision overruled *Plessy,* one might have expected that neither the now-discredited majority opinion nor the dissent would play any role in further Supreme Court decisions.

But in the half century following *Brown,* the country and the Court grappled with the meaning of equal protection for minorities such as women and gays but especially for people of color. The early cases were relatively simple, as the Court struck down one state law after another that mandated segregation and it upheld federal laws protecting civil rights and the right to vote for African Americans. But then the road to equality grew trickier, and the country and the Court debated the wisdom of affirmative action and so-called majority-minority election districts. Beginning in the 1960s, justices started referencing Harlan's *Plessy* dissent as they wrestled with ever more complicated questions of civil rights. They also took into account his broad views on what constituted governmental action.

---

* Justice Harlan's opposition to segregation did not abate, and in 1908 he penned another strong dissent in *Berea College v. Kentucky*. Berea had been established in 1859 to promote Christian values and sometime after the Civil War began admitting black students. In 1904, Kentucky passed a law prohibiting the education of children of different races in the same school. The school sued and argued that the law prevented it from pursuing a lawful occupation, but the same Court that had decided *Lochner* said that the college's right to teach depended on the state. Harlan's dissent invoked the notion of substantive due process and denounced the legislation as "an arbitrary invasion of the rights of liberty and property guaranteed by the Fourteenth Amendment against state action." Few people paid attention to the case or the dissent at the time. While there had been some outcry against *Plessy* in northern newspapers, the decision in this case occasioned little comment and no protest.

The most influential part of Harlan's *Plessy* dissent has been the simple phrase "Our Constitution is color-blind." Clearly this was not true in 1896, nor had it been in 1787 or 1868. A number of clauses in the original Constitution referred to slavery, providing for how slaves would be counted for purposes of taxation and representation in the House of Representatives, and for the recapture of runaways. The Reconstruction amendments, no matter how later interpreted, had been passed with race clearly in mind. Harlan's assertion, however, was neither ignorant of history nor naive, but rather aspirational: in a society of equal rights for all people, no group should be either favored or disfavored.

In the first affirmative action case, *Regents of the University of California v. Bakke* (1978), four of the justices believed that affirmative action violated both the Equal Protection Clause of the Fourteenth Amendment and the 1964 Civil Rights Act and argued that neither permitted the favoring of one race over another. Justice Brennan, speaking for himself and three other justices, supported affirmative action and declared—correctly—that "no decision of this Court has ever adopted the proposition that the Constitution must be colorblind." Brennan might have been right, but from that time forward the phrase became a rallying cry for conservatives on the Court who believed that preferential treatment based on race violated the Constitution.

In a 1980 case, a 6–3 majority sustained a law requiring contractors on federal projects to sublet a certain percentage of the work to minority businesses. Justice Potter Stewart dissented, claiming that the minority business provision denied the equal protection of the law, because it barred one class of business owners from the opportunity to secure a government benefit on the basis of the owners' racial and ethnic attributes. He wrote,

"Our Constitution is color-blind, and neither knows nor tolerates classes among citizens. . . . The law regards man as man, and takes no account of his surroundings or of his color. . . ." Those words were written by a Member of this Court 84 years ago. His colleagues disagreed with him, and held that a statute that required the separation of people on the basis of their race was constitutionally valid because it was a "reasonable" exercise of legislative power and had been "enacted in good faith for the promotion [of] the public good. . . ." Today, the Court upholds a statute that accords a preference to citizens who are "Negroes, Spanish-speaking, Orientals, Indians, Eskimos, and Aleuts," for much the same reasons.

I think today's decision is wrong for the same reason that *Plessy v. Ferguson* was wrong, and I respectfully dissent.

Within a few years, the Court looked more askance at affirmative action, and the justices often cited Justice Harlan's dissent. In the 1980s, the city of Richmond, Virginia, tried to implement a minority business provision in its contracts, only to have the Court strike it down. In a concurring opinion, Justice Antonin Scalia saw the law as a racial quota that might benefit blacks, but at the expense of whites, and argued that "even 'benign' racial quotas have individual victims, whose very real injustice we ignore whenever we deny them enforcement of their right not to be disadvantaged on the basis of race." "Our Constitution is colorblind," he declared, quoting Harlan, "and neither knows nor tolerates classes among citizens."

HARLAN'S DISSENT often came up in the Court's efforts to deal with majority-minority districting. The Voting Rights Act of 1965 aimed at ensuring not only access to the ballot box for blacks but also that the minority vote would not be diluted by districting. Section 5 provided that in states with a history of past discrimination, district lines might have to be redrawn to give minorities proportional representation in the total makeup of a state's congressional delegation. For example, a state with eight congressional seats and a 25 percent African American population might be required to so draw district lines that two "majority-minority" districts would be created in which blacks constituted a majority of the electorate.

Ever since 1960, gerrymandering districts along racial lines had been illegal, but in 1982 the Court approved a plan for single-district seats for county commissioners in Burke County, Georgia, to ensure that some districts would have black majorities. During the 1980s, the Court routinely approved majority-minority districts on the rationale that Congress had the power to ensure fair representation under the Enforcement Clause of the Fifteenth Amendment. However, as a majority of justices came to see affirmative action as unconstitutional, they also questioned the validity of majority-minority districting.

In the first case it heard, *Shaw v. Reno* (1993), the Court abandoned its deference to the Justice Department's policies regarding racial districting. Opponents of the plan cited Justice Harlan in their brief, but although they ultimately won in this case, Justice Sandra Day O'Connor made it clear that the color-blind phrase did not automatically doom a racially conscious plan. "This Court never has held that race-conscious state decision-making is impermissible in *all* circumstances." In this case, the plan was so weirdly drawn that, as one state legislator noted, "if you drove down the interstate with both car doors open, you'd kill most of the people in the district."

The Court did not say that all majority-minority districts were invalid, and in fact Justice O'Connor declared that some could be upheld. But the Court did not lay down clear guidelines, and it heard a whole series of cases in which plans varied and in which the color-blind phrase appeared as often as not. The justices were well aware of the tension that existed between the history of racial discrimination and denial of the ballot in southern states, on the one hand, and the desire to have a society where, at least in law, race did not matter. Finally, the Court essentially washed its hands of the issue by declaring that if there were adequate political reasons for drawing district lines, the Court would not review those decisions.

One might think that over a century after the *Plessy* decision, its reversal in *Brown,* the legislative achievements of the civil rights movement, and the election of an African American president the Court would have no need to keep going back to Harlan's dissent. Racism, however, is far from extinct in twenty-first-century America, and while less frequent than in decades immediately following *Brown,* questions of race are still debated in our society and come before the Court.

In 2005, for example, the Court overturned a California policy that segregated new and transferred inmates on the basis of race until regular housing assignments could be made. The state claimed that this was not a question of prejudice but a means to prevent gang violence while the newcomers were being processed. In an opinion by Justice O'Connor, the Court declared the policy invalid. All questions of racial classification had to be subject to a standard of strict scrutiny, because "the Constitution is color-blind, and neither knows nor tolerates classes among citizens."

Two years later, in a highly controversial decision, Chief Justice John Roberts again invoked Harlan in two cases involving resegregation of public schools. The Louisville school system had been segregated during the Jim Crow era and was for a number of years under court supervision to end those practices. The courts eventually cleared the system, but as in many urban areas officials worried about resegregation due to housing patterns and instituted a plan whereby race would be a factor in assigning students to schools in an effort to maintain racial diversity. The Seattle schools had never been segregated by law and therefore had not been under court order to desegregate. But officials also worried about housing patterns and used race as a tiebreaker when assigning students to schools where one race or the other predominated. Parent groups in both cities sued, and the Court combined the cases for hearings.

Chief Justice Roberts declared that "the way to stop discrimination on the basis of race is to stop discriminating on the basis of race." He believed the majority view, in striking down the two school systems' plans, was faithful to *Brown,* which he claimed had repudiated the notion of using race to assign children to schools. He seemed annoyed by the Seattle system Web site that described "emphasizing individualism as opposed to a more collective ideology" as a form of "cultural racism"; the district declared that it had no intention "to hold onto unsuccessful concepts such as a . . . colorblind mentality." To which Roberts cited Harlan, and for him and for Justices Scalia, Thomas, and Alito, the only standard that should apply would be that of a "color-blind Constitution" in which race could never be a factor in school assignments, hiring, or contract allocation. Justice Clarence Thomas, more than any other member of the Court, wrapped himself in Harlan's dissent and wrote,

> Most of the dissent's criticisms of today's result can be traced to its rejection of the color-blind Constitution. The dissent attempts to marginalize the notion of a color-blind Constitution by consigning it to me and Members of today's plurality. But I am quite comfortable in the company I keep. My view of the Constitution is Justice Harlan's view in *Plessy:* "Our Constitution is color-blind, and neither knows nor tolerates classes among citizens." And my view was the rallying cry for the lawyers who litigated *Brown.* . . . "Thurgood Marshall had a 'Bible' to which he turned during his most depressed moments. The 'Bible' would be known in the legal community as the first Mr. Justice Harlan's dissent in *Plessy v. Ferguson.* I do not know of any opinion which buoyed Marshall more in his pre-*Brown* days."

There is a certain irony here that Harlan's dissent against segregation is being used, it would seem, to permit resegregation of schools. The earlier apartheid, however, had been mandated by the state, and to Harlan that clearly ran against the command of the Fourteenth Amendment. In the twenty-first century, he might well have said that the Constitution does not protect social rights, and it cannot be used to thwart residential patterns where people are living, if not completely by their own choice, certainly not because the state is making them do so. Carried to a logical end, a color-blind Constitution would not allow racial classification even for benign purposes. Harlan probably did not consider that when he wrote, but his argument has continued to be part of the constitutional dialogue on race, even as our understanding of race in our society has changed and continues to change.

As a final note on the influence of Harlan's *Plessy* dissent, we turn to the first breakthrough case for gay rights, *Romer v. Evans* (1996). The case involved a Colorado referendum that nullified various laws prohibiting discrimination against gays in housing, employment, and other areas. Justice Anthony Kennedy began his opinion for a 6–3 majority by declaring, "One century ago, the first Justice Harlan admonished this Court that the Constitution 'neither knows nor tolerates classes among citizens.' Unheeded then, those words now are understood to state a commitment to the law's neutrality where the rights of persons are at stake." Kennedy noted that it was a dissenting opinion but treated it as if it were an authoritative statement of the law, although it had never been accepted as such by the Court. In his dissent, Justice Antonin Scalia did not object to the authority of the Harlan dissent, only to Justice Kennedy's spreading its mantle over a new group. Few, if any, dissents in the Court's history, and few phrases, have had an impact on the constitutional dialogue comparable to that of Justice Harlan in *Plessy*.

HARLAN'S DISSENTS in the segregation cases are his best known, but he also participated in other constitutional dialogues, and these deserve to be noted as well. At a time when many of his colleagues seemed obsessed with the protection of business and property rights, Harlan, who also cared about them, nonetheless saw with a clearer eye the impact of industrialization.

Harlan has been described as a giant of a man, standing over six feet two and weighing near 240 pounds. He had a robust nature and also a temper that at times boiled over, occasionally even in the courtroom. He allowed his feelings to get the better of him in two cases, one of them the *Income Tax Case* of 1895. He reportedly shook his finger and shouted angrily while delivering his dissent, looking at Justice Stephen Field as he did so. The future attorney general Philander Knox remarked, "I should hate to use any such language about the Court as it said about itself yesterday."

The original Constitution did not provide for an income tax, and the federal government, until the Civil War, had lived on the tariffs imposed on imported goods and the sale of western lands. The costs of the war had far exceeded this income, and Congress, among other measures, had imposed an income tax. The Court sustained this tax in 1881, ruling that the direct taxes prohibited by the Constitution consisted only of capitation (a head tax) and real estate taxes. Economic hard times, especially the depression of 1893, and a decline in tariff receipts, led to a series of government deficits. Reformers, especially the Populists, had been clamoring for an income tax, especially on the wealthy, and in 1894, as part of the Wilson-Gorman Tariff, Congress enacted a 2 percent tax on all corporate and individual incomes, with a $4,000 exemption for the latter.

Conservatives reacted as if there had been a revolution. Joseph Choate, who argued against the tax, called it "communistic in its purposes and tendencies, and is defended here upon the principles as communistic, socialistic—what shall I call them—populistic as ever have been addressed to any political assembly in the world." Had the Court followed legal precedent, it would have had to uphold the tax. Chief Justice Melville Fuller, however, dismissed all of the precedents as "a century of error" and by a vote of 6–2 invalidated the main tax as a direct but unapportioned tax on land. But the justices split 4–4 on three other questions related to the tax.

Normally, when the high court splits, the decision of the lower court stands, and on these questions the lower courts had upheld the tax. Fuller would have none of this, so he scheduled new hearings. Justice Howell Jackson had missed the first round because of illness. He took part in the second hearing, and although he voted to sustain the tax, one of the dissenters in the first case changed his mind, and by a 5–4 vote the Court invalidated all sections of the tax. Fuller's opinion again distorted history and precedent. The rights of property, not a strict construction of the Constitution, informed his opinion.

The issue was less about the constitutionality of the income tax than about who would make policy—the Court or Congress. Justice Henry Billings Brown—who could hardly be considered a radical—openly attacked the political rather than the judicial concerns that had motivated the majority. In words that any Populist could have cheered, Brown declared that "the decision involves nothing less than a surrender of the taxing power to the moneyed class."

Harlan entered a very long dissent, far longer than the majority opinion, quite unlike his normally restrained manner. According to reporters present, Harlan "pounded the desk," "shook his finger under the noses of the Chief Justice and Mr. Justice Field," and spoke in a tone "more appropriate to a stump speech at a Populist barbecue than to an opinion

on a question of law before the Supreme Court of the United States."
When the American people, Harlan declared, "come to the conclusion
that the judiciary of this land is usurping to itself the functions of the
legislative departments of the government and by judicial construction
only, is declaring what shall be the public policy of the United States,
we shall find trouble."

In his dissent, Harlan exhaustively examined the history of taxation
in the country, what the Framers had said at the Philadelphia convention, the practices not only of the colonies but of the mother country,
and the Court's various decisions going back for a century and completely demolished Fuller's history and analysis. He also attacked Field,
who had agreed with Choate that the Court had to "stand in the breach"
against such radical ideas. Indeed, Field had warned that if the Court
upheld the tax, the "present assault upon capital is but the beginning.
It will be the stepping-stone to . . . a war of the poor against the rich."
Harlan dismissed such arguments. "With the policy of legislation of this
character, the court has nothing to do." If the decision stood, then "the
American people cannot too soon amend their Constitution."

As Harlan charged, the Court had overreached itself, and the extent
of the Court's action astonished even conservative opinion. Although
the major eastern and midwestern papers applauded, the majority of
the country reacted in disbelief and anger. Within a few months, Harlan's suggestion of a constitutional amendment took hold with the
public, and a proposed amendment was introduced in every Congress
starting that fall, along with bills to reduce the power of the courts
and give Congress the authority to override Court decisions. Conservative senators managed to block the tax amendment until 1909, when
under threat from insurgent Republicans and Democrats the conservative bloc allowed it to go through Congress, because, as Senator Nelson
Aldrich predicted, it would surely be defeated in the states. Aldrich
badly misread the temper of the country, and by early 1913 forty-two
states had ratified the Sixteenth Amendment, six more than necessary,
giving Congress the power that Harlan had maintained it possessed all
along. The Wilson administration immediately tacked on an income tax
to the Underwood Tariff of that year and would rely heavily on it to help
finance World War I. Academic circles have echoed Harlan's scornful
dismissal of Fuller's opinion ever since.

THE INABILITY OF THE GOVERNMENT under the Articles of Confederation to control interstate or foreign commerce had been one of
the primary reasons for the drafting and adoption of the Constitution,

and up to the Civil War the Court had taken a rather broad view of the extent of that power. Harlan, like his namesake, the great chief justice, believed the commerce power plenary in nature and broad in scope. Conservative justices following the Civil War, however, took a far more restrictive view of what interstate commerce meant and the reach of the federal government's authority in regulating it. Harlan opposed this narrowing of what he considered one of the national government's most important powers.

There are two laws that we need to look at briefly—the Interstate Commerce Act of 1887 and the Sherman Antitrust Act of 1890. Both statutes attempted to deal with the realities of the new industrial era by setting up a regulatory scheme to govern the nation's railroads in the first case and to prevent the monopolization of markets by giant corporations in the second.

The first law established the Interstate Commerce Commission (ICC), and initially a majority of the Court found the new agency not only a puzzle but in some ways threatening as well. The Constitution makes no mention of administrative agencies, especially those that are independent of either the president or Congress. Today, of course, we are all familiar with what some have termed the fourth branch of government, the many administrative agencies that oversee everything from air traffic safety to the quality of the foods and drugs we use. These agencies, however, are hybrids unknown to the founding generation. They can hold hearings and draft regulations (a legislative function), implement and enforce those rules (an executive role), and punish those who violate the rules (a judicial task). We now understand that given the ever more complex nature of the industrial economy, the complicated technical work of, for example, determining rates that would be fair both to the railroads and to their customers (shippers and passengers) is far beyond the knowledge or ability of Congress. Setting up agencies which would have that expertise made good sense.

Conservatives on the Court like Field and Fuller, however, opposed the ICC because it both trenched on the judicial prerogative and violated their belief that the government should have no role in regulating the economy. Although they could find no grounds on which to declare the ICC unconstitutional, a majority on the Court managed to hamstring the agency by denying it powers granted by Congress or requiring judicial review of rates. In one of the first cases, the Court ruled that the ICC had no power to impose on railroads moving goods in foreign trade the same rates they charged for similar goods moving in domestic commerce. Harlan dissented and pointed out that such an interpretation would leave such a wide loophole in the act that it would be ineffective; Congress could not have intended such a result.

The following year, the Court went even further in two cases in its efforts to strip the ICC of meaningful powers, declaring that it had no authority at all to prescribe rates; it could only hold hearings after the railroad had put whatever rates it wanted into effect. (This, of course, sounds very much like the majority opinion in the *Civil Rights Cases* that held Congress could act under the Fourteenth Amendment only after a state had deprived blacks of rights.) Harlan's dissent pointed out the obvious, that the ruling left the ICC practically powerless to accomplish its purpose:

> Taken in connection with other decisions defining the powers of the Interstate Commerce Commission, the present decision, it seems to me, goes far to make that commission a useless body, for all practical purposes, and to defeat many of the important objects designed to be accomplished by the various enactments of Congress relating to interstate commerce. The Commission was established to protect the public against the improper practices of transportation companies engaged in commerce among the several States. . . . It has been shorn, by judicial interpretation, of authority to do anything of an effective character. It is denied many of the powers which, in my judgment, were intended to be conferred upon it.

Between 1897 and 1906, the ICC won only one major case out of sixteen before the high court. The demand for regulation, however, could not be stopped. Progressives and agrarian interests believed that the railroads charged overly high rates to shippers, and there is evidence that the railroads, finding rate wars too expensive, also sought regulation. Congress passed revisions to the law and in the Hepburn Act of

Standard Oil plant in Indiana, 1910

1906 attempted to clarify the ICC's authority and restore some of the powers taken away by court decisions. The Court, however, refused to budge and struck down a key provision prohibiting railroads from handling goods, especially coal, made in companies they owned, because they could then charge favorable rates that would put other manufacturers at a disadvantage. In a Jesuitical opinion, Justice Edward Douglass White held that the law was not intended to apply to ownership of stock, although he failed to explain how else one company could own another.

Harlan took the brethren to task for allowing the railroad companies, "by one device or another, to defeat altogether the purpose which Congress had in view." He then invited Congress to in effect overrule the Court. The majority opinion, he declared, was not a constitutional judgment but a matter of statutory interpretation, and if Congress had intended a different result, then it should reenact the measure with clearer wording so that the courts could not misinterpret congressional intent.

Congress did that, and within a few years the Court vindicated Harlan's interpretation of the commerce power. In one case after another, the Court approved of ICC powers to investigate and to set rates and in 1914 even allowed it to set intrastate rates when they directly affected interstate commerce. The Court, however, would remain enmeshed in rate making for nearly a half century. In a case in which Harlan joined the majority, *Smyth v. Ames* (1898), the Court ruled that while a state legislature could prescribe rates for intrastate carriers, these rates were subject to judicial review. As a result, the courts were besieged with cases in which railroads, introducing "new" evidence, constantly appealed state rate making. The Court finally abandoned its review of rates in 1944.

THE OTHER IMPORTANT ASPECT of the commerce powers involved congressional efforts to curb the powers of monopolies. In the decades

after the Civil War, not only did industrialization produce large corporations, but many of them merged to form giant trusts that dominated their fields. To take one example, by 1879 John D. Rockefeller's Standard Oil empire controlled between 90 and 95 percent of the nation's oil-refining capacity. In the 1880s, five other nationwide trusts came into being, each essentially controlling its industry.

There had long been a common-law tradition opposed to monopolies, and as early as 1602 judges in Britain's *Monopolies Case* had accepted the economic arguments that monopolies led to higher costs and poorer quality for the consumer while cutting off entrepreneurial opportunity. In response to the public outcry against Standard Oil and other monopolistic companies, several states tried to codify the common law in statutory form in the 1880s. But no one state could hope to control the problem, and Congress, under increasing public demand, finally acted in 1890. Congress could have decided to require federal incorporation of all companies doing interstate business and then set up strict prohibitions against certain types of behavior in their charters. Instead, it chose a weaker model.

The Sherman Antitrust Act of 1890, which remains the basis for nearly all federal antitrust prosecutions to this day, outlawed every "contract, combination in the form of trust or otherwise, or conspiracy in restraint of trade or commerce." The act nowhere defined what any of these terms meant, nor did it set up any specialized agency to enforce the law, leaving it in the hands of the Justice Department. The wording is so vague because Congress did not really know what it wanted to do. The act embodied the traditional common-law proscription against restraint of trade, yet the legislators knew that in the highly competitive atmosphere of the late nineteenth century all successful businesses restricted trade to some extent. Moreover, did the act outlaw *every* combination or only *some*? In retrospect, it is clear that Congress did not have any coherent economic theory but merely wanted to assuage an angry public and hoped that the courts would somehow make sense of it—or perhaps even nullify it.

That certainly appeared to be the result in the first major antitrust case to come before the Court. The government sought dissolution of the American Sugar Refining Company, a combination of four Philadelphia firms that controlled over 90 percent of the nation's sugar-refining capacity. The Justice Department argued that the agreements used to establish this monopoly substantially restrained trade and caused higher prices for the consumer.

Chief Justice Melville Fuller found against the government and drew a sharp line between manufacturing and commerce. "Commerce succeeds to manufacturing," he declared, "and is not a part of it." The Sherman Act applied only to firms in interstate commerce, and while the defendants had conspired to monopolize the production of sugar, under the terms of the law that by itself could not be held illegal. Fuller conceded that Congress might be able to reach manufacturing that had a direct impact on interstate commerce, but it did not spell out what that meant; federal power could certainly not be used to control indirect effects.

Harlan entered a powerful but lone dissent. The majority essentially gutted the law, he charged, and took issue with Fuller's definition of commerce. "It is the settled doctrine of this court that interstate commerce embraces something more than the mere physical transportation of articles," he declared. Commerce "includes the purchase and sale of articles that are intended to be transported from one state to another—every species of commercial intercourse among the states and with foreign nations." The activities of a manufacturing monopoly could not realistically be said to have only an "incidental" effect on commerce. After all, the whole aim of manufacturing is sale of its goods, and sales constitute commerce.

The force of Harlan's logic proved too strong for the brethren. In no succeeding case did the Court accept the *Knight* doctrine fully but attempted to distinguish it, and within a decade, with Harlan still on the bench, it all but disappeared. In 1899, the Court heard a case in which six companies had entered a compact to divide up the cast-iron pipe market. All nine justices voted that the companies had violated the Sherman Act, and Justice Peckham tried to distinguish the case from *Knight* by finding that the sugar company had only an indirect effect on commerce, while the pipe makers had a direct effect, a bit of sophistry that must have made Harlan smile. In 1905, the Court ruled that Swift & Company, the giant meatpacker, had also engaged in monopolistic practices. In his opinion for the Court, Holmes ignored *Knight* and its manufacturing/commerce distinction by inventing the "stream of commerce" theory to demonstrate the effect of monopolies on interstate commerce. The stockyards, controlled by Swift and its allies, constituted a "throat" through which commerce passed, and therefore came within the reach of the Commerce Clause. But while history and the Court have vindicated Harlan's broad view of commerce, they have rejected his views on what constituted the type of restraint prohibited by the Sherman Act.

In 1904, Harlan spoke for a 5–4 majority in holding the Northern Securities Company had violated the law. The James J. Hill and J. P. Morgan group owned the Northern Pacific and Great Northern rail lines and had just bought the Burlington line to secure a terminal in Chicago. E. H. Harriman, who controlled the Union Pacific line, had been rebuffed in his effort to join in the Burlington line, so he launched an effort to buy a controlling interest in the Northern Pacific. This sent the railroad securities market into a spin, and to resolve the issue, Hill, Morgan, and Harriman formed the Northern Securities Company, capitalized at $400 million, to operate the Great Northern, Northern Pacific, and Burlington lines as an integrated system.

When Theodore Roosevelt embarked on his trust-busting crusade, he and Attorney General Philander Knox decided that in spite of the decision in *Knight,* the Sherman Act still retained some vitality. Looking for a test case, they decided to challenge the formation of Northern Securities and won a suit for dissolution in the lower courts.

Northern Securities, relying on *Knight,* claimed that the merger represented nothing more than a stock transfer, which did not constitute commerce. Second, the corporation had done nothing illegal under the terms of its New Jersey charter, and because state law controlled the incorporation of businesses, application of the Sherman Act would violate the Tenth Amendment by unconstitutionally intruding federal power into a domain reserved for the states.

Justice Harlan wrote for the 5–4 majority and rejected both propositions. Whatever the technical aspects of the stock arrangement, the purpose had been to restrain competition in the railroad industry. The Sherman Act outlawed *all* contracts, combinations, or conspiracies that directly or indirectly restrained competition in interstate commerce. As for the states' rights argument, Harlan dismissed the notion that a state could grant immunity from a federal law. The idea that a state could prevent the national government from exercising its constitutional power could not "be entertained for a moment."

Although the government won the case, and Harlan seemed vindicated and wrote the opinion, the narrowness of the vote indicated that the Court had not yet found a comfortable means of evaluating the Sherman Act. Harlan's opinion reiterated his belief that Congress had plenary and broad powers, and his opinion in *Northern Securities* helped drive another nail into the narrow and unrealistic view of commerce that had been put forward in *Knight* less than a decade earlier. But while Harlan grasped the notion that commerce included nearly every aspect of a national economy, he seemed not to understand the nature of economic transactions, a surprising failure for a man who had been a lawyer and managed an estate.

In this case, the way of the future lay not in Harlan's opinion but in the dissent of Oliver Wendell Holmes Jr., who questioned the intent of Congress. Clearly the legislature wanted to protect competition from overweening power, but he did not think Congress wanted to lose all of the benefits of consolidation. Although the statute said "every" combination, Holmes believed it unlikely that Congress actually meant that, because such an absolute prohibition would "disintegrate society so far as it could into individual atoms." All business, he noted, to some extent "monopolizes whatever business it does," whether within one state or between states. Once a buyer enters a contract with a seller, it freezes out all other sellers. In an attempt to discern what Congress intended, Holmes suggested a rule of reason—that the law should apply only to those contracts, combinations, or conspiracies that *unreasonably* restrained trade and not those where restraint was merely a consequence of securing greater efficiency.

Holmes, who did not even believe in the efficacy of antitrust laws, had the better of the practical argument, even if Harlan had the better of the legal argument. In the dialogue on the Court, Holmes won out, and his triumph came in 1911 at the end of Harlan's career. Harlan agreed with the Court's decision to break up both the Standard Oil Company and the American Tobacco Company but dissented in both cases because the Court had adopted the rule of reason, and it did so in a casuistic opinion in which the new chief justice, Edward White (whom Harlan heartily disliked), declared that the rule of reason had never been rejected by the Court. Harlan might not have been as annoyed that the Court rejected his interpretation as that White denied that it had done any such thing. In his dissents in *Standard Oil* and in the tobacco case, Harlan pointed to the decision in the *Trans-Missouri* case as clearly holding the direct opposite of what White had said.

Logically, Harlan had the better argument, because there is no doubt that the Court in at least three cases had rejected the rule of reason, and White's history convinced no one. But the rule of reason had a great deal of support. Although Theodore Roosevelt had criticized Holmes for not voting to dissolve Northern Securities, the president's antitrust policy only targeted those companies he believed had acted unreasonably in restraining trade. It also fit into the general mood of a Court that from the 1890s until the 1930s had no problem substituting its views of reasonableness for those of the legislature. Even when antitrust prosecutions, which languished in the 1920s, were revived in the 1930s and 1940s, neither the Justice Department nor the courts rejected the rule of reason, even as the whole body of antitrust law took on economic technicalities to determine what constituted a restraint of trade.

ONE COULD WRITE a great deal more about Harlan and his dissents. He suggested, for example, the idea of incorporation—that the Due Process Clause of the Fourteenth Amendment "incorporates" the first eight amendments to the Constitution and makes them applicable to the states—a process that did not get started until fifteen years after his death. In the *Insular Cases,* the first series of cases in which the Court dealt with the acquisition of overseas lands in the Spanish-American War, the Court held in general that the federal government did not have to observe the Constitution's fair trial provisions, or any of the guarantees of civil liberties, in these new territories. Harlan dissented from these holdings, arguing that procedures such as a grand jury indictment and a jury trial are essential components of American legal culture and must be applied to all peoples under the national government, either in existing states or in unincorporated territories. Congress eventually came around to Harlan's views and extended basic rights to all people living in its territories. Similarly, when the Supreme Court heard cases involving the Bush administration's detention of foreign nationals at Guantánamo Naval Base, Harlan's view prevailed over that of his colleagues.

As with any dissenter, even one whose views prevail afterward, not all dissents affect future courts. Harlan, however, had a great influence in areas of interstate commerce, labor law, and of course civil rights. First, he had a clear and unwavering faith in a strong national government, and while some of his colleagues feared and opposed any effort by government—state or national—to regulate the economy, Harlan understood that large-scale industrialization and the creation of a truly national market required that the federal government had ample powers to do the job assigned to it by the Constitution. The course that economic development has taken, including major recessions, validated his belief. Second, in an era that turned its back on the plight of African Americans freed from bondage, Harlan—southern-born and a onetime slave owner—showed himself as the one person on the nation's highest court who cared about the welfare and treatment of the former slaves. According to one biographer, his "great humanitarian heart led him to a belief in human dignity and freedom surpassing that held by any other justice of his day." He set the terms for the great constitutional dialogue that would eventually find the Court reversing its course and confirming the rights of people of color.

HARLAN AND HOLMES IN
LOCHNER V. NEW YORK (1905)

The industrialization of the United States after the Civil War brought great wealth to the nation but also opened up a Pandora's box of social ills and economic disparities unknown in an earlier and mostly agrarian country. The growth and prosperity did not come without a human price. Working in mines, mills, and factories was often dangerous. Owners hired women and children, some as young as six, not only because of their nimbler fingers but also because they worked for lower wages than men. In many industries, workers toiled ten or more hours a day, six or seven days a week; in the steel industry, for example, a twelve-hour day remained the norm until after World War I. The sick or the injured simply lost their jobs and, if they had no resources of their own, relied on family, friends, neighbors, or local charities to survive. A network of laws protected owners not only from efforts by workers to unionize but even from paying damages to laborers hurt on the job. While life certainly improved for those in the middle and upper classes, it did so on the backs of laboring men, women, and children who seemingly had no voice in either society or politics.

The era of reform we call Progressivism arose in response to the evils that industrialization spawned. Reformers tried to secure laws, mostly at the state level (because it was unclear if a federal police power existed), to do away with child labor, limit the number of hours a person could work each day, establish safety standards in the workplace, set minimum wages, and create a safety net of employer liability and workmen's compensation to help those injured on the job. Although successful in a number of areas, the final accomplishment of many of these goals would not come until the New Deal in the 1930s. In the early part of the century, reformers not only had to work to get their programs enacted by state legislatures but had to fight for judicial approval as well. In the courts, the story of protective legislation is a battle between conservative advocates of substantive due process and freedom of contract, on the one hand, and reform proponents of the police power, on the other.

The case of *Lochner v. New York* (1905) grew out of efforts to reform the baking industry in New York. Baking was a growth industry in the second half of the nineteenth century. Prior to the Civil War, most baking was done in the home, but industrialization drew many women to work in factories, and as fewer found the time to bake at home they turned to local bakeries for their bread. Urbanization contributed to this trend, because tenements usually had no ovens. Even in those apartments with ovens, the cramped conditions with two or more families sharing quarters made home baking impossible.

Although there had been some inventions such as a mechanical mixer in 1880 and a molding machine in 1905, bread baking remained highly labor intensive. A boss baker essentially needed only an oven and a

Eleven-year-old bakery worker outside cellar bakery

place to put it. Profit margins were low, and lacking any form of mass production, few opportunities existed to improve efficiency. About the only costs over which the boss baker had any sort of control were the wages he paid, how many hours he could work his men, and the rent he paid for his work space. In cities, the tenement cellars constituted the cheapest places available. Because they could not normally be rented out for residence, cellars often went unused, and building owners eagerly accepted the additional income from the bakers. The majority of New York bakers—about 87 percent as late as 1912—worked out of tenement house cellars.

From the bakers' view, the rent was cheap and the floors, whether of wood, dirt, or occasionally concrete, were sturdy enough to support the weight of an oven. These spaces, however, had never been intended for commercial use; in fact, they had not been designed for any use other than storage. Whatever sanitary facilities the tenements had—sinks, baths, and toilets—all drained down to a sewer pipe in the cellar. In the 1880s, when many of the tenements had been constructed, the drainpipes had been made of clay and brick, and even the more modern iron pipes leaked and smelled foul, especially in the heat generated by the baking ovens. In the cellar bakeries, the sewer pipes were often encased in wood and used for benches, storage, or even cooling racks for the loaves.

One could hardly imagine a worse place in which to prepare food, or even in which to work. The cellar floors were often damp, from either leaky sewers or rain seepage; dirt walls were the norm, and ceilings usually low. A factory inspector in 1895 reported that ceilings in cellar bakeries ran from a high of eight feet to as low as five and a half feet, a height in which most men would have to stoop to work. There were few windows, so even in daytime little light came in, and ventilation might often be no more than horizontal grates on the outside sidewalk. In the summer, workers suffered intense heat, and in winter even the heat of the oven could not keep the place warm. The lack of ventilation also meant that flour dust and fumes, natural in any baking, could not escape. The cellar bakery in 1900 bore no resemblance to the modern bakeshop, with its light, airy work space and clean, stainless-steel implements, or even to Grandma's kitchen. Everyone who visited these workplaces agreed that they were filthy and that the bread they produced posed a health hazard to consumers. Something had to be done.

In May 1895, the New York Assembly enacted a bakeshop law modeled on a British measure that included prohibitions against keeping domestic animals in bakeries and workers sleeping in the bake room, and also sought to establish minimum sanitary standards. The key provision from labor's standpoint was a clause limiting biscuit, cake, and bread workers to ten hours of labor a day and sixty per week. A front-page editorial in the *Bakers' Journal* proclaimed that this day "will stand forth as one of the most memorable days in the history of the great struggle of American bakers for better and more humane conditions."

The scene now shifts from the Lower East Side of New York, the site of so many of the cellar bakeries, to upstate Utica and Lochner's Home Bakery, which produced cookies, bread, and cakes primarily for early-morning customers on their way to work. A 1908 photograph of the bakery shows a relatively airy and mechanized shop on the first floor of a commercial building, one quite unlike the cellar bakeries of New York City.

Like most bakery owners, Joseph Lochner opposed the act, and in the years after its passage he simply ignored it. His employees often had to work late into the night, sometimes sleeping in the bakery before getting up early to prepare for the morning rush. An inspector, probably through the Bakers Union (which had a long-standing feud with Lochner), learned that one of Lochner's employees, Aman Schmitter, worked more than sixty hours one week and swore out a complaint against the bakery owner. Apparently, this was not Lochner's first violation, but this time he decided to fight. No one was going to tell him how to run his business—not the workers, nor their union, nor the State of New York. Although Lochner lost in the trial court and at all levels of the state's appellate process, it seems he had always planned to get the case to the U.S. Supreme Court, and in this he succeeded.

THE JUSTICES HEARD oral argument on 23 February 1905 and handed down their decision on 17 April. Given the Court's recent history in upholding police power regulations, it came as a surprise when Lochner won, albeit by a close 5–4 vote. (There is evidence that in the initial vote the Court had sided 5–4 with New York, and Justice John Marshall Harlan had been assigned the opinion. Then one of the justices changed his mind, throwing the case to Lochner, and Harlan's opinion became a dissent.) Chief Justice Melville Fuller, David Brewer, and Rufus Peckham, as anticipated, voted to void the law; these three men had never met a labor law they considered constitutional. More surprisingly, they were joined by Henry Brown and Joseph McKenna, neither of whom had previously voted to invalidate protective legislation. Why they did so in this case has been attributed by some to the creativity of the brief filed by Lochner's attorneys, Frank Field and Henry Weismann, especially the appendix, arguing that baking was not an unhealthful profession.

Rufus Wheeler Peckham, associate justice,
1896–1909

Peckham delivered the majority opinion employing a fundamental rights/due process analysis. The hours provision clearly interfered with the right of contract, he declared, which the Court had recognized in *Allgeyer v. Louisiana* (1897) as part of the liberty protected by the due process clause of the Fourteenth Amendment. Under *Holden v. Hardy* (1898), which upheld protective laws for miners, this liberty could be infringed to protect the public health or the health of workers at risk, but the law always favored liberty of contract. The Bakeshop Act could be sustained only if in fact it protected workers' health, and Peckham clearly did not believe that it did. "Clean and wholesome bread," he asserted, "does not depend on whether the baker works but ten hours a day or only sixty hours per week."

Unlike children, women, or the miners in *Holden,* bakers could not be considered a "necessitous" group needing special protection. So unless the state could prove that the hours provisions had been intended to address particular unhealthful aspects of bakery work, the law unconstitutionally violated the fundamental right of liberty of contract. Peckham then asked whether any proof existed to show baking as a dangerous or unhealthful trade and concluded it did not; in fact, the scientific evidence seemed to say just the opposite.

Because the law clearly failed to qualify as a health measure, it could not be maintained as a valid exercise of the police power. The act is not, he declared, "within any fair meaning of the term, a health law, but is an illegal interference with the rights of individuals, both employers and employees, to make contracts regarding labor upon such terms as they may think best, or which they may agree upon with the other parties to such contracts." While the sanitary provisions of the law might be valid, the hours regulations definitely were not. He ended by warning state legislatures that the courts would determine whether purported health laws were in fact related to legitimate concerns of the state and that merely describing a measure as a health law did not make it so. In other words, it did not matter whether state legislatures thought they were enacting health measures or not; that judgment would be made by the courts.

What one finds not only in this decision but in many cases at this time is the assumption that the Court had the power—indeed the duty—to determine not only the constitutionality of a measure but its wisdom as well. Stephen Field's demand that the courts act as "censors" on the state legislatures had been fulfilled. Peckham and other conservative jurists from the late 1880s through 1937 argued that judges had the power to pass on the wisdom of legislation, and if they disagreed with the policy, that by itself made it unconstitutional. *Lochner* has come to stand for that proposition, but it is far from the only case in which the high court set itself up as the ultimate arbiter not only of constitutionality but of legislative wisdom as well.

By Peckham's reasoning, the field of activity for the state police power was very narrow and at all times had to be justified; beyond its bounds, freedom of contract reigned supreme. The police power for the states was what the commerce power was for the federal government, and both were to be narrowly interpreted. In *Lochner,* he wrote that "both property and liberty are held on such reasonable conditions as may be imposed by the governing power of the State," and he clearly meant it would be the courts, not the political branches, that would determine "reasonable conditions."

He conceded that "it is unfortunately true that labor, even in any department, may possibly carry with it the seeds of unhealthiness. But are we all, on that account, at the mercy of legislative majorities?" While not denying that a nexus might exist between hours of labor and health, he would set the bar very high before he would allow the legislature, under the guise of the police power, to interfere with liberty of contract.

Peckham did speak approvingly of state laws that authorized sanitary inspections of bakeries and required improvements in bakeries for the sake of health, such as washrooms, water closets, proper drainage, adequate ceiling heights, and cementing and tiling of floors. New York could, therefore, protect the health not only of the public but of bakery workers as well, not through maximum hours, but by requiring a cleaner workplace.

THERE WERE TWO DISSENTS, and very different ones indeed. The first, by John Marshall Harlan, is all but forgotten today; the other, by Oliver Wendell Holmes Jr., is on every list of iconic opinions studied in law schools. Harlan's, joined by Justices William Day and Edward White, is in some ways a better opinion, in that it tries to respond directly to Peckham's arguments and in fact accepts nearly all of the underlying philosophy of the majority: the state police power is not boundless, it must relate directly to the health and safety of its citizens, and courts have the final say on whether it meets the standards not just of constitutionality but of wisdom as well. In Harlan's view, the New York Bakeshop Act met these criteria. If one is looking for dialogue, it is to be found in Peckham's majority opinion and Harlan's well-crafted dissent.

Harlan, like Peckham, agreed that "health" was the only allowable end that the Court should consider in assessing the statute, and he also agreed that there had to be a direct relation—"real and substantial"—between the law and bakers' health. But he employed the same test as did Peckham: "In determining the question of power to interfere with liberty of contract, the court may inquire whether the means devised by the State are germane to an end which may be lawfully accomplished and have a real or substantial relation to the protection of health, as involved in the daily work of the persons, male and female, engaged in bakery and confectionery establishments."

The only difference between Peckham's majority opinion and Harlan's dissent turned on whether the necessary justification had been established tying the statute's provisions on hours to the health of bakery workers. Given the evidence, Harlan, unlike Peckham, stood willing to accept that health had been the motivation guiding the New York Assembly. He noted the existence of scientific evidence supporting the belief that baking was an unhealthy profession, and he reminded his colleagues that there were many reasons supporting the theory that "more than ten hours' steady work each day, from week to week, in a bakery or confectionery establishment, may endanger the health and shorten the lives of the workmen." Given that such reasons existed, "that ought to be the end of this case." The Court should not invalidate state statutes unless they are "plainly, palpably, beyond all question, inconsistent with the Constitution."

Harlan's language is strong, but he clearly accepted the majority's basic premise and then diverged from it on how it should be applied. Harlan and Peckham might have disagreed on many things, and they certainly differed on what they saw as the legitimate reach of the police power in this case. But it is a distinction, not a difference. Harlan is using the same rationale and criteria as Peckham; the issue is one of application, not philosophy. Just a few years later, Harlan wrote for the majority in *Adair v. United States,* striking down a federal labor statute on liberty of contract grounds, and this time he spoke for Peckham and the other members of the *Lochner* majority still on the Court. In *Adair,* he quoted at length and approvingly from Peckham's *Lochner* opinion and accepted Stephen Field's view on the limited nature of the police power. Harlan saw the liberty of contract espoused in *Lochner* as belonging to both employer and employee, and both should be unfettered in their negotiations by the state. In *Adair,* he saw the employer's right to fire for any reason as the reciprocal of an employee's right to quit for any reason. "In all such particulars the employer and the employee have equality of right, and any legislation that disturbs that equality is an arbitrary interference with the liberty of contract which no government can legally justify in a free land." This liberty and the consensual nature of the employment contract were protected—against interference from the federal government by the Fifth Amendment and from the states by the Fourteenth Amendment. There could, of course, be some interference when the state used the police power legitimately to protect health, but Harlan, like Peckham, believed that the courts, not the legislature, would decide the statute's legitimacy.

THE OTHER, lone dissent came from Oliver Wendell Holmes Jr., and it is that opinion which shaped the future. It is difficult, in some ways, to say there is a dialogue here, because neither Peckham nor Harlan understood or responded to the arguments Holmes put forth, first, that judges should not be in the business of determining the wisdom of legislative measures and, second, that the state should be given the widest possible latitude in using its power, even if that meant favoring one economic class or social group over another. Holmes's opinion at the time was not taken seriously in orthodox legal circles, but then Holmes did not take legal orthodoxy too seriously.

If there is any agreement among both Holmes's admirers and his critics, it is that he was a skeptic. "When I say that a thing is true I mean that I can't help believing it—and nothing more," he once explained. "But as I observe that the cosmos is not always limited by my 'can't helps' I don't bother about absolute truth or even inquire whether there is such a thing, but define the truth as the system of my limitations." Holmes did not mistrust his "can't helps," but he did distrust dogma, in the law and elsewhere. He recognized that his own principles did not limit the search for truth, which, because of ever-changing conditions, would best be found by a free play of ideas—the position he would expound in his dissents in the speech cases. Thus he suspected any "first principles," because a blind faith to them subverted the search for truth. Because of this skepticism, Holmes has been accused of lacking morality and of draining the law of its moral base, but this is not true. He did insist that immutable beliefs of any kind prevented judges and others from recognizing all of the factors that played into the law. As early as 1881 in his famous lectures on the common law, Holmes had proclaimed that the life of the law had been not logic but experience, and in 1913 he would declare that "all law embodies beliefs that have triumphed in the battle of ideas and then have translated themselves into action." But as long as any doubt remained and opposing beliefs still battled, "it is a mistake if a judge reads his conscious or unconscious sympathy with one side or the other prematurely into law, and forgets that what seems to him to be first principles are believed by half of his fellow men to be wrong."

In his very first opinion on the high court, Holmes had declared that "considerable latitude must be allowed for differences of view. Otherwise a constitution, instead of embodying only relatively fundamental rules of right, would become the partisan of a particular set of ethical or economical opinions which by no means are held *semper ubique et ab omnibus*" (what has been believed always, everywhere, and by all).

Peckham had been insistent that redistribution of power and wealth was not a legitimate end of the police power and only health could be a permissible rationale. All of the members in the majority, as well as Harlan and the two who signed on with him, shared this view. Holmes did not. He essentially dismissed the efforts that Peckham had gone to in order to show that the New York law was not a health measure by simply stating, "A reasonable man might think [the statute] a proper measure on the score of health." As for the redistribution that Peckham and the others feared, Holmes was equally dismissive: "Men whom I certainly could not pronounce unreasonable would uphold [the Bakeshop Act] as a first instalment of a general regulation of the hours of work. Whether in the latter aspect it would be open to the charge of inequality I think it unnecessary to discuss."

Holmes went even further a few years later when, again alone, he dissented in *Adair.* "It cannot be doubted that to prevent strikes, and, so far as possible, to foster its scheme of arbitration, might be deemed by Congress an important point of policy," he declared, "and I think it impossible to say that Congress might not reasonably think that the provision in question would help a good deal to carry its policy along."

In both cases, he denied that the Court had a right to second-guess legislative wisdom. "Reasonable men"—the traditional common-law rule for rational judgment—might well believe that certain measures made good sense, and it did not really matter whether judges agreed or not. Unless a clear constitutional prohibition existed, legislatures ought to be free to pursue any policy they desired. "The Fourteenth Amendment," he declared in one of the most quoted epitaphs in American constitutional history, "does not enact Mr. Herbert Spencer's *Social Statics.*" In that one sentence, Holmes exposed the basic premises of both the majority opinion and the Harlan dissent—a belief that the Constitution existed to protect property rights, and anything threatening those rights was clearly invalid.

A few years later, Learned Hand wondered why the validity of the bakeshop law had ever become a matter of health and suggested that in *Lochner* the majority (and one could even include Harlan and his dissenters) had finally adopted Stephen Field's very narrow definition of the police power. It had, according to Hand, embraced a laissez-faire, social Darwinist interpretation of the Constitution. Although this did not rule out all governmental involvement in the economy, only those regulations that fit into this very narrow framework would be acceptable. In *Lochner,* the majority argued that the bakeshop law stood outside acceptable parameters, while Harlan argued that it fit. Holmes completely rejected the framework of judges passing on legislative policy decisions, and he did so in one of the most memorable sentences in American constitutional history.

Harlan, like Holmes, would have preferred that the Court start from a presumption of the statute's validity, but for different reasons. Harlan declared, "The state is not amendable to the judiciary, in respect of its legislative enactments, unless such enactments are plainly, palpably, beyond all question, inconsistent with the Constitution of the United States." But who would judge the inconsistency? Harlan, like Peckham, had no doubt that this responsibility and the judgment should be in the hands of the courts. Holmes recognized that courts had to make judgments, but he wanted these judgments to be limited to strictly legal questions. In essence, courts did not have to look at anything regarding the reasons why a legislature adopted a certain policy. If a reasonable person could see merit in the policy, that was enough. The only question courts should ask would be, "Is there a constitutional prohibition?"

In a letter written while he served on the Massachusetts high court, Holmes suggested (a view, he quickly noted, that his brethren on the state court did not share) that "a state legislature has the power of Parliament, i.e., absolute power, except so far as expressly or by implication is prohibited by the Constitution—that the question always is where do you find the prohibition—not, where do you find the power." The power, he believed, existed, and it ranged broadly.

Holmes would make this explicit in a few years when he declared that the police power "may be put forth in aid of what is sanctioned by usage, or held by the prevailing morality, or strong and preponderant opinion to be greatly and immediately necessary to the public welfare." In *Lochner,* he declared, "I think that the word liberty in the Fourteenth Amendment is perverted when it is held to prevent the natural outcome of a dominant opinion, unless it can be said that a rational and fair man necessarily would admit that the statute proposed would infringe fundamental principles as they have been understood by the traditions of our people and our law."

His colleagues on the Court clearly did not understand Holmes's dissent, and neither Peckham nor Harlan made any effort to address the issues he raised. Some have suggested that Holmes had little influence on the Court, because he was not—certainly in 1905—speaking the same language of jurisprudential discourse as the majority. Yet within a relatively short time, the notion of judicial restraint would gain hold, if not among conservative jurists, certainly among reformers with whom, ironically, Holmes never identified. Gradually, a sense of internal limits on the state police power would disappear, and the question would become, as Holmes had asked in 1893, not "Where do you find the power?" but "Where do you find the prohibition?" The triumph of these ideas came following the constitutional crisis of the 1930s.

Holmes, it should be noted, did not oppose judicial review, and he believed that courts need to exercise judgment. For him, however, the parameters of that judgment were far narrower than for Field, Peckham, or even Harlan. While he would not give a legislature carte blanche, unless he found the statute in question arbitrary, he would not strike it down, no matter how much he might disagree with its policy. Thus, if a "reasonable" person could find sense in a law, then judges had no business saying otherwise.

AS ONE MIGHT EXPECT, reaction varied according to where one stood in relation to protective legislation. Bakery owners and other businessmen applauded, while organized labor denounced Peckham's opinion as reactionary, confirming their view of the judiciary as a handmaiden to capitalist entrepreneurs and an enemy of working people. Legal scholars then and later condemned the majority opinion as mechanical jurisprudence, as abstract reasoning that did not take into account the facts of real life. Here they overlooked the presence of the factual appendix about bakers' mortality rates in Field and Weismann's brief, one that Peckham clearly relied on, and the fact that the State of New York made no effort to prove its assertion that the hours provision was in fact a health measure. *Lochner* was destined to become a symbol of judicial interference with the democratic process, where judges substituted their own judgment of policy choices for those of the people's elected assemblies. Holmes's dissent became a rallying cry for Progressives, and even though subsequent scholars have tried to show that a legitimate jurisprudential theory undergirded Peckham's opinion, "Lochner" and "Lochnerism" never lived down this odor. It has ever since been used in the larger societal dialogue as the worst-case example of judicial interference with policy making, a prerogative that belongs to the people and their elected representatives.

Three years later, however, many reformers believed that the justices had recognized their "error" when a unanimous Court upheld a ten-hour-a-day, sixty-hour-week law for women in *Muller v. Oregon*. The noted Boston attorney and future Supreme Court justice Louis D. Brandeis submitted a brief designed to answer Peckham's arguments. Where Field and Weismann had put factual material into an appendix, Brandeis made it the heart of his brief—nearly one hundred pages of abstracts from state and medical reports and only two pages of legal citation. The State of Oregon believed that limiting the number of hours women worked was a legitimate health measure, and Brandeis gave the Court proof that it was—proof that New York had failed to advance in support of the Bakeshop Act.

Although Brandeis did not ask the Court to overrule *Lochner*—merely to distinguish the two cases—*Muller* seemed a turning point, and in the following decade the Court rarely voided state statutes regulating labor. By the time the United States entered World War I, most people thought of *Lochner* as a dead letter. In 1917, the Court upheld a maximum-hours law applying to all workers, men as well as women, and *Lochner* seemed to have faded away. In the 1920s, though, it came roaring back when the Taft Court, dominated by conservatives opposed to protective regulation, invalidated one reform law after another, narrowing the scope of the police power and how that power affected the public interest. In 1923, the Court struck down a federal minimum-wage law that applied to the District of Columbia, and Justice George Sutherland ignored nearly two decades of precedent to revive *Lochner* and the primacy of freedom of contract. This freedom, Sutherland proclaimed, is "the general rule and restraint the exception." Even Chief Justice Taft, who rarely dissented, could not agree to this. He noted the long line of cases after *Lochner* upholding protective legislation and declared, "I have always supposed that the Lochner Case was thus overruled *sub silentio.*" *Adkins* set the stage for the ongoing fight between reformers and conservatives that would reach its peak in the constitutional crisis of the mid-1930s.

Debate continues today over *Lochner* and its jurisprudence, with the notion of substantive due process—once thought dead and buried—reincarnated to protect rights other than property. Much of the revolution in civil liberties, including the Court's enunciation of a right to privacy, found its origin in liberty interests in the Fourteenth Amendment, and this presents a paradox for scholars who support those rights but denounce the *Lochner* Court as activist.

In this dialogue, however, one often finds a gulf as wide as that between Holmes and the other justices, with one side arguing that a particular right does not exist because a proper reading of the Constitution precludes it, while the other side supports the right but with a completely different interpretation of what particular constitutional provisions mean. "The question always is where do you find the prohibition—not, where do you find the power."

CHAPTER 6

HOLMES AND BRANDEIS DISSENTING

I am a philosopher, and if people cannot stand the truth, no concern of mine.

— OLIVER WENDELL HOLMES JR.

*Now I think the opinion is persuasive, but what
can we do to make it more instructive?*

— LOUIS DEMBITZ BRANDEIS

In February 1928, Justice Oliver Wendell Holmes Jr. wrote to his friend the great English legal scholar Sir Frederick Pollock, noting that his colleague Louis Brandeis had dissented from one of his opinions. "We are so apt to agree that I am glad he dissents," Holmes noted. "It will indicate that there is no preestablished harmony between us." Holmes felt it important to point this out because he recognized that many people believed Brandeis had great sway over him. Chief Justice William Howard Taft, for example, complained that Holmes was "so completely under the control of Brother Brandeis that it gives to Brandeis two votes instead of one."

In the 1920s, one of the most fecund periods in American constitutional development, there were indeed many cases with the notation "Holmes and Brandeis dissenting." There had, of course, been earlier periods when two justices voted together on most issues. John Marshall and Joseph Story had a high rate of agreement, but they were nearly always in the majority. Stephen Field and Joseph Bradley also held similar views, especially of what the Fourteenth Amendment should mean, but they tended to dissent separately. From the time Brandeis came on the Court in 1916 until Holmes retired in 1932, the two men forged an alliance not seen before. They did, as Holmes reported to Pollock, differ from time to time and did not always vote together, but their ideas and philosophies proved complementary.

The liberals who rejoiced when they saw "Holmes and Brandeis dissenting" rarely recognized that Holmes's soaring rhetoric and Brandeis's inexorable fact-laden logic arose from different worldviews. Both men believed in judicial restraint, that is, that judges should not second-guess the policy-making prerogatives of the legislative branch. Holmes, however, voted as he did out of skepticism, not believing in the reform measures or, other than as an intellectual matter, in rights either. Brandeis, even when he disagreed with a program, believed fervently that the people should make policy through their elected representatives, that they should even have the opportunity to make mistakes, and he valued rights, especially speech, as essential components of a free society. For all of Holmes's wit and marvelous style, Brandeis's dissents would lay the foundation for the future and are the great examples of how one can engage in and affect not just the constitutional dialogue but the larger question of what rights we value as a free society.

OLIVER WENDELL HOLMES JR. (1841–1935) is the most colorful—and best-known—character ever to occupy a seat on the Supreme Court, and legal scholars consistently rank him, along with John Marshall and Louis Brandeis, as one of the greatest justices ever to sit on the Court. While many of the men and women who have served on the high court came there with prior experience as judges, only a few have brought with them a fully developed philosophy of law. Holmes must be deemed foremost among them. By the time Theodore Roosevelt named him to the Supreme Court in 1902, Holmes enjoyed a reputation as America's finest legal philosopher, and much of this renown rested upon a series of lectures he had given and published as *The Common Law* in 1881.

William Blackstone, whose *Commentaries on the Laws of England* greatly influenced the development of American law, had seen divine authority as the source of law and assumed that law reflected morality. As such, it had to be somewhat subjective so that judges could apply the correct moral rule to find the proper legal solution. Holmes wanted to do away with subjectivity in the law and replace it with objectivity, rules

Oliver Wendell Holmes Jr., associate justice, 1902–1932

that ignored the mental or moral conditions of the actors. He dismissed natural rights theory (the basis of the opening lines of the Declaration of Independence) and asserted that law served the general good as defined by the state. "The life of the law," he wrote in the famous opening paragraph of *The Common Law,* "has not been logic; it has been experience. The felt necessities of the time, the prevalent moral and political theories, intuitions of public policy, avowed or unconscious, even the prejudices which judges share with their fellow-men, have a good deal more to do than the syllogism in determining the rules by which men should be governed."

Holmes's assertion that law had to reflect the conditions of the time became the basis for "sociological jurisprudence," the belief that judges had to take into account economic, social, and political facts in addition to legal theory when determining a case, as well as for the later school of "legal realism," which argued that many factors influenced legal outcomes, of which the law itself was but one. Holmes's ideas not only influenced progressive reformers but greatly reshaped American law. Today the laws of contract and tort very much reflect what Holmes wrote, and *The Common Law* is considered the greatest American work on legal thought.

As a judge, both on the Massachusetts court and on the United States Supreme Court, Holmes earned a reputation as a progressive, not because he fervently supported reform, but because he believed that policy should be left in the hands of the legislature. Whatever judges thought of that policy should make no difference, and as he wrote in one case, "judges should be slow to read into the [Constitution] a *nolumus mutare* as against the law-making power." One historian has put it that Holmes saw his role as a judge more as a sentry than as a navigator. Unless the Constitution specifically prohibited a program, it should be considered valid. Holmes himself had little use for reform and thought most of the efforts championed by Progressives ineffective. At one point he wrote, "Of course I know and every sensible man knows that the Sherman Law is damned nonsense, but if my country wants to go to hell, I am here to help it." Holmes saw law as a social creation, one that embodied the nation's history. Law, therefore, grew organically, and he rejected classical legal thought that saw law as eternally fixed and that ignored the realities of everyday life.

Holmes from the beginning made it clear that judges should not impose their policy preferences over those of the legislature and announced this position in his very first opinion for the Court, *Otis v. Parker* (1903). California had prohibited contracts for the sale of corporate stocks on margin, that is, by putting up only a small percentage of the sale price and gambling that the stock would go up and then be sold to cover the debt and make a profit. "It is by no means true that every law is void which may seem to the judges who pass on it excessive, unsuited to its ostensible end, or based on conceptions of morality with which they disagree." This posture of judicial restraint marked nearly all of his dissents in matters of economic regulation. He did protest, often forcefully, against judicial use of "liberty of contract" to invalidate social legislation, and these dissents quickly became a key element in the constitutional dialogue. At a time when conservative justices often struck down efforts by the states to ameliorate the worst aspects of industrial life, the fact that Holmes was willing to allow these laws won him a reputation as a progressive that he neither deserved nor wanted.

Judge Richard Posner has noted that "the primary vehicles of Holmes's innovations were dissenting opinions that, often after his death, became and remained the majority position." He might have sounded the clarion call for the coming constitutional era, but his dissenting opinions did not have great influence until after his death. This certainly is the case with the *Lochner* dissent, which did not assume canonical status until the 1930s, the era of the New Deal. Scholars talk about both a canon of important majority opinions—such as *Brown v. Board of Education* (1954)—and a canon of dissents. The method for determining these canons is fairly simple: after looking at all the major casebooks on constitutional law, scholars list those cases and dissents that are included in all or nearly all of them. According to one scholar, the Holmes dissent in *Lochner* was the first to be canonized, and that was due as much to the judicial crisis of the 1930s as to the intrinsic merits of the opinion.

Following the constitutional controversy that ended in 1937, the demonized majority holding in *Lochner* gained a new status as a symbol of all that was wrong with the older classical school of jurisprudence, one in which justices used a rigid method of analysis to uphold their own policy views. Although legal scholars and progressive reformers had long cited Holmes, the first judicial citation came in the late 1940s. By then, the law schools, the people, and the courts had all rejected the use of due process to protect economic rights, and Holmes's view had been vindicated. Interestingly, the first two cases actually to cite the opinion were dissents by Felix Frankfurter, who claimed to be the intellectual and judicial heir of Holmes.

In the two dozen or so cases that followed in which the *Lochner* dissent is cited, we see a variant of the constitutional dialogue. Justices did not look to Holmes as a justification for overturning *Lochner*-era opinions; those had gone by the board in the late 1930s and early 1940s. Rather, they cited Holmes as a vindication of the new jurisprudence and also as an admonition against repeating the errors of ideologically conservative justices. They seemed to say that judges had to be careful not to read their own biases into the Constitution and not let "the ghost of *Lochner v. New York* walk again." Both conservatives and liberals looked to Holmes's warning against judges placing themselves above the legislative will and often quoted the line "a constitution is not intended to embody a particular economic theory.

Aside from the reversal of *Lochner,* Holmes won in other ways. Judge Learned Hand, considered by many one of the great appellate judges of the twentieth century, declared, "Courts know today that statutes are to be viewed, not in isolation or *in vacuo,* as pronouncements of abstract principles for the guidance of an ideal community, but in the setting and the framework of present-day conditions, as revealed by the labors of economists and students of the social sciences in our own country and abroad." Moreover, the test that Holmes suggested was finally adopted by the Court.

After 1937, the Court rarely struck down a measure of economic regulation, deferring to the legislature as the proper policy-making authority. In a 1955 case, *Williamson v. Lee Optical Co.,* Justice William O. Douglas adopted Holmes's rational basis test as the standard the Court would henceforth use in evaluating economic regulations. The statute in question made it unlawful for anyone except a licensed optometrist or ophthalmologist to fit eyeglass lenses or duplicate or replace lenses. The measure represented the interests of the optometrists and ophthalmologists at the expense of opticians, who could clearly and safely do all this work. Douglas admitted that might be so, but if the legislature perceived an evil, the law would stand if "it might be thought that the particular legislative measure was a rational way to correct it."

Holmes, like Brandeis, was not a great dissenter because of the quantity of opinions; one tabulation suggests that Holmes actually dissented in writing less frequently during his tenure than did the average of his brethren, only once in every thirty-three cases. His renown, aside from the eloquence of his style, rests on the fact that he so often got it right. In the constitutional dialogue, he might not have been speaking the language of his contemporaries in the early twentieth century, but he played a major role in defining the discourse that would follow. Although never formally overruled, and even resurrected for a short time, the majority opinion in *Lochner* is no longer law, while Holmes's dissent has been canonized, and the test he proposed accepted by the Court.

In 1918, the Court struck down the 1916 Child Labor Act by a 5–4 vote. The opinion by Justice Day went back to what many had thought the discredited view of interstate commerce in the *Knight* decision. Most people thought that Holmes's more expansive view of what constituted interstate commerce—a view that really harked back to John Marshall's opinions—had carried the day in *Swift.* In *Hammer v. Dagenhart,* Day held that Congress could not regulate factories, which were local in nature and therefore not part of interstate commerce. Once the goods left the factory, child labor was not involved in the shipment or sale of the products, and the government could not use its commerce power to reach backward into the factories to ban the labor of children.

Holmes in his dissent conceded that the factories could not be regulated directly, but because the Constitution granted Congress power over interstate commerce, its use of that power could not be fettered by any indirect effects it had on production. Precedent, he argued, clearly

Children making artificial flowers at eight cents a gross;
the youngest child working is five years old

supported a broad reading of the Commerce Clause. As for Day's contention that the goods produced by child labor were not intrinsically
harmful, Holmes noted that all civilized countries agreed that "prema-
ture and excessive child labor" constituted an evil. The majority's reasoning struck him as saying that prohibition "is permissible as against
strong drink but not as against the product of ruined lives." Holmes also
denied Day's contention that only the states could exercise police power
over manufacturing, asserting that "the national welfare as understood
by Congress may require a different attitude within its sphere from that
of some self-seeking State. It seems to me entirely constitutional for
Congress to enforce its understanding by all the means at its command."

With the child labor case, the Court majority set up a no-man's-land,
known as "dual federalism," that effectively blocked both state and federal reform measures throughout the 1920s and well into the 1930s. On
the one hand, it used the Due Process Clause of the Fourteenth Amendment, with its implied freedom of contract, to block state efforts, and it
used a very narrow definition of interstate commerce to thwart congressional proposals. That barrier remained in place until *United States v.
Darby* in 1941.

Justice Harlan Fiske Stone's opinion in that case in one stroke wiped
away the doctrine of dual federalism. First, he invoked Holmes's dis-

sent in *Dagenhart* to declare that it and other cases relying on the constricted view of interstate commerce had all been departures from well-established rules regarding the definition of commerce and were now overruled. Stone made it clear, again following Holmes's argument, that Congress had the power to reach individual manufacturers, and that henceforth the Court would apply a broad and generous interpretation of what constituted interstate commerce.

Although he did not declare it as a rule, Stone also applied the rational basis test that Holmes had suggested in *Lochner*. Courts would not question the wisdom of legislative acts so long as the power to legislate in that area existed. By limiting the authority of the courts to review such legislation, the opinion destroyed the argument of substantive due process, which went into a decline until the 1960s, when it resurfaced to be used on behalf of individual liberties.

One can cite other areas in which Holmes's dissents became law. He objected when a bare majority of the Court struck down a New York State law regulating the prices that ticket vendors could charge to no more than fifty cents above the retail price. New York argued that theaters are of public interest and could be regulated, while Tyson & Brother claimed that the law violated liberty to contract. In his dissent, joined by Brandeis, Holmes noted that the courts "fear to grant power and are unwilling to recognize it when it exists." The police power, he conceded, is often used "to apologize for the general power of the legislature to make a part of the community uncomfortable by a change. I do not believe in such apologies. I think the proper course is to recognize that a state legislature can do whatever it sees fit to do unless it is restrained by some express prohibition in the Constitution." He responded to the majority's declaration that theaters were not in the public interest by baldly telling his colleagues that this was a policy decision to be made by the legislature, not by judges. A legislature may regulate any business, he claimed, when it has sufficient force of public opinion behind it. In 1965, the Court affirmed a district court ruling that followed Holmes's reasoning and formally overturned *Tyson*.

In the notorious *Adair* case of 1908, the majority struck down a federal statute outlawing yellow-dog contracts, in which job applicants had to swear they did not belong to a union and if hired would not join one. Following the reasoning in *Lochner*, the opinion by Justice Harlan (who had dissented in *Lochner*) held not only that the law violated freedom of contract but that labor was a local matter and therefore beyond the reach of the commerce power. The decision was but one in a long line in which the Court showed an unwavering hostility to unions.

Holmes dissented, repeating much of what he had said in his *Lochner* dissent. Labor clearly had a substantial connection to commerce, and if Congress believed that helping labor unions would facilitate interstate commerce, then it also had the power to do so, and the courts had no business second-guessing the wisdom of the means. Whether or not unions did any good was a question on which "intelligent people may differ . . . but I could not pronounce it unwarranted if Congress should decide that to foster a strong union was for the best interest, not only of the men, but of the railroads and the country at large."

With the federal government now barred from regulating labor relations, several states stepped into the breach. But in *Coppage v. Kansas* (1915), the Court, relying on *Adair,* struck down a state law prohibiting yellow-dog contracts. Holmes entered a short but powerful dissent: "In present conditions a workman not unnaturally may believe that only by belonging to a union can he secure a contract that shall be fair to him. If that belief, whether right or wrong, may be held by a reasonable man, it seems to me that it may be enforced by law in order to establish the quality of position between the parties in which liberty of contract begins. Whether in the long run it is wise for the workingmen to enact legislation of this sort is not my concern, but I am strongly of opinion that there is nothing in the Constitution of the United States to prevent it."

Not until the New Deal would labor have powerful friends both in Congress and in the White House, and in 1935 Congress passed the National Labor Relations Act recognizing the right of workers to join unions and to bargain collectively—positions at odds with a whole string of high court decisions. The Court by a 5–4 majority upheld the law, as well as the mechanisms it created to enforce labor rights. A few years later, in a sweeping and unanimous decision, the Court abandoned the freedom of contract argument it had used to void federal and state prohibitions against yellow-dog contracts, which as a result passed into history. *Adair* and *Coppage,* according to Justice Frankfurter, no longer had any authority.

While a number of his dissents are worth noting, in one particular case Holmes gave us a new definition of what a basic right means. Rosika Schwimmer came to the United States from Hungary in 1921 and shortly afterward stated her intention to become a citizen. Five years later, she filed her petition for naturalization. An intelligent woman who lectured on politics, she declared that she understood the principles of and fully believed in the American form of government. But the district court denied her petition, because as a pacifist she could not swear that she would defend the government by force of arms.

*Rosika Schwimmer, Hungarian-born pacifist,
feminist, and suffragist*

The majority opinion affirmed the district court's ruling. In a mechanistic opinion by Justice Pierce Butler, the 6–3 majority held that the Constitution had assigned control over immigration and naturalization to Congress; Congress had prescribed the necessary oath of allegiance; it had a legitimate interest in ensuring that those who came here would be willing to fight in the nation's defense; ergo, if a person could not take the oath, that person could not become a citizen. For once, the majority deferred to legislative intent, most probably because it did not like pacifists any more than anarchists.

Holmes pointed out the total illogic of the majority argument. At that time, women were not allowed in the armed forces, and as "a woman over fifty years of age, [Schwimmer] would not be allowed to bear arms if she wanted to." While he did not share her belief that war would eventually disappear, she could hardly be considered a radical, and everything that was known about her indicated she would make a good citizen. The fact that some, perhaps many, people disagreed with her views made no difference. "If there is any principle of the Constitution that more imperatively calls for attachment than any other it is the principle of free thought—not free thought for those who agree with us but freedom for the thought that we hate." The Quakers, he concluded, had done their share to build the country, and "I had not supposed hitherto that we regretted our inability to expel them because they believe more than some of us do in the teachings of the Sermon on the Mount."

Possibly because of Holmes's dissent, in which Brandeis joined, the government did not move to expel her. She remained in the United States, working for pacifist causes and trying to establish an archive of women's history, a project that came to naught when she could not raise the necessary funds in Depression-era America. She died in New York of pneumonia in 1948 at age seventy. The Court specifically overruled the *Schwimmer* decision in 1946, with Justice William O. Douglas citing Holmes's avowal that the Constitution exists to protect free thought—not for the thought with which we agree, but "for the thought that we hate."

There is a matter of dialogue here that should be considered. While the majority opinion in *Schwimmer* might have been mechanistic, it was also correct in that the Constitution gives Congress plenary power over immigration and naturalization, and both Holmes and Brandeis joined the majority in other cases during the 1920s that took this view. The majority, in fact, did exactly what Holmes had been calling for since *Lochner,* leaving policy decisions to the legislature, even while Holmes was declaring that the policy decision was wrong. *Schwimmer,* however, involved a question of statutory interpretation, not constitutional power. In cases of statutory interpretation, the dissent is saying to Congress, "Did you really mean this? Because if you did not, then the power is in your hands to overrule this decision by the simple process of amending the naturalization law."

Congress, however, did not act, which would normally be interpreted to mean that it approved of what the Court said, and in fact the dissenters took this position in the *Girouard* case in 1946. Chief Justice Stone believed the lower court had correctly applied the law, governed by the high court's previous decisions, "whose construction Congress has adopted and confirmed."

But as William O. Douglas pointed out, even if Congress had not acted, conditions had changed a great deal over the past sixteen years. First of all, James Girouard had indicated his willingness to serve in the armed forces, but because he was a Seventh-Day Adventist, he would not bear arms or engage in killing others. He would be more than willing to serve in a noncombatant capacity as a medic. This option had been extended to American citizens who were pacifists since the draft had been initiated in World War I. According to Douglas, if natural born citizens enjoyed the religious liberty of refusing to participate in combat, then naturalized citizens should have the same right.

But what about Congress? If the Court had been wrong in *Schwimmer* and other cases, why had not Congress stepped in to remedy the Court's error? Unlike Stone, who took congressional silence and inaction as assent, Douglas believed that such silence did not necessarily mean consent and that Congress should not always be responsible for reversing an error by the Court. Douglas, as he did in so many cases, asked the right questions and ignored the traditional procedures when they did not yield the right answers or, as some critics have charged, the answers he wanted.

LOUIS D. BRANDEIS (1856–1941) dissented in every one of the opinions cited above that came after he went onto the bench in 1916. Like Holmes, he brought a mature legal philosophy with him, but one far more pragmatic and attuned to the political currents of the Progressive Era.

When Woodrow Wilson nominated Louis Brandeis to the high court in January 1916, he touched off a firestorm that lasted four months and remains one of the most bitter confirmation fights in our history. He was the first Jew named to the Court, and there is no doubt that anti-Semitism played at least some role in the animosity toward him. But the conservative opposition to him came primarily from his political philosophy and his approach to the law, both of which important segments of the business and legal communities considered unacceptable.

If Holmes and, to a lesser degree, Dean Roscoe Pound of the Harvard Law School were the intellectual proponents of sociological jurisprudence, Brandeis was its great practitioner. He claimed that judges could be relied upon to know the law, but not the facts, and that law had to be responsive to the facts—the real social, political, and economic conditions of daily life. As social needs changed, laws had to follow, and judges had to take these conditions into account. In defending Oregon's ten-hour law for women, he submitted a brief consisting almost entirely of data on the effects of long hours on women's health, to prove to the justices that the state had a legitimate interest in using its police powers to limit the number of hours a woman could work in a day. The "Brandeis brief" is still used today by advocates trying to justify why a certain policy should be allowed.

Louis Dembitz Brandeis, associate justice, 1916–1939

Unlike Holmes, who cared very little for politics and reportedly did not even read a newspaper, Brandeis might have been one of the best-informed men of his time regarding politics at both the state and the national levels, a product of his own experience as well as the huge network of friends and correspondents who provided him with information. Even after he went on the bench, he kept up with happenings in government and in the world, and reformers and administration officials high and low came to his weekly teas to ask his advice and to keep him posted on their progress.

His zeal for facts seemed boundless, and it is unlikely that any other member of the high court ever read government reports from agencies in the Departments of Commerce and Agriculture or the Federal Trade and Interstate Commerce Commissions so regularly. Facts not only informed him but served as a tool, perhaps even a weapon. Where many justices assign the statement of facts in an opinion to their clerks, Brandeis did this himself. He had to know the facts in the case, he explained, and if he got the facts right, it would be that much harder to deny the logic of his legal analysis. He believed in judicial restraint, as did Holmes, and unless the Constitution clearly barred certain actions, courts should defer to the policy-making prerogatives of the legislature. This combination of judicial restraint, a belief in what he termed "a living law"—one responsive to the times—and the need for facts to explain why certain laws were necessary can be seen in nearly all of his judicial opinions. (In a draft for one dissent, Brandeis called the Constitution a "living organism . . . capable of growth . . . and of adaptation to new conditions," one of the first references I have seen to the notion of a living Constitution.)

Brandeis did not dissent that often, although more so than Holmes. In his twenty-three terms on the bench, he wrote 454 opinions speaking for the Court. When he wrote the majority opinion, he recognized that he spoke for at least four others besides himself and so kept the rulings as narrow as possible, a trait that also fit into his philosophy of judicial restraint.

He felt no such compunction when he wrote in opposition, and in his seventy-four dissenting opinions we find all of Brandeis's distinguishing characteristics: attention to the context in which a law had been passed, the factual situation that the legislature had relied on in enacting the law, the necessity for the judiciary to defer to the legislative branch in policy making, the attention to individual liberties, and especially the role that speech played in a democratic society. To make his case, Brandeis relied not only on precedent—cases decided earlier by the Court—but on non-case materials as well, such as government reports.

One of his clerks, Dean Acheson, later recalled that "very early in our association I awakened to the fact that the law library did not contain all the tools of our trade." He and all of the justice's clerks spent much of their time at the Library of Congress looking up statistical reports, history books, and other sources. Just as Brandeis had used all sorts of non-case materials in his *Muller* brief, so he utilized them in his Court opinions. His lengthy dissents led the political scientist Harold Laski to suggest to Holmes, "If you could hint to Brandeis that judicial opinions aren't to be written in the form of a brief it would be a great relief to the world."

They are, however, legal briefs—Brandeis briefs written to explain to the bench, the bar, and the public why the majority had erred. Brandeis intended them to be convincing, and therefore they needed not just legal citations but facts as well. Above all, they had to teach, and a number of clerks reported a similar story. After justice and clerk had labored over a dozen or more drafts of a dissent, Brandeis would say, "Now I think the opinion is persuasive, but what can we do to make it more instructive?" In his remarks at Brandeis's memorial service, Dean Acheson noted that for the justice "truth was less than truth unless it was expounded so that people could understand and believe."

This is what makes Brandeis the acknowledged master of the judicial dissent. Holmes, perhaps the greatest stylist ever to sit on the Court, often seemed more concerned with philosophy than with jurisprudence. George Harrison, who served as clerk to Holmes in 1913–1914, recalled an occasion when, after reading the draft of an opinion, he could not see how Holmes had addressed a point in contention. When he said as much to Holmes, the justice replied that perhaps he should reread the opinion. After doing so, Harrison still could not see that it addressed the point and returned to the justice. Holmes pointed to a word in the opinion. Harrison looked it up in the dictionary and found a secondary meaning that made it possible to construe the sentence in such a way as to dispose of the contention. The law clerk returned to Holmes and said, "All right, Mr. Justice, but I still think that there isn't one man in a thousand who would understand the sentence that way." To which Holmes replied, "I write for that man."

One cannot even think of Brandeis writing this way—he wrote to educate. He hoped to teach his brethren but understood that success with them would be a rare thing. So he kept up collegial relations with them and worked on educating others, especially lawyers and teachers. This "teaching" is a key part of an ongoing constitutional dialogue, and while other justices since Brandeis have acknowledged this function, no one did before him. In reaching out to these other constituencies, Brandeis made sure that his ideas would be heard in the larger debate that we have mentioned before—the discussion by the people and their representatives as to what the proper public policy should be.

Brandeis also pioneered another form of constitutional discourse in his efforts to encourage law schools, and especially law reviews, to engage in the dialogue through the form of articles discussing and criticizing Supreme Court opinions. Brandeis had helped to found the *Harvard Law Review* and for many years served as a treasurer and trustee of the journal. His interest in law reviews continued after he went onto the bench, and he became the first justice to cite a law journal article in an opinion, a practice that is now commonplace. He once commented that "much of the best and original legal thinking in America during the last generation is to be found in the law journals." He also encouraged Professor Felix Frankfurter of the Harvard Law School to set his students at work on law review articles that would examine Supreme Court decisions, and when they wrote such articles, he cited them whenever he could. In one dissent, as he told Frankfurter, "I thought this a good occasion to let the law journal contributors know they are helping." He also prodded the law school to expand its curriculum to include federal law. Brandeis provided funding so that Frankfurter could hire research assistants to help him in preparing the first casebook on administrative law, a subject that is now taught in all law schools.

Although Brandeis certainly ranks as one of the great dissenters, perhaps the greatest, from the time he joined the Court, he believed justices should refrain from dissenting except when necessary. He drew a distinction between cases involving constitutional questions and those involving common legal matters. (One needs to recall that prior to the Judges' Bill of 1925, the Court had little discretion or control over its docket; it had to take numerous cases on appeal that it could—and did—refuse after 1925.) "In ordinary cases," he told Frankfurter, "there is a good deal to be said for not having dissents. You want certainty & definiteness & it doesn't matter terribly how you decide, so long as it is settled." It is usually more important "that a rule of law be settled than that it be settled right."

One also had to weigh the effect of dissents on relations with other justices. "There is a limit to the frequency with which you can [dissent] without exasperating men." Silence did not mean concurrence, but one had to husband resources, and dissenting too often would weaken the force of a dissent when it became important to write. So "I sometimes endorse an opinion with which I do not agree. 'I acquiesce'; as Holmes puts it 'I'll shut up.'" There might be an important case in which you want cooperation, and so "you do not want to antagonize [other justices] on a less important case." And, he might well have added, if a judge dissents too often, then the bench, bar, and public will not pay attention; they will not learn when an important dissent comes down. Beyond that, Brandeis at times would suppress a dissent. He might have gotten the majority to modify its opinion or even, at times, to come over to his side.

Both the court of appeals judge Jerome Frank and the Supreme Court justice Ruth Bader Ginsburg have commented on this practice. According to Frank,

Brandeis was a great institutional man. He realized that . . . random dissents . . . weaken the institutional impact of the Court and handicap it in the doing of its fundamental job. Dissents . . . need to be saved for major matters if the Court is not to appear indecisive and quarrelsome. . . . To have discarded some of [his separate] opinions is a supreme example of Brandeis's sacrifice to the strength and consistency of the Court. And he had his reward: his shots were all the harder because he chose his ground.

To which Ginsburg added, "In the years I am privileged to serve on the Court, I hope I will be granted similar wisdom in choosing my ground."

While Brandeis hoped to educate the other justices, during nearly all of his tenure he found the conservative majority intractable, and so he put his hope in the people. While working on dissents in speech cases, he told Dean Acheson, "The whole purpose, and the only one, is to educate the country. . . . The only hope is the people; you cannot educate the Court." Brandeis understood that the constitutional dialogue extended far beyond the walls of the courtroom, and he in many ways made the country, and especially the law schools, his classroom.

In his first few years on the Court, Brandeis set the pattern for his tenure—short majority opinions, but longer dissents designed to educate the public, especially the legal profession and the law schools. The partnership with Holmes reached full fruition in the dissents they wrote on speech, starting in 1919 and going through Brandeis's extraordinary concurrence in *Whitney v. California* in 1927.

IN WAGING THE WAR "to make the world safe for democracy," the Wilson administration triggered one of the worst invasions of civil liberties in the nation's history. While the government clearly had to protect itself from subversion, the laws it secured seemed aimed more at suppressing criticism of government policy than at ferreting out spies. The worst measure, the 1918 Sedition Act, struck at a variety of "undesirable" activities and forbade "uttering, printing, writing, or publishing any disloyal, profane, scurrilous or abusive language."

While these laws would be challenged in the courts, there had been little jurisprudence about the First Amendment's speech clause, and the few cases pretty much followed the traditional view of Blackstone that free speech meant little more than absence of prior restraint. In other words, the government could not stop people from saying or writing things, but it could punish them for the content of their speech afterward, especially if the courts found that the speech had a "bad tendency." In the fifty years prior to World War I, both state and federal courts had rejected free speech claims and clung to this doctrine. Holmes had written the leading high court opinion on speech in *Patterson v. Colorado* (1907), relying primarily on Blackstone's view that the truth or falsity of the statement had nothing to do with criminal libel—"the provocation [that is, the bad tendency], and not the falsity, is the thing to be punished criminally."

The first case to reach the high court testing the Sedition Act centered on the conviction of Charles Schenck, general secretary of the Socialist Party, for printing and distributing a leaflet attacking the draft. Its "impassioned language," wrote Holmes for a unanimous Court, "intimated that conscription was despotism in its worst form and a monstrous wrong against humanity in the interest of Wall Street's chosen few." But what about the First Amendment? Holmes drew what most people considered a commonsense conclusion: "The character of every act depends upon the circumstances in which it is done, and when a nation is at war many things that might be said in time of peace are such a hindrance to its effort that their utterance will not be endured so long as men fight and that no Court could regard them as protected by any constitutional right."

In order for courts to evaluate the speech, Holmes set forth the "clear and present danger" test: "The question in every case is whether the words are used in such circumstances and are of such a nature as to create a clear and present danger that they will bring about the substantive evils that Congress has a right to prevent. It is a question of proximity and degree." This was in many ways a more speech-protective approach than the "bad tendency test" that the Court had used and would in fact use for several more years. The clear and present danger test quickly became the established standard by which courts would judge free speech tests for the next half century, and it immediately caused concern among free speech advocates who recognized its subjectivity. In the hands of conservative jurists, almost anything that questioned the status quo or criticized the free enterprise system could be considered clearly and presently dangerous. Holmes had thought the terms so clear and obvious that he had never defined "clear" or "present" or "danger."

Brandeis joined the Court in these cases, but "I have never been quite happy about my concurrence," he later told Felix Frankfurter. "I had not then thought the issues of freedom of speech out—I thought at the subject, not through it." Thinking "at the subject" meant relying on the state of First Amendment jurisprudence in 1919; thinking "through it" would lead to the modern notions of what free speech entails in a democratic society.

The *Schenck* decision came down on 3 March 1919, near the end of the Court's term, and over the summer both Holmes and Brandeis were besieged by friends and civil libertarians objecting not just to the clear and present danger test but also to what they saw as the continuing suppression of speech and other rights. In June 1919, the *Harvard Law Review* published Zechariah Chafee's "Freedom of Speech in War Time," the first part of what would be his classic treatise on free speech in the United States. Both Holmes and Brandeis read the article (the latter would cite it in a 1920 dissent), and Harold Laski arranged a meeting between Holmes and Chafee. Holmes, who had been stung by the fierce criticism of his *Schenck* opinion, listened carefully. He also exchanged a series of letters with Judge Learned Hand, who supported a more speech-protective interpretation of the First Amendment. Here one finds a different but not unique form of constitutional dialogue, between members of the high court and legal scholars, a discourse that became more common as the years went by, and a dialogue that Brandeis greatly encouraged.

That fall, the Court affirmed the conviction of Jacob Abrams and his colleagues for publishing leaflets in English and Yiddish calling for a general strike to protest the American attempt to destroy the Russian Revolution. Writing for the seven-man majority, Justice John Clarke dismissed the free speech claim and in a rather mechanical manner applied the clear and present danger test. Holmes, joined by Brandeis, dissented, and his short opinion—just twelve paragraphs—is one of his most famous and still resonates as a call for intellectual freedom. The first ten paragraphs summarize the charges and conclude that none of the actions posed any threat. Holmes had no use for the ideas that Abrams and others put forth, but they were of no danger, and their beliefs—as opposed to their actions—should never have been taken into consideration.

The First Amendment supported the free exchange of ideas, not their suppression. "When men have realized that time has upset many fighting faiths, they may come to believe . . . that the ultimate good desired is better reached by free trade in ideas—that the best test of truth is the power of the thought to get itself accepted in the competition of the market; and that truth is the only ground upon which their wishes may be safely carried out. That, at any rate, is the theory of our Constitution. It is an experiment, as all life is an experiment."

The clear and present danger test, as explained by Holmes in *Abrams,* has had a long history. Even after the Court nominally abandoned it as part of its Speech Clause analysis, it has continued to resonate among justices who employ it as an ideal rather than as a yardstick in a continuing dialogue over the meaning of free speech. (See table 1.) Holmes went back to it in 1925, discussing and reaffirming his *Abrams* dissent in a case involving the American Communist leader Benjamin Gitlow. In 1941, Justice Black, who would arguably become the strongest defender of free speech on the Court during his tenure, said the test still "afforded practical guidance in a great variety of cases" and noted that it had been used by both majorities and minorities in deciding convictions under a variety of laws that in one way or another restricted speech.

Table 1. Abrams v. United States, *250 U.S. 616 (1919) (Holmes dissenting)*

CASE	DISCUSSION
Bridges v. California, 314 U.S. 252, 262 (1941)	Cited for restatement of the clear and present danger test
Hartzel v. United States, 322 U.S. 680, 686 (1944)	Cited for importance of construing strictly legislation that regulates speech
Thomas v. Collins, 323 U.S. 516, 528 (1945)	Cited during discussion of the clear and present danger test
Winters v. New York, 333 U.S. 507, 540 (1948) (Frankfurter dissenting)	Cited for the proposition that even valid legislation may sometimes impinge on protected speech
American Communications Ass'n v. Douds, 339 U.S. 382, 396n11 (1950)	Referenced the idea of free speech in a marketplace of ideas
Dennis v. United States, 341 U.S. 494, 543 (1951) (Frankfurter concurring in the judgment)	Referred to briefly in comparison of Justice Holmes's views in several cases
Konigsberg v. State Bar of California, 366 U.S. 36, 51n11 (1961)	Cited for importance of reconciling immunity for free speech and governmental objectives
Communist Party of the United States v. Subversive Activities Control Bd., 367 U.S. 1, 148 (1961) (Black dissenting)	Cited for the importance of allowing a marketplace of ideas
Garner v. Louisiana, 368 U.S. 157, 201 (1961) (Harlan concurring in the judgment)	Cited for the importance of allowing a marketplace of ideas
Bell v. Maryland, 378 U.S. 226, 344 (1964) (Black dissenting)	Cited for the importance of allowing a marketplace of ideas
New York Times Co. v. Sullivan, 376 U.S. 254, 276 (1964)	Cited as assuming the unconstitutionality of the Sedition Act
Brown v. Louisiana, 383 U.S. 131, 147 (1966) (Brennan concurring)	Cited for the importance of allowing a marketplace of ideas

CASE	DISCUSSION
Curtis Pub. Co. v. Butts, 388 U.S. 130, 149 (1967)	Cited as a "fountainhead opinion" in the law regulating free speech
Brandenburg v. Ohio, 395 U.S. 444, 451 (1969) (Douglas concurring)	Cited for argument that speech may be restricted only in the face of a clear and present danger
Red Lion Broadcasting Co. v. FCC, 395 U.S. 367, 390 (1969)	Cited for the importance of allowing a marketplace of ideas
Norton v. Discipline Committee of East Tennessee State University, 399 U.S. 906, 907 (1970) (Marshall dissenting)	Identified as the source of much modern free speech law
Monitor Patriot Co. v. Roy, 401 U.S. 265, 275 (1971)	Cited for the principle of protecting even objectionable speech
Columbia Broadcasting System Inc. v. Democratic Nat'l Committee, 412 U.S. 94, 183 (1973) (Brennan dissenting)	Cited for the importance of allowing a marketplace of ideas
Gertz v. Robert Welch Inc., 418 U.S. 323, 387n23 (1974) (White dissenting)	Cited for the proposition that the First Amendment does not protect seditious libel
Rogers v. United States, 422 U.S. 35, 47 (1975) (Marshall concurring)	Cited for the proposition that regulating pure speech is unwise
Greer v. Spock, 424 U.S. 828, 864 (1976) (Brennan dissenting)	Cited for argument that speech may be restricted only in the face of a clear and present danger
First National Bank of Boston v. Bellotti, 435 U.S. 765, 780n31 (1978)	Cited for assertion that the First Amendment rejects a paternalistic approach
Consolidated Edison Co. v. Public Serv. Comm'n, 447 U.S. 530, 534 (1980)	Cited for the importance of allowing a marketplace of ideas
Central Hudson Gas & Elec. Corp. v. Public Service Comm'n, 447 U.S. 557, 592 (1980) (Rehnquist dissenting)	Cited for the importance of allowing a marketplace of ideas
Perry Educ. Ass'n v. Perry Local Educators' Ass'n, 460 U.S. 37, 71 (1983) (Brennan dissenting)	Cited in a discussion of the importance of preserving a free market of ideas
FEC v. Massachusetts Citizens for Life Inc., 479 U.S. 238, 257 (1986)	Cited for the importance of allowing a marketplace of ideas
Shapero v. Kentucky Bar Ass'n, 486 U.S. 466, 483 (1988) (O'Connor dissenting)	Cited for the proposition that the Constitution is premised on a theory of a marketplace of ideas
Texas v. Johnson, 491 U.S. 397, 419 (1989)	Cited for the proposition that the speech at issue would not have an unduly pernicious effect
Austin v. Michigan State Chamber of Commerce, 494 U.S. 652, 689 (1990) (Scalia dissenting)	Cited for importance of restricting speech only in the face of a clear and present danger
McIntyre v. Ohio Elections Comm'n, 514 U.S. 334, 349 (1995)	Cited for the importance of allowing a marketplace of ideas
Board of County Commissioners v. Umbehr, 518 U.S. 668, 681 (1996)	Cited for the proposition that constitutional principles trump tradition

CASE	DISCUSSION
Denver Area Educational Telcommunications Consortium v. FCC, 518 U.S. 727, 740 (1996)	Cited for the importance of allowing a marketplace of ideas
Virginia v. Black, 538 U.S. 343, 358 (2003)	Cited for the importance of allowing free trade in ideas
McConnell v. FEC, 540 U.S. 93, 265, 274 (2003) (Thomas concurring in part and dissenting in part)	Cited for the importance of allowing a marketplace of ideas
Johanns v. Livestock Marketing Ass'n, 544 U.S. 550, 575 (2005) (Souter dissenting)	Cited for the importance of allowing a marketplace of ideas
Morse v. Frederick, 551 U.S. 393, 442 (2007) (Stevens dissenting in part)	Cited for the importance of protecting expression and recognized as supplanting the decision in *Abrams*
N.Y. State Bd. of Elections v. Lopez Torres, 552 U.S. 196, 208 (2008)	Cited for the importance of allowing a marketplace of ideas
United States v. Williams, 553 U.S. 285, 321 (2008) (Souter dissenting)	Cited as the beginning of a revolution in First Amendment jurisprudence that culminated in *Brandenburg v. Ohio*
Holder v. Humanitarian Law Project, 130 S. Ct. 2705, 2733 (2010) (Breyer dissenting)	Cited for the importance of safeguarding essential liberties
Sorrell v. IMS Health Inc., 131 S. Ct. 2653, 2674 (2011) (Breyer dissenting)	Cited for the importance of allowing a marketplace of ideas
Arizona Free Enterprise Club's Freedom Club PAC v. Bennett, 131 S. Ct. 2806, 2837 (2011) (Kagan dissenting)	Cited for the importance of allowing truth to be tested in the "market" of ideas

A few years later, Justice Frank Murphy picked up the dialogue and utilized the test in a case strikingly reminiscent of the World War I convictions. Three men had been charged and convicted under the 1917 Espionage Act for disseminating antiwar pamphlets to men eligible for the draft or already in the military. Speaking for a 5–4 majority, Murphy reversed the conviction and declared that while the clear and present danger test was the correct standard, it had to be construed narrowly, or as Holmes had put it in *Abrams,* the words had to be understood in "a strict and accurate sense."

During the Red Scare following World War II, the Court heard a number of cases of admitted or alleged communists charged with a variety of offenses, and the justices split over exactly what clear and present danger meant. In reviewing the loyalty oath cases that came before it during the McCarthy era, the Court showed that the judiciary, like the other branches of government, was caught up in the anticommunist fever of the times. In 1950, a 5–1 majority upheld a provision of the 1947 Taft-Hartley Act denying access to the National Labor Relations Board to unions whose officers had refused to swear they were not communists. Although citing both Holmes and Brandeis, Chief Justice Fred Vinson dismissed their speech-protective views as inapposite to the danger posed by communism, a view that both men would have found insulting.

Just one year later, the Court fully vindicated the fears of Zechariah Chafee and others that the clear and present danger test could be used to restrict speech. Eleven top leaders of the American Communist Party had been convicted for violating the Smith Act, which prohibited the organization of people to teach and advocate the overthrow of the government, as well as the teaching of such a doctrine. The government never claimed that any revolutionary acts had taken place other than teaching and discussion, and the men were not even charged with conspiring to overthrow the government. As Justice Douglas noted in his dissent, they had been prosecuted for speaking.

Once again, Chief Justice Vinson paid lip service to clear and present danger and again said communism posed a far greater danger than Holmes and Brandeis could have imagined. Clear and present danger could not possibly mean that before the government could act, it had to wait "until the *putsch* is about to be executed, the plans have been laid and the signal is awaited." The Court used the formula of "the gravity of the 'evil,' discounted by its improbability," a clear throwback to the bad tendency test in *Gitlow,* about words that "are used in such circumstances and are of such a nature" that they cannot be sanctioned. By this line of reasoning, the government could silence any speech that not only directly incited unlawful action but also conspired to promote such action or even taught that such action could be a good thing.

Felix Frankfurter, who always claimed to be the great disciple of Holmes, concurred in the judgment. He personally disagreed with the policy of the Smith Act and feared its heavy-handedness would silence not only communists but honest and loyal critics of government policy as well. He declared that the clear and present danger test became a simplistic and useless tool unless it took into account numerous factors, including the relative seriousness of the danger, the availability of other forms of control, and the specific intent of the speaker. This, he claimed, is what the Court had done, and he echoed Vinson in his belief that neither Holmes nor Brandeis had ever faced such dangerous foes. The serious threat of communism far outweighed the "puny anonymities" that Holmes had defended in *Abrams* or the "futile" advocacies in

Gitlow. Alas, here and elsewhere the man who claimed to have inherited the mantle of Holmes and Brandeis failed to display their fortitude in protecting speech and other rights. By this time, all the weaknesses in the test had become apparent, and critics of the *Schenck* decision had been proven right: the notion of a clear and present danger could, in the hands of those frightened by radical ideas, become an instrument of speech suppression rather than speech protection.

Eventually, the Court abandoned the clear and present danger test and substituted in its place a fairly stringent set of speech-protective criteria. However, in a number of cases, various justices have mentioned it not as the proper test but for the importance of allowing a marketplace of ideas. This began in the early 1960s, in a case in which the second justice Harlan concurred in overturning the conviction of lunch-counter sit-in protesters and, citing *Abrams,* declared that their actions deserved protection as part of the "free trade in ideas." This notion of civil rights activism as a form of speech, and therefore deserving of protection in the intellectual marketplace, appeared in several other cases.

In more recent years, the notion of a free market of ideas has not lost favor on the high court, with both liberal and conservative jurists appealing to it. Justices Clarence Thomas, David Souter, John Paul Stevens, Stephen Breyer, and Elena Kagan have all utilized this concept in dissenting from opinions they believed restricted the free exchange of ideas in one form or another.

THIS DEVELOPMENT would certainly have appealed to Holmes, who valued free speech in an abstract way and for its intellectual challenge. His marketplace of ideas, while certainly a great improvement over Blackstone's bad tendency test, also appealed to the idealist in Brandeis as a theory but did not satisfy him from a pragmatic stance. The test allowed too much subjectivity on the part of judges and juries; worse, the marketplace analogy gave lower courts no guidance in establishing criteria for First Amendment protection. Brandeis began working on the problem in a series of dissents culminating in the great concurring opinion in *Whitney v. California* in 1927. Just as in his economic cases, he grounded his opinions in facts. "Knowledge is essential to understanding," he wrote, "and understanding should precede judging." His first effort came in *Schaefer v. United States,* a few months after the *Abrams* case.

Peter Schaefer owned and published a German-language newspaper in Philadelphia and allegedly printed pro-German articles and false news reports about the war; the government charged Schaefer and his co-defendants with violating the 1917 Espionage Act. The chief charge centered on the claim that some of the articles they printed and/or translated differed from the original. The Court, speaking through Justice McKenna, upheld the guilty verdict and ruled that the First Amendment does not protect any speech during wartime that tends to weaken patriotism, raise skepticism, support the enemy, or in some way deflate the will to fight. Virtually any such speech creates a clear and present danger of unlawful activity by citizens against America's involvement in the war.

Brandeis, who had grown up in a household speaking both German and English, analyzed the four reprinted articles and then went back and read both the original German pieces and those published by Schaefer. He discovered that the government translator had made errors, there had been an omission of a sentence, and one word, "breadlines," had been mistranslated as "bread riots." The content of the articles from a Berlin newspaper resembled those circulated by American patriotic societies to arouse "American fighting spirit," and their "coarse and heavy humor" could in no way be considered a threat to the war effort. Brandeis did not fully agree with the Holmes clear and present danger test, but he had to use it. Holmes took great pride in it and saw it as a progressive step in speech protection. Brandeis had no alternative to offer at this time, but he warned that clear and present danger was a "rule of reason," one that could only be applied by the exercise of good judgment. He then took an important step, one that the majority had rejected, and one that would take years to be accepted: "The constitutional right of free speech has been declared to be the same in peace and in war. In peace, too, men may differ widely as to what loyalty to our country demands; and an intolerant majority, swayed by passion or by fear, may be prone in the future, as it has often been in the past, to stamp as disloyal opinions with which it disagrees. Convictions such as these, besides abridging freedom of speech, threaten freedom of thought and of belief."

Brandeis, joined by Holmes, was now trying to educate the Court and the country on how regulations of speech should be judged. Holmes's test as a "rule of reason," therefore, had to be applied in a reasonable manner. The fierce sentiments of war should not color the judgment of what had been said. Although it would be difficult to ignore the passions of an intolerant majority, the same criteria should be applied in wartime as during peacetime. In a second 1920 case, Brandeis moved much closer to a modern understanding of what the First Amendment meant both for speech and for the press.

A clergyman, Clinton Pierce, had been arrested and convicted for distributing a four-page pamphlet written by a prominent Episcopal church leader who charged that the war had been started by the capitalists. The leaflet had come from Socialist Party headquarters, but Pierce and his associates did not distribute it until a Maryland judge ordered an acquittal in another case involving the same pamphlet. Pierce, like Schaefer, had been convicted under the falsity provisions of the Espionage Act. Speaking for a 7–2 majority, Justice Mahlon Pitney held that the First Amendment did not protect any form of antiwar speech.

Brandeis, again joined by Holmes, argued that to punish a person for a false statement, the government had to prove the passage to be false in fact and that the defendant had known it to be false at the time of publication. An expression of opinion, however, can never be false, because the accuracy of an opinion is indeterminate. No matter how "grossly unfair as an interpretation of facts or even wholly unfounded in fact," an opinion represented what a person believed, and belief could not be made criminal.

The justice and his clerk found the one precedent that supported this distinction, a case in which the Court had held claims by Christian Scientists to be "mere matters of opinion upon subjects which are not capable of proof as to their falsity." The roots of war can rarely be identified precisely, Brandeis argued, and even historians, with training and hindsight, often disagree. Moreover, at the time President Wilson had asked Congress for a declaration of war in April 1917, many senators and representatives had disagreed with the president's justification and expressed views very similar to that for which Pierce had been prosecuted. If such statements were indeed criminally false, Brandeis implied, then a number of high-ranking government officials should have been indicted as well.

(Eventually, the Court adopted this view not just in speech cases but for free exercise of religion claims as well. In a 1944 case involving the "I AM" movement, the leader of the movement, Edna Ballard, had been convicted of mail fraud. Justice William O. Douglas, writing for a 5–4 majority, ruled that the sincerity of a religious belief, no matter how bizarre, could not be used as the basis for determining guilt for another offense. The case is famous for the idea that there can be no heresy trials in the United States.)

In *Abrams,* Holmes had tried to clarify what he had meant in a way to protect speech but had been unable to say what was wrong in *Schenck.* Because Holmes was his natural ally on the Court, Brandeis would have to extend First Amendment speech protection without abandoning the clear and present danger test. In *Schaefer,* he had described the test as a "rule of reason" that required judges to apply it in "calmness" and using "good judgment." He then added two other qualifications, immediacy and gravity.

The danger complained of could not be theoretical or remote or merely possible; it had to be about to happen, and to justify this assertion, he cited Chafee's article in the *Harvard Law Review*. He also turned to Judge Learned Hand's opinion in the *Masses* case regarding direct incitement. To limit speech, the government had to prove that the speech in question posed an immediate danger and would also be the proximate cause of that danger. Speech that merely discussed violence but did not call for it in a specific circumstance could not be deemed a danger. To this, Brandeis added the rule of gravity—the feared action could not be trivial, and even possible destruction of property or trespass did not qualify. The danger had to be the "probability of serious injury to the State."

Brandeis was clearly "thinking through" the issue of free speech, but in his efforts to educate, he had a very pragmatic purpose. An important function of Supreme Court opinions is to provide guidance to lower courts. It is not enough to merely state a principled test, such as "clear and present danger"; judges need to know how to apply that rule to cases in their own courtrooms. Here Brandeis continued what he had always done, instruct the courts in the facts. Judges had to read the material closely and in a calm and rational manner. Freedom of speech should be the rule, and any restrictions based on the clear and present danger test should be the rare exceptions.

In a third 1920 case decided in the fall, Holmes and Brandeis disagreed. A Minnesota statute made it a crime to urge people not to enlist in the military and prohibited pacifist speech not only in wartime but in peacetime as well. Joseph Gilbert, a pacifist, had spoken out against the war and the draft and also believed that in a democracy the citizens should be allowed to vote on whether there should even be a draft. Gilbert had been arrested and convicted under the state statute, and in his appeal he argued that a state cannot abridge the First Amendment's protection of speech.

McKenna spoke for a 7–2 majority in upholding both the conviction and the constitutionality of the state law. States could override the First Amendment because it did not apply to them. He also rejected the claim that the Fourteenth Amendment made the First Amendment applicable to the states; the Fourteenth Amendment protected only the ability to acquire and enjoy property. McKenna also relied on supposed war powers and repeated what he had said earlier in *Schaefer,* that courts had no jurisdiction over state repressions of speech in wartime. Holmes concurred without opinion, and Brandeis dissented without Holmes.

Brandeis quickly dismissed the war powers argument; if a measure related to war, then only the federal government, not the states, could act. (This was the basis for Chief Justice White's dissent.) He spent the bulk of his dissent on speech. Unlike the federal Espionage Act, the Minnesota statute applied in peacetime as well as during war and was designed to "prevent teaching that the abolition of war is possible." This point failed to move Holmes at all. The statute, he told a friend, was a "war statute—it was passed and applied in time of war. It was none of the defendant's business whether it would or would not be applied in time of peace, or would or would not be repealed then." Repeating an earlier warning from *Schaefer,* Brandeis contended that allowing suppression of speech in wartime only made it easier to restrict free expression afterward. The law made the teaching of pacifism itself illegal, and therefore "Father and mother may not follow the promptings of religious belief, of conscience or of conviction, and teach son and daughter the doctrine of pacifism."

Despite the "judicial" language he used, there is no doubt of Brandeis's anger in this case, an anger that led him to invoke the Fourteenth Amendment's Due Process Clause as justification for protecting the right of a parent to teach a child and of a free man to speak his mind. Referring to the many times that the Due Process Clause had been used to strike down economic regulations, he vehemently declared,

> I have difficulty in believing that the liberty guaranteed by the Constitution, which has been held to protect the right of an employer to discriminate against a workman because he is a member of a trade union, the right of a businessman to conduct a private employment agency, or to contract outside the state for insurance of his property, although the Legislature deems it inimical to the public welfare, does not include liberty to teach, either in the privacy of the home or publicly, the doctrine of pacifism. . . . I cannot believe that the liberty guaranteed by the Fourteenth Amendment includes only liberty to acquire and enjoy property.

The *Gilbert* dissent is an important milestone in the history of modern jurisprudence. Brandeis's suggestion that the Fourteenth Amendment could be used to protect other rights soon found an unlikely champion in James Clark McReynolds, who used exactly this argument in two important rights cases just a few years later. More important, the opinion is a significant step on the road to the doctrine of incorporation, which would be at the very heart of the rights revolution in the 1950s and 1960s. Ever since the 1833 case of *Barron v. Baltimore,* the Bill of Rights had been held applicable only to the federal government ("*Congress* shall make no law . . ."), not to the states. The Fourteenth Amendment, and especially its Due Process and Equal Protection Clauses, had been intended to rein in state power following the Civil War, and from time to time the argument had been raised that the Due Process Clause "incorporated" the Bill of Rights and applied it to the states. John Marshall Harlan had argued this earlier, but no one had paid attention at that time; Brandeis's claim that it did so would start bearing fruit in only a few years.

Beyond that, Brandeis took an important step in *Gilbert* toward identifying an intellectual rationale for free speech in a democracy. In *Schaefer* and *Pierce,* he had shown himself sensitive to protecting free expression but had not explained the importance of doing so. A free marketplace of ideas is very well for a philosopher, but how, if at all, did it apply to the daily life of a citizen?

A citizen, he explained, cannot participate in the affairs of a democratic society without the right of free speech, and he has a corresponding duty to speak out on matters of importance, "to endeavor to make his own opinion concerning laws existing or contemplated prevail, and to this end, to teach the truth as he sees it." Therefore, the exercise of the right of free speech is also a citizen's duty, "for its exercise is more important to the nation than to himself. . . . In frank expression of conflicting opinion lies the greatest promise of wisdom in governmental action; and in suppression lies ordinarily the greatest peril."

Holmes in this case could not go along with Brandeis (on the return he wrote, "I think you go too far"), even though he "heartily disagreed with the reasoning of the majority." Holmes might have objected to the radical idea that the Fourteenth Amendment limited state action, a step that the full Court would not take for another five years.

In the next important speech case, Holmes wrote the dissent, joined by Brandeis. Benjamin Gitlow, a leading figure in the American Communist Party, had been convicted under New York's 1902 Criminal Anarchy Act for publishing a radical newspaper and other allegedly subversive activities. In a now familiar scenario, a seven-member majority sustained the conviction. But, seemingly from left field, Justice Edward Sanford, without elaboration, announced that "for present purposes we may and do assume that freedom of speech and of the press—which are

Edward Terry Sanford, associate justice,
1923–1930

protected by the First Amendment from abridgment by Congress—are among the fundamental personal rights and 'liberties' protected by the due process clause of the Fourteenth Amendment from impairment by the States." With this bare-bones statement, the Supreme Court for the first time put forward, as the majority view, what came to be known as the doctrine of incorporation, by which the Due Process Clause of the Fourteenth Amendment applied the liberties protected in the Bill of Rights to the states. This doctrine, hinted at by Harlan and begun in Brandeis's *Gilbert* dissent, would be at the heart of the constitutional revolution that transformed American law after World War II.

Sanford's opinion in *Gitlow* is not a knee-jerk reaction to radical ideas, such as McKenna's was in *Gilbert*. It is a workmanlike product, and while we may no longer subscribe to its jurisprudence, he took the time to examine what Gitlow had said in the documents and did not dismiss the American Civil Liberties Union argument about the First Amendment applying to the states; in fact he agreed with it. But ironically, he practiced what Brandeis and Holmes had called for in property and labor cases—deference to the legislative judgment. The New York legislature had determined that this type of speech fomented rebellion and violence. Sanford explored different types of speech and concluded that when a statute proscribed a class of speech that contained general advocacy of violence, the boundaries of free speech had been reached. Holmes in his dissent dismissed the speech as having no chance of inciting anything, and Sanford responded to it. He agreed that the state had presented no evidence that Gitlow's speech would incite anyone, but that did not matter. The state had the power to define categories of expression that might provoke violence. The bad tendency of such speech justified the state's restriction.

Like Sanford, Holmes utilized clear and present danger but came to the conclusion that no danger existed. "It is said that this manifesto was more than a theory, it was an incitement. Every idea is an incitement [and] eloquence may set fire to reason. But whatever may be thought of the redundant discourse before us it had no chance of starting a present conflagration." As he told Felix Frankfurter, "I gave an expiring kick . . . (Brandeis was with me) in favor of the right to drool on the part of believers in the proletarian dictatorship."

Holmes, however, did not deal with a critical question—namely, whether the Court should simply accept a legislative judgment that some types of speech were dangerous and could therefore be proscribed. There is no indication in his very brief dissent that the New York statute might be unconstitutional. He also did not address Sanford's notion that the courts should accept legislative determination, a position Holmes and Brandeis had long held in economic cases. If a case concerned civil liberties, did that put it into a different category or give judges greater responsibilities? These questions would concern Brandeis in the next speech case to come to the Court, *Whitney v. California.*

A NIECE OF THE FORMER JUSTICE Stephen Field's, Charlotte Anita Whitney, at the time of her arrest was described as a woman nearing sixty, a Wellesley graduate long known for her philanthropic work. She had been convicted under the California Criminal Syndicalism Act of 1919 for helping to organize the Communist Labor Party in the state. The law made it a felony to organize or to knowingly become a member of an organization founded to advocate the commission of crimes, sabotage, or acts of violence. Whitney denied that the communist group had ever intended to become an instrument of crime or violence, and the state offered no evidence at her trial that the party had ever engaged in violent acts. Nonetheless, the trial court found her guilty, and on appeal Justice Sanford, utilizing the bad tendency test of *Gitlow,* upheld the conviction. The 1919 act, he ruled, clearly lay within the purview of the state legislature in its efforts to prevent the violent overthrow of society, and the Due Process Clause did not protect one's liberty to destroy the social and political order.

Because of technical issues, Brandeis chose to concur rather than dissent. Because free speech issues had not been raised at the trial, and Whitney presented only due process and equal protections claims in her appeal, the Supreme Court could not reach the First Amendment grounds. But because the Court had not yet fixed a standard by which to determine when a danger shall be deemed clear, Brandeis found it necessary to discuss the issue. His opinion, joined by Holmes, has never been seen as anything other than a protest against the Court's restrictive interpretation of free speech, and some scholars have declared it the greatest "dissent" in the Court's history. In it, Brandeis identified the scope of First Amendment protection for speech and did so with a rhetoric as powerful as anything Holmes ever wrote. According to Mark Tushnet, one of our leading constitutional scholars, the Brandeis opinion in *Whitney* "is the best example we have of what a dissent can do."

Since he had first joined Holmes in the wartime cases eight years earlier, Brandeis had given a great deal of thought to speech and the necessity of protecting it in a free society. Holmes's "marketplace of ideas" struck Brandeis as not going far enough to protect speech in a positive manner; surely the Framers had more in mind than simply letting people engage in rancorous debate. His thought, which has been described as republican "civic virtue" or "civic courage," summed up his ideas not only on speech but also on the nature of democratic society, and in it he achieved an eloquence rarely matched in the annals of the Court:

> Those who won our independence believed that the final end of the State was to make men free to develop their faculties; and that in its government the deliberative forces should prevail over the arbitrary. They valued liberty both as an end and as a means. They believed liberty to be the secret of happiness and courage to be the secret of liberty. They believed that freedom to think as you will and to speak as you think are means indispensable to the discovery and spread of political truth; that without free speech and assembly discussion would be futile; that with them, discussion affords ordinarily adequate protection against the dissemination of noxious doctrine; that the greatest menace to freedom is an inert people; that public discussion is a political duty; and that this should be a fundamental principle of the American government. . . .
>
> To courageous, self-reliant men, with confidence in the power of

free and fearless reasoning applied through the processes of popular government, no danger flowing from speech can be deemed clear and present, unless the incidence of the evil apprehended is so imminent that it may befall before there is opportunity for full discussion. If there be time to expose through discussion the falsehood and fallacies, to avert the evil by the processes of education, the remedy to be applied is more speech, not enforced silence. Only an emergency can justify repression. Such must be the rule if authority is to be reconciled with freedom. Such, in my opinion, is the command of the Constitution. It is therefore always open to Americans to challenge a law abridging free speech and assembly by showing that there was no emergency justifying it.

Although Brandeis paid lip service to the older clear and present danger test, he in essence abandoned it in *Whitney.* Even the destruction of property, the bugaboo of conservatives, did not justify restricting speech; speech could be shut off only in the case where the social and political order itself faced imminent danger and no time existed to reason or debate. Otherwise, the cure for "bad" speech must be more speech.

But why should society put up with ideas it found offensive? For Brandeis, the most important position in a democratic society belonged not to any elected or appointed official but to the individual citizen. Citizenship in a democracy conferred privileges but also carried responsibilities, especially the need to participate in debate over public policy. From the time he had been a local reformer, Brandeis had believed that no reform could succeed unless the people understood it and supported it. But citizens could not make informed judgments unless they understood all sides of an issue, and this meant that opposing speakers had to have the right to lay out their ideas; conversely, the citizenry had the right to hear conflicting views. This included not just questions of whether a street railway should get a franchise but more fundamental questions about the nature of government and the economy. Brandeis never subscribed to any of the doctrines brought to the Court in the speech cases starting in 1919, but he thought that their merits or lack of merits had to be decided by people who could hear both sides of the question.

How did this differ from Holmes's marketplace analogy? For Holmes, the entire question was an abstraction, a means of philosophical inquiry; all his life he remained aloof from the political process, not even reading newspapers. For Brandeis, who devoured not only the daily news but dry corporate and governmental reports, free speech and an informed citizenry had practical purposes. After the debate, the people could, through their elected representatives, translate these ideas into specific policies. Citizens had the civic *duty* to participate in politics, to deliberate important questions. Only in that way could the state provide conditions of freedom that were "the secret of happiness."

Implicit in the opinion is a notion of civic virtue that derives from classical Greek theory, and in *Whitney* one can easily discern Brandeis's long fascination with ancient Greece. The sentence "they believed liberty to be the secret of happiness and courage to be the secret of liberty" comes almost directly from Pericles, and much of the paragraph is fashioned after the Funeral Oration. There is a great idealism in this passage, a belief that if men and women can learn and make informed decisions, they can create a better society. But it is not just idealism here but pragmatism as well. Political liberty is at best a fragile construct, and it will fail if citizens become inert.

Brandeis, like his colleagues, wanted to maintain public order. But where Sanford would allow the government to clamp down on any speech that had a "bad tendency," Brandeis believed this policy would be counterproductive. "Those who won our independence," he declared, "knew that order cannot be secured merely through fear of punishment." It is not simply a "safety valve" that Brandeis talks about, the idea that if the state allows dissidents to let off steam they will do little harm. Rather, he wanted the debate; he wanted people with radical ideas to challenge the mainstream, to make people think about the values they cherished and not be complacent about them.

Perhaps more than any other of his opinions, Brandeis's *Whitney* concurrence has shaped American constitutional law. In it, he developed a legal doctrine identifying the scope of protection that the First Amendment affords, a doctrine that eventually became the law. Its influence can be seen in the powerful First Amendment opinions later penned by Justices Hugo Black, William O. Douglas, William Brennan, and John Marshall Harlan II. Gradually, the Court abandoned Sanford's "bad tendency" standard and also moved away from Holmes's clear and present danger test. Although the test continued to be used in the 1940s and 1950s, the Warren Court abandoned it in the 1960s. In *Bond v. Floyd* (1966), the Georgia legislature tried to prevent the seating of the civil rights activist Julian Bond because of his antiwar views. In his opinion for a unanimous Court, Chief Justice Warren did not even mention the Holmes test. Legislators, like citizens, had to have the widest latitude to express their views on controversial policy matters.

A few years later, the Court unanimously overturned an Ohio law very similar to the California one that had ensnared Whitney. In a *per curiam* opinion, the Court said that the majority opinion in *Whitney* had "been thoroughly discredited by later decisions." In their concurring opinions, Hugo Black and William Douglas emphasized one point, that "clear and present danger" no longer had any place in First Amendment jurisprudence. A few years later, in *Grayned v. City of Rockford,* the outlines of modern First Amendment standards are clearly visible—questions of vagueness, overbreadth, and a higher standard of judicial scrutiny.

Brandeis's *Whitney* opinion continues to be cited in the dialogue over the meaning and especially the extent of First Amendment protection and also for the notion that the Speech Clause favors more rather than less speech. In a 1980 case, Justices Blackmun and Stevens, in concurring opinions, and Justice Rehnquist in a dissent, all cited the *Whitney* concurrence as the standard for free speech adopted by the Court. In June 2011, Justice Elena Kagan, the successor to the Brandeis seat, cited her predecessor's opinion for the proposition that the Free Speech Clause always favors more speech rather than less.

Debate about the reach of the First Amendment continues, questions such as whether it embraces only political discourse or if it takes in other forms of expression such as commercial and artistic speech. But *Whitney* continues to be the touchstone, not only for the rationale it provides for the First Amendment, but also for the unusual eloquence of a man known for his detached, fact-laden, and lawyerly opinions. That rare eloquence showed up in another seminal dissent Brandeis wrote in 1928, in which he established the constitutional basis for a right to privacy.

WHITNEY IS GENERALLY CONSIDERED Brandeis's greatest opinion, but his dissent in *Olmstead v. United States* (1928) runs a close second. The case and the dissent are treated extensively in the next mise-en-scène, so we will just look at a few salient features here.

In the case, Brandeis objected to two things. First, he considered the use of a wiretap without a proper search warrant a violation of the Fourth Amendment as well as a lawless act on the part of the government. The fact that the wiretap had been in aid of law enforcement was immaterial. "Experience should teach us to be most on our guard when the Government's purposes are beneficent. . . . The greatest dangers to liberty lurk in insidious encroachment by men of zeal, well-meaning but without understanding."

Second, he wanted to call attention to what he considered a fundamental right—that of privacy or, as he put it, the right to be let alone.

This triggered an ongoing debate on whether a constitutional right can exist if it is not spelled out in the document itself. Again, Brandeis's views have come to be accepted by nearly all Americans, because in an age of increasing governmental surveillance in the name of national security, the right to be let alone has resonated very strongly with many Americans. Here, too, Brandeis changed our understanding of what the Fourth Amendment means.

His arguments about both wiretapping and privacy were not accepted overnight, but after the *Olmstead* decision it proved impossible to deal with Fourth Amendment issues without taking his views into account. The dissent joined the canon and became part of the ongoing constitutional dialogue and also part of the wider discussion. The news that the National Security Agency (NSA) had secretly eavesdropped on millions of phone and e-mail conversations, and without a warrant, led to a massive public debate over the meaning of privacy in a technical age, the balances that needed to be struck between individual rights and national security, and the question of who would make those decisions. If nothing else, this debate surely confirmed Brandeis's opinion of privacy as the right most prized by free men.

HOLMES RETIRED from the Court in January 1932; Brandeis would serve another seven years. His last great dissent came down just two months after Holmes left, in *New State Ice Co. v. Liebmann,* one of the first of the Great Depression cases to come before the Court.

An Oklahoma statute treated the manufacture of ice as a public utility and required a certificate of convenience and necessity for anyone wishing to start such a business. The state justified its law on the grounds that too many competitors would drive the price down, causing many companies to go out of business and thus deprive the public of needed ice. By limiting the number of ice companies, the state hoped to stabilize the market; the practical effect, however, was to shut out new enterprises and give existing companies a monopoly. When Ernest Liebmann opened an ice business without a certificate, New State Ice, which had a certificate, sued to stop him.

By a vote of 6–2, the majority, speaking through Justice Sutherland, denied that ice could be considered affected with a public interest, and therefore it could not be legitimately regulated by the state. Furthermore, the law tended to foster monopoly.

With his well-known antipathy toward monopoly, Brandeis might have been expected to vote against the statute as well; instead, he entered a powerful dissent. He criticized the majority for failing to take

account of the economic conditions that had led the Oklahoma legislature to view ice making as affected with a public interest. "The true
principle," he wrote, "is that the State's power extends to every regulation of any business reasonably required and appropriate for the public
protection." In a depression, it might be necessary to limit certain types
of businesses, and the state legislature had decided to try this approach.
Whether it would work, he did not know; nor did it matter. "It is one of
the happy incidents of the federal system that a single courageous State
may, if its citizens choose, serve as a laboratory, and try novel social and
economic experiments without risk to the rest of the country."

Brandeis ended with an eloquent plea for judicial restraint. The Court,
he said, had the power to prevent experiments because the Due Process
Clause had been interpreted to include substantive as well as procedural
rights. "But in the exercise of this high power," he warned, "we must be
ever on our guard, lest we erect our prejudices into legal principles. If
we would guide by the light of reason, we must let our minds be bold."

Although *New State Ice* is still defended by some scholars as an effort
to protect consumers from special interest legislation and has never been
specifically overruled, it has in effect been abandoned. Subsequent courts
have recognized a broad range of legislative discretion, both for states
and for the federal government. In terms of a constitutional dialogue,
its impact was almost immediate, not with the brethren, but with the
public. Brandeis always wanted to educate, and he got his lesson across
quickly to people who recognized that the severest depression ever to
afflict the country required experimentation, even if some bold new programs did not work out.

The New York Times had already begun commenting on Brandeis's
"logic, his learning, the lucid order of his reasoning, the exactness of his
language, his extraordinary penetration of facts." Others joined in the
praise, hailing him as "an analyst of the processes of his own times" and
lauding his concern with the social, economic, and political ramifications of proposed legislation in times of great economic hardship. No
doubt Franklin D. Roosevelt read the dissent, and there is an echo in
his speech at Oglethorpe University in May 1932: "The country needs,
and unless I mistake its temper, the country demands bold, persistent
experimentation. It is common sense to take a method and try it. If it
fails, admit it frankly and try another. But above all, try something."

The notion of states as laboratories of democracy became ingrained in
the discourse on federalism. Where the Framers had seen the federalist
system as a means of dividing sovereignty and preventing the national
government from becoming too powerful, Brandeis saw the system as a

means of attacking the problems of modern life. A man who had always opposed big government, he saw action by the states (even policies with which he might have personally disagreed) as a far better approach than the national government imposing a one-size-fits-all solution. It was even better when he could defend a state policy in which he believed, such as Florida's higher tax on chain drugstores. In *Liggett v. Lee,* decided one year after *Liebmann,* Brandeis dissented from a majority that struck down the tax on due process grounds. He repeated what he had said earlier: "Whether the citizens of Florida are wise in seeking to discourage the operation of chain stores is, obviously, a matter with which this Court has no concern." He then went on, in the best Brandeis brief style, to explain why the legislature believed big corporations posed a danger and contributed to the current economic distress. Six decades later, Justice Sandra Day O'Connor would be citing Brandeis's view of the states as laboratories for economic and social experiments in dealing with a new and difficult issue, the right to die.

The *Liebmann* and *Liggett* dissents became rallying cries for New Dealers and led *The New York Times* to cite them as proof for the proposition that Brandeis was a "vigorous defender of many New Deal measures and social experimentation." There is a great deal of unconscious irony in this statement, because, although Brandeis voted to support many of the New Deal measures that came before the Court, he did not approve of all of them. He agreed with Roosevelt that failures in the capitalist system, especially in the banking sector, lay at the root of the country's ills, and his analysis of the problem led Roosevelt and many New Dealers to call Brandeis "Isaiah." But Isaiah did not think that regulation by the national government was the solution.

WHAT STRIKES ONE when looking at the Brandeis record is how often the arguments made in dissent would become the accepted jurisprudence of the Court. In some instances, it happened while the justice still sat on the bench; other times, his position would not be adopted until decades had passed. He saw his dissents as part of a constitutional discourse, a view that other judges have since recognized. He did not feel the need to win so much as to start the dialogue, one that would be picked up in the law journals, where arguments could be dissected and refined. "You and Holmes set the pace," Benjamin Cardozo wrote to him in gratitude. "The rest of us are merely imitators who try to keep in line." If judges like Cardozo, Julian Mack, and Learned Hand recognized and joined in this effort, then his faith, as he said so many times, was great in time, and by all measures time has justified that faith.

Brandeis had a great impact on a number of areas, and while not every one of his views has been accepted, many have been. The most influential antitrust scholar of the twentieth century, Milton Handler, believed that no one on the Court affected this field of law more than Brandeis. Of course Brandeis went onto the Court with fairly well-defined views on big business and monopoly; he had written extensively on the subject, testified before congressional hearings, advised Wilson, and helped draft the Clayton Act. His views on bigness as a curse and monopoly as inefficient were well-known by the time he went onto the bench. Brandeis's contribution to antitrust law, however, came not in his opposition to bigness but in his sophisticated development of the "rule of reason," first suggested by Holmes in *Northern Securities* and then elaborated upon by Chief Justice Edward White in the 1911 *Standard Oil* case. A combination by itself, or even actions that restrained trade, would not be considered illegal if reasonable. The courts then had to deal with what constituted a "reasonable" combination or action in restraint of trade.

The first cases in which Brandeis wrote on antitrust amazed some of his reform colleagues. He spoke for a unanimous Court in holding that the Chicago Board of Trade's rules on futures trading, which essentially locked out a group of warehousemen, did not violate the antitrust law. Then Brandeis dissented when his colleagues held that an association of hardwood manufacturers violated the antitrust law, arguing that the group had legitimate reasons for sharing pricing and other information and that their cooperation fostered rather than limited competition. As one might expect, Brandeis wanted the courts to examine the facts. Courts must "consider the facts peculiar to the business to which the restraint is applied; its condition before and after the restraint was imposed; the nature of the restraint; and its effect, actual or probable. The history of the restraint, the evil believed to exist, the reason for adopting the particular remedy, the purpose of or end sought to be attained, are all relevant facts."

Thirteen years later, in the so-called *Cracking Oil* case, Brandeis presented a highly sophisticated analysis of competition that still governs antitrust jurisprudence. He developed what Professor Handler called the "concentric circle rule of reason." The fact that a combination eliminated competition among a small group of companies (the inner circle) did not matter if the quality of competition in the market as a whole (the outer circle) remained unimpaired. In that case, Brandeis spoke for the Court in reversing a government conviction of four major gasoline producers using a new "cracking" or refining technology. The companies had established a horizontal price agreement on royalties for pooled patent sublicenses, which the government claimed violated the antitrust law. Brandeis looked at various dimensions of competition in the industry and determined that while the merger effectively ended competition among the four producers, it did not have a negative effect on competition in the larger gasoline market. The companies had done what many companies in changing markets do—join together to take advantage of and to share new technology. The companies did not prevent other firms from utilizing the new cracking methods but established a rational and fair system by which their patents could be licensed.

Although Brandeis emphasized the finding of facts relating to various layers of the market and the actions of the companies, the facts by themselves did not tell the Court enough. It then had to evaluate these facts in light of the total market; *per se* rules would not do. In the early twenty-first century, this type of multidimensional analysis is the beginning of all antitrust law.

IN ONE ADDITIONAL AREA, Brandeis helped to transform American law. According to one scholar, "The contributions of one man, Justice Louis D. Brandeis, reoriented the focus of administrative law toward the appropriate allocation of functions and power between courts and agencies." Courts had been leery of federal administrative agencies ever since the creation of the Interstate Commerce Commission in 1887. The ICC seemed to violate one of the cardinal tenets of the Constitution, the separation of powers, because it had executive and legislative as well as judicial functions. Initially, the Supreme Court hamstrung the ICC through a series of decisions that either took a very narrow view of its delegated authority or permitted extensive judicial review of its findings. Not until the Progressive Era, when Congress significantly strengthened the ICC and lawyers became more comfortable with administrative regulation, did the Supreme Court begin to allow the agency leeway to operate. In one of his first administrative law decisions, Brandeis upheld the doctrine of primary jurisdiction, in which federal rate making took precedence over state judicial scrutiny.

In 1923, Brandeis entered a dissent in *Pennsylvania v. West Virginia,* a suit by Pennsylvania and Ohio to enjoin West Virginia from enforcing a state law designed to divert or retain, for the benefit of its own citizens, natural gas in an interstate pipeline passing through the state that would otherwise have gone to neighboring states. West Virginia created a public service commission that had the power to limit the amount of gas going through the state and to divert it to West Virginia consumers. A majority of the Court held the statute unconstitutional as interference with interstate commerce.

In his dissent, Brandeis maintained that the determination of an equitable allotment of natural gas required an investigation into production, demand, reserves, and the business practices of the various companies, all requiring expert knowledge and experience and beyond the abilities of the courts. The situation would change regularly, thus requiring constant adjustment and fact-finding, duties properly exercised by an administrative agency. To determine what the responsibilities of an agency should be and what the courts should do, Brandeis developed four criteria:

1. Did the problem's complexity require expert knowledge?
2. Was the question one that could be conclusively resolved in one sitting (a court case) or that required continued involvement over time by the regulatory body?
3. Were the problems presented, by their very nature, "administrative" in scope?
4. Were the particular issues ones of "fact" or of "law"?

Responses to the first two provided the criteria to answer the third; only in the fourth area, where questions of law arose, should the courts get involved. Otherwise, courts were simply not equipped to make the continual investigations into the constantly changing economic variables involved. These standards became the primary criteria for allocating power between courts and administrative agencies in modern America and came into full flower with the great explosion of administrative agencies during the New Deal, during World War II, and in postwar America.

A majority of the Taft Court, however, had no desire to turn over what it considered a judicial function to administrative agencies, even though it was becoming increasingly clear that judges lacked the expertise to establish rates, much less review complex administrative findings. In addition, conservative justices disliked the idea of a federal agency regulating business practices. Although the Taft Court tended to support national power vis-à-vis the states, it had no love for the Federal Trade Commission (FTC), and the FTC had no worse enemy than Justice McReynolds, who had helped draft the measure creating it.

In *FTC v. Gratz* (1920), he spoke for the majority in denying the commission the power to determine "unfair methods of competition," because the statute had not defined what this phrase meant. Three years later, McReynolds again delivered an opinion overturning a cease-and-desist order after extensive investigation and held that the courts had the power to look at the evidence *de novo.* If a judge agreed with the agency's findings, then they would be considered conclusive; if not, the court could make its own determination. Brandeis dissented in *Gratz* and in several more cases during the decade, trying to get the Court to recognize administrative agencies not only as legitimate but also as entrusted with particular duties requiring expert knowledge that the courts lacked.

While willing to give administrative agencies broad discretion in matters of economic regulation, Brandeis held them to a higher standard when individual rights came into play. Although *The Milwaukee Leader* is normally discussed as a speech case, it was also a case testing the power of the postmaster general to award and retract valuable mailing privileges, a decision often considered administrative in nature. When agency decisions affected individual liberties, Brandeis could be just as insistent as his colleagues on judicial review. In *Ng Fung Ho v. White* (1922), two Chinese immigrants had been summarily deported by an immigration official, and they challenged his action, claiming they were American citizens. Writing for a unanimous Court, Brandeis held that their claim of citizenship was entitled to judicial review, because the immigration agency's power to deport a person depended solely on the fact of that person being an alien. To refuse to review a claim of citizenship would be a denial of due process.

Brandeis's concern with delineating the powers of administrative agencies led Felix Frankfurter to offer one of the first courses in administrative law at Harvard, and when Frankfurter decided to edit a book of cases for use as a text, Brandeis put additional money at his disposal to hire a student and also to get out a book on the related subject of federal jurisdiction.

During the New Deal, Brandeis's dissents began to bear fruit, and following the 1937 Court fight open resistance to the idea of administrative agencies collapsed. In 1939, just a few months after he stepped down, Brandeis learned that the Court, after several hearings, had finally decided *United States v. Morgan,* a case that had been going back and forth between the high court and a Missouri district court for three years, involving the administrative power of the secretary of agriculture to dispose of money held in escrow following a controversy involving stockyard fees. The Court said that while there had been procedural irregularities, the secretary could correct his own missteps without further judicial scrutiny. In his opinion, Justice Stone essentially followed the criteria that Brandeis had set up fifteen years earlier.

STARE DECISIS, the practice by which courts base their current decisions on past rulings, plays an important role in our jurisprudence. Some judges, even if they disagree with an earlier holding, will often feel bound by it; this is especially true on lower courts, which have to take guidance on the meaning of the Constitution from the Supreme Court. In general, the doctrine provides continuity and stability, and lawyers can assume that courts, once having established a doctrine, will follow it. But there is also the argument that when a court makes a wrong decision, following it blindly merely leads to the compounding of error. Moreover, in a complex legal society, one can often cite precedents in support of both sides. This gives the Court a great deal of leeway in determining which precedents to follow.

Although it is quite common now for justices to say that *stare decisis* ought not to be followed blindly, and perhaps not even at all in constitutional cases, Brandeis was the first justice to suggest that the Court not feel completely bound by precedent. On the one hand, he knew that many of the precedents took a narrow and restrictive view of what the state could do and bent over to protect property rights. While *Muller* might have overcome *Lochner* in 1908, he had seen how the *Lochner* precedent informed the decision in *Adkins*.

So in a 1932 case, *Burnet v. Coronado Oil and Gas Co.,* he listed over one hundred cases in which the Court had overruled itself and cataloged the Court's overruling practices in such a powerful manner that his analysis has, according to some scholars, assumed canonical authority. Brandeis wanted the Court to constantly reevaluate the law, to take into account changing conditions, a theme that, as we have seen, proved a constant throughout his career. It is not that he disapproved of precedent but that he believed that like all aspects of the law it had to be viewed through the light of changing conditions. One scholar says that this dissent, although lesser known than *Whitney* or *Olmstead,* should also be considered canonical, because it led the Court to adopt a far more flexible and pragmatic view of how it would treat the *stare decisis* doctrine.

DURING THEIR YEARS on the Court, Brandeis and Holmes fought the rigidity of a conservative majority's attachment to legal classicism, with its emphasis on unyielding rules that ignored social and economic facts. Both men believed that law divorced from factual reality could only be sterile, and the more separated it became, the greater a threat to society. This was especially true for Brandeis, whose dissents at times seemed too concerned with facts. But he had a reason: to drive home the sins of the majority in refusing to recognize that law had to fit the conditions of society. Although seemingly voices in the wilderness during much of their tenure, in the end the Court and the society accepted their views. The decisions of the majority, with their rigidity and formalism, have been overturned. The Holmes and Brandeis dissents, and the discourse they engendered, pointed the way to the future.

BRANDEIS IN *OLMSTEAD V. UNITED STATES* (1928)

R oy Olmstead rose to prominence because of the great failed experiment of Prohibition, a legacy of the Progressive reform ferment that marked American society in the two decades leading up to the nation's entry into World War I. Soon after the ratification of the Eighteenth Amendment in January 1919, it became apparent that many people in the country had little use for Prohibition. In rural areas, moonshine and hard cider abounded, while the cities stood overwhelmingly opposed to the ban on drink. Before long, the "Noble Experiment" in social reform turned into a national nightmare of failed law enforcement and a widespread disdain for federal and state agencies trying to enforce the ban.

The American people, who took pride in their ingeniousness, came up with one device after another to get what the law said they could not have. Sophisticated chemical laboratories, hidden in warehouses, redistilled industrial alcohol. Compliant druggists wrote prescriptions for alcohol that could then be blended with other ingredients. Many people brewed at home, and hardware stores openly displayed and sold the equipment needed. Boats smuggled in premium liquors from Europe and the Caribbean along New Jersey's Rum Row, while ice sleds easily crossed over from Canada in midwinter.

Criminals quickly adapted the new technologies of telephones and automobiles to help them circumvent Prohibition. In Seattle, a police

Roy Olmstead, the "King of the Bootleggers," and his wife, Elise, in Seattle

lieutenant named Roy Olmstead learned all about the bootlegging business while making arrests and realized that the main problem of running an illegal business was lack of organization. There were too many unconnected pieces, too many mistakes arising from lack of information and communication and lack of leadership. Olmstead left the police department and proceeded to put together a highly efficient organization to import and distribute liquor in violation of the Volstead Act.

The "Olmstead Ring" could serve as a case study at the Harvard Business School. At its peak, the organization employed between fifty and seventy people and leased two seagoing vessels to bring the liquor from British Columbia to Seattle and several smaller boats to distribute alcohol up and down the Washington State coast. The ring ran out of a central office manned by telephone operators, salesmen, deliverymen, dispatchers, bookkeepers, collectors, and even an attorney. As a former police officer, Olmstead had contacts—including two brothers—in the Seattle Police Department who kept him apprised of possible raids and also helped him to arrange the release of any of his men who might be arrested.

From early morning to late at night, operators manned the phones at the main office, and either Olmstead or one of his managers would then take the orders and give them to a deliveryman, who would go to one of the local caches, pick up the requested items, and take them to the customers. On some days, the operation delivered as many as two hundred cases of liquor. As the court records showed, even in a bad month sales amounted to $176,000, and annual income easily topped $2 million (equivalent to more than $25 million in current dollars). Little of this was secret. The local press dubbed Olmstead the "King of the Puget Sound Bootleggers," and Olmstead made no effort to maintain a low public profile.

Federal agents utilized their own technology. They ran taps on the phones into the ring's main office as well as the lines at Olmstead's home and the residences of some of his partners. At the main office, they set up a listening post in the basement of the building and attached earphones to the telephone wires using alligator clips. At the private residences, they attached the wires either in the basements of apartment buildings or on telephone poles outside houses. At no time did they enter the premises, nor did they have a warrant to eavesdrop—because neither police nor prosecution believed a warrant necessary. One needed a warrant to enter a premise, but federal agents never actually did so; they listened from outside the office and the homes.

Over the course of the investigation, the agents compiled 775 pages of transcriptions of telephone calls and on that basis secured arrest warrants for Olmstead and seventy other people. Some escaped, and at trial a few were acquitted. But juries in the federal court for the Western District of Washington found Olmstead and seventeen of his partners and managers guilty, and the Court of Appeals for the Ninth Circuit affirmed the convictions and jail sentences. From there, Olmstead appealed to the U.S. Supreme Court.

From the beginning, Olmstead's lawyers had argued that the use of wiretap evidence obtained without a search warrant violated the Fourth Amendment to the Constitution. His lead attorney, John F. Dore, claimed that the rights guaranteed under the Constitution are "indispensable to the full enjoyment of personal security, personal liberty, and private property," and therefore may not be trampled upon by the government. If the government used fraud or subterfuge to secure evidence, then it could not be admitted as evidence in a case. Dore also tried to convince the Court that even if there had not been an actual invasion of the physical premises, if the results were to force a person to furnish evidence against himself, then it violated the Fifth Amendment's prohibition against self-incrimination.

American Telephone & Telegraph, the nation's largest provider of phone service, as well as a number of smaller telephone firms, filed briefs as *amici curiae* or friends of the court, protesting against the use of private conversations, secured through wiretaps, as violations of the Fourth and Fifth Amendments. Their arguments sound eerily prescient in terms of current NSA eavesdropping.

When the justices heard the case in February 1928, there had only been a few Fourth Amendment cases before the Court—and none involving wiretaps—but the Court had been firm in its insistence that federal agents needed a warrant to search a suspect's premises. Just a few years earlier, the Court had heard a case in which the Justice Department, without a warrant, had ransacked the office of the Silverthorne Lumber Company, removing books, papers, and other documents. Justice Holmes spoke for a 7-2 majority in labeling the government's action an "outrage" and blocked any use of the illegally seized material in legal proceedings. Holmes's insistence that the documents "shall not be used at all" helped expand the "exclusionary rule" that the Court had expounded in *Weeks v. United States* (1914). In *Weeks, Silverthorne,* and other cases, the Court stressed two themes: the exclusionary rule provided the only effective means of protecting Fourth Amendment rights, and judicial integrity required that the courts not sanction illegal search by admitting the fruits of this illegality into evidence. In fact, that previous fall, Brandeis, speaking for a unanimous Court, reinforced the exclusionary rule, holding that evidence illegally seized in a warrantless search could not be used in a federal court.

Given this line of precedents, one would have thought that the Court in Olmstead's case would have excluded the warrantless wiretap evidence. A bare majority of the Court, however, refused to accept the Fourth Amendment argument and instead agreed with the government that wiretapping did not constitute an unreasonable search and seizure within the meaning of the Fourth Amendment.

CHIEF JUSTICE William Howard Taft wrote the majority opinion and tried to limit the decision to what he termed was the sole question that the Court had agreed to hear in accepting the case—whether "the use of evidence of private telephone conversations between the defendants and others, intercepted by means of wire tapping, amounted to a violation of the Fourth and Fifth Amendments."

In what can only be described as a wooden opinion, Taft went over all of
the Supreme Court's prior Fourth Amendment opinions and found them
irrelevant to Olmstead's case. The precedents had all involved physical
intrusion into the defendants' homes or offices, and in this instance the
federal agents had done no more than listen in on conversations from
positions outside the premises. "There was no evidence of compulsion
to induce the defendants to talk over their many telephones. They were
continually and voluntarily transacting business without knowledge of
the interception." As for the alleged violations of the Fourth Amendment, Taft declared, "The Amendment does not forbid what was done
here. There was no searching. There was no seizure. The evidence was
secured by the use of the sense of hearing and that only. There was no
entry of the houses or offices of the defendants."

Taft could find no means by which this activity violated the Fourth
Amendment. "The language of the Amendment can not be extended
and expanded to include telephone wires reaching to the whole world
from the defendant's house or office. The intervening wires are not part
of his house or office, any more than are the highways along which they
are stretched." Then Taft, who in other cases had no problem in reaching out to make new law, adopted the posture of strict judicial restraint.
Congress could, he noted, make evidence secured by wiretap inadmissible in federal trials, but "courts may not adopt such a policy by attrib-
uting an enlarged and unusual meaning to the Fourth Amendment."

The Taft opinion elicited dissents from Butler, Holmes, and Brandeis.
In a well-reasoned historical analysis, the generally conservative Butler
repudiated Taft's sterile interpretation of what the Fourth Amendment
meant, although he agreed with Taft that the only question properly
before the Court was whether the evidence itself could be used. Stone,
who concurred in all of the dissents, did not agree with this part of
Butler's writing. Although the grant of certiorari accepting the appeal
identified a single issue, he believed that the Court was always free to
consider any matter in the record and in this regard found himself in
agreement with Holmes and Brandeis.

Holmes took a different tack from Butler and, in a comment that
soon caught the liberal imagination, condemned wiretapping as a "dirty
business." He identified two "objects of desire," noting that one could
not have both. "It is desirable that criminals should be detected, and
to that end all available evidence should be used. It also is desirable
that the government should not itself foster and pay for other crimes,
when they are the means by which the evidence is to be obtained." We
have to choose, he declared, "and for my part I think it less evil that

some criminals should escape than that the government should play an ignoble part." Holmes had originally not intended to write an opinion at all, because "my brother Brandeis has given this case so exhaustive an examination," but he did so for two reasons. First, Brandeis had privately asked him to do so, and, second, he did not completely agree with all that Brandeis said, especially that the Fourth and Fifth Amendments created a right of privacy.

HOLMES AND BRANDEIS had bowed to the will of the people in accepting Prohibition, although in practice Holmes continued to enjoy his drink and to receive bottles from his friends. Brandeis had liked his beer and an occasional whiskey, and for many years at dinner he had served guests the good Kentucky bourbon that his brother, Alfred, regularly sent from Louisville. His views on democratic governance led him to support Prohibition after ratification, and in time he even came to be a fervent supporter of the ban on alcohol, believing it could improve the lives of working people.

In *Olmstead,* Brandeis did not attack or defend Prohibition, but rather the means the government had chosen to enforce it, and his dissenting opinion had a profound and lasting impact on Fourth Amendment jurisprudence. Brandeis wanted to drive home several points. He clearly abhorred the methods used by the federal agents, and the reason for his

Prohibition agents dump illegal alcohol into sewer in New York.

antipathy is one that should be read every day by government officials, including presidents:

> Decency, security and liberty alike demand that government offi-
> cials shall be subjected to the same rules of conduct that are com-
> mands to the citizen. In a government of laws, existence of the
> government will be imperilled if it fails to observe the law scru-
> pulously. Our Government is the potent, the omnipresent teacher.
> For good or for ill, it teaches the whole people by its example.
> Crime is contagious. If the Government becomes a lawbreaker, it
> breeds contempt for law; it invites every man to become a law unto
> himself; it invites anarchy. To declare that in the administration of
> the criminal law the end justifies the means—to declare that the
> Government may commit crimes in order to secure the conviction
> of a private criminal—would bring terrible retribution. Against
> that pernicious doctrine this Court should resolutely set its face.

But Brandeis had another argument to make, one that he had been advocating for nearly four decades—the right to privacy. In an 1890 article he had written with his law partner, Samuel D. Warren, Brandeis had argued that a common-law right to privacy existed. At the time, he had relied on private action and tort law, because the alleged violators of privacy had been the press and commercial actors. Now, because the government had been involved, he identified personal privacy as a matter of constitutional law and married his earlier notion of the right to be let alone with the Fourth Amendment's ban on unreasonable search and sei- zure and the Fifth Amendment's protection against self-incrimination. To justify reading privacy into these amendments, he assigned his law clerk that term, Henry J. Friendly, to research the circumstances sur- rounding the drafting of the Fourth Amendment. Brandeis expected his clerks to argue with him, and when they did make a convincing argu- ment, he would listen. At first, the justice wanted to base his dissent on the violation of the Washington State statute against wiretapping, but Friendly convinced him that it should rest on a constitutional basis. The result is one of the landmark dissents in constitutional history.

Taft had emphasized that the Framers had nothing more in mind than the general warrants used by the British in the 1760s and 1770s, and the Fourth Amendment applied to little else. Brandeis cited Chief Justice Marshall's reminder that "we must never forget that it is a constitution we are expounding." Times had changed since 1791, and Brandeis cited case after case as well as historical treatises to show that the Court had constantly read constitutional provisions to take into account conditions never envisioned by the Framers. The technical nature of the federal agents' entry onto the defendant's property did not matter as much as the intent of the amendment to protect people in their homes and businesses. "Time works changes, brings into existence new conditions and purposes. Subtle and more far-reaching means of invading privacy have become available to the Government. Discovery and invention have made it possible for the Government, by means far more effective than stretching upon the rack, to obtain disclosure in court of what is whispered in the closet." (At this point, Brandeis wanted to refer to a new device recently developed by the General Electric Company called "television," but he removed the note in deference to Friendly's skepticism.)

He then went on to write one of the most eloquent—and most quoted—passages in American law.

> The makers of our Constitution undertook to secure conditions favorable to the pursuit of happiness. They recognized the significance of man's spiritual nature, of his feelings and of his intellect. They knew that only a part of the pain, pleasure and satisfactions of life are to be found in material things. They sought to protect Americans in their beliefs, their thoughts, their emotions and their sensations. They conferred, as against the Government, the right to be let alone—the most comprehensive of rights and the right most valued by civilized men. To protect that right, every unjustifiable intrusion by the Government upon the privacy of the individual, whatever the means employed, must be deemed a violation of the Fourth Amendment.

Brandeis dismissed Taft's mechanistic view that no intrusion had occurred, because it did not matter where the actual physical connection with the telephone wires took place: "And it is also immaterial that the intrusion was in aid of law enforcement. Experience should teach us to be most on our guard to protect liberty when the Government's purposes are beneficent. Men born to freedom are naturally alert to repel invasion of their liberty by evil-minded rulers. The greatest dangers to liberty lurk in insidious encroachment by men of zeal, well-meaning but without understanding."

In the *Olmstead* dissent, Brandeis reinvented Fourth Amendment jurisprudence. Taft's majority opinion, as well as prior search and seizure cases, had been grounded in conceptions of property, whether or not police had actually entered the home or business. Brandeis shifted the emphasis from where the alleged wrong took place to how it affected the individual's rights. While Brandeis disliked the "dirty business" of wiretapping as much as Holmes, for him the more important issues were the conduct of the police and the individual's right to be let alone. If the police had probable cause to suspect a person of wrongdoing, the Constitution required that a warrant be secured. Warrantless searches, except in very special circumstances, could not be allowed.

Chief Justice Taft reacted furiously to the dissents. "If they think we are going to be frightened in our effort to stand by the law and give the public a chance to punish criminals," he told his brother, "they are mistaken, even though we are condemned for lack of high ideals." Holmes had written "the nastiest opinion," and Taft claimed that Holmes had voted the other way "till Brandeis got after him and induced him to change." But, he told Justice Sutherland, "I hope that ultimately it will be seen that we in the majority were right."

BRANDEIS UNDERSTOOD the role that dissent played in constitutional discourse, and in *Olmstead* he wanted the justices to talk not only about privacy and respect for the law but also about how the Due Process Clause of the Fourteenth Amendment should be interpreted. If nothing else, he told Felix Frankfurter, reviewers of the opinion would see that "in favor of property the Constitution is liberally construed—in favor of liberty, strictly." He especially wanted to advance the idea that the Fourteenth Amendment incorporated the Bill of Rights to the states, a position that made Holmes uncomfortable, especially the notion that one could find a constitutional right of privacy in the Fourth and Fifth Amendments.

Taft's prediction, of course, proved wrong. Brandeis lived to see Congress prohibit wiretapping evidence in federal courts in the Communications Act of 1934 and the Court vote to partially reverse *Olmstead* in 1937. But it took a while for the Court to fully adopt Brandeis's views on the applicability of the Warrant Clause to eavesdropping and that the Fourth Amendment applied to the states.

In 1942, the majority ruled that a detectaphone placed against an outer wall to record conversations inside an office without a warrant did not violate the Fourth Amendment, with Justice Owen Roberts following the reasoning in Taft's *Olmstead* opinion. Justice Murphy dissented, following what he called "Mr. Justice Brandeis's memorable dissent in Olmstead." Chief Justice Stone and Justice Frankfurter also dissented, noting, "Had a majority of the Court been willing to overrule the Olmstead case, we should have been happy to join them. But as they have declined to do so, and as we think the case is indistinguishable in principle from Olmstead's, we have no occasion to repeat here the dissenting views in that case with which we agree."

Ten years later, the majority of the Court allowed as admissible a secretly recorded conversation between a federal agent and On Lee in the latter's laundry. Once again, Brandeis's opinion was cited, this time by Frankfurter in his dissent, when he charged that "the law of this Court ought not to be open to the just charge of having been dictated by the 'odious doctrine,' as Mr. Justice Brandeis called it, that the end justifies reprehensible means." Justices Douglas and Harold Burton also dissented, and both noted Brandeis's "powerful dissent" in *Olmstead.*

Then, in the 1960s, the tide began to change. In *Silverman v. United States* (1961), the government had driven a spike microphone through an outside wall until it came into contact with the air-conditioning and heating ducts, which served as a natural amplifier of all conversations taking place throughout the house. In an opinion by Justice Potter Stewart, eight members of the Court held that the use of this "spike mike" did not constitute a violation of the 1934 Communications Act but that its use without a warrant violated the Fourth Amendment. Justice Douglas concurred, pointing out the inconsistencies of the Court's record in this area. A detectaphone had been ruled permissible in *Goldman,* but a similar device was not permissible here. As far as he was concerned, the type of device should make no difference. Any type of eavesdropping without a warrant constituted a violation of the Fourth Amendment.

In 1967, the Supreme Court fully adopted Brandeis's position and overturned *Olmstead* completely, bringing wiretapping within the ambit of Fourth Amendment protection. That same year, Justice Stewart explained the Court's new philosophy in words that grew directly out of Brandeis's dissent: "The Fourth Amendment protects people, not places." Stewart, in fact, based his opinion on Brandeis's argument.

In a 2001 case, Justice Antonin Scalia used the logic of Brandeis's dissent to hold that federal agents could not use a new technology, thermal imaging, to look through the walls of Danny Lee Kyllo's house to determine if the occupant was raising marijuana. Even though the agents used the machine outside the premises, they had secured information about the inside and could not use that evidence without a warrant. Then, in 2013, a drug-sniffing dog was brought to the front door of Joelis Jardines's house and reacted strongly to the odor of marijuana. Based on this, the police secured a warrant, found cannabis plants in the house, and arrested Jardines. After he was convicted of drug trafficking,

Jardines appealed, and once again Justice Scalia, following the reasoning of Brandeis's opinion but without citing it, held that the use of a dog, like a thermal-imaging device, required a warrant before any evidence it produced could be used in court. Scalia did not cite the Brandeis dissent, because, as a textualist, he objected to the idea of a constitutional right to privacy, which is at the heart of the Brandeis opinion.

WINNING THE FIGHT on the necessity for a warrant proved the easier battle, even though it took forty years before victory was complete. The Court had long before *Olmstead* ruled that the Fourth Amendment required federal agents to get a warrant prior to searching premises or seizing records or contraband. In many ways, business-related conversations, even if they related to an illegal business, correlated to business records, the type of property the Court had always held protected by the Fourth Amendment. Once the Court accepted that premise, the debate in the years following *Olmstead* focused on whether electronic eavesdropping—either through a phone tap, a detectaphone, or a spike mike—constituted the type of entry onto premises that required a warrant. Although privacy played a role here—the Fourth Amendment protects people, not places, and people speaking on their phones had an expectation of privacy—that did not mean that a separate constitutional right to be let alone existed.

Brandeis, however, spoke about more than mere business transactions. "The makers of our Constitution," he explained, "sought to protect Americans in their beliefs, their thoughts, their emotions and their sensations. They conferred, as against the Government, the right to be let alone—the most comprehensive of rights and the right most valued by civilized men." He meant that the government had no business inquiring in private decisions that people made—what books they read, whom they loved, how they raised their children—so long as the activity did not violate any legal prohibition.

Privacy as a constitutional right means that government cannot proscribe those decisions that men or women make to shape their own lives. Certain choices are so fundamental that they may properly be said to be totally outside the reach of the state's power. Over the years, the Court has come to recognize areas of procreation, marriage, family life, health, and more recently sexual preference. Despite great pressure from religious and social conservative groups, the Court and the country have accepted Brandeis's notion that the Constitution embodies a right to be let alone. Debate has not ceased, but the arguments are less on whether the right to privacy exists and more on what its limits are.

James Clark McReynolds, associate justice, 1914–1941

Even before Brandeis wrote in *Olmstead,* the Court had struck down a state statute, passed in the anti-German fervor of World War I, that forbade the teaching of foreign languages in elementary school. The statute had been challenged on the grounds that it violated liberties guaranteed under the Fourteenth Amendment's Due Process Clause. Justice McReynolds agreed and declared that liberty "denotes not merely freedom from bodily restraint but also the right of the individual to contract, to engage in any of the common occupations of life, to acquire useful knowledge, to marry, to establish a home and bring up children, to worship God according to the dictates of his own conscience, and generally to enjoy those privileges long recognized at common law as essential to the orderly pursuit of happiness by free men."

To be sure, McReynolds based his argument on the types of property rights enunciated in the *Lochner* case, not in any specific right to privacy. In the next case that came before the Court that implicated private decisions, the Court in 1942 unanimously struck down an Oklahoma statute that mandated sterilization for "compulsory criminals." One might have expected challenges to this law on the basis of either the Equal Protection or the Due Process Clause of the Fourteenth Amendment. But the former had been so narrowly interpreted by the Court that it had become practically moribund, while the abuse of the latter by conservative jurists to strike down reform legislation in the 1920s and 1930s had made the Roosevelt appointees extremely reluctant to use it.

Justice William O. Douglas cut through this Gordian knot by noting that the law did not apply equally to all felons, because it made an exception for embezzlers. This opened the door to equal protection analysis, and Douglas charged through. He defined marriage and procreation as "basic civil rights . . . fundamental to the very existence and survival of the race" and thus subject to strict scrutiny by the courts.

Douglas also wrote the opinion in the case that specifically recognized an independent and fundamental constitutional right to privacy, *Griswold v. Connecticut* (1965). The case involved a state statute that prohibited the use of contraceptives by married people and forbade doctors to prescribe contraceptive medicines or devices. Because the notion of substantive due process still labored under the odium of the *Lochner* era, Douglas engaged in jurisprudential gymnastics, cobbling together justifications from various parts of the Bill of Rights that, he said, "have penumbras, formed by emanations from those guarantees that help give them life and substance." These emanations together (joined in what one wit described as Amendment 3½) form a constitutionally protected right of privacy, and no privacy could be more sacred, or more deserving of protection from intrusion by the state, than that of the marital chamber.

Interestingly, Douglas did not cite Brandeis in *Olmstead,* but Justice Arthur Goldberg in his concurrence did, and he would have located a right to privacy in the Ninth Amendment, which averred that "the enumeration in the Constitution, of certain rights, shall not be construed to deny or disparage others retained by the people." For Goldberg, the fact that the word "privacy" is not mentioned in the Constitution was irrelevant, because he considered it, as did Brandeis, a fundamental right rooted in the history of the people.

Neither Douglas's Amendment 3½ nor Goldberg's Ninth Amendment argument would, in the end, provide the vehicle needed to embed privacy firmly in the constitutional dialogue. Rather, Justice John Marshall Harlan II located it in the personal liberties protected by the Due Process Clause. Harlan certainly knew about the history of due process, and its abuse in earlier days, but unlike other members of the Court did not feel constrained to ignore what he considered a powerful and all-encompassing clause to guarantee personal liberties such as privacy.

Over the next few years, the Court expanded the right to use contraceptives to unmarried people; struck down antimiscegenation laws, holding that the right to choose whom to marry is a fundamental privacy right; said that states could not put financial barriers in the way of a divorce, which Justice Harlan described as a "precondition to the adjustment of a fundamental human relationship"; held that a man had the right to view pornography in the privacy of his home; and held that the notion of privacy extended to a woman's right to terminate a pregnancy.

The abortion decision touched off a firestorm of public criticism not seen since the *Dred Scott* case prior to the Civil War, although it had the strong support of the burgeoning feminist movement. While we need not go into the full details of this debate, it should be noted that even before *Roe* was decided, some influential academics, such as Robert H. Bork, criticized the Court for "creating" a constitutional right of privacy. Bork did not oppose privacy but could not find any mention or justification for it in the Constitution. On the Court itself, William H. Rehnquist steadfastly opposed *Roe* and its progeny but eventually came around to supporting privacy, albeit by calling it a different name.

In *Cruzan v. Director, Missouri Department of Health* (1990), the Court, speaking through Rehnquist, held that the right to die is not a fundamental privacy right but acknowledged a constitutionally protected liberty interest in a competent person's right to refuse life-sustaining medical treatment. This liberty interest could be found in the Due Process Clause of the Fourteenth Amendment, just as Justice Harlan had suggested in his *Griswold* concurrence.

Perhaps the most recent area to be included within the right to be let alone involves the right of homosexuals to love whom they please and even to marry them. When the issue first came before the Court in 1986, a slim 5–4 majority held that no right to privacy existed that would give gays the right to sex. Such conduct had always been illegal, wrote Justice Byron White, and nothing in the Constitution changed that history. By any standards, White had written a harsh, even a homophobic, opinion.

Over the next few decades, the mood of the country became far more tolerant of gays and lesbians, and this in turn no doubt influenced several justices when the issue came back to the Court in 2003. In addition to denouncing White's opinion in the earlier case, Justice Anthony Kennedy declared that a fair-minded understanding of the basic constitutional right of privacy would take seriously, in gay as well as straight sexual relations, the accompanying integrity of the connection between sexual expression and companionate friendship and love. The state, he concluded, "cannot demean [homosexuals'] existence or control their destiny by making their private sexual conduct a crime."

For those who argued that the Constitution mentioned neither privacy nor rights given to gays, Kennedy responded that the Framers had not drafted the document in specific terms. They did not claim to know "the components of liberty in its manifold possibilities" but were themselves open—as the Court needed to be—to new arguments and experiences. In words Brandeis might himself have used, Kennedy concluded that the Framers "knew times can blind us to certain truths and later generations can see that laws once thought necessary and proper in fact serve only to oppress. As the Constitution endures, persons in every generation can invoke its principles in their own search for greater freedom."

CHAPTER 7

THE RETURN OF SERIATIM

Mr. Justice Black delivered the opinion of the Court.
For concurring opinion of Mr. Justice Frankfurter, see post, p. 593.
For concurring opinion of Mr. Justice Douglas, see post, p. 629.
For concurring opinion of Mr. Justice Jackson, see post, p. 634.
For concurring opinion of Mr. Justice Burton, see post, p. 655.
For opinion of Mr. Justice Clark, concurring in the judgment of the Court,
see post, p. 660.
For dissenting opinion of Mr. Chief Justice Vinson, joined by Mr. Justice Reed
and Mr. Justice Minton, see post, p. 673.

— *YOUNGSTOWN SHEET & TUBE CO. V. SAWYER* (1952)

During the 1920s, the vast majority of Supreme Court decisions came down without separate opinions. During the thirty years that Holmes served on the high court (1902–1932), the justices agreed unanimously in 91 percent of the cases. Twenty years later, only 22 percent—roughly one in five—had the support of all nine justices. This sea change resulted from a number of factors, among which we can count (1) the Judges' Bill of 1925; (2) the increasing complexity of the cases, especially those involving constitutional issues; (3) the transition from the strong leadership of Taft and Hughes to the inability of Stone and Vinson to manage the Court; (4) the presence of powerful and disruptive personalities on the bench; and (5) the growing role of clerks in the justices' chambers. While there were certainly some important dissents between 1932 and 1953, the growing babble on the Court often disguised important jurisprudential principles. Thomas Jefferson, however, might well have approved.

THE JUDGES' BILL OF 1925. William Howard Taft disliked dissents, yet ironically, one of his great accomplishments as chief justice played a key role in destroying the justices' willingness to suppress dissents for the sake of institutional solidarity. The Judiciary Act of 1925, commonly known as the Judges' Bill, which Taft lobbied Congress to enact, fundamentally redefined the high court's role. Prior to the law, the Court had to accept a whole host of cases under the right of appeal, and most of these cases dealt not with constitutional issues or even matters of statutory interpretation.

A look at the dockets of prior courts shows that in the nineteenth century only a handful of cases each term required constitutional interpretation. In 1899, for example, the five volumes of *U.S. Reports* show that the Fuller Court that year dealt mostly with issues of federal equity receiverships, diversity mortgage foreclosures, diversity suits against railroads for personal injuries, and the like. Diversity simply means that the parties came from different states, a jurisdictional requirement for standing in a federal court, but aside from the residential distinction, mortgage foreclosures and personal injury suits heard by the nation's highest court differed little from what today would be heard in state courts. In the early nineteenth century, however, Congress had decreed that the Supreme Court would be a court of last resort and had created large categories of cases that the Court had to take on appeal, the types of cases that Brandeis said were "better that they be decided than that they be decided right."

Amendments to the jurisdiction laws in 1891 and again in 1916 helped cleanse the docket of some of these cases so that by 1923 the Taft Court had far fewer appeals of right. Nonetheless, in the October 1923 term, the Court heard cases involving creditor suits against a local bank, a dispute between two insurance companies over liability of a policy, and a suit to determine jurisdiction in a case where a bank was suing to be paid on a contract, not to mention numerous bankruptcy cases. Taft, who transformed the role of chief justice into something analogous to that of chief executive of the judicial branch of government, had a broader vision of what the Supreme Court should be—namely, a constitutional court dealing only marginally with nonconstitutional matters. The 1925

William Howard Taft, chief justice, 1921–1930

law sharply constricted the Court's mandatory jurisdiction—those cases it had to take—and gave the justices the opportunity to take only those cases that raised important constitutional issues or questions of federal statutory interpretation.

The act succeeded, as Taft had intended, in transforming the Court from a forum that corrected errors in ordinary private litigation—such as personal injury suits—into a constitutional tribunal that decided policy issues of national importance. The Court's decisions changed from a conversation between the justices and the litigants before the bar into an ongoing dialogue with Congress, the president, and, most important, the public.

One unintended consequence, especially from Taft's point of view, is that as the docket filled with important questions of constitutional significance, the justices began to emphasize the principles that went into their opinions and their differences with other members of the Court. While, as Brandeis claimed, it did not really matter how one resolved a foreclosure suit so long as it was settled, one had to get a constitutional question right. The justices no longer solved legal matters between two parties but articulated legal rules that affected the entire country, and their views on their roles changed dramatically.

To give an idea of how greatly the act changed the Court's docket, before its passage three out of every four cases had been taken under its obligatory jurisdiction, while the remaining 25 percent were taken only when four justices voted to accept the matter. Immediately following its enactment, the ratios reversed, and then the number of discretionary cases soon took over almost the entire docket. The year before the act, unanimous opinions accounted for 91.6 percent of the Court's decisions; in the year after passage, that number fell to 85.2 percent.

As the justices dealt with ever more complex and controversial topics, they had more incentive to express dissent and to abandon the chimera of institutional unity. This new discretion in choosing cases, however, meant that individual members of the Court had to develop and articulate coherent individual judicial philosophies. Where with lesser cases they might well have "shut up," they now felt not only that constitutional questions required a fuller exposition but that the exposure of internal disagreements within the Court might well be a good thing. Holmes and Brandeis, like Harlan and Field before them, had always felt that in important matters they had an obligation to speak out. After 1925, other members of the Court also started to do this, and institutional unity began to evaporate.

THE GROWING COMPLEXITY OF CONSTITUTIONAL CASES. Writing about difficult cases that come before a court, Benjamin Cardozo observed, "In a sense it is true of many of them that they might be decided either way. By that I mean that reasons plausible and fairly persuasive might be found for one conclusion or another." William H. Rehnquist also believed "that the nature of constitutional adjudication invites, at least, if it does not require, more separate opinions than does adjudication of issues in law in other areas." Moreover, he added, "because so many of our cases are in the area of constitutional law, the conclusions we reach are bound to be less certain and more subject to debate than were the conclusions reached by the Fuller Court in the kinds of cases it decided."

Constitutional adjudication may indeed invite or even require more opinions, but one should also note the increasing complexity of the cases that came before the Court after 1925. This is not to say that nineteenth-century courts did not face difficult issues, but as the nature of society changed due to a national industrialized economy, as the country became more involved with the rest of the world, and as minorities began to use the courts to assert civil rights and civil liberties, it is not surprising that the justices would take differing views on what the Constitution meant when confronting these issues.

—How far, for example, could the federal government go in regulating intrastate commerce when that activity impacted on interstate commerce? Could Congress, under the aegis of the Commerce Clause, regulate guns in school yards, make assaults on women a federal crime, or require individuals to buy health insurance?
—The Constitution designates the president as commander in chief, but what specific powers does this give the executive in wartime? What happens when there is a "war on terror"? Does the president have the power to designate prisoners as "enemy combatants" and subject them to harsh treatment?
—What does the Fourteenth Amendment's Equal Protection Clause mean in terms of how states treat minorities, or women, or gays? Can a governmental entity, such as a state university, create preference for minority admissions to compensate for past discrimination, even if that school itself had never discriminated?

None of these questions are simple, and while the facts in some cases may make it easier for the courts to decide, the truly easy cases are nearly always resolved in the lower courts. Given the complexity of many of the questions that come to the high court, the multiplication of opinions is easily understood.

David O'Brien points out another aspect of Court life at this time that contributed to the growth of dissent. Throughout the nineteenth century, the author of the Court's opinion did not circulate any drafts of that opinion. Instead, the drafts were read at conference, where the other members of the Court could offer suggestions. In the 1920s and 1930s, with the technological innovation of the typewriter, the Court began the practice of circulating drafts prior to conference. Justices now had more time to study the wording, make suggestions for change, or decide to write separately. Threats of a dissent carried more weight when the consensus norm prevailed. The author of the Court's opinion would accommodate as much as possible, and in return other justices would not publish dissents, even if they still disagreed with the results. As the constitutional cases grew more complex and the norm for institutional unity eroded, threats of dissent carried less force, and the institutional pressure against dissents collapsed.

The problem, however, is whether multiple opinions really facilitate a dialogue on public policy, or have they become a babble making it difficult, if not impossible, for the constitutional dialogue to take place? When the Court is so fractured that every justice feels it incumbent to write an opinion, one may forgive the public for failing to understand the issues involved. Dissents, once reserved for only the deepest jurisprudential disagreements, are now commonplace.

LEADERSHIP OF THE COURT. Early in his tenure as chief justice, William Howard Taft declared that dissents "are a form of egotism. They don't do any good and only weaken the prestige of the Court. It is much more important what the Court thinks than what any one [justice] thinks." In the eight terms he served as chief justice, he wrote 294 opinions for the Court, dissented in only 17, and filed only three written dissents. Moreover, he suppressed some two hundred dissenting votes; once the justices voted on a case, he felt it his obligation to stand with the majority for the sake of the institution.

As chief, Taft worked hard to bolster the institutional solidarity of the Court. He could not, of course, prevent any justice from dissenting, but he demonstrated patience, tact, and flexibility—all traits notably lacking during his tenure as president—in an effort to bring his colleagues to full agreement. Taft took the comments of his colleagues on his opinions seriously and willingly changed or even deleted parts of draft opinions to accommodate their views. Sometimes if the draft of an opinion looked as if it might split the Court, Taft used his office as chief to reassign the case. On more than one occasion, he was able to take the insights of a threatened dissent and incorporate them into an opinion that ultimately commanded the votes of the entire Court.

Needless to say, Taft found the dissents by Holmes and especially Brandeis frustrating and maddening. One of the leading scholars of the Taft Court, Dean Robert Post, points out that these dissents—especially the heavily fact-laden and footnoted opinions by Brandeis, threatened to undermine not so much a "norm of consensus" as a "norm of acquiescence," something Taft painstakingly nurtured. Taft strongly believed that even if the justices privately disagreed with each other, those differences should be put aside so that the Court could display a united front to the public, one that presented "the impact of monolithic solidarity" that Taft believed so necessary to the credibility of the Court's judgments. A good example of this is seen in a note from Pierce Butler to Harlan Fiske Stone: "I still think a reversal would be better. But I shall in silence acquiesce. Dissents seldom aid us in the right development or statement of the law."

While it is true that prior to the Judges' Bill the vast majority of cases that came before the Court involved minor, nonconstitutional issues, Taft nonetheless deserves credit as a strong leader of the Court whom liberals like Brandeis and Holmes respected. Whether Taft could have maintained the high level of unanimity once the Court actually became a true constitutional tribunal is difficult to say; while more than willing to tailor his own opinions, he only did so if the results comported with his rather conservative views.

Taft also presided at a time when the entire government—the executive, the legislative, and the judiciary—was dominated by conservatives devoted to property rights. On the bench, Taft could always count on at least five other votes on nearly every issue and rarely found himself in the minority. He could "mass the Court" because on the main issues his voice did in fact represent majority opinion. Although we note the dissents of Holmes, Brandeis, and later Stone, in the vast preponderance of cases these three men voted *with* the majority.

While president, Taft had nominated Charles Evans Hughes as an associate justice of the Court, a position Hughes resigned from in order to run as the Republican nominee for the White House in 1916. An ailing Taft rejoiced when he learned that Hughes would succeed him in early 1930, believing him to be the best man to keep the Court on a conservative path. Although the Great Depression had already begun when Hughes took the oath of office, no one at the time anticipated how severe the economic downturn would be or how the Court would get caught up in the politics of recovery.

Hughes proved the ideal person to lead the Court in the 1930s. He understood the great changes occurring in American society and the economy and that there would have to be adjustments in the law to deal with these changes. He also believed strongly in the need for social and political order—both threatened by the turmoil of the Depression—and the importance of preserving the integrity of the Court. Unlike Taft, Hughes was not a staunch judicial conservative, and his record on civil liberties as a private citizen quickly translated into a new sensitivity on the Court to questions of free speech and press.

Hughes had a commanding presence, and people spoke of his "Jovian" appearance. He kept strict control of the Court's business, and when time ran out on a lawyer during oral argument, it was said that Hughes could cut him off in the middle of the word "and." Where Taft in his

*Charles Evans Hughes, associate justice, 1910–1916;
chief justice, 1930–1941*

later years had let the weekly conference drag on for hours, Hughes had a simple, direct manner. He would summarize the facts of the case, and while the justices had time to discuss the merits, Hughes moved things along briskly so that the Saturday conference rarely ran past 4:30. Although some of the justices growled at the chief's hyper-efficiency, others, such as Brandeis, welcomed it. He told a friend that Hughes was the greatest executive genius he had ever encountered in law, in business, or in government. William O. Douglas, who came onto the bench in 1939 and served two terms with Hughes, also admired Hughes's efficiency in running the conference.

Given the sharp ideological divisions on the Court and the constitutional complexities that New Deal measures presented, one could hardly expect that Hughes could have maintained the high level of unanimity that had hitherto been the norm. In fact, during the eleven and a half terms that Hughes led the Court, the rate of nonunanimous opinions rose from 11 percent in the 1930 term to more than 28 percent in the 1940 term, and in some years exceeded 30 percent. Looked at the other way, however, the percentage of unanimous opinions still stayed relatively high, 89 percent in 1930 and 72 percent in 1940. After the new Roosevelt appointees started coming on the bench in 1938, Hughes found it difficult to keep them in line, and the last two years of his tenure saw his control of the brethren eroding.

When Hughes stepped down in July 1941, Franklin Roosevelt nominated associate justice Harlan Fiske Stone to replace him. The appointment of Stone, a Republican who had nonetheless been a clear ally of Holmes and Brandeis, drew cheers from liberals. Moreover, the famous footnote 4 he wrote in an otherwise obscure 1938 regulatory case would have great impact on the Court's jurisprudence in the 1940s and 1950s. There he had suggested that while courts ought to give deference to laws regulating economic matters, they should impose a higher level of scrutiny in cases involving civil liberties and "prejudice against discrete and insular minorities." But while Stone should deservedly be remembered as an important, perhaps even a great, associate justice, he was a weak and ineffective chief. During his five-year tenure, the rate of dissent climbed from 36 to 56 percent and in two terms stood at 58 percent.

Hughes had the stature, experience, and presence to make his colleagues respect him and, in most instances, follow his lead. People liked Stone and they respected his jurisprudential thought, but he lacked the authority to guide the Court as Taft and Hughes had done. William O. Douglas wrote to his friend and ally Hugo Black that while he liked Stone, unless Stone proved to be a stronger person than he seemed, the Court "will not be a particularly happy or congenial atmosphere in which to work." Douglas's words proved prophetic.

There are several reasons for Stone's inability to lead the Court. First of all, although he had been a successful Wall Street lawyer, his greatest pleasure before joining the Court had been as a professor and dean of the Columbia Law School. A good teacher, he enjoyed the intellectual discourse among his colleagues. Stone had chafed at Hughes's tight control

Harlan Fiske Stone, associate justice,
1925–1941; chief justice, 1941–1946

of the conference and believed that there ought to be more opportunities
for the justices to debate matters. As Douglas noted, Stone was "first,
last, and always a professor" who "wanted to search out every point and
unravel every skein." In Hughes's last years, Stone started having rump
conferences in which he, Felix Frankfurter, Owen Roberts, Douglas, and
occasionally Frank Murphy would spend hours debating the fine points
of cases before the Court.

As for "massing the Court" as Taft had done, Stone confessed that he
did not believe it either desirable or even possible. Stone had dissented
frequently as an associate justice, even when strong majorities were
against him, and would continue to do so after his promotion; he would
be the first chief justice who did not encourage unanimity over dissent.
If unity rested upon fully considered judgments, all well and good, but
agreement secured at the cost of "strongly held convictions" would be
disastrous. During the Taft era, James McReynolds had taken Stone to
task for being too willing to dissent rather than going along with the
majority to build institutional unity. Stone had heatedly replied that the
Court had made too many mistakes "which would not have been made
had it not been for the disposition of the majority to rush to conclusions
without taking the trouble to listen to the views of the minority."

A chief justice, he believed, should recognize the value of dissents and

Frederick Moore Vinson, chief justice,
1946–1953

should seek a fine line that would permit dissent without anarchy. As chief, Stone dissented in 95 of the 704 cases heard during his tenure, a rate of 1 3 percent—higher than that of any other occupant of the center chair. Stone also abandoned the tight control Hughes had exercised over the conference; even if he had wanted to continue, it is unlikely he could do so. Stone liked discussion, but without a firm hand of leadership the Saturday conferences soon degenerated into endless debates. All sides were surely discussed, but very often the justices would have to meet at least once during the week for several hours to complete business left over from Saturday, business that under Hughes would have been finished. Most scholars blame Stone's failure of leadership as a primary cause of the end of the norm of consensus.

The rate of dissent increased even more under Stone's successor, Frederick Moore Vinson. The quotation from the headnote of the *Youngstown* case that begins this chapter gives some idea of the dissentious nature of the Court in those years, and President Harry Truman, well aware of the increasingly bitter infighting on the Court, hoped that his friend Fred Vinson would be able to restore some order. Vinson, although he had some judicial experience on a circuit court of appeals, had primarily been an executive. He directed the Office of Economic Stabilization during the war, and had also been Truman's Treasury secretary. He was used to directing a bureaucracy and could not translate that into leading a court where he was, at best, first among equals. Fred Rodell speculated that the "one-man power he held in his high administrative posts perhaps led him to believe that he could boss the Supreme Court in the same firm-but-gentle way." Where the "scorpions," as one scholar has described the Roosevelt appointees, had at least respected Stone's intellectual abilities, they had nothing but scorn for Vinson or for the other Truman appointees, nearly all of whom have been dismissed by historians as third-rate. Vinson himself left practically no mark on American jurisprudence. The nonunanimous rate climbed from 64 percent in Vinson's first year to 78 percent in his last.

The growth of dissent, while it dismayed some, elated others. In 1948, Justice William O. Douglas gave an impassioned defense of courts that had been "severely criticized for tolerating" individual opinions. In the puppet courts of the totalitarian world, unanimity was not only possible but "indispensable." In contrast, he saw legal uncertainty as a necessary condition of democracy. That "judges do not agree . . . is a sign that they are dealing with problems on which society itself is divided. It is the democratic way to express dissident views." Dissent is essential for a free people, he argued, because dissent is dialogical; the proliferation of dissent provides political legitimacy by assuring the public of a reasoned discourse.

Even had Vinson been a strong leader, he presided over a Court that faced some very complex issues—the nature and limit of presidential powers, the extent of freedom of expression during the McCarthy Red Scare, the reach of the Commerce Clause, and several civil rights cases that would lead to *Brown v. Board of Education.* In fact, the Court heard *Brown* argued the first time during Vinson's last term and, because it could not come to agreement, scheduled it for reargument in the fall of 1953. Vinson, however, died in September before the Court reconvened.

I am not suggesting that dissents are bad, but the earlier opinions by Field, Harlan, Holmes, and Brandeis stood out and mattered so much because there were far fewer dissents. When the Court spoke in one voice nine out of ten times, people paid attention when it did not. Stone had said that a chief justice had to walk a fine line between fostering dissent and yet preventing anarchy. In the twelve terms between Stone's appointment to the center chair and Vinson's death, many observers of the Court would have said that anarchy had won.

DISSENTIOUS PERSONALITIES. Nearly every scholar who has looked at the Court starting in the late 1930s has commented on the change in nature of the men who were appointed by Franklin D. Roosevelt and the collapse of consensus when they arrived at the Marble Palace. The new justices represented a generation of liberals who had revolted against the legal formalism of the old conservative order and embraced legal realism and liberal legalism. Unlike classic legal thought, with its emphasis on property rights, laissez-faire, and an anti-union prejudice, legal realism was less a well-defined school of thought than an intellectual movement that encompassed diverse, generally progressive, and especially pragmatic notions of judging and legal reform. Legal realism emphasized the indeterminacy of law, and held that judges had to be pragmatic in balancing competing values. Many ideas, some of them contradictory, crowded into the tent known as legal realism. The Roosevelt appointees certainly agreed on some matters, but in the end their differences proved more important.

Raymond Moley, one of Franklin Roosevelt's early advisers who later broke with him, had this to say in *Newsweek* about the Court in July 1946: "The present majority has neither good sense nor dignity. We are reaping a harvest of twenty years of failing judicial statesmanship aggravated by outside interference and poor appointments. . . . President Roosevelt unquestionably appointed a series of men who should not be on the Court. Most of the Roosevelt appointees were partisans. Some of the men appointed had undisguised political ambitions which apparently they still harbor." The editors of *Time* charged that personal rivalries and enmities had poisoned the well of collegiality, while *Collier's* asserted that the Court is "unfortunately divided by the most damaging factors of ambition and personal politics." By the end of the war, the normal level of polite give-and-take within the Court had been seriously poisoned by the ongoing feuding between Frankfurter, Owen Roberts, and Robert H. Jackson, on one side, and Hugo Black, William O. Douglas, and Frank Murphy (often joined by Wiley Rutledge), on the other. The extent of this bitterness can be seen in two events, one involving a retirement letter and the other a case. The former for the most part stayed within the walls of the Marble Palace; the latter feud made it into the newspapers.

Owen Roberts, weary of the continuous infighting on the bench, resigned at the end of the 1944 term. Although he and Frankfurter disagreed on certain issues of law, they had found themselves united in their dislike of Black and Douglas and the latter's willingness to ignore precedents. Following Court custom, Chief Justice Stone drafted a farewell letter that, in light of the Court's rancorous division, sounded a relatively neutral tone.

Stone sent the letter to the senior justice, now Hugo Black, asking him to sign it and pass it on to the next senior member of the Court. But Black objected to two phrases, one of which expressed the regret that the remaining brethren supposedly felt at Roberts's departure, and the other of which read, "You have made fidelity to principle your guide to decision." Black wanted to delete both phrases. Stone reluctantly agreed to the deletions, but Frankfurter did not, and he protested. In the end, only Douglas agreed fully with Black's draft. Murphy, Reed, and Rutledge were willing to sign either version in order to secure agreement, while Frankfurter and Jackson took an uncompromising stand and insisted on retaining the sentence on "fidelity to principle." Black would not budge, and as a result Roberts received no letter. This incident mirrored the pettiness and personal animosities that marred the Court during the Stone and Vinson years.

The other brouhaha grew out of a case requiring an interpretation of the 1938 Fair Labor Standards Act, also known as the Black-Connery bill, one of Hugo Black's last legislative accomplishments before his appointment to the bench. Robert Jackson had demanded that Black, as the co-author of the law, recuse himself, and Black refused. The press soon learned of the battle between the two men and had a field day discussing one of those rare instances when conflict within the Court became known. Jackson then went off to Nuremberg to serve as chief Allied prosecutor at the war trials, leaving the Court shorthanded for several months. While he was in Germany, Jackson received news that Stone had died and also rumors that Truman might appoint Black chief, a position he believed Roosevelt had promised to him. Jackson sent off an intemperate telegram to the president threatening to resign if Black received the appointment, an act that led Truman to name Vinson.

There had been blocs on the Court before, most notably the Four Horsemen—Sutherland, Butler, Van Devanter, and McReynolds—in the 1930s. There had been men of genius with strong egos—witness Marshall and Taney, Field and Harlan. There had, however, with the exception of James McReynolds, been no one who treated his colleagues with disdain and who actively sought strife rather than cooperation. The era of the Roosevelt appointees, or as Stone called them, his "wild horses," has never been matched—either before or since—for the high level of personal antagonism and bitter infighting among the justices, a situation that carried over and mixed with jurisprudential differences and thus contributed a great deal to the demise of the consensus norm. Unlike their predecessors, the Roosevelt appointees had no inclination to suppress dissents and took every opportunity to mark their disagree-

Table 2. Opinion Distribution of Roosevelt Appointees

JUSTICE	YEARS ON THE COURT	CASES HEARD	OPINIONS FOR THE COURT	DISSENTING OPINIONS	CONCURRING OPINIONS
Stanley Reed	19	2,215	228	79	21
Hugo Black	34	3,754	481	310	88
Felix Frankfurter	23	2,681	247	251	132
William O. Douglas*	36	4,157	524	486*	154
Frank Murphy	9	1,336	132	66	18
Harlan Fiske Stone[†]	21	3,392	456	93	37
Robert H. Jackson	13	1,441	150	107	47
Wiley Rutledge	6	873	65	59	34

* Douglas's rate of dissent went up sharply in the last six terms he served on the Court under Chief Justice Warren Burger. Between 1969 and 1974, he wrote 231 dissenting opinions, an average of 38.5 per term.
[†] Harlan Fiske Stone includes years as an associate justice (1925–1941) and as chief justice (1941–1946).

ment. This would, unfortunately, set a pattern that many of their successors would follow.

One can note how often they wrote separate opinions. During their careers on the high court, Holmes in thirty years had written 873 majority opinions for the Court and 72 dissenting opinions, an average of 2.4 dissents per term, while Brandeis in twenty-three years had 455 opinions for the Court and 65 dissents, an average of 2.8 per term. Compare those numbers with those of the Roosevelt appointees.

In addition, all of these justices wrote "separate opinions" and "statements," the latter sometimes only a sentence or so explaining their votes. For example, Earl Warren, Hugo Black, and William O. Douglas noted in one case that they "concur in the result for reasons set out in their dissents in *Yates v. United States,* 355 U.S. 66, 76, and *Green v. United States,* 356 U.S. 165, 193, but under constraint of the Court's holdings in those cases they acquiesce in the opinion here." Justices had made statements ever since John Marshall's time, but the rate picked up in the early 1940s. John Marshall had made 5 statements in thirty-five years, Holmes 11, and Brandeis 20. Black made 201 and Douglas 164.

A separate opinion served the same purpose but was longer and more elaborate. For example, in *Bell v. Maryland* (1964), one of the sit-in cases, the Court vacated the criminal trespass conviction of a dozen civil rights protesters. Brennan delivered the opinion for a 6–3 majority, Douglas and Goldberg concurred separately, and Black wrote the dissent. Then Douglas added a separate, data-laden appendix bolstering his argument that instead of being freed on a legal technicality, the protesters should have had their convictions nullified because it was their constitutional right to be served in a public place and all of the stores and restaurants involved were part of national chains. Douglas set forth the old common-law notion that public accommodations could not discriminate, the exact position that would soon be adopted by Congress in the 1964 Civil Rights Act.

The Roosevelt appointees—the scorpions—who sat on the Court during the Stone and Vinson years were very unlike the justices who preceded them. Even the great dissenters like Field, Harlan, Holmes, and Brandeis valued institutional unity, and the rate of unanimous opinions in their time remained quite high. Granted, many of the cases they heard were garden-variety private suits on which the justices could easily agree or, if they were in a minority, "shut up" because the substance was not worth the expenditure of energy needed for a dissent. The Roosevelt appointees—including Chief Justice Stone—felt no need for unanimity and indeed welcomed dissent. They disagreed among themselves over a wide number of issues, especially how they should treat the new claims of individual rights that were beginning to crowd out the older questions of economic regulation. Personality conflicts, to say the least, very much exacerbated the doctrinal differences.

CLERKS. One final development also contributed to the explosion in separate writing. In early 1925, as the Judges' Bill moved toward passage in Congress, Louis Brandeis wrote to his friend and disciple Felix Frankfurter: "U.S.S.C.—venerated throughout the land. Despite the growth of population, wealth and governmental functions, & development particularly of federal activities, the duties of the Court have, by successive acts passed from time to time throughout a generation, been kept within such narrow limits that nine men, each with one helper, can do the work as well as can be done by men of their caliber, i.e., the official coat has been cut according to the human cloth."

Brandeis did not share Taft's passion for the Judges' Bill nor his enthusiasm for erecting a grand building in which to house the Court. He saw justices, each with one clerk, as the right way to conduct the business of government and thought poorly of people in the executive and legislative branches who had so many aides they really did not know their own responsibilities or perform their duties well.

The "one helper" was a clerk, an institution dating back to 1882, when Justice Horace Gray hired a recent Harvard Law School clerk to assist him for one year. Gray had started using clerks when he served as chief justice of the Supreme Judicial Court of Massachusetts in 1875, and in fact Louis Brandeis had been one of what he then termed his "secretaries." Holmes, who took Gray's place on the high court, followed this practice, as did Brandeis. Originally, justices who hired clerks paid for them out of their own pockets, but the 1922 Appropriation Act allowed each justice to employ one clerk at an annual salary of $3,600 to be paid by the government. In 1924, Congress made law clerk positions at the Court permanent.

Holmes and Brandeis took their clerks from Harvard, and after Felix Frankfurter joined the Harvard Law School faculty, he chose the clerks for the two of them. Harlan Fiske Stone, the former dean of Columbia Law, took his clerks from that institution, and Professor Walter Gellhorn chose them. William O. Douglas took his from West Coast law schools and, like several other members of the Court, relied on law school faculty members or committees that often included past clerks to make the selection. Most justices kept their clerks for one year, but some clerks had a longer tenure. Pierce Butler, for example, had the same clerk from the time he came onto the Court in 1923 until his death in 1939; Owen Roberts also had only one clerk, who was with him from 1930 until his retirement in 1945.

Samuel Williston, Gray's first secretary and later a famed professor of law at Harvard, said that Gray "employed clerks exclusively as sources of inspiration and criticism . . . contributing ideas but not documents to Gray's work." Brandeis also expected his clerks to think aloud with him but used them mainly for research and to cite check his opinions. As the Court's caseload increased, so too did the number of clerks and the responsibilities their justices assigned to them. Congress increased the number of clerks to two in 1946, then to three in 1974. Today each justice may have as many as seven people working in his or her chambers—four clerks, two secretaries, and a messenger. Their duties will include not just research and cite checking, but screening certiorari petitions, preparing bench memoranda for cases that will be argued before the Court, and even—in some chambers—preparing a first draft of an opinion, be it majority, concurring, or dissenting.

Some scholars have suggested that the rise in the number of clerks in each chamber is a significant cause of the increase in concurring and dissenting opinions. By itself, the number of clerks might or might not be causal, but taken together with the other factors mentioned here, additional clerks make it far easier for justices not only to write separately but also to write more often. One clerk can easily work on three or four opinions at a time in terms of doing research and drafting arguments. The justice, of course, is responsible for the final product, but how much easier it is to produce a separate opinion if a clerk does much of the basic preparatory work.

John P. Frank, a close friend of both William O. Douglas and Hugo Black, reported that by the 1940s clerks were making substantive contributions to Court opinions. During this time, "sometimes clerks are allowed to do the bulk of serious writing for the Justice." This practice, of course, varied from justice to justice. William O. Douglas wrote his own opinions, although at the end of the term he would often let his clerk draft a minor decision. Robert Jackson would allow his clerk to write one opinion during the clerkship. Chief Justice William Rehnquist made no bones about the fact that his clerks were responsible for the first draft of nearly all opinions. Thurgood Marshall relied heavily on his clerks to help in the writing. Sean Donahue, a former clerk to Justice John Paul Stevens, reported that the justice allowed his clerks a large amount of autonomy and influence in the opinion writing. Donahue estimated that "well over half of the text the Court now produces" came from clerks. He described the "common practice" of having "a clerk write the first draft of an opinion, followed by editing, rewriting and perhaps reorganization by the Justice."

This practice does not sit well with some critics. Judge Richard Posner believes that clerks have usurped functions that judges ought to be doing themselves: "What are these able, intelligent, mostly young people doing? Surely not merely running citations in Shepard's and shelving the judges' law books. They are, in many situations, 'para judges.' In some instances, it is to be feared, they are indeed invisible judges, for there are appellate judges whose literary style appears to change annually."

Again, it should be noted that the clerks, no matter how great a role they play in the decision and opinion writing in chambers, are not the sole or even primary cause of the growth in concurring and dissenting opinions. The increased support they provided, however, certainly played a role in tearing down institutional consensus.

CHAPTER 8

THE PRIMA DONNAS I

PERSONALITIES AND ISSUES OF WARTIME

If I had to go into a classroom, and explain these {past five} years, I would have to say:

1. Never before in the history of the Court were so many of its members influenced in decisions by considerations extraneous to the legal issues that supposedly control decisions.

2. Never before have members of the Court so often acted contrary to their convictions on the governing legal issues in decisions.

3. Never before has so large a proportion of the opinions fallen short of requisite professional standards.

—FELIX FRANKFURTER TO FRANK MURPHY, 10 JUNE 1946

Given these institutional developments, one could understand why there would be an increase in separate opinions and how, in some difficult or complex cases, one might have six, seven, or even nine opinions. The strong personalities and abrasive tempera-ments of some of the Roosevelt appointees drove the disintegration of institutional unity. Noah Feldman has described Hugo Black, Felix Frankfurter, William O. Douglas, and Robert Jackson as "scorpions in a bottle," and others have called them prima donnas. Not only did the

United States Supreme Court in 1943. SEATED FROM LEFT, *Stanley Reed,*
Owen J. Roberts, Chief Justice Harlan Fiske Stone, Hugo L. Black,
and Felix Frankfurter; STANDING FROM LEFT, *Robert H. Jackson,*
William O. Douglas, Frank Murphy, and Wiley B. Rutledge

number of nonunanimous decisions skyrocket—reaching 75 percent in
1948 and then 78 percent in 1952—but the abrasive tone of the opinions and the clear lack of necessity for many of the concurrences contributed to the low level of constitutional dialogue.

At the same time, the Court during this period managed to accomplish a great deal, and while the level of discourse at times might have
been petty, it nonetheless went on. The Court took the first steps that
would lead to the overturning of racial segregation, continued the incorporation of the Bill of Rights, and dealt with important issues arising
out of World War II and the Korean conflict. During this time, the
justices split into two opposing forces, one led by Felix Frankfurter and
the other by Hugo Black. Their disputes and conflicting jurisprudential theories are in large measure responsible for the multiple opinions,
but they also helped sharpen the issues and pointed the way toward the
modern agenda of the Court.

The large number of separate opinions made it almost impossible at
the time to pick out which if any of them carried the seeds for future
growth and the transformation of judicial doctrine. Of course, the passage of time helps, and six decades later we can identify some important

Hugo Lafayette Black, associate justice,
1937–1971

opinions: Black in *Betts v. Brady* (1942), Jackson in *Korematsu v. United States* (1944) and *Youngstown Sheet & Tube* (1952), Wiley Rutledge in *In re Yamashita* (1946), and Douglas in *Dennis v. United States* (1951) have all had enduring significance. Despite the internal bickering and nastiness, the demands of the time made the Court respond, and in many ways it responded well.

WHEN HUGO BLACK went onto the Court in 1937, he had relatively undeveloped constitutional ideas that would mature during his tenure. While in the Senate, Black had undertaken an intensive reading program of works on history and government, starting with the Greek and Roman philosophers. Upon his appointment to the Court, he recognized his weaknesses in constitutional history and theory and read through the entire series of *United States Reports.* He believed in the superiority of the Constitution as a philosophical as well as a governance document and carried a copy in his pocket the rest of his life.

At the heart of Black's philosophy lay a populist belief in the Constitution as an infallible guide. He opposed judicial subjectivity; the Constitution did not empower judges to select from competing alternatives. Black was not an originalist in that he considered works such as *The Federalist* or the records of the ratifying conventions to be authoritative guides to constitutional meaning. He interpreted the Constitution broadly in some areas, such as the Commerce Clause, believing it gave the federal government power to regulate the economy and respond to emergencies. The First Amendment, however, said that Congress shall make no law abridging freedom of speech, and not only did he take that prohibition literally, but he believed the First Amendment and the rights of expression it protected held a "preferred position" in the constitutional panoply. On the other hand, he could not find the word "privacy" in the Constitution and voted against constitutionalizing such a right. This philosophy narrowed the scope of judicial discretion, but it also helped to make the judiciary the prime vehicle for guaranteeing the values of those absolutes.

Part of Black's effectiveness derived from the considerable political skills he had honed in the Senate. More than any other justice of his time, Black proselytized, "working" the other justices as he had once worked his senatorial colleagues in order to gain a majority. He liked to tell the story about an unnamed senator who said that when he wanted to accomplish something, he would introduce two bills—the one he wanted passed and another that made the first seem conservative. Robert Jackson disdainfully noted that while these methods were appropriate in a legislative body where one deals with adversaries, he considered them unsuited to a court, in which the members were supposed to be colleagues. But Jackson must surely have known that for the entire time he sat on the bench, its members often saw each other as ally or opponent rather than colleague.

The chief fomenter of this anarchy was Felix Frankfurter, although that was never his intention. He wanted to instruct his brethren on the proper interpretation of the Constitution and to lead the Court intellectually. He never understood that in large measure he caused the chaos, but rather blamed it on the stubbornness of his colleagues in failing to heed his teachings. When the majority handed down decisions with which he disagreed, he felt it his duty to dissent. And even if he agreed with the results but thought the rationale failed to meet his standards, he wrote separately. Worst of all, he wrote law review articles disguised as judicial opinions. In his twenty-three years on the bench, Frankfurter wrote 247 opinions for the Court, 132 concurring opinions, and 251 dissents. He might have been the Court's most forceful voice for judicial restraint, but he showed no moderation in spewing out opinions, few of which are remembered today. Thanks in large measure to his example, the size of Court opinions doubled in length, and four out of five cases saw multiple opinions.

Felix Frankfurter, associate justice, 1939–1962

Moreover, they had little lasting influence. A number of his majority opinions have been overturned, and his dissents are studied, if at all, only for their futility. One analysis of Frankfurter concurrences showed that in almost no instance did they have any impact. Lower courts would apply the majority opinions but did not use the concurrences or even treat the majority opinion as in any way modified by the concurrence. Moreover, aside from some acolytes at the Harvard Law School, the legal literature also ignored much of what Frankfurter wrote. As one unsympathetic critic declared, the various Frankfurter opinions, "for all practical purposes, might as well have been written on paper airplanes and thrown out a Supreme Court window."

Frankfurter went onto the Court at the beginning of 1939 with a well-developed judicial philosophy centered on the notion of judicial restraint, the result, as he explained, of years of studying the Court and its decisions at the Harvard Law School. Unless a judge could find a clear constitutional prohibition against an act, courts should defer to legislative judgment and uphold the statute. Frankfurter's chief rival on the

Court throughout his tenure, Hugo Black, also believed strongly in judicial restraint. But Black—like Holmes and Brandeis—saw a difference between economic regulation and restrictions on individual liberties, which he believed required a higher standard of scrutiny. Frankfurter considered all legislation equal and all parts of the Constitution identical in value. The debate between these two views would fragment the Stone and Vinson Courts, making them the most contentious in history.

Frankfurter took a condescending approach to his colleagues, lecturing them as if they were slow students in one of his Harvard classes. "It is the lot of professors to be often not understood by pupils," he told one. "So let me try again." He suggested that one of the justices follow the advice he had given his students, that in order to construe a statute correctly, they should read it not once but thrice. When William O. Douglas had been a professor at Yale, he had admired Frankfurter, who looked on him as an acolyte, and so when Douglas took Brandeis's seat on the Court, Frankfurter assumed that Douglas would follow his lead. Douglas, however, had enjoyed a very successful career on his own merits, first at Yale, and then as a member and ultimately head of the Securities and Exchange Commission (SEC). He felt confident about his abilities and had long passed the stage where he needed to bask in Frankfurter's praise. Other members of the Court, whose careers owed nothing to Frankfurter and who had confidence in their own abilities, also resented the professor's condescending manner. As his dream of leading the Court slipped away, Frankfurter grew nastier and his temper shorter. The papers of the justices who served with him are littered with notes from Frankfurter accusing them of everything from stupidity to the inability to understand the law; what he said behind their backs, and in his diary, usually went much further.

By the 1942 term, nearly half of the cases were nonunanimous, and the following term, for the first time in history, more than half—58 percent—were decided by a divided Court. "I have had much difficulty in herding my collection of fleas," Stone told a friend and complained that he himself had to write an excessive number of opinions because the brethren were "so busy disagreeing with each other." *The Wall Street Journal* remarked that the justices tended "to fall into clamorous argument even on the rare occasions when they agreed on the end result." Within the Court, Frankfurter began talking about "enemies" on the bench and once yelled at a clerk, "Don't you get the idea that this is a *war* we are fighting." He referred to Black, Douglas, and Frank Murphy as "the Axis" and counted Douglas as one of the "two completely evil men I have ever met."

The legal historian G. Edward White identified two "principal twentieth-century devices designed to constrain subjective judicial lawmaking: fidelity to constitutional text or doctrine, and institutional deference." By the latter, he meant paying attention to precedent and justifying one's position primarily through legal argument. There is no question that the great advocate of these two devices was Felix Frankfurter.

Holmes rarely wrote a lengthy opinion and believed that he could say all that was needed in just a couple of pages. Brandeis's opinions for the Court are short, but his lengthy dissents, while acknowledging relevant precedents, are not heavily laden with case citation after case citation. Like Brandeis briefs, they emphasize facts and the reasons why a legislature saw fit to enact certain legislation. Harlan Stone could and did write opinions parsing the precedents when necessary, but he believed that short opinions should be the norm. Not so Frankfurter, who essentially wrote opinions—whether for the Court, in concurrence, or in dissent—that ran on for pages and read more like densely noted law review articles than the types of opinions written by the men he claimed were his judicial heroes, Holmes, Brandeis, and Cardozo. On more than one occasion, he informed his colleagues that he had researched every case on a particular subject going back to medieval English precedents.

Roosevelt named the third of the scorpions, William O. Douglas, to take Brandeis's seat in 1939. Douglas had worked his way through Whitman College and the Columbia Law School and after a brief stint in private practice (which he hated) had wound up at the Yale Law School and became one of the stars of the new Legal Realism, which attempted to understand development in the law through psychological and economic insights. When Roosevelt came to the presidency in 1933 and began the New Deal, Douglas grew restive in New Haven and the following year secured an assignment from the newly created Securities and Exchange Commission to study protective committees, the agencies stockholders use during bankruptcy reorganization to protect their interests. His work caught the attention of the SEC chair, Joseph P. Kennedy, who arranged for the thirty-seven-year-old Douglas to be appointed to the commission in 1935. Two years later, Roosevelt named him chair of the SEC.

During these years in Washington, Douglas became part of Roosevelt's inner circle, often joining the weekly poker games at the White House. There was a good deal of speculation that Douglas had political ambitions, but in fact by early 1939 he had begun negotiating a return to Yale. Then Roosevelt named him to the Court, the youngest person

William O. Douglas, associate justice, 1939–1975,
walking to the Court on opening day of the 1941 term

ever appointed, and he would establish a record for longevity of service
before illness forced him to retire in late 1975.

No other justice has ever engaged in so extensive and public a nonjudicial life. Douglas always claimed that the work of the Court never
took more than three or four days a week; he read petitions rapidly, rarely
agonized over decisions, could get to the heart of an issue instantly, and
wrote his opinions quickly. This left him time for other activities, such
as traveling, lecturing, writing, climbing mountains, and, as some critics claimed, getting into trouble. His writings, however, need to be seen

as part of the dialogue. In many ways, Douglas was the first justice to take his ideas out of the Court and to the people. While other justices had from time to time done so (such as John Marshall in his defense of *McCulloch v. Maryland,* albeit anonymously), Douglas went much further. In books like *An Almanac of Liberty* (1954) and *Being an American* (1971), he spoke directly to the public about the values he held and what he thought should be the proper response to issues confronting the nation.

Jurisprudentially, Frankfurter and Douglas—who took their seats within three months of each other—seemed to have the same values. The shifting agenda of the Court, with its growing emphasis on individual rights and liberties, soon highlighted the differences between them, and within a few years of going on the bench, Douglas aligned himself with Hugo Black. In the October 1943 term, for example, Black and Douglas voted together in 86 percent of the nonunanimous cases, the highest pairing of any two justices on the Court. Eventually, Douglas became the more activist, but he proved himself an able second to Black in the battles shaping up over which direction the Court should take.

If Frankfurter epitomized the characteristics that G. Edward White considered the hallmarks of modern jurisprudence, then Douglas was, in White's words, the "anti-judge," a man who had little use for either precedent or the normal modes of constitutional interpretation. A better way to look at Douglas's tenure on the high court is as a common-law judge. It is true that he had little use for precedent, once declaring that he would rather make a precedent than follow one. But he asked the right questions, ones that would never have been asked had he slavishly followed precedent and narrow modes of logic. In doing so, he breathed life back into the Equal Protection Clause, giving the Court the tool it needed to tackle segregation and developing the right to privacy as a constitutional protection.

A good example involves a dissent from a Frankfurter opinion in 1959, in a case in which a city health inspector had entered premises without a search warrant. Nearly everyone except Douglas thought it a simple matter, because the Warrant Clause had previously been held to apply only in criminal situations. Although supposedly an easy case, Frankfurter wrote a lengthy opinion tracing the origins of the Warrant Clause in colonial times and its history ever since. Douglas disagreed and set his clerk, Charles Miller, to work on materials for a dissent. Miller got a number of books from the library but could not find any materials to oppose Frankfurter's interpretation.

Finally, Douglas got very frustrated and told him to bring all the books in, and he would see what he could do. Douglas holed himself up in his office and, working off the materials that Miller had gotten, scratched out a ten-page opinion, arguing that the right to privacy implicit in the Fourth Amendment applied to civil searches as well as to criminal. On its circulation, Chief Justice Warren and Justices Black and Brennan left Frankfurter, who now had a bare 5–4 majority, and that would have evaporated had he not brought a great deal of pressure on Justice Charles Whittaker not to abandon ship. Eight years later, the Court overruled the Frankfurter opinion and adopted Douglas's view.

When it came to nastiness, Douglas could dish it out with just as much venom and force as Frankfurter, and especially at Frankfurter, who in conference would often speak for fifty minutes, the exact length of a lecture at the Harvard Law School. After one of these disquisitions, Douglas noted, "When I came into this conference, I agreed with the conclusion that Felix has just announced. But he's just talked me out of it." When bored during one of Frankfurter's talks, he would leave the conference table and go over to the sofa to read his mail.

On the same day that he nominated Harlan Stone as chief justice, Roosevelt named Robert Houghwout Jackson to take Stone's place as associate justice. Jackson is, unfortunately, one of the lesser-known members of the Roosevelt Court, although he had a notable career and a facile pen and helped create the modern doctrinal rules for judicial review of economic regulation.

Born on a western Pennsylvania farm, Jackson was self-educated; he briefly attended Albany Law School but then qualified for the bar by reading law as an apprentice in a lawyer's office, the last Supreme Court justice to do so. He set up a thriving and varied practice in western New York and became active in state politics as an adviser to Governor Franklin D. Roosevelt. After Roosevelt entered the White House in 1933, he brought Jackson to Washington, where the New York lawyer advanced from general counsel of the Internal Revenue Service to solicitor general and then attorney general. Jackson later described his tenure as solicitor general as the happiest part of his life, and he won high marks for his role as the government's chief litigator; Louis Brandeis once commented that Jackson should have been named solicitor general for life.

Many people considered Jackson a possible presidential candidate, and his name was frequently mentioned for the 1940 Democratic nomination until Roosevelt decided to run for a third term. The president had promised Jackson a seat on the Supreme Court at the time he had asked him to head the Justice Department; the next vacancy, however, occurred with Hughes's resignation. With war on the horizon, Roosevelt

Robert Houghwout Jackson, associate justice, 1941–1954

felt that for the sake of national unity he should promote the Republican Stone to the center chair. It appears, however, that Roosevelt did not expect the sixty-eight-year-old Stone to serve that long and promised to name Jackson chief justice when Stone left the bench.

Had Jackson been chief justice, he might have been happier on the Court, but his activist nature chafed at the restrictions of judicial propriety. During the war, he felt cut off from the great events going on around him and remarked that the Monday after Pearl Harbor the Court heard arguments about the taxability of greens fees. While he, like Frankfurter and Douglas, continued privately to advise Roosevelt, Jackson wanted to do more. Thus he leaped at the opportunity when President Harry S. Truman asked him to head the American prosecutorial team at the Nuremberg trial of Nazi war criminals.

Jackson tended to join Frankfurter on most issues, but he could not be considered a predictable vote for the conservatives. He parted from Frankfurter in the second flag salute case and in one of the Japanese relocation cases. His decision in *Wickard v. Filburn* (1942) is a ring-

*William Francis "Frank" Murphy,
associate justice, 1940–1949*

ing endorsement of an all-encompassing congressional power over commerce, yet he took a far more restricted view of presidential power during the Korean conflict, and his concurring opinion in the 1952 steel seizure case remains the definitive guide to determining the limits of executive authority.

Roosevelt made his fifth appoint to the Court in early 1940, when he named Frank Murphy to replace Pierce Butler, and in doing so sealed the constitutional revolution triggered by the New Deal. In Murphy, Roosevelt got a thoroughgoing liberal, one who had little use for technical questions and believed that the objectives of the law should be justice and human dignity. Murphy cared even less for precedent than Douglas and Black and openly relied on what one commentator has called "visceral jurisprudence." The law knows no finer hour, Murphy wrote, "than when it cuts through formal concepts and transitory emotions to protect unpopular citizens against discrimination and persecution."

Murphy had won his spurs as a strong supporter of New Deal labor policy while governor of Michigan, backing the autoworkers during the 1937 sit-down strikes. It cost him reelection in 1938, and the following year Roosevelt named him attorney general. He held that office for just a year but during that time set up a civil liberties bureau that for the first time employed the power of the federal government to protect individual rights. This activity did not sit well with many people, especially southerners, and to some extent Roosevelt's sending him to the high court amounted to kicking him upstairs. He certainly did not want to go, and many people thought he had his sights set on the presidency.

Even Murphy's admirers make no claim that he had special talents as a jurist, and he recognized his own limitations. He felt inferior in the company of Stone and Black, Douglas and Frankfurter. He knew little constitutional law, and his prior judicial experience had been on a small municipal criminal bench. But he learned and relied on bright clerks to draft his opinions.

Murphy did, however, develop a jurisprudence, one based on Stone's *Carolene Products* footnote 4 that restrictions on individual liberties required strict scrutiny by the courts. He also adopted Hugo Black's notion that the liberties protected by the First Amendment held a "preferred position" in the constitutional firmament. New jurists may pick their first opinion, and Murphy chose a case overturning a state law that banned virtually all picketing by union members. Although Brandeis had earlier suggested that picketing might be a form of protected speech, this notion did not become law until Murphy's opinion in *Thornhill v. Alabama* (1940). There the new justice extended First Amendment protection to peaceful picketing and forcefully cited the *Carolene Products* footnote to justify the judiciary's overturning of a law that invaded civil liberties. The *Thornhill* opinion proved to be both influential and enduring; it has been cited in more than three hundred subsequent cases, and in 1969 the former justice Tom Clark wrote that the opinion was "the bedrock upon which many of the Court's civil rights pronouncements rest." Murphy, along with Black and Douglas, fought consistently for greater protection of individual rights.

Wiley Rutledge Jr., the former dean of the law school at Washington University in St. Louis, became Roosevelt's last appointment to the Court in early 1943. In the early 1930s, Rutledge had solved a tense racial situation at a conference of black and white lawyers. Because Missouri enforced segregation, African American lawyers could not sit at the same table as white participants; Rutledge invited all the minority members to join him at the dean's table. Rutledge's name figured prominently whenever an opening occurred on the high court, and Roosevelt did name him to the prestigious Court of Appeals for the District of Columbia in 1939. There he made a reputation for himself as consistently voting for labor unions in the many National Labor Relations Board cases.

Unfortunately, Murphy and Rutledge died within two months of each other in the summer of 1949, and their short tenures have led scholars to overlook them because of the giant shadows cast by Black, Douglas, Frankfurter, and Jackson. This is a shame because both men contributed a great deal to the 1940s Court. Rutledge like Murphy carved out a consistently liberal position, one that took its cue from the double standard enunciated in Stone's *Carolene Products* footnote, and provided the fifth vote necessary to begin the expansion of protected freedoms under the First Amendment. Moreover, he was willing to go beyond Black's position regarding the meaning of the Fourteenth Amendment's Due Process Clause. Where Black believed the clause included just the rights enunciated in the first eight amendments and no more, Rutledge tended to agree with Murphy and Douglas that it included at least those protections and possibly more. The area in which he had the most impact involved the religion clauses of the First Amendment, and he played a key role in the Jehovah's Witnesses cases the Court heard during the war. At his death, articles appeared in law reviews in a quantity one would associate with a justice who had far longer service on the bench. Part of this resulted from his open and friendly nature, but at least part of it grew out of a belief that had Rutledge lived longer, he would have been a great justice. As two of his former clerks put it, "Death met him . . . after he had completed his apprenticeship but before he had proceeded far in a master's work."

THE PERSONALITIES of the prima donnas certainly contributed to the friction, but as Thomas Reed Powell, a very astute observer of the Court, noted, laymen should "not draw too broad conclusions from any reportorial propensity to play up judicial disagreements as contests like those in war or sports." It is true that what we remember, and what is most important, are the jurisprudential divisions. The Court passed on important issues at this time, and the differences among the justices laid out the key arguments that would govern major cases for the next three decades. Personal pettiness nonetheless contributed a great deal to the lack of unanimity on the high court.

One can see this division in an early case in the spring of 1940, when Chief Justice Hughes assigned Frankfurter the opinion in *Minersville School District v. Gobitis.* A Pennsylvania school board had expelled Jehovah's Witnesses children because they refused, on grounds of religious conscience, to salute the flag during morning exercise. In Witnesses belief, the practice violated the biblical command against bowing down to graven images. (At the time, it should be noted, the salute used was a straight arm out, similar to that used by the Nazis.) The question of whether schools could compel students to salute the flag had been an issue in twenty states between 1935 and 1940, as well as the subject of major litigation in seven. Prior to *Gobitis,* the Supreme Court had four times upheld state court decisions validating compulsory flag salutes.

The Witnesses claimed that the compulsory salute violated their rights under the First Amendment to a free exercise of religion. Frankfurter saw no trampling of First Amendment rights in the case and during oral argument passed a note to Frank Murphy questioning whether the Framers of the Bill of Rights "would have thought that a requirement to salute the flag violates the protection of 'the free exercise of religion'?" In his ten-page opinion for the 8–1 majority, Frankfurter framed the "precise" issue in terms of judicial restraint and called upon the Court to defer to the wisdom and prerogatives of local school authorities. Aware that Harlan Stone was planning to dissent, Frankfurter sent him a five-page letter declaring his intention "to use this opinion as a vehicle for preaching the true democratic faith of not relying on the Court for the impossible task of assuring a vigorous, mature, self-protecting, and tolerant democracy by bringing the responsibility for a combination of firmness and toleration directly home where it belongs—to the people and their representatives themselves."

The Frankfurter opinion was consistent with his long-held views that the judiciary should not interfere with the formation of public policy absent any clear violation of a constitutional provision. This is the essence of judicial restraint, the policy that had been preached by his idols Holmes and Brandeis. But Frankfurter, an immigrant who fervently loved America, had another agenda. In June 1940, with France about to fall to the Nazis, many people understood that it would be nearly impossible for the United States to avoid being drawn into a second world war, and he considered it essential that there not be the types of divisions that had rent the country in 1917 and 1918.

The question the Court had to decide, he said, "is whether the legislatures of the various states and the authorities in a thousand counties and school districts of this country are barred from determining the appropriateness of various means to evoke the unifying sentiment without which there can be no liberties, civil or religious." Framed this way, the question could have only one answer: "The wisdom of training children in patriotic impulses by those compulsions which necessarily pervade so much of the educational process is not for our independent judgment. Even were we convinced of the folly of such a measure, such a belief would be no proof of its unconstitutionality." He concluded that "to the legislature no less than to courts is committed the guardianship of deeply cherished liberties."

Frankfurter always believed that questions of public policy, no matter what the issue, could and eventually would be properly resolved through the political process. Holmes and Brandeis, and in this case Stone, understood that when the rights of minorities are involved, they usually lack the political influence to secure relief. A majority, comfortable with the status quo, has no incentive to change. Surely the most obvious proof of this lies in the racial segregation practiced in the South, a practice that would never have altered had it been left to southern state legislatures. Although Harlan Stone believed that courts should not second-guess legislative policy decisions in economic matters, he had also said in 1938 that "prejudice against discrete and insular minorities may be a special condition, which tends seriously to curtail the operation of those political processes ordinarily to be relied upon to protect minorities, and which may call for a correspondingly more searching judicial inquiry."

This idea, put forth in what became the most consequential footnote in Court history, captured the notion that courts had a special role to play in protecting the rights of minorities. The question of a higher level of scrutiny, and what that level should be, would be debated again and again in the Court over questions of civil rights for African Americans and equality for women, homosexuals, and other minorities. But in 1940, footnote 4 was still just that, a footnote, and Stone took the first step to make it into a constitutional doctrine in his dissent in the flag salute case.

Stone had decided early that he would not vote with the majority, but he still believed it unnecessary to file a dissenting opinion every time he found himself outvoted. After some indecision, however, he wrote a dissent and then took the rather unusual step, for him, of reading it aloud from the bench. The law that is thus sustained, he wrote,

is unique in the history of Anglo-American legislation. It does more than suppress freedom of speech and more than prohibit the free exercise of religion, which concededly are forbidden by the First Amendment and are violations of the liberty guaranteed by the Fourteenth. For by this law the state seeks to coerce these children to express a sentiment which, as they interpret it, they do not entertain, and which violates their deepest religious convictions.

Responding directly to Frankfurter's claim that schools needed to inculcate patriotism, he continued,

> The Constitution may well elicit expressions of loyalty to it and to the government which it created, but it does not command such expressions or otherwise give any indication that compulsory expressions of loyalty play any such part in our scheme of government as to override the constitutional protection of freedom of speech and religion. And while such expressions of loyalty, when voluntarily given, may promote national unity, it is quite another matter to say that their compulsory expression by children in violation of their own and their parents' religious convictions can be regarded as playing so important a part in our national unity as to leave school boards free to exact it despite the constitutional guarantee of freedom of religion. The very terms of the Bill of Rights preclude, it seems to me, any reconciliation of such compulsions with the constitutional guaranties by a legislative declaration that they are more important to the public welfare than the Bill of Rights.

Much to Frankfurter's dismay, his majority opinion received almost universal condemnation, both in the daily press and in the law journals. The *Harvard Law Review* pointedly did not comment on it, but in a note it had published prior to the Court's decision, it had declared that "regardless of the constitutionality of the compulsory flag salute, however, the advisability of imposing it upon religious objectors seems extremely questionable." *The New Republic,* to which Frankfurter had been a major contributor from its founding until his appointment to the Court, printed both opinions and then editorialized that the Court appeared to be verging on hysteria when it "says in effect that we must imperil religious liberty in the interest of the American state, which is worth preserving because it guarantees religious liberty." Stone's dissent, moreover, received widespread approval. One hundred and seventy-one newspapers in nearly all of the major cities in the country promptly condemned the decision. Harold Laski, a close friend of Frankfurter's, wrote to Stone from London, "I want to tell you how right I think you are . . . , and, to my deep regret, how wrong I think Felix is. [Yours] was a noble decision, nobly written."

Patriotic organizations welcomed the decision and used it to justify physical attacks on the Witnesses. In the two weeks following the ruling, the Justice Department received reports of literally hundreds of attacks on the Witnesses. In many communities, school boards made the flag salute requirement even more stringent, sending Witnesses children who refused to participate to reform schools as delinquents. When the Court convened after its summer recess, Douglas told Frankfurter that Black had been having second thoughts about his *Gobitis* vote. "Has Black been reading the Constitution?" Frankfurter sarcastically asked. "No," Douglas responded, "he has been reading the newspapers."

Black, Douglas, and Murphy had gone along with Frankfurter's opinion, albeit reluctantly. Murphy had originally planned to dissent in *Gobitis,* but pressure from Chief Justice Hughes and his insecurity as a freshman led him to join the majority. Black originally saw the problem as one of due process, not free exercise. He did not like the law, but saw nothing in the Constitution to invalidate it. Douglas later claimed that if Stone's dissent had not come down at the very last minute, he would have joined it. Over the next few years, these four began to dissent in a number of Witness-related cases, and in one they declared that the majority had been wrong in *Gobitis.* The increasing number of attacks on Witness adherents, often justified by the *Gobitis* opinion, led the justices to accept another flag salute case, *West Virginia State Board of Education v. Barnette,* in early 1943. The justices' abhorrence of the violence directed against the Witnesses, as well as changes on the Court, led to a decision upholding the right of schoolchildren not to be forced to participate in the salute.

Because the religion clauses of the First Amendment had not yet been incorporated and applied to the states, Justice Jackson shifted the emphasis of the case from religious freedom to freedom of speech. He did this not by overruling *Gobitis* but by distinguishing it and then redefined the "broader issue" to be the value of political speech. (He did, however, unmercifully refute all of the major points Frankfurter had made; where Frankfurter had extolled the democratic nature of school boards, Jackson called them "village tyrants.") Although many scholars have continued to look at *Barnette* in Jackson's terms, in fact it really is a free exercise case. In one of the most memorable phrases in the Court's history, Jackson declared, "If there is any fixed star in our constitutional constellation, it is that no official, high or petty, can prescribe what shall be orthodox in politics, nationalism, religion or other matters of opinion or force citizens to confess by word or act their faith therein." That certainly addresses religious values far more than simple political speech.

Although six members of the Court supported Jackson's majority opinion, Black, joined by Douglas, concurred separately; Murphy concurred separately from them; Frankfurter dissented, but Owen Roberts and Stanley Reed would not join his opinion and dissented without an opinion. Only Stone and Wiley Rutledge joined Jackson's majority opinion without writing separately. The fissures on the Court were now there for all to see.

Frankfurter's impassioned dissent began, "One who belongs to the most vilified and persecuted minority in history is not likely to be insensible to the freedoms guaranteed by our Constitution." He went on, "Were my purely personal attitude relevant I should wholeheartedly associate myself with the general libertarian views in the Court's opinion, representing as they do the thought and action of a lifetime. But as judges we are neither Jew nor Gentile, neither Catholic nor agnostic."

Frankfurter's dissent, if taken literally, nearly denies the Court any role in enforcing the Bill of Rights. Douglas's denunciation of that dissent in his memoirs seems to be warranted: "The Frankfurter philosophy was fully exposed. Although free exercise of religion was guaranteed by the First and Fourteenth Amendments, the legislature could nonetheless regulate it by invoking the concept of due process, provided they stayed within reasonable limits." Indeed, despite the comment that he belonged to the "most vilified and persecuted minority in history," he dismissed judicial protection of minorities. The Framers of the Bill of Rights, he said, "knew that minorities may disrupt society."

Frankfurter worked for weeks on the dissent; in apologizing to Jackson for holding up the decision, he described his dissent as "the expression of my credo regarding the function of this Court in invalidating legislation." He reiterated the formula he had used in an earlier decision: "This Court's only and very narrow function is to determine whether within the broad grant of authority vested in legislatures they have exercised a judgment for which reasonable justification can be offered." Frankfurter could not pass over Jackson's eloquent depiction of the meaning of free exercise of religion as lightly as he had Stone's dissent in *Gobitis,* but he took a minimalist approach. The First Amendment provides "freedom from conformity to religious dogma, not freedom from conformity to law because of religious dogma." Claims of conscience by themselves can never justify exemption from valid laws that have a reasonable basis. This meant that because a state could always create the nexus of a reasonable justification for its action, the courts would never impose any serious review on state action.

Frankfurter's pride in his dissent and the importance he attached to it led him to an active extrajudicial campaign to publicize his views. He sent copies to the retired chief justice Hughes and suggested to President Roosevelt that a copy be placed in the Hyde Park library, because it would "furnish to the future historian food for thought on the scope and meaning of some of the Four Freedoms—their use and misuse." He also wrote to friends in the press, trying to get them to run articles favorable to his point of view, but they all refused. Even Frankfurter's friends sensed that the man who had been such a towering liberal champion in the 1920s and 1930s had come down on the wrong side of history. Whatever hopes Frankfurter had of leading the Court essentially vanished after the second flag salute case.

Interestingly enough, Frankfurter's argument in *Gobitis* that religious beliefs do not excuse a citizen from obeying valid laws received a new airing in Justice Antonin Scalia's majority opinion in the so-called peyote case nearly fifty years later. Two men had been fired from their jobs and then denied unemployment benefits because they had smoked peyote as part of a Native American religious ceremony. Although many states permitted the use of peyote as part of a religious ritual, Oregon did not. A majority of the Court upheld the state's actions, and Scalia quoted Frankfurter's *Gobitis* opinion, and its exceptions holding, although in fact the distinction between belief (always protected) and action (which can be regulated) goes back to the Mormon polygamy case *Reynolds v. United States.* For the most part, in the intervening years since *Gobitis* and *Barnette,* Frankfurter's opinion in the former and dissent in the latter have generally been derided as blind to the meaning of the First Amendment.

WITH THE EXCEPTION OF SLAVERY, the worst example of racist invasion of civil liberties in American history is the forcible transfer of 120,000 persons of Japanese ancestry—70,000 of them American citizens—away from their homes, jobs, and property to detention centers, ostensibly because they posed a security threat to the West Coast during World War II. Three cases resulting from the relocation reached the Supreme Court. The first case, *Hirabayashi v. United States,* involved Gordon Hirabayashi, a native-born American citizen and a senior at the University of Washington, who had been arrested for failing to report to a control center and for violating the curfew. After conviction, he appealed on the grounds that the military had exceeded its constitutional authority. Both the district and the appeals courts upheld the conviction, and the case came to the Supreme Court in the spring of 1943.

There is an old legal adage, *inter arma silent leges*—"in wartime the law is silent"—and this surely described the Japanese internment cases. In the *Hirabayashi* case, Chief Justice Stone strongly supported the army's

Tule Lake internment camp for Japanese Americans

actions and used all his persuasive power to mass the Court to back the government. After his first draft, he willingly accepted Frankfurter's suggestion that "we decide nothing that is not before us." *Hirabayashi* dealt only with the curfew, and so should the Court's decision. Stone revised his opinion and included much of Frankfurter's language.

Stone wanted a united Court, but at least two members—William O. Douglas and Frank Murphy—had grave doubts. Although Douglas supported that part of Stone's opinion that the justices should not be second-guessing the military, he had grown up in the Pacific Northwest with Japanese American friends, and he knew that not all of them, as Stone had insisted in his draft, had strong racial attachments to Japan. The lack of due process also troubled Douglas, but he said he would be willing to concur in an opinion that approved the military orders as a temporary expedient, and he urged Stone to limit the Court's decision to that holding. In addition, he wanted the Court to issue a requirement that individuals had to have an opportunity to be classified as loyal citizens. Murphy seems to have been the only member of the Court willing to face the issue of racism head-on. He termed the discrimination "so utterly inconsistent with our ideals and traditions, and in my judgment so contrary to constitutional sanctions, that I cannot lend my assent."

Frankfurter hit the roof and urged Stone not to give in to Douglas; in fact, he wanted Stone to alter his language so as to close off the *habeas corpus* option Douglas suggested. Douglas ought to be pulling along with everyone else instead of acting as if he were "in a rival grocery business." He won't change his mind because he wants "to make the spread eagle speech." Frankfurter pleaded with Murphy to think of the good of the country and of the Court and not play "into the hands of the enemy."

In the end, Stone got all the other justices to join his opinion upholding the curfew, but Douglas, Murphy, and Wiley Rutledge entered concurring opinions that came close to dissents. All indicated that they had agreed to what they considered an unconstitutional program because of the allegedly critical military situation. "Detention for reasonable cause is one thing," Douglas wrote. "Detention on account of ancestry is another." He also stood by his suggestion that individuals be permitted an opportunity to establish their loyalty. Although Murphy quashed his dissent, he put some of those ideas into the concurrence and insisted that "distinctions based on color and ancestry are utterly inconsistent with our traditions and ideals." The tone of their opinions indicated that it would be far more difficult to get unanimity when another challenge reached the Court.

That challenge came sixteen months later, and this time the justices would not be able to avoid the larger constitutional issues. Fred Korematsu had been charged with failing to report to an assembly center for relocation. His attorneys claimed that the entire exclusion order violated the Constitution by depriving citizens of their freedom without trial or any other aspect of due process. Moreover, the mass expulsion of an entire group based solely on a racial classification constituted a cruel and unusual punishment forbidden by the Eighth Amendment.

At conference in October 1944, Stone tried to limit the discussion to a narrow technical question. Korematsu had been convicted of violating the exclusion order, designed to keep Japanese out of certain militarily designated areas. The only question the Court had to answer, according to the chief justice, was the constitutionality of the exclusion order. Framed this way, the case could be decided on narrow grounds similar to those in *Hirabayashi*.

Stone turned to the senior justice, Owen Roberts, who had endorsed the earlier opinion, only to find Roberts dead set against the chief's plan. Roberts had been a member of the first commission looking into the attack at Pearl Harbor, and he knew that there had been absolutely no evidence of Japanese American sabotage on the West Coast. The combination of exclusion and prohibition orders gave Japanese Americans a cruel choice: defy the order and be imprisoned, or report to an assembly point and be relocated to a concentration camp. Black and Frankfurter supported Stone, as did Rutledge and Reed. But four justices—Roberts, Douglas, Murphy, and Jackson—planned to dissent on grounds that the military had overstepped its constitutional bounds of authority. Jackson, normally a supporter of strong government, declared, "I stop with *Hirabayashi.*"

Stone assigned the decision to Black, who tried to write it in as limited a fashion as possible. Black's effort to lure Douglas away from the dissenters, hold on to Rutledge, who was not that strong for the decision, mollify Frankfurter's insistence on judicial restraint, satisfy Stone's strong support of the military, and write something that would stand up to the dissents led to "an almost schizophrenic opinion, unpersuasive in its arguments and ambiguous in its ultimate impact." According to some scholars, *Korematsu* "was the worst judicial opinion that Justice Hugo Black wrote in his thirty-four years on the Court. . . . It was a philosophically incoherent defense of broad government power by one of the most influential civil libertarians in the Court's history. Although Black did not say so, he had given the military a license to trample on individual rights at will during wartime."

The three dissents tore Black's opinion apart. Owen Roberts provided a detailed history of the army orders and showed that Korematsu and others like him had been put into a bind from which they could not escape. The military orders, "one which commanded him to stay and the other which commanded him to go, were nothing but a cleverly devised trap to accomplish the real purpose of the military authority, which was to lock him up in a concentration camp." Roberts also derided what he termed "a new doctrine of constitutional law that one indicted for disobedience to an unconstitutional statute" had to suffer the "disgrace of conviction" and imprisonment before he could challenge the law's validity.

Frank Murphy ripped into what he saw as the blatant racism of the entire relocation program. The exclusion of Japanese Americans from the West Coast "goes over the very brink of constitutional power and falls into the ugly abyss of racism." While courts had to defer to military judgment, limits existed on that deference. Martial law had not been declared, and no proof had ever been offered that the men, women, and children who had been taken from their homes and sent to concentration camps—all because of their race—had posed any threat to American security.

Jackson took the most lawyerly approach, worrying what the decision would mean in the future if the Court approved a policy based entirely on racial classification. Whatever the military necessity might be, Jackson warned, once the Court approved that action, it would become a precedent ready to be used—and abused—in the future: "The principle then lies about like a loaded weapon ready for the hand of any authority that can bring forward a plausible claim of an urgent need. . . . All who observe the work of the courts are familiar with what Judge Cardozo described as 'the tendency of a principle to expand itself to the limit of its logic.' A military commander may overstep the bound of constitutionality, and it is an incident. But if we review and approve, that passing incident has become the doctrine of the Constitution."

Frankfurter, of course, had to express his own views, even though Black had tried to meet his demands. He tried to exonerate himself from the result by noting that a finding of constitutionality did not imply approval of congressional or presidential policy. "That is their business, not ours," he declared.

In wartime, there is always pressure on the courts to uphold the executive and military authority, and the reasoning is somewhat valid. Those in charge of the day-to-day security of the country and who determine its military policies in the midst of war have access to important information that is not and should not be public, and they have to respond quickly, without having to go into court for judicial approval. In most wars, the Court has managed to defer ruling on all but a handful of cases. In World War I, for example, the government wanted the Court to rule on the validity of the draft. If the justices had found it unconstitutional, then other ways would have to be found to raise an army. Nearly all matters relating to economic regulation, such as rent control, were delayed. If the courts then found the government to have been wrong, the plaintiffs could have been made whole by monetary compensation.

Had martial law been declared on the West Coast, it is likely that the relocation cases would not have come to the high court. But it had not, and so the Court could not really refuse a civilian challenge to what was clear even then: that many people had been singled out for detention on no other basis than their ancestry and the color of their skin. The dissents made this very clear. The majority, as they knew then and as history has confirmed, abdicated judicial responsibility in the name of patriotism. Here the dialogue on the Court, especially the dissents, very much mirrored a larger debate going on in society. The full disapproval of the relocation program did not come until after the war, and at that time commentators began to see it as tied very much to the desires of another group, African Americans, to escape the racist bonds under which they suffered.

ALTHOUGH WE HAVE primarily been concerned with dissent and its role in the constitutional dialogue, mention has been made from time to time of concurrences. In some cases, such as Brandeis in *Whitney,* the concurrence is really a dissent. In other instances, the concurrence may deprive the plurality of a fifth vote to make a particular legal rule a binding precedent. In one case, however, the dialogue can be seen not so much in dissent as in the majority and concurring opinions.

In the spring of 1952, the United Steelworkers threatened to strike after the Wage Stabilization Board failed to negotiate a settlement between the union and the mill owners. Harry Truman believed that with American troops fighting in Korea, he had the same broad authority to mobilize the country that Roosevelt had used between 1941 and 1945. In early April 1952, Truman issued Executive Order 10340 directing Secretary of Commerce Charles Sawyer to seize and operate the nation's steel mills to assure continued production of steel for defense needs.

Although the president had no statutory authority for this action, he did have another option, one with express legislative approval, which he could have used to forestall the strike. The Taft-Hartley Act of 1947 included procedures by which the government could secure an eighty-day cooling-off period to postpone any strike that might adversely affect the public interest. Truman, however, had vetoed the measure, only to have the Republican Congress override his veto. Taft-Hartley would not have provided a permanent solution, but at least it enjoyed statutory legitimacy and might have bought time in which a settlement could be negotiated. Truman did not want to use a law that he had vetoed, so he simply seized the steel mills, informed an astounded Congress of what he had done, and invited it to take legislative action if it thought it necessary.

The steel operators immediately appealed the action, but at the time few people thought they stood a chance. After all, both the lower benches and the Supreme Court were staffed by judges appointed by either Roosevelt or Truman, men (and a handful of women) who believed that the government had few limits in terms of its own powers to regulate pri-

Harry S. Truman, thirty-third president
of the United States

vate property. Yet even at the time, a number of people recognized that a strike would not mean that ammunition factories would have to close or that Detroit would have to stop making tanks and trucks. This lack of true urgency would affect how the justices viewed the case.

Moreover, the steel companies framed their argument in a manner that allowed the Court an easy way to avoid deciding the case on its merits. The steel operators conceded that an emergency existed and that in an emergency the government had the right and the power to take over their businesses. They objected *that the wrong branch of government had proceeded against them.* In essence, they complained that the executive had unconstitutionally infringed upon the powers of the legislative branch. Rarely does a private party sue on behalf of a branch of government, and the courts could easily have dismissed the suit for lack of standing.

Nonetheless, the steel companies secured an injunction against the seizure in federal district court, at least in part because of the Justice Department's poor handling of the case. Judge David A. Pine ruled that the government lacked any authority to seize the mills, either in statutory or in constitutional form. The government immediately went to the Court of Appeals seeking a stay of the restraining order, and in an unusual step the entire nine-member court heard arguments by the government and the steel companies. By a bare 5–4 vote on 2 May, the appeals court granted a forty-eight-hour stay so that both sides could appeal to the Supreme Court.

Although the rules of the Supreme Court allow a direct appeal for certiorari from a district court ruling, in practice the justices prefer not to hear a case until it has traversed the full gamut of lower court hearings and a so-called final decision has been handed down. In unusual cases, however, the Court will accept an appeal when the issues are "of such imperative public importance as to justify the deviation from normal appellate processes as to require immediate settlement in this Court." At its regular Saturday conference on 3 May 1952, less than a month after Truman had ordered the seizure, the Court granted certiorari by a vote of 6–2; only Frankfurter and Burton voted against hearing the case, and Jackson passed.

Truman might well have been forgiven if he assumed that the government would easily triumph in the high court. He had based his decision to seize the mills in part on a memorandum prepared at an earlier time by Justice Clark, then attorney general, which spoke expansively about the "inherent" powers of the presidency. Truman had also met with his old friend Fred Vinson before issuing the executive order, and Vinson had said the president could go forward; there were sufficient legal grounds to justify the seizure. With four members of the Court his own appointees, Truman assumed that a majority would bless his expansive use of presidential authority as Roosevelt's nominees had blessed his.

On Monday, 12 May, the Court heard oral argument and at conference on Friday, 16 May, spent an unusual four hours debating the case. Harold Burton thought initially that he might be the only one to vote against the president, but by the end of the discussion he could note that the justices had discussed the steel case "with a most encouraging result."

According to Justice Douglas's extensive conference notes, a clear majority emerged fairly quickly on the view that the president had overstepped his authority, but no consensus developed as to what limits actually existed on presidential authority. Only Chief Justice Vinson, who had privately told Truman he had the power, joined by Stanley Reed and Sherman Minton, supported the government. Felix Frankfurter suggested that everyone write in this case, and for once the brethren took his advice; every member of the majority issued a separate opinion, while the minority all joined in the chief justice's dissent.

The Court handed down its decision in *Youngstown Sheet & Tube Co. v. Sawyer* on 2 June 1952, barely a month after it had voted to grant certiorari and three weeks after it heard oral argument. Four members of the Court agreed that Congress had prohibited the seizure. The legislative history of the Taft-Hartley Act showed that Congress had rejected a proposed amendment that would have authorized seizure of plants in national emergencies in favor of a provision to enjoin strikes. According to Justice Frankfurter, "The authoritatively expressed purpose of Congress to disallow such power to the President could not be more decisive if it had been written into . . . the Labor Management Relations Act."

Justice Black, as the senior member of the majority, assigned himself the opinion of the Court and took a broader approach. In his view, neither statute nor constitutional provision gave the president power to act as he had done; the constitutional provisions of the commander in chief, which had always been used by executives to justify wartime acts, did not extend this far. While Black's strict constructionist interpretation of the Constitution led to an expansion of the protections guaranteed in the Bill of Rights, here it led to a narrow view of presidential power. In essence, Black took a Jeffersonian position: if neither the Constitution nor an act of Congress specifically gave the chief executive the power, then it did not exist. The "President's power, if any," Black asserted, "must stem either from an act of Congress or from the Constitution itself." Power to authorize seizure of the mills did exist, but in the legislative branch, and when the president acted on his own authority in this manner, he encroached on congressional responsibility and violated the separation of powers. Douglas, who joined Black's opinion, also developed the separation-of-powers argument. The seizure of the mills constituted a taking of private property for which the owners had to be compensated. Only Congress could authorize such expenditures, and a seizure not authorized by statute would go against the express constitutional requirement of congressional appropriation of funds to compensate the taking.

If in Black's view the president could do only what statute or Constitution authorized, Chief Justice Vinson in dissent took the exact opposite stance: the president could, in response to a national emergency, do everything except what the Constitution specifically prohibited. Taking an expansive—indeed a Hamiltonian—reading of Article II, Vinson read broad authority into the Constitution's delegation of the "executive power," which he interpreted to go far beyond the few examples the Framers had enumerated. Truman himself, writing a few years later, took a similar position in justifying his actions. "The President must always act in a national emergency. A wise President will always work with Congress, but when Congress fails to act or is unable to act in a crisis, the President, under the Constitution, must use his power to safeguard the nation."

The most important opinion is Justice Jackson's concurrence, which Professor Louis Jaffe called "a most brilliant exposition of 'undefined presidential powers' and their relation to legislation." For Jackson, the issue was not whether specific statutory authority or implied constitutional power existed to justify the seizure; in this case, Congress had specifically said that it did not want to delegate such power to the president. While this had not been spelled out in the Taft-Hartley Act and other laws, the legislative history clearly showed congressional intent. By consciously omitting giving the president this power, Congress intended that he should not have it.

Presidential authority, Jackson held, stood at its height when the chief executive acted at the direct or implied command of Congress, and in such situations the president relied on his own powers as well as those given to him by the legislature. In circumstances in which Congress had not acted, the president might act relying on his own powers, but here a twilight zone existed in which it would not be clear who had the ultimate responsibility. Presidential authority was weakest, Jackson said, when the president acted in defiance of either express or implied legislative intent, and in such circumstances the Court could uphold the president only by ruling that Congress lacked power to legislate on the subject. In this instance, Congress did have the power, and it had spoken quite clearly as to its intent.

Although none of the six justices in the majority signed on to another's opinion, Frankfurter's concurrence played nicely into elaborating on Jackson's. Where Jackson set out a spectrum on which one could evaluate the strength of presidential authority, Frankfurter's comments rightly caught the practice of government as well as its theory. In many instances, he noted, Congress had been silent but acquiesced in presidential actions. If there had been a tradition of the legislature's going along with a particular policy, then such acceptance added a "historical gloss" on the Constitution, and the Court had often relied in the past on the understanding of the other two branches to evaluate the constitutionality of specific actions. He had his clerks compile a fifty-two-page tabulation of prior presidential seizures and from that review concluded that "abstract analysis" of checks and balances or separation of powers was pernicious because it did not take into account how government actually worked. But while there had been a number of presidential seizures in the past, there had only been three prior to 1952 similar to that of the steel mills, a number insufficient to provide the "gloss." He then, of course, went on to repeat his usual call for judicial restraint: "The Framers . . . did not make the judiciary the overseer of our government." Therefore, the Court should avoid grand pronouncements on the president's power, of the sort, he implied, in Black's opinion.

One might say that the wide range of opinions in the steel seizure case reflected the complexity of the problem, and to some extent it did. But while six members of the Court agreed that Truman lacked the authority, no two of them agreed on exactly why. Although Frankfurter managed to get in a little nit-picking to the extent that he considered Black's separation-of-powers argument simplistic, in this case there is clearly a dialogue going on—among the members of the Court, between the Court and the other two branches of government, and with the public. There is a spectrum, with Black at one end saying if the power is not explicit in statute or Constitution, it does not exist. At the other end is Vinson, with a perfectly good argument redolent of both Hamilton and John Marshall, that if the end be legitimate and there be no specific prohibition, then the means are legitimate. Douglas shades off into the idea of a taking and concludes that for this taking to be legitimate, Congress must be involved, because the Takings Clause requires it to be. Jackson's is the most nuanced and explores the question of presidential legitimacy in terms of congressional action or lack of it, while Frankfurter's notion of a historical gloss makes eminent good sense because that is in fact how Congress and the president work when the subject matter is not directly centered on a constitutional provision.

How, then, is this case different from one with seriatim opinions? It is not, except that here the dialogue is clearer, we can differentiate between the different positions, and it is not a matter of parsing small and perhaps insignificant differences. John Marshall and William Howard Taft would not have approved, but it seems that in this instance the airing of competing views proved worthwhile.

WILEY RUTLEDGE AND
IN RE YAMASHITA (1946)

I t sometimes takes many years until the argument of a dissent becomes
adopted as the proper rule in the dialogue. The argument not only
has to win over a majority of the Court but also has to be accepted
in the larger conversation. This is certainly true of Wiley Rutledge's
opinion in the *Yamashita* case, which continues to gain importance as
we shift from the arguably clearly defined parameters of a conventional
war to far less certain lines of a conflict within which terrorists wage
their "battles" against civilian targets. There is a broad dialogue occurring here involving not just the Court but a wider group of participants,
including the president, Congress, the military, and even special foreign
courts.

THE CASE OF General Tomoyuki Yamashita (pronounced "Yah-*mosh*-
i-tah") has troubled legal scholars and others concerned with the principles of military justice from the time the Court handed down its
decision in early 1946. On the face of it, the atrocities committed by
Japanese soldiers during their occupation of the Philippines in 1944
and 1945 certainly warranted punishment as much as did the actions of
the Germans. Murder, rape, mutilation, torture, beheadings, live buri-
als, and starvation—with the victims often women and children—were
indeed horrific. Many of these acts occurred as Allied forces under General Douglas MacArthur tried to recapture the islands.

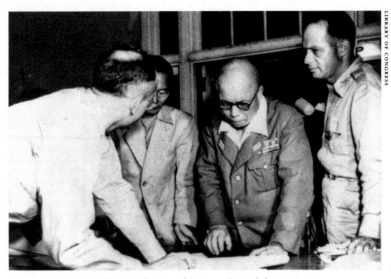

General Tomoyuki Yamashita consults with his attorneys.

Yamashita, the second son of a country doctor, did not show much promise as a youth, and in order to instill discipline, his parents sent him to a school operated by a former samurai warrior. The experience gave the boy the direction he needed, and he then enrolled in a military academy in Hiroshima where he excelled. He joined the army and slowly worked his way up the ranks, gaining a reputation as a capable officer. Two stints as a military attaché in Europe gave him a broader and more sophisticated perspective, and when war broke out in late 1941, Yamashita commanded Japan's Twenty-Fifth Army, with orders to take Singapore. This he did in a manner that has consistently been described as brilliant, and the supposedly impregnable fortress fell in early February 1942.

After taking Singapore, however, Yamashita spent two and a half years exiled to a post in Manchukuo; he had opposed the war, and Tojo did not trust him. When the fighting turned against Japan, Tokyo recalled Yamashita and assigned him to the Philippines, where he commanded Japan's besieged and dispersed forces in that final year of the war, the year of unspeakable atrocities. Although the prosecution conceded that the Japanese general had neither directed nor taken any part in these crimes, MacArthur, who ordered the trial on his own authority, charged Yamashita with the crime—unknown in military law—of having "failed to control" his troops. The military commission he convened consisted of five American generals, none of them versed in law. It was the first prosecution in history of a military commander for such a "crime," and in the turbulent trial both the judges and the prosecution disregarded the army's own rules. The trial was so flawed from start to finish that the international correspondents covering it voted 12–0 that he would be acquitted. The generals delivered the verdict they knew MacArthur wanted, and then Yamashita's lawyers sought review by the U.S. Supreme Court. Much to everyone's surprise, the justices agreed to hear the case.

TO UNDERSTAND Yamashita's case, one has to briefly revisit *Ex parte Quirin* (1942), which followed the arrest of eight Nazis put ashore from submarines on Long Island and Florida with orders to sabotage bridges, industrial plants, and military installations. The plan failed miserably, and authorities quickly apprehended the saboteurs and their few American confederates. President Roosevelt named a special military tribunal of seven generals to try the men, with orders to transmit the record of the trial—and the verdict—directly to him. At the same time, he closed the civilian courts to "all persons who are subjects, citizens, or residents of any nation at war with the United States . . . and are charged with committing or attempting . . . to commit sabotage."

The army lawyers appointed to defend the captured Germans tried to get their clients a civilian trial on the basis of the Civil War case of *Ex parte Milligan* (1866). In that decision, the Court had held that in areas apart from the battle zones in which civilian courts remained open, the government could not preempt the civil judiciary through military tribunals, a holding that became known as the "open court" doctrine. When the army refused this request, the defense lawyers appealed to the Supreme Court and convinced the justices that given the nature of the presidential order there could be no other forum for review. The Court's decision to hear the case was seen at the time and later as highly unusual, because the existing rules of military justice did not mention appeal to civilian courts.

When the justices met in conference after oral argument, apparently no one suggested that the Court deny the legitimacy of the proceedings. They agreed they needed to hand down a decision, to do it quickly, and that it should be unanimous in order to demonstrate that the Court had absolutely no reservations about the government's conduct. To do this, Chief Justice Stone managed to limit the issues to whether or not the Court had jurisdiction to hear the petition for *habeas corpus* and whether the president had the authority to order the saboteurs tried by a military panel. Even deciding these questions required extensive debate in the conference over whether the saboteurs were spies or prisoners of war, because treatment of the latter was specifically provided for by Congress in the Articles of War, a body of law that rarely came before the Court. Hugo Black's notes summed up the consensus: "Constitution makes President Supreme Commander and Congress can carry on war. Time out of mind it is within the power of the Commander-in-Chief to hang a spy. . . . By all usages they were not prisoners of war. Bound to give some play to Executive as to an administrative agency."

On 31 July 1942, less than forty hours after it heard the case, the Court issued a brief *per curiam* opinion upholding the power of the military commission to try the saboteurs and announcing that a formal opinion would be filed later. Within a few days, the eight men had been found guilty; six were executed, a seventh was sentenced to life imprisonment, and the eighth was given thirty years at hard labor.

While all eight justices who sat on the case (Murphy, then in uniform, recused himself) agreed that the president had the authority, they disagreed on the jurisprudential reasons to support the finding. Stone, for judicial as well as political reasons, believed it would be bad if the Court divided and took upon himself the task of crafting as narrow an opinion as possible. By the time the Court convened in October, he had succeeded.

The rather elaborate opinion said, in essence, that under the executive war powers the president could establish military commissions to try such cases. Stone took pains to rebut all of the points raised by defense counsel, pointing to thirteen separate clauses in the Constitution supporting executive war powers. In addition, he ruled that the constitutional guarantee of grand jury indictment and petit jury trial did not apply to defendants appearing before a military tribunal on charges of offenses under the law of war. The opinion avoided the validity of the presidential proclamation as well as a number of questions regarding interpretation of the Articles of War.

The decision in *Quirin,* and the justices' reluctance to interfere in military policy then and in the Japanese relocation cases, would play an important role when the Court, in late 1945, had to rule on the validity of the military trial of Tomoyuki Yamashita. It would also, in terms of the ruling that enemy combatants had no rights under the Constitution, be a key justification during the George W. Bush administration in determining how prisoners captured in Iraq and Afghanistan would be treated.

THE COURT in *Quirin* and the relocation cases consisted almost entirely of justices committed to judicial restraint. While that normally meant deference to legislative policy decisions, it also included—especially in wartime—deference to the president's direction of military affairs. The Court had rarely involved itself in cases arising out of the Articles of War, but when it did, it had usually taken the position that it had little power or authority to intervene. The justices who heard *Yamashita* had changed only slightly from the *Quirin* Court; Owen Roberts and James Byrnes had departed, replaced by Harold Burton and Wiley Rutledge. Although the details regarding the authority to order the trial differed considerably, the majority of the Court had essentially the same mind-set: the judiciary had little to do with matters arising out of military law. The justices also had to consider whether Douglas MacArthur would even recognize the Court's review power.

On this, they had legitimate concerns. When the Court received the habeas petition from Yamashita's lawyers, Chief Justice Stone called the solicitor general to see if the army would defer any execution until the Court could decide what to do. The solicitor general called the secretary of the army, who in turn called MacArthur, suggesting that he defer, and MacArthur refused. The Supreme Court had no jurisdiction, he told the secretary, and thus there was no reason to delay anything. The only review would be his. The secretary immediately ordered MacArthur to take no action while the Court considered the matter. To be doubly sure that Yamashita would survive until after the hearing, the Court ordered a stay of all proceedings in the case, and not even MacArthur dared disregard a direct order of the nation's highest court.

Once again Stone, seconded by Frankfurter, wanted to endorse the military's action, but unlike *Quirin* this case raised doubts among several of the brethren. There had been no question that the German saboteurs had been landed from an enemy submarine, intent on inflicting damage to American plants making war materials as well as to military installations. But as Yamashita's lawyers put it,

> In essence, therefore, the petitioner is not charged with having done something or with having failed to do something. He is charged merely with having been something, to wit: a commanding officer of a Japanese force whose members offended against the law of war. The heart of the charge is the proposition that commanding officers are rendered criminally liable regardless of fault

for the acts of their troops. But it is a basic premise of all civilized criminal justice that punishment is adjudged not according to status, but according to fault, and that one man is not held to answer for the crime of another.

The strongest legal argument involved the use of depositions in the case, taken from Filipino civilians who had either suffered from or witnessed the Japanese atrocities. Article of War 25 specifically prohibited the prosecution's use of depositions in capital cases. This was not a question of whether or not constitutional safeguards should apply, or even one of what safeguards would be considered fair in such a trial. It was in direct contravention of the Articles of War that Congress, under the Constitution, clearly had the power to make.

There was also a clear distinction between the trial of a Japanese general in the Philippines and those of the Nazi hierarchy in Nuremberg. No question existed that the genocide against the Jews and other crimes committed by German troops had been ordered by the Nazi leaders. In the Philippines, an army on the run, demoralized, and often not even in contact with headquarters, had run amok. While no one could or would excuse their actions, it was clear that Yamashita had never ordered, approved, or perhaps even known of the atrocities.

The solicitor general, J. Howard McGrath, had strong legal points to make as well, including the long line of precedents in which the Court had said it would not get involved in questions of military justice. In 1829, the great chief justice, John Marshall, had announced the principle that the judiciary had no authority under the Constitution to act on the government's "interests against foreign powers." In any event, McGrath argued, the Court had always abided by the "ancient doctrine" that nonresident enemy aliens had no access to American courts at all. But, he concluded, if the Court did not dismiss the case, as it should, and decided to hear the arguments, it ought to go no further than to satisfy itself that the military commission had been properly convened and that it had jurisdiction to try Yamashita for war crimes.

The Court heard arguments on 7 and 8 January 1946, and when the justices met in conference, Stone and Frankfurter, citing judicial restraint, argued that the Court should not interfere with what the military had done, a position later backed by Douglas, Burton, and Reed after they had seen a draft of Stone's opinion. (Jackson took no part because he was off in Europe prosecuting the Nuremberg trials.) In his opinion, Stone backed away from the position he had implied in *Quirin* that enemy combatants had at least some constitutional rights. Because the United States was technically still at war with Japan (a peace treaty would not be signed until 1952), the Articles of War allowed military commissions to operate without regard to the due process requirements of the Constitution.

On the more troublesome question of the alleged violation of Article 25 regarding depositions, Stone held that the Articles of War applied to "persons subject to military law." Article 25, therefore, applied only to "members of our own Army" and to people who "accompany the army," not to "enemy combatants." As for Article 63 of the Geneva Convention, also cited by Yamashita's lawyers to show how illegal the trial had been, Stone acknowledged that it applied to enemy prisoners but pertained only to offenses committed while in captivity, not to war crimes before capture. Finally, Stone summarily dismissed the Due Process Clause of the Fifth Amendment as inapplicable, declaring that only the military officials, not the courts, had authority to review the trial commission's rulings on evidence and "mode of conducting these proceedings."

Stone had gotten the necessary votes and upheld the military, without ever really addressing the important challenges raised by Yamashita's attorneys. Perhaps, as some have suggested, he believed that any other result would have led either President Truman or General MacArthur to just ignore the Court's decision. The Court believed, then and later, in deference to the military, both in peacetime and during a war.

IN RESPONSE TO Stone's draft, Wiley Rutledge suggested to Frank Murphy, the other dissenter, "You take the charge; I'll take the balance."

Murphy had a far more intimate knowledge of the Philippines than any of his colleagues, having served as governor-general for three years. He apparently earned the respect and affection of the islanders because of his vigorous advocacy for their interests as well as the generous support he gave local projects. No one empathized more with the hardships they had suffered, but that did not justify the way Yamashita had been treated.

He began his dissent by noting the very feature that had also disturbed Hugo Black, "whether a military commission . . . may disregard the procedural rights of an accused person as guaranteed by the Constitution, especially by the due process clause of the Fifth Amendment." (Ironically, Felix Frankfurter, who talked constantly about due process, had no interest in it in this case.) Due process, Murphy declared, applies to "any person," including an enemy belligerent. No serious attempt had been made to charge Yamashita "with a recognized violation of the laws of war." He had not been accused of personally participating in the acts of atrocity, he had not ordered or condoned them, and in fact

Wiley Blount Rutledge Jr., associate justice,
1943–1949

it appeared he had not even known about them. He had, according to
the military commission, been guilty of failing to control troops under
his command, a "crime" without the slightest precedent in international law, especially in the context of a defeated army in disarray and
under "constant and overwhelming assault." "In no recorded instance,"
Murphy asserted, "has the mere inability to control troops under fire or
attack by superior forces been made the basis of a charge of violating the
rules of war." Murphy essentially accused the majority of allowing the
commission to create an *ex post facto* law, "to make the crime whatever it
willed, dependent upon its biased view as to the petitioner's duties and
his disregard thereof, a practice reminiscent of that pursued in certain
less respected nations in recent years."

Murphy's sermon, for that was what it was, relied not only on those
rights in the American Constitution but on the notion of natural rights.
"The immutable rights of the individual, including those secured by
the due process clause of the Fifth Amendment, belong not alone to the
members of those nations that excel on the battlefield or that subscribe
to the democratic ideology. They belong to every person in the world,
victor or vanquished, whatever may be his race, color or beliefs. They
rise above any status of belligerency or outlawry." Because prisoners of
war lack direct access to the courts, judicial review through a habeas

proceeding "must be wider than usual in order that proper standards of justice may be enforceable."

As the judge and historian John Ferren noted, Murphy "overstated his case." Stone had cited international conventions that offered a substantial basis, although with little precedent, to charge criminal liability for breach of command responsibility. And despite the passionate rhetoric, some of Murphy's analysis tended toward assertion rather than documentation. Murphy had begun writing his dissent before Stone had passed around the draft of his opinion, so it never really grappled with the majority's argument. It would be up to Rutledge to dissect Stone's opinion, and it is Rutledge's dissent, not that of Murphy, which has influenced the military code of justice since. He delivered his dissent orally, and some observers noted a tone of bitterness whenever he glanced at the chief justice. "More is at stake," he began,

> than General Yamashita's fate. There could be no possible sympathy for him if he is guilty of the atrocities for which his death is sought. But there can be and should be justice administered according to law. In this stage of war's aftermath it is too early for Lincoln's great spirit, best lighted in the Second Inaugural, to have wide hold for the treatment of foes. It is not too early, it is never too early, for the nation steadfastly to follow its great constitutional traditions, none older or more universally protective against unbridled power than due process of law in the trial and punishment of men, that is, of all men, whether citizens, aliens, alien enemies or enemy belligerents. It can become too late. . . .
>
> With all deference to the opposing views of my brethren, whose attachment to that tradition needless to say is no less than my own, I cannot believe in the face of this record that the petitioner had had the fair trial our Constitution and laws command.

Rutledge then proceeded to dissect Stone's opinion point by point. Unlike *Quirin,* which took place during wartime and therefore justified a military commission, the cessation of hostilities had rendered a military trial unnecessary. Yamashita should have been tried in civilian court and accorded full due process of law.

At the heart of his opinion, Rutledge argued that the law of war allowed conviction of a commander for failure to control his troops only if proof existed that the commander knew of the crimes his troops had committed in time either to stop them or to punish them afterward. (We now call this command accountability.) The majority opinion, however, would uphold Yamashita's conviction—and that of any other military officer in a similar position—on the ambiguous assertion that he had failed his duty simply by "permitting" the troops to commit atrocities. But did "permit" mean that the troops had acted with his approval or that he had failed to discover what they were doing through the military chain of command? If the former, then he was guilty of a crime, but if the latter, the most that could be charged would be negligence. Given the disarray of Japanese troops in the last weeks and months of the war, it would have to be the latter. The charge before the military commission authorized conviction on the latter interpretation and was fatally defective because negligence was not a law-of-war violation.

In addition to the defective nature of the charges, the commission's findings were themselves inadequate. Nowhere in the commission's report were any allegations, based even on circumstantial evidence, that Yamashita had actually known of his troops' actions. Instead, the commission, without citing any facts, offered "inferential findings" that the general "had knowledge." The crimes had been so extensive that Yamashita must have "willfully permitted" or "secretly ordered" them. There was no credible evidence, Rutledge believed, to back up these findings. Indeed the conclusions of law on which the commission found guilt did not even mention knowledge, a condition that any form of due process required for culpability.

The matter, he declared, is not just a question of what evidence could be admitted:

It goes to the very competency of the tribunal to try and punish consistently with the Constitution, the laws of the United States made in pursuance thereof, and the treaties made under the nation's authority. . . . Whether taken singly in some instances as departures from specific constitutional mandates or in totality as in violation of the Fifth Amendment's command that *no* person shall be deprived of life, liberty, or property without due process of law, a trial so vitiated cannot withstand constitutional scrutiny. I cannot conceive any instance of departure from our basic concepts of fair trial, if the failures here are not sufficient to produce that effect.

As to MacArthur's directive that allowed any evidence to come in, "a more complete abrogation of customary safeguards relating to the proof could hardly have been made. So far as the admissibility and probative value of evidence was concerned, the directive made the commission a law unto itself. It acted accordingly." For all of the "evidence" accumulated in the trial, the "commission's ultimate findings draw no express conclusion of knowledge, but state only two things: (1) the fact of widespread atrocities and crimes; (2) that petitioner 'failed to provide effective control . . . as was required by the circumstances.' " At most, all one could fairly read into the commission's final report was that Yamashita had no knowledge of what had happened, and because he had failed to find out, he was negligent and therefore should be hanged.

If Yamashita had received a fair trial, then its conduct would have had to comply with the Articles of War passed by Congress, the Geneva Convention of 1929, and the Due Process Clause of the Fifth Amendment. If the majority agreed with that contention, then the Court should have reversed the conviction and ordered a retrial. Stone had said these safeguards did not apply, and Rutledge went about refuting his analysis point by point. Where Stone had said that the Articles of War, especially Articles 25 and 38, only applied to American military personnel and not enemy combatants, Rutledge argued that was not true. After Congress had revised the Articles in 1920, it had for the first time recognized military commissions as agencies to try not only courts-martial but also enemy belligerents. As such, the commission trial of enemy belligerents had to follow the same due process requirements as trials of American personnel.

Stone's opinion relied on a textual analysis of the Articles of War and the Geneva Convention, a skill normally considered one of Stone's strengths. But Rutledge's reading and explication of the same texts came to a far different conclusion, and one that proved far more convincing. Rutledge's dissent, refuting Stone's argument point by point, ran to forty pages in *U.S. Reports*, longer than Stone's twenty-one and Murphy's sixteen combined. He concluded, "I cannot accept the view that anywhere in our system resides or lurks a power so unrestrained to deal with any human being through any process of trial. What military agencies or authorities may do with our enemies in battle or invasion, apart from proceedings in the nature of trial and some semblance of judicial action, is beside the point. Nor has any human being heretofore been held to be wholly beyond the elementary procedural protection by the Fifth Amendment. I cannot consent to even implied departure from that great absolute."

He then quoted, as had Yamashita's counsel, from Thomas Paine: "He that would make his own liberty secure must guard even his enemy from oppression; for if he violates this duty he establishes a precedent that will reach to himself."

As many people who have examined the cases have noted, aside from

General Douglas MacArthur

the procedural and due process deficiencies of the trial, the Court could have, indeed should have, followed Rutledge. He was arguing not that there could not be military trials but only that they had to adhere to basic American tenets. All Congress had to do was adopt new rules for military tribunals, a step it ultimately took. Why the rush to hang Yamashita? He was not going anyplace. What harm would there have been to have given his defense counsel time to prepare adequately? The result might well have been the same. Yamashita might well have been found guilty. But then his trial would not have gone down in history as the travesty it was.

IN FAIRNESS, the case presented a number of difficulties, not the least of which was the fear of the justices that if they ruled in Yamashita's favor, Truman or MacArthur would simply ignore the result. In fact, four days after the Court handed down its decision on 4 February 1946, Truman denied executive clemency, and MacArthur ordered Yamashita hanged before sunrise on 23 February. Beyond that, however, this was a case of first impression before the Court and raised a number of issues. Could failure to control troops, could negligence, be a crime under the applicable American and international rules? Should the Court even review the judgments of military commissions? If it did, what standards ought to be used? Although Rutledge and Murphy did not argue that the due process applicable to civilian criminal cases should be applied, they did insist that there be some substantive level of due process.

What is perhaps most notable about the three opinions is how differently the justices approached the case, and not just on specific points. Stone and the majority saw a legitimate military tribunal attempting to deal with one of the more horrible events of the war. Murphy and Rutledge, on the other hand, saw MacArthur and the five military judges misapplying American law and disregarding the Constitution's majestic command that no person suffer loss of life without due process of law. The majority could not honestly deal with that issue and at the same time uphold the legitimacy of the trial—so it ignored it.

Criticism of the opinion began almost immediately. Edward S. Corwin, perhaps the nation's leading constitutional scholar, called the decision "a complete retreat, as well as a completely *silent* retreat," from *Ex parte Quirin,* where Stone had held that even enemy combatants were entitled to constitutional safeguards. Charles Fairman, an expert in military and constitutional law, wrote that "Mr. Justice Rutledge would seem to have the better of the argument." Whether one agrees with him or not, Fairman declared, "one must respect the ideal of justice" for which Rutledge was striving. As time has passed, criticism of the majority opinion has increased. In a recent book, Allan Ryan asserts, "The lasting significance of the Court's convoluted and erroneous reasoning is . . . that the justices were faced with a conviction that was obtained in violation of the laws of the United States and should therefore have been invalidated, and they did not do it."

Needless to say, Douglas MacArthur did not appreciate either of the dissents and issued a statement: "No trial could have been fairer than this one, no accused was ever given a more complete opportunity of defense, no judicial process was ever freer from prejudice." Much mail flowed into Rutledge's office, some condemning him as a "Jap coddler," but more, including from a number of military men, applauded his "courageous defense" of due process. Even the clerk of the Court, C. E. Cropley, who by tradition did not comment on cases, told Rutledge, "Though you do not subscribe to the new law made in the heat of today—your contribution to the classics of American philosophy will be recognized in a cooler tomorrow, and, I hope, not too late."

THE NEXT CASE involving enemy combatants, *Johnson v. Eisentrager,* came to the Court after both Rutledge and Murphy had died in 1949. German soldiers had been seized in China and tried and convicted by a military commission for violation of the laws of war. Afterward, they were transported to the American-occupied part of Germany and imprisoned there in the custody of the U.S. Army. They then filed a habeas appeal in American courts. The district court dismissed because the men were technically not within the jurisdictional limits of the United States, but the appeals court reversed, ruling that being held by the American army constituted being under American jurisdiction. The Supreme Court, by a 6–3 vote, held that because the Germans were enemy aliens who had never entered the United States and were captured, tried, convicted, and imprisoned on enemy soil for offenses outside the United States, they had no right to seek habeas review in American courts. The Bush administration relied heavily on this decision to argue that prisoners taken in the Iraqi and Afghan wars and held at the Guantánamo Naval Base in Cuba had no recourse to American courts.

Hugo Black, joined by Douglas and Burton, dissented and argued that the government could not evade the civil courts' jurisdiction by detaining and trying enemy combatants on foreign soil. If the detainees were effectively under American control, then the courts had power to entertain a habeas petition. Interestingly, Black cited both *Quirin* and *Yamashita* for the proposition that courts could hear appeals from enemy combatants, but neither he nor Justice Jackson, who wrote for the majority, discussed questions of due process. *Eisentrager* was not about the conduct of the commission but about the reach of the Court's jurisdiction.

Shortly after the Court decided *Eisentrager,* Congress enacted the Uniform Code of Military Justice, which went into effect in 1951. Among other provisions, the code established an appellate court of military review within each service and, more important, created the U.S. Court of Appeals for the Armed Forces, its members to be drawn not from military ranks but from civilian life. Some of its other provisions could be read as a sharp rebuke to the *Yamashita* majority, such as the applicability of its terms to trials of enemy combatants as well as American military personnel and the due process provisions to protect defendants. Article 77 also makes explicit the command responsibility of officers whose subordinates commit a crime. Anyone who "aids, abets, counsels, commands, or procures" the commission of a crime "is a principal."

THE CONCEPT OF "command accountability" is difficult both to define and to administer. The army's manual of regulations of war had shifted several times and began with the question of a soldier's liability for following his superior's orders. In the first iteration (1914), individuals "will not be punished for [violations of the law of war] in case they are committed under the orders or sanctions of their government or commanders." The commanders, however, could be punished "by the belligerent into whose hands they may fall." Of course, if they were not captured or defeated, neither commanders nor soldiers would be brought to account.

The 1934 and 1940 editions of the regulations repeated these provisions, but in November 1944 the army deleted them, because preparations for the postwar trial of Nazi officials could not afford to have everyone saying he was just following Hitler's orders. So now "individuals and organizations who violate the accepted laws and customs of war may be punished therefor." The trial judges, however, could take into account if a person was following orders in determining culpability and punishment. When Robert Jackson drafted the Charter of the International Military Tribunal at Nuremberg, he removed this discretion. "The fact that the defendant acted pursuant to orders of his Government or of a superior shall not free him from responsibility." The Nuremberg charter said nothing about command accountability, nor did the Allies rely on it in the cases against high Nazi officials. Under the Nuremberg rules, it would have been possible to prosecute any of the Japanese soldiers who took part in the atrocities, but because Yamashita had not ordered those actions, nor had he been given orders to allow his troops to rampage, he would have been acquitted.

The army again revised its manual in 1956, the edition still in effect today, and severely limited the "just following orders" defense. Also, for the first time it explicitly provided for command accountability. The responsibility of a commander for crimes committed by those under him "arises directly when the acts in question have been committed in pursuance of an order of the commander concerned. The commander is also responsible if he has actual knowledge, or should have knowledge, through reports received by him or through other means, that troops or other persons subject to his control are about to commit or have committed a war crime and he fails to take the necessary and reasonable steps to insure compliance with the law of war or to punish violators thereof."

Rutledge and Murphy would have had no problem with that definition, which surely went beyond mere "negligence," had it been rigorously applied by the Yamashita tribunal. The prosecution would have had to prove that the general actually knew about the actions of his troops and with that knowledge had failed to take the necessary steps. This would probably have been impossible to do in Yamashita's circumstances, where the Japanese troops were in disarray and few if any messages got through between the command position and troops in the field, and had Yamashita learned of the atrocities, the question then would have been whether he could, in fact, have done anything to stop them.

Knowledge, as Rutledge had argued, had to be an essential component of accountability, and that standard was adopted not at the primary Nuremberg trials, where Jackson served, but in the twelve sets of trials that followed afterward for lower-ranking German officers and Nazi officials. Many field commanders claimed they knew nothing of the hostage taking or reprisal killings committed by their subordinates, and the judges took this defense seriously. They eventually rejected it because German generals in the Balkans knew or should have known from reports sent to their headquarters that the crimes were taking place. German organization and efficiency ensured that field commanders had reports at least twice a day, with ten-day and monthly reports recapitulating previous actions and laying out plans for future operations. Army commanders, the judges categorically ruled, will not be permitted to deny knowledge of reports received. The judges did take into account the claim that commanders did not receive reports when away from their posts, but the defendant still had the burden of showing that he lacked the knowledge required for culpability. Moreover, upon receiving information, the officer had to prove that he had not authorized the actions of the field soldiers and either did something or tried to act to restrain these excesses when he found out.

This formulation was the first meaningful analysis of command accountability by any military court and continues to influence the concept, its meaning, and its application. In these trials the judges made no reference to either the majority or the dissenting opinions in *Yamashita,* but their emphasis on knowledge as a critical element of accountability clearly tracked Rutledge's dissent. Moreover, in the trials known as the *Hostage Cases,* the judges noted that in modern warfare there is a fair amount of decentralization, and a high commander may not be fully informed of what every soldier under his command is doing. He has the right to assume, moreover, that subordinates will carry out their assignments lawfully. To prove guilt, therefore, prosecutors have to show "personal neglect amounting to a wanton, immoral disregard of the action of his subordinates amounting to acquiescence." Again, this is a criterion the dissenters could have accepted as providing a standard in which due process could be achieved.

THE IMPACT OF Wiley Rutledge's ideas in *Yamashita* has been felt internationally in dialogues over modern war crimes. In 1993, the United Nations created a new court charged with bringing to justice those responsible for the brutalities of the war in Serbia. The UN gave the International Criminal Tribunal for the Former Yugoslavia (ICTY) jurisdiction to prosecute war crimes, crimes against humanity, genocide, and violations of the Geneva Convention that had occurred since the country splintered following the death of Marshal Tito in 1980. The following year, the UN established a similar court to deal with the genocide in Rwanda, known as ICTR.

The legal experts drawn from several countries who drafted the ICTY statute did something highly unusual: they wrote in a provision defining command accountability and authorized prosecutors to apply it to people in positions of authority. They did not write on a blank slate. In 1974, after several years of discussion triggered by both the postwar trials and Vietnam, protocols had been added to the Geneva Convention requiring nations that subscribed to the convention to take appropriate steps to punish "grave breaches which result from a failure to act when under a duty to do so," that is, war crimes and a concomitant command accountability. They spelled out commanders' duties to act to prevent such acts when possible or to punish the guilty parties after the fact. The protocols provided that commanders are not to be absolved from responsibility for the crimes of subordinates "if they knew, or had information which should have enabled them to conclude in the circumstances of the time," that subordinates were about to act illegally.

In *Yamashita,* the majority seemingly adopted MacArthur's view that commanders had a duty to prevent war crimes; the 1974 protocol for the first time wrote this explicitly into international law. The protocol also took a step that the majority—but not the dissenters—had avoided, addressing the question of the commander's knowledge as an element in fixing responsibility. Granted, the protocol is a treaty, not a criminal statute, but had its standard of accountability been applied to General Yamashita—as the dissent had demanded—it would have made his conviction well-nigh impossible.

The charters for the ICTY and ICTR, however, are rules to be applied in criminal trials to determine command accountability, and they make clear distinctions between those who order and/or participate in crimes and those whose accountability depends on what their subordinates did and what knowledge they had or should have had about those events.

WHAT IS LEFT OF *Yamashita,* both the majority and the dissenting opinions? The answer for the majority opinion is very little. Justice Stevens did cite it in the first of the terrorist cases, *Rasul v. Bush* (2004), for the proposition that federal courts, despite the efforts of the executive, always retain the power to review habeas appeals, in wartime as in peacetime and from insular possessions. In *Hamdan v. Rumsfeld* (2006), Justice Stevens declared that the military commissions created by the Bush administration failed to pass muster and that any trials of the detainees would have to follow the rules set forth in the Uniform Code of Military Justice. In addition, he held that "the Government must make a substantial showing that the crime for which it seeks to try a defendant by military commission is acknowledged to be an offense against the law of war. That burden is far from satisfied here." The Court has not been involved with any war crimes trials in several decades, but aside from the jurisdictional issue it is clear that the ideas expressed by Wiley Rutledge—in terms of both due process and command accountability—have triumphed. The due process provisions in the Uniform Code of Military Justice are far stricter than those in the old Articles of War; they apply to both American military personnel and foreign combatants tried by U.S. military courts, and judicial review of sentences and proceedings is available through both military courts of appeals and civilian courts. The far more difficult question of defining command accountability has made its way into the code, into an additional protocol of the Geneva Convention, and into the charters of courts hearing war crimes trials from Rwanda and the former Yugoslavia.

The dialogue here is, admittedly, more difficult to detail than the rather straightforward progress of Justice Brandeis's dissent in *Olmstead* to its triumph in the 1960s. Rutledge's influence, however, cannot be gainsaid. It is to the questions he raised in his *Yamashita* dissent, not the assertions made by Douglas MacArthur and seconded by Harlan Fiske Stone, that the drafters of the subsequent national and international documents paid attention. Issues before the Court growing out of the war on terror have moved on to a different level, one involving unlawful combatants, and raise questions unknown to the Court that decided *In re Yamashita.* But in their efforts to answer these questions, the justices have been guided by Wiley Rutledge's dissent, not by the majority opinion.

CHAPTER 9

THE PRIMA DONNAS II

INCORPORATION, CRIMINAL
PROCEDURE, AND FREE SPEECH

*It is our business not to decide constitutional issues, not to enter the
domain of political conflicts as to power, which Constitutional issues are,
by the most rigorous application of traditional procedural restrictions.
That's not "avoiding jurisdiction," that's being observant of our
constitutional duty as formulated from the beginning of our history.*

—FELIX FRANKFURTER TO STANLEY REED, 1941

*No higher duty, no more solemn responsibility, rests upon this Court, than
that of translating into living law and maintaining this constitutional
shield deliberately planned and inscribed for the benefit of every human
being subject to our Constitution—of whatever race, creed or persuasion.*

—HUGO BLACK, *CHAMBERS V. FLORIDA* (1940)

While Frankfurter and Black were often on the same side in
the wartime cases, the debate between them continued
and emerged full-blown shortly after the war. In March
1946, the Court heard argument in a suit brought by Professor Kenneth W. Colegrove of Northwestern University, who sought to invali-

date all elections held under Illinois's antiquated apportionment system, which, despite massive population shifts to urban areas, had not been revised since 1901. Legislative power remained entrenched in the rural districts, efforts to secure reform through state judicial and political methods had failed, and Colegrove appealed to the federal courts. He argued that the Illinois system, which affected the election of congressmen as well as state representatives, violated the Fifteenth Amendment ban against the abridgment of the right to vote as well as guarantees in Article I regarding apportionment of congressmen and Article IV, which decrees that the United States "shall guarantee to every State in this Union a Republican Form of Government."

Colegrove pointed to recent decisions protecting the right to vote, but those decisions had involved the special case of discrimination against blacks. The Court in 1932 had specifically denied that the Constitution required compactness, contiguity, or equality of population in congressional districts. Moreover, a majority of the Court had expressed its belief that such issues comprised "political" questions and were therefore nonjusticiable.

The political question doctrine dates back to the Dorr Rebellion of 1842, when defeated rebels attacked the legitimacy of the old Rhode Island state government under the guaranty clause. Chief Justice Roger Taney denied their claim and held that enforcement of the Article IV clause "belonged to the political power and not to the judicial." In such situations, the courts would not intervene because the judicial branch had neither the authority to resolve the dispute nor the means to enforce such a decision. The doctrine allowed the Court to evade certain types of cases. For an advocate of judicial restraint, such as Frankfurter, the political question doctrine could be invoked as an absolute bar to judicial involvement in the Illinois dispute.

A "bobtailed Court" of seven justices handed down its decision on 10 June 1946. (Harlan Stone had died a month after oral argument, and Robert Jackson, still in Nuremberg, had not taken part.) Frankfurter, speaking for himself, Harold Burton, and Stanley Reed, declared, "The petitioners ask of this Court what is beyond its competence to grant. This is one of those demands on judicial power which cannot be met by verbal fencing about 'jurisdiction.' It must be resolved by considerations on the basis of which this Court, from time to time, has refused to intervene in controversies. It has refused to do so because due regard for the effective working of our government revealed this issue to be of a peculiarly political nature and therefore not meet for judicial determination."

The Constitution, Frankfurter concluded, had conferred sole authority in Congress to assure fair representation among the states in the House of Representatives. Courts, he warned in a famous phrase, "ought not to enter the political thicket." Frankfurter got his fourth vote, and the majority, through the concurrence of Wiley Rutledge, who, although he disagreed about the nonjusticiability of such issues, voted to dismiss for want of equity. With the next elections so close, Rutledge believed, it would be impossible to implement any workable remedy.

Black, Douglas, and Murphy dissented. Black believed a clear constitutional violation existed and that federal courts had not only the power but the obligation to protect rights secured by the Constitution, including the right to a "Republican Form of Government." Legislative malapportionment violated Black's beliefs in the popular sovereignty implicit in the Constitution that he considered had been the basis for its adoption. No one, he asserted in his dissent, "would deny that the equal protection clause would also prohibit a law that would expressly give certain citizens a half-vote and others a full vote." Why, then, should courts tolerate a system that gave certain citizens a vote only one-ninth as effective as that of other citizens in choosing their state and congressional representatives? "Such discriminatory legislation," he concluded, "seems to me exactly the kind that the equal protection clause was intended to prohibit."

Although only three members of the Court actually believed apportionment nonjusticiable, the case served as a barrier to election reforms in the states for the next sixteen years. For Frankfurter, *Colegrove* stood for exactly the type of restraint the Court should exercise. But malapportionment also fit the sort of issue that Stone in footnote 4 said required heightened judicial scrutiny, not the judicial abdication implicit in the political question doctrine. People living in the malapportioned states—even if they constituted a majority of the population—could not get reform past the entrenched rural minorities that controlled the legislatures.

Ironically, an opinion by Frankfurter himself led to the eventual abandonment of the *Colegrove* decision. When the civil rights movement burst onto the national stage, the NAACP went to court to challenge various southern devices to deprive blacks of their votes. In *Gomillion v. Lightfoot* (1960), blacks challenged a gerrymandering scheme in Tuskegee, Alabama, that redrew the city boundaries from a square into "an uncouth twenty-eight-sided figure" that had the effect of disenfranchising all but four or five of Tuskegee's registered black voters without depriving a single white of the franchise. In briefs and in oral argument, Alabama claimed that the *Colegrove* doctrine barred jurisdiction.

Speaking for a unanimous Court, Frankfurter rejected this claim completely. The facts in *Colegrove* had affected all citizens; in Tuskegee, "the inescapable human effect of this essay in geometry and geography is to despoil colored citizens, and only colored citizens, of their theretofore enjoyed voting rights. That was not *Colegrove v. Green.*" The Fifteenth Amendment spoke directly to the issue of black suffrage, and that fact removed the case from the realm of political questions into direct constitutional litigation.

Despite Frankfurter's best efforts to distinguish *Gomillion* from *Colegrove,* the inherent contradiction could not be hidden. If black citizens could secure judicial redress because their votes had been diluted, then why should not white citizens, suffering from a different form of the same ailment, be able to seek similar relief? No matter how Frankfurter had phrased it, a "dilution" of the vote had the same effect as a "deprivation."

One week later, the Court noted probable jurisdiction in a case challenging Tennessee's apportionment scheme. The state legislature had not been reapportioned since 1901, and the challengers claimed that because of the malapportionment they could not secure redress through the traditionally preferred manner of legislative reform. Before the Court could decide whether to grant or deny relief, it had to decide whether it had the power to do so. *Baker v. Carr,* therefore, was the first of a two-step process, and the justices well understood what they were taking on in this case. If the Court decided it did not have the power, if the justices followed *Colegrove* as Frankfurter urged them to do, that would be the end of the matter, and the petitioners would have to find some other way to break out of their trap. If the Court decided it had the authority, then it would hear subsequent cases to determine what sort of relief should be given, and such relief would one way or another affect the makeup of every state legislature. To affirm jurisdiction required overruling *Colegrove.*

Because of the importance of the issue, the Court heard oral argument over two days in April 1961. At the conference on the twenty-first, Frankfurter spoke for ninety minutes, darting around the room and gesticulating as he pulled one volume of *U.S. Reports* after another off the shelves. He warned the Court would "rue the result" if it got involved in reapportionment; even taking the case would be an error akin to the Bay of Pigs invasion of Cuba the previous week. William Brennan disagreed, saying that "the purpose of the Fourteenth Amendment was to give equality," and the remedies were not insoluble. After going around the table, the justices split 4–4, with Potter Stewart undecided. He asked if they could hold the case over until the following term, and reargument was set down for the following October.

Over the summer, Frankfurter had his clerks hard at work, and one day after the reargument on 9 October he circulated a sixty-page memorandum detailing why the Court should stay out of the issue. Once again he warned of the dire consequences to the Court if it should decide to force reapportionment. Brennan responded with an eleven-page chart one of his clerks had drawn, showing in stark detail the disparities among Tennessee counties. When it came time to vote, Potter Stewart agreed that the malapportionment required judicial intervention, but, he added, in this first case he would refuse to go beyond agreeing that courts could hear the issue and would oppose any particular remedy.

On 26 March 1962, Justice Brennan announced the opinion for a 6–2 majority. Justices Douglas, Clark, and Stewart added concurring opinions, while Frankfurter and Harlan dissented. Simply put, Brennan believed that questions of apportionment were in fact justiciable, that is, open to challenge and remedy in the courts, and that citizens who believed their votes had been diluted had standing to sue in federal court. He did not prescribe any particular remedy but declared that "we have no cause at this stage to doubt that the District Court will be able to fashion relief if violations of constitutional rights are found." In this, the Court did as it had in the civil rights cases a decade earlier, assigning the power and responsibility to hear and decide cases to the lower courts, with the results reviewable on appeal.

The opinion is one of Brennan's best, closely reasoned and sensitive to the great issues involved. Brennan also knew there would be a dissent from his former teacher, although it is doubtful if Frankfurter appreciated how well his student had done. Brennan did not ignore the political question doctrine but distinguished it from apportionment. In all other cases, either the Constitution explicitly or implicitly assigned the issue to another branch of government, or the Court had refused jurisdiction because the question lacked "judicially discoverable and manageable standards for resolving it." In *Colegrove,* Brennan correctly noted, a majority of the Court had believed the issue justiciable, and in *Gomillion* it had specifically asserted judicial power and the ability to resolve the problem.

An obviously angry Frankfurter prefaced his lengthy dissent by declaring, "Today the Court begins a process of litigation that it requires no prophet to say—and Cassandra was sometimes right—will outlast the life of the youngest member of this Court." The decision would plunge the Court into a task that it had neither the experience nor the

ability to handle—devising "what should constitute the proper composition of the legislatures of the fifty states." After reviewing and prais-
ing the wisdom of the political question doctrine, he predicted direly
that the Court had plunged itself into a morass from which it would
be impossible to emerge, a quagmire lacking judicially discoverable or
administrable standards, an area infected by partisan politics.

This was Frankfurter's last major opinion; a month later, he suffered a
stroke and retired from the Court in August. One wishes he might have
gone out on a better note, perhaps a decision in which he could have
reinforced his concerns for Fourth Amendment rights or the separation
of church and state. Instead, his dissent in *Baker* has the same tone as
the one he wrote two decades earlier in *Barnette,* namely, "I am right
and why don't you people listen to me." And once again, he was wrong.
His prophecies of a judicial nightmare never materialized. Although the
entrenched state legislatures fought to prevent reapportionment, once it
happened and a majority population controlled a majority of legislative
seats, opposition died out. Justice Douglas provided a judicially manageable standard, "one man, one vote," which Chief Justice Warren then
applied in *Reynolds v. Sims* (1964), a suit against the Alabama apportionment scheme. The obvious justness of the decision, and the equally
obvious facility with which it could be implemented, made Frankfurter's opinion seem, in subsequent readings, more and more paranoid and
unrealistic. Compared with the democratic majesty of Warren's opinion
in *Reynolds,* Frankfurter's claim that "there is not under our constitution a judicial remedy for every political mischief" sounds crabbed and
visionless. Warren, Brennan, Black, and Douglas spoke to the possibilities of democracy; Frankfurter could apparently see only its limits.

MUCH OF THE DEBATE between Black and Frankfurter involved
the question of incorporation, or what rights listed in the first eight
amendments to the Constitution, and designed to restrict Congress, also
applied to the states through the Due Process Clause of the Fourteenth
Amendment. Their positions framed the larger discussion on this topic
that occupied the Court for three decades.

Frankfurter championed the position taken by Benjamin Cardozo in
Palko v. Connecticut (1937), that the Fourteenth Amendment did not
automatically subsume the entire Bill of Rights. It did incorporate
all the protections of the First, for freedom of thought and speech is
"the matrix, the indispensable condition, of nearly every other form of
freedom." But as for the Second through the Eighth Amendments, the
Court should apply only those that are "of the very essence of a scheme

of ordered liberty" and "so rooted in the traditions and conscience of our people as to be ranked as fundamental." This "selective incorporation" appealed to Frankfurter because it required judges to evaluate what constituted a fundamental right.

Frankfurter's philosophy grew out of his earlier opposition to the use of substantive due process to strike down reform legislation, a concern Black shared. The answer to this abuse of power, according to Frankfurter, lay in judicial restraint and appropriate deference to the policy decisions of the political branches. But the Due Process Clause clearly meant something, and judges had to determine what that something was.

Black had just gone onto the Court when *Palko* came down, but he grew increasingly uncomfortable with the whole notion of selective incorporation and especially the great power it lodged in the courts. By 1946, Black could identify this judicial discretion as the core of his difference with the Frankfurter-Cardozo approach. If judges could strike down state laws that failed to meet "civilized standards," then courts had reverted to a "natural law concept whereby the supreme constitutional law becomes this Court's view of 'civilization' at a given moment." Such a philosophy made everything else in the Constitution "mere surplusage" and allowed the Court to reject all of the provisions of the Bill of Rights, and substitute its own idea as to what legislatures could or could not do.

He realized, of course, that there had to be some standards that judges could apply, but he did not fully articulate his position until a California murder case in 1947. The defendant, Admiral Dewey Adamson (his real name, not a rank) had been in and out of prison for seventeen years when police arrested him for the murder of an elderly widow. On the advice of his counsel, he did not take the stand, because he could then have been questioned about his prior arrests. But the prosecutor, as allowed under California law, pointed out to the jury Adamson's failure to testify. If he had been innocent, the prosecutor declared, it would have taken fifty horses to keep him off the stand. The jury convicted Adamson, and his lawyer on appeal challenged the California statute as violating the Fourteenth Amendment's Due Process Clause. Allowing comment on the failure to testify was equivalent to forcing a defendant to take the stand, and both violated due process.

At conference, Frankfurter convinced a majority of the brethren that the issue had already been decided correctly in *Twining v. New Jersey* (1908), when the Court held that a state law permitting comment on a defendant's refusal to take the stand did not violate procedural fairness. In his majority opinion, Justice Reed conceded that such behavior by a prosecutor in a federal proceeding would be unacceptable and a violation of the Fifth Amendment. But well-settled law held that the self-incrimination clause did not apply to the states and was not one of the fundamental principles inherent in a scheme of well-ordered liberty. "For a state to require testimony from an accused," Reed concluded, "is not necessarily a breach of a state's obligation to give a fair trial."

Black dissented, joined by Douglas, and Murphy dissented, joined by Rutledge. Frankfurter filed a concurrence, and in the opinion, concurrence, and dissents we see one of the great dialogues of modern constitutional jurisprudence. For the majority, Reed adhered to precedent, both the holding in *Twining* and the criteria of selective incorporation laid down by Cardozo in *Palko*. It is a well-reasoned opinion, logical and deferential to state policy choices.

In his dissent, Black set forth his view of "total incorporation" of the first eight amendments by the Fourteenth. Just as the Bill of Rights applied objective standards to the behavior of the federal government, so its application to the states would provide equally ascertainable criteria by which to judge state action. He dismissed *Twining* as the first and only decision of the Court to hold that states "were free, notwithstanding the Fifth and Fourteenth Amendments, to extort evidence from one accused of a crime," and *Twining* should not be reaffirmed.

In a lengthy appendix, Black presented the historical evidence he had assembled to support his position, an essay that most scholars have found less than convincing. As might be expected from a former senator, he relied almost entirely on the congressional history of the Fourteenth Amendment, the debates and concerns expressed in the House and the Senate during the drafting. But amending the Constitution requires ratification by the states, and Black neglected to look at the debates there, nor at the abolitionist antecedents. As one of his biographers noted, "Black's was an advocate's history: he proved too much and ignored or swept away all doubtful evidence."

What is most interesting in Black's rationale is that it resembled Frankfurter's own views on limiting judicial power. Black rejected Cardozo's criteria as too vague because phrases like "civilized decency" and "fundamental liberty and justice" could be interpreted by judges to mean many things. This "natural law" theory gave judges far too much power, much more than the Framers of the Constitution had envisioned. The only way to avoid this abuse of judicial power would be to carry out the original intent of the framers of the Fourteenth Amendment and apply all of the protections of the Bill of Rights to the states.

Frankfurter had already written a brief concurrence but now set to work to respond to Black. The results must surely rank as one of his most forceful and important opinions. In probably no other statement, either for the Court or in dissent, do we get such a clear exposition of Frankfurter's philosophy of judging, one that scholars have termed "process jurisprudence." Relying on his own historical research, Frankfurter denied that the framers of the Fourteenth Amendment had intended to subsume all of the Bill of Rights. He also responded to what he took as the most serious of Black's charges, that the vague criteria of *Palko* left judges too much discretion, and as a result protection of rights relied on the mercy of individual subjectivity. The real issue, he declared,

> is not whether an infraction of one of the specific provisions of the first eight Amendments is disclosed by the record. The relevant question is whether the criminal proceedings which resulted in conviction deprived the accused of the due process of law to which the United States Constitution entitled him. Judicial review of that guaranty of the Fourteenth Amendment inescapably imposes upon this Court an exercise of judgment upon the whole course of the proceedings in order to ascertain whether they offend those canons of decency and fairness which express the notions of justice of English-speaking peoples even toward those charged with the most heinous offenses. These standards of justice are not authoritatively formulated anywhere. . . . The fact that judges among themselves may differ whether in a particular case a trial offends accepted notions of justice is not disproof that general rather than idiosyncratic standards are applied. An important safeguard against such merely individual judgment is an alert deference to the judgment of the State court under review.

Frankfurter portrayed judging as a process removed from the fray of daily pressures. Protected in their sanctum, justices may engage in that process of discovery that will yield *the* right answer—not an objective, eternally fixed answer, but the right answer for the time—which they will then explain through "reasoned elaboration." He did not espouse a moral relativism but believed that judges in their decisions should reflect the advances that society has made so that the Due Process Clause means not fairness in terms of 1868 but fairness today. Courts thus help keep the Constitution contemporary, but they must do so cautiously, always following strict intellectual processes and always deferring to those who are in the thick of the battle—the state courts and legislatures—who must in turn be left free to reform their procedures according to their standards of fairness. If the judge adheres to certain methods and standards, it does not matter what the result will be in a particular case, because the process will assure ultimate fairness across the spectrum of cases. The *process,* not a particular *result,* is the desideratum of judging and will assure the public that judges are acting fairly and adhering to a common set of principles.

Yet can judging ever be quite this impersonal? Would scientific analysis really produce the right results? Holmes had declared that the prejudices of judges had as much if not more to do with determining the law than the logic of the syllogism. As Black asked, how did one objectively determine the "canons of decency and fairness" that everyone would accept? While one might say that due process is meaningful over a whole gamut of cases, individuals are on trial; individuals must cope with the criminal justice system; individuals must pay the penalties if found guilty; individuals suffer if deprived of their rights.

In total incorporation, Black offered a partial answer in that judges would no longer subjectively determine what rights met the "canons of decency and fairness." There were, however, still questions to answer. Even if one applied the Fourth Amendment to the states, for example, one still had to determine what constituted an "unreasonable search." But the basic rights, the ones enshrined in the Constitution, would be in force and not dependent upon whether a handful of appointed judges determined that they met the canon.

Neither approach is without merit, and neither is without flaw, and this made the ensuing dialogue more complex and far richer in nuance. If Frankfurter's method refused to face up to the fact that process jurisprudence involved subjective evaluation, it did have the virtue of recognizing an acceptable diversity in a federal system and acknowledging that one could have more than one model of a fair and workable system. Its open-ended approach to fairness also permitted judges—always exercising caution—to help keep basic constitutional guarantees current with the times.

Black's approach did do away with some but not all subjectivity, and debates over the reach of the exclusionary rule and expectations of privacy show that interpreting the "canons of decency and fairness" is an ongoing judicial function. Moreover, in many ways Black's rigid adherence to the text led to a cramped view of individual liberty. He would take an uncompromising stand that the First Amendment permitted no abridgment of speech, but since he could find no mention of privacy in the Constitution, he could not support the judicial claim that such a right existed.

Because Black and Frankfurter spoke in such loud and authoritative voices, commentators overlooked Frank Murphy's approach. Murphy filed a separate dissent in which he for the most part agreed with Black. He told Black he had found his essay "exciting reading," but, he said, "I think you go out of your way—as you always do—to strike down natural law." Murphy wanted to incorporate all of the Bill of Rights, as Black proposed, but he objected to what he saw as the rigidity in Black's approach. There were times when one had to be flexible, when a strict reading of the first eight amendments would not suffice to provide justice. In those instances, Frankfurter's use of due process would allow judges to secure justice. Murphy's reading of Black's opinion was not that wrong.

In the end, Murphy's approach prevailed. Although the Court has continued to use the Cardozo-Frankfurter approach of selective incorporation, since World War II nearly all of the first eight amendments have been applied to the states. (As of this writing, only the Third Amendment, prohibiting the quartering of troops, and the Seventh, guaranteeing jury trials in civil suits, have not been incorporated.) Black's approach proved too rigid, as Murphy had argued, and Frankfurter's notion of due process as fundamental fairness became a useful tool for judges confronting new and unusual situations.

Adamson did not resolve the issue but was merely the opening scene of an ongoing dialogue. Less than a year later, the Court heard a Michigan case in which a local judge had sat as a one-man grand jury, indicted the suspect, and then convicted him in a secret trial without giving the defendant any opportunity to defend himself. The Court almost unanimously condemned this travesty in *In re Oliver* (1948), and Justice Rutledge pointed out that much of the problem lay in the *Adamson* doctrine of allowing the states to experiment without hindrance. He declared that "so long as the Bill of Rights is regarded here as a strait jacket of Eighteenth Century procedures rather than a basic charter of personal liberty, like experimentation may be expected from the states."

Interestingly enough, in another Bill of Rights case a few years later, Black joined with Frankfurter to hold that the exclusionary rule did not apply to the states. The Court had begun to hold federal agents to a strict accountability under the Fourth Amendment when it imposed the exclusionary rule in *Weeks v. United States* (1914). The rule prohibited the use of evidence seized illegally, thus providing a simple preventive standard. As a result, the government, especially the Federal Bureau of Investigation, trained its officers in constitutionally acceptable procedures.

The Fourth Amendment, however, does not mention an exclusionary rule; in fact, it makes no mention of any means by which to enforce the ban against unreasonable or warrantless searches and seizures. Justice William Day, in his opinion for a unanimous Court, explicitly noted that the exclusionary rule applied only to federal agents, not to state or local police. Many states, such as New York, declined to adopt the exclusionary rule because, in Benjamin Cardozo's memorable phrase, it allowed the criminal "to go free because the constable has blundered."

In 1949, the Court heard the case of Dr. Julius Wolf, convicted for conspiring to perform abortions. The indictment was based partly on the list of patients contained in his appointment books, which police seized during a warrantless arrest. In conference, Frankfurter claimed, "I am nuts about [the Fourth Amendment], because there is [no] provision of the Constitution more important to be nuts about. Nothing more important in Bill of Rights than search and seizure." In his opinion for a 6–3 majority, Frankfurter, using the idea of selective incorporation, applied the Fourth Amendment to the states through the Fourteenth Amendment. Unreasonable searches and seizures on the part of state officials ran afoul of the Constitution because such searches violated the test for due process.

But if the core of the Fourth Amendment—the ban against unreasonable searches and seizures—now applied to the states, that did not mean that the methods used to enforce that right also applied. Even though the provision "calls for more alert enforcement by this Court," Frankfurter still saw the exclusionary rule, effective as it might be, as judge-made law, not part of the Fourth Amendment, and unnecessary to secure due process. States could, therefore, develop their own minimal standards. They could, it seemed clear, ignore the Fourth Amendment, even though it now supposedly applied to them, provided they did not act so unreasonably as to shock the conscience.

Black joined Frankfurter's opinion and wrote a brief concurrence. He repeated what he had said earlier about the full incorporation of the Fourth Amendment, but his literalness argued that there was nothing in the constitutional text about an exclusionary rule. He thought that protection ought to be had from overzealous state and local police just as much as from overzealous federal officials, but judges should not be adding their own glosses to the text.

Douglas, Murphy, and Rutledge dissented, and Douglas argued that even without judicial articulation of the exclusionary rule, it existed implicitly in the Fourth Amendment by a simple commonsense reading: if the amendment protected against search and seizure without an appropriate warrant, then it could only do so by making any evidence seized—even incontestably reliable evidence—inadmissible. Murphy, joined by Rutledge, agreed, that "the conclusion is inescapable that but one remedy exists to deter violations of the search and seizure clause. That is the rule which excludes illegally obtained evidence." The voice of the dissenters eventually prevailed, and a dozen years later the Warren Court explicitly overruled *Wolf* in *Mapp v. Ohio*.

Police came to the home of Dollree Mapp in Cleveland, claiming they had information that a person wanted in connection with a bombing was hiding in her house. She refused to let them in without a warrant, and three hours later police officers forced open a door and waved a piece of paper they claimed was a warrant, which they refused to let her read. She grabbed the paper and "placed it . . . in her bosom," and in the ensuing scuffle police manhandled and handcuffed her for, as Justice Clark noted in the Court's opinion, resisting the policemen's "official rescue of the 'warrant' from her person." After subduing her, the police searched the house and found a cache of pornographic items in a trunk in the basement. She claimed the trunk belonged not to her but to a former tenant, for whom she was storing it.

The state courts conceded there had probably never been a warrant, but the prosecution correctly claimed that under existing law it could use evidence obtained by a warrantless and unreasonable search. On appeal, an amicus brief from the American Civil Liberties Union suggested that the case offered an opportunity to ask whether the Fourteenth Amendment applied all of the Fourth Amendment to the states, and if so, did that mean it also applied the exclusionary rule? Five justices seized on the idea, and although neither Ohio nor Mapp's lawyer had briefed or argued the exclusionary rule, the Court overruled *Wolf* and applied all of the Fourth Amendment protections to the states and with them the exclusionary rule. The majority essentially adopted Justice Day's reasoning in *Weeks* that the rule provided the only means to enforce the Fourth Amendment.

Justice Black said that while at the time of *Wolf* he had seen no justification for the exclusionary rule, recent cases coming to the Court dealing with both the Fourth and the Fifth Amendments had convinced him that "a constitutional basis . . . not only justified but actually requires the exclusionary rule." Justice Douglas joined the Court's opinion but in his concurrence sought to show how difficult it would be to enforce the Fourth Amendment by means other than the exclusionary rule. Harlan, joined by Frankfurter and Whittaker, dissented, believing that the *Wolf* ruling should not have been overruled. In words that surely appealed to

.ter, Harlan wrote, "The Court, in my opinion, has forgotten the ⱴf judicial restraint."

ᴇʟᴀᴛᴇᴅ ᴛᴏ ᴛʜᴇ ᴅᴇʙᴀᴛᴇ over incorporation was that over due process. Here the key question is not whether the framers of the Fourteenth Amendment intended to apply the Bill of Rights to the states but the meaning of the phrase itself, used in both the Fifth and the Fourteenth Amendments. Both Frankfurter and Black had rebelled against the conservative use of so-called substantive due process to protect property rights and defeat reform legislation. In regard to *procedural* due process, most often associated with criminal prosecutions, the two men also differed, and the debate between them and the dialogue it spawned shaped the modern dialogue.

Due process is critical in criminal procedure because if the police are not restrained by procedural safeguards, then people suspected or accused of crimes are at the mercy of the state. To prevent police abuse, the Bill of Rights spelled out restrictions on the national government; one did not have to overtly incorporate those protections, Frankfurter believed, because the Fourteenth Amendment's Due Process Clause by itself governed state police practices. Relying on Cardozo's *Palko* opinion, Frankfurter spoke often of "those canons of decency and fairness which express the notions of justice of English-speaking peoples even toward those charged with the most heinous offenses." The courts should not tolerate police tactics that "offend the community's sense of fair play and decency" or conduct that "shocks the conscience."

Due process, then, equated with fundamental fairness, but one can argue that fairness, like beauty, may be in the eye of the beholder, and that is what upset Hugo Black. If judges had the discretion to determine fairness on the basis of what shocked them, then due process would vary from judge to judge and court to court. The guarantees of the Constitution had to be absolute, not dependent upon any one judge's notions of fairness. For Frankfurter, the Due Process Clause by itself provided a sufficient limit on state abuses. Judges "knew" what was fundamentally fair and what was not and had the power and the duty to affirm fairness and denounce practices that offended fairness.

But as Frankfurter knew, not everyone, not even all judges, defined "fairness" in precisely the same way, and so within rather broad parameters he stood ready to defer to state legislatures in their determination of proper procedure. The Fourteenth Amendment, he argued in one dissent, should not be applied "so as to turn this Court into a tribunal for revision of criminal convictions in the State courts." Due process did not restrict the states "beyond the narrow limits of imposing upon them standards of decency deeply felt and widely recognized in Anglo-American jurisdictions." The problem with this approach is that it had few if any objective standards. And by the time he said this in 1953, enough cases, especially ones from southern states where the defendants were black, showed that the Anglo-American standards he lauded were notoriously absent.

The problem, as Black pointed out, is that the rigorous analysis Frankfurter called for required some objective criteria, and as Frankfurter admitted in his opinion, "these standards of justice are not authoritatively formulated anywhere." Is there a scientific means of determining what society, or even a large part of it, considers civilized behavior? Looking at the not too distant past, we cannot but be shocked at the large number of what we would consider petty crimes that could be punished by death in England, or the tortures routinely applied to suspected "enemies of the state," or the inanity of imprisonment for debt. At what point did society determine that such punishment violated civilized standards?

To take one example, Frankfurter personally opposed the death penalty, and yet in a 1947 case he exercised the restraint he considered an essential limit on judicial interpretation of due process. Willie Francis, a young black man, had been convicted of murder and sentenced to death in Louisiana. He had been strapped into the electric chair, the switch had been closed, and the device malfunctioned. Francis then sued to block Louisiana from trying again, on grounds that a second attempt would violate due process. Although little of the debate appears in the opinions, the question of whether a second trip to the chair would violate the Eighth Amendment also implicated important questions of federalism—should the Court intervene in state criminal justice processes?—as well as incorporation, and what, if any, constitutional provision applied.

The Court voted 5–4 to send Francis back to the electric chair (Reed wrote the majority opinion, joined by Vinson, Black, Frankfurter, and Jackson). In conference Frankfurter declared that the state's actions, while hardly defensible, did not shock his conscience. To Harold Burton, who prepared a powerful dissent, Frankfurter wrote an anguished letter noting his opposition to the death penalty and explaining why he could not join the dissent:

> I am prevented from doing so only by the disciplined thinking of a lifetime regarding the duty of the Court. . . . Holmes used to

express it by saying he would not strike down state action unless the action of the state made him "puke." . . . And that being so, I cannot say it so shocks the accepted, prevailing standards of fairness not to allow the state to electrocute. . . . And when I have that much doubt I must, according to my view of the Court's duty, give the state the benefit of the doubt and let the state action prevail.

Although voting with the majority, Frankfurter wrote separately after Reed made several concessions to Black regarding the applicability of Fifth and Eighth Amendment standards to the state. Moreover, Burton's dissent rested primarily on due process grounds, and Frankfurter found it awkward that it used some of the same criteria he had been proposing. He began by stating that when four members of the Court find that a state has denied due process, "it seems to me important to be explicit regarding the criteria" to be used, especially when a life is at stake. He implied he did not approve of Louisiana's actions, but "I would be enforcing my private view rather than the consensus of society's opinion, which for purposes of due process, is the standard enjoined by the Court."

The noted political scientist and Court scholar Herman Pritchett found Frankfurter's entire due process rationale in this case untenable. Frankfurter claimed to rely on society's consensus. "But how did he know what the consensus of opinion was on a subject that had never risen before?" Pritchett went on, "Instead of the result at which he arrived, could he not have assumed with equal validity that his own personal aversion at sending this man on a second trip to the electric chair was what any normally sensitive human being would have felt?"

A few weeks later, Frankfurter again cast the fifth and deciding vote in a capital punishment case, but this time to overturn the conviction. A fifteen-year-old black youth had confessed to murder after police had subjected him to hours of intense interrogation without allowing him to see a lawyer, friends, or even family. Douglas wrote an opinion joined by Black, Murphy, and Rutledge, in which he cited several cases leading to the conclusion that "the Fourteenth Amendment prohibits the police from using the private, secret custody of either man or child as a device for wringing confessions from them."

Although Frankfurter voted to reverse the conviction, he objected to Douglas's use of due process as something that was developed through a series of cases and could then be automatically applied. Just because the Court had acted consistently in prior cases with similar fact situations, it could not do so in each new case. "If the rationale of those cases ruled this, we would dispose of it *per curiam* with the mere citation of the cases. [But] they do not rule it." He went on sanctimoniously in tones of congratulatory self-righteousness: "Humility in this context means an alert self-scrutiny so as to avoid infusing into the vagueness of a Constitutional command one's merely private notions. Like other mortals, judges, though unaware, may be in the grip of prepossessions. The only way to relax such a grip, the only way to avoid finding in the Constitution the personal bias one has placed in it, is to explore the influences that have shaped one's unanalyzed views in order to lay bare prepossessions."

One seeks in vain in these two concurrences any hint of an objective standard by which to make the appropriate judgment. If Frankfurter found Black's reliance on the protections of the first eight amendments too rigid, Black was absolutely correct in that Frankfurter's due process jurisprudence essentially left it up to what the judge considered appropriate. Frankfurter's nonsense, and there is no other word for it, that by rigorous training he had rid himself of all bias, is a claim that few judges could or would make. If nothing else, the Legal Realists of the 1920s had taught that judges' personal views played an important role in the decision process.

Certainly Frankfurter's due process jurisprudence combined with judicial restraint made it far more likely that he would defer to state policy even if, as in the Willie Francis case, he found it abhorrent. Black's insistence on incorporating the Bill of Rights might have been, as some critics have charged, too rigid. In the end, the Court adopted an amalgam of the two philosophies. It incorporated, one by one, nearly all of the provisions in the first eight amendments, yet in those cases where these guarantees did not provide clear guidance (a position Black refused to recognize), the justices employed a case-by-case, fact-specific due process analysis. It is a very workable process, and it grew out of the Black-Frankfurter dialogue in the 1940s and 1950s.

ONE OTHER AREA of dialogue to examine is that of speech where Black and Frankfurter had very differing views. When the two men went on the Court in the late 1930s, the dominant test for speech regulation remained Holmes's clear and present danger test (discussed in chapter 6), although Brandeis's *Whitney* opinion pointed the way toward a far more speech-protective doctrine. The case that epitomized their differences proved to be one of the most controversial decisions of the Vinson Court, *Dennis v. United States* (1951).

In *Palko,* Justice Cardozo had called the protections of the First

Amendment "the matrix, the indispensable condition, of nearly every other form of freedom." Hugo Black agreed with this, and he, and to a lesser extent Douglas, began to develop a jurisprudence that viewed the First Amendment, particularly the Speech Clause, as occupying a "preferred" position among constitutionally protected rights. They also argued for an "absolutist" interpretation of the First Amendment's prohibition against the abridgment of speech. The Speech Clause, in their view, barred all forms of governmental restriction on speech, so "there was no place in the regime of the First Amendment for any 'clear and present danger' test." The reason, as Black explained elsewhere, was that the test "can be used to justify the punishment of advocacy." Clear and present danger can only function as a balancing test, and rights protected under the First Amendment cannot be balanced. Thus it had become "the most dangerous of the tests developed by the justices of the Court."

For Frankfurter, the evaluation and balancing implicit in the clear and present danger test fit perfectly with his conception of the judicial function. Just as in due process cases, by applying rigorous tools of analysis and clearheadedly evaluating the circumstances, judges would be able to say with reasonable certainty when a clear and present danger existed and warranted state action and when it did not. In this view, explicating First Amendment issues differed not at all from any other constitutional question, and he rejected the view that First Amendment rights held a "preferred" position, requiring an absolutist interpretation of the ban against infringing free speech.

Douglas claimed that Frankfurter saw the First Amendment not as a protection against state regulation of speech but as an invitation to limit speech, with "the constitutional mandate being construed as only a constitutional admonition for moderation." There is a great deal of truth to this charge, and one can see it in a letter Frankfurter wrote to his old friend and Cambridge neighbor the great Harvard historian Samuel Eliot Morison, who had questioned the extent to which the First Amendment protected speech. Frankfurter recalled the time when he had led the fight to free Sacco and Vanzetti in the 1920s:

> Whether the Commonwealth of Massachusetts, through its appropriate organ, should have put Sedgwick and me in durance vile for The Atlantic article on the Sacco-Vanzetti case is one thing; whether Massachusetts would have been forbidden to do so by the Constitution of the United States quite another.
>
> The main function of law is drawing lines. Should an American state really be denied those standards and practices of judicial

administration which are commonplaces of an England which is more alert to civil liberty even during time of war than we are as a matter of national habit in time of peace.

Black and Douglas are fairly consistent in their speech decisions, nearly always coming down on allowing the speech. Even when the Court decided against restrictions, they would often enter concurrences indicating their belief in the absolute protection offered by the First Amendment. Frankfurter's opinions are more ambiguous. In one of his first opinions involving speech, Frankfurter wrote for a 6–3 Court upholding an injunction against peaceful picketing, even though one of his mentors, Louis Brandeis, had held picketing protected as a form of speech. Frankfurter not only believed in deference to state legislatures but also urged courts not to second-guess the officials—police, prosecutors, judges, and juries—who had been on the scene; the Court should defer to the state court's knowledge of local conditions rather than impose an "abstract or doctrinaire" interpretation of the Fourteenth Amendment. Black, joined by Douglas, dissented on the grounds that the Illinois injunction was far too sweeping. Reed's dissent, however, pointed the way, noting that one should not allow the fear of disorder to limit speech; rather, the answer lay in keeping the peace and not penalizing speech.

In all of these speech cases, even while repeatedly declaring that the Court should defer to state policy decisions, Frankfurter also warned the states that if they went too far, then "while this Court sits," it would step in to halt abuses. But what did "too far" mean? What constituted an "abuse"? None of these opinions provided the slightest shred of an objective standard that could be used either by the legislatures or by lower courts hearing challenges to state laws. Surely Black was right in charging that here as elsewhere Frankfurter would leave it to judges to make the call on defining civilized behavior and abuses. Although as overly rigid as Frankfurter was overly flexible, the Black standard gave legislatures and courts a much clearer notion of what the Speech Clause meant. Out of the dialogue between these two positions, a First Amendment jurisprudence would later emerge. But at the time, the Vinson Court proved unable to articulate a clear standard for the protection of speech, and this in part explains the train wreck of the *Dennis* case.

THE BACKGROUND for the case is the great Red Scare of the late 1940s and early 1950s. Communism certainly posed a danger to the United States, as one could plainly see in the arrests and trials of Julius and Ethel Rosenberg, Judith Coplon, Klaus Fuchs, and others as spies. But with the exception of Alger Hiss (who was convicted for perjury, not spying), the House Un-American Activities Committee (HUAC) contributed nothing to the exposure of espionage or subversion. The Federal Bureau of Investigation, not HUAC, uncovered the major post-war spy rings. The committee, and then Senator Joseph McCarthy, kept repeating undocumented charges that communists had infiltrated government and society and demanded that Truman "do something."

In response to this pressure, Truman issued Executive Order 9835 in March 1947, instituting the Federal Loyalty-Security Program. The attorney general would compile a list of subversive organizations, defined as "totalitarian, Fascist, Communist or subversive . . . or approving the commission of acts of force or violence to deny to others their constitutional rights." Membership in any group on the attorney general's list by itself constituted "reasonable doubt" as to an employee's loyalty and could be grounds for dismissal. The massive investigation of federal workers that followed included the collection of a great deal of unverified information from numerous sources, which could be the basis for an individual's dismissal as a security risk. In the end, the Justice Department named 82 organizations, and although the list carried a disclaimer that the government of the United States did not believe in "guilt by association," right-wing groups and private employers often considered membership in any one of the proscribed organizations evidence of disloyalty. The House Un-American Activities Committee condemned the attorney general's list as wholly inadequate and issued its own report, naming 624 groups that were allegedly communistic or dedicated to the overthrow of the government.

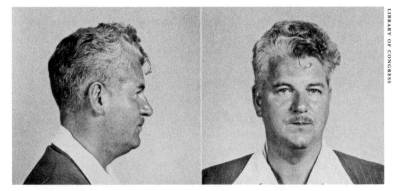

Eugene Dennis, one of the leaders of the American Communist Party

LIBRARY OF CONGRESS

Leaders of the Communist Party USA. TOP FROM LEFT, *Benjamin Davis,
William Z. Foster, and Eugene Dennis;* BOTTOM FROM LEFT,
John Williamson, Henry Winston, and Jacob Stachel

To further demonstrate its opposition to communism, the administration went after twelve leaders of the American Communist Party
under the 1940 Smith Act, which made it a crime to conspire to teach
or advocate the overthrow of the government by force or to belong to a
group advocating such overthrow. It thus departed drastically from the
classic civil liberties position of proscribing only those words or actions
posing a clear and present danger to society. Before 1948, the government had invoked the Smith Act only twice, against a Trotskyite faction
of a Teamsters union local in Minnesota and once against a group of
thirty-one alleged fascists. But as early as 1945, the FBI had begun com-
piling information on the Communist Party; its dossier reached over
eighteen hundred pages within two years. Under pressure from HUAC,
Attorney General Tom Clark finally initiated prosecution. In July 1948,
a federal grand jury returned indictments against twelve national leaders; because of ill health, the case of one of the communist officials was
severed from the others.

.d not go into the travesty, or farce as some would have it, of the
ᴐnth trial of the other eleven—the "Battle of Foley Square"—that
ᴌ in January 1949. Suffice it to say that both the government and
defense turned it into a circus, a process aided by the heavy-handed
ᴌlings of Judge Harold Medina, who then imposed contempt citations
on the five lawyers who represented the defendants.

In *Sacher v. United States* (1952), a majority of the Supreme Court,
speaking through Justice Jackson, upheld the contempt conviction,
noting that the lawyers had violated professional decorum in the face of
repeated warnings from the bench. Justices Black, Douglas, and Frankfurter dissented. Black believed that given the behavior of both the
judge and the attorneys, due process entitled the lawyers to a trial, with
a jury, before another judge. Medina had called the lawyers "brazen,"
"mealy-mouthed," and "liars," and no one should be tried by a judge
who had so publicly attacked them.

Frankfurter entered a separate opinion that alone dealt with the real
issue. It was true that the lawyers had been abusive, but "the contempt
of the lawyers had its reflex in the judge," and in a long appendix Frankfurter laid out a bill of particulars against Medina's conduct of the trial,
a conduct, he charged, that made him totally unfit to pass on the lawyers' contempt. There is no question that Frankfurter, who valued due
process and the rule of law, found the whole trial as handled by Medina
to have been a perversion of all he held noble in the law.

By the time the lawyers' appeal had reached the high court, that of
their clients had already been decided. The eleven defendants claimed
that the government had not proven that either their words or their
deeds met the clear and present danger test. They had good reason to
believe they could win on this argument, because the Supreme Court
had used it frequently in the 1940s to strike down a variety of restrictions on various forms of expression. There had, however, been growing
criticism of that standard from a number of sources. Strict advocates of
free speech protested the "balancing" of speech against other, and supposedly lesser, values. On the other hand, some critics believed that the
test restricted the government too much and prevented it from taking
the necessary measures to protect against subversion. A middle position condemned clear and present danger as oversimplified, because the
whole problem of freedom and order required the consideration of many
other variables.

The convicted communists certainly hoped for victory in the first level
of appeal, to the Court of Appeals for the Second Circuit, where Judge
Learned Hand presided. Hand had wrestled with the problem of free

speech and its relationship to social order since World War I. Despite his skepticism that substantive constitutional rights could be enforced by courts, he had tried to articulate judicial standards for speech cases and had won a reputation as a defender of speech because of his opinion as a district court judge in the 1917 *Masses* case. Hand had displayed considerable solicitude for speech in his opinion and would have allowed all but speech that directly incited unlawful action.

Now, as chief judge of the Second Circuit, he heard the initial appeal of the Smith Act defendants in 1950, and he tried to distinguish their situation from former cases, such as *Gitlow v. New York* (1925), which dealt primarily with verbal protests against some governmental activity. "It is one thing to say that the public interest in keeping streets clean, or in keeping a register of union leaders, or in requiring solicitors to take out licenses, will not justify interference with freedom of utterance," he wrote, upholding the convictions. "It is quite another matter to say that an organized effort to inculcate the duty of revolution may not be repressed." Although some of Hand's defenders have argued to the contrary, it seems inescapable that Hand had retreated from his original speech-protective stance in *Masses* and even to have diluted the speech-protective aspects of Holmes's clear and present danger test. Because of the high regard that several members of the high court had for Hand, his opinion would play an important role in their decision.

For all that we are now aware of how important unfettered speech is in a free society, we need to keep in mind that the Supreme Court at the time of *Dennis* had relatively little Speech Clause jurisprudence, aside from the clear and present danger test developed by Holmes and Brandeis in the 1920s. (The full implications of Brandeis's opinion in *Whitney v. California* would not be recognized and developed until the Warren era.) But Holmes's famous aphorism about falsely shouting fire in a theater is not a very useful analytical tool to determine when a danger is real, and if real, when it is proximate, and if proximate, if it is of the magnitude that justifies state intervention.

In addition, the members of the Court were well aware of the anticommunist hysteria sweeping the country and were not immune to it, as just a few years earlier the Court had given in to the anti-Japanese sentiment on the West Coast. Justice William J. Brennan Jr. (who served on the Court during the latter part of the Red Scare) observed in 1987 that the country "has a long history of failing to preserve civil liberties when it perceived its national security threatened." After the security crisis ended, "the United States has remorsefully realized that the abrogation of civil liberties was unnecessary. But it has proven unable to prevent itself from repeating the error when the next crisis came along." The Court, for the most part, has been as guilty as the country of this practice. As William O. Douglas noted, "The Court is not isolated from life. . . . Its members [share] the fears, anxieties, cravings and wishes of their neighbors. . . . The state of public opinion will often make the Court cautious when it should be bold." From the October 1949 through the October 1961 term, the Court issued decisions in roughly one hundred "communist" cases, and in the first half of this period it for the most part acquiesced in the repressive practices of the government's loyalty program and the prosecution of communist leaders.

The *Dennis* case is in many ways the final judicial validation of the government's loyalty and security program. Unions had been purged of known or admitted communists under section 9(h) of the Taft-Hartley Act, a policy sustained by the Court in *American Communications Association v. Douds* (1950), and large parts of the government program had been upheld in *Bailey v. Richardson* (1951). In *Dennis,* the Court pondered the constitutionality of the Smith Act as applied to leaders of the Communist Party. They had been indicted for (1) conspiracy to organize as an assembly of people who teach and advocate the overthrow and destruction of the government of the United States by force and violence, and (2) advocating and teaching the duty and necessity of overthrowing the government by force and violence.

The government never claimed that any revolutionary acts other than teaching and advocacy had taken place, and although "seditious conspiracy" remained a crime on the statute books, the Justice Department did not charge the eleven men with conspiring to overthrow the government. The government recognized that it would have been unable to show that the speech itself had raised a clear and present danger, so it resorted to the conspiracy charge. In essence, the men had been tried and convicted for conspiring to form a party to teach and advocate the overthrow of the government. The First Amendment, as articulated by Holmes and Brandeis, declared that the government had to wait for the evil to mature before acting, but the conspiracy doctrine "enables the government 'to move the clock back' so as to reach a prior stage of preparation to speak." Thus all the government had to show was that the speech *might* be dangerous, an easy task in the Cold War atmosphere, and the parties would then be guilty of conspiracy to bring about that evil, even if they had never actually spoken. By a vote of 6–2 (with the former attorney general Tom Clark not participating), the Court confirmed the convictions.

The central issue involved reconciling the constitutional guarantee of free speech with a conviction for no more than speaking and teaching. The trial judge, Harold Medina, had solved the problem by the bridge of intent and had instructed the jury that it could find the defendants guilty if it believed they intended to overthrow the government as soon as the opportunity arose. The highly respected Learned Hand had sustained the convictions on appeal, arguing that the courts had to balance a number of factors in applying a version of the clear and present danger test. "In each case they must ask whether the gravity of the 'evil,' discounted by its improbability, justified such invasion of free speech as to avoid the danger." Given recent events in Europe and Asia, as well as the memory of the Nazi rise to power in Germany, it seemed evident that Russia intended to conquer the world, and the American Communist Party, as a highly disciplined arm of the international movement, stood ready to act at a moment's notice. The conspiracy existed, and the government claimed that it could and should act to avert the evil.

The conference saw little acrimony among the brethren because, as Douglas noted, "those wanting to affirm had minds closed to argument or persuasion. The conference discussion was largely *pro forma*. It was the more amazing because of the drastic revision of the 'clear and present danger' test which affirmance requires." The task of modifying, or perhaps even abandoning, the Holmes-Brandeis test fell to the chief.

Fred Vinson closely followed Learned Hand's reasoning in his plurality opinion for the Court, which was joined in full only by Burton, Minton, and Reed. Although he paid lip service to the Holmes test, Vinson pointed out that communism posed a far different and more menacing danger than the anarchism and socialism Holmes and Brandeis had dealt with in the 1920s cases. Therefore, the clear and present danger test could not possibly mean that before the government could act, it had to wait "until the *putsch* is about to be executed, the plans have been laid and the signal is awaited." By this line of reasoning, the government could not only reach speech directly inciting unlawful action, or conspiring to promote such action, or teaching that such action should occur, but also penalize conspiring to organize a group that would teach that such action should occur. The justices might well have remembered Brandeis's powerful caution that clear heads had to prevail in (cold) wartime as well as peacetime and that suppression was impermissible while there was time for discussion.

Frankfurter realized that the modifications utilized by both Hand and Vinson to the clear and present danger test could produce harmful results, and not just to speech by communists, so he refused to join the plurality opinion. He did not object to affirming the convictions but disagreed strongly with Vinson's reasoning. Frankfurter personally detested the Smith Act and feared its heavy-handedness would silence not only those who sought to overthrow the government but anyone, no matter how loyal or honest, who criticized government policy. The justice, however, found himself in a bind. His devotion to judicial restraint, his refusal to accept Black's notion of a preferred position for speech, and his denial of a special role for the judiciary in protecting civil liberties left him very little room for maneuver. So he fell back on his due process position, namely, that the courts retained the right to review the application of laws that, while facially valid, might have been used in an unconstitutional manner.

The Court, Frankfurter declared, had done just that in the *Dennis* case, and he emphasized that the seriousness of the communist danger far outweighed the "puny anonymities" that Holmes had defended in *Abrams* or the "futile" advocacies in *Gitlow.* The Communist Party, with its extensive organization, membership, and discipline, constituted a serious threat to the nation. On the other hand, of course, one valued freedom of speech. But not "every type of speech occupies the same position on the scale of values," and "it is not for us to decide how we would adjust [this] clash of interests. . . . Congress has determined that the danger created by advocacy of overthrow justifies the ensuing restriction of freedom of speech." Frankfurter's long opinion, with an equally long appendix (forty-two pages in all), tried to show that the history of First Amendment jurisprudence led not to Black's view of absolutism but to a more pragmatic sense of allowing government to protect itself from evils. He charged Black with the sin of formalism: "such literalness treats the words of the Constitution as though they were found on a piece of outworn parchment" or as "barren words found in a dictionary."

Frankfurter knew that the American Communist Party posed no threat to the country and that its leaders were basically harmless, but he wanted to evade the question of whether they should be in jail. His opinion tried to uphold both the Smith Act and the convictions without endorsing a crude anticommunism. As Noah Feldman noted, "He wanted to believe he was following Holmes, who had patented the trick of saying that a given law was a bad one while simultaneously upholding it as constitutional. But there was a catch. In all his writings on the freedom of speech, Holmes had never said that courts should defer to the legislature. Neither had Brandeis." Frankfurter's *Dennis* concurrence, read in the light of history, smacks more of judicial abdication of responsibility than measured deference and restraint. It is an awkward opinion, because the long shadow of the Holmes and Brandeis dissents clearly called for a far different result and reasoning.

Had Rutledge and Murphy (both of whom died in 1949) still been on the Court, *Dennis* might have gone the other way because there would have been four solid votes against the government's position. Instead, conservatives now held those seats, and Jackson, after his experience at Nuremberg, looked on potential dictatorial groups with far less tolerance than he had displayed in his earlier First Amendment opinions. He dismissed the defendants' claim that their activities presented no clear and present danger. That formula was devised to combat the "anarchistic terrorism that plagued this country about the turn of the century, [and] which lags at least two generations behind Communist Party techniques."

Nuremberg certainly shaped Jackson's belief in the reality of the communist threat, but it also led him to what he saw as the cure, namely, put the leaders on trial for conspiracy. "The basic rationale of the law of conspiracy," he wrote, "is that a conspiracy may be an evil in itself, independently of any other evil it seeks to accomplish." At Nuremberg, Jackson had claimed that Nazism amounted to the greatest criminal conspiracy in history.

Black and Douglas tried in vain to tone down the Court's opinion, pointing out the fallacies in Vinson's reasoning and the fact that the dreaded communist plot was, in Black's words, a "ghost conspiracy." Every time Vinson raised the specter of a communist putsch, Black would respond, "The goblin'll get you!" Black lashed out at Vinson's draft in vicious marginal comments. The new formulation of clear and present danger, he noted, "permits courts to sustain anything." "In other words courts can approve suppression of free speech at will and despite 1st Amendment." "Now puts 'speech' and 'armed internal attack' in same category." "How can one explain without fear that he will be charged with advocating?" "Emergency, crisis, always the plea of those who would give dictatorial power to rulers." Next to Vinson's comment that the government should not have to wait until the putsch begins, Black scribbled "good semantic emotionalism and ghost conjuring." On a copy of Jackson's concurrence, his last comment summed up his view: "1st Amendment presumes that free speech will preserve, not destroy, the nation."

Although Douglas voted against the plurality opinion, it remained unclear to Black in the spring of 1951 whether Douglas would write. Given the mood of Congress, impeachment did not strike Black as fanciful if he dissented alone. He also worried whether Douglas still had presidential ambitions, and if so, whether that might dissuade him from writing. In the end, Douglas did write, and that made Black's decision easier. Even before the Court heard oral argument, he knew he would lose, and he now had to decide whether to write a long or a short dissent. By now, he believed, his basic disagreements with his colleagues were so well-known that expressing them at length would serve no useful purpose. "A reasonable legal opinion," he said, referring to the type of writing favored by Frankfurter and Jackson, "is not a persuasive document. That's why I put rhetoric in my opinions. The most effective dissents are short ones."

Black's dissent ran two pages, but it summed up his views quite clearly. The indictment for conspiracy amounted to a "virulent form of prior censorship of speech and press." Referring in particular to Frankfurter's concurrence, Black said he could not believe that the First Amendment "permits us to sustain laws suppressing freedom of speech and press on the basis of Congress' or our own notions of mere 'reasonableness.'" Such a doctrine "waters down the First Amendment to little more than an admonition to Congress." In *Dennis,* Black came closer than ever before to declaring the right to free speech as absolute:

> To the Founders of this Nation, however, the benefits derived from free expression were worth the risk. They embodied this philosophy in the First Amendment's command that "Congress shall make no law . . . abridging the freedom of speech, or of the press. . . ." I have always believed that the First Amendment is the keystone of our Government, that the freedoms it guarantees provide the best insurance against destruction of all freedom. At least as to speech in the realm of public matters, I believe that the "clear and present danger" test does not "mark the furthermost constitutional boundaries of protected expression" but does no more than recognize a minimum compulsion of the Bill of Rights.

The Smith Act prohibited speech, and the First Amendment did not allow that. As for Holmes's clear and present danger test, Black for the first time indicated his willingness to jettison it and to go further.

Black finished in what might have been a paraphrase of Brandeis's plea that such cases be considered with a cool head. "Public opinion being what it now is, few will protest the conviction of these Communist petitioners. There is hope, however, that in calmer times, when present pressures, passions, and fears subside, this or some later Court will restore the First Amendment liberties to the high preferred place where they belong in a free society."

Black and Douglas did not join each other's dissent, probably because Douglas at that point had not yet come around to Black's absolutist position, and Black disagreed when Douglas said that "the freedom to speak is not absolute." But Black could not have disagreed with anything else in Douglas's powerful dissent.

In *Dennis,* Douglas searched the voluminous record to find evidence— *any* evidence—that the defendants had engaged in actual acts of terror or seditious conduct that would be outside the ambit of First Amendment protection. He found none, only that they had attempted to teach Marxist-Leninist doctrine, and the First Amendment, he believed, fully protected instruction. Teaching, as he pointed out, might have been the reason communism had been rejected in the United States:

> Some nations less resilient than the United States, where illiteracy is high and where democratic traditions are only budding, might have to take drastic steps and jail these men for merely speaking their creed. But in America they are miserable merchants of unwanted ideas; their wares remain unsold. The fact that their ideas are abhorrent does not make them powerful. . . . The First Amendment reflects the philosophy of Jefferson "that it is time enough for the rightful purposes of civil government, for its officers to interfere when principles break into overt acts against peace and good public order."

Douglas drew a clear distinction between thought and speech, on the one hand, and action, on the other: the first enjoyed almost complete protection; the second did not. *Dennis* involved only speech, not "speech plus acts of sabotage or unlawful conduct. Not a single seditious act is charged in the indictment." He did not deny that communism posed a threat on the world stage, but the witch hunt launched against the U.S. Communist Party leaders constituted an even greater threat to American values. "The crime," he charged, "depends not on what is taught but on who the teacher is. That is to make freedom of speech turn not on what is said, but on the intent with which it is said. Once we start down that road we enter territory dangerous to the liberties of every citizen."

GIVEN THE COMPLEX as well as highly politicized issues that are coming to the Court (patenting of genes, gay marriage, civil rights), it is highly unlikely that we will ever see the type of institutional unity that prevailed from the time of John Marshall through the tenure of Charles Evans Hughes. Even with a greater sense of collegiality on the Court, there are several historical developments that most scholars believe mean we will continue to have three out of four cases decided by a split vote.

What happened that no one could foresee at the height of the constitutional fight over the New Deal is that within a very short time the agenda of the Court would change from concentration on economic rights to concerns over civil rights and civil liberties. Unlike Commerce Clause powers, there was no agreement among the Roosevelt justices over what the "right" position should be on these issues. On the one hand, Frankfurter, Reed, and Jackson took that aspect of legal liberalism inherited from Holmes and emphasized judicial restraint. For them, legislative enactments limiting speech should be assessed in the same light, and with the same criteria, as laws regulating the market. Over time, all of these men became more conservative in their views. Black, Douglas, Murphy, and Rutledge, on the other hand, followed the form of legal liberalism inherited from Brandeis, who used judicial restraint as a tool to champion progressive legal reforms. This group pushed constantly toward greater liberal activism, especially in terms of incorporating the Bill of Rights and protecting freedom of expression.

Even with their constant arguing and bad manners and petty fights, dialogue took place, and sometimes at a high intellectual level. While most scholars believe that the Frankfurter concurrence in *Adamson* is a better historical analysis than Black's dissent, all are agreed that they crystallized two important points of view on the question of incorporation and that this dialogue quickly spread into the legal academy. The dissents by Black in *Betts,* Stone in *Gobitis,* Jackson in *Korematsu,* Rutledge in *Yamashita,* and Douglas in *Dennis* all had effect, and the arguments they made are still studied and discussed. While Frankfurter was often the foil for these dissents, he posited a jurisprudential philosophy that, even while it might have been eclipsed in the short run, is still debated regarding just how deferential or how activist a justice should be. In terms of dialogue, one has to have two sides, and Frankfurter provided a strong defense of legal liberalism as he understood it, and for a while his conservatism managed to withstand the growing demand for the Court to be a more active advocate of rights. He did not oppose these rights. He had been an outspoken champion of civil rights and free speech before he became a judge, but unlike some of his peers he believed that as a judge he could not go so far as he had as a private citizen. That notion has also become part of the dialogue.

The legacy of the Stone and Vinson Courts—of great disunity and little institutional consensus—which seemed so terrible at the time to many, has now become the norm. It is clear, however, that a dialogue is still taking place; what is not clear is whether the dissent in the modern Court is as powerful an agent of dialogue as it was in the days of Holmes and Brandeis, especially in terms of conversing with the larger society.

BLACK IN *BETTS V. BRADY* (1942)

In May 1939, Smith Betts, an unemployed farmworker, found himself in the circuit court of Carroll County, Maryland, about an hour northwest of Baltimore. Forty-three years old and on relief, he was charged with the armed robbery of a country store on Christmas Eve 1938. When arraigned before Judge William H. Forsythe Jr., he said he could not hire an attorney and requested that the court appoint a lawyer to represent him. Judge Forsythe said this could not be done except in prosecutions for murder and rape.

No stranger to the court system—in 1935, he had been sentenced to three years in prison after a larceny conviction—Betts did not waive his right to counsel, pleaded not guilty, and asked to be tried without a jury. He gave the court a list of witnesses he wanted called in his behalf, cross-examined the state's witnesses, and examined his own in trying to show he had an alibi. Betts did not, however, take the stand in his own behalf, because then his prior conviction could have been entered into testimony. After hearing the evidence, the judge found Betts guilty and sentenced him to eight years in prison.

While serving his sentence, Betts filed a petition for habeas corpus with the chief judge of the Maryland Court of Appeals, Carroll T. Bond, claiming he had been denied the right of counsel guaranteed to him by the Fourteenth Amendment. The state's highest court recognized the importance of the issue and directed an attorney to help Betts with the appeal and at the hearing. Although Judge Bond had issued the writ, he nonetheless denied Betts relief and remanded him to prison. In his opinion, Bond declared that the trial had been simple and routine, and "in this case it must be said there was little for counsel to do on either side." Betts had been able "to take care of his own interests."

Subsequent examination of the case reveals that a lawyer could have made a great difference. Betts did not protest, as any good defense attorney would have, the police station identification of him without a lineup and with him wearing clothing similar to that described by the store attendants. Neither did he demand that the prosecution witnesses be kept out of the courtroom so they would not hear and repeat each other's testimony. It also appears that the police had shown the witnesses photographs of Betts as a convict. As Professor Yale Kamisar, a leading authority on criminal procedure noted, "The Betts record cries out for the talents of trained defense counsel."

Betts no doubt had heard of the decision in *Johnson v. Zerbst* (1938), in which the Supreme Court had ruled that defendants in federal courts had a right to counsel guaranteed by the Sixth Amendment. He might also have heard about an earlier ruling of the Court in the Scottsboro case, in which the Court had held that state defendants in capital cases were entitled to counsel, and if they could not afford it, the state would have to provide a lawyer. Despite these two cases, at the time states did not have to provide counsel for indigents in criminal cases other than those carrying the death penalty.

From there, and apparently with the approval of Judge Bond, Betts applied to the U.S. Supreme Court, which heard arguments on 13 and 14 April 1942. According to Justice Owen Roberts, who wrote the 6–3 majority opinion, the Court first had to decide two questions, one jurisdictional and the other to determine whether Betts had exhausted all of his state remedies before applying to the high court. The jurisdictional question centered on whether Judge Bond had acted, in issuing the writ, as a proper court, and the Court quickly concluded he had. Although Betts had not properly gone through the state procedures, the fact that Judge Bond as a member of the state's highest court had ruled on the matter allowed the case to come to the Supreme Court. Roberts then got to the real meat of the issue, "whether due process of law demands that in every criminal case, whatever the circumstances, a State must furnish counsel to an indigent defendant." The Sixth Amendment had been interpreted to mean that in all federal criminal cases counsel had to be supplied for indigent defendants. But "the Amendment lays down no rule for the conduct of the States," Roberts noted, so the question must be whether the constraint laid upon federal courts "expresses a rule so fundamental and essential to a fair trial, and so to due process of law, that it is made obligatory upon the States by the Fourteenth Amendment."

After reviewing the history of the Sixth Amendment as well as the history of the original thirteen colonies and state actions after the Constitution had been adopted, Roberts found that while a defendant had the right to an attorney, this did not mean that the state had to provide one in all cases. He quoted from Judge Bond's opinion: "Charges of small crimes tried before justices of the peace and capital charges tried in the higher courts would equally require the appointment of counsel. Presumably it would be argued that trials in the Traffic Court would require it." Furthermore, Roberts warned, if one interpreted the Fourteenth Amendment to protect property as well as life and liberty, "logic would require the furnishing of counsel in civil cases involving property."

In his conclusion, Roberts did leave the door slightly ajar. Due process, he declared, would prohibit "the conviction and incarceration of one whose trial is offensive to the common and fundamental ideas of fairness and right, and while want of counsel in a particular case may result in a conviction lacking in such fundamental fairness, we cannot say that the Amendment embodies an inexorable command that no trial for any offense, or in any court, can be fairly conducted and justice accorded a defendant who is not represented by counsel." Although it is doubtful that Roberts recognized it at the time, this statement practically invited a flood of appeals from indigents who had been denied counsel, with claims that there had been unusual circumstances that could be construed as "offensive to fundamental ideas of fairness."

Justice Hugo Black dissented, joined by the two most liberal members of the Court, William O. Douglas and Frank Murphy. Black's law practice in Birmingham had included a fair amount of criminal work; he had also served as a police court judge for two years and a county solicitor for three and was the only member of the Court at that time with actual trial experience in criminal cases. Black's first major opinion on the Court involved the Sixth Amendment, *Johnson v. Zerbst*. Two marines, on leave, had been charged with the felony offense of possessing and passing counterfeit $20 bills. They had pleaded not guilty and had been tried and convicted without the assistance of counsel. The Court overturned the conviction, and Black wrote, "The Sixth Amendment stands as a constant admonition that if the constitutional safeguards it provides are lost, justice will not 'still be done.' It embodies a realistic recognition of the obvious truth that the average defendant does not have the professional legal skill to protect himself when brought before a tribunal with power to take his life or liberty, wherein the prosecution is presented by experienced and learned counsel. That which is simple, orderly and necessary to the lawyer, to the untrained layman may appear intricate, complex and mysterious."

Owen Roberts had joined this opinion, and despite Black's language that a fair trial could only be had with the representation of an attorney, Roberts nonetheless argued in *Betts* that the right to counsel did not, in Cardozo's words, constitute a fundamental right "of the very essence of a scheme of ordered liberty."

Black began his dissent in *Betts* by dismissing Roberts's assertion that if the Court granted Betts the right to counsel, then defendants in every type of case would have to be granted a lawyer. Rather, he suggested that just looking closely at the trial of Smith Betts would show that he had been denied the procedural protection guaranteed by the Fourteenth Amendment. The court below had found that Betts had "at least an ordinary amount of intelligence." To Black, it was clear from his examination of witnesses "that he was a man of little education."

Had the case come from federal court, there would have been no question that the conviction would have been reversed on the grounds that the defendant had been deprived of his right to counsel. "I believe that the Fourteenth Amendment made the Sixth applicable to the states." This view, however, had never been supported by a majority of the Court, nor had it been in the *Betts* decision, so he would not argue that today. Rather, Black believed that Betts's trial had not met the Court's prevailing view of what constituted due process, and therefore the conviction should be reversed.

Black then quoted from various Supreme Court opinions, including his own in *Zerbst,* as well as from a number of state court decisions to support his assertion that even "the intelligent and educated layman . . . lacks the skill and knowledge adequately to prepare his defense, even though he have a perfect one." Defendants in criminal trials, he concluded, needed a lawyer. "Any other practice seems to me to defeat the promise of our democratic society to provide equal justice under the law." He then appended a list of states that through either constitutional provision, statute, or judicial decision required that indigent defendants in noncapital as well as capital cases be provided with counsel on request.

CRITICISM BEGAN not long after the *Betts* decision came down. In a lengthy letter to *The New York Times,* Benjamin V. Cohen, the noted New Deal lawyer, and Erwin N. Griswold, then a professor and later dean of the Harvard Law School, harshly attacked the Roberts opinion. The decision comes at "a singularly inopportune time. Throughout the world men are fighting to be free from the fear of political trials and concentration camps. From this struggle men are hoping a bill of rights will emerge which will guarantee to all men certain fundamental rights." Most Americans, lawyers and laymen alike, would have thought prior to this decision that the right to counsel in "a serious criminal case was unquestionably a part of our own Bill of Rights." Although the *Journal* of the American Bar Association accepted the majority opinion as reasonable, most law reviews—the publications that Louis Brandeis believed should always be critiquing court decisions—condemned it. The *Columbia Law Review* picked up on Roberts's assertion that the circumstances in some cases might warrant counsel. "It would seem that a supposed constitutional guaranty should not be made dependent on distinctions that are at best difficult of ascertainment and often tenuous." The criticism continued when it became unclear just what criteria—other than if the defendant had been charged with a capital crime—the Court employed.

In the early cases that followed, the Court relied on *Betts* and denied that any special circumstances had been present. In 1947, Felix Frankfurter asserted that the Court in all noncapital cases would follow the rule of *Betts* except when special circumstances could be shown. "It does not militate against respect for the deeply rooted systems of criminal justice in the states," he wrote, that "such an abrupt innovation as recognition of the constitutional claim [to assistance of counsel] would furnish opportunities hitherto uncontemplated for opening wide the prison doors of the land." Frankfurter here expressed a fear, also held by some of the other justices, that if the Court overruled *Betts,* and the ruling were made retroactive, thousands of prisoners who had not been given an attorney would demand either release or retrial. But even at this point, four members of the Court dissented—Black, Douglas, Murphy, and Rutledge—and had the latter two not died in 1949 and been replaced with more conservative justices, the life span of *Betts* might have been much shorter. Black responded to Frankfurter's worry: "I do not believe that such a reason is even relevant to a determination that we should decline to enforce the Bill of Rights."

But the *Betts* ruling, and Black's continuing dissents, kept troubling the members of the Court. In 1944, the Court adopted Rule 44 of the Federal Rules of Criminal Procedure, which stated unequivocally that "if the defendant appears in court without counsel, the court shall advise him of his right to counsel to represent him at every stage of the proceeding." This rule, however, only applied in federal courts; the vast majority of criminal prosecutions took place in the states, and there counsel could only be provided in special circumstances.

What, however, constituted these special circumstances? Justice Stanley Reed tried to answer this question in 1948: "Where the gravity of the crime and other factors—such as the age and education of the defendant, the conduct of the court or prosecuting officials, and the complicated nature of the offense charged, and the possible defenses thereto—render criminal proceedings without counsel so apt to result in injustice as to be fundamentally unfair . . . the accused must have legal assistance." In other words, if the defendant was so legally illiterate or mentally impaired as not to comprehend the charges, or if the judge and prosecutors prejudicially abused their authority, or if the nature of the law was very complex, then counsel had to be provided.

The problem, of course, is that Reed's criteria, except at the self-evident extremes, were remarkably subjective and relied upon judicial interpretation as to whether these conditions actually existed in a particular trial. According to one study of state practices, courts "rarely if ever bothered to find out whether the circumstances were 'special.' " This offended Black as well, who throughout his career opposed judges' making such evaluations. The law should be clear and not subject to whether one judge thought conditions warranted a lawyer while another, looking at the same facts, did not.

What Black objected to could be seen in two cases decided the same day, 14 June 1948. Frank Gryger claimed that he had been given a life sentence because the trial judge thought that state law required him to do so. Gryger had no attorney who could have disputed this and shown the judge that another sentence was possible under Pennsylvania law. In the other case, also from Pennsylvania, Townsend said the judge in his case had imposed a sentence on the mistaken belief that he had been convicted on two prior charges, when in fact he had been acquitted. In the two majority opinions, both written by Justice Robert Jackson, the Court by a 5–4 vote affirmed Gryger's conviction but by a 6–3 vote reversed that of Townsend. Nothing in the majority opinions indicates why a majority of the Court found that due process had been violated in one case but not the other. In the *Gryger* decision, Justice Wiley Rutledge dissented, joined by Black, Douglas, and Murphy, the same trio that had dissented in *Betts.* Little wonder that one academic critic could write that the cases decided under *Betts* "are distinguished neither by the consistency of their rules nor by the cogency of their argument."

Cases kept coming to the Supreme Court with the claim that one of the special circumstances delineated in Justice Reed's opinion applied to them. At the same time, one state after another enacted legislation to provide counsel to indigents in all felony cases. Academic criticism also continued, and somehow, according to Anthony Lewis, the Court began to retreat from *Betts* "almost invisibly, paying it lip service but never really allowing it to stand in the way of desired results." In 1950, the Court affirmed—for the last time—a state court conviction in which the defendant had been refused counsel. From 1950 on, whenever a case involved denial of an attorney, the Court found "special circumstances" and reversed the conviction.

In all of these cases, Justice Black's dissent, even when not cited, hovered over the decisions like Banquo's ghost, reminding the justices that the right to counsel was fundamental in ensuring a fair trial and that the most straightforward way to ensure fairness was by a rule applied to all cases: indigent defendants had to have a lawyer.

Starting in 1960, it seemed as if the justices were paying attention. In that year, Justice Potter Stewart found counsel required, not due to a special circumstance, but on constitutional grounds. Midway through a trial of two men in North Carolina, with no counsel appointed, one of the defendants struck a bargain and changed his plea to guilty, a fact that could easily have prejudiced the jury against the other defendant. Justice Clark dissented that the Court's opinion, "without so much as mentioning *Betts v. Brady,* cuts serious inroads into that holding." It would be the last dissent in a denial of counsel case before the Court changed its mind completely.

BY THE EARLY 1960S, the conditions seemed ripe to tackle *Betts* head-on. Forty-five of the fifty states required that counsel be provided to indigents in felony cases; the other five were in the South and generally ignored *Betts.* In 1956, Black had managed to establish the right of an indigent defendant to an effective hearing on appeal by holding, for a closely divided Court, that a state must furnish a free transcript of the trial to a defendant in a noncapital case. He also began to work actively to ensure that when a pauper case came to the federal courts, one of his former clerks—who knew and agreed with his views on representation—would be assigned the case. Although none of these cases challenged *Betts* directly, Black wanted to attack it on the fringes until the day that a frontal assault would be possible.

In 1961, the Court reversed an assault conviction of Elijah McNeal because of the "complex and intricate legal questions" in his case that "were obviously beyond the ken of a layman." Justice Douglas, joined by Justice Brennan, concurred and called for the abandonment of *Betts,* which, he wrote, "is so at war with our concept of equal justice under law that it should be overruled." Shortly afterward, Brennan gave a lecture at New York University in which he emphasized what had been implied in the concurrence: that equal protection demanded assistance of counsel as much as did due process. He cited Black's opinion in *Griffin v. Illinois* (1956) that a state could not distinguish between rich and poor in allowing appeals. The denial of counsel to an indigent at the trial, Brennan averred, "seems almost to me to be an *a fortiori* case of the violation of the guarantee of equal protection of the laws."

By the beginning of the 1961 term, several members of the Court, including Felix Frankfurter, Black's archfoe through most of the 1940s and 1950s, seemed ready to overrule *Betts.* "I think I'm prepared," Frankfurter told William Brennan, "in view of the change of climate and of legislation to spell out my view of due process and overrule Betts and Brady." By this time, Chief Justice Warren had his clerks scouring the *in forma pauperis* petitions (those filed by indigent prisoners who did not have the money either to have a lawyer make the appeal or to pay the filing fees) to find the "right" case to overturn *Betts.* In his choice of that case, we can see another part of the constitutional dialogue—that between the Court and the public.

In 1962, the Court heard two cases in which the defendants claimed they had been denied due process because they had no attorneys. An illiterate man, Willard Carnley, had been convicted of incest and sexual assault upon a child, and given the evidence produced by the state, there was no question of his guilt. The witnesses against him included his thirteen-year-old daughter, his fifteen-year-old son, and another minor whom he had sexually assaulted. But he had not been given assistance of counsel at the trial. The Court could have overruled *Betts* here, but as Frankfurter explained, it was impossible to "imagine a worse case, a more unsavory case to overrule a long standing decision." Warren was eager to get rid of *Betts* but not with this defendant. So in an opinion by Brennan, the high court reversed, on the grounds that due process required assistance of counsel unless intelligently waived, one of the special circumstances tests from *Betts* and its progeny. Clearly the defendant lacked the intelligence to make that decision. Black concurred in the results but once again called upon the Court to make the Sixth Amendment applicable to the states.

In the other case, Bennie Will Meyes and William Douglas had been jointly tried and convicted in a California court for thirteen felonies. Under California law, they were entitled to a lawyer, and the court

appointed a public defender to represent them. Then Meyes did, as prosecutors like to call it, the "right thing"—admitted his guilt and ratted
out Douglas. At this point, the overworked and inexperienced public
defender was in over his head, but the trial court refused to appoint a
second lawyer so that each defendant was separately represented. Douglas claimed that he had in effect been deprived of a lawyer, because he
and Meyes now had competing interests. Again, the facts of this case
would have supported overturning *Betts,* because none of the usual special circumstances applied. But just as the justices did not want to make
a major criminal law decision in favor of an obviously guilty sex preda-
tor and child molester, neither did they want to do it for someone clearly
guilty of thirteen felonies. So they ordered the case held, because on the
morning of 8 January 1962 the clerk of the Court had accepted a large
envelope from Clarence Earl Gideon, then resident at the Florida State
Prison in Raiford.

THANKS TO ANTHONY LEWIS'S classic work—and the Henry Fonda
movie based on it—the public probably knows as much about Gideon's
case as it does about any of the Court's criminal procedure decisions.
A drifter, Gideon had been in and out of prison and had been arrested
on charges of breaking and entering a pool hall and stealing change, a
misdemeanor under Florida law. From the Warren Court's point of view,
he provided the ideal case. He was neither a child molester nor someone
convicted of thirteen felonies. He might have been innocent, but even
if guilty, his crime would not lead the critics of the Warren Court to
charge the justices with setting a vile and dangerous man free.

As is normal with pauper cases, the Court asked an attorney to represent the indigent in preparing a brief, and in oral argument and in
this case specifically asked both sides to argue whether *Betts* should be
reconsidered, that is, overruled. If one seeks a clue as to what the Court
wanted to do, then its appointment of Abe Fortas to represent Gideon
is as clear as anything. One of the most able lawyers in Washington,
Fortas could be depended upon to make a strong argument on Gideon's
behalf that depriving him of an attorney violated his rights under the
Sixth Amendment. Moreover, twenty states had filed amicus—friend
of the court—briefs urging the Court that *Betts* was "an anachronism
when it was handed down" and that it should be overruled; only two
states, both from the South, filed briefs supporting Florida. The Court
heard oral argument on 15 January 1963 and handed down its opinion
two months later, on 18 March. Aware of Hugo Black's long crusade to

incorporate the Sixth Amendment, Chief Justice Warren assigned the opinion to him.

After noting the facts of the case, Black observed that "the facts upon which Betts claimed he had been unconstitutionally denied the right to have counsel appointed to assist him are strikingly like the facts upon which Gideon here bases his federal constitutional claim." If judged by the *Betts* holding, Gideon's claim would have to be denied. "Upon full reconsideration we conclude that *Betts v. Brady* should be overruled."

No one could ever accuse Hugo Black of being unfocused, and his reasoning in *Gideon* is essentially the same as that of his dissent in the earlier case: the Fourteenth Amendment incorporates the guarantees of the Sixth and applies them to the states. *Betts* had been wrongly decided, and the time had long since come to be rid of it. "In deciding as it did," he wrote, the Court "made an abrupt break with its own well-considered precedents." He rehearsed all of the cases prior to *Betts* that supported this conclusion and quoted with approval Justice Sutherland's opinion in the Scottsboro case that "the right to be heard would be, in many cases, of little avail if it did not comprehend the right to be heard by counsel. . . . Without it, though he be not guilty, he faces the danger of conviction because he does not know how to establish his innocence." In returning to these older precedents, in *Gideon* the Court is doing nothing more than "restor[ing] constitutional principles established to achieve a fair system of justice."

Seven justices signed on to the opinion, including William O. Douglas, who entered a separate opinion briefly elaborating on the relationship between the Bill of Rights and section 1 of the Fourteenth Amendment. Justice Clark concurred in the result but based his decision on due process rather than right to counsel. John Harlan also concurred but did so both to protest that *Betts* was "entitled to a more respectful burial than has been accorded" and to emphasize that the majority opinion did not automatically extend every protection of the Bill of Rights to the states.

Following the ruling, the State of Florida retried Clarence Earl Gideon, but this time with the assistance of a lawyer the jury found him not guilty.

THERE IS NO QUESTION that Hugo Black's dissent in *Betts v. Brady* and his repeated objections in cases where the Court followed the *Betts* rule had a great deal to do with the result in *Gideon v. Wainwright*. One can see the dialogue taking place in the two decades between the decisions, not only within the Court, but in the states as well. By the early

1960s, only two members of the original *Betts* Court remained, Black and Douglas, but they had been joined by men like Earl Warren and William Brennan. Even Felix Frankfurter had come around, and shortly after the *Gideon* decision Black had visited the ailing Frankfurter to tell him about the conference votes and discussion. Black said he believed that Felix, true to his own view of due process, would have voted to reverse Gideon's conviction. Frankfurter said, "Of course I would."

More than simple personnel changes had taken place. With the advent of Earl Warren as chief justice and the Court's decision in *Brown v. Board of Education* in 1954, a major jurisprudential shift took place, one that had been building since the early 1940s. While the Court that heard *Betts* had been deferential to federalism and reluctant to interfere with state prerogatives, the justices who heard the segregation and apportionment cases were far more concerned with individual civil rights and liberties. The fact that Clarence Earl Gideon had not had a lawyer for his trial meant far more than the fact that Florida had never provided counsel except in capital cases.

In addition, the Court's experience in those two decades showed that the flexible, case-by-case evaluation that Owen Roberts had proposed, and the special circumstances described by Stanley Reed, did not work well. The criteria were so imprecise and so open to differing interpretations as to create chaos in the lower courts. In the 1950s, in the cases that came before them, the justices found in every instance that the accused had been the victim of "special circumstances" and needed counsel. And as Hugo Black kept reminding them, it would be far simpler to adopt the protection of the Sixth Amendment and apply it to the states. According to law professor Lucas Powe, "*Betts* was so out of step that had Fortas lost, then a retirement with his beloved violin would have been fitting. . . . Gideon could have argued *Gideon* and won 9–0."

For the most part, the reception of *Gideon* proved positive, in part because nearly all of the states had already adopted the rule, and so it made little difference to them. The five states that had not—Florida, North Carolina, South Carolina, Alabama, and Mississippi—quickly enacted laws to set up public defender offices. Even in these states, the reaction to *Gideon* was for the most part positive. The head of the Wake County Bar Association in North Carolina, R. Mayne Albright, said, "I think few lawyers would disagree with the principle enunciated by the Supreme Court. It was time we recognized the need for the defendant who is indigent to have a lawyer." Some people grumbled that the costs were prohibitive, especially to lawyers in private practice who had no choice when courts appointed them to serve as counsel to indigents. In some areas, legal aid and the public defender's offices were overwhelmed, but eventually the system reached equilibrium.

Interestingly, the justices carried on the dialogue with the public, something they had not done after either the segregation or the apportionment decisions. Justice Tom Clark called *Gideon* historic, a case that would "possibly have more physical impact on the administration of justice than any decided by the Court," and urged law schools to upgrade the study of criminal law. State and local bar associations also had a role to play, and Clark urged them to establish programs to make lawyers available to the courts for indigent cases. Chief Justice Warren told the Conference of Judicial Councils that *Gideon* would "amount almost to a revolution in some states," and judges had to make sure that the spirit of the Sixth Amendment was carried out. Whatever expenses the states incurred, said Warren, they would be more than repaid not only in fairer treatment of indigent defendants but also in criminal courts that would work more efficiently and effectively with lawyers' help.

For many people, as Barry Friedman concluded, "*Gideon* crystallized all that was good in the Warren Court's activism: equal justice for all, the furthering of national values against foot-dragging states; the Court acting because others would not." Without the Supreme Court, Clarence Earl Gideon said, "it might have happened sometime, but it wouldn't have happened in {Florida} soon."

One of his law clerks that term, now a law professor, A. E. Dick Howard, said that for Black "*Gideon* was real exuberance. The Judge knew he was summing up thirty years of cases, knitting up in this area. It gave him special pleasure." In many cases, the Court does not adopt the dissenting position for many years, usually long after the dissenter has left the bench. A few weeks after the decision came down, Hugo Black told a friend, "When *Betts v. Brady* was decided, I never thought I'd live to see it overruled."

CHAPTER 10

LOWER FEDERAL COURTS, THE STATES, AND FOREIGN TRIBUNALS

I always had a high regard for your Honor's judicial wisdom, but not any more. While I am not qualified to interpret legal excerpts, I did believe that what was sauce for the goose was good for the gander. It is shocking that one like you, who has read so many volumes of decisions, could have written as you did in People v. Shaw. *Thank God it was a dissent!*

— INMATE AT DANNEMORA STATE PRISON TO JUDGE STANLEY H. FULD, NEW YORK STATE COURT OF APPEALS

While our focus has naturally been on the U.S. Supreme Court, dissent plays an important, albeit different, role in the lower federal courts, while within their jurisdictions state supreme courts often follow a pattern similar to that of the high court. Overseas, the story is quite different, although in recent years dissent has become a feature in many courts that previously had handed down only a single opinion. In each of these areas, however, dissent is part of an important ongoing dialogue.

JUSTICE ROBERT JACKSON once said of the Supreme Court, "We are not final because we are infallible, but we are infallible because we are final." Decisions in lower federal courts, on the other hand, are neither infallible nor final, because all are subject to review by the high court.

Article III of the Constitution vests the judicial power of the United States "in one supreme Court, and in such inferior Courts as the Congress may from time to time ordain and establish." In the Judiciary Act of 1789, Congress created the Supreme Court as well as one district court in each state, and a court of appeals consisting of one member of the high court sitting with one or more district court judges. There are currently nearly seven hundred judges sitting in ninety-four federal judicial districts, which hear criminal and civil cases brought under federal law, as well as bankruptcy and so-called diversity suits, civil suits involving litigants from different states. These trials are the first stop in the process that may eventually bring an issue to the Supreme Court.

In 1891, Congress created a separate court of appeals for each judicial circuit. Today there are twelve judicial circuits, and all except that for the District of Columbia are composed of at least three states. In addition, the Court of Appeals for the Federal Circuit is a semi-specialized court that handles all appeals in patent cases as well as appeals from civil service personnel, veterans, and people with financial claims against the federal government. There are also courts of special jurisdiction—including the Court of Appeals for the Armed Forces, the Court of Federal Claims, the Court of International Trade, and the Foreign Intelligence Surveillance Court. With the exception of the last, which operates in secret, all federal court decisions are appealable. The jurisdiction for each court is established through a congressional statute.

In the district courts, an individual judge will preside over trials (either bench or jury) arising under federal criminal and civil laws, and they are not much different from trials conducted in a state court. If the constitutionality of a federal statute or administrative regulation is challenged, this will be the first forum in which it is heard, so district court judges may from time to time write an opinion on constitutional questions. Technically, all decisions of a district court may be appealed, but not all of them will be heard.

In the appeals courts, the senior judge assigns each case to a three-judge panel. The vast majority of these cases are decided unanimously, but there are dissents in a fair number of them. Following a decision, the losing party may appeal to have the case reheard *en banc,* that is, by all of the judges assigned to that court. This motion is rarely granted, and when it is, it indicates that some of the judges believe it might have been wrongly decided. While the panel usually confirms the original decision, in this instance there may be one or more dissents.

The losing party may now appeal to the Supreme Court, but the chances of getting review are slim. In the October 2012 term, the Court received thousands of petitions for certiorari but only heard and handed down decisions in 79 cases. One study of civil liberties cases in a five-year period during the Warren Court era showed that out of 649 cases heard in three courts of appeals, 252 were appealed to the Supreme Court, which granted cert in only 24. When William Rehnquist became chief justice, he set about cutting down the number of cases accepted, so in the last quarter century the high court has handed down roughly 75 written decisions a term, compared with 125 or more in previous years.

The vast majority of cases from the appeals courts are denied cert because the justices believe that they either have been correctly decided or raise no new federal issue. (Under the rule of four, four justices must vote to grant cert.) The high court will, however, act when there is an important issue that has been decided differently in separate circuits or when a lower court has found a federal statute unconstitutional, even if a majority of the justices believe the lower court decided correctly.

From this brief review, one can see that decisions in the lower federal courts are determinative in the vast majority of cases. Moreover, as two early scholars of the Court noted many years ago, the work of the Supreme Court "is largely predetermined by the jurisdictional ambit of the lower courts." It is in the appeals courts that we need to look to see how judges use dissent and how those dissents affect the law as well as the docket of the high court.

HIGHER COURTS, of course, occasionally reverse lower courts. When a court of appeals reverses a district court ruling, it may in turn find its decision overturned by the Supreme Court; this is a dialogue, with the high court having the last word. At the appeals court level, a dissent may serve somewhat different purposes from one by a member of the Supreme Court.

The power of reversing a district court ruling is critical in the oversight of the federal judiciary. Just as the Supreme Court rides herd, in a way, on the appeals courts, so too do they keep an eye on the district courts. The Supreme Court sets down the criteria by which the requirements of the Constitution, and especially of the Bill of Rights, shall be implemented. If a district court judge fails to follow that mandate, he or she will find that the court of appeals will reverse the decision. Conversely, should trial judges be faced with a factual situation in which the current rules do not seem applicable, they will try to determine what guidance can be found in prior decisions. If they get it right, the court of appeals, and ultimately the Supreme Court, will affirm; if not, then they will have to fashion another rule.

For all practical purposes, the decisions of the courts of appeals are final. Very few appeals court decisions are accepted for review, so a majority ruling, for example, in the Fifth Circuit, is binding upon all of the district courts within that circuit and also serves as a guiding precedent for the three-judge panels at the appeals level. To give one example, in 1996 the Court of Appeals for the Fifth Circuit handed down a decision in *Hopwood v. Texas,* ruling that the prestigious University of Texas Law School could not use admissions standards for minority students different from those it used for white applicants. The Supreme Court decided not to grant cert in this case, meaning that the *Hopwood* ruling applied to the three states in the district—Texas, Louisiana, and Mississippi—but nowhere else in the country. Not until 2003 did the high court accept an affirmative action case, and in *Grutter v. Bollinger* it held that the University of Michigan Law School could take race into account for purposes of diversity, providing that race was just one of several considerations.

Judge Richard Posner, a member of the Court of Appeals for the Seventh Circuit, has written about what he calls "dissent aversion" on the appeals court level and claims that—with the exception of Supreme Court justices—most judges do not like to dissent. Among the reasons he gives are caseload, because courts of appeals judges handle far more cases than do members of the higher court, and dislike of stirring up personal animosities that will fray collegiality. In addition, he says that because judges do not like dissents from their own majority opinions, they will refrain from dissenting from those of others. How true this may be is problematical, because Posner himself is a frequent dissenter, one whose vivid prose style has garnered considerable attention.

One goal that all dissenters on the appeals courts have in common is to secure review by the Supreme Court, in the hope that the high court will take their side. Frank M. Coffin, for many years a judge on the Court of Appeals for the First Circuit, notes that many of the cases that come before appellate panels are not easy. There are cases, he writes,

> in which the issue is both important and evenly balanced and, while the court may be divided, both the majority and the minority can see the reason in the other's opinion. . . . Often, in such a situation, all the judges will welcome a dissent in order to reflect

the closeness of the issue, to advance reasoned analysis, and perhaps even to stimulate the Supreme Court to accept the case for review. On such occasions, it happens that even judges on the majority side do not hesitate to make suggestions that help strengthen the dissent.

On the high court, justices have often said that dissents help sharpen the majority opinion, but I have not found anything in which they say that members of the majority aid in improving a dissent, so this may be something unique about dissent on the appeals court. Unless the high court takes the case for review, the majority opinion will have limited force, applying only to that circuit. If the Supreme Court affirms the majority, then the rule of law pronounced by the majority will have nationwide application. Similarly, should the Court reverse, the dissenter's views will become the law of the land.

Judge Helen Wilson Nies, the late chief judge of the Court of Appeals for the Federal Circuit, believed that dissent at the circuit court level "more likely will pique the [Supreme] Court's interest than lawyers disputing a point." A student of appellate argument has explained that for a high court to take a case, the attorneys for the losing side have to be able to document procedural and/or substantive flaws in the trial. But "it is always helpful if there is a dissent in the lower court ruling. Attorneys can use dissents. . . . Sometimes a dissenting judge's opinion will give an attorney the clues needed to formulate a better argument."

According to Justice Scalia, the dissent on an appeals court can eventually bring the issue to the high court in other ways:

When a judge of one of our Circuit Courts of Appeals dissents from an opinion of his colleagues, he warns the Courts of Appeals of the other twelve Circuits (who are not bound by the *stare decisis* effect of that opinion) that they should not readily adopt the same legal rule. And if they do not, of course—if they are persuaded by the view set forth in his dissent, pressed upon them by counsel in some later case—a "conflict" among the Circuits will result, ultimately requiring resolution by the Supreme Court's grant of a petition for certiorari.

Judge Evan A. Evans of the Seventh Circuit declared that he knew "of at least four cases where dissenting opinions were written largely in the belief that their pronouncement would result in the Supreme Court's granting certiorari, and in all four cases the dissenter's hopes were realized." Evans wrote in 1938, so dialogue between appeals courts and the high court has been going on for a long time.

There is a rather unique case in which a sharp dissent led the government to drop charges against Juan Ramirez-Lopez, accused of leading fifteen other illegal immigrants from Mexico through the mountains in eastern San Diego County. A freak spring snowstorm led to the death of one of the party from hypothermia and the arrest and detainment of the others. Two of the group claimed Lopez was the leader, but twelve others said he was not, and Lopez denied being a smuggler. Despite the overwhelming evidence that he was not responsible, Lopez was arrested and charged with multiple counts of alien smuggling. After the government interviewed the detainees, nine witnesses—all of whom had cleared the defendant of any wrongdoing—were returned to Mexico and were unavailable for the defense at his trial. The government detained the two witnesses who inculpated Lopez and three who testified as to his innocence.

At his trial, the jury never heard that twelve of the fourteen members of the group had exonerated Lopez. He was found guilty and sentenced to six and a half years in prison. Although the appeals court noted procedural irregularities, a majority concluded that these did not constitute clear error. As for the defense's inability to question the witnesses who had been returned to Mexico, the majority held that there had been no abuse of government discretion because Lopez had failed to show that their statements carried sufficient indicia of reliability and trustworthiness.

Judge Alex Kozinski shredded the majority opinion and began his dissent with an imaginary conversation between Lopez and his lawyer. The attorney is explaining to his client that although Lopez had lost an opportunity to have counsel promptly appointed—counsel who could have been expected to interview and take notes or statements from the nine witnesses who had been sent back to Mexico—it was really all right, and no harm had occurred because the government's agents had taken exhaustive notes:

Ramirez-Lopez: No kidding, man. They did all that for me?
Lawyer: They sure did. Is this a great country or what?
Ramirez-Lopez: OK, I see it now, but there's one thing that still confuses me.
Lawyer: What's that, Juan?
Ramirez-Lopez: You see, the government took all those great notes to help me, just so we'd know what all those guys said.

Lawyer: Right, I saw them, and they were very good notes. Clear, specific, detailed. Good grammar and syntax. All told, I'd say those were some great notes.

Ramirez-Lopez: And twelve of those guys all said I wasn't the guide.

Lawyer: Absolutely! Our government never hides the ball. The government of Iraq or Afghanistan or one of those places might do this, but not ours. If twelve guys said you weren't the guide, everybody knows about it.

Ramirez-Lopez: Except the jury. I was there at the trial, and I remember the jury never saw the notes. And the officers who testified never told the jury that twelve of the fourteen guys that were with me said I wasn't the guide.

Lawyer: Right.

Ramirez-Lopez: Isn't the jury supposed to have all the facts?

Lawyer: Not all the facts. Some facts are cumulative, others are hearsay. Some facts are both cumulative and hearsay.

Ramirez-Lopez: Can you say that in plain English?

Lawyer: No.

The force of Kozinski's argument, and the devastating manner in which he laid out how the government's actions had made a fair trial impossible, did not convince his fellow jurists, but it led the government to dismiss Lopez's case, release him from prison, and send him back to Mexico. As his lawyer might have said, "Is this a great country or what?"

ONE FINAL OBSERVATION on the appeals courts is a practice unique to them. Increasing numbers of circuit judges are writing concurrences in, or dissents from, orders denying rehearing *en banc,* practices known colloquially as "concurrals" and "dissentals," a phrase we will use to differentiate the practice from regular dissents. Although the practice of petitioning for a rehearing *en banc* dates back many years, the normal practice had been that if the request were denied, it would simply be noted. But over the last seventy-five years or so, judges who believe a petition for rehearing should have been granted have taken to writing dissentals.

Although dissents are normally associated with published opinions, they are not so limited. On the court of appeals level, many actions are taken that do not involve a full opinion, and federal reports include dissents against procedural orders, jurisdictional orders, dismissal for mootness, the grant (or denial) of a certificate of probable cause, certificates of applicability, and referral to a state court for resolution of a state law issue.

The first known dissental came in 1943 from the pen of Judge William Denman, a highly respected member of the Ninth Circuit, and it protested against what was then the normal practice, that *en banc* calls could only be made by one of the judges who decided the case. Denman argued that this was the equivalent of the fox guarding the henhouse. Denman kept up his campaign, and after his death his position was vindicated by adoption of Federal Rule of Appellate Procedure 35, which allows all active-service judges on a circuit court to deliberate and vote on a rehearing petition.

In 1960, Judge Charles E. Clark, after losing an *en banc* vote, wrote a dissental chiding the Second Circuit for not taking the case. Judge Henry J. Friendly responded and attacked the legitimacy of a practice that would enable "any active judge to publish a dissent from any decision, although he did not participate in it. More recently, Judge Rosemary S. Pooler reiterated Friendly's complaints and dismissed dissentals as "oddities [with] as much force of law as if those views were published in a letter to the editor [of the authors'] favorite local newspaper."

Despite the disparagements of Friendly and Pooler, the practice seems to be growing in the appeals courts, and dissentals and concurrals have gained some strong voices in the legal academy. Commentators see dissentals as akin to dissents, although unlike dissents they are written by judges who have not taken a role in the case. The point that Friendly and Pooler seem to have missed is that the judge writing the dissental is dissenting not from the panel's opinion on the merits but from the order of the full court declining to take the case *en banc*. Of course, the writer of the dissental is probably opposed to either the panel's conclusion or its reasoning, and the dissental necessarily touches on these matters. But so does an order granting *en banc* rehearing. A judge may even agree with the results but believe the case should be reheard. A judge is telling his or her colleagues, "I think the issue here is important, and I think all of us—not just a three-person panel—ought to be looking at it."

How many dissentals and concurrals there are across the twelve circuits is impossible to determine, but to some critics of the practice there are far too many. Judge James Hill of the Eleventh Circuit claims that dissentals have proliferated "to the point where the practice may be said to have become institutionalized." That is, as judges write more rehearing dissents, they become part of the normal workload of an appeals court judge. Judge Hill also believes that the growing number of dissentals is at least partially a result of the increasing number of dissents from certiorari on the Supreme Court. If it is good enough for the justices, it is good enough for the judges.

While the total number of such dissentals is small, so was the number of dissents on the high court—many without opinion—through the Taft era, yet some of those dissents proved very influential and formed a key part of the constitutional dialogue. The court of appeals judge who writes a dissental is telling his colleagues—and the public—that he believes an error has been committed and should be rectified.

STATE COURTS SYSTEMS function in most ways the same as the federal judicial system. There are a series of local courts, an intermediate appellate tribunal, and a supreme court, although the latter has different names in some states (in Maryland, for example, it is called the Court of Appeals). Local state courts are often differentiated by the type of case they hear—traffic offenses, domestic relations, probate, criminal, and civil. In some states, there is still a division between courts of law (which provide monetary damages) and courts of equity (which provide nonmonetary relief, such as an injunction). The overwhelming majority of all court cases in the country occur in state courts.

One very important difference between state and federal judges is that the latter are appointed for "good behavior," that is, life tenure. In most states, judges are either elected or appointed to fixed terms, and if they hand down unpopular decisions, they may be voted out of office or fail to be reappointed. Chief Justice Rose Bird of California and two of her colleagues, Cruz Reynoso and Joseph Grodin, were voted out of office after a well-financed campaign in 1986 because of their opposition to the death penalty.

State judges, moreover, labor under a dual mandate. Unlike federal courts, which take their guidance from the Constitution, state courts are guided by both the federal Constitution and their own state constitutions. In some areas, the state constitution and laws are all that matter; there is no federal question raised by a speeding ticket in a school zone. There are, however, areas where federal law dominates, and state judges—who take an oath to preserve and protect the federal Constitution as well as their state charters—must be aware of these. The Supremacy Clause (Article VI) clearly states that the Constitution and federal laws are the supreme law of the land, "any Thing in the Constitution or Laws of any State to the Contrary notwithstanding."

Therefore the interpretation given by the U.S. Supreme Court to the meaning of a federal statute or a provision of the Constitution binds state judges as well in the occasional case in which a federal right is claimed. This happens most often in regard to the rights afforded to those accused of crimes in the Fourth, Fifth, and Sixth Amendments. The general rule is that states must provide at the least the same amount of protection that the Supreme Court says the Constitution provides, but they may go further. Some states, for example, hold that access to basic education is a fundamental right protected by the state constitution, even though the Supreme Court has ruled that under the federal Constitution it is not.

If a federal issue is involved, a plaintiff may choose to fight it out in a federal court or, because of jurisdictional considerations, take it through the state courts. Once a final decision has been entered by the state's highest court, the parties may then appeal directly to the U.S. Supreme Court. If no federal provision is violated, and the state court has framed its opinion based on state constitutional considerations, then the high court will deny review on the basis of the "independent and adequate state grounds" doctrine. The doctrine was stated first in 1875, but the modern statement derives from a 1935 ruling: "Where the judgment of a state court rests upon two grounds, one of which is federal and the other non-federal in character, our jurisdiction fails if the non-federal ground is independent of the federal ground and adequate to support the judgment."

As in the federal courts, there are few if any dissents in the local courts, but we begin to see them in the intermediate courts of appeals, and they serve the same function as in federal appeals courts—to bring to the attention of the supreme court a view different from that of the majority opinion. At the state supreme court level, dissents function much as they do in the U.S. Supreme Court dialogue: they point out errors, limit the reach of the holding, appeal to the legislature, and try to convince the wider audience of academics, lawyers, and the public of their rightness. In addition, if a federal issue is involved, dissenters on state courts are seeking the attention of the justices, hoping that four of them will consider their argument worthwhile enough to grant cert. Moreover, just as in federal courts, the frequency of dissent has increased over the years.

The stories that come out of state courts are remarkably similar to those that come out of Washington. State court judges who dissent talk about the respect they feel for and from their colleagues, and they often tell charming stories. Judge Stanley H. Fuld of the New York Court of Appeals (the state's highest court) wrote about how he hoped his dissents would impress law school professors, lawyers, or the public, and then he got the letter from a prison inmate that is quoted at the beginning of this chapter. Fuld also quoted approvingly a statement attributed to Lord Justice Asquith, that his colleagues on the English Court of Appeal "are such nice and accomplished men, that it is almost a pleasure to be dissented from by them."

Chief Justice Leroy Rountree Hassell Sr. of the Supreme Court of Virginia clearly described the impact of a well-reasoned dissent on the internal dialogue of his court:

A dissent can have the immediate impact of persuading a judge or justice to change his or her views. I can recall that on a few occasions, I felt compelled to change my views and, thus, changed the outcome of cases because I was persuaded to join dissents that ultimately became the majority opinions of the court. I must confess that on one occasion I authored a majority opinion, yet I was persuaded to change my views and embrace the position of the dissent. Parenthetically, I teased my colleague, whose dissent became a significant portion of my majority opinion, by informing him that he was the best, and cheapest, law clerk I have ever had.

Just as William Howard Taft labored to discourage dissents, so too did some state chief justices. A study of the fifty state supreme courts found that in 1964 thirty-one had two or fewer dissents that term and eleven had no dissents; that same year, the U.S. Supreme Court had seventeen. Seymour Simon of the Illinois Supreme Court related how when he went onto the bench, his dissents, although not numerous, always riled his colleagues. One judge of the Pennsylvania high court compared dissents to homicides, in that they fell into three categories—"excusable, justifiable, and reprehensible"—and clearly felt most belonged in the latter group. The Louisiana Constitution of 1898 actually forbade the publication of dissenting opinions.

Dissents on state courts have grown more frequent. Among the judges who have won the admiration of the legal community (if not always the appreciation of their colleagues) are Martha B. Sosman of the Massachusetts Supreme Judicial Court, Carmen Beauchamp Ciparick and Robert S. Smith of the New York Court of Appeals, Jesse W. Carter of the California Supreme Court, and Charles Austin O'Niell of the Louisiana Supreme Court. All of them wrote dissents that in one way or another helped shape state constitutional and statutory law.

WHEN HOLMES AND BRANDEIS wrote their famous dissents, the unanimity rate on the Court stood at 95 percent or more, and their colleagues, as they made clear, frowned on separate opinions. By the time the men and women who have been sitting on state and federal courts went to law school in the 1960s and after, dissents not only had become common on the high court but showed up in the leading texts used not only in Con Law but in criminal procedure, contracts, torts, antitrust, and state law courses as well. Students read *Abrams* not for the majority opinion but for Holmes's dissent, just as they read *Olmstead* for the Brandeis dissent. Teachers used the dissents to show students the weaknesses and fallacies of the majority opinions, a skill they could then apply to other decisions. Law students also imbibed the notion that dissenting opinions spoke to more than one audience, that they had to be not only well reasoned but educational.

To take one example, Leroy Hassell, the first African American chief justice of the Virginia Supreme Court, graduated from the Harvard Law School in 1980, where he was exposed to this type of education. He practiced law for only seven years before his appointment to the court in 1989; his peers elected him chief in 2002, and he served in that position until his death in 2011. When he spoke about dissent and its audiences, he used the type of language that Brandeis would have recognized and applauded.

An appellate judge's first audience is his or her colleagues on the bench. The dissent is trying to persuade them, either to a different conclusion or to a different mode of reasoning. Majority and dissenters are participating in the decision-making process together. This is, of course, the type of dialogue we have been talking about throughout this book. A dissent in one case may form the basis of a majority opinion later. A Hassell dissent in 1996 became the basis of the majority opinion just two years later.

The second audience consists of the litigants before the court. There is always a losing side, and the dissent serves to reassure those who have lost that their arguments had been heard. Another issue to address for this audience is that the parties have framed the legal principles of the case, and therefore both the majority opinion and the dissent have to be careful to stay within those parameters. To go beyond the specific question brought by the parties is to invade the domain of the legislature.

Third, there is the bar and members of the public at large. Lawyers advise their clients to undertake or to refrain from certain acts based on judicial decisions. Similarly, the public is greatly affected by court decisions, and Hassell cited *Brown v. Board* as a case with profound social consequences. If a major decision does not command a clear majority of the court, this can be disruptive. A dissent informs the bar that perhaps the majority opinion is not as rigid a rule as it may seem or that perhaps it would be possible to challenge the rule.

To Hassell's list, one should add the legal academy. How legal scholars treat opinions will also have consequences, especially in the treatment of the next generation. For all the outcry by some groups against the activism of the Warren Court, the law schools embraced the move toward greater equality and, at the same time, damned the property-conscious decisions of the old Court. The courts talk to many audiences, and in the dialogue those audiences respond as well.

Like the Supreme Court, state high courts speak to the legislatures. In a recent case, the Maryland Court of Appeals upheld the state's long-standing "all or nothing" approach to assessing liability in civil suits, although nearly all other states have adopted a system in which the relative fault of both parties is taken into account. The majority said the court has the power to rewrite the rules, which are generally considered antiquated, but because the General Assembly has not done so, the court will not act. The dissent by Judge Glenn T. Harrell Jr. (joined by the recently retired chief judge, Robert M. Bell) ran fifty-one pages, and Harrell compared the current standard to a dinosaur that should be rendered extinct with "the force of a modern asteroid strike," and he urged the legislature to rid the state of an "unjust and outmoded" law.

Finally, a well-written dissent will expose the perceived errors or weaknesses in the majority opinion, and if there is a federal issue involved, the dissent is a clear call to the U.S. Supreme Court to take the case. The example Judge Hassell uses is that of Daryl Renard Atkins, convicted of capital murder and sentenced to death. The first jury trial was set aside for a procedural irregularity; in a second trial, a new jury also found him guilty and recommended the death penalty, and the judge imposed it. Atkins appealed to the Virginia Supreme Court, which affirmed the verdict and the sentence.

But two judges dissented—Hassell and Lawrence L. Koontz Jr. Evidence presented to the jury showed that Atkins had the mental age of a child between nine and twelve and that he was mentally retarded. In their dissents, they argued that "the imposition of the sentence of death upon a mentally retarded defendant with an I.Q. of 59 is excessive . . . considering both the crime and the defendant." Atkins's attorney used the dissents as a basis for an appeal to the U.S. Supreme Court, which in its opinion specifically noted that it had granted cert in part because of the powerful dissents of Justices Hassell and Koontz. The Court then overruled its previous holding allowing states to execute mentally retarded defendants convicted of crimes and held that the execution of such a defendant violated the Eighth Amendment's ban on cruel and unusual punishment.

State court judges, perhaps even more than members of the high court, are aware of the tension between a powerful dissent and the consistency in law that derives from *stare decisis*. The majority of cases heard in state courts are not constitutional in nature but deal with questions of state law—both public and private. Judge Christian Compton of Virginia wrote, "The doctrine of *stare decisis* is more than a mere cliché. That doctrine plays a significant role in the orderly administration of justice by assuring consistent, predictable, and balanced application of legal principles. And when a court of last resort has established a precedent, after full deliberation upon the issue by the court, the precedent will not be treated lightly or ignored, in the absence of flagrant error or mistake." The key here, of course is whether a majority of a court recognizes "flagrant error or mistake," and the dissenter's role—and obligation—are to show his or her colleagues that in fact the precedent either was wrong or is no longer properly applicable.

IN A SPEECH to the *Columbia Law Review* board in April 1962, Judge Stanley H. Fuld of the New York Court of Appeals took out a newspaper clipping that had aroused his curiosity a few years previously:

> The Italian Constitutional High Court, which corresponds roughly to the Supreme Court of the United States, accepted today the resignation of its president, Senator Enrico de Nicola.
> The reasons for Judge de Nicola's resignation were not given, [but] . . . it is understood . . . that . . . he was . . . irritated by the fact that some of the fourteen judges who sit with him on the High Court had dissented from some of his decisions.

The customs of foreign courts have often puzzled American jurists. In part, this is due to the differing historical circumstances and legal systems from which they grew and which still dominate current practices. In return, American procedures appear just as confusing to foreigners. In the summer of 1989, Justices Sandra Day O'Connor, Antonin Scalia, and Ruth Bader Ginsburg went to Paris to exchange views with the Conseil d'État. A multifunctional institution established in Napoleonic times, one of its sections serves as the supreme court of France for administrative law cases.

Justice O'Connor described the doctrine of deference that courts owe to decisions or rules made by expert administrative agencies and officials. American courts are bound to accept an agency's construction of its authorizing statute so long as the agency's reading is a plausible one, even if not the only plausible reading or even, in the judges' view, the more or most plausible reading.

How can that be? one of the French officials asked. How can the law have more than one meaning? Even more important, how can a court openly acknowledge that there are multiple and legitimate readings? The law is the law, there can be only one officially correct reading, and it is the court's responsibility, through public announcements, to assure the public of that. As Justice Ginsburg noted, this exchange laid bare one of the fundamental differences between the two systems. The French, and most civil law systems, see judicial decisions as providing the inexorable result demanded by the law. There is a right answer to every legal question; it should be expressed in a unanimous opinion and written up in a formal and impersonal manner. In France, the author of a court ruling is neither named nor in any other way identified. In the French tradition, the judgment is precisely composed, and according to some commentators the ideal judgment "is considered all the more perfect for its concise and concentrated style, so that only experienced jurists are able to understand and admire it."

Aside from jurisprudential considerations, the status of continental judges is far different from that of judges in the United States. One of Justice Scalia's children spent a semester in Europe with a family, and when she told them that her father was a law professor, this was greeted by great respect and approval. When his daughter returned a few years later and told the same family that her father had become a judge, the change bewildered them. Why would a tenured professor want to become a judge? One of the reasons for the unanimous and anonymous style of judging in civil law countries is the civil service character and mentality of the judiciary.

The highest court in France, the Cour de Cassation, has over eighty members, while the highest civil court in what was then West Germany had over one hundred judges. Whereas in common-law countries—Great Britain, the Commonwealth members, and the United States—judges are appointed from among practicing attorneys who have excelled in their profession, in civil law countries one takes what is essentially a civil service exam and, upon passing, begins one's career as a judge. Advancement is very slow and essentially depends upon one's evaluation by superiors. Finally, as Justice Ginsburg notes, there is no such thing as *stare decisis* in civil law regimes. Courts look not to prior decisions as precedents but to the statute itself, with its supposedly one inexorable interpretation. Naturally, there are no dissents and no indication of whether a law panel was divided in its reasoning.

There is disagreement on whether there ever existed a tradition of separate opinions in Europe. Under early Germanic as well as Roman procedure, courts reached their decisions in public. Secrecy as to both deliberation and vote on the judgment seems to have had its origin in later Roman and church practice. The courts of the Catholic Church for centuries have kept individual votes in secret archives. In Spain, in the Ordinance of Medina of 1489, Ferdinand and Isabella directed the secular courts, shortly after the introduction of the Inquisition, to enter the results of the vote in a special book that was to be kept secret.

According to Judge Dieter Grimm, a former justice on the Federal Constitutional Court of Germany, any tradition of separate opinions came to an end with the rise of absolute monarchs. They concentrated all power in their hands, including the judicial, and judges served the king and rendered judgments in his name. Because the king could not govern in multiple voices, his judges—who spoke for him—had to speak in one voice. Even after absolute monarchy faded away, the basic understanding survived. It is the *court,* not the *judge,* that decides a case. Even the term "opinion" is not relevant, because the court does not have an opinion. Because the law in nearly all of continental Europe is based on statutory code rather than judge-made common law, precedent has no place in judicial decisions. Although Holmes once famously said that the law is not a great brooding omnipresence waiting to be discovered, in European countries that is exactly the case. There can be only one correct interpretation, and any opinion by a member of the court disagreeing with the proper conclusion would be seen not as an alternative interpretation but as an error. If the interpretation of the court wreaks hardship, then the solution lies in the hands of lawmakers, not judges.

After World War II, many European countries established constitutional courts, and the judges on those tribunals won the right, like their counterparts in the United States and the British Commonwealth, to file separate opinions. But while individual judges may file separate opinions, this does not mean that the court will publish them. (This right, it should be noted, was given by the legislatures and only to the constitutional courts. Regular courts still speak in one voice.) In Germany, dissenting opinions were introduced in 1970, two decades after the establishment of the Federal Constitutional Court. Spain followed the German example in its post-Franco constitution, and so did many of the former socialist countries after the dissolution of the Soviet Union. Austria, France, and Italy still do not have dissents. While the European

Court of Human Rights allows dissents, the European Union Court of Justice does not, nor have its judges sought that right. Even in those countries that allow it, many individual judges still believe that it is better not to dissent. Grimm's predecessor on the German Constitutional Court, whom Grimm describes as "a highly respected and very influential judge," made it a principle for himself never to file a dissenting opinion.

Apparently, only the presence of dissenting opinions in the German reports will indicate that a decision is not unanimous. The actual votes are not announced, so if dissenting members choose not to file an opinion, there is no way the public will know how they voted. Only when the court splits 4–4 has it become customary to present the opinions of both sides with the names of the justices.

Practices vary from court to court. The International Court of Justice in The Hague has both dissenting and concurring opinions, because unlike national systems of codified law international law remains plastic and therefore open to differing interpretations. According to Sir Percy Spender, if the answers to the questions that came before the fifteen members of the court were simple, there would be no need for them to adjudicate those questions. But "in the nature of things different minds approach problems in different ways. The approach to a legal problem is no exception. What is to be solved will be solved according to the manner of him who solves it." Another member of the court, Sir Gerald Fitzmaurice, echoed what many American jurists have said, that a decision can only be properly appreciated in the light of a contrary opinion, especially if it is a difficult case.

In England, early judging was traditionally in public, with each judge stating what he thought the decision should be. Even in the sinister Star Chamber, opinions were given seriatim, and that tradition remains today in English, Scottish, and Irish courts. (In the Irish Republic, however, no dissent may be announced in cases where the Supreme Court decides a question of the constitutional validity of a law.) The exception has been the Judicial Committee of the Privy Council, which serves as a court of review for dominion and colonial appellate courts and for decisions of the English ecclesiastical tribunals. Only "the judgment of the Privy Council" is published, because technically the decision is merely a recommendation to the monarch, and indications of differences would therefore be improper.

Many countries in Latin America—with the exception of Haiti and the Dominican Republic, which kept the French system—drew heavily on the American model after they won their independence from Spain in the nineteenth century. While the actions of courts during times of military dictatorships are not representative, in the functioning democracies of Central and South America the right of a dissenting judge to announce his opinion is accepted, although practices have varied about the publication of a dissent. When Cuba and Puerto Rico were occupied by American forces in the Spanish-American War in 1898, one of the first acts of the military governments was to put an end to the Spanish system of the secret book, a practice that had lasted more than four centuries.

Our neighbors to the north have a somewhat different system of constitutional review, especially in regard to individual rights. The Canadian Charter of Rights and Freedoms, enacted in 1982, gave courts a greater say in defining individual liberties when confronted by government action. But any Supreme Court decision on constitutionality does not end the matter, as it does in the United States. As Justice Allen Linden has explained it, "We have created a unique system of 'legislative review of judicial review.' To maintain our respect for the supremacy of Parliament, the drafters of the Charter have given our legislatures the last word on constitutional matters." The charter, Linden continues, has created a dialogue between the courts and the legislatures. In four out of five cases where courts have nullified all or parts of either provincial or federal statutes as contrary to the charter, the legislature has responded with some alternative means of reaching its original objective without violating the charter.

Canadian courts do have dissents, and according to another judge of that country's Supreme Court, Claire L'Heureux-Dubé, the tradition of dissent in the courts is deeply embedded and has "encouraged a blossoming of legal concepts and solutions." Although Canada was originally a French colony, the English captured it before the Napoleonic institution of the law code, and as a result Canadian courts have inherited the traditions of the British common-law courts. A partial exception is the court system of Quebec, which is a hybrid of French and English culture due to the province's unique view of itself. Nonetheless, unlike French courts, those in Quebec allow dissents. With the establishment of the Supreme Court in 1877, judges delivered their opinions—including dissents—seriatim until the early 1960s, when Chief Justice Bora Laskin, borrowing from John Marshall, persuaded his colleagues to adopt the unanimous and anonymous "decision of the Court" for certain important cases, in which unanimity was both possible and desirable. These cases, however, constitute less than one in ten of the court's decisions.

Dissents in the Canadian high court have, from time to time, borne fruit once the ideas became part of the dialogue. Chief Justice Laskin often found himself in dissent, especially in his early years on the court. Justice L'Heureux-Dubé notes approvingly Laskin's dissent in a case involving an ancient concept of English property law, the "constructive trust," in an effort to find a more equitable result in family law. He argued that the constructive trust should allow for the recognition of the right of a spouse, who has contributed to family property through unpaid labor, to share in that same property upon divorce. His dissent, in 1975, became part of a plurality opinion in 1978 and was then adopted by the majority in 1980. In retrospect, according to Justice L'Heureux-Dubé, it seems clear that the Laskin dissent was also part of the dialogue with the emerging social and political awareness of the demand by women for equality.

As in the United States, dissenting opinions are an important part of the dialogue among judges, academics, legislative assemblies, and lawyers. The law reviews of Canada comment frequently on opinions of the high court, both majority and dissenting opinions, and according to Justice L'Heureux-Dubé the members of the court read these critiques carefully. She also notes that dissents have played a very important role in the dialogue between courts and legislatures concerning the criminalization and prosecution of sexual offenses. A number of questions were raised about the shielding of a victim's prior sexual history, and a majority of the court held that withholding this information violated the right of the accused to make full answer and defense. Over the next few years, similar questions arose in sexual assault cases about how much of a victim's medical and therapeutic records should be made available, and in each instance Justice L'Heureux-Dubé, and then others, dissented, until Parliament adopted the dissenters' approach and enacted legislation more protective of the victims' privacy. When a challenge to that law came to the high court, the justices unanimously agreed that the dissenting opinions had been correct and validated the new law.

Although the Australian Constitution to some extent follows the plan of our Article III, the U.S. and Australian supreme courts have different practices. To take just one example, oral argument before the Australian High Court may take as many as five days. More important, there is no explicit Bill of Rights in the Australian constitution, and the High Court, unlike its American counterpart, is part of the legal system of the states that constitute the federation. Its docket is thus dominated by appeals in civil and criminal matters. Until the 1990s, according to the former justice Michael McHugh, the High Court generally decided cases in accordance with a theory of legal positivism, similar to the French notion that a single correct answer can be found by working out the logical implications of relevant legal rules and principles deriving from the statute in question.

There were relatively few dissents when the High Court first sat at the start of the twentieth century, just four in the years 1903 to 1906. This might have been because a majority of the justices had been framers of the new Australian constitution. Like their American equivalents, justices often expressed regret at disagreeing with their colleagues. In *Duncan v. Queensland* (1916), Justice Edmund Barton wrote, "To say that one regrets to differ from one's learned brethren is a formula that often begins a judgment. I end mine by expressing heavy sorrow that their decision is as it is." Over the years, the rate of disagreement rose, reaching a high of 72 percent in 1944, and then dropped down, only to rise again in later years.

According to one student of the Australian High Court, "Most dissenting judgments do not have long-term impact. While the Court is not strictly bound by precedent, adherence to past decisions, even if only majority decisions, promotes certainty and stability; thus majority opinions inescapably command more respect." Yet Professor Andrew Lynch reluctantly admits that some dissenting opinions "have later assumed a much greater importance" and notes that "whether there is a causal connection between those dissents and the subsequent shifts in the law is hotly debated." Moreover, while the courts may declare some laws unconstitutional, actual changes in the constitution can only take place through popular referenda. As a result, despite strong dissents, in only a few cases have the dissenting voices had an impact on the court's later development.

Since the 1990s, there has been a continuing debate inside the court as well as in the public over the role of the court and its shift in emphasis. According to Justice McHugh, starting around 1990 the justices adopted a broader approach to interpreting the constitution and the common law. They rejected the literalism that was a feature of legal positivism and began looking at contemporary social and economic conditions, as well as historical purpose. Moreover, some justices have held that the Australian Constitution implicitly guarantees the equality of all people under the law and before the courts, even in the absence of the warranties found in the Fifth and Fourteenth Amendments to the U.S. Constitution. So far, only a minority of the court has taken this view, and it has run into serious criticism, much of which sounds like the cry raised against "judicial activism" in the United States.

THIS ADMITTEDLY BRIEF DIGRESSION into lower federal, state, and foreign courts shows that in all of these areas dissent plays an important role in the constitutional dialogue. The exceptions, of course, are those foreign courts that do not allow dissent, not because of a lack of democracy, but because they have legal traditions that are rooted in legal positivism.

One could do a detailed study of some of the American state courts and discover that dissent over the years has played a critical role in helping to define the contours of the state constitutions. But state courts, like the federal appeals courts, are not completely autonomous. Both are governed by the supremacy of the federal Constitution, and while the Supreme Court is final, even looking at this brief discursion, one can see how important dissents are in framing the questions that ultimately end up on the high court's docket.

Overseas, the role of dissent has also been changing, especially since the end of World War II. Many of the countries that gained independence, either from their colonial masters or from the Soviet Union, have looked to the American judiciary as a model, not to be slavishly copied, but as a critical player in the constitutional governance of their countries. Time after time, writers on foreign courts have declared, much as Justice Douglas did, that dissent is crucial in a democratic society and in fact fosters that very democracy.

CHAPTER II

CONTINUING THEMES, FROM
WARREN TO ROBERTS

Justice John Paul Stevens was once asked, "If you could fix one thing about the American judicial system, what would it be?" He replied, "I would make all my dissents into majority opinions."

Historians find it easier to place events in an appropriate context when sufficient time has passed so they can be fairly certain that their judgments take into account the social, economic, political, or—in the case of this book—judicial developments that have ensued. As Mark Tushnet has noted, "The fate of a dissent lies in the hands of history." Justice James McReynolds's dissents in the New Deal cases have been considered "wrong" because history validated the majority opinion, while Justice John Marshall Harlan's *Plessy* dissent was eventually endorsed. As Tushnet notes, "Justice Scalia's dissents *might* be prescient, but he is not yet a great dissenter because we do not know how the story will turn out." In place of Antonin Scalia's name, we could easily substitute that of William J. Brennan, Ruth Bader Ginsburg, or John Paul Stevens.

Since 1953, we have had, using the customary terminology, four "courts," named after the chief justices who headed them—the Warren Court (1953–1969), the Burger Court (1969–1986), the Rehnquist

Court (1986–2005), and the Roberts Court (2005–). The Court's agenda began changing in the 1940s, as the justices grappled more and more with issues of civil rights and civil liberties. Looking back, cases like *Brown v. Board of Education* (1954), *Gideon v. Wainwright* (1963), and *New York Times v. Sullivan* (1964) were obviously "right" and in some ways "easy." By this, I do not mean that the justices who decided these cases lacked courage or did not have to grapple with difficult questions, but in historical hindsight we can say, "Of course, how else could they have decided? It was wrong then and remains wrong to segregate people on the basis of race, or deny a person accused of a crime the assistance of counsel, or penalize a newspaper for criticizing the conduct of public officials." But once past the foundational cases, the outgrowths of these decisions involved difficult matters of public and jurisprudential policy whose resolution proved far from easy or perhaps even right. Questions of affirmative action, majority-minority districting, and measures to avoid resegregation have split the country, no matter how strongly we believe that the Court decided *Brown* correctly. Privacy, abortion, health, women's equality, the death penalty, and many other issues have led to strongly divided courts.

It is not just the Court that is torn over these issues but the country at large as well. Just as political blocs have solidified in Congress and the electorate, so too we have seen a Supreme Court divided into conservative and liberal factions, with the balance of power often found in one person in the middle—Lewis F. Powell Jr., then Sandra Day O'Connor, and most recently Anthony Kennedy. The "prophetic" dissent—Harlan I in *Plessy,* Brandeis in *Olmstead,* Black in *Betts*—seems to have disappeared, although we cannot be sure, because, as Tushnet reminds us, we have to await history's judgment. The dialogic value of dissent when a reversal occurs may at times be less a factor than a change in personnel on the Court. The retirement of Justice O'Connor, who tended to defer to congressional judgment, and her replacement by Samuel Alito, who is less deferential, played a greater role in reversing some decisions than did earlier dissents in those cases. This is certainly true in cases involving campaign finance, where O'Connor tended to defer to legislative judgment, while Alito views any effort to regulate campaign finance as an abridgment of First Amendment rights.

WE TEND TO THINK of the Warren Court as one of the most "active" in history, deciding momentous issues of racial discrimination, apportionment, free speech, privacy, and rights of the accused. The phrase "judicial revolution" is often used, and whether one is conservative or liberal, a great sea change in jurisprudential philosophy did occur. Although the Court stood united in some of the great cases—*Brown v. Board of Education I* and *II* and nearly all of the racial discrimination cases, *Gideon v. Wainwright, New York Times v. Sullivan, Epperson v. Arkansas* (1968), and *Brandenburg v. Ohio* (1969)—in most of the Warren-era decisions some members of the Court dissented, and some of the "great" cases were far from unanimous.

If one looks at the statistics, the rate of unanimity on the Warren Court ranged from a high of 46 percent in the October 1965 term to a low of 28.9 percent in the 1957 term. Some members of the Court were certainly prolific dissenters. Over their careers, Hugo Black wrote 310 dissents, William Brennan 457, William O. Douglas 486, Felix Frankfurter 251, and John Marshall Harlan II 313. Brennan, Frankfurter, and Harlan II actually wrote more dissents than majority opinions during their tenures on the Court. The number of dissenting votes (as opposed to written opinions) is even higher: Black 660, Brennan 998, Douglas 982, Harlan II 465, and even Earl Warren voted in the minority 202 times. The work of the Roosevelt justices came to fruition in the Warren Court in terms of the complete abandonment of the desire for unanimity; the notion of consensus had been transformed into one of individual expression. "Unanimity is an appealing distraction," Felix Frankfurter once said, but "a single Court statement on important constitutional issues and other aspects of public law is bound to smother differences that in the interest of candor and of the best interest of the Court ought to be expressed." The one area where Earl Warren insisted on unanimity—and the brethren agreed—involved the desegregation cases.

Nearly all of the dissents filed in the Warren years have been forgotten, because, except in a few instances, the public accepted and validated the majority decisions. Hugo Black's dissents in the sit-in cases were swept aside by the 1964 Civil Rights Act, which adopted Justice Douglas's argument that public accommodations—such as hotels and restaurants—cannot discriminate on the basis of race. Justice Brennan's dissents in the Sunday closing law cases were adopted by the Court within two years, when he delivered the majority opinion in *Sherbert v. Verner* (1963) requiring states to make reasonable accommodation to an individual's need for religious observance. While the many decisions in the area of criminal procedure have been modified, their essential holdings continue to be accepted by the Court. Even the *Miranda* decision, which evoked so much criticism at the time, came to be accepted as a "constitutional rule," a judgment handed down by William Rehnquist,

HARRIS & EWING, COLLECTION OF USSC

Earl Warren, chief justice, 1953–1969

who had earlier been one of the most forceful critics of the case. The controversy over the apportionment decisions, which generated so much heat at the time and even led rural state representatives to try to override the Court by constitutional amendment, faded away once reapportionment took place and the new urban/suburban majorities took power.

Not all of the Warren-era decisions, however, became easily—or fully—accepted. The civil rights decisions generated great resistance in the Jim Crow states, and not until after the passage of the 1965 Voting Rights Act and the eventual election of African American local officials—including sheriffs—did those decisions supplant decades of state-sponsored apartheid. The school prayer (*Engel v. Vitale* [1962]) and the Bible-reading (*Abington School District v. Schempp* [1953]) cases led to a firestorm of criticism. One newspaper headline screamed, "COURT OUTLAWS GOD." An outraged Billy Graham thundered, "God pity our country when we can no longer appeal to God for help." The tenor of the criticism had been anticipated by Justice Potter Stewart's dissent. "We are," he said, quoting an earlier opinion by Douglas, "a religious people whose institutions presuppose a Supreme Being." The practice of school prayer did no more than recognize "the deeply entrenched and highly cherished spiritual traditions of our Nation," as did the opening of Court and Congress with prayer.

Stewart's dissent anticipated the opposition to the school prayer case. The Court received more mail denouncing *Engel* than for any other decision, including *Brown.* Polls showed this ruling the most unpopular of any Warren Court decision, with 80 percent of the American people favoring prayer in schools. "They put Negroes into the schools and now they have driven God out of them," ranted Representative George W. Andrews of Alabama. Within a few days, senators and members of the House submitted three dozen proposed constitutional amendments to overturn the decision. While the more liberal churches accepted the ruling, conservative and evangelical groups, especially in the rural South, refused to do so and in many instances have continued to do so until today. When teaching these cases, I will invariably get a student from a small southern town who tells me that in his elementary or high school they still start the day with a prayer. In those areas with few Jews, Catholics, or other non-Protestant families, the prayers used are openly sectarian.

THERE IS ONE AREA, however, where the dissents continue to echo, and that is in the privacy decisions of the Warren Court. Normally, when we think of the Warren Court and privacy, we look to the landmark decision in *Griswold v. Connecticut* (1965), but there is a predecessor case in which the Court refused to decide the merits. Justice Harlan's dissent in *Poe v. Ullman* (1961) has become an important part of the constitutional dialogue, primarily for what it says about finding new constitutional rights.

John Marshall Harlan, often known as Harlan II, was the fourth generation of lawyers in his family and was named after his grandfather, the first justice Harlan. In November 1954, Dwight Eisenhower named him to succeed Robert Jackson, who had died the month before.

Harlan served until 1971 and through most of his years on the Court stood as the conservative resistance to the liberal motifs of the Warren

John Marshall Harlan II, associate justice,
1955–1971

Court. Yet he also played an important role in some of the Court's liberal decisions, especially those involving the First Amendment's Speech Clause. Harlan devised the means by which the Court could move away from the judicial morass it had created in the 1951 *Dennis* case. According to one of his law clerks, Norman Dorsen, Harlan's two principal judicial values were federalism and proceduralism, both directed to keeping the delicate balance of state-federal relations in good working order. He dissented in all of the reapportionment cases for the simple reason that he believed the courts had no business in an area that the Constitution left to state discretion. Proceduralism meant the Court should only decide those questions properly within the judicial power. "The Constitution is not a panacea for every blot on the public welfare, nor should this Court, ordained as a judicial body, be thought of as a general haven for reform movements."

Most scholars talk of "two" Warren Courts. The first dates from the appointment of Earl Warren in 1953 to when Felix Frankfurter retired in August 1962, to be replaced by Arthur Goldberg. Until then, the liberal tendencies of Warren, Black, Douglas, and Brennan were kept in check by a conservative coalition led by Frankfurter that included at different times Sherman Minton, Tom Clark, Stanley Reed, Charles Whittaker, Harold Burton, and Harlan II. Once Frankfurter left, Goldberg joined with the four liberals to give them a working majority, and many of the most activist decisions identified with the Warren Court came in the years 1962–1969. During those years, Harlan, often joined by Byron White and Potter Stewart, served as the conservative loyal opposition.

However much Harlan and Frankfurter agreed on jurisprudential issues, they were quite different. Everybody liked Harlan, who had none of the acerbity that marked Frankfurter's personality and poisoned his relations with other members of the Court. William O. Douglas, who often voted against Harlan's opinions, nonetheless had nothing but nice things to say about him in his memoirs and put Harlan on the roster of the great judges with whom he had served. Harlan's legal knowledge, like that of Brandeis, came from nearly three decades of successful practice. He had been a "lawyer's lawyer," and on the bench he became a "judge's judge," one whose opinions, either for the Court or in dissent, merited careful appraisal by the other justices.

In 1961, the Supreme Court voted to hear the case of *Poe v. Ullman.* The plaintiffs included a married couple who had lost three babies born with multiple birth defects (the pseudonymous Paul and Pauline Poe), a married woman who had recently undergone a pregnancy that caused illness and unconsciousness and had left her partially paralyzed, and a doctor legally unable to counsel his patients about contraception. Under Connecticut law, a physician could not dispense advice about birth control, even when the life of the mother was in danger. The plaintiffs sought declaratory relief from the Supreme Court, asking it to declare the law unconstitutional. They claimed that the law violated the Fourteenth Amendment's protection of life and liberty without due process of law and said that they feared prosecution if they violated the law. They also believed that the state's attorney intended to prosecute them, but in fact he had not done so nor even threatened them with prosecution.

The Connecticut law had been enacted in 1879, but the state had never prosecuted anyone for its violation. As such, the Court concluded, the Poes were in no danger of prosecution if they received contraceptive advice from their physician. Warren assigned the case to Frankfurter, who avoided the constitutional issue, declaring the case nonjusticiable for lack of a case or controversy. The state's policy of nonenforcement posed no danger to people seeking birth control information; the case was therefore nonjusticiable, and to decide the merits would, in effect, be an advisory opinion, which the Court never issued.

Black dissented without opinion, merely stating that he thought the constitutional issue should be reached and decided. Brennan concurred in the result only because of the jurisdictional issue. Douglas entered a strong dissent, arguing that the Connecticut statute ought to be invalidated on its face, while Stewart joined both Black and Harlan.

One might have thought that a jurisdiction hound like Harlan would have joined the opinion. Article III of the Constitution requires that a real case or controversy exist for a federal court to hear a matter, and it seemed clear from the record that no controversy existed. While Connecticut argued that it had the power to enact such a law, the facts showed that it had not been enforced, and without enforcement the Poes' alleged rights had not been infringed. Beyond that, the Fourteenth Amendment's Due Process Clause had been in ill repute because of how conservative jurists had used substantive due process to strike down reform legislation. The plaintiffs were essentially asking the Court to revivify substantive due process, an idea that justices like Frankfurter, with memories of the bad old days, found frightening.

Although Harlan well knew the struggles that substantive due process had caused, he had no antipathy toward it. He saw the notion of inherent rights as useful and not to be discarded simply because it had been misused three and more decades earlier. Beyond that, Frankfurter's argument that the Poes should not worry because the law had never been enforced offended the lawyer in Harlan. So long as the law remained on the books, it *could* be enforced; every lawyer worth his salt knew that and would not in good conscience advise a client to simply ignore the statute. "I think it is pure conjecture, and indeed conjecture which to me seems contrary to realities, that an open violation of the statute by a doctor (or more obviously still by a birth-control clinic) would not result in a substantial threat of prosecution."

While he "unreservedly subscribed" to Frankfurter's general argument regarding nonjusticiability, that doctrine allowed the Court to decide cases when certain conditions existed, and he believed such conditions existed here. Constitutional claims had been put forward by the plaintiffs, and the fact that there had been no actual prosecution did not mean that the issue was not "ripe" for judicial consideration. "I cannot see what further elaboration is required to enable us to decide the appellants' claims, and indeed neither the plurality opinion nor the concurring opinion . . . suggests what more grist is needed before the judicial mill could turn." There was, as far as he was concerned, a true controversy that deserved settlement.

The most substantial claim which these married persons press is their right to enjoy the privacy of their marital relations free of the enquiry of the criminal law, whether it be a prosecution of them or of a doctor whom they have consulted. And I cannot agree that their enjoyment of this privacy is not substantially impinged upon, when they are told that if they use contraceptives, indeed whether they do so or not, the only thing which stands between them and being forced to render criminal account of their marital privacy is the whim of the prosecutor. Connecticut's highest court has told us in the clearest terms that, given proof, the prosecutor will succeed if he decides to bring a proceeding against one of the appellants. . . . All that stands between the appellants and jail is the legally unfettered whim of the prosecutor and the Constitutional issue this Court refuses to decide.

Harlan differed from Frankfurter in the nonjusticiability argument because he believed that the constitutional rights allegedly infringed by the state were substantial and deserving of judicial protection. This, he said, was the core of his disagreement with the majority. To him, the Connecticut statute outrageously interfered with personal privacy and in effect punished marital relationships that did not result in procreation. "I can hardly believe," he wrote to a friend, "that such a statute would be deemed constitutional."

The word "privacy" had not been mentioned in too many Court cases in the previous three decades, and in part 2 of his dissent Harlan laid down a constitutional basis for the right of privacy grounded in the Fourteenth Amendment. Contrary to his normally conservative and restrained opinions, his *Poe* dissent, in the words of one scholar, was "an activist, value-oriented, free-wheeling piece of judicial lawmaking."

To understand Harlan's dissent, we must see it in the context of ongoing jurisprudential debates that preceded his appointment to the Court and would continue after his tenure. One is the question of incorporation, whether and to what extent the Fourteenth Amendment's Due Process Clause incorporated the protections of the Bill of Rights. Another argument concerned the concept of substantive due process, whether the Due Process Clause contained inherent rights that protected people in ways not spelled out in the first eight amendments to the Constitution. Because of the abuse of that notion by conservative jurists in the *Lochner* era, New Deal justices like Black, Douglas, and Frankfurter shied away from any effort to revitalize substantive due process.

Harlan rejected Black's theory of total incorporation, but even if he had accepted it, nothing in the Constitution or the Bill of Rights explicitly prohibited the Connecticut legislation. To invalidate the state's law would require finding that it violated some substantive right found buried in the Fourteenth Amendment's Due Process Clause. According to some accounts, one of his law clerks that term, Charles Fried, argued that due process included substantive rights, defined not by the first eight amendments but by history and tradition, and his argument proved decisive. "I believe," Harlan wrote, "that a statute making it a criminal offense for married couples to use contraceptives is an intolerable and unjustifiable invasion of privacy in the conduct of the most intimate concerns of an individual's personal life." The Fourteenth Amendment, not the Bill of Rights, put limits on how far the state could invade privacy in the name of public health.

Due process, Harlan argued, could not be reduced to a formula, but he looked at prior decisions to conclude that it "represented the balance which our Nation, built upon postulates of respect for the liberty of the individual, has struck between that liberty and the demands of organized society." Whatever the original meaning of due process, it had progressed far beyond Magna Carta's "law of the land" and in the United States had become a bulwark against arbitrary legislation.

Harlan understood that one of the criticisms of the old due process was that it had been used arbitrarily, and he hastened to say that he saw it in a quite different light:

> Due process has not been reduced to any formula; its content cannot be determined by reference to any code. The best that can be said is that through the course of this Court's decisions it has represented the balance which our Nation, built upon postulates of respect for the liberty of the individual, has struck between that liberty and the demands of organized society. If the supplying of content to this Constitutional concept has of necessity been a rational process, it certainly has not been one where judges have felt free to roam where unguided speculation might take them. The balance of which I speak is the balance struck by this country, having regard to what history teaches are the traditions from which it developed as well as the traditions from which it broke. That tradition is a living thing. A decision of this Court which radically departs from it could not long survive, while a decision which builds on what has survived is likely to be sound. No formula could serve as a substitute, in this area, for judgment and restraint.

This statement is key to understanding Harlan's view, and to some extent it mirrors some of what earlier conservative judges had said, namely, that due process subsumed those rights treasured by a free people. But where they had concentrated on property rights, Harlan, reflecting the changing agenda of the Court, looked to personal liberties, such as a right to privacy. He went on to explicate how important a right that was, especially in the context of married life and sexuality, and why there could be no justification for state involvement. Harlan quoted from Brandeis's great dissent in *Olmstead,* that the Framers had "conferred, as against the Government, the right to be let alone—the most comprehensive of rights and the right most valued by civilized men."

What Harlan did, however, was far more than use the older notion of substantive due process to find that it included a right to privacy. He provided a conceptual framework to house modern rights—often described as "liberty interests"—not subsumed within the first eight amendments. Let us leave Harlan for a moment and look at the next phase in the fight against the Connecticut law.

Following the decision in *Poe,* the Connecticut Planned Parenthood League stepped up its activities. Estelle Griswold, the executive director, recognized that it would take an arrest to get the Court to decide the merits, so she and her colleagues went about practically daring the state to enforce the law. Eventually, Connecticut did just that, arresting her and the League's medical director in New Haven, Dr. C. Lee Buxton, and in 1965 the state's prohibition against birth control came back to the Marble Palace in *Griswold v. Connecticut.*

The Court that heard *Griswold* differed significantly from that which had decided *Poe* four years earlier. Frankfurter was gone, replaced by Arthur Goldberg, and Byron White had taken Whittaker's seat. More important, the nonjusticiability argument no longer applied: the law had been enforced, and arrests had been made. The decision this time would have to reach the merits. After hearing oral argument on 29 March, the justices agreed that the Connecticut law violated the Constitution, and Chief Justice Warren assigned the opinion to William O. Douglas, who had dissented in *Poe.*

In the earlier case, Douglas had tried to build a right to privacy on anything but due process, and he continued that theme in *Griswold,* where he delivered one of the most creative and innovative opinions in his thirty-six years on the bench. He cobbled together justifications for privacy from various parts of the Bill of Rights. These amendments, he said, "have penumbras, formed by emanations from those guarantees that help give them life and substance." These emanations together (joined in what one wit described as Amendment 3½) form a constitutionally protected right of privacy, and no privacy could be more sacred or more deserving of protection from intrusion by the state than that of the marital chamber.

Even if one believes that a right to privacy exists, Douglas's argument is a weak reed on which to support it. Arthur Goldberg (joined by Warren and Brennan) concurred in the result but would have relied on the rarely cited Ninth Amendment, which reserves to the people all unenumerated rights. The right to privacy, Goldberg maintained, predated the Constitution, and the Framers intended for all such ancient liberties to also enjoy constitutional protection. At this point, he too quoted from Brandeis's *Olmstead* opinion, whose power seemed to grow as the years went on.

The notion that privacy existed within due process was again put forth, this time in a concurring opinion by Justice Harlan. A revealing glimpse into Harlan's view is at the beginning, where he says that the majority opinion is very much like the dissents of Black and Stewart, namely, that the Due Process Clause does not touch the Connecticut statute unless it can be shown that the law somehow violates either a specific provision of the Bill of Rights or a penumbra emanating from it. The incorporation doctrine, he argued, cannot be used to restrict the reach of due process, any more than it can impose all of the provisions of the Bill of Rights on the states.

Borrowing from Cardozo's language, he asked whether the Connecticut law violated basic values "implicit in the concept of ordered liberty," and as he had argued in *Poe,* he concluded that it did. The Court, he said, needed to reinterpret constitutional essentials such as equal protection and due process so that the Constitution grows with the times. Harlan saw Black's approach as too rigid; both the states and the federal government needed the flexibility to experiment in means to expand the protection of individual rights. Harlan's concurrence is as good a statement of the "living Constitution" philosophy as any.

Although polls show that most people in this country believe that there is a right to privacy, Douglas's penumbral opinion did not impress many constitutional scholars. People like Robert Bork agreed with the dissents of Black and Stewart that because the Constitution did not mention privacy, there could be no constitutional right embodying it. The dissenters had no use for the law, but they would have left it to Connecticut voters to deal with their "uncommonly silly" statute. Both Stewart and Black demanded something—anything—in the Constitution on which to rest a decision. They dismissed the Ninth Amendment as saying nothing, a sentiment that Bork picked up when he described the amendment as saying, "People shall have the right," with the rest of the sentence obscured by an inkblot.

Harlan made it possible to bring privacy within constitutional protection, making it part of the individual's "liberty interests" protected by the Fourteenth Amendment. When the Court decided *Cruzan,* its first right-to-die case in 1990, Chief Justice Rehnquist held that an adult has a right to refuse medical treatment even if that decision would lead to death. Rehnquist based this finding not on privacy but on the common-law principles of bodily autonomy and the liberty interests found in the Fourteenth Amendment's Due Process Clause.

Beyond that, Harlan's contribution to the constitutional dialogue made it possible to create new rights beyond those specifically listed in the Constitution. A good example of this influence is in the concurring opinion of Justice David Souter in the 1997 assisted-suicide cases, *Washington v. Glucksberg* and *Vacco v. Quill.*

Following the *Cruzan* decision, advocates of physician-assisted suicide stepped up their political and legal efforts and won a major victory in 1994 in Oregon, which became the first state to legitimate the practice. In the same year, physicians and patients in New York and Washington filed suits in federal court seeking to overturn their state laws prohibiting physician-assisted suicide on due process and equal protection grounds. The Ninth Circuit agreed that the Washington law violated due process, while the Second Circuit overturned the New York law on equal protection ground. The Court took both cases, and everyone expected the justices to reverse the findings, which they did.

Rehnquist wrote a fairly narrow opinion, stressing the long history of laws banning suicide and assisting suicide, so one could not argue that the Framers had considered this a right under the original Constitution or Bill of Rights. He did note that a profound national debate was then going on, and he noted approvingly Oregon's experiment with legal physician-assisted suicide and concluded, "Our holding permits the debate to continue, as it should in a democratic society." Although technically Rehnquist spoke for a unanimous Court, only four justices joined his opinion fully; O'Connor qualified her support by saying that the ruling would not prevent a physician from prescribing painkilling medication even if it hastened death. The concurrences of four other justices—John Paul Stevens, David Souter, Ruth Bader Ginsburg, and Stephen Breyer—amounted to dissents and essentially said that they would go along with the ruling now, but if states narrowed end-of-life choices too much, they would be willing to revisit the issue.

The most interesting opinion came from David Souter, whose

JOSEPH BAILEY, NATIONAL GEOGRAPHIC SOCIETY, COURTESY OF USSC

David Hackett Souter, associate justice,
1990–2009

eighteen-page concurrence, according to one commentator, appeared to be channeling Harlan II. This is not surprising, because on several occasions Souter expressed admiration for Harlan. At his confirmation hearings, when asked about Harlan's separate opinion in *Griswold,* Souter forthrightly said he agreed that "the due process clause . . . does recognize and protect an unenumerated right of privacy."

In *Glucksberg,* Souter explored the history of due process from its early days in the Republic to its repudiation after abuse by conservatives attacking economic regulation. But he also noted that substantive due process had been used to defend individual liberties as well as property rights, and he considered Harlan's *Poe* dissent the most important statement of the types of rights subsumed under due process. Souter found three elements of Harlan's opinion necessary for any analysis of Fourteenth Amendment liberty interests. First, he noted Harlan's "respect for the tradition of substantive due process review" and the necessity for the courts to undertake that review. The very text of the Due Process Clause imposes on courts "nothing less than an obligation to give substantive content to the words 'liberty' and 'due process of law.' "

Harlan's second point in *Poe* reminded the Court that the purpose of such review "is not the identification of extratextual absolutes but scrutiny of a legislative resolution (perhaps unconsciously) of clashing principles, each quite possibly worthy in and of itself, but each to be weighed within the history of our values as a people." Here judges cannot impose their own values or substitute their views for that of the legislature unless the assembly has clearly exceeded constitutional parameters. This led to Harlan's third point, the necessity to pay attention to detail, to determine specific facts in order to understand the competing claims of both sides.

Souter went into this extended buildup because he found Rehnquist's opinion devoid of compassion or awareness of the claims of terminally ill patients. The majority had found no historical basis for recognizing assisted suicide as a liberty interest and therefore determined it did not exist. But Harlan had shown that new rights could be created using the due process clause, provided that the necessity of the times demanded that the courts recognize the liberty interests of the individuals involved. Souter, like Harlan, recognized that due process had in the past been used to create or at least recognize hitherto latent rights. While not prepared at that time to create a right to assisted suicide, he wanted to emphasize that even if the legislature had been well within its powers to make the choice it did, and even if judicial deference required courts to respect that decision, those seeking the right also had a claim that the courts needed to hear even if they did not agree with it. Souter indicated that the majority had been far too rigid in its analysis, and he quoted from Harlan in *Poe* that appropriate review of substantive due process claims comes not from drawing arbitrary lines but from understanding the historical bases of those claims as well as the recognition of shared social values.

Souter did not invent a new right in *Glucksberg,* but he indicated that assisted suicide might be a latent liberty interest, ready to emerge and be recognized by courts when the times made such an interest necessary for individual liberty. Harlan's *Poe* dissent pointed the way—and provided a logically far more coherent analysis than Douglas's penumbras—to recognizing how the Constitution could embody a right to privacy. In *Poe* and again in *Griswold,* John Marshall Harlan II resuscitated the idea of substantive due process. As the Roosevelt appointees left the Court, taking with them their antipathy to substantive due process, Harlan's view of the Due Process Clause as a source for newly emerging liberty interests has proven a powerful and influential argument.

IN 1985, justices on the U.S. Supreme Court filed 400 opinions in the 150 cases decided that term, a high for a forty-year period. Chief Justice Warren Burger complained about the increase in plurality opinions

LIBRARY OF CONGRESS

Warren Earl Burger, chief justice, 1969–1986

where the majority lacked the fifth vote to make it a binding precedent. Between 1800 and 1900, only 10 opinions of the Court had the support of less than a majority. Between 1901 and 1969—the last year of the Warren Court—51 cases were decided by a plurality opinion. By contrast, during the Burger years, 1969 to 1986, the Court handed down 116 plurality opinions, nearly twice the total that had been rendered in the entire prior history of the Court. The chief justice blamed the "proliferation of concurring opinions and even some dissenting opinions" on the increasing caseload and the lack of time to hammer out differences.

That made for a nice, simple explanation, except the caseload provided only part of the reason for the growing dissensus on the Court.

In May 1969, Nixon named Burger to succeed Earl Warren. In his seventeen years in the center chair, Burger never did succeed in bringing the Court around to the strict constructionist posture that Nixon had envisaged. Most scholars believe that Burger never actually led the Court—in any direction. Much of the blame, then and since, has fallen on Burger himself, a man who greatly enjoyed the title and trappings of chief justice of the United States but who might have been one of the more inept chiefs in the twentieth century. Like Fred Vinson, Burger showed far greater interest in administration than in jurisprudence, and a number of his colleagues reported that at conference he was "the least prepared member of the Court." Like Harlan Stone, Burger let the brethren talk on and on, and confusion often resulted over who voted how and whether any votes had changed. Technically, the chief is only "first among equals" and like the other justices has only one vote. He can only lead if he demonstrates superior intellectual, legal, or political skills, none of which Burger had. Douglas and Brennan respected Earl Warren and so would often—but not always—follow the lead of the man Brennan called "Super Chief." They had little respect for Burger. By the early 1980s, the Burger Court was becoming increasingly dysfunctional, with no real leadership. Thus the four hundred separate opinions.

There were many dissents—hundreds in fact—but did any of them matter in the sense that they contributed to the constitutional dialogue? We can pick a few out, but one should note that for the most part the dissents often tended to be fractious, indicating the justices' annoyance as much as a strong jurisprudential objection. One study of the Burger Court shows that in about one case in twenty a justice who had indicated he or she would join the majority eventually wound up voting on the other side. At the same time, a higher percentage utilized threats of either changing votes or writing separately to try to shape the majority decision. We have no comparable figures for other courts, but it is fair to say that given the lack of leadership and hostile relations that marred the Burger Court, these numbers are on the high side.

Three cases decided during the Burger years are all high profile and should be seen in the context of broad policy debates within the country. In each of these cases, both the majority and the dissenting opinions contributed to the constitutional—and political—dialogue and at the same time reflected changes occurring within the country. The three cases are *Roe v. Wade* (1973), *Regents of the University of California v. Bakke*

Harold Andrew "Harry" Blackmun, associate justice,
1970–1994

(1978), and *Bowers v. Hardwick* (1986), and the issues they raised continued well into the eras of William Rehnquist and John Roberts.

THERE HAS BEEN so much written about *Roe v. Wade,* and so much
public and political debate about abortion, that the story is probably
familiar to most Americans. Briefly, at a time when many states were
abandoning or modifying their nineteenth-century prohibitions against
abortion, the Supreme Court, in a case involving an older Texas statute,
declared that a woman had a constitutional right to decide to have an
abortion.

   In *Roe,* Justice Harry Blackmun's opinion for the 7–2 Court relied on
the concepts of privacy and autonomy first suggested in *Griswold.* But
Blackmun boldly ventured to what Douglas had skirted in the earlier
case: he identified a new substantive due process right as the basis for
noneconomic individual rights. Conceding that "the Constitution does
not explicitly mention any right of privacy," Blackmun cited a dozen

or so cases going back more than eighty years to assert that the Constitution protected privacy in a variety of ways. He asserted that "the Court has recognized that a right of personal privacy, or a guarantee of certain areas or zones of privacy, does exist under the Constitution." In support of this view, Blackmun cited, among other cases, the Brandeis dissent in *Olmstead* and concluded that "this right of privacy, whether it be founded in the Fourteenth Amendment's concept of personal liberty and restrictions upon state action, as we feel it is, or, as the district court determined, in the Ninth Amendment's reservation of rights to the people, is broad enough to encompass a woman's decision whether or not to terminate her pregnancy."

In addition to the majority opinion, Chief Justice Burger and Justices Douglas and Stewart submitted concurring opinions. Stewart essentially echoed the Harlan dissent in *Poe* and acknowledged that the right to privacy on which the Court had relied could not be found specifically in the Constitution but was indeed protected by the Due Process Clause. Ironically, he also cited from a dissenting opinion by Justice Frankfurter—a man who wanted nothing to do with substantive due process or the creation of new rights: "Great concepts like . . . 'liberty' . . . were purposely left to gather meaning from experience. For they relate to the whole domain of social and economic fact, and the statesmen who founded this Nation knew too well that only a stagnant society remains unchanged."

Douglas's concurrence grew out of a lengthy memo he had prepared after he found an early draft of Blackmun's opinion unsatisfactory. Comments from Douglas, Brennan, and Thurgood Marshall, however, had strengthened the majority opinion significantly, although Douglas would have gone further. He again emphasized the place of a right to privacy in a free society, and he went on to list certain freedoms that he considered essential and beyond the interference of the state: the autonomous control over the development of one's intellect, interests, and personality; freedom of choice in basic decisions such as marriage, divorce, procreation, contraception, and raising children; freedom in health decisions and from bodily restraint; "freedom to walk, stroll, or loaf." The concurrence may be the best articulation of Douglas's libertarian views, his belief that government should be kept off the backs of the people.

Rehnquist, after acknowledging the "extensive historical fact and a wealth of legal scholarship" and saying that "the opinion thus commands my respect," nonetheless dissented. He questioned whether a real plaintiff existed, because by the time the case came to the Court, Jane Roe had presumably had her baby. (Blackmun had responded to this issue by noting that pregnancy fell into the category of "capable of repetition, yet evading review," and that the issue needed to be decided for future Jane Roes.) While he agreed that the liberties in the Fourteenth Amendment included others than found in the Bill of Rights, the Constitution did not make any of those rights absolute but provided only that they could not be restricted without due process of law. The only test that the Court should impose here was that of rational basis: Did the Texas statute have a legitimate and rational relation to a legitimate state objective?

He then charged that the Court had engaged in just the sort of behavior that had been so vilified when undertaken by earlier courts—substituting judicial preferences for legislative judgment. Although Blackmun had quoted from Holmes's *Lochner* dissent, Rehnquist charged, "the result it reaches is more closely attuned to the majority opinion of Justice Peckham in that case." Here even Blackmun's defenders had to agree, and Tinsley Yarbrough noted that "as an exercise in judicial lawmaking, Justice Blackmun's abortion opinions put to shame the judicial legislators of the *Lochner* era."

The fact that a majority of states had restrictions on abortions for at least a century stood as a strong indication that abortion could not be considered a historical right "so rooted in the traditions and conscience of our people as to be ranked as fundamental." Rehnquist noted that a public debate on abortion was then going on, but the very existence of such a debate proved that abortion could not be considered a fundamental right. To reach its decision, he charged, the majority had to find within the Fourteenth Amendment a right completely unknown to its drafters. In fact, the Texas statute at issue had been enacted in 1857, eleven years before the ratification of the Fourteenth Amendment.

If Rehnquist maintained an air of civility in his dissent, Byron White found nothing in the language or history of the Constitution to support the essential holding of the Court. The Court "apparently values the convenience of the pregnant mother more than the continued existence and development of the life or potential life that she carries."

Ironically, in light of the later furor, the decisions in the two cases were not particularly controversial at the time. More amici filed briefs in support of a woman's right to choose than in support of the state laws. A few states, like California and New York, had already reformed their laws along the lines set out by Blackmun, and in 1973 there were more legal abortions in New York than live births. As Rehnquist noted, there was a debate going on, and other states were then considering revising their statutes. Ruth Bader Ginsburg said, both at her confirmation hearings and since, that she objected not to the holding per se but to the timing. By issuing the ruling, a group of "unelected old men" stopped the momentum that was building among the states. "That was my concern, that the Court had given opponents of access to abortion a target to aim at relentlessly. . . . My criticism of *Roe* is that it seemed to have stopped the momentum that was on the side of change."

Indeed within a few years the climate had changed. Some religious groups—most notably Roman Catholics and fundamentalist Protestants—began a vocal campaign against the decision, declaring that a fetus was a person and therefore entitled to full protection against abortion/murder. (In his opinion, Blackmun had said that science had no way of determining when life began; that was a theological question that the Court would not discuss. English common law treated the fetus as property, with life beginning at birth.)

The charges raised by Rehnquist and White in their dissents have continued to reverberate in the public attack on *Roe:* the Court had substituted its judgment for that of duly elected legislators; it had created a new right, the Constitution did not recognize any right to privacy; the Court had elevated the convenience of some women over the Constitution and life itself. Various states have tried to limit *Roe* by placing ever more difficult conditions upon securing abortions or allowing doctors to perform them; in some southern state-sponsored medical schools, for example, students cannot even learn how to perform the procedure.

The abortion decisions would remain at the center of the political and judicial landscape for more than two decades, and as more and more abortion cases came to the Court testing state restrictions, White and Rehnquist remained adamantly in support of state laws and against the basic holding of *Roe* and over the years picked up support as Reagan and George H. W. Bush appointed ever more conservative jurists to the Court. At confirmation hearings, conservative senators peppered nominees with questions about judicial activism, whether a right to privacy existed, and the constitutional basis for *Roe.* By 1992, it appeared to be only a matter of time until the Court overruled *Roe.*

A Pennsylvania law seemed to include every restriction that abortion opponents could think of to burden the procedure to the point of making an abortion impossible to obtain. The statute required minors to get parental consent and wives to notify their husbands before obtaining an abortion; doctors had to inform women about potential medical complications; women had to wait twenty-four hours after requesting an abortion before a doctor could perform the procedure; and doctors had to follow up with onerous reporting requirements. The district court had invalidated the law, but the Third Circuit Court of Appeals reinstated

*William Hubbs Rehnquist, associate justice, 1972–1986;
chief justice, 1986–2005*

it and then declared that, contrary to *Roe,* abortion would no longer be considered a fundamental right. By this logic, courts would accept any restrictions the legislature thought reasonable.

The Court announced it would take the case on 21 January 1992, the eve of *Roe*'s nineteenth anniversary, and tens of thousands of anti-abortion demonstrators were gathering in Washington for what had become an annual march. The justices heard the case on 22 April, and a few weeks following conference Chief Justice Rehnquist circulated a twenty-seven-page draft upholding all of the Pennsylvania restrictions and finding that "the Court was mistaken in *Roe* when it classified a woman's decision to terminate her pregnancy as a 'fundamental right' that could be abridged only in a manner that withstood 'strict scrutiny.'" Once again he argued that states may regulate abortion procedures in any way rationally related to a legitimate state interest. If Rehnquist actually spoke for a majority, this would be the end of *Roe.* Blackmun prepared to write a dissent.

Then he received a handwritten note from Anthony Kennedy, asking to see him. Kennedy, along with Sandra Day O'Connor and David Souter, proposed to keep the essential holding of *Roe* and would have the majority if Blackmun and John Paul Stevens agreed. The three took the unusual step of co-authoring an opinion that sustained some but not all of the Pennsylvania restrictions, but then reaffirmed three components of *Roe:* the right of a woman to choose to have an abortion before viability and to obtain it without undue interference from the state; the state's power to restrict abortion after viability, providing the law contains exceptions for pregnancies that endanger the woman's life; and the state's legitimate interests in protecting the health of the woman and the life of the fetus that may become a child. "These principles do not contradict one another, and we adhere to each." The opinion did not, however, reaffirm the strict scrutiny standard that *Roe* had established for evaluating restrictions, and it added a new test—whether the restrictions unduly burdened a woman in securing a legitimate abortion.

Because the majority had upheld several of the Pennsylvania statutes, Rehnquist and White, joined by Scalia and Thomas, concurred in that part of the judgment but dissented from the part reaffirming *Roe*. Essentially, Rehnquist repeated what he and White had said in the earlier cases, and their arguments are still at the heart of the debate over abortion and the law, part of the dialogue both inside the Marble Palace and in the public arena.

THE SECOND Burger Court decision involved affirmative action, an issue that lacks some of the fiery vitriol that marks the abortion debate but still has split the country in two.

In the 1970s, civil rights advocates, while still fighting over discrimination, began to look at ways by which blacks could truly become equal members of society. The strategy they chose became and has remained one of the most divisive issues in our society. The reasoning behind affirmative action is simple, perhaps even simplistic. Because society discriminated against blacks in so many ways for three centuries, it is unrealistic to assume that mere removal of the old fetters made African Americans suddenly equal and able to avail themselves of all opportunities. Something had to be done to compensate for prior discrimination so that eventually blacks could take full advantage of equal opportunities.

One answer would be to grant African Americans some preference in jobs and college admissions. Employers would make special efforts to recruit minority members and perhaps even hold aside a certain percentage of jobs. By Executive Order 11246, promulgated by Lyndon Johnson and then greatly strengthened by Richard Nixon, federal contractors had to take affirmative steps to hire more women and minorities, or they would run the risk of being barred from future government work.

On the surface, affirmative action sounded like a great idea, but in fact it forced society to make some very difficult choices. By providing preferential treatment to one group, it penalized another. If giving a job to a black man or woman that might have otherwise gone to a white person helped the black overcome a legacy of persecution, who paid for it? The white denied a job might never have discriminated against blacks; his or her ancestors might have come to this country after the end of slavery. What some people called affirmative action others called reverse discrimination. There is no tradition of group rights in the United States. The Civil Rights Act of 1964, in several provisions, bars discrimination against *persons,* that is, individuals, because of race, color, or national origin.

The issue first came to the Court in 1974, and the Court ducked. Marco DeFunis had been accepted by several law schools, but he wanted to live and practice in Seattle, and the University of Washington Law School had twice turned him down. The school had a separate admissions process for blacks, Hispanics, Indians, and Filipinos, and DeFunis learned that of the thirty-seven minority candidates accepted for the fall of 1971, all but one had combined test and grade scores below his. Believing federal courts too sympathetic to minorities, DeFunis sued in state court on claims of racial bias; he won, and the trial court ordered him admitted to the law school. The Washington State Supreme Court reversed and upheld the university's plan, and then the Supreme Court granted cert. In the meantime, DeFunis had been attending law school and, thanks to a stay of judgment issued by Justice Douglas, had been registered for his last term by the time the high court heard the case in early 1974.

Because DeFunis would graduate regardless of the outcome, five members of the Court—Burger, Stewart, Blackmun, Powell, and Rehnquist—declared the question moot in a *per curiam* opinion and thus avoided having to rule on the substantive issues surrounding affirmative action. Four justices—Douglas, Brennan, White, and Marshall—dissented, arguing that the constitutionality of special admissions programs ought to be resolved. "The constitutional issues which we avoided today," Brennan declared, "concern vast numbers of people, organizations and colleges and universities. . . . Few constitutional questions in recent history have stirred as much debate, and they will not disappear." Brennan only argued that the Court should have decided the question, without giving any hint as to how he himself would have voted. William O. Douglas made his views quite clear.

Although Douglas was now in his thirty-fifth year on the Court, and some observers thought he had grown bored and sloppy, his dissent in this case is one of his best—sharp, well reasoned, and well written. What he said would be at the heart of the affirmative action debate for years to come. "The key to the problem is the consideration of each application *in a racially neutral way.*" Because the standard Law School Admission Test (LSAT) admittedly had cultural biases, the admissions committee acted properly in setting minority applications aside. But

> the melting pot is not designed to homogenize people, making them uniform in consistency. . . . Minorities in our midst who are to serve actively in our public affairs should be chosen on talent and character alone, not on cultural orientation or leanings. . . . There is no constitutional right for any race to be preferred. The years of slavery did more than retard the progress of blacks. Even a greater wrong was done the whites by creating arrogance instead of humility and by encouraging the growth of the fiction of a superior race. There is no superior person by constitutional standards. A DeFunis who is white is entitled to no advantage by reason of that fact; nor is he subject to any disability, no matter what his race or color. Whatever his race, he had a constitutional right to have his application considered on its individual merits in a racially neutral manner.

Douglas went on to ridicule the notion that some form of "compelling state interest" required that there be a proportion of minority students in the law school reflecting the minority in the general population. By that reasoning, one would have to divide up every college and law school class, every public service such as buses and trains, every public works undertaking, to ensure that there was the right ratio of blacks, Hispanics, Poles, Jews, Irish, and what have you represented. "The Equal Protection Clause commands the elimination of racial barriers, not their creation in order to satisfy our theory as to how society ought to be organized." One other assumption, he declared, "must be clearly disapproved—that blacks or browns cannot make it on their own individual merit. That is a stamp of inferiority that a State is not permitted to place on any lawyer."

As Brennan predicted, the issue would not go away, and it returned to the high court just four years later in a case that could not be considered

Lewis Franklin Powell Jr., associate justice,
1972–1987

moot. Allan Bakke was twice denied admission to the University of California at Davis Medical School, which set aside sixteen of its entering hundred places for minority students who could have lower test scores than the white students who made up the bulk of the class. Bakke's test scores were higher than those of the sixteen minority students, and thus as a white person he had been discriminated against on the basis of his race. He claimed that the admissions program violated his rights under the Civil Rights Act. The university conceded that race-based admissions programs were constitutionally problematic but asserted that the program served to remedy the effects of past discrimination.

A deeply fractured Court, speaking (sort of) through Justice Lewis Powell, ruled that universities could not constitutionally use numerical quotas in their admissions program but could use race as one of many criteria. The only part of his ruling joined by any other justice was the one-paragraph statement of fact. Powell flatly rejected the use of quotas and noted that the Court had upheld racial quotas in only a few instances where they had supplied a discrete remedy to specified prior discrimination, as determined by an appropriate judicial, legislative, or executive authority. At Davis, there had been no record of prior discrimination, and it exceeded the medical faculty's competence or authority to establish a remedial program. The faculty, however, was well within its competence as an educational group in seeking to diversify the student body along as many lines as possible—including racial lines. To use race flexibly, within the context of a comprehensive admissions policy with an educational rather than a societal goal—as Harvard did—would be permissible. The Davis plan failed, and Powell ordered Bakke admitted; Davis and other schools, however, would be able to take race into account, but only as one of several considerations.

From this opinion, the other eight members of the Court dissented. Four of the justices—Chief Justice Burger, Stewart, Rehnquist, and Stevens—took a strict statutory approach, holding that the Davis plan violated Title VI of the 1964 Civil Rights Act, which prohibited discrimination against any person—that is, an individual—because of race, color, or national origin in any institution or program receiving federal assistance. They therefore supported Powell's conclusion that Bakke should be admitted and that quota plans were bad, but they refused to go along with his argument that race could be considered as a factor in admissions. Brennan, White, Marshall and Blackmun, on the other hand, agreed that race could be considered in admissions. They did not believe that the Davis program violated either Title VI or the Fourteenth Amendment and dissented from ordering Bakke's admission.

There have, of course, been plurality opinions, in which five members of the Court may agree on the result but not on the reasoning, but there is no other instance in the Court's history of a plurality opinion of one. Some commentators, such as the *New York Times* columnist Anthony Lewis, praised Powell for striking an astute political compromise. One might well call it a transitional decision, one that satisfied neither side but at the same time did not alienate them either. Clearly, no majority existed on the Court on this matter, and while a 5–4 decision is as binding as a 9–0 vote, the Court has long realized that on major issues unanimity carries greater legal as well as moral weight. The "somewhat fuzzy" nature of Powell's *Bakke* decision, declared Paul Freund of the Harvard Law School, "leaves room for development, and on the whole that's a good thing."

If the Court as a whole did not reach the merits, eight of the justices did so, and as in *Roe* the voices of the dissenters—and in this case there were dissents on both sides—would play an important role in the dialogue over affirmative action for the next thirty-five years.

Brennan, joined by White, Marshall, and Blackmun, would have upheld the Davis plan against both Title VI and equal protection challenges. Choosing that part of Powell's opinion with which they agreed, they claimed the "central meaning" of the decision was that "government may take race into account when it acts not to demean or insult any racial group, but to remedy disadvantages cast on minorities by past racial prejudice." Brennan's group took a very limited view of Title VI, saying it did no more to prohibit racial discrimination than the Fourteenth Amendment, and they saw both as permitting affirmative action plans to remedy past discrimination.

According to Brennan, "No decision of this Court has ever adopted the proposition that the Constitution must be colorblind." Second, even if one argued that in 1964 the "Constitution might conceivably require color blindness," Congress in the Civil Rights Act looked more to voluntary compliance in attempting to remedy past wrongs, and the program at Davis surely fit that description. As the Court had said earlier, "Just as the race of students must be considered in determining whether a constitutional violation has occurred, so also must race be considered in formulating a remedy." Congress could not have conceived of eliminating race as a consideration in programs designed to counter or compensate for discrimination. Finally, Congress "eschewed any static definition of discrimination in favor of broad language that could be shaped by experience, necessity, and evolving judicial doctrine."

For justices who throughout their careers showed sensitivity to the plight of underdogs, minorities, and the poor, the opinion strikes a discordant note in its almost dismissive treatment of how individual whites, like Allan Bakke, would fare—yes, it would hurt a little, but not as much as segregation had hurt African Americans. His biographers argue that Brennan was trying to hold together a fragile coalition that supported affirmative action, not all of them for the same reasons, and he was trying to lay a strong enough foundation to support similar programs in the future. His colleagues, especially Thurgood Marshall and Byron White (who had been involved with civil rights in the Kennedy Justice Department), strongly supported affirmative action, and Harry Blackmun was getting there.

A memorandum by Thurgood Marshall to the brethren made it quite clear that how one looked at the issue determined its outcome: "If you view the programs as admitting qualified students who, because of this Nation's sorry history of racial discrimination, have academic records that prevent them from effectively competing for medical school, then this is affirmative action to remove the vestiges of slavery and state imposed segregation by root and branch. If you view the program as excluding students, it is a program of quotas which violates the principle that the Constitution is color-blind."

The Brennan group saw it as the former, while Justice John Paul Stevens, who wrote the other concurrence/dissent, joined by Burger, Stewart, and Rehnquist, saw it as the latter.

Where Brennan had tried to paint in broad strokes, Stevens hewed to the particular: The case involved two specific parties, Allan Bakke and the Davis Medical School. Both sides had asked for a judgment based on the Constitution; "our settled practice, however, is to avoid the decision of a constitutional issue if a case can be fairly decided on a statutory ground." While a constitutional issue existed, it need not be decided, because the statutory claim proved dispositive: The University of California at Davis Medical School had clearly violated the 1964 Civil Rights Act. Title VI held that "no person in the United States shall, on the ground of race, color, or national origin, be excluded from participation in, be denied the benefits of, or be subjected to discrimination under any program or activity receiving federal financial assistance." Davis excluded Bakke on the grounds of his race, it was receiving federal money, and so "the plain language of the statute requires" that the lower court's ruling in support of Bakke be affirmed. Having narrowed the question to this one issue, Stevens wrote a short but pointed opinion that, unlike Brennan's, did not try to deal with large issues of why affirmative action ought to be encouraged. All he needed to know was whether there had been a violation of the law.

At the time the act was drafted, Congress had little concern about "reverse discrimination" or "affirmative action" but a great deal about the "glaring discrimination" against African Americans. The drafters of Title VI did not say, however, that only certain groups would be protected from discrimination, and indeed did not even talk about groups. They wrote, and Congress enacted a law directing, that "no *person*" shall be subject to exclusion on the basis of race. The facts in this case made it quite clear that Allan Bakke had been denied admission to the school for no reason other than his race, and indeed at the trial the university admitted that it could not show that, absent the special program, he would have been denied acceptance.

Over the next several years, the Court heard a number of cases involving affirmative action. Brennan, utilizing arguments he had set forth in *Bakke,* got the Court to approve a voluntary private sector plan in 1979, on the grounds that Title VI did not apply to private agreements. A year later, he also wrote for the Court in sustaining the minority business enterprise clause of the 1977 Public Works Employment Act, requiring that 10 percent of federal funds appropriated for local public works projects be subcontracted for goods and services supplied by minority-owned businesses. The high point in the Court's approval of affirmative action came in a California case involving not race but gender discrimination.

By then, however, the arguments of the Stevens group had begun to pick up steam. Byron White became less enamored of affirmative action, and the addition of Sandra Day O'Connor and Antonin Scalia gave the Court a slim majority that looked askance at affirmative action, at the same time that the Reagan Justice Department took a decidedly hostile approach to these plans. Attorney General Edwin Meese went so far as to try to pressure city governments that had signed consent decrees establishing hiring plans for women and minorities to rescind them.

The Rehnquist Court could not be accused of indifference to civil rights when confronted with overt evidence of state-sponsored discrimination. But a majority of justices seemed to be searching for a new paradigm of equal protection analysis, and this became apparent in their affirmative action decisions. In the first case the Rehnquist Court heard—the California plan to hire and promote more women—even though Brennan managed to get six votes, there really was not that much support. O'Connor signed on to the judgment but not the reasoning, and only because she saw the numbers proving there had been no women in key positions in the transportation agency—ever. Scalia, joined by White and Rehnquist, filed a strong dissent. Instead of making the law gender-blind or color-blind to do away with all forms of discrimination, the majority, they charged, had done just the opposite. In the name of affirmative action, individuals who had not violated the law in any way would be penalized so that minority members who might never have suffered individual discrimination could receive a preference. When Powell, Marshall, and Brennan left the Court in the next few years, to be replaced by Anthony Kennedy, Clarence Thomas (who personally despised affirmative action), and David Souter, the tide quickly shifted. In *City of Richmond v. J. A. Croson Co.* (1989), Justice O'Connor spoke for a 6–3 Court in striking down a city minority business set-aside plan modeled on the federal program. Congress, she noted, had provided extensive evidence regarding discrimination in federal contracting; the city, on the other hand, had offered nothing but anecdotal evidence. One could still have an affirmative action plan, but now one would have to justify it on the basis of real evidence of past discrimination.

Six years later, O'Connor again spoke for the Court, but this time a highly splintered one, holding that under the Due Process Clauses of the Fifth and Fourteenth Amendments any action involving racial classification, including set-asides, by *either* the states or the federal government would be judged by a standard of strict scrutiny, the same standard

Rehnquist had suggested at the time of *Bakke.* Just as the courts frowned on measures that discriminated because of race, they would now frown with equal fervor on measures that favored on the basis of race.

If one looks at the dozen or so affirmative action cases that followed *Bakke,* even with changes of the Court's personnel, one finds the same arguments put forth in that earlier case. Affirmative action is constitutional because it is necessary to compensate minorities for past discrimination, as opposed to the belief that any program that discriminates against any individual, whatever his or her color or gender, violates both the Equal Protection Clause and the Civil Rights Act. The dialogue on the Court reflected similar conversations in statehouses and among the public. A poll at the end of the twentieth century found that 77 percent of the people surveyed believed that affirmative action programs discriminated against whites; even 66 percent of the black respondents answered the same way.

Justice Powell's *Bakke* compromise allowed colleges and universities to continue their programs to attract minorities, even if some of them had scores below those of white applicants. But as years went by, some schools began not only to take race into account but in some instances to make it a major factor in admissions, and this led to attacks on these plans. In California, a voter referendum stopped the University of California and all of its branches from taking race or ethnicity into account in admissions, and within a year minority numbers at elite schools like Berkeley and UCLA dropped precipitously. In 1996, the Court of Appeals for the Fifth Circuit struck down the University of Texas plan that favored black and Hispanic minorities. In *Hopwood v. Texas,* the appeals court told the prestigious University of Texas Law School that it could not use admissions standards for minority students different from those it used for white students, a ruling that overtly ran counter to *Bakke.* The Supreme Court denied *certiorari,* thus leaving *Bakke* in place everywhere but in the Fifth Circuit.

The Court gave no reason for denying cert, but it is possible that it wanted a case that would make the options clearer. If so, it found them in two cases coming out of Michigan in 2003, one concerning undergraduate admissions and the other the law school. Given the thousands of undergraduate applications it received each year, the university could not provide individualized evaluation and instead used a scoring system that awarded up to 150 points. Students who came from underrepresented areas of the state (such as the Upper Peninsula), were the children of Michigan graduates (legacies), or fell into other categories (such as veterans) received additional points; minorities could receive up to

20 points. A white student from Detroit had little to rely on other than her grade point average and SAT scores.

The law school at Michigan is an elite, national institution consistently ranked in the first tier of American law schools. It had decided that diversity in the classroom was necessary to provide a good legal education. The school did not establish any quotas and did not use any numerical formulas but did take race into account, as one factor among many. The admissions policy seemed to follow Justice Powell's *Bakke* opinion but led to situations where white students with higher GPAs and LSAT scores found themselves denied admission while the school accepted minority students with lower scores.

The Court upheld the law school plan in *Grutter v. Bollinger,* because race had clearly been just one factor. Justice O'Connor made it a point—and sent a message to the Fifth Circuit—that despite the strange vote in *Bakke,* Justice Powell's opinion was the law. Moreover, the 5–4 majority recognized that diversity in the classroom could be the type of compelling state interest that on occasion could justify some racial classification.

In the undergraduate case, O'Connor and Breyer joined the dissenters in *Grutter.* Chief Justice Rehnquist wrote the majority opinion in *Gratz v. Bollinger,* and while he conceded that the law school case demonstrated that the government had a compelling interest in diversity, the rigid point system for undergraduate admissions, with twenty points automatically awarded for race, failed the strict scrutiny test applicable in racial classification cases.

If one read the *Bakke* opinions and then those in the Michigan cases, one would find that little had changed. Only Rehnquist and Stevens remained from the Burger Court, and while Stevens had changed his views, Rehnquist had not. The various opinions—seven in the law school case and five in the other—rehearsed the same arguments from a quarter century earlier. Did programs that supposedly benefited large groups and addressed past discrimination warrant constitutional approbation when, at the same time, they in effect discriminated against individual nonminority applicants? How much leeway is there in the wording of the Equal Protection Clause and the Civil Rights Act? Should they be taken literally or in the context of a nation still trying to heal from three centuries of slavery and then apartheid?

And that dialogue continues. In 2013, the Court heard a challenge to the University of Texas, which after *Grutter* made race one factor in its admissions policy. The district court had found for the university, and the Fifth Circuit, after its rebuke in the Michigan case, had affirmed.

The Supreme Court, by a 7–1 vote, sent the case back to the Fifth Circuit, which "did not hold the University to the demanding burden of strict scrutiny articulated in *Grutter* and *Bakke*." But, the Court went on, *Bakke* and the Michigan cases are "taken as given for purposes of deciding this case." In other words, if one reads Justice Kennedy's opinion properly, Texas may take race into account if it does so as one of several factors in a carefully tailored program. The case will probably come back to the Court in a few years, and at the time we will no doubt hear the same arguments rehearsed as we heard in the two concurrence/dissents in *Bakke*.

Before that could happen, though, the Court heard another case from Michigan. Following the *Gratz* and *Grutter* decisions, the voters in that state had passed a constitutional amendment that forbade any state college or university to take race, gender, ethnicity, and other factors into account in its admissions policy. When the case came to the high court, a majority of the justices spoke not to the merits of affirmative action but to the question of whether the electorate could enact a policy that was race and gender neutral. In a 6–2 decision, Justice Kennedy said it could, which may now allow voters in other states to end affirmative action by insisting on race-neutral policies, in effect carrying out Justice Harlan's admonition that "the Constitution is color-blind." Justice Sonia Sotomayor, joined by Ruth Bader Ginsburg, entered a passionate dissent defending affirmative action and charging that the voters, in what would appear to be a facially race-neutral proposal, had in fact now placed additional burdens on minorities.

ONE OF THE VERY LAST opinions of the Burger Court tested the limits of a privacy right in a new area, and the debate within and outside the Court has reverberated to the present. *Bowers v. Hardwick* (1986) involved the constitutionality of sodomy laws, statutes that prohibited sexual relations between members of the same sex. Prior to this case, the Court had never addressed the extent to which states could constitutionally regulate sexual practices per se. The Court had earlier, by a 6–3 vote, summarily affirmed a lower court decision that rejected a challenge to Virginia's statute outlawing sodomy, but while such affirmances bind lower courts, they have little or no precedential value.

The fact that sexual relationships usually take place in the privacy of one's home complicated matters, because it brought not only *Griswold* into play but also *Stanley v. Georgia,* one of the last of the Warren Court decisions. There a unanimous Court, speaking through Justice Marshall, had ruled that a combination of First Amendment values and the right

Byron Raymond White, associate justice, 1962–1993

of privacy gave constitutional protection to read or view sexually ori-
ented materials within the privacy of one's home, even if the state could
legally ban the sale of such materials as obscene.

Hardwick involved a Georgia statute that criminalized consensual
sodomy and provided up to twenty years' imprisonment for anyone
who "performs or submits to any sexual act involving the sex organs of
one person and the mouth or anus of another." Michael Hardwick was
arrested in his own home when a police officer entered his bedroom to
serve a warrant for drinking in public. The district attorney, who had
been trying to improve relations with the gay community in light of
the growing gay rights movement, refused to prosecute, but Hardwick
brought an action in federal court to challenge the constitutionality of
the Georgia statute. The Court of Appeals for the Eleventh Circuit held
the Georgia statute violated rights to privacy under the Ninth and Fourteenth Amendments.

Five justices voted to overturn the lower court—Burger, White, Powell, Rehnquist, and O'Connor. Justice White stated the question clearly:

"The issue is whether the Federal Constitution confers a fundamental right upon homosexuals to engage in sodomy and hence invalidates the laws of the many States that still make such conduct illegal and have done so for a very long time." Given this long history of antisodomy laws, the right claimed by Hardwick as either "deeply rooted in the Nation's history" or "implicit in the concept of ordered liberty" was, "at best, facetious." No such right existed, and White noted that the Court's prior statements recognizing the right of privacy all dealt with family rights, child rearing, and procreation. These cases bore no "resemblance to the claimed constitutional right of homosexuals to engage in acts of sodomy," because there is "no connection between family, marriage, or procreation on the one hand and homosexual activity on the other."

There were two dissents. One by Harry Blackmun, which Brennan, Marshall, and Stevens joined, and the other by Stevens, joined by Brennan and Marshall. Blackmun's opening statement captured the message: "This case is no more about 'a fundamental right to engage in homosexual sodomy,' as the Court purports to declare, than *Stanley v. Georgia* was about a fundamental right to watch obscene movies, or *Katz v. United States* was about a fundamental right to place interstate bets from a phone booth. Rather this case is about 'the most comprehensive of rights and the one most valued by civilized men,' namely, 'the right to be let alone.' " (Citing the Brandeis dissent in *Olmstead*.)

For Blackmun it was all about privacy, and he disputed White's interpretation of what the Court's previous cases had been about. "In construing the right to privacy, the Court has proceeded along two somewhat distinct, albeit complementary, lines. First, it has recognized a privacy interest with reference to certain *decisions* that are properly for the individual to make. Second, it has recognized a privacy interest with reference to certain *places* without regard for the particular activities in which the individuals who occupy them are engaged. The case before us implicates both the decisional and the spatial aspects of the right to privacy." No mention of the activity involved, just who would get to make the decision and where the activity took place. "In a variety of circumstances," he explained, "we have recognized that a necessary corollary of giving individuals freedom to choose how to conduct their lives is acceptance of the fact that different individuals will make different choices. . . . A way of life that is odd or even erratic but interferes with no rights or interests of others is not to be condemned because it is different. The Court claims that its decision today merely refuses to recognize a fundamental right to engage in homosexual sodomy; what the Court really has refused to recognize is the fundamental interest all individuals have in controlling the nature of their intimate associations with others."

By this time in his career, Blackmun had become a strong advocate of the right of privacy. He was devoting a portion of his annual lecture at the Aspen Institute to defending the views of the British legal scholar H. L. A. Hart that, based on the philosophy of John Stuart Mill, the government had no business interfering with private acts that inflicted no harm on others merely because society considered such conduct "immoral."

He concluded his dissent by noting that during World War II the Court had at first upheld and then overturned compulsory flag salutes in public schools, deciding that one could not compel orthodoxy. "I can only hope that here, too, the Court soon will reconsider its analysis and conclude that depriving individuals of the right to choose for themselves how to conduct their intimate relationships poses a far greater threat to the values most deeply rooted in our Nation's history than tolerance of nonconformity could ever do. Because I think the Court today betrays those values, I dissent."

To show how strongly he felt, Blackmun decided to read aloud part of his dissent, including the line "It is precisely because the issue raised by this case touches the heart of what makes individuals what they are that we should be especially sensitive to the rights of those whose choices upset the majority." When he had finished, Thurgood Marshall passed him a note. When Blackmun had first come on the bench, Marshall had chided his junior colleague for failing to understand how other people—people who were different—lived. The note read, "You was great."

In these opinions, and especially in Blackmun's dissent, we get the major arguments that would determine the debate and dialogue over gay rights and the law for the next quarter century. During that time, public understanding and acceptance of homosexuality increased significantly, especially among younger people. The gay rights movement, however, had to suffer a few setbacks on the Court before it would triumph.

In 1995, the Court unanimously held that a state law forbidding discrimination on the basis of sexual orientation could not be applied to the expressive decisions of a private parade. The free speech rights of the organizers of the annual St. Patrick's Day parade in Boston permitted them to include or exclude whom they wanted.

Then came *Romer v. Evans* in 1996, giving gay activists their first real glimmer of hope that the Supreme Court might be moving away from

Anthony McLeod Kennedy, associate justice, 1988–

its earlier and more hostile stance. The political activism of gay and lesbian advocacy groups in Colorado had met with success in the form of numerous municipal ordinances banning discrimination in housing and jobs on the basis of race, gender, or sexual orientation, and the state legislature had repealed its sodomy statute. Then a socially conservative evangelical Christian group, opposed to homosexuality as a sin, managed to get a constitutional amendment on the ballot specifically repealing any state or local law that protected people who were "Homosexual, Lesbian or [of] Bisexual Orientation" and prohibited the passage of any legislation in the future to protect these people in their "conduct, practices, or relationships." In November 1992, 53 percent of the electorate approved Amendment 2. Richard Evans, a city official in Denver, sued Roy Romer, then governor of Colorado, to have Amendment 2 nullified as a violation of the Fourteenth Amendment. The Colorado Supreme Court agreed with the trial court that Amendment 2 was unconstitutional, in that it named a specific class and penalized it. The state appealed to the high court.

At oral argument on 10 October 1995, Justice Anthony Kennedy appeared visibly appalled by Amendment 2, which in effect closed off all of the normal political venues by which any citizen or groups of citizens could seek redress of grievances. Moreover, Kennedy, according to one of his clerks, was impressed with a brief filed by Professor Laurence Tribe of the Harvard Law School, suggesting that the Court could strike down Amendment 2 without revisiting *Hardwick;* the debate over Amendment 2 dealt not with sexual practices but with political and social rights.

In a clear departure from the heavily moralizing tone of the majority in *Hardwick,* Kennedy spoke for six of the justices—himself, Stevens, O'Connor, Souter, Ginsburg, and Breyer—in striking down Amendment 2 and affirming the state supreme court. The opening sentence showed exactly where the majority was heading: "One century ago, the first Justice Harlan admonished this Court that the Constitution 'neither knows nor tolerates classes among citizens.' Unheeded then, those words now are understood to state a commitment to the law's neutrality where the rights of persons are at stake. The Equal Protection Clause enforces this principle and today requires us to hold invalid a provision of Colorado's Constitution."

Kennedy seemed particularly outraged by the notion that the law prevented homosexuals from seeking political or judicial recourse against discrimination. Moreover, a fair reading of Amendment 2 could lead to the conclusion that "it deprives gays and lesbians even of the protection of general laws and policies that prohibit arbitrary discrimination in governmental and private settings." Quoting from an earlier opinion of Justice Brennan's, Kennedy wrote that the constitutional idea of equal protection unequivocally tells us this "cannot constitute a *legitimate* government interest." Not once in his opinion did Kennedy refer to *Hardwick,* although he referenced many of the leading cases in civil rights.

Justice Antonin Scalia, joined by Chief Justice Rehnquist and Justice Clarence Thomas, referred almost immediately to *Hardwick,* and he saw no harm in what he described as "a modest attempt by seemingly tolerant Coloradans to preserve traditional sexual mores against the effort of a politically powerful minority to reverse those mores through use of the laws." That objective, as far as he was concerned, was "unimpeachable under any constitutional doctrine." The Court should not "take sides in the culture war." Because the Constitution says nothing about this subject, "it is left to be resolved by normal democratic means, including the democratic adoption of provisions in state constitutions. This Court has no business imposing upon all Americans the resolution favored by an elite class from which the Members of this institution are selected, pronouncing that 'animosity' toward homosexuals is evil." Scalia felt that *Hardwick* should have been the deciding precedent, not the civil rights cases cited by Kennedy.

He then attacked Kennedy's opinion on a point-by-point basis, but underlying the entire dissent was a belief that what was really at issue was not an unconscionable effort to deny some group equal rights but the vile nature of that group's sexual practices, which offended many people. Because, unlike religious freedom and racial equality, the Constitution did not specifically protect homosexuals, it ought to be left up to the people to treat them as they wished. This theme, of course, underlay the various initiatives and ordinances that in many states treated gays as inferior people, men and women tainted by a perverse sexuality that sinned against God's rule. While Scalia did not invoke the deity, he clearly shared the disdain that the supporters of Amendment 2 had taken no pains to hide.

Romer v. Evans is seen by many as a major turning point in the battle for gay rights. Kennedy gave advocates what they had been seeking all along: recognition that prejudice on the basis of sexual orientation was no more acceptable under the Constitution than discrimination because of race or religion. The dissenters in *Hardwick* had provided one part of the constitutional argument, namely, that what consenting adults did in their bedrooms was no business of the government but stood protected by the right of privacy. Now Kennedy gave them an even stronger basis, equal protection. No group, Kennedy argued, could be made inferior and discriminated against under the Equal Protection Clause.

Two years later, gays won another victory when Justice Scalia, speaking for a unanimous Court, held that the sexual harassment provisions of Title VII of the 1964 Civil Rights Act applied to men as well as women. Even though a closely divided Court in 2000 upheld the right of the Boy Scouts—supposedly a private organization—to keep gays out of leadership positions, *Romer* showed that a majority of the Court no longer shared the homophobic sentiment that had seemingly animated *Hardwick*. Gay and lesbian advocacy groups now believed they could secure a reversal of *Hardwick* and set about looking for the right test case. They found it in the case of John Geddes Lawrence and Tyron Garner, arrested in their Houston apartment for violating the Texas sodomy law.

The justices accepted the case and heard oral argument on 26 March 2003. Paul Smith, the lawyer who represented Lawrence, had once been a law clerk to Lewis Powell and later in life had come out of the closet to announce himself as gay. The Court asked counsel for both sides to address three questions:

1. Whether the petitioners' criminal convictions under the Texas Homosexual Conduct law—which criminalized sexual intimacy by same-sex couples but not identical behavior by different-sex couples—violated the Fourteenth Amendment guarantee of equal protection of the laws;
2. Whether the petitioners' criminal convictions for adult consensual sexual intimacy in their home violate their vital interests in liberty and privacy protected by the due process clause of the Fourteenth Amendment; and
3. Whether *Bowers v. Hardwick* should be overruled.

When lawyers for both sides read these questions, it became clear not that the Court would definitely reverse *Hardwick* but that at least a majority stood ready to do so. (When the Court heard *Gideon v. Wainwright,* they had similarly asked counsel whether *Betts v. Brady* should be overturned.) Unlike the Georgia statute in *Hardwick,* which penalized sodomy no matter who committed it, the Texas law applied only to same-sex practices and thus targeted homosexuals. If the Court had meant what it said in *Romer,* this by itself should have been enough to invalidate the Texas law as well as similar prohibitions in twelve other states. The justices also recognized that unlike in *Romer* they could not strike down the Texas law and leave *Hardwick* in place. The question mark would be Sandra Day O'Connor, who had been in the majority in both *Hardwick* and *Romer.* She would probably be willing to strike down the Texas law because it was so discriminatory, but would she be willing to override *Hardwick?*

In conference, five members of the Court—Stevens, Kennedy, Souter, Ginsburg, and Breyer—agreed that the Texas law should be struck down and *Hardwick* overruled. O'Connor agreed with the first point but not the second, while Rehnquist, Scalia, and Thomas would have upheld the law. With the chief justice in the minority, John Paul Stevens as the senior justice in the majority had the authority to assign the case and might well have kept it for himself, because he had written such a forceful dissent in *Hardwick.* He chose Anthony Kennedy for two reasons. First, Kennedy's opinion in *Romer* formed the jurisprudential basis for the decision in the Texas case, and, second, Kennedy was considered a moderate conservative. A decision sure to upset social conservatives and evangelical Christians would be better received if it came from a conservative rather than a liberal (although Stevens never saw himself as a liberal). In the end, Stevens got exactly what he hoped for—an analytically powerful opinion that also rang with moral fervor.

Courts as a rule are reluctant to overturn precedent, especially in cases that have been decided recently. *Hardwick* was less than two decades old, and three of the justices in that case still sat on the bench. Kennedy understood that in order to justify such a step, he had to show that the earlier opinion failed on jurisprudential as well as societal grounds. He began with what is the boldest statement of a right of privacy articulated by a modern Court (some of whose members denied the existence of such a right): "Liberty protects the person from unwarranted government intrusions into a dwelling or other private places. In our tradition the State is not omnipresent in the home. And there are other spheres of our lives and existence, outside the home, where the State should not be a dominant presence. Freedom extends beyond spatial bounds. Liberty presumes an autonomy of self that includes freedom of thought, belief, expression, and certain intimate conduct. The instant case involves liberty of the person both in its spatial and more transcendent dimensions."

The only way the Court could agree that the sexual conduct of two consenting adults fell within the liberty provisions of the Due Process Clause was to reexamine *Hardwick*. Kennedy questioned Byron White's framing of the issue as whether the Constitution "confers a fundamental right upon homosexuals to engage in sodomy" and charged that how White had phrased the issue "discloses the Court's own failure to appreciate the extent of the liberty at stake." The very wording "demeans the claim of the individual put forward, just as it would demean a married couple were it to be said marriage is simply about the right to have sexual intercourse."

A fair-minded understanding of the basic constitutional right of privacy, Kennedy declared, would take seriously gay as well as straight sexual relations and the accompanying integrity of the connection between sexual expression and companionate friendship and love. "When sexuality finds overt expression in intimate conduct with another person," he wrote, anticipating another important opinion a decade later, "the conduct can be but one element in a personal bond that is more enduring. The liberty protected by the Constitution allows homosexual persons the right to make this choice." The state, he declared, "cannot demean [homosexuals'] existence or control their destiny by making their private sexual conduct a crime." The dissenters' analysis in *Hardwick* "should have been controlling . . . and should control here."

For those who argued that the Constitution mentioned neither privacy nor rights given to gays, Kennedy responded that the Framers had not drafted the document in specific terms, because they did not claim to know "the components of liberty in its manifold possibilities," but were themselves open—as the Court needed to be—to new arguments and experiences. "They knew times can blind us to certain truths and later generations can see that laws once thought necessary and proper in fact serve only to oppress. As the Constitution endures, persons in every generation can invoke its principles in their own search for greater freedom."

Justice Scalia (joined by Rehnquist and Thomas) entered one of his bravura dissents, charging the majority with signing on to the "homosexual agenda," without ever defining what that meant, and attacking the majority for its inconsistency. It had refused to overturn *Roe v. Wade,* a bad decision, but had no qualms in reversing a perfectly good precedent in *Hardwick.* Essentially, Scalia, like White, did not believe in a constitutional right to privacy in general or its application to support either abortion or sodomy in particular. He dismissed Kennedy's careful historical analysis that showed how attitudes toward homosexuals had changed over the years, because he considered such history constitutionally irrelevant. Original intent was all that mattered, and a strict construction of the Constitution and the intent of its Framers would make clear that laws prohibiting abortion as well as sodomy were perfectly acceptable. Only a change in the Constitution could alter that fact. The Court, he charged, found the "fact that the governing majority in a State has traditionally viewed a particular practice as immoral is not a sufficient reason for upholding a law prohibiting the practice." Scalia defended a reliance on tradition. "The Texas statute undeniably seeks to further the belief of its citizens that certain forms of sexual behavior are 'immoral and unacceptable.'" What Texas had chosen to do, he argued, was "well within the range of traditional democratic action, and its hand should not be stayed . . . by a Court impatient of democratic change." Should attitudes change in the future, then the people, acting through the democratic process, could change their laws.

In many ways, Scalia's dissent in *Lawrence* is a continuation of his remarks in *Romer.* He opposes a so-called right of privacy; he is against the Court finding new rights of liberty and autonomy in the Due Process Clause; if a right is not in the Constitution, it does not exist; he ignores history as a constitutional consideration but is quite willing to accept "tradition" when it suits his purpose; there is no consideration at all of the individual; and if a majority of the population finds a group's behavior offensive, they can criminalize it.

Toward the end of his dissent, Scalia penned a dire and what proved to be a prescient warning. The majority's logic, he declared, would inevitably lead to the judicial imposition of same-sex marriage. Although the Court had assured the public that *Lawrence* did "not involve whether the government must give formal recognition to any relationship that homosexual persons seek to enter," Scalia scathingly said, "Do not believe it." He found "more illuminating than this bald, unreasoned disclaimer . . . the progression of thought displayed by an earlier passage in the Court's opinion, which notes the constitutional protections afforded to 'personal decisions relating to *marriage,* procreation, contraception, family relationships, child rearing, and education,' and then declares that 'persons in a homosexual relationship may seek autonomy for these purposes, just as heterosexual persons do.' " The Court, he charged, had just dismantled "the structure of constitutional law that has permitted a distinction to be made between heterosexual and homosexual unions." Because moral disapprobation of homosexual conduct was no longer considered by the Court a legitimate reason to proscribe that conduct, it would just be a matter of time before the Court would inevitably confer "the benefits of marriage to homosexual couples."

Scalia is one of the most activist judges in the Court's history in terms of getting his views out to the public and especially to conservative groups. In the months following the *Lawrence* decision, he criticized the ruling in other venues. In a speech to the conservative Intercollegiate Studies Institute, for example, he adopted a mocking tone as he read from Kennedy's opinion striking down the Texas sodomy law. According to an Associated Press account, Scalia said the ruling "held to be a constitutional right what had been a criminal offense at the time of the founding and for nearly two hundred years thereafter."

Scalia's many appearances allowed him to speak to people beyond the Court and outside the legal profession. According to one of his admirers, his dissents were not designed to try to pick up votes from colleagues for a similar case the next time around. Rather, according to David Forte in the *National Review,* Scalia "speaks less to his own—the courts and the legal fraternity—and more to those in other parts of our political system. He casts up a dire warning that not only has the Supreme Court in many ways removed the Constitution from the Framers, it is also removing the democratic process from the people and their representatives." Yet Scalia showed himself so angry that he had little impact except among the true believers. The mood in the country was changing, and in that dialogue the views of Harry Blackmun and Anthony Kennedy seemed to be winning.

ALTHOUGH JUSTICE KENNEDY had not in fact mentioned same-sex marriage, Scalia's warning triggered a backlash as several states adopted so-called defense of marriage acts or even constitutional amendments defining marriage as between a man and a woman. (Congress had passed such a law in 1996.) On 3 October 2003, President George W. Bush proclaimed 12–18 October "Marriage Protection Week" and declared that marriage is "a union between a man and a woman." His administration, he promised, would work to support that institution.

Then, on 18 November 2003, the worst fears of conservatives seemed to come to life as the Supreme Judicial Court of Massachusetts ruled that the commonwealth had failed to "identify any constitutionally adequate reason" to deny gay and lesbian couples the right to marry. In the ensuing legal conflict, both sides looked to *Lawrence* for either confirmation of their claims for equality or evidence of the moral disintegration of the nation. Over the next several years, courts in some other states reached the same conclusion, and then some states began adopting statutes or referenda legitimizing same-sex marriage. So long as all this took place in state courts and state legislatures, and relied on state constitutional provisions, federal judges could breathe a sigh of relief: the issue of same-sex marriage would not be in their courts. Then two cases arose that had to be handled under the federal Constitution, and both reached the Marble Palace in the spring of 2013.

Edith Windsor and Thea Spyer married in Canada in 2007, a marriage recognized at the time by New York, where they resided and which later became one of the states that enacted legislation providing for same-sex marriage. Spyer died in 2009, leaving her estate to Windsor, who sought to claim the federal estate tax exemption for surviving spouses, but the Internal Revenue Service denied her claim under section 3 of the Defense of Marriage Act (DOMA), which was passed by Congress in 1996 and which altered the Dictionary Act to define marriage as between a man and a woman. (All told, DOMA's definition affected more than one thousand federal laws.) Windsor paid $363,053 in estate taxes and then sought a refund. When the IRS refused, she went to court suing for a refund, claiming that DOMA violated the equal protection principles incorporated in the Fifth Amendment. She won her suit in both the district court and the Court of Appeals for the Second Circuit. At this point, Attorney General Eric Holder notified the Speaker of the House that the Obama administration Justice Department would not defend the law, believing it unconstitutional. In response, the Bipartisan Legal Advisory Group of the House (which was in fact dominated by the majority Republicans) voted to intervene to defend section 3's constitutionality.

At the same time, the Court accepted a case from the Ninth Circuit. After the California Supreme Court held that limiting the official designation of marriage to opposite-sex couples violated the California Constitution's equal protection clause, California voters passed a ballot initiative known as Proposition 8, amending the state constitution to define marriage as solely between a man and a woman. Two same-sex couples who wished to marry then sued in federal district court, challenging Proposition 8 under the Due Process and Equal Protection Clauses of the federal Constitution. Governor Arnold Schwarzenegger and his successor, Jerry Brown, both refused to defend the law, and eventually the California courts allowed the original backers of the initiative to defend it. Both the district court and the Court of Appeals for the Ninth Circuit found Proposition 8 unconstitutional. Judge Stephen Reinhardt based his opinion entirely on *Romer,* noting that once the state had given gays and lesbians the right to marry, it could not then take that right away. The Supreme Court took the case but asked both sides to argue whether the petitioners—the group defending Proposition 8—had standing under Article III.

Although many commentators, especially after the oral argument, expected the Court to strike down DOMA, it did so by a bare 5–4 majority. Had Sandra Day O'Connor still been on the Court, her commitment to equal protection—the basis for her vote in *Lawrence*—might have led her to join the majority. Her replacement, Samuel Alito, filed a dissent, as did Chief Justice Roberts and Justice Scalia; Justice Thomas joined the Roberts and Alito opinions.

There were several aspects to the case, and which ones the Court emphasized would make a big difference. If it decided solely on equal protection, it might well be interpreted as ruling that states could not bar same-sex marriage, a step no one on the Court was prepared to take. So Kennedy emphasized federalism. "By history and tradition the definition and regulation of marriage has been treated as being within the authority and realm of the separate States." Yet, as he had to acknowledge, Congress in exercising its legitimate authority also had the power to affect marriage. DOMA, however, affected numerous federal laws and impinged on the laws of the twelve states that recognized and allowed same-sex marriage. Looking at history, at the time of the drafting of the Constitution states possessed full power over marriage, and in the area of domestic law the federal government had always deferred to state law policy. DOMA thus goes against two centuries of state governance of marriage, and it does so to impose restrictions and disabilities.

Kennedy looked at the legislative history of DOMA, where its sponsors explained that the law expresses "both moral disapproval of homosexuality, and a moral conviction that heterosexuality better comports with traditional (especially Judeo-Christian) morality." The brief filed by the House of Representatives committee reinforced the idea that the law opposed homosexuality. "This," Kennedy said, "raises a most serious question under the Constitution's Fifth Amendment."

His opinion then went into an extended detailing of the harm that DOMA posed to gays, lesbians, and their children—lack of access to health care, disqualification from certain provisions of the bankruptcy code, tax penalties, no protection under federal law if the spouse is attacked, no survivors benefits under Social Security, penalties in determining student aid. "Under DOMA same-sex married couples have their lives burdened, by reasons of government decree, in visible and public ways. . . . What has been explained to this point should more than suffice to establish the general purpose and the necessary effect of this law are to demean those persons who are in a lawful same-sex marriage. This requires the Court to hold, as it now does, that DOMA is unconstitutional." So although Kennedy based most of his opinion on federalism—states should be the ones determining marriage—he finished by noting all the disabilities heaped upon same-sex marriages as a violation of equal protection.

Justice Scalia's dissent picked up on the same themes he had belabored in *Romer* and *Lawrence:* "This case is about power in several respects. It is about the power of our people to govern themselves, and the power of this Court to pronounce the law. Today's opinion aggrandizes the latter, with the predictable consequence of diminishing the former. We have no power to decide this case. And even if we did, we have no power under the Constitution to invalidate this democratically adopted legislation. The Court's errors on both points spring forth from the same diseased root: an exalted conception of the role of this institution in America."

Scalia would have had the Court dismiss for lack of a case or controversy. Windsor won in the lower court, and the Justice Department did not defend the law, so where is the controversy necessary for Article III courts? (He ignored the House committee, which the majority accepted as a legitimate party.) "Having gotten the jurisdiction wrong," he charged, "the majority gets the merits wrong as well." The rest of his opinion attempted to refute points Kennedy had made, but at its heart was the argument he had made earlier: government has the power to enforce traditional moral and sexual norms. (At this point, he cited his own dissent in *Lawrence*.) "The Constitution neither requires nor forbids our society to approve of same-sex marriage, much as it neither requires nor forbids us to approve of no-fault divorce, polygamy, or the consumption of alcohol." He then attacked Kennedy for describing the law as "mean-spirited," although he implied that by itself that would not invalidate a law.

Scalia read his dissent from the bench. "I only do it in really significant cases," he had explained earlier that year, "where I think the court's decision is going to have a really bad effect upon the law and upon society, a really, really big case." He saw *Windsor* as such a case, and what worried him was less the immediate ruling—Edith Windsor would get her tax refund—than the implications for the future. In the last sentence of Kennedy's opinion, he declared that "this opinion and its holding are confined to those lawful marriages." In other words, the federal government had to recognize same-sex marriages in states that legalized them but not elsewhere.

Scalia interpreted the majority opinion as opening the gates to a legal assault that could end state bans on same-sex marriage. "By formally declaring anyone opposed to same-sex marriage an enemy of human decency, the majority arms well every challenger to a state law restricting marriage to its traditional definition." Just prior to this statement, he edited a few lines from the majority opinion so as to make it read that all bans on same-sex marriages would have to fall. (This comment upset Chief Justice Roberts, who in his dissent declared that the question of whether states can ban same-sex marriage was not before the Court; it was an issue for another day. The logic of the DOMA decision, he argued, did not support Justice Scalia's sky-is-falling approach.)

Scalia, however, may once again be prescient, even as he appears to be on the wrong side of history. Every poll shows a growing acceptance of same-sex marriage, especially among the young, and a decline in hostility to and disapproval of homosexuality per se. Within days of the decision, the American Civil Liberties Union and other groups filed suits in Virginia, Illinois, and other states to overturn laws barring same-sex marriages. In Pennsylvania, the attorney general announced she would not defend the statute, because she believed it unconstitutional. Within a year, bans against same-sex marriage in Utah, Oklahoma, Tennessee, Michigan, Idaho, Oregon, and Pennsylvania had been struck down in federal courts, with judges relying on the majority opinion in *Windsor* as their rationale.

The majority of justices on the high court clearly had no desire to go down the path of declaring same-sex marriage a constitutionally protected right. The continuing reverberations of *Roe v. Wade* stand as a clear reminder of what happens when the Court gets out ahead of the curve of public opinion. While more than 50 percent of the populace supports same-sex marriage (the number is upwards of 70 percent for those under thirty), there are still large parts of the country, especially in rural areas and southern states, where opposition is high.

(With gay rights advocates successfully challenging state laws and state constitutional provisions in federal courts, the justices found a number of cert petitions awaiting them at the beginning of the October 2014 term. Much to everyone's surprise, the high court refused to take any of these cases, leaving intact the holdings in the lower courts striking down the bans. According to several commentators, the reason is that neither side knew how Anthony Kennedy would vote on a direct equal protection challenge. The conservatives thought that, in light of the DOMA decision, he might well vote with the liberal bloc to support same-sex marriage. The moderates feared that Kennedy might not be willing to go that far and thus join the conservatives in overturning the lower courts. Then, in early 2015, the Court accepted appeals from two appeals court decisions, one supporting same-sex marriage and the other upholding a state ban. This is the typical case in which the Court has little choice but to accept cases and to resolve differences between circuits.)

It would have been more difficult to avoid the issue of constitutionality in the California case, and from the time the Court had voted to take it, there had been misgivings. During oral argument, Justice Kennedy had suggested that the Court dismiss the case. Justice Scalia responded with, according to witnesses, a note of glee in his voice: "It's too late for that now, isn't it? We have crossed that river." Later Kennedy was heard to say, "I just wonder if the case was properly granted." Court observers immediately began predicting that in the end the case would be dismissed, and they were right.

Chief Justice Roberts announced that the Court would not reach the merits of the case. "We have never before upheld the standing of a private party to defend the constitutionality of a state statute when state officials have chosen not to. We decline to do so for the first time here." Although the California Supreme Court had said the defenders of Prop 8 had standing to defend it, Roberts said that standing in federal court was a different matter from standing in state court. This was, at best, a disingenuous statement. The Court of Appeals for the Ninth Circuit had certified a question to the California Supreme Court as to whether those parties had standing, and the California court had said yes. Usually, in matters such as this involving state law, the federal courts accept the state court rulings. But Roberts, joined by the odd coalition of Scalia, Ginsburg, Breyer, and Kagan, wanted to avoid the hard questions. It was, as one reporter noted, a technical decision involving "a carefully negotiated compromise with the goal of steering a dangerous vehicle off the judicial fast track and down an exit ramp."

The dissenters were an equally mixed lot—Kennedy, a centrist who wrote the opinion, Thomas and Alito, both conservatives, and Sotomayor, a liberal. They said that the majority "disrespected" the California court's ruling that the litigants had standing, and they agreed that the Court should have answered the main question and decided on the merits. But the dissent said nothing about how its four signers would have voted on that question.

THERE ARE NUMEROUS other issues that one could have looked at whose themes run through successive courts, but these areas of privacy, abortion, affirmative action, and gay rights will have to stand in for them. Other scholars have looked into questions of women's equality, criminal procedure, civil rights, religious freedom, federal preemption, and many others. Indeed, one could go back a century or more and find themes such as property rights, regulation of labor, and other issues that came up before the high court, term after term, for decades.

This is part of the dialogue. The common-law tradition requires that justices decide no more than is necessary, not give advisory opinions, and rely on prior decisions—including dissents—in formulating the proper answers to cases before the bar. Sometimes we can follow the line easily enough, such as when Justice Kennedy in *Lawrence* said that the dissenters in *Hardwick* had gotten it right. Other times the lines are blurry, and this is especially true in ongoing issues. Certainly the Roberts Court, and at least its immediate successor, will be hearing cases on affirmative action, gay rights, and privacy, as well as some of the other issues mentioned. Some scholars are predicting that within a few years we will once again see a wholesale shift in the Court's docket. Just as in the 1940s the Court moved from a preoccupation with property rights to cases implicating civil rights and liberties, so we should expect to see more and more cases dealing with technology and the legal and moral implications thereof. New issues will bring new ideas and new dissents. And while only history and time can tell which dissents will prevail, the dialogue itself will go on.

MARSHALL, BRENNAN, AND CAPITAL PUNISHMENT

One writer has referred to a particular type of opinion as a "perpetual dissent," one where the author knows that the position advocated has little or no chance of adoption by the majority—not in the near future and perhaps never. The most extensive examples of perpetual dissents are those filed by William Brennan and Thurgood Marshall against the death penalty.

AT THE TIME British settlers created colonies in North America, the "bloody code" of the mother country included some 220 crimes punishable by death, including "being in the company of Gypsies for one month," "strong evidence of malice in a child aged 7–14 years," and "blacking the face or using a disguise whilst committing a crime." To protect the property of the wealthy classes, the Black Act of 1723 created 50 capital offenses for various acts of poaching and theft, including pickpocketing. Men and women convicted of murder, burglary, and robbery usually went to the gallows, but for lesser offenses—even when the law provided for execution—the sentence could usually be commuted or permanently postponed for reasons such as benefit of clergy, pardon, pregnancy of the offender, or voluntary transportation to the colonies. Between 1770 and 1830, courts in England and Wales handed down thirty-five thousand death sentences, of which one-fifth were actually carried out.

The colonists brought the English code with them, but in practice the death penalty applied to only a few crimes. The first recorded death sentence in British North America occurred in 1608, with the execution by firing squad of Captain George Kendall in Jamestown for allegedly spying for Spain. Although some reformers wanted to abolish the death penalty, they made little headway until well after World War II. In 2013, Maryland became the eighteenth state, along with the District of Columbia, to abolish capital punishment.

The Supreme Court's modern jurisprudence on the death penalty began in October 1963, when Justice Arthur Goldberg circulated a memorandum questioning the value of the death penalty as a deterrent and noting growing evidence of the mistaken execution of innocent defendants. He noted that "most civilized nations of the western world" had done away with capital punishment and that "the world-wide trend is unmistakenly [*sic*] in the direction of abolition." Goldberg believed the death penalty constituted cruel and unusual punishment and as such violated both the Eighth and the Fourteenth Amendments. His memorandum also reflected the thinking at the NAACP's Legal Defense Fund, and he wanted his colleagues to consider the constitutionality of the death penalty for rape because of "the well-recognized disparity in the imposition of the death penalty for sexual crimes committed by whites and non-whites." According to one study, from the 1880s on almost all executions for rape took place in the South, and 85 percent of those executed were African American.

Around this time, the Legal Defense Fund mounted a full-scale attack on the death penalty, challenging nearly every aspect, from the method of choosing jurors through various aspects of administration, as well as judicial discretion in determining who would be executed. The result was a virtual moratorium on executions beginning in 1967, because states could not be sure how the Court would eventually decide these challenges and did not want to take the chance of executing someone under challenged procedures that might be declared unconstitutional. When Thurgood Marshall joined the Court that year, he found the justices ready to work through the various challenges and reach a decision on the constitutionality of the death penalty.

The members of the Court differed widely on the issue, on whether the Court could or should impose standards on the states over selection of juries, whether there should be a two-stage procedure (one to determine guilt and the second to determine punishment), and over what types of reviews—if any—to require when a person had been sentenced to death. Then Warren Burger became chief justice in 1969 and saw no way to define standards, because jury decisions rested on "the sum total of the life experience of the jurors." John Harlan, who had wrestled with the issue, finally decided that a one-stage trial was "one of [the] clearest cases of denial of fundamental fairness," because "if the sentence is committed to [the] unrestricted judgment of [the] jury," the trial could not restrict what the defendant wanted the jury to consider, which might include evidence of diminished responsibility even while acknowledging guilt. Potter Stewart thought the Constitution required neither standards nor a two-stage trial, but if the majority found two stages were required, then standards were also necessary.

Law clerks for William Brennan, Byron White, and Harry Blackmun worked through the pending appeals to see if they could identify cases that presented the basic questions clearly and without legal distractions from these issues. The justices finally picked four appeals for review: a murder and a rape case from Georgia and a rape case from Texas. (A murder case from California was mooted when the California Supreme Court reversed the conviction.) In all three, the defendant was an African American and had been sentenced to death, and the conviction had been upheld by the state's highest court.

The Court issued a *per curiam* opinion representing the views of five justices (Douglas, Brennan, Stewart, White, and Marshall), leaving the finding of guilt intact but reversing the imposition of the death penalty and remanding each case for further proceeding. The opinion held that the imposition of the death sentence in these particular cases constituted cruel and unusual punishment in violation of the Eighth and Fourteenth Amendments. Each of the five wrote a separate concurring opinion, while the four dissenters (Burger, Blackmun, Powell, and Rehnquist) also wrote separately.

Three of the opinions are of interest here. The Brennan and Marshall opinions can be characterized as reflecting the jurisprudence of a "living Constitution." Whatever the rationale and popular acceptance of the death penalty in the eighteenth century, times had changed. Enlightened opinion in the United States and Europe had come to see execution not only as cruel but also as fruitless, in that it served none of the traditional rationales for punishment, such as deterrence and rehabilitation, and satisfied only the need for retribution. The meaning of the Eighth Amendment prohibition of cruel and unusual punishment had to be interpreted in terms not of 1791 but of 1972. Harry Blackmun in many ways agreed, as he wrote, "I yield to no one in the depth of my distaste, antipathy, and, indeed, abhorrence, for the death penalty. . . . That distaste is buttressed by a belief that capital punishment serves no useful purpose that can be demonstrated." But for him judicial restraint meant that policy decisions of this magnitude should be left to the legislative and executive branches.

BRENNAN HAD PUT one of his clerks, Loftus Becker, at work in the spring of 1971 to lay out the arguments why the death penalty constituted cruel and unusual punishment. Until then, Brennan had shown no special interest in death penalty cases, but Becker knew that even before his justice had gone onto the Court, Brennan had considered "simple human dignity" one of the core values of American society. In a 1961 speech, he had called "the dignity and worth of the individual . . . the supreme value of our American democracy."

It is impossible to determine exactly when Brennan began to embrace human dignity as a core value, and there is no evidence that he read the writings of Immanuel Kant or Father John A. Ryan, both of whom placed great importance on the concept. The phrase "human dignity" does not appear in the Constitution or in any Court decisions prior to the 1940s. Then Frank Murphy began employing it, notably in his dissent in the Japanese American internment cases. Hugo Black, William O. Douglas, and Earl Warren also began talking about human dignity, especially in decisions condemning coerced criminal confessions and improper police searches.

In a 1985 talk, Brennan explained he had come to his position on the death penalty "over many years and after much troubling thought. . . . The calculated killing of a human being by the state involves, by its very nature, an absolute denial of the executed person's humanity. The most vile murder does not, in my view, release the state from constitutional restraints on the destruction of human dignity. . . . For me, then, the fatal constitutional infirmity of capital punishment is that it treats members of the human race as nonhumans, as objects to be toyed with and discarded. It is, in other words, 'cruel and unusual' punishment in violation of the Eighth Amendment."

During the unusually long four hours devoted to oral argument in *Furman,* Brennan said little, but at conference he told his colleagues he would reverse all the convictions, and he cited Goldberg's 1963 memorandum as well as the strong arguments put forth by Professor Anthony Amsterdam against the death penalty. Although Potter Stewart hoped that there might be a unified opinion, the views of the five justices varied too much. Brennan listened carefully and then prepared his own opinion, defining cruel and unusual punishment as one that "does not comport with human dignity." But what did comport with human dig-

William Joseph Brennan Jr., associate justice,
1956–1990

nity? Here Brennan relied on four principles that Stewart had suggested in earlier discussions before the Court heard *Furman.* Punishment could not be too severe, arbitrarily inflicted, unacceptable to contemporary standards, or excessive.

If human dignity constituted Brennan's guiding principle, he did not offer much insight into what he meant, apparently assuming it was self-evident. While the idea had been widely discussed in philosophy and in the Catholic Church, there is a great gulf between stating broad concepts and then making them specific in legal terms so that they can serve as a guide to lower court judges. Brennan had little to go on in the way of precedent, and in only one decision could he find any justification for invoking human dignity in terms of the Eighth Amendment. In a 1958 case, Chief Justice Earl Warren had written that "the basic concept underlying the Eighth Amendment is nothing less than the dignity of man." In the years ahead, Brennan's critics would single out his use of human dignity as the worst-case example of judicial activism. Raoul Berger, a Harvard legal historian and fierce critic of the Warren Court, declared, "Respect for 'human dignity' clearly is spun out of thin air." Others claimed that Brennan set out a moral vision rather than a legal standard, and one critic charged that with the dignity concept "Brennan's humanistic activism runs amok."

Brennan then and later rejected as "utterly groundless" the notion that the idea of human dignity either was too subjective or lacked standards, and his defenders argued that it was no more difficult to discern standards for human dignity than for the due process requirements of the Fourteenth Amendment, which, of course, justices had been doing for years. In 1985, Brennan would tell students at Georgetown University that "if the interaction of this justice and the constitutional text over the years confirms any single proposition, it is that the demands of human dignity will never cease to evolve."

Brennan, of course, could not ignore a history that showed widespread acceptance of capital punishment or the fact that the Constitution apparently endorsed it in the Fifth and Fourteenth Amendments. ("Nor shall life . . . be taken without due process of law.") Rather, he argued that the Framers had put forward not practices that had to be unwaveringly followed but rather principles of justice that each generation had to reexamine in the light of contemporary ideas and needs. The argument could be made that because the Constitution provided the power to inflict capital punishment, if it complied with due process, the death penalty could not be proscribed, and the Eighth Amendment's "cruel and unusual" phrase applied only to noncapital offenses.

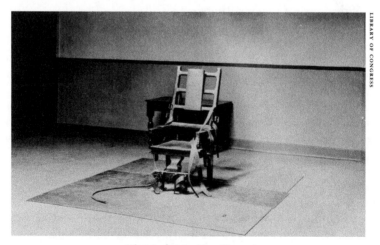

Electric chair at Sing Sing prison

Brennan, however, argued that the Eighth Amendment circumscribed both the Fifth and the Fourteenth and that the Framers actually looked to a future in which constitutional protections would be expanded. Just because the Constitution mentioned capital punishment did not mean that the states had to adopt it or that the Court had to approve it. Again, looking at *Trop v. Dulles,* Brennan agreed that the words of the Eighth Amendment "are not precise, and that their scope is not static. The Amendment must draw its meaning from the evolving standards of decency that mark the progress of a maturing society."

Marshall's opinion was the longest, and there is no question it was informed by his years as the head of the NAACP's Legal Defense Fund and his personal knowledge of how southern states used the death penalty as a means of keeping African Americans subjugated. University of Vermont Law School professor Michael Mello tells this story:

A few years back I researched the history of the death penalty for juveniles. In the National Archives I came across the certiorari petition filed in the United States Supreme Court on behalf of two black teenage murderers in a Mississippi case in 1947. The petition had weak legal claims—the papers seemed desperate, and succeeded only in postponing that double execution for a few months. I think I can imagine the sense of humiliation and defeat that their lawyer must have felt the night of the execution, when he watched the clock and knew he had failed so completely to stop the inexorable grinding of that racist system. The signature at the bottom of that cert petition was Thurgood Marshall's.

But Marshall could not tell stories like this, no matter how illustrative they might have been of the racist use of the death penalty. He did, however, point out how the death penalty fell most heavily on "the poor, the ignorant, and the underprivileged members of society": "Their impotence leaves them victims of a sanction that the wealthier, better-represented, just-as-guilty person can escape. . . . Legislators are content to maintain the *status quo.* . . . Assuming knowledge of all the facts, the average citizen would, in my opinion, find it shocking to his conscience and sense of justice. For this reason alone, capital punishment cannot stand." He would have to do more, however, than simply appeal to the conscience. He began by acknowledging the brutality of the crimes but pointed out that the question before the Court was whether the death penalty constituted a cruel and unusual punishment prohibited by the Eighth Amendment.

Thurgood Marshall, associate justice,
1967–1991

He reviewed the amendment's history and earlier Court decisions interpreting it. The fact that capital punishment had been permitted, even by the Framers, did not answer the argument that by the latter part of the twentieth century it had become cruel and unusual. "Evolving standards" invalidated excessive and unnecessary punishments and those "abhorrent to currently existing moral values."

Society, of course, had to punish crime, and the standard reasons given for punishing felons included deterrence, rehabilitation, and retribution. Clearly the death penalty lacked any value in rehabilitation, and studies showed it had little or no deterrent value. That left only one reason, and "retaliation, vengeance, and retribution have been roundly condemned as intolerable aspirations for a government in a free society." Otherwise the Eighth Amendment ban would be drained of any meaning, for any punishment could be justified as a form of retribution for a crime. Marshall noted that "there is a demand for vengeance on the part of many persons in a community against one who is convicted of a particularly offensive act," but the Eighth Amendment "is our insulation from our baser selves."

The death penalty was excessive because unnecessary, but the gravamen of Marshall's opinion lay in his claim that it was also "morally unacceptable to the people of the United States at this time in their history."

For Marshall to make this statement meant he had to ignore the fact that legislatures in three-fourths of the states, representing the views of their citizens, found the death penalty morally acceptable, and public opinion polls also found a vast majority of the populace approving capital punishment. He disregarded both the legislation and the polls by declaring that most people "know almost nothing about capital punishment," and if "people were fully informed" about the death penalty, a majority of them would find it "shocking, unjust, and unacceptable." He could not believe "that at this stage in our history, the American people would ever knowingly support purposeless vengeance."

Aside from the intrinsic wrongness of the death penalty, it had been used in a discriminatory manner against "the poor, the illiterate, the underprivileged, the member of the minority group—the man who, because he is without means, and is defended by a court-appointed attorney—who becomes society's sacrificial lamb." The bare statistics tell the story. A total of 3,859 persons had been executed since 1930, of whom 1,751 were white and 2,066 were Negro. Of these executions, 3,334 were for murder; 1,664 of the executed murderers were white and 1,630 were Negro; 455 persons, including 48 whites and 405 Negroes, were executed for rape. "It is immediately apparent that Negroes were executed far more often than whites in proportion to their percentage of the population. Studies indicate that while the higher rate of execution among Negroes is partially due to a higher rate of crime, there is evidence of racial discrimination." Racial or other discriminations should not be surprising, because in *McGautha v. California* the Court held "that committing to the untrammeled discretion of the jury the power to pronounce life or death in capital cases is [not] offensive to anything in the Constitution." This was an open invitation to discrimination.

As one of Marshall's biographers noted, here as in virtually all of his decisions the justice presented what he saw as the simple common sense of the solution. There is no indication that Marshall struggled to overcome uncomfortable facts, such as the widespread approval of the death penalty not only throughout American history but in 1972 as well. He practically ignored the proposition that an executed person will commit no further crimes and that most people, and probably most potential murderers, want to live. He concluded with a paragraph of unabashed patriotism, noting the inherent goodness of the American people and the great principles embodied in the Constitution, if we could just understand it properly.

According to several sources, nearly all of the justices thought that *Furman*—even though it did not declare the death penalty unconstitutional per se, but only how it had been applied—would end capital punishment in the United States. But Chief Justice Warren Burger in his dissent (joined by Blackmun, Powell, and Rehnquist, who also wrote separately) correctly pointed out that only two members of the Court—Brennan and Marshall—believed that the Eighth Amendment prohibited the death penalty as a "punishment for all crimes and under all circumstances." He suggested that statutes providing for capital punishment could meet constitutional scrutiny if they addressed the issues raised by Justices Stewart and White: the lack of standards, the arbitrary and often discriminatory imposition of the death penalty, and the need to ensure fairness and consistency in its use.

With an unsurprising alacrity, the state legislatures in every one of the thirty-seven states that had previously imposed the death penalty redrafted their laws to meet these objections. For the most part, the reformed statutes fell into two categories. One group made the death penalty mandatory for certain crimes. The other followed the provisions of the Model Penal Code of the American Law Institute, which had two important features. First, it set out a list of aggravating circumstances that could justify the death penalty in the absence of any mitigating circumstances. Second, it provided for a two-part trial, the first to establish guilt and the second for sentencing, at which time the jury would hear arguments for leniency as well as evaluate aggravating and mitigating circumstances. In states where it did not exist before, the new legislation required examination of all capital sentences by appellate courts.

In 1976, the Court began reviewing these revised statutes and upheld the first of them in *Gregg v. Georgia*. Justices Stewart, Powell, and Stevens announced the judgment of the Court, with the chief justice and Justices White, Blackmun, and Rehnquist concurring. While the seven members of the majority differed on a number of points, they all agreed that capital punishment per se did not violate the Eighth or the Fourteenth Amendment. As the Court pondered these cases, Brennan announced to the conference on 2 April 1976 that he would never again vote to sustain a death sentence. "I'm absolutely convinced that it's 'cruel and unusual,' and that's where I'm going to be from now on." Over the next ten years, the Burger Court handed down several other decisions clarifying its views on particular issues raised by state laws. In each and every one, William Brennan and Thurgood Marshall reiterated their view that the death penalty was unconstitutional. Brennan adopted the formula noting his view that "the death penalty is in all circumstances cruel and unusual punishment prohibited by the Eighth and Fourteenth Amendments." Marshall would write, "I adhere to my consistent view that the death penalty is under all circumstances cruel and unusual punishment forbidden by the Eighth and Fourteenth Amendments." They appended these statements not only to cases heard by the Court but to denials of cert in death row appeals. When the Court reversed a conviction, they would concur in the result but emphasize their continuing opposition to capital punishment. They were always together, because they both believed that the death sentence constituted a cruel and unusual punishment.

To get a sense of the extent to which Marshall went, we can look at a memo written by one of his clerks in February 1991, just a few months before he retired:

> With respect to cert. [petitions], you have issued approximately 2095 standard dissents from denial in which you say that you would grant [cert] in order to vacate the death sentence. You have issued an additional 98 dissents from denial on substantive grounds that also include your standard "adhering" language.
>
> In argued capital cases, since *Furman v. Georgia* was decided, you have joined or written majority opinions 19 times. On each occasion the majority disposition was favorable to the capital [defendant]. I could not find a single case in which you joined a majority opinion that disposed of the case in a manner adverse to the capital [defendant]. In one case you even emphasized that you could not join a portion of the majority opinion that suggested that the death penalty might be imposed in other circumstances.

In a somewhat complicated case that spring in which due process claims were raised under the Sixth, Eighth, and Fourteenth Amendments, Marshall found himself voting in a way that would have upheld the death sentence and then being assigned to write the opinion. When his clerk pointed out this inconsistency, Marshall sent a note to Chief Justice Rehnquist asking him to reassign the opinion, "since I cannot bring myself to endorse the death penalty under the Eighth Amendment." Rehnquist wrote back that at the conference the vote had been 5–4 to affirm. If Marshall now voted to reverse, then there would be a 5–4 vote to do so. Because the chief would now be in the minority, Marshall as the senior justice should proceed to assign the case. But Marshall's opposition to the death penalty was a far different reason to reverse from that held by the other four, and as he told them, he did not feel right making the assignment. Eventually, Justice Stevens wrote the opinion.

There were cases, however, in which Brennan and Marshall were able to forge an alliance to spare a prisoner's life by essentially forgoing the Eighth Amendment argument. Mark Kelman has called this a "one-sided acceptance" of the reasoning in *Furman*. By this, he means that when the two men provided their votes to reprieve a prisoner's life in a particular situation, they could tacitly accept the abstract constitutionality of the death sentence and establish an ad hoc alliance with three other justices who were willing to invalidate the death penalty in those circumstances.

In *Enmund v. Florida* (1982), Marshall and Brennan provided the majority for an opinion by Byron White that found the death penalty unconstitutionally severe as a punishment for an armed robber who neither took a life nor intended nor contemplated that a life would be taken. Marshall did not write separately, because, although White did not declare all capital sentences unconstitutional, he did hold it to be invalid in these circumstances, and Marshall might have wanted to strengthen the opinion. Brennan, however, while joining the Court's opinion, noted, "I adhere to my view that the death penalty is in all circumstances cruel and unusual punishment prohibited by the Eighth and Fourteenth Amendments."

Another example is in the important case of *Ford v. Wainwright* (1986), which held that the Constitution forbids execution of the insane. Alvin Ford had been convicted of murder in 1974, and at that time there had been no indication of incompetence at the trial or at sentencing. In 1982, however, he began to manifest significant changes in his behavior, indicating a severe loss of sanity. (He referred to himself as Pope John Paul III and claimed to have appointed nine justices to the Florida Supreme Court.) Marshall, as senior justice in the majority, took the opinion himself and was joined by Brennan, Blackmun, Powell, and Stevens. Powell, however, agreed with only part of the opinion and concurred separately to say so. O'Connor and White disagreed with the majority but agreed with the result in part and dissented in part. Rehnquist filed a straight-out dissent, joined by Burger.

The opinion was straightforward. "For centuries," Marshall wrote, "no jurisdiction has countenanced the execution of the insane, yet this Court has never decided whether the Constitution forbids the practice. Today we keep faith with our common-law heritage in holding that it does." Marshall could have written that the Eighth Amendment forbade all executions, but he would not have had any vote other than William Brennan's. So he concentrated on the very narrow question of whether the Eighth Amendment prevented Florida from executing the insane and what process was due between the time of sentencing and the time of execution should there be, as in this case, evidence of an onset of insanity. In essence, he had to assume that the entire body of law decided since *Furman* had been decided correctly; the death penalty was not per se invalid but in this case was clearly unconstitutional.

LOUIS BRANDEIS said on a number of occasions, "My faith in time is great." He believed in the rightness of his dissents but also recognized that he was often swimming against the current of the dominant conservative jurisprudence. At some point—years, perhaps even decades later—he believed his views would be validated, and, as it happened, they have been.

Surely William Brennan and Thurgood Marshall must have shared at least some of that philosophy, believing that one day the American people would agree with them that the execution of criminals, no matter what the offense, constituted cruel and unusual punishment. But for them, time took a great toll. Whether the government required a warrant for wiretapping might mean some people went to jail; the continuation of capital punishment meant that hundreds of men (and some women) would die. Yet they persevered, and in the last quarter century their battle has shown some small but significant gains.

First, they got Harry Blackmun. Although Blackmun in *Furman* had said he personally opposed the death penalty, he had kept a quotation from his old law professor Felix Frankfurter, who also did not believe in capital punishment. "But as a judge I could not impose the views of the very few States who through bitter experience have abolished capital punishment upon all other States, by finding that 'due process' proscribes it." Blackmun's jurisprudence in the 1970s in this area is notable only for his willingness to grant review of death penalty cases, but if they did come to the Court, he voted on the legal issues presented, not on his personal opposition to the death penalty.

Then, in the mid-1980s, Blackmun found himself allied with Brennan, Marshall, and Stevens to bring the appeal of a convicted Florida murderer to the Court. The four had the votes to bring the case up on cert, but they needed a fifth vote to get Willie Darden a stay of execution. At one minute to midnight, they managed to get a reluctant Lewis Powell to agree to the stay, and this triggered a debate within the Court on what procedures needed to be followed. The experience shook Blackmun, because without Powell there would have been enough votes to grant cert but not to save a man's life, even for the period in which the case could be reviewed. As he told the conference, "I think allowing an execution under such circumstances would do far more to discredit this Court than any delay in allowing a proper execution could ever entail." The Court heard the case and by a 5–4 vote affirmed the judgment; Blackmun, joined by Brennan, Marshall, and Stevens, dissented. But in September 1986, Blackmun, whatever his personal feelings, still did not consider capital punishment unconstitutional.

A few months later, the Court heard arguments in *McCleskey v. Kemp*, a challenge to Georgia's administration of capital punishment that was based on a statistical analysis showing sharp racial disparities. People who killed whites were 4.3 times more likely to receive a death sentence than defendants accused of killing blacks. In prior cases, Blackmun and a majority of the Court had rejected such evidence, arguing that an individual had to show that he had been the victim of this discrimination. Now he disagreed and accused the Court of failing its duty and sanctioning the execution of a man "despite his presentation of evidence that establishes a constitutionally intolerable level of racially based discrimination."

Then came *Herrera v. Collins* (1993), in which the Court ruled that a state death row inmate presenting belated evidence of innocence is not ordinarily entitled to *habeas corpus*. Blackmun, joined by Stevens and Souter, dissented and announced his opinion from the bench to underscore his anger. In addition to his legal analysis, he ended with this bitter paragraph:

> I have voiced disappointment over this Court's obvious eagerness to do away with any restriction on the States' power to execute whomever and however they please. I have also expressed doubts about whether, in the absence of such restrictions, capital punishment remains constitutional at all. Of one thing, however, I am certain. Just as an execution without adequate safeguards is unacceptable, so too is an execution when the condemned prisoner can prove that he is innocent. The execution of a person who can show that he is innocent comes perilously close to simple murder.

Blackmun here came close to disavowing the death penalty, as had Brennan and Marshall, but he did not do so. That summer, however, one of his law clerks, Andrew Schapiro, put together a memorandum tracing the Court's tortuous post-*Furman* journey and concluding that the efforts to achieve a fair and nondiscriminatory system of capital punishment had failed. In essence, Schapiro suggested that Blackmun take the logical next step, and the justice agreed. At the beginning of the next term, the eighty-five-year-old justice told his clerks to start drafting a "death penalty" dissent and then to find the case in which to use it. It had to be a fairly straightforward case, one that raised no exotic or extraneous issues.

On 22 February 1994, the Court denied review of the murder conviction of Bruce Edwin Callins, allowing his scheduled execution to go forward the next day. The opinion read, "The petition for the writ of certiorari is denied." Blackmun dissented. "Twenty years have passed," he noted, "since this Court declared that the death penalty must be imposed fairly, and with reasonable consistency, or not at all, and despite the efforts of the States and the courts to devise legal formulas and procedural rules to meet this daunting challenge, the death penalty remains fraught with arbitrariness, discrimination, caprice, and mistake."

Unlike Marshall and Brennan, Blackmun still found capital punishment theoretically acceptable, but in terms of practice it could not be made to operate in a constitutionally acceptable manner. "Rather than continue to coddle the Court's delusion that the desired level of fairness has been achieved and the need for regulation eviscerated, I feel morally and intellectually obligated simply to concede that the death penalty experiment has failed. It is virtually self-evident to me now that no combination of procedural rules or substantive regulations ever can save the death penalty from its inherent constitutional deficiencies."

Perhaps one day the Court would develop procedural rules that would provide consistency, fairness, and reliability, but Blackmun doubted that day would ever come. He was more optimistic, quoting Marshall, that the Court and the nation would one day recognize its failure so that "the death penalty must be abandoned altogether." But for himself, "from this day forward, I no longer shall tinker with the machinery of death."

After the opinion had been released, Justice Brennan, now frail and four years retired from the bench, called Blackmun's chambers and left a message: "Thank you for the present." The clerk's office asked Blackmun how he wished to phrase the standard dissent he would now use in every death penalty case. Unlike Brennan and Marshall, who reiterated their view of the innate unconstitutionality of capital punishment, Blackmun wrote, "Adhering to my view that the death penalty cannot be imposed fairly within the restraints of the Constitution, I dissent."

SINCE BLACKMUN'S RETIREMENT at the end of that term, no one on the Court has believed that the death penalty violates the Eighth and Fourteenth Amendments. Cases arose, however, that have made a majority of the justices uncomfortable.

In *Atkins v. Virginia* (2002), Daryl Atkins had been convicted of murder. His attorney hired a psychologist, who evaluated Atkins and found he had an IQ of 59. The state supreme court affirmed the death sentence on the basis of *Penry v. Lynaugh* (1989), in which the Supreme Court held that executing a mentally retarded person did not violate the Eighth Amendment. The Supreme Court reversed the Virginia sentence as well as its own precedent. By a vote of 6–3, the Court, speaking through Justice John Paul Stevens, held that a national consensus had formed that executing the mentally retarded did constitute cruel and unusual punishment. In 1989, when *Penry* had been decided, only two of the thirty-eight states with capital punishment had outlawed the execution of the mentally incompetent; by the time the Court heard *Atkins,* the number had grown to eighteen. Stevens held that a national consensus had formed on the subject, but in an opinion that struck many as surprisingly activist, he held that the Supreme Court would bring its own judgment to bear by asking whether there is reason to agree or disagree with the judgment reached by the citizenry and its legislators. Stevens found growing agreement that the objectives of capital punishment—deterring murder and exacting retribution—do not apply when imposed on people of significantly below-average intelligence.

Aside from overturning a relatively recent precedent, the Court's decision came amid a growing national debate over the death penalty. The use of DNA testing had led to a reversal of several convictions of people on death row for murders that they had not committed, and flaws in the system of capital punishment led the Illinois governor George Ryan to suspend execution until a full-scale review could take place. Following that study, the state legislature abolished the death penalty, and Governor Pat Quinn commuted the sentences of the fifteen men left on death row to life imprisonment.

Atkins set the stage for the Court to review its 1989 decision in *Stanford v. Kentucky,* in which a majority had upheld the constitutionality of executing juveniles older than fifteen. The case, *Roper v. Simmons,* arose after the Missouri Supreme Court, ignoring the rule in *Stanford,* voted 4–3 to vacate the death sentence for Christopher Simmons for a murder he committed when he was seventeen and changed his sentence to life imprisonment. The state appealed the decision, saying that because Missouri law allowed for the execution, the state court could not ignore the Supreme Court's ruling in the Kentucky case.

In oral argument, the former solicitor general Seth Waxman, appearing for Simmons, noted the trend both in the nation and in the world against executing juveniles. "We are literally alone in the world," he claimed. Although four of the justices had been under attack by conservative groups for consulting international law with respect to questions arising before American tribunals, Waxman's argument led to a 5–4 decision striking down the death penalty for those under eighteen. Justice Anthony Kennedy cited moral imperatives as well as a growing consensus in the United States and overseas against executing minors and declared that "from a moral standpoint, it would be misguided to equate the failings of a minor with those of an adult, for a greater possibility exists that a minor's character deficiencies will be reformed." Then, in words that brought down the opprobrium of conservative groups, Kennedy noted that most other countries in the world had stopped executing juveniles. It was relevant, albeit not controlling, to recognize that the United States "now stands alone in a world that has turned its face against the juvenile death penalty."

About this time, the Court also began looking at death cases involving charges of ineffective counsel. Ever since *Powell v. Alabama* in 1932, people accused of capital crimes in state courts had to have counsel and, if they could not afford it, to have the state appoint someone to represent them. The poor quality of counsel in death penalty cases had become a major source of public concern, with perhaps the most notorious example being a Texas lawyer who slept through much of his client's trial. It offended the justices when court-appointed counsel failed to provide a minimally acceptable level of assistance. In 2003, the Court threw out the death sentence of a Maryland man because the court-appointed lawyers failed to look into easily accessible information about his troubled background that might have led the jury to give him life imprisonment rather than death. A few years later, the Court set aside the death penalty for a Pennsylvania man because his lawyers had failed to search files on his past convictions for mitigating evidence. His public defender lawyers had elicited character witness testimony but did not review court records that would have revealed his past mental illness and alcoholism, as well as a childhood lived in poverty—all of which could have been taken into account as mitigating factors in sentencing.

In June 2008, the Court ruled against Louisiana's death penalty for child rapists, saying, "There is a distinction between intentional first-degree murder on the one hand and nonhomicide crimes against individual persons." The Court went further, ruling out the death penalty for any crime against an individual (as opposed to "offenses against the state," such as treason or espionage) "where the victim's life was not taken." Justice Kennedy's opinion for the most part tracked that of

Justice Byron White in *Coker v. Georgia* (1977), one of the post-*Furman* cases, that the death penalty for rape was excessive.

In some ways, the evolution of death penalty cases seems to mirror the decisions between *Betts v. Brady* and *Gideon v. Wainwright,* in that the Court has nibbled at the edge of the problem, finding "special circumstances" in cases involving minors, the mentally retarded, and lack of effective counsel. Moreover, a number of states have in recent years rescinded their capital punishment statutes.

In 1984, Rhode Island became the first state to repeal the death penalty after *Gregg,* and since then has been followed by New Jersey and New York in 2007, New Mexico in 2009, Illinois in 2011, Connecticut in 2012, and Maryland in 2013. At the present time, eighteen states and the District of Columbia do not have a death penalty statute. On the other hand, in states such as Texas and Virginia with large death row populations and strong support for enforcement, the death penalty remains entrenched in the criminal justice system.

In his opinion in *Furman,* Justice Marshall said that if the American people knew more about the death penalty, they would oppose it. That was forty years ago, and so far—despite all the publicity about the Supreme Court's cases, the information about faulty convictions, the innocence of men on death row for years—public opinion has not changed greatly. The Gallup poll first asked about the death penalty for convicted murderers in December 1936, when 59 percent of the respondents said they favored it and 38 percent opposed. Support of execution of murderers reached its high point in September 1994, when four out of every five persons said they believed in it. The most recent poll in March 2014 showed that 55 percent of the sample supported the death penalty, down from a high of 78 percent in 1996, and even lower than the 62 percent in 2011. Marshall might have taken heart that although half the people believed the death sentence was imposed fairly, 41 percent said "unfairly."

The faith in time of Brennan, Marshall, and Blackmun may be great, but the changes, great as they have been in some areas, still leave capital punishment on the books in nearly two-thirds of the states. The decades-long opposition to capital punishment, expressed in their dissents, surely fits Chief Justice Hughes's description of dissents as "appeal{s} to the brooding spirit of the law, to the intelligence of a future day."

CHAPTER 12

CODA

The dissenter is one who speaks to the future with a voice pitched
to a key that will carry through the years.

—BENJAMIN NATHAN CARDOZO

After the Court had decided its final cases of the term in June 2013, Robert Barnes, the Supreme Court reporter for *The Washington Post,* noted some of the recent criticism aimed at the nation's highest tribunal and its members:

The high court this term proved itself to be a "black-robed supremacy" infected by an "exalted conception" of its role in American life. It "egregiously" trampled on the power that the Constitution bestows on the people's elected representatives.

One of its decisions was a "betrayal of the court's precedents and of federal statutes." Another was based on an understanding of the law "that is nowhere to be found in the annals of Anglo-American jurisprudence."

A third ruling was so vague in its prescriptions that even the person to whom the decision was directed "would have no idea—no idea" what was required of him.

"Who dares," Barnes continued, "to so harshly bad-mouth the thoughtful and hardworking members of the Supreme Court?" The answer—themselves: Antonin Scalia ("supremacy"), Ruth Bader Ginsburg ("egregiously"), Elena Kagan ("betrayal"), Samuel Alito ("nowhere"), and Chief Justice John Roberts ("no idea"). And, Barnes noted, it would not take very much effort to find similar statements by the other four members of the bench. Where did one find these scathing comments? In the dissents, those "fusillades of objection" that usually, but not always, conclude with the message that the justice "respectfully dissents."

The strong language used by some members of the Court may capture the public's attention, but the fact remains that it is a dissent, and unless it can show convincingly how wrong the majority is, it will never—no matter how well it may be written—be more than an angry tirade or enter into the constitutional dialogue. There is no question, for example, that one of the best stylists on the current Court, Antonin Scalia, writes marvelous dissents in terms of literary felicity. No other member of the current Court has had a book published collecting his dissents. His dissents have not won over many adherents, and in some areas, despite the force of his protest, he may well be on the wrong side of history. Scalia wrote a blazing protest against the majority's determination that the Defense of Marriage Act was unconstitutional, calling Justice Anthony Kennedy's reasoning in the decision "legalistic argle-bargle." But same-sex marriage already enjoys popular support, and as several commentators noted, Scalia's "rant" was as much a cry against change of which he disapproves as a dissection of what he considers faulty reasoning.

MUCH OF THE DIALOGUE we have looked at has taken place within the Court, and every justice will attest to its importance one way or another. Justice Ginsburg says that about four times a term an opinion starting out as a dissent is so well reasoned that it persuades enough justices to join and transform it into a majority decision. "I had the heady experience once," she told the Harvard Club of Washington at the end of 2009, "of writing a dissent for myself and just one other justice; in time, it became the opinion of the Court from which only three of my colleagues dissented."

All of the justices agree that dissents, if well reasoned, almost invariably make the majority opinion stronger. In a talk at the Aspen Institute in July 2013, Justice Stephen Breyer reiterated this point. Because both the majority and the dissenting opinions circulate among the justices, he said, the person writing for the majority will try to answer the strongest points. "You never see the best points the dissent makes," he suggested, "because they've been written out of the majority opinion, so there is no need to make that dissenting point anymore."

Other conversations are also taking place—with Congress, with the president, and, especially in recent years, with the public. The Supreme Court does not give advisory opinions; that is, it will not decide the constitutionality of a congressional bill or a proposed executive action until after the bill has been passed or the president has done something. There has to be, according to the Constitution, a real case or controversy, not just a possibility of one. So when Congress or the president engages in a policy, the Court will only become involved when someone who has a grievance because of that policy challenges its constitutionality in the courts.

With Congress, and correspondingly with state legislatures, the Court's response may take several forms. First of all, it can uphold the law and dismiss the suit. Second, it can declare the law unconstitutional, and between 1801 and 2004 the Court overturned 173 acts of Congress and invalidated 967 state laws. (It also, during this period, reversed 223 of its own precedents.) In such cases, both the majority and the dissenters are talking to legislators. In constitutional cases, of course, if the Court says that Congress or the state does not have the power to do something, that is pretty much the end of the discussion. But in other instances, the Court may in effect say, "We only have the statute and its wording in front of us, and all we can look at is what is within the four corners of the writing. You may have the power to achieve what you want, but in order to do so, you have to take a different approach."

A recent example is the decision by the Court striking down a key provision of the landmark Voting Rights Act of 1965. Section 5 required that those states with a clear history of racial discrimination get prior approval from the Justice Department in order to change district voting lines or take any action that might conceivably dilute minority voting. Congress in a near-unanimous vote extended the law in 2006, and President George W. Bush signed the measure.

A small utility district near Austin, Texas, challenged the measure and claimed that changes in society and voting patterns made the preclearance requirements of section 5 no longer necessary or constitutional. Although an 8–1 majority upheld the law, Chief Justice Roberts made plain that the fact that Congress had not changed its criteria for jurisdictions covered by the law upset him. If Congress ignored the validity of changing social and demographic patterns, then the viability of section 5 could be called into question.

John Glover Roberts Jr., chief justice, 2005–

Congress either did not hear this message, chose not to make adjustments in the formula, or, perhaps most likely, proved unable to do so. In any event, the question came back before the Court four years later, and this time a 5–4 majority suspended the oversight provision, saying that the data Congress used to identify the states covered by the law were outmoded and thus unfair. The Court very clearly told Congress that it had the power to act under the Enforcement Clause of the Fifteenth Amendment but that it had to base that action on the realities of 2013, not 1965. Whether Congress, given its current polarization and gridlock, can come up with a new formula is far from clear.

Similarly, the Court and the executive branch interact. One example will suffice for now, and that involves the president's authority to remove executive officers. While the Constitution provides for presidential appointments, it is silent on whether or how the chief executive may get rid of unsatisfactory members of the administration. As early as 1803, Chief Justice John Marshall suggested in *Marbury v. Madison* that once the appointment process had been completed, the appointee had to be allowed to take office. Since then, of course, Congress has created myriad federal offices and agencies, and in some of the enabling statutes there is clear language that allows the president to remove a person for cause, such as poor performance. But what about other reasons, such as political differences? This debate began almost as soon as the new government convened in 1789, when the House of Representatives discussed the process for removing executive officials from office, and members of the House divided over whether that authority resided solely in the executive or required legislative participation as well. James Madison defended sole executive prerogative, and for the most part Congress over the next eight decades deferred to the president on personnel matters. The Supreme Court did not get involved until the end of the nineteenth century, when it upheld the president's authority to terminate executive appointments that did not require Senate confirmation.

The key issue arose after the Civil War, when Congress passed the Tenure of Office Act in 1867. The statute is part of the congressional Reconstruction, when a Republican Congress with broad support in the North faced opposition from a racist and politically obtuse Andrew Johnson. The president wanted to let the southern states back into the Union immediately and to leave the question of how the former slaves would be treated to their former owners. Eventually, the House of Representatives impeached Johnson, and the Senate came within one vote of convicting him. Prior to that, however, Congress tried to restrict Johnson by taking away much of his discretion and authority in Reconstruction matters, and under the Tenure of Office Act a president could not, without Senate approval, discharge any officer whose appointment had been approved by that chamber. Johnson's defiance of that law in his efforts to get rid of Secretary of War Edwin Stanton proved to be a key cause of impeachment.

After Reconstruction, the law pretty much fell into disuse. Aside from cabinet members, ambassadors, and judges, very few government positions required Senate confirmation. In most instances, department heads and foreign ministers understood they served at the president's pleasure and resigned when asked to do so. By the 1920s, however, there were literally thousands of government employees in a vast range of positions. Many were covered under the Civil Service Act and therefore beyond presidential control, but independent agencies, beginning with the Interstate Commerce Commission in 1887, had proliferated, and appointees to these bodies not only required Senate confirmation but enjoyed fixed terms. Could a president remove any of these people?

In 1920, Woodrow Wilson removed Frank S. Myers as postmaster of Oregon (at that time, a patronage position requiring Senate confirmation) without the consent of the Senate. A short time later, Myers died, and his wife, as executor of the estate, sued for damages and lost wages, claiming that Wilson had needed the Senate's approval before firing her late husband. The case represented an issue near and dear to Chief Justice William Howard Taft, who as an ex-president strongly believed in presidential prerogative. Relying on history going back to the Constitutional Convention, Taft wrote a seventy-one-page opinion for the 6–3 majority to prove that the Framers had intended to create a strong executive power that—at least in the area of appointments—Congress could not limit.

Both Louis Brandeis and James McReynolds tore the Taft opinion apart. McReynolds, in a sixty-two-page dissent, ridiculed the idea of any inherent presidential power to remove government employees. The Constitution gave Congress the power to place the appointment of lesser officials in hands other than the president's and to provide a means by which they could be removed. The power given by the Constitution to appoint certain officials did not deprive Congress of the power to place limits on their removal.

Had Taft not stretched his opinion to include the commissioners of the regulatory agencies, Brandeis might well have gone along with McReynolds. But Brandeis believed that if Taft's ruling were fully implemented, it would undermine the independent agencies. Where Taft had framed the question broadly—"Whether under the Constitution the President has the exclusive power of removing executive officers of the United States whom he has appointed"—Brandeis structured his argument far more narrowly: "May the President, having acted under the statute in so far as it creates the office and authorizes the appointment, ignore, while the Senate is in session, the provision which prescribes the condition under which a removal may take place?" Like Taft and McReynolds, Brandeis relied heavily on history in his fifty-five-page dissent. He dismissed Taft's separation-of-powers argument and claimed instead that the checks and balances among the three branches constituted the most important principle involved. That is why the Framers had refused to give the president an unlimited removal power. Separation of powers had been established "not to promote efficiency but to preclude the exercise of arbitrary power." For Brandeis, Congress, in protecting government employees from arbitrary dismissal, acted also to protect democracy.

Unlike with some of his other dissents, Brandeis lived to see this one vindicated and in fact still sat on the Court nine years later when the justices heard *Humphrey's Executor v. United States* in 1935. Relying on *Myers,* Franklin Roosevelt had forced William Humphrey, a conservative advocate of big business, to resign from the Federal Trade Commission. The Court, in a unanimous opinion by Justice Sutherland, held that it had been the intent of Congress to make the regulatory commissions independent of the executive and subject only to the legislature and the judiciary. A president could remove a commissioner only for cause, and an unqualified power of removal violated the separation of powers.

The Court's dialogue with the public takes many forms. The justices, even if they do not admit to it, are tuned in to public opinion. There have been very few instances in the past 225 years when the Court has pursued a jurisprudential path that runs contrary to public opinion. Textualists like Antonin Scalia will proclaim that what the public thinks should have no bearing on the work of the Court, which is to interpret the constant meaning of the Constitution. But Scalia is an outlier on this issue, and more moderate conservatives—such as Anthony Kennedy on the current Court and Sandra Day O'Connor and Lewis Powell Jr. on earlier courts—have been sensitive to changing mores. In some instances, it will be the majority that invokes these changes; in others, it may be the minority.

Moreover, in recent years several justices have taken their views directly to the public in the forms of books, speeches, law review articles, and interviews. William O. Douglas started the trend, interspersing thoughts on jurisprudence among his various books and then writing a volume of memoirs on his Court years. More recently, William Rehnquist, John Paul Stevens, Sandra Day O'Connor, Antonin Scalia, Anthony Kennedy, Clarence Thomas, and Stephen Breyer have all published books on constitutional topics. Thomas and Scalia have been frequent speakers at conservative gatherings, while Scalia and Breyer have on several occasions debated each other over constitutional interpretation.

PART OF THE DIALOGUE with the public includes how the citizenry views the members of the nation's highest court, and for better or worse politics often intrudes in the equation. Throughout the 225 years that the Court has sat, all of its justices have proclaimed that they try to reach decisions based on constitutional precepts, not partisan considerations. Yet because the constitutional dialogue on the Court reflects the larger public policy debates in the nation, it is perhaps inevitable that those people and groups unhappy with the Court's decisions will charge that politics, not law, has determined the results. Thomas Jefferson and his followers continually attacked the Court for its Federalist opinions, even after a majority of the bench consisted of men appointed by Jefferson, Madison, and Monroe. The *Dred Scott* decision brought widespread denunciation in the North that the justices had sided with the Democratic slaveholders of the South. During the 1930s, supporters of the New Deal charged the conservative majority that thwarted Franklin Roosevelt's program as carrying the political standard of the Old Guard, which, of course, meant the Republican Party. Richard Nixon and southern Democrats claimed that the Warren Court represented the political beliefs of the liberal left wing of the Democratic Party, even though two of its most liberal members—Earl Warren and William Brennan—had been appointed by a Republican president.

The Supreme Court, as one of the three branches of government, is of course political; it takes part not only in policy making but in interacting with the other parts of the federal government, the states, and the people. But ever since the 2000 election, the volume of charges that the Court is also partisan has increased exponentially. Part of this is due not only to the decision in *Bush v. Gore* but to the fact that so many of its most important decisions have been decided by a 5–4 vote, with alleged Republicans (conservatives) lined up against Democrats (liberals). The appointments made by Ronald Reagan, George H. W. Bush, and George W. Bush, with the exception of David Souter, have been consistently conservative, with some, like Antonin Scalia, Clarence Thomas, and Samuel Alito, more so than others, like Sandra Day O'Connor and Anthony Kennedy. Those named by Bill Clinton and Barack Obama have certainly been more moderate, if not liberal in the Douglas/Brennan/Goldberg category.

We expect presidents to name men and women to the federal bench who agree with their political philosophy. George Washington expected his appointees to share a particular view of the Constitution, a view that later became known as Federalist. Franklin Roosevelt wanted men who believed the Commerce Clause gave the federal government power to deal with the economic problems caused by the Depression. Ronald Reagan and his attorney general Edwin Meese set up a questionnaire system to ensure that judicial appointees held the correct Republican views on issues such as abortion and affirmative action. It should therefore come as no surprise that people like Scalia and John Roberts, or Stephen Breyer and Elena Kagan, share many of the beliefs of the presidents who nominated them.

Justice Stephen Breyer is one of the members of the Court who has done a great deal of speaking at universities and law schools, and he says there are two preconceived notions that he faces at each meeting: one is that the justices only take cases they find interesting, and the other is that the justices are less objective interpreters of the law than "junior-league politicians." He says he finds it much easier to refute the first than the second, even though he can cite case after case where the lineup had supposed conservatives voting with alleged liberals and 5–4 decisions are really a minority of the Court's opinions.

The moderator at one of these sessions, Professor Jeffrey Rosen of the George Washington Law School, agreed with Breyer in general but noted that at the end of every term there will be 5–4 decisions that precisely confirm the Court's ideological divide. Rosen told Breyer that he instructs his students that if they believe it is all about politics, they will "miss everything that's beautiful about constitutional law." But guess what, Rosen said, "They don't believe me. They think it's all politics." That is a view that, rightly or wrongly, is shared by many people.

Breyer, however, is right, in that on any number of issues that come before the Court, there is no "Democratic" or "Republican" position. In the October 2013 term, for example, Scalia, joined by Ginsburg, Sotomayor, and Kagan, wrote a powerful dissent against an opinion by Thomas, regarding the validity of an anonymous 911 tip as a cause to stop and search a car. In a second case, Elena Kagan, considered the most liberal member of the current Court, joined with the conservatives in turning down a death row inmate's claim that his case deserved additional review. The Court actually split three ways in trying to decipher a fuzzy law passed by Congress ordering restitution to victims of child pornography.

It would be difficult to determine when—or if—partisan consideration plays a role in decision making, and one should also keep in mind that agendas change. Franklin Roosevelt named justices who he believed—and rightly so—would uphold his view of broadly interpreted Commerce Clause powers, yet within a few years questions of economic and property rights practically disappeared from the Court to be replaced by cases involving civil rights and liberties, on which the Roosevelt appointees differed widely. The Reagan and Bush appointees have been fairly consistent in their decisions regarding business claims and opposition to affirmative action, but there is no "Republican" position on questions of right to die, patent law, and the Internet.

A number of scholars have suggested that we are in the midst of another significant change in the Court's agenda, where the hot-button issues of race and abortion will be replaced by questions growing out of the technological revolution. The Court has already begun to hear some of these cases, and the divisions on the bench clearly reflect intellectual and jurisprudential considerations.

AS NOTED EARLIER, "the fate of a dissent lies in the hands of history." While contemporaries who agree with a dissent may proclaim it

Elena Kagan, associate justice, 2010–

prophetic and bound for glory, for the most part we cannot tell at the time whether or not a dissent will succeed in its call to future generations. There is no evidence that Stephen Field's dissent in *Slaughterhouse,* the first Harlan's in the *Civil Rights Cases* or *Plessy,* Holmes in *Abrams,* Brandeis in *Olmstead,* and Black in *Betts v. Brady* made any great impression on those who read them at the time. All have now entered the canon of great dissents, written by "prophets with honor."

Those of us who work in the field of constitutional and legal history are as aware as our colleagues in social, economic, or political history of the difficulties in trying to assess what is happening today as part of a long-term trend. A half century ago, one of my teachers told me that French schools avoided this problem by declaring that anything after the French Revolution in 1789 was not history but current events. One assumes that date has moved forward somewhat, but there is a certain wisdom in making sure that sufficient time has elapsed so that one can make a balanced judgment.

When I lecture, I am invariably asked how I think the Court will act in some future case or controversy. Just as consistently, I say, "I am a historian, not a prophet, and while I trust my judgment on things past, I have no idea how the Supremes will decide." Certainly one could not have predicted in 2008, for example, that in five years the Court would take not one but two cases on same-sex marriage and rule that homo-sexuals could not be denied the equal protection of the laws.

Yet despite the caution that I and other historians share, we do venture to make assessments, even on some things that are less than fifty years old. I decided to ask my colleagues in the field of constitutional history what dissents they thought would have staying power, opinions that might one day be part of the canon and, if not justified, at least enshrined in constitutional law casebooks. The answers varied enormously and reflected the respondents' professional as well as personal interests, which is to be expected.

Three dissents stood out: those of William Brennan in *McCleskey v. Kemp* (1987), Antonin Scalia in *Morrison v. Olson* (1988), and Ruth Bader Ginsburg in *NFIB v. Sebelius* (2012).

WILLIAM J. BRENNAN. In 1978, a jury in Atlanta, Georgia, convicted Warren McCleskey, an African American, of killing a white policeman during a robbery. The jury recommended the death penalty. After unsuccessful appeals in state courts, McCleskey sought habeas relief in federal court, arguing that in Georgia the death penalty was applied in a manner that discriminated against blacks. He supported this position with research done by David C. Baldus showing that 11 percent of defendants charged with killing whites, but only 1 percent of defendants charged with killing blacks, received the death penalty. The Baldus study showed many other discrepancies between how whites and blacks accused of murder were sentenced, with harsher penalties always meted out to African Americans. The district court and the court of appeals rejected this argument, and so did the Supreme Court. Writing for the Court, Justice Lewis Powell held that even if these statistics were accurate, they did not prove that McCleskey's death penalty had been the result of racial bias. Death penalty decisions were made on an individual, case-by-case basis, and each judgment rested on a variety of interconnected facts. The decision makers—the jurors—were different in each case. "At most," Powell concluded, "the Baldus study indicates a discrepancy that appears to correlate with race. Apparent disparities in sentencing are an inevitable part of our criminal justice system."

Brennan began his dissent with the familiar statement that he adhered to the view that "the death penalty is in all circumstances cruel and unusual punishment forbidden by the Eighth and Fourteenth Amendments." The statistics McCleskey had presented clearly impressed Brennan, who quoted them extensively throughout his dissent and said they "demonstrated precisely the type of risk of irrationality in sentencing that we have constantly condemned in our Eighth Amendment jurisprudence." Had Warren McCleskey at some point in the proceedings asked his lawyer whether a jury would be likely to convict him, a "candid reply . . . would have been disturbing." Yet the majority found no fault in a system in which race clearly affected sentencing.

Under the majority opinion, no matter how prevalent a role racial considerations played in the criminal justice system, no one defendant would ever be able to prove that general prejudice had affected his particular case. Brennan, however, argued that this did not matter, because a whole string of death sentence cases going back to *Furman v. Georgia* (1972) had emphasized not the specific case but the *risk* of arbitrariness in the system. The Baldus study did just that; it showed not that McCleskey had been the victim of racial prejudice but that the system itself was flawed. Defendants challenging death sentences have never had to prove that "impermissible considerations actually infected sentencing decisions," only that the system under which they had been sentenced "posed a significant risk of such an occurrence." Here the Baldus study, despite the majority opinion, clearly showed not only that the risk existed but that in fact it played a role in hundreds of decisions. Brennan tore apart the majority opinion for its blindness to the fact that African Americans faced real prejudice in the Georgia criminal justice system, especially in capital cases. He concluded,

> It is tempting to pretend that minorities on death row share a fate in no way connected to our own, that our treatment of them sounds no echoes beyond the chambers in which they die. Such an illusion is ultimately corrosive, for the reverberations of injustice are not so easily confined. "The destinies of the two races in this country are indissolubly linked together," and the way in which we choose those who will die reveals the depth of moral commitment among the living.
>
> The Court's decision today will not change what attorneys in Georgia tell other Warren McCleskeys about their chances of execution. Nothing will soften the harsh message they must convey, nor alter the prospect that race undoubtedly will continue to be a topic of discussion. McCleskey's evidence will not have obtained judicial acceptance, but that will not affect what is said on death row. However many criticisms of today's decision may be rendered, these painful conversations will serve as the most eloquent dissents of all.

Antonin Scalia, associate justice, 1986–

Since *McCleskey,* the Court has refused to accept statistical evidence of discrimination against groups, and insisted—in death penalty as well as in many affirmative action cases—that proof of individual impact must be shown. If, and when, changes on the Court lead to accepting the type of proof found in the Baldus study, then Justice Brennan's dissent will guide them in how they use these materials.

ANTONIN SCALIA. A little over a year later, the Court handed down its decision in *Morrison v. Olson,* dealing with the constitutionality of special prosecutors. In the aftermath of the Watergate scandals, Congress enacted the Ethics in Government Act of 1978. A provision in the law allowed for a court, called the Special Division, to appoint independent counsel to investigate and prosecute high-ranking government officials for violations of federal criminal laws. In 1985, the House Judiciary Committee accused Theodore Olson, assistant attorney general for the Office of Legal Counsel, of providing false and misleading testimony. The committee chair requested that an independent counsel be appointed to investigate the allegations. The Special Division appointed James McKay independent counsel, and he was later replaced by Alexia Morrison, who instructed a grand jury to serve subpoenas on Olson and two others.

All three moved to quash the subpoenas, claiming that the independent counsel provisions of the act were unconstitutional. In July 1987, the district court upheld the constitutionality of the law, but the court of appeals reversed. The majority ruled that the independent counsel provision violated several parts of the Constitution, including separation of powers, Article III delegation authority, the Appointments Clause, and the Take Care Clause (Article II, section 3). Morrison appealed to the Supreme Court, which heard the case on 26 April 1988.

At conference, Chief Justice Rehnquist said he believed the special prosecutor provision to be constitutional. The 1978 law gave only limited responsibility to judges to choose prosecutors upon a request by the attorney general. It did not usurp executive powers, because the independent counsel remained subordinate to the attorney general and could indeed be fired by him, albeit only with good cause. All the other justices (Kennedy did not participate) agreed with Rehnquist, except Antonin Scalia, for whom the provision violated everything he believed about the constitutional separation of powers. Scalia, the last justice to speak around the table, claimed that the law, in his opinion, sanctioned prosecutorial powers outside the executive branch. Under the Constitution, the president's duties included complete control over investigations and prosecutions of violations of federal law. Scalia changed no votes at the conference and during the drafting process actually turned off some of his colleagues. Harry Blackmun objected to Scalia's hard line and strident tone.

In Rehnquist's opinion for the 7–1 majority, he conceded that "there is no dispute that the functions performed by the independent counsel are executive" in nature, but that did not unduly trammel on the president's authority. The chief justice acknowledged that "it is undeniable that the Act reduces the amount of control that the Attorney General and, through him, the President exercises over investigation and prosecution," but this limitation did not "sufficiently deprive the President of control over the independent counsel to interfere impermissibly with his constitutional obligation to ensure the faithful execution of the laws." Nor did it disrupt "the proper balance between the coordinate branches by preventing the Executive Branch from accomplishing its constitutionally assigned functions." Separation of powers, Rehnquist argued, does not require "that the three Branches of Government operate with absolute independence."

Although he had only been on the Court less than two years, Scalia's dissent in the case, according to Ralph A. Rossum, "remains his most fully developed and powerful statement on his textualist understanding of the principle of separation of powers." It did not matter that the law could be sustained on the majority's understanding of separation of powers. Did the act violate "the text of the Constitution and the division of power that it established"? That division, which Scalia described as "the equilibrium the Constitution sought to establish," mandated that all purely executive power had to remain under the president's control, not what "the majority thinks, taking all things into account, . . . *ought*" to be under the president's control.

Scalia has normally called for deference to the political branches, but not in separation of powers. As he explained,

> Where a private citizen challenges action of the Government on grounds unrelated to separation of powers, harmonious functioning of the system demands that we ordinarily give some deference, or a presumption of validity, to the actions of the political branches in what is agreed, between themselves at least, to be within their respective spheres. But where the issue pertains to separation of powers, and the political branches are (as here) in disagreement, neither can be presumed correct. The reason is stated concisely by Madison: "The several departments being perfectly co-ordinate by the terms of their common commission, neither of them, it is evident, can pretend to an exclusive or superior right to settling the boundaries between their respective powers. . . ." *Federalist* No. 49. The playing field for the present case, in other words, is a level one. As one of the interested and coordinate parties to the underlying constitutional dispute, Congress, no more than the President, is entitled to the benefit of the doubt.

Without any compulsion to presume the constitutionality of the independent counsel law, Scalia charged that Congress had "effectively compelled a criminal investigation of a high-level appointee of the President in connection with his actions arising out of a bitter power dispute between the President and the Legislative Branch." Moreover, Congress had deprived the president and his subordinates of their power to control the nature and extent of investigations. The constitutional text made very clear that the " 'executive Power shall be vested in the President of the United States' (Art. II) and this does not mean some of the executive power, but all of it."

Scalia went on to outline ways in which abuse of executive power could be controlled by Congress and the courts, and ultimately the people would decide when executives and their lieutenants abused their power. The independent counsel, on the other hand, was not accountable to the public in any way, shape, or form. He conceded that in the actual workings of government situations arose where bright lines of separation might be blurred, but in this instance there had been a deliberate effort to avoid the constraints envisioned by the Constitution. Moreover—and here Scalia showed that he, too, understood the workings of government—the act took away the power of the president to protect his high-level assistants from partisan sniping by Congress.

Scalia in many ways anticipated the major criticisms that would be hurled at Kenneth W. Starr's investigation of the Clinton White House in the 1990s, when a partisan Republican majority in the House of Representatives seemed hell-bent on bringing the president down. What Scalia did not anticipate is that both President Clinton and Attorney General Janet Reno had resources to withstand the partisan importuning of the House Republicans. Nor did Scalia address the question of whether the wrongdoing in the Nixon administration related to the Watergate scandal might have remained hidden had there been no independent counsel.

The dissent shows both a strength and a weakness of Scalia's jurisprudence. His textualism is impressive, and whether one agrees or disagrees with his jurisprudence, in this case and elsewhere his views require one to go back and read the text and question whether Congress and the president have overstepped the authority granted them by the Constitution vis-à-vis their relations to each other. The weakness is his unbending adherence to a literal reading of the text and his insistence that a document drafted in 1787 will provide all the answers necessary to resolve issues that are the products of conditions two centuries after the Philadelphia convention.

RUTH BADER GINSBURG. The third opinion that won the admiration of legal scholars was that of Justice Ginsburg in *National Federation of Independent Business v. Sebelius,* the case involving President Obama's signature achievement in his first term, the Patient Protection and Affordable Care Act (ACA). At issue were two key provisions: first, the individual mandate that all Americans secure health insurance by 2014, and, second, a required expansion by the states of the Medicaid program. A splintered Court held that the individual mandate provision of the ACA exceeded Congress's power under the Commerce Clause, but because it involved a penalty collected by the Internal Revenue Service, the fine could be construed as a "tax," and the mandate thus passed constitutional muster under the congressional taxing authority. A different majority struck down the provision that allowed the federal government to withhold Medicaid funds unless a state agreed to implement certain expansions of the program under terms of the ACA.

Ruth Bader Ginsburg, associate justice, 1993–

Justice Ginsburg helped give Chief Justice Roberts the majority he needed to uphold the ACA under the taxing power, but she, along with Justices Sotomayor, Breyer, and Kagan, would have upheld the ACA under the Commerce Clause and approved the Medicaid expansions under the Spending Clause.

She began with a long justification for the ACA, discussing the size of the nation's health-care industry, the amount of money spent, the number of people left uncovered by the current system, and efforts by Congress over the past half century to provide health care to the elderly and the poor. The problems of health-care costs and the number of uninsured exceeded what any one state could do to resolve the matter, even within its own borders. Even in Massachusetts, which had a comprehensive health-care plan for its citizens, out-of-state residents sought and received millions of dollars of uncompensated medical and hospital care. Because these problems were national in scope, only the federal government had the power to deal with them. The ACA thus "address[ed] an economic and social problem that has plagued the Nation for decades." Moreover, "whatever one thinks of the policy decision Congress made, it was Congress' prerogative to make it. Reviewed with appropriate deference [the ACA's components] should survive measurement under the Commerce and Necessary and Proper Clauses."

She then launched into a history of the Commerce Clause, from its inception in Philadelphia, and the Framers' intent that, as Alexander Hamilton wrote in *Federalist* 34, "there ought to be a CAPACITY to provide for future contingencies." The Commerce Clause, therefore, should be read—as the Court had done for most of its history—in an expansive manner. Prior cases had held that Congress could regulate not only interstate economic activities but also intrastate actions that, "viewed in the aggregate, have a substantial impact on interstate commerce." After going through numerous examples of how broadly the Court had interpreted the Commerce Clause, she declared that the chief justice had relied on a "newly minted constitutional doctrine. The commerce power does not permit Congress to 'compel individuals to become active in commerce by purchasing a product.'"

Ginsburg lacerated Roberts's reasoning. The chief justice admitted that all Americans participate in the market for health services over the course of their lives but then claimed that the uninsured cannot be considered "active in the market for health care," because one could not determine the proximity between their status today and their future needs. This, Ginsburg pointed out, had been one of the reasons for congressional action: one could not know when health care would be needed, and so it was important that when the need arose, individuals have the necessary insurance coverage. Beyond the fallacy of Roberts's reasoning, this was not a decision for him to make: policy making belonged in Congress, not in the Court. She concluded her section on the Commerce Clause by noting,

> In the early 20th century, this Court regularly struck down economic regulation enacted by the peoples' representatives in both the States and the Federal Government. The Chief Justice's Commerce Clause opinion, and even more so the joint dissenters' reasoning, bear a disquieting resemblance to those long-overruled decisions. Ultimately, the Court upholds the individual mandate as a proper exercise of Congress' power to tax and spend "for the . . . general Welfare of the United States." I concur in that determination, which makes the Chief Justice's Commerce Clause essay all the more puzzling. Why should the Chief Justice strive so mightily to hem in Congress' capacity to meet the new problems arising constantly in our ever-developing modern economy? I find no satisfying response to that question in his opinion.

WHY DID MY COLLEAGUES in the profession choose these three? It is too early to know whether any of them will be part of the canon, but all three do have certain traits in common, traits that are found in many of the prophetic dissents that have played such an important role in the constitutional dialogue. First, they set out the problem before the Court in a clear manner but in such a way as to support both their jurisprudential disagreement with the majority and what they consider the "correct" argument. It is not so much that the dissenters and the majority are looking at different scenarios: Warren McCleskey was, in fact, convicted of murder; Congress did enact a statute providing for a special counsel who did not answer to the president; and the Affordable Care Act did require an individual mandate and Medicaid expansion.

But Brennan told the McCleskey story in the context of a criminal justice system that consistently penalized African Americans more harshly than white defendants. Scalia talked about the special counsel within the broad ideas of separation of powers as he divined that theory in the constitutional text. Ginsburg looked at the individual mandate and Medicaid provisions within the larger story of the health-care crisis in America.

All three forcefully explained why they believed the majority reasoning to be wrong and, more important, then provided what they considered a better constitutional argument. They laid out their conclusions convincingly, with great reliance on prior decisions and a strong rationale for why their views should be adopted.

Whether these dissents will eventually become the law is unknown. The fact that a majority of the country still supports capital punishment makes it unlikely that the efforts of Brennan, along with Thurgood Marshall, will prevail in the near future. But should the justices at some point begin to question the application of the death penalty, as they did in the late 1960s, Brennan's opinion will be there, ready to guide them.

Congress allowed the independent counsel law to expire, but situations are always arising that appear to blur the lines between executive and legislative authority. In such instances, there will undoubtedly be challenges, and as of now Scalia's dissent remains the strongest case yet made for a textualist approach to understanding separation of powers.

Justice Ginsburg's dissent argued convincingly that the majority misunderstood the full parameters of the Commerce Clause and had turned away from its history and a century of expansive interpretation of the commerce power. While it is unlikely that the ultraconservative wing of the Republican Party will endorse any large new government program, political fortunes vary, and in time a more liberal Congress may be elected that will have an activist agenda. When those laws, whatever they may be, are challenged, the *Sebelius* dissent will be there to explain why and how the Commerce Clause empowers Congress to act.

Each of the three is, in the words of Charles Evans Hughes, "an appeal to the brooding spirit of the law, to the intelligence of a future day."

IN NOVEMBER 1985, Justice William Brennan gave the Tobriner Memorial Lecture at the University of California Hastings College of the Law and titled it "In Defense of Dissents." By then, Brennan had sat on the high court for nearly three decades, and after the liberal Warren Court had transmuted into the conservative Burger Court, he had become one of the leading dissenters. As he told his audience, in his first term on the bench he had written sixteen opinions, not one of them a dissent. In the October 1984 term, he had written fifty-six opinions, forty-two of them dissents. In a thoughtful and at times introspective mood, Brennan then explained to his audience why he believed so strongly in dissents and their importance.

Borrowing from George Orwell, he characterized dissent as an act "of saying I, of imposing oneself upon other people, of saying *listen to me, see it my way, change your mind.*" Aside from pointing out what the author believes are flaws in the majority opinion, the dissent "safeguards the integrity of the judicial decision-making process by keeping the majority accountable for the rationale and consequences of its decision." Even the legal philosopher Karl Llewellyn, who for the most part opposed separate opinions, conceded that dissents helped "ride herd on the majority." In a similar manner, the dissent may strengthen the limits of the majority, preventing it from sweeping too broadly—a form of damage control.

Brennan's most intriguing comment came when he asked what made certain dissents enduring, such as Harlan I in *Plessy* and Brandeis in *Olmstead*. These are the dissents, he said, "that often reveal the perceived congruence between the Constitution and the 'evolving standards of decency that mark the progress of a maturing society,' and that seek to sow seeds for future harvest. These are the dissents that soar with passion and ring with rhetoric. These are the dissents that, at their best, straddle the worlds of literature and law."

Probably no other member of the Court fought so hard for the idea of a living Constitution as did Brennan, because he strongly believed that as society evolved, the Constitution had to take into account changes not only in the economic and physical aspects of society but in its moral attitudes as well. Not all dissents, of course, are addressed to this issue, but Brennan is right that the great dissents, ones that we have looked at in this book, have been markers on the road from the past to the present and the future:

Stephen J. Field, seeking to expand the meaning of due process to include a wide variety of rights available both to the individual and to business.

John Marshall Harlan I, objecting to the segregation that flowed directly from slavery and urging that the Constitution is color-blind, an ideal yet to be achieved.

Oliver Wendell Holmes Jr., breaking from a past that allowed constraints on free speech and arguing for a freedom of expression that knew few bounds.

Louis D. Brandeis, reaching back into the origins of the Fourth Amendment to find a right to privacy to protect individuals in a world where the right to be let alone was endangered on all sides.

Wiley Rutledge, demanding that the victor's treatment of the vanquished adhere to traditional ideas of due process.

Hugo L. Black, drawing on his own experience as a lawyer, and arguing that in order to have a fair trial, a defendant needed the benefit of counsel.

In all these instances, the dissenter spoke for a future that not only had not arrived but in some cases could not even be guessed at. It is not, as Mark Tushnet tells us about a great dissent, that "it anticipates some social or political change that will make its doctrine seem the right one, but because its vision of democracy and the Constitution and its rhetoric themselves contributed to making its doctrine seem correct." Although they did not use the phrase "evolving standards of decency"—a term that Brennan used often—they might have done so, because in each of those dissents we see a justice trying to limn how the Constitution should be interpreted in light of changing social conditions. For Brennan and others, the Constitution's vitality depends on an interpretation that addresses the immediate needs of the community. "When a justice perceives an interpretation of the text to have departed so far from its essential meaning, that justice is bound by a larger constitutional duty to the community, to expose the departure and point toward a different path." The great dissents, the ones examined in this book, have all pointed "toward a different path," and in so many instances that has ultimately been the path the Court and the country have taken.

ACKNOWLEDGMENTS

As with any work of scholarship, I could not have completed this book without the help of many people. Librarians at American University, the Washington School of Law, and the Library of Congress, especially the Law Division, aided me at every step of the research, and I am grateful to them. I was able to try out some of the ideas and themes at various roundtables, as well as in talks at various law schools, including the Universities of Arkansas and Oklahoma, as well as the Washington Area Consortium on Legal History.

One of the most satisfying parts of the academic life is the give and take among scholars, and one way in which this takes place is the reading and commenting upon one another's works-in-progress. The volume you hold in your hand is a far better book thanks to the close reading and suggestions of three friends—William R. Casto of the Texas Tech University Law School, Mark R. Killenbeck of the University of Arkansas Law School, and Jonathan Lurie of Rutgers University. Many others answered questions on H-LAW, or responded to specific queries I sent to them. It does, indeed, take an academic village to write a book, and I am grateful to all of them.

Around the time I finished the manuscript my good friend and agent, Loretta A. Barrett, died. I first met Loretta more than forty years ago, and she was my editor for several books before becoming my agent, and during all that time she was a good friend to Susan and me. Her successor, Nick Mullendore, took over the last part of the process, and I look forward to working with him in the future.

At Pantheon I have been lucky to work with one of the best editors in the business, Victoria Wilson. She and her colleagues—Audrey Silverman and Iris Weinstein— transformed a rather large manuscript into the book. In my acknowledgments in the Brandeis biography, I wrote that I would gladly have Ingrid Sterner copyedit any future book, and so consider myself fortunate that she was assigned to this one as well.

My wife Susan over the years has come to recognize the various emotional stages in my work, from the laid-back early research on up to the intense writing and then almost frenetic revision, and not only keeps calm herself, but usually quiets me down as well. I am so lucky to be married to her.

NOTES

CHAPTER I: DISSENT AND THE CONSTITUTIONAL DIALOGUE

4 not least, the public: Barry Friedman, *The Will of the People* (2009). Friedman tellingly subtitles his work "How Public Opinion Has Influenced the Supreme Court and Shaped the Meaning of the Constitution."

5 of the majority: Pamela C. Corley, *Concurring Opinion Writing on the U.S. Supreme Court* (2010).

5 safeguard of democracy: William O. Douglas, "The Dissent: A Safeguard of Democracy," 32 *Journal of the American Judicature Society* 104, 105 (1948).

6 never be made public: See, for example, Kurt H. Nadelmann, "The Judicial Dissent: Publication v. Secrecy," 8 *American Journal of Comparative Law* 415 (1959), which traces the historical roots for suppressing dissent on the Continent, and Dieter Grimm, a German judge, "Remarks on the Use of Dissenting Opinions in Continental Europe," material for a comparative constitutionalism course made available through the courtesy of Dean Robert Post of the Yale Law School and used with the kind permission of Dr. Grimm.

7 "to express their dissent": *Rhode Island v. Massachusetts,* 37 U.S. 657, 752 (1838) (Taney dissenting).

7 at a later date: Robert H. Jackson, *The Supreme Court and the American System of Government* (1955), 18.

8 "fundamental canons": Irving Dilliard, ed., *The Spirit of Liberty: Papers and Addresses of Learned Hand* (1959), 211.

8 "and new rules": Benjamin N. Cardozo, *The Nature of the Judicial Process* (1921), 84, 100.

9 "which compose this": Marshall in *Mitchel v. United States,* 34 U.S. 711, 723 (1835); Johnson in *Martin v. Hunter's Lessee,* 14 U.S. 304, 364 (1816).

9 "difficult legal questions": Address to the American Law Institute, 1936, quoted in Felix Frankfurter, *Of Law and Men* (1956), 42.

9 "is disastrous because": Learned Hand, *The Bill of Rights* (1958), 72.

9 "When unanimity can be obtained": Charles Evans Hughes, *The Supreme Court of the United States* (1928), 67–68.

10 **"ought to be weakened"**: Quoted in Loren P. Beth, "Justice Harlan and the Uses of Dissent," 49 *American Political Science Review* 1085, 1086 (1955).

10 **a prior decision**: *Burnet v. Coronado Oil & Gas Co.,* 285 U.S. 393, 406 (1932) (Brandeis dissenting). William O. Douglas eventually came to believe that "*stare decisis* has . . . little place in American constitutional law." *We the Judges* (1956), 429.

10 **"doctrine of *stare decisis*"**: *Florida Dept. of Health v. Florida Nursing Home Ass'n,* 450 U.S. 147, 151, 155 (1981) (Stevens concurring). Justice Stevens was far more supportive of the doctrine than have been other modern justices.

11 **"ought to be"**: Henry Wollman, "Evils of Dissenting Opinions," 57 *Albany Law Journal* 74–75 (1898). Hampton Carson, "Great Dissenting Opinions," 50 *Albany Law Journal* 120 (1894).

11 **"abolished by law"**: "Dissenting Opinions," 20 *American Law Review* 428 (1886).

11 **"only of disrespect"**: A sampling of how the different law journals felt about dissent can be found in an editorial note, *id.* The lawyers are quoted in Alexander Simpson Jr., "Dissenting Opinions," 71 *University of Pennsylvania Law Review* 205, 206 (1923). For an overview of the late-nineteenth-century attitude among lawyers, see Hunter Smith, "Personal and Official Authority: Turn-of-the-Century Lawyers and the Dissenting Opinion," 24 *Yale Journal of Law and the Humanities* 507 (2012).

11 **"minority said it meant"**: Jackson, *Supreme Court,* 18–19.

11 **"community against dissent"**: J. Louis Campbell III, "The Spirit of Dissent," 66 *Judicature* 305 (1983).

12 **"A dissent in a court"**: Hughes, *Supreme Court,* 68.

12 **"The voice of the majority"**: Benjamin N. Cardozo, *Law and Literature and Other Essays and Addresses* (1931), 36.

13 **"in other areas"**: Tom C. Clark, "Internal Operation of the United States Supreme Court," 43 *Journal of the American Judicature Society* 45, 51 (1959–1960); William H. Rehnquist, "The Supreme Court: Past and Present," 59 *American Bar Association Journal* 361, 363 (1973).

13 **Why do judges dissent?**: There has been a great deal of literature by political scientists on why justices dissent. These include matters such as legal culture, organizational and institutional factors, and individual personality. While I am aware of this literature, for the most part it does not address the question I am concerned about, the role of the dissent itself in the constitutional dialogue. A very good summary of political science research on the non-jurisprudential factors leading to dissent is Steven A. Peterson, "Dissent in American Courts," 43 *Journal of Politics* 412 (1981).

13 **not wholly wrong**: *Federal Maritime Commission v. South Carolina State Ports Authority,* 535 U.S. 743, 788 (2002) (Breyer dissenting); Antonin Scalia, "The Dissenting Opinion," 19 *Journal of Supreme Court History* 33 (1994).

13 **legislative apportionment**: *Perry v. United States,* 294 U.S. 330, 361 (1935) (McReynolds dissenting); *Baker v. Carr,* 369 U.S. 186, 266 (1962) (Frankfurter dissenting).

13 **members of the Court**: Roscoe Pound, "*Cacoethes Dissentiendi:* The Heated Judicial Dissent," 39 *American Bar Association Journal* 794 (1953).

13 **"among the justices"**: Lewis F. Powell Jr., "Myths and Misconceptions About the Supreme Court," 61 *American Bar Association Journal* 1347 (1975).

13 **"feeling was reciprocated"**: Quoted in Ruth Bader Ginsburg, "Dissent Is an

'Appeal' for the Future," 32 *Alaska Bar Rag* 1 (2008). Justice Ginsburg goes on, "The same might be said today about my close friendship with Justice Scalia."

14 **and will change it:** Brian Lamb, Susan Swain, and Mark Farkas, eds., *The Supreme Court* (2010), 28.

14 **"unnoticed by dissent":** Quoted in Alexander M. Bickel, *The Unpublished Opinions of Mr. Justice Brandeis: The Supreme Court at Work* (1957), 18.

15 **"the heightened phrase":** Jackson, *Supreme Court,* 17.

15 **"write the opinion":** Lamb, Swain, and Farkas, *Supreme Court,* 97.

15 **members of the majority:** Paul J. Wahlbeck, James F. Spriggs II, and Forrest Maltzman, "Marshalling the Court: Bargaining and Accommodation on the United States Supreme Court," 42 *American Journal of Political Science* 294 (1998), explores this process and sets out several hypotheses, based on data drawn from an examination of majority circulations for 2,295 cases decided by the Burger Court.

16 **applied to racial categories:** *Califano v. Goldfarb,* 430 U.S. 199 (1977).

16 **the opposite result:** *Martin v. City of Struthers,* 319 U.S. 141 (1943). The other members of the former majority—Roberts, Reed, Frankfurter, and Jackson—now dissented.

16 **or joined a dissent:** Walter F. Murphy, *Elements of Judicial Strategy* (1964), 44. Forrest Maltzman, James F. Spriggs II, and Paul J. Wahlbeck, *Crafting Law on the Supreme Court: The Collegial Game* (2000), 69.

16 **"course of the law":** Cited in Jacob M. Lashley and Paul B. Rava, "The Supreme Court Dissents," 28 *Washington University Law Quarterly* 191, 192n11 (1943).

17 **some of his objections:** See Bickel, *Unpublished Opinions of Mr. Justice Brandeis,* esp. chap. 5, dealing with *United Mine Workers of America v. Coronado Coal Co.,* 259 U.S. 344 (1922).

17 **accommodated his views:** David O'Brien, *Storm Center: The Supreme Court in American Politics,* 7th ed. (2005), 265.

17 **"her point of view":** William A. Fletcher, "Dissent," 39 *Golden Gate University Law Review* 291, 296 (2009).

17 **"minority could agree":** David Danelski, quoted in *id.*

17 **"in-house impact":** Ginsburg, "Dissent Is an 'Appeal' for the Future," 1. The case is *United States v. Virginia,* 518 U.S. 515 (1996).

18 **"Though the fact":** Scalia, "Dissenting Opinion," 41.

18 **"strengthen the dissent":** Frank M. Coffin, *The Ways of a Judge: Reflections from the Federal Appellate Bench* (1980), 186.

18 **the decisional process:** Lamb, Swain, and Farkas, *Supreme Court,* 27–28 (Roberts), 142 (Breyer), 156 (Alito).

19 **the initial draft:** In his study of the Court in the 1940s, Professor Howard concludes that "hardly any major decision in this decade was free from significant alteration . . . before announcement to the public." J. Woodford Howard Jr., "On the Fluidity of Judicial Choice," 62 *American Political Science Review* 43, 44 (1968).

19 **"unconstitutional detention":** *Stone v. Powell,* 428 U.S. 465, 502, 517 (1976) (Brennan dissenting).

19 **the concurrence argues:** See, for example, *Citizens and Southern National Bank v. Bougas,* 434 U.S. 35, 45 (1977) (Stewart concurring).

20 **"alienate another judge":** Murphy, *Elements of Judicial Strategy,* 57. Murphy is

the classic study, but I have also relied on Maltzman, Spriggs, and Wahlbeck, *Crafting Law on the Supreme Court.*

20 **pedantic separate opinions:** See Melvin I. Urofsky, *Felix Frankfurter: Judicial Restraint and Individual Liberties* (1991), especially for relations between Frankfurter and the other justices.

20 **not in the reasoning:** *Johnson v. Transportation Agency, Santa Clara County,* 480 U.S. 616 (1987). For the case and Brennan's efforts, see Melvin I. Urofsky, *A Conflict of Rights: The Supreme Court and Affirmative Action* (1991), esp. chap. 9.

20 **opinion of the Court:** William J. Brennan, "State Court Decisions and the Supreme Court," 31 *Pennsylvania Bar Association Quarterly* 393, 405 (1960).

20 **circulation of a dissent:** William H. Rehnquist, *The Supreme Court: How It Was, How It Is* (1987), 303.

20 **concurring in the judgment:** The Rehnquist memo was in regard to *Ruckelshaus v. Monsanto Co.,* 467 U.S. 986 (1984); the Burger note to Marshall was for *Berkemer v. McCarty,* 468 U.S. 420 (1984); and the O'Connor message is from *United States v. Karo,* 468 U.S. 705 (1984). The examples are from Maltzman, Spriggs, and Wahlbeck, *Crafting Law on the Supreme Court,* 65.

21 **"on major points":** Scalia, "Dissenting Opinion," 41.

22 **"has less leverage":** Rehnquist, *Supreme Court,* 302.

22 **no one else joined him:** *Marrese v. American Academy of Orthopaedic Surgeons,* 470 U.S. 373 (1985). Maltzman, Spriggs, and Wahlbeck, *Crafting Law on the Supreme Court,* 67.

22 **"we accommodate":** William H. Rehnquist, "Remarks on the Process of Judging," 49 *Washington and Lee Law Review* 263, 270 (1992); H. W. Perry Jr., *Deciding to Decide: Agenda Setting in the United States Supreme Court* (1991), 144.

23 **medical treatment:** *Cruzan v. Director, Missouri Department of Health,* 497 U.S. 261 (1990).

23 **might be discovered:** The Ninth Circuit case is *Washington v. Glucksberg,* 521 U.S. 702 (1997), and that from the Second Circuit is *Vacco v. Quill,* 521 U.S. 793 (1997).

24 **by the Warren Court:** *Rochin v. California,* 342 U.S. 165 (1952). When police entered Rochin's apartment, he swallowed several pills to hide the evidence. The officers then took him to a hospital where, against his will, doctors pumped his stomach and retrieved evidence used against him at his trial. Black's concurrence is at 174 and that of Douglas at 177.

24 **"in the court's opinion":** Murphy, *Elements of Judicial Strategy,* 60; Ginsburg, "Dissent Is an 'Appeal' for the Future," 143.

25 **"to the future":** Quoted in Henry J. Abraham, *The Judicial Process,* 5th ed. (1986), 213. See also Fletcher, "Dissent," 295.

25 **this may be true:** See Charles Fried, "Five to Four: Reflections on the School Voucher Case," 116 *Harvard Law Review* 163 (2002).

25 **favor of its measures:** See Marian C. McKenna, *Franklin Roosevelt and the Great Constitutional War: The Court-Packing Crisis of 1937* (2002).

25 **next seven years:** See L. A. Scot Powe, *The Warren Court and American Politics* (2000).

26 **lower court litigation:** The Court upheld McCain-Feingold in *McConnell v. Federal Election Commission,* 540 U.S. 93 (2003); the ban on corporate expenditures was *Austin v. Michigan Chamber of Commerce,* 494 U.S. 652 (1990).

26 **during an election cycle:** *Citizens United v. Federal Election Commission,* 558 U.S. 310 (2010); *McCutcheon v. Federal Election Commission,* 134 S. Ct. 1434 (2014). For the latter case, as well as a good overview of the Court's history relating to campaign finance, see Ronald Collins and David Skover, *When Money Speaks . . .* (2014).

27 **"which pervades society":** See Thomas O. Mason and Sophie A. James, eds., *Campaign Finance and the Citizens United Supreme Court Case* (2011); Robert H. Jackson, *The Struggle for Judicial Supremacy* (1941), 312–13.

27 **unconstitutional in 1895:** *Pollack v. Farmers' Loan & Trust Co.,* 158 U.S. 601 (1895).

28 **with the remedy:** *Cary v. Curtis,* 44 U.S. 236, 257 (1845) (Story dissenting).

29 **29 January 2009:** *Ledbetter v. Goodyear Tire & Rubber Co.,* 550 U.S. 618 (2007).

29 **defects of the law:** *Paroline v. United States,* 134 S. Ct. 1710 (2014).

30 **handle the matter:** *Youngstown Sheet & Tube Co. v. Sawyer,* 343 U.S. 579 (1952). For details of the case, as well as an analysis of the seven opinions, see Maeva Marcus, *Truman and the Steel Seizure Case: The Limits of Presidential Power* (1977).

30 **jurisdiction of the high court:** The literature on the war on terror, the various court cases, and the role of the courts is constantly expanding, but a good place to start is Louis Fisher, *The Constitution and 9/11: Recurring Threats to America's Freedom* (2008). See also Richard M. Pious, *The War on Terrorism and the Rule of Law* (2006); and Jesse Bravin, *The Terror Courts: Rough Justice at Guantánamo Bay* (2013).

31 **history of habeas corpus:** *Boumediene v. Bush,* 553 U.S. 723 (2008).

32 **"law-school professors":** The citation is in *Adams v. Tanner,* 244 U.S. 590, 613n21 (1917) (Brandeis dissenting); Melvin Urofsky, *Louis D. Brandeis: A Life* (2009), 504 (regarding law review articles); Taft to Henry Taft, 8 June 1928, quoted in Alpheus Thomas Mason, *William Howard Taft: Chief Justice* (1965), 228.

32 **members of the organization:** *Sierra Club v. Morton,* 405 U.S. 727 (1972). The vote was 4–3, with the two newest members of the Court, William Rehnquist and Lewis Powell, not voting.

32 **"part of it":** *Id.* at 743 (Douglas dissenting).

33 **American public:** Adam M. Sowards, *The Environmental Justice: William O. Douglas and American Conservation* (2009).

33 **majority of racism:** *Schuett v. Coalition to Defend Affirmative Action.* 134 S. Ct. 1623 (2014). Justice Kagan, who had been involved in an earlier phase of this case as solicitor general, recused herself.

34 **from the bench:** *Town of Greece v. Galloway.* 134 S. Ct. 1811 (2014).

34 **"of a future day":** Michael Mello, *Against the Death Penalty: The Relentless Dissents of Justices Brennan and Marshall* (1996); Linda Greenhouse, *Becoming Justice Blackmun: Harry Blackmun's Supreme Court Journey* (2005), chap. 7.

35 **articles, and interviews:** For a list, see Ronald K. L. Collins, "Books by Supreme Court Justices," 38 *Journal of the Supreme Court Historical Society* 94 (2013).

35 **constitutional interpretation:** See, for example, the transcript of their debate at American University, 13 January 2005, posted at www.freerepublic.com /focus/news/1352357/posts. More recent debates are available at different sources, including one before the Federalist Society on 14 May 2012, on www.youtube.com/watch?v=_4n8gOUzZ81.

35 "what the law means": Lamb, Swain, and Farkas, *Supreme Court,* 69.

35 to public sentiment: Barry Friedman, "Dialogue and Judicial Review," 91 *Michigan Law Review* 577 (1993).

35 fairly wide support: *Bowers v. Hardwick,* 478 U.S. 186 (1986); *Boy Scouts of America v. Dale,* 530 U.S. 640 (2000).

36 seen as reactionary: *Lawrence v. Texas,* 539 U.S. 558 (2003). The best single volume covering the legal debate from *Bowers* to *Lawrence* is David A. J. Richards, *The Sodomy Cases* (2009).

36 he did not agree: *United States v. Windsor,* 133 S. Ct. 2675 (2013). Scalia's dissent is at 2697. For the same-sex marriage cases, see Adam Liptak, *To Have and Uphold* (2013).

CHAPTER 2: FROM SERIATIM TO THE OPINION OF THE COURT

38 "its relative unimportance": Bernard Schwartz, *A History of the Supreme Court* (1993), 33.

39 collusion with the Crown: M. Todd Henderson, "From Seriatim to Consensus and Back Again: A Theory of Dissent," *Supreme Court Review* 283, 293 (2007).

40 "to the present day": James Oldham, *English Common Law in the Age of Mansfield* (2004), 10.

41 an occasional dissent: William R. Casto, *The Supreme Court in the Early Republic: The Chief Justiceships of John Jay and Oliver Ellsworth* (1995), 110.

41 with Great Britain: *Id.,* 90–95.

42 a divided Court: See, for example, *West v. Barnes,* 2 U.S. 401 (1791), and *Jones v. LeTombe,* 3 U.S. 384 (1798). John P. Kelsh, "The Opinion Delivery Practices of the United States Supreme Court, 1790–1945," 77 *Washington University Law Quarterly* 137, 140 (1999).

42 agreed on the decision: Chase in *Bas v. Tingy,* 4 U.S. 37 (1800), and Wilson in *Talbot v. Janson,* 3 U.S. 133, 168 (1795).

42 "the contrary opinion": *Hayburn's Case,* 2 U.S. 409 (1792).

43 "my opinion particularly": *Sims v. Irvine,* 3 U.S. 425, 457 (1799) (Iredell concurring).

43 of reverse seniority: *Georgia v. Brailsford,* 2 U.S. 415 (1793).

43 clause actually meant: *Calder v. Bull,* 3 U.S. 386 (1798).

43 "the Court's decisions": David P. Currie, *The Constitution in the Supreme Court: The First Hundred Years, 1789–1888* (1985), 45, 55. William Casto, on the other hand, sees *Calder* as a good example of judicial dialogue.

44 drive of the amendment: *Chisholm v. Georgia,* 2 U.S. 419 (1793). For the Eleventh Amendment, see John V. Orth, *The Judicial Power of the United States: The Eleventh Amendment in American History* (1987).

44 "confidence and respect": Quoted in Henderson, "From Seriatim to Consensus," 309, 310.

44 "a Holt or a Mansfield": Adams apparently also considered other possible names for the post. See Kathryn Turner, "The Appointment of Chief Justice Marshall," 17 *William and Mary Quarterly* 143 (1960).

45 secretary of state: For Marshall, see R. Kent Newmyer, *John Marshall and the Heroic Age of the Supreme Court* (2001); and Charles F. Hobson, *The Great Chief Justice: John Marshall and the Rule of Law* (1996).

45 his distant cousin: Joseph Ellis, *American Sphinx: The Character of Thomas Jefferson* (1997), 175.

45 *Marbury v. Madison:* 5 U.S. 137 (1803).

45 in time of war: *Talbot v. Seeman,* 5 U.S. 1 (1801).

46 in one voice: Kevin M. Stack, "The Practice of Dissent in the Supreme Court," 105 *Yale Law Journal* 2235, 2238–40 (1996).

46 "the opinion of all": Percival E. Jackson, *Dissent in the Supreme Court* (1969), 3.

46 a unanimous court: *Marbury,* 5 U.S. at 1; *Fletcher v. Peck,* 10 U.S. 87 (1810); *McCulloch v. Maryland,* 17 U.S. 316 (1819); *Gibbons v. Ogden,* 22 U.S. 1 (1824).

46 had been established: Peter Bozzo, Shimmy Edwards, and April Christine, "Many Voices, One Court: The Origin and Role of Dissent in the Supreme Court," 36 *Journal of Supreme Court History* 193, 199–200 (2012).

46 "assumption of power": Albert J. Beveridge Jr., *The Life of John Marshall* (1919), 16, cited in Henderson, "From Seriatim to Consensus," 313.

46 involving constitutional questions: Donald M. Roper, "Judicial Unanimity and the Marshall Court—a Road to Reappraisal," 9 *American Journal of Legal History* 118, 119 (1965).

47 speak in one voice: See G. Edward White, *The Marshall Court and Cultural Change, 1815–1835* (1988), chap. 3.

47 1804 insurance case: *Head & Amory v. Providence Insurance Co.,* 6 U.S. 127, 169 (1804) (Chase concurring).

47 "inconsiderately given": *United States v. Fisher,* 6 U.S. 358, 397, 397–98 (1805).

47 "of my brethren": *Ex parte Bollman,* 8 U.S. 75, 101 (1807).

47 the Court's history: S. Sidney Ulmer, "Exploring the Dissent Patterns of Chief Justices: John Marshall to Warren Burger," in *Judicial Conflict and Consensus: Behavioral Studies of American Appellate Courts,* ed. Sheldon Goldman and Charles M. Lamb (1986), 50, 53.

47 jurisprudential right hand: R. Kent Newmyer, *Supreme Court Justice Joseph Story: Statesman of the Old Republic* (1985).

47 reciprocated these views: Ellis, *American Sphinx,* 175; Charles F. Hobson et al., eds., *The Papers of John Marshall,* 12 vols. (1974–2006), 6:46.

48 "independent judiciary": James F. Simon, *What Kind of Nation: Thomas Jefferson, John Marshall, and the Epic Struggle to Create a United States* (2002), 9.

49 "despotism of an oligarchy": Jefferson to William C. Jarvis, 18 September 1820, in Walter F. Murphy and C. Herman Pritchett, *Courts, Judges, and Politics: An Introduction to the Judicial Process* (1961), 557. It should be noted that the Marshall Court never again declared an act of Congress unconstitutional, and the next time the Court did so was in the *Dred Scott* case.

49 an independent judiciary: The Jeffersonian "war" on the judiciary is the subject of several books. See especially Richard E. Ellis, *The Jeffersonian Crisis: Courts and Politics in the Young Republic* (1971), and Simon, *What Kind of Nation.*

49 "his own reasoning": Jefferson to Thomas Ritchie, 25 December 1820, quoted in Karl M. ZoBell, "Division of Opinion in the Supreme Court: A History of Judicial Disintegration," 44 *Cornell Law Quarterly* 186, 194 (1959).

49 "I could have wished": *McCulloch v. Maryland,* 17 U.S. 316 (1819); James Madison to Spencer Roane, 2 September 1819, quoted in Henderson, "From Seriatim to Consensus," 332.

49 **opposed to a single opinion:** I am indebted to Mark R. Killenbeck, who graciously shared with me the manuscript of his article " 'No Bed of Roses': Johnson, Jefferson, and the Court, 1822–1823," which ultimately appeared in 37 *Journal of Supreme Court History* 95 (2012).

49 **"talent to be useful":** Donald G. Morgan, *Justice William Johnson: The First Dissenter* (1954), vii; Albert Gallatin to Thomas Jefferson, 15 February 1804, cited in Killenbeck, " 'No Bed of Roses,' " 95.

50 **criminal jurisdiction:** *United States v. Hudson and Goodwin,* 11 U.S. 32 (1810).

50 **and his integrity:** In addition to Morgan, *Justice William Johnson,* see A. J. Levin, "Mr. Justice William Johnson, Creative Dissenter," 43 *Michigan Law Review* 497 (1944), and Sandra F. VanBurkleo, "In Defense of 'Public Reason': Supreme Court Justice William Johnson," 32 *Journal of Supreme Court History* 115 (2007).

50 ***Gibbons v. Ogden:*** 22 U.S. 1 (1824); Johnson's concurrence is at 223. For the case, see Maurice G. Baxter, *The Steamboat Monopoly: Gibbons v. Ogden* (1972).

50 **denouncing South Carolina's action:** *Elkison v. Deliesseline,* 8 F. Cases 493 (1823).

51 **"any form they please":** Mark R. Killenbeck, "William Johnson, the Dog That Did Not Bark?," 62 *Vanderbilt Law Review* 407 (2009). The "wax" comment is in a letter from Jefferson to Spencer Roane, 16 September 1819, regarding the decision in *McCulloch v. Maryland,* which like all the great nationalist opinions was unanimous.

51 **done in *McCulloch:*** *Anderson v. Dunn,* 19 U.S. 204 (1821).

52 **over state authority:** Jefferson to Johnson, 27 October 1822. This and the following letters are cited in Killenbeck, " 'No Bed of Roses.' "

52 **"not ad libitum":** Johnson to Jefferson, 10 December 1822.

53 **"value him for honesty":** Jefferson to Johnson, 4 March 1823.

53 **the Court had erred:** Johnson to Jefferson, 11 April 1823.

53 **"of their principles":** Jefferson to Johnson, 12 June 1823.

CHAPTER 3: FROM MARSHALL TO *DRED SCOTT*

56 **any man could do it:** There are numerous books on Jackson and Jacksonian democracy, but a good overview is Daniel Walker Howe, *What Hath God Wrought: The Transformation of America, 1815–1848* (2007).

56 **"the page of history":** Carl Brent Swisher, *Roger B. Taney* (1935), 581–82.

56 **banking, commerce, and transportation:** See Paul Finkelman, " 'Hooted Down the Page of History': Reconsidering the Greatness of Chief Justice Taney," 19 *Journal of Supreme Court History* 83 (1994). Chief Justices Charles Evans Hughes and William H. Rehnquist have both lauded Taney as a "great" chief justice, not, of course, for *Dred Scott,* but for his other opinions.

56 **power of the Court:** See, for example, *Ableman v. Booth,* 62 U.S. 506 (1859).

57 **take Duvall's seat:** There is no good modern biography of Taney, and the classic remains Swisher, *Roger B. Taney,* but see also his *Taney Period* (1974), in the Holmes Devise history of the Court, and R. Kent Newmyer, *The Supreme Court Under Marshall and Taney,* 2nd ed. (2006).

58 **"from that of the Court":** *Briscoe v. Bank of Kentucky,* 36 U.S. 257, 328 (1837) (Story dissenting).

58 **nonconstitutional cases:** Currie, *Constitution in the Supreme Court,* 201 ff.

58 **from Marshall's day:** Between 1833, when the Court first heard these cases, and Taney's confirmation in March 1836, the Marshall Court literally fell

apart. Marshall and William Johnson died, and Gabriel Duvall resigned. The Jackson appointees who took their places did not share their assumptions about many legal matters, and for that reason the Court could not reach a decision on several cases argued before it, and they were held over.

58 **jurisdiction of Congress:** *Gibbons v. Ogden,* 22 U.S. 1 (1824).

59 **law was unconstitutional:** *Mayor of New York v. Miln,* 36 U.S. 102, 153, 161 (1837) (Story dissenting).

59 *Craig v. Missouri:* 29 U.S. 410 (1830).

59 **Kentucky scheme unconstitutional:** *Briscoe v. Bank of the Commonwealth of Kentucky,* 36 U.S. 257, 324, 350 (1837) (Story dissenting).

60 **reasonable investor expectations:** *Charles River Bridge v. Warren Bridge,* 36 U.S. 420, 583 (1837) (Story dissenting). See R. Kent Newmyer, "Justice Joseph Story, the Charles River Bridge Case and the Crisis of Republicanism," 17 *American Journal of Legal History* 232 (1973). The notion of "reasonable investor expectations" would have a significant modern parallel in the takings and zoning rules articulated by the Court. See, for example, *Penn Central Transportation Co. v. New York City,* 438 U.S. 104 (1978).

61 **by ceaseless change:** Morton J. Horwitz, *The Transformation of American Law, 1780–1860* (1977).

62 **long-established practice:** *Cary v. Curtis,* 44 U.S. 236, 257 (1845) (Story dissenting).

62 **"against a collector":** 5 Stat. 349 (1845). George Stewart Brown, "A Dissenting Opinion of Mr. Justice Story Enacted as Law Within Thirty-Six Days," 26 *Virginia Law Review* 759 (1940).

62 **collection of customs duties:** See, for example, *DeLima v. Bidwell,* 182 U.S. 1 (1901), one of the first of the important *Insular Cases.*

62 **"occupying so much time":** *Inglis v. Trustees of the Sailor's Snug Harbor,* 28 U.S. 99, 145 (1830) (Story dissenting).

62 **associated with the majority's opinion:** Kelsh, "Delivery Practices," 157.

63 **planters in Mississippi:** *Groves v. Slaughter,* 40 U.S. 449 (1841).

63 **federal Commerce Clause:** The complicated matter of slavery in the courtroom is examined in Paul Finkelman, *An Imperfect Union: Slavery, Federalism, and Comity* (1981).

63 **interstate slave trade:** *Groves,* 40 U.S. at 503, 508 (McLean concurring in part and dissenting in part).

63 **only to protect slavery:** *Id.* Taney at 508 and Baldwin at 510. Both Justices Story and McKinley dissented, but without opinion.

64 **blacks in the United States:** *Prigg v. Pennsylvania,* 41 U.S. 539 (1842). The case should never have been heard by the high court, because it was a collusive arrangement with no real case or controversy. Maryland and Pennsylvania had contrived to have Edward Prigg, a slave catcher, kidnap a supposed runaway slave in Pennsylvania to test the states' laws regarding runaways. The problem is that Margaret Morgan and her children were in fact free blacks. For the case and its various opinions, see Earl M. Maltz, "Majority, Concurrence, and Dissent: *Prigg v. Pennsylvania* and the Structure of Supreme Court Decision-Making," 31 *Rutgers Law Journal* 345 (2000). For the facts about the principles, see Paul Finkelman, "Sorting Out *Prigg v. Pennsylvania,*" 24 *Rutgers Law Journal* 605 (1993).

64 **"the [majority] doctrine":** *Ohio Life Ins. & Trust Co. v. Debolt,* 57 U.S. 416, 422 (1853) (Catron concurring).

64 "my own consistency": *The Propeller Monticello v. Mollison,* 58 U.S. 152, 156 (1854) (Daniel dissenting).

64 "the opinion just delivered": *United States v. Vallejo,* 66 U.S. 541, 545 (1861) (Grier dissenting).

64 justices and their views: Kelsh, "Delivery Practices," 158–59.

64 "I wholly dissent": *Gaines v. Hennen,* 65 U.S. 553, 631 (1860) (Grier dissenting).

65 "chiefly to free myself": *Fountain v. Ravenel,* 58 U.S. 369, 396 (1854) (Daniel dissenting). For examples of similar sentiments, see *Gelpke v. City of Dubuque,* 68 U.S. 175, 207 (1864) (Miller dissenting), and *United States v. Boisdore,* 52 U.S. 63, 103 (1850) (Wayne dissenting). None of these cases involved the issues of slavery.

66 Scott was still a slave: *Dred Scott v. Sandford,* 60 U.S. 393 (1857). The classic work remains Don E. Fehrenbacher, *The Dred Scott Case: Its Significance in American Law and Politics* (1978); see also Paul Finkelman, *Dred Scott v. Sandford: A Brief History with Documents* (1997).

67 the major issues: For one effort to parse the nine opinions, see William A. Bowen, "Dissenting Opinions," 17 *Green Bag* 690 (1905). A more sophisticated examination of the concurrences and dissents is Fehrenbacher, *Dred Scott,* chap. 17, and a chart showing where the justices agreed is on p. 405.

68 very bad law: Currie, *Constitution in the Supreme Court,* 264.

69 be free or slave: Some scholars note that the Douglas-sponsored Kansas-69 Act of 1854 had in many ways repealed the Missouri Compromise, because if a majority of a people in a territory—even one above the Missouri border— voted to have slavery, they could have it. Therefore it was unnecessary to even mention the earlier law, much less invalidate, other than Taney's obsession with protecting slavery.

69 Scott remained a slave: *Dred Scott,* 60 U.S. at 459–68. On this narrow point, Nelson had the support of three other justices—Wayne, Grier, and Daniel—as well as a Supreme Court precedent that spoke to this very issue, *Strader v. Graham,* 51 U.S. 82 (1851), in which the Court, speaking through Taney, had refused to review a Kentucky statute holding that a trip to Ohio had not freed Kentucky slaves. Had one more justice signed on, this decision would not have unleashed the firestorm of Taney's opinion.

69 Nonetheless, McLean, who for most: The only biography is Francis P. Weisenburger, *The Life of John McLean: A Politician on the United States Supreme Court* (1937), which is dated and emphasizes his political interests rather than his work on the Court.

71 *American Insurance Co. v. Canter:* 26 U.S. 511 (1828).

72 the right to vote: *Dred Scott,* 60 U.S. at 529 (McLean dissenting).

72 "constitutional opinion-writing": Currie, *Constitution in the Supreme Court,* 273.

74 rules regarding territory: *Dred Scott,* 60 U.S. at 564 (Curtis dissenting).

74 "When a strict interpretation": *Id.* at 621.

75 most part polemical: Fehrenbacher, *Dred Scott,* 414.

75 dialogue with the public: John Marshall had, of course, written a defense of the Court's opinion in *McCulloch v. Maryland,* but he did so using the nom de plume Amphictyon, and his authorship of the two essays was at the

time known only to a few close friends. See Gerald Gunther, *John Marshall's Defense of McCulloch v. Maryland* (1969).

75 **outrightly rejected it:** For the response to the case, see Paul Finkelman, "Dred Scott v. Sandford," in *The Public Debate over Controversial Supreme Court Decisions,* ed. Melvin I. Urofsky (2006), 24–33.

75 **"slaveholding community":** Quoted in Garrett Epps, "The Antebellum Political Background of the 14th Amendment," in *Infinite Hope and Finite Disappointment: The Story of the First Interpreters of the Fourteenth Amendment,* ed. Elizabeth Reilly (2011), 24.

76 **"Illinois a slave state":** Quoted in Melvin I. Urofsky and Paul Finkelman, *A March of Liberty,* 2 vols., 3rd ed. (2011), 1:439.

76 **"black as well as white":** Speech at Springfield, Illinois, 26 June 1857, in *Collected Works of Abraham Lincoln,* ed. Roy P. Basler, 8 vols. (1953–1955), 2:399, 405, 407.

77 **"source of authority":** *Id.,* 402.

77 **established the Constitution:** For Lincoln's analysis of the decision, and his familiarity with and reliance on the dissents, see Lucas E. Morel, "The *Dred Scott* Dissents: McLean, Curtis, Lincoln, and the Public Mind," 32 *Journal of Supreme Court History* 133 (2007), and Sanford Levinson, "Abraham Lincoln, Benjamin Curtis, and the Importance of Constitutional Fidelity," 4 *Green Bag* 419, n.s. (2001).

78 **life on the Court intolerable:** His son, in a memoir of his father, said that the "controlling reason" was financial but added that Curtis "no longer felt that confidence in the Supreme Court which was essential to his useful co-operation with its members." Cited in Currie, *Constitution in the Supreme Court,* 273n274.

80 **"land of his birth":** See *Congressional Globe,* 35th Cong., 2nd sess., 10–11 February 1859, 987.

80 **settle the controversy:** *Congressional Globe,* 39th Cong., 1st sess., 30 January 1866, 504.

80 **"citizens of the United States":** *Id.,* 1 March 1866, 1116.

CHAPTER 4: FIELD, *SLAUGHTERHOUSE,* AND *MUNN*

83 **reentry into the Union:** Johnson's political ineptitude, and the blame he carries for the failure of Reconstruction, are well explicated in Eric L. McKitrick, *Andrew Johnson and Reconstruction* (1960).

83 **use them for decades:** The best overview of the Civil War period is James M. McPherson, *Battle Cry of Freedom,* 2nd ed. (2003). For constitutional development, see Harold M. Hyman and William M. Wiecek, *Equal Justice Under Law: Constitutional Development, 1835–1875* (1982).

83 **legitimacy of secession:** *Ex parte Milligan,* 71 U.S. 2 (1866) (military trial of civilians); *Cummings v. Missouri,* 71 U.S. 277 (1867), and *Ex parte Garland,* 71 U.S. 333 (1867) (test oaths); *Mississippi v. Johnson,* 71 U.S. 475 (1867), and *Georgia v. Stanton,* 73 U.S. 50 (1868) (federal jurisdiction); and *Texas v. White,* 74 U.S. 700 (1869) (legitimacy of secession).

84 **"abolition of slavery meant":** *Blyew v. United States,* 80 U.S. 581, 595 (1872) (Bradley dissenting). For more on the Court and the Civil War amendments, see Robert J. Kaczorowski, *The Politics of Judicial Interpretation: The Federal Courts, Department of Justice, and Civil Rights, 1866–1876* (1985).

85 **Crescent City Slaughterhouse:** The best study is Ronald M. Labbé and Jonathan Lurie, *The Slaughterhouse Cases: Regulation, Reconstruction, and the Fourteenth Amendment* (2003).

85 **fit that category:** Paul Kens, *Justice Stephen Field: Shaping Liberty from the Gold Rush to the Gilded Age* (1997), 118–19.

86 **New Orleans butchers:** The only full-length biography is Robert J. Saunders Jr., *John Archibald Campbell: Southern Moderate, 1811–1899* (1997).

86 **"obligations and duties":** Jonathan Lurie, "Ex-justice Campbell: The Case of the Creative Advocate," 30 *Journal of Supreme Court History* 17, 20–21 (2005).

87 **"before the law":** *Cummings,* 71 U.S. at 321–22.

88 **five-man majority:** *Slaughterhouse Cases,* 83 U.S. 36 (1873).

89 **"which ratified them":** *Id.* at 70–71, 72, 78–79.

90 **not been present before:** For a convincing argument that the framers of the Fourteenth Amendment intended to apply the Bill of Rights to the states, see Akhil Reed Amar, *The Bill of Rights: Creation and Reconstruction* (1998), part 2.

90 **power of the state:** See, for example, *Missouri Pacific Railway Co. v. Humes,* 115 U.S. 522 (1885), requiring railroads to erect fences, and *Jacobson v. Massachusetts,* 197 U.S. 11 (1905), which upheld a state's compulsory vaccination law.

91 **"in pursuance of it":** *Knox v. Lee,* also known as the *Second Legal Tender Case,* 79 U.S. 457, 634, 680 (1871) (Field dissenting).

92 **"position of the plaintiffs":** The Field dissent is at *Slaughterhouse Cases,* 83 92.S. at 83.

95 **racially motivated wrongs:** *Blyew v. United States,* 80 U.S. 581, 596 (1872) (Bradley dissenting). According to Jonathan Lurie, Bradley never reiterated this view in his remaining two decades on the Court.

97 **to be lawyers:** *Bradwell v. Illinois,* 83 U.S. 130 (1873). Only Chief Justice Chase dissented, but without opinion. For more on this case, see Jane M. Friedman, *America's First Woman Lawyer: The Biography of Myra Bradwell* (1993).

97 **right to vote:** *Minor v. Happersett,* 88 U.S. 162 (1875).

97 **rights, particularly voting:** See, for example, *United States v. Reese,* 92 U.S. 214 (1876); *United States v. Cruikshank,* 92 U.S. 542 (1876); and *Ex parte Siebold,* 100 U.S. 371 (1880) (Field dissenting). Field also dissented from two of the few decisions during this era in which the rights of blacks were upheld, *Strauder v. West Virginia,* 100 U.S. 303 (1880), and *Ex parte Virginia and J. D. Coles,* 100 U.S. 339 (1880).

97 ***Bartemeyer v. Iowa:*** 85 U.S. 129 (1874).

97 **"No one has ever":** *Id.* at 137–38 (Field concurring).

98 **"in the Fourteenth Amendment":** *Davidson v. New Orleans,* 96 U.S. 97, 104 (1877).

98 **regulation of business:** *Munn v. Illinois,* 94 U.S. 113 (1877). Although the *Granger Cases* figure prominently in most studies of the Gilded Age, there is no single book devoted to them. Good analyses, though, can be found in George H. Miller, *The Railroads and the Granger Laws* (1971), and Morton Keller, *Affairs of State: Public Life in Late Nineteenth Century America* (1977).

99 **"revert to the polls":** Waite upheld state railroad regulation again nearly a decade later in the *Railroad Commission Cases,* 116 U.S. 307 (1886), yet

in both cases he appended statements that would eventually be invoked to justify judicial review of rates.

100 "majority of its legislature": *Munn,* 94 U.S. at 140 (Field dissenting).

101 "life and liberty": *Id.* at 141.

101 "his personal liberty": *In re Jacobs,* 98 N.Y. 98, 105 (1885).

101 as did natural people: *Santa Clara County v. Southern Pacific Railroad,* 118 U.S. 394 (1886).

101 "effect to the Constitution": *Mugler v. Kansas,* 123 U.S. 623, 661 (1887).

101 violate the Fourteenth Amendment: *Powell v. Pennsylvania,* 127 U.S. 678 (1888).

102 oppose any such policy: *Id.* at 687 (Field dissenting).

102 without due process of law: *Chicago, Milwaukee & St. Paul Railroad Co. v. Minnesota,* 134 U.S. 418 (1890).

102 not a judicial, prerogative: *Id.* at 461 (Bradley dissenting).

102 *Allgeyer v. Louisiana:* 165 U.S. 578 (1897).

102 "In the privilege of pursuing": *Id.* at 589, 591.

103 "enjoyment of the other": *Boston Gazette,* 22 February 1768. The best study of the interconnectedness of liberty and property is James W. Ely Jr., *The Guardian of Every Other Right: A Constitutional History of Property Rights,* 3rd ed. (2008).

104 "when either is uncertain": Stephen Field, "The Centenary of the Supreme Court," 4 February 1890, reprinted in 134 U.S. 729, 745 (1890). See James W. Ely Jr., "Property Rights and the Supreme Court in the Gilded Age," 38 *Journal of Supreme Court History* 330 (2013).

104 infringing on individual liberties: *Gideon v. Wainwright,* 372 U.S. 335, 346 (1963) (Douglas concurring).

104 "citizens of any free government": *Shapiro v. Thompson,* 394 U.S. 618, 668 (1969) (Harlan dissenting).

104 Privileges or Immunities Clause means: Justice Alito wrote the majority opinion in *McDonald v. City of Chicago,* 130 S. Ct. 3020 (2010), while Justice Scalia spoke for the majority in *Brown v. Entertainment Merchants Association,* 131 S. Ct. 2729 (2011).

CHAPTER 5: JOHN MARSHALL HARLAN: THE FIRST GREAT DISSENTER

105 at least three colleagues: ZoBell, "Division of Opinion," 199.

105 next half century: *Adamson v. California,* 332 U.S. 46, 59, 62 (1947) (Frankfurter concurring); Richard F. Watt and Richard M. Orlikoff, "The Coming Vindication of Mr. Justice Harlan," 44 *Illinois Law Review* 13, 15n7 (1949).

106 Many of those views: Harlan has been fortunate in having several good biographers. The most recent is Linda C. A. Przybyszewski, *The Republic According to John Marshall Harlan* (1999), who also edited his wife's memoir, Malvina Shanklin Harlan, *Some Memories of a Long Life, 1854–1911* (2002). See also Tinsley E. Yarbrough, *Judicial Enigma: The First Justice Harlan* (1995). Przybyszewski has an appendix listing the opinions that Harlan suggested be included if anyone ever did a book on him, and many of these are dissents.

106 "enemy of our free institutions": Linda Przybyszewski, "The Dissents of John Marshall Harlan I," 32 *Journal of Supreme Court History* 152, 156 (2007).

108 a constitutional right: 165 U.S. 173 (1897).

108 action regarding property: *Chicago, Burlington & Quincy Railroad Co. v. Chicago,* 166 U.S. 226 (1897).

108 "dissent from the opinion": *Brenham v. German American Bank,* 144 U.S. 173, 197 (1892) (Harlan dissenting).

108 "justice and righteousness": Edward F. Waite, "How 'Eccentric' Was Mr. Justice Harlan?," 37 *Minnesota Law Review* 173, 180–81 (1953).

109 rather than the states: For this and other Reconstruction measures, and the constitutional changes they wrought, see Robert J. Kaczorowski, *The Nationalization of Civil Rights: Constitutional Theory and Practice in a Racist Society, 1866–1883* (1987).

110 both blacks and whites: *Strauder v. West Virginia,* 100 U.S. 303 (1880), *Virginia v. Rives,* 100 U.S. 313 (1880), and *Ex parte Virginia and J. D. Coles,* 100 U.S. 339 (1880), all dealing with state laws that excluded blacks from juries. *Neal v. Delaware,* 103 U.S. 370 (1881) (juries). *Pace v. Alabama,* 106 U.S. 583 (1883). The miscegenation decision would not be overturned until *Loving v. Virginia,* 388 U.S. 1 (1967).

110 *Civil Rights Cases:* 109 U.S. 3 (1883). The cases came from Kansas, California, Missouri, New York, and Tennessee. Two were for denying blacks services at an inn or hotel, two for denying blacks access to theaters, and the fifth for refusing to allow a woman of color a seat in the ladies' car of a train.

111 "history of our country": Mark V. Tushnet, ed., *I Dissent: Great Opposing Opinions in Landmark Supreme Court Cases* (2008), 64. The Conkling letter is quoted in George R. Farnum, "John Marshall Harlan: Portrait of a Great Dissenter," 30 *American Bar Association Journal* 576, 578 (1944).

111 "the substance and spirit": *Civil Rights Cases,* 109 U.S. at 26 (Harlan dissenting).

112 "The Thirteenth Amendment": *Id.* at 34.

112 "The citizenship thus acquired": *Id.* at 46.

113 "Congress may prevent": The majority quite correctly pointed out that nearly all the businesses covered by the 1875 statute were already extensively regulated, but they would leave that regulation to the states, not to the federal government.

114 re-enslaved some blacks: *Bailey v. Alabama,* 219 U.S. 219 (1911); *United States v. Reynolds,* 235 U.S. 133 (1914).

114 publicly owned building: *Burton v. Wilmington Parking Authority,* 365 U.S. 715 (1961).

114 equal protection grounds: *Lombard v. Louisiana,* 373 U.S. 267 (1963).

114 "duties to the public": *Id.* at 281 (Douglas concurring), citing Harlan's dissent, *Civil Rights Cases,* 109 U.S. at 58–59.

114 received by a white person: *Bell v. Maryland,* 378 U.S. 226, 302 (1964) (Goldberg concurring).

115 Thirteenth and Fourteenth Amendments: *Heart of Atlanta Motel v. United States,* 379 U.S. 241 (1964), and its companion case, *Katzenbach v. McClung,* 379 U.S. 294 (1964).

116 do away with it: *Jones v. Alfred H. Mayer Co.,* 392 U.S. 409 (1968).

116 regarding congressional authority: *United States v. Guest,* 383 U.S. 745 (1996), 774, 783 (Brennan concurring in part and dissenting in part).

116 extent of governmental power: *Adickes v. S. H. Kress & Co.,* 398 U.S. 144,

179 (1970) (Douglas dissenting in part); *Moose Lodge No. 107 v. Irvis,* 407 U.S. 163, 183 (1972) (Douglas dissenting).

116 **been enacted to secure:** *Regents of the University of California v. Bakke,* 438 U.S. 265, 387, 392 (1978) (Marshall concurring in part).

118 **and took him to jail:** The best single book remains Charles A. Lofgren, *The Plessy Case: A Legal and Historical Interpretation* (1988), but see also Thomas Brook, ed., *Plessy v. Ferguson: A Brief History with Documents* (1996), and William James Hull Hoffer, *Plessy v. Ferguson: Race and Inequality in Jim Crow America* (2012). The starting point for any discussion of segregation is C. Vann Woodward's classic, *The Strange Career of Jim Crow,* which first appeared in 1955.

118 **with interstate commerce:** *Hall v. DeCuir,* 95 U.S. 485 (1878); *Louisville, New Orleans & Texas Railway v. Mississippi,* 133 U.S. 587 (1890).

118 **"of involuntary servitude":** *Plessy v. Ferguson,* 163 U.S. 537, 543 (1896). Justice Brewer did not participate in the case.

119 **"The white race deems":** *Id.* at 552, 559 (Harlan dissenting). Many scholars have noted how racist this statement is—the white race as dominant, no caste system, and so on. Harlan is of course right about what the law should be but not about the realities of late-nineteenth-century America.

120 **"in the race of life":** Przybyszewski, *Republic According to Harlan,* 69.

120 **"Among the forms":** Bowen, "Dissenting Opinions," 697.

120 **"It is eighty-six years":** *New York Times,* 23 May 1954, sec. 4, p. 10E.

121 **"established by the Constitution":** Henry Billings Brown, "Dissenting Opinions of Mr. Justice Harlan," 46 *American Law Review* 336, 338 (1912), cited in Pearson, "Plessy v. Ferguson," 82. However, J. Morgan Kousser suggests that Harlan might not have supported the result in *Brown* because of his opinion in *Cumming,* "Separate but *Not* Equal: The Supreme Court's First Decision on Racial Discrimination in Schools," 46 *Journal of Southern History* 17 (1980).

121 **further Supreme Court decisions:** For the NAACP strategy, see Mark V. Tushnet, *Making Civil Rights Law: Thurgood Marshall and the Supreme Court, 1936–1961* (1994); the Texas law school case is *Sweatt v. Painter,* 339 U.S. 629 (1950).

121 **questions of civil rights:** For example, Justice Douglas noted his agreement with Harlan's views in *Garner v. Louisiana,* 368 U.S. 157, 177 (1961) (Douglas concurring), as did Hugo Black in *Harper v. Virginia State Board of Elections,* 383 U.S. 663, 678n7 (1966) (Black dissenting). In *Oregon v. Mitchell,* 400 U.S. 112, 275 (1970), Justice William J. Brennan's dissent called on Harlan to support his view regarding the scope of Fourteenth Amendment protections.

122 **"must be colorblind":** *Regents of the University of California v. Bakke,* 438 U.S. 265 (1978). Four justices, Stevens, Burger, Stewart, and Rehnquist, opposed affirmative action as unconstitutional. Four justices, Brennan, White, Marshall, and Blackmun, supported it. Justice Lewis Powell wrote what became the opinion of the Court by saying that racial quotas were unacceptable but that race could be one factor in college and university admissions procedures. See Terry Anderson, *The Pursuit of Fairness: A History of Affirmative Action* (2004). The Brennan quotation is at 336.

122 **to minority businesses:** *Fullilove v. Klutznick,* 448 U.S. 448 (1980).

Notes to Pages 122–128

122 " 'Our Constitution is color-blind' ": *Id.* at 522 (Stewart dissenting).

123 **"classes among citizens":** *City of Richmond v. J. A. Croson Co.,* 488 U.S. 469, 521 (1989) (Scalia concurring). The Court heard a few more affirmative action cases and upheld a federal plan to ensure more minority-owned radio and television stations. In his dissent in that case, Justice Kennedy also invoked the color-blind phrase. *Metro Broadcasting Inc. v. Federal Communications Commission,* 497 U.S. 547, 637 (1990) (Kennedy dissenting).

123 **Fifteenth Amendment:** *Gomillion v. Lightfoot,* 364 U.S. 339 (1960); *Rogers v. Lodge,* 458 U.S. 613 (1982); *Thornburg v. Gingles,* 478 U.S. 30 (1986). The complicated story of the Court's wrestling with this issue is well told in Tinsley E. Yarbrough, *Race and Redistricting: The Shaw-Cromartie Cases* (2002).

124 **"people in the district":** *Shaw v. Reno,* 509 U.S. 630, 642 (1993).

124 **appeared as often as not:** *Shaw v. Hunt,* 517 U.S. 899 (1996); *Bush v. Vera,* 517 U.S. 952 (1996).

124 **review those decisions:** *Easley v. Cromartie,* 532 U.S. 234 (2001).

124 **"classes among citizens":** *Johnson v. California,* 543 U.S. 499, 513 (2005).

125 **or contract allocation:** *Parents Involved in Community Schools v. Seattle School District No. 1,* along with *Meredith v. Jefferson County Board of Education,* 551 U.S. 701, 731n14 (2007). The absolute ban these four proposed did not become binding precedent, because Justice Kennedy, who concurred in the result, wrote that there might be circumstances in which race could legitimately be a factor in student assignment.

125 **"Most of the dissent's criticisms":** *Id.* at 772. The quotation about Marshall is from the proceedings in the Supreme Court marking Marshall's death.

126 ***Romer v. Evans:*** 517 U.S. 620 (1996).

126 **as such by the Court:** Although *Brown* had overruled *Plessy,* no case in the hundred years between *Plessy* and *Romer* had ever declared that "the opinion of Justice Harlan is hereby adopted as an authoritative statement of law." Richard Primus, "Canon, Anti-canon, and Judicial Dissent," 48 *Duke Law Journal* 243, 246 (1998).

126 **over a new group:** *Romer,* 517 U.S. at 636, 650 (Scalia dissenting).

126 **"said about itself yesterday":** Beth, "Justice Harlan and the Uses of Dissent," 1092. Harlan denied that he had used strong language, but he also claimed that Field had deliberately whispered, shuffled papers, and in general acted discourteously during the delivery of Harlan's opinion.

127 **real estate taxes:** *Springer v. United States,* 102 U.S. 586 (1881). In several other cases, the Court upheld varieties of taxes not mentioned in the Constitution and took a very narrow view of the prohibited direct tax.

127 **exemption for the latter:** The fight over the income tax can be followed in Robert Stanley, *Dimensions of Law in the Service of Order: Origins of the Federal Income Tax, 1861–1913* (1993).

127 **related to the tax:** *Pollock v. Farmers' Loan & Trust Co.,* 157 U.S. 429 (1895).

127 **informed his opinion:** *Pollock v. Farmers' Loan & Trust Co.,* 158 U.S. 601 (1895).

127 **"the moneyed class":** *Id.* at 695 (Brown dissenting).

128 **"Supreme Court of the United States":** David G. Farrelly, "Justice Harlan's Dissent in the Pollock Case," 24 *Southern California Law Review* 175, 177 (1951).

128 **"we shall find trouble":** *Pollack* at 638, 674 (Harlan dissenting).

129 **expertise made good sense:** Good overviews of the beginning of the regulatory state include Thomas K. McCraw, *Prophets of Regulation* (1984), and the relevant chapters in Stephen Skowronek, ed., *Building a New American State: The Expansion of National Administrative Capacity, 1870–1916* (1982). The standard history of the ICC is Ari Hoogenboom and Olive Hoogenboom, *A History of the ICC: From Panacea to Palliative* (1976). The Court's response is detailed in Owen M. Fiss, *Troubled Beginnings of the Modern State, 1888–1910* (1993).

130 **intended such a result:** *Texas and Pacific Railway Co. v. ICC,* 162 U.S. 197, 239 (1896) (Harlan dissenting). Harlan's ICC opinions are examined in Thomas Jefferson Knight, "The Dissenting Opinions of Justice Harlan," 51 *American Law Review* 481 (1917).

130 **"Taken in connection":** *ICC v. Alabama Midland Railway Co.,* 168 U.S. 144, 176 (1897) (Harlan dissenting); in the other case, *ICC v. Cincinnati, New Orleans, and Texas Pacific Railway Co.,* 167 U.S. 479 (1897), Harlan dissented without opinion.

130 **also sought regulation:** Gabriel Kolko, *Railroads and Regulation, 1877–1916* (1965), first set forth this thesis.

131 **misinterpret congressional intent:** *United States v. Delaware and Hudson Co. et al.,* 213 U.S. 366, 418 (Harlan dissenting).

131 **affected interstate commerce:** *Shreveport Rate Cases,* 234 U.S. 342 (1914). There are several reasons for this turnabout, one of which is the appointment of seven new justices to the bench between 1902 and 1912, men who recognized the need for railroad regulation and who, like Charles Evans Hughes and Oliver Wendell Holmes Jr., were more sympathetic to national power.

131 **review of rates in 1944:** *Smyth v. Ames,* 169 U.S. 466 (1898); *Federal Power Commission v. Hope Natural Gas Co.,* 320 U.S. 591 (1944).

133 **control indirect effects:** *United States v. E. C. Knight Co.,* 156 U.S. 1 (1895).

133 **sales constitute commerce:** *Id.* at 18 (Harlan dissenting).

133 **made Harlan smile:** *Addystone Pipe & Steel Co. v. United States,* 175 U.S. 211 (1899), affirming the circuit court opinion of William Howard Taft. In a later case, Justice Wiley Rutledge, in a long survey of commerce cases, held that the *Knight* case had long been ignored and had been a "dead letter" since 1937. *Mandeville Island & Farms v. American Crystal Sugar Co.,* 334 U.S. 219 (1948).

133 **reach of the Commerce Clause:** *Swift & Co. v. United States,* 196 U.S. 375 (1905).

134 **rejected both propositions:** *Northern Securities Co. v. United States,* 193 U.S. 197 (1904).

135 **securing greater efficiency:** *Id.* at 400 (Holmes dissenting). Loren Beth suggests that the dislike between Holmes (who had taken his seat on the Court at the end of 1902) and Harlan may date from this dissent. Harlan resented Holmes's intellectual arrogance, and Holmes had little respect for Harlan, whom he characterized as "the last of the tobacco spittin' judges." Beth, "Harlan and the Uses of Dissent," 1098.

135 **rejected by the Court:** *Standard Oil Co. v. United States,* 221 U.S. 1 (1911). For more on this and other cases, and evolving doctrine, see William Letwin, *Law and Economic Policy in America* (1965), and James May, "Antitrust in the Formative Era . . . ," 50 *Ohio State Law Journal* 257 (1989).

135 **opposite of what White had said:** *Standard Oil Co.,* 221 U.S. at 82 (Harlan, concurring in part and dissenting in part); *United States v. American Tobacco Co.,* 221 U.S. 106, 189 (1911) (Harlan concurring in part and dissenting in part).

136 **after his death:** *Patterson v. Colorado,* 205 U.S. 454, 463 (1907) (Harlan dissenting). In his dissent, Harlan not only suggested incorporation but also put forward a far more speech-protective view than Holmes did in his opinion for the Court. An even earlier suggestion hinting at incorporation came in Harlan's dissent in *Hurtado v. California,* 110 U.S. 516 (1884).

136 **unincorporated territories:** *Hawaii v. Mankichi,* 190 U.S. 197, 227 (1903) (Harlan dissenting); *Dorr v. United States,* 195 U.S. 138, 154 (1904) (Harlan dissenting). See Bartholomew H. Sparrow, *The Insular Cases and the Emergence of American Empire* (2006).

136 **that of his colleagues:** See, for example, *Boumediene v. Bush,* 553 U.S. 723 (2008).

136 **"other justice of his day":** Beth, "Harlan and the Uses of Dissent," 1104.

MISE-EN-SCÈNE I

HARLAN AND HOLMES IN *LOCHNER V. NEW YORK* (1905)

137 **society or politics:** The literature on this era is enormous, but see Naomi R. Lamoreaux, *The Great Merger Movement in American Business, 1895–1904* (1985); Robert H. Wiebe, *The Search for Order, 1877–1920* (1967); and Morton Keller, *Regulating a New Economy: Public Policy and Economic Change in America, 1900–1933* (1990).

137 **industrialization spawned:** There are a number of good works on Progressivism, including Steven J. Diner, *A Very Different Age: Americans in the Progressive Era* (1998); Michael McGerr, *A Fierce Discontent: The Rise and Fall of the Progressive Movement in America, 1870–1920* (2003); and Samuel P. Hays, *The Response to Industrialism, 1885–1914,* 2nd ed. (1995).

138 **police power, on the other:** For the struggle in state courts, see Melvin I. Urofsky, "State Courts and Protective Legislation in the Progressive Era: A Reevaluation," 72 *Journal of American History* 63 (1985); for the Supreme Court, see John E. Simonche, *Charting the Future: The Supreme Court Responds to a Changing Society, 1890–1920* (1978).

138 **baking industry in New York:** *Lochner v. New York,* 198 U.S. 45 (1905). The best analysis of the case is Paul Kens, *Judicial Power and Reform Politics: The Anatomy of Lochner v. New York* (1990). David E. Bernstein has written a highly controversial book that not only attempts to "set the record straight" but argues that the majority opinion was jurisprudentially correct. *Rehabilitating Lochner: Defending Individual Rights Against Progressive Reform* (2011). A well-balanced perspective on the case and its long shadow can be found in Howard Gillman, *The Constitution Besieged: The Rise and Fall of Lochner Era Police Power Jurisprudence* (1993).

138 **home baking impossible:** There are few works on the history of baking, but see William G. Panschar, *Baking in America,* 2 vols. (1956).

139 **tenement house cellars:** This section on working conditions is drawn from Kens, *Judicial Power,* chap. 1, aptly titled "Not Like Grandma Used to Bake."

139 **The cellar bakery:** Roy Lubove, *The Progressives and the Slums: Tenement House Reform in New York City, 1890–1917* (1962).

140 "more humane conditions": *Bakers' Journal,* 11 May 1895.

140 state's appellate process: *People v. Lochner,* 73 App. Div. N.Y. 120 (1902); *People v. Lochner,* 177 N.Y. 145 (1904).

141 *Allgeyer v. Louisiana:* 165 U.S. 578 (1897).

141 *Holden v. Hardy:* 169 U.S. 366 (1898).

141 "sixty hours per week": *Lochner,* 198 U.S. at 57.

142 made by the courts: *Id.* at 45, 64.

142 "reasonable conditions": *Id.* at 53.

143 a cleaner workplace: *Id.* at 62.

143 "In determining the question": *Id.* at 66, 69 (Harlan dissenting).

143 New York Assembly: *Id.* at 73.

144 "inconsistent with the Constitution": *Id.* at 72.

144 still on the Court: *Adair v. United States,* 208 U.S. 161 (1908), striking down the Erdman Act, which prohibited yellow-dog contracts, in which employees had to swear they did not belong to nor would they join a union.

144 the Fourteenth Amendment: *Id.* at 175. See the discussion of Harlan's dissent in Fiss, *Troubled Beginnings of the Modern State,* 165–72.

144 the statute's legitimacy: One of Harlan's biographers, Linda Przybyszewski, believes that Harlan differed significantly from Peckham and others in the extent to which he accepted Field's view of the limits of the police power. *Republic According to John Marshall Harlan,* 150–52. This is not clear in his *Lochner* dissent.

144 orthodoxy too seriously: G. Edward White, "Holmes and American Jurisprudence: Revisiting Substantive Due Process and Holmes's Lochner Dissent," 63 *Brooklyn Law Review* 87 (1997).

145 "system of my limitations": Holmes to Learned Hand, quoted in Kens, *Judicial Power,* 123. He also told Hand that truth is "the majority vote of that nation that can lick all others."

145 of its moral base: This charge is made most strongly by Albert W. Alschuler, *Law Without Values: The Life, Work, and Legacy of Justice Holmes* (2000).

145 "men to be wrong": Oliver Wendell Holmes Jr., *Collected Legal Papers* (1921), 291, 295–96.

145 and by all: *Otis v. Parker,* 187 U.S. 606, 608–9 (1903).

146 "unnecessary to discuss": *Lochner,* 198 U.S. at 76 (Holmes dissenting).

146 "carry its policy along": *Adair,* 208 U.S. at 191 (Holmes dissenting).

146 would be acceptable: Learned Hand, "Due Process and the Eight Hour Day," 21 *Harvard Law Review* 495, 503 (1908).

146 "Constitution of the United States": *Lochner,* 198 U.S. at 72–73.

147 "you find the power": Holmes to James B. Thayer, 2 November 1893, cited in Fiss, *Troubled Beginnings of the Modern State,* 181.

147 "necessary to the public welfare": *Noble State Bank v. Haskell,* 219 U.S. 104, 111 (1911).

147 "I think that the word": *Lochner,* 198 U.S. at 76.

147 Holmes never identified: See Brad Snyder, "The House That Built Holmes," 30 *Law and History Review* 661 (2012). His good friend Harold Laski recognized Holmes's conservatism, especially in regard to economic matters, and declared that "the basis of Holmes's economic faith would have been rejected neither by Adam Smith nor Ricardo." Quoted in Kens, *Judicial Power,* 122.

148 **no business saying otherwise:** See the discussion of Holmes's view of judicial review and his stance in *Lochner* in G. Edward White, *Justice Oliver Wendell Holmes: Law and the Inner Self* (1993), 324ff.

148 **enemy of working people:** A good sampling of the reaction to the case is Paul Kens, "Lochner v. New York," in Urofsky, *Public Debate over Controversial Supreme Court Decisions,* 95–103.

148 **people's elected assemblies:** For a far different interpretation of the case, see Bernstein, *Rehabilitating Lochner.*

148 **Muller v. Oregon:** 208 U.S. 412 (1908). One can find useful information about the case and the Brandeis brief in Nancy Woloch, *Muller v. Oregon: A Brief History with Documents* (1996).

149 **have faded away:** *Bunting v. Oregon,* 243 U.S. 426 (1917).

149 **freedom of contract:** *Adkins v. Children's Hospital,* 261 U.S. 525 (1923).

149 **"restraint the exception":** *Id.* at 546.

149 **"overruled *sub silentio*":** *Id.* at 562, 564 (Taft dissenting). In point of fact, Taft had long regarded *Lochner* as wrongly decided and had written so to a friend more than ten years before *Adkins.*

CHAPTER 6: HOLMES AND BRANDEIS DISSENTING

150 **"harmony between us":** Holmes to Pollock, 17 February 1928, in *Holmes-Pollock Letters,* ed. Mark DeWolfe Howe, 2 vols. (1941), 2:215; the case was *Casey v. United States,* 276 U.S. 413 (1928).

150 **"two votes instead of one":** Mason, *William Howard Taft,* 220.

151 **ever to sit on the Court:** Holmes has engendered more literature than any other justice, as well as a play and a motion picture. The best single biography is White, *Justice Oliver Wendell Holmes.* Mark DeWolfe Howe edited two of the most important of Holmes's correspondence series, the *Holmes-Pollock Letters* and the *Holmes-Laski Letters,* 2 vols. (1953). Howe was also at work on what might have been the definitive life of Holmes and published two volumes before his death in 1967. Alschuler, *Law Without Values* is a stinging attack on Holmes's alleged lack of morals in his jurisprudence.

152 **"men should be governed":** Oliver Wendell Holmes Jr., *The Common Law* (1881), 5.

153 **"the law-making power":** *Noble State Bank v. Haskell,* 219 U.S. 104, 110 (1911). The Latin phrase means "we shall not be changed," or, as Holmes uses it here, "the judges will not allow any change."

153 **be considered valid:** Paul Kens, *Lochner v. New York: Economic Regulation on Trial* (1998), 141.

153 **"I am here to help it":** Henry J. Abraham, *Justice and Presidents,* 3rd ed. (1992), 160.

153 **"with which they disagree":** *Otis v. Parker,* 187 U.S. 606, 608 (1903).

153 **"the primary vehicles":** Quoted in Bernard Schwartz, *Decision: How the Supreme Court Decides Cases* (1996), 163.

154 **nearly all of them:** Jack M. Balkin and Sanford Levinson, "The Canons of Constitutional Law," 111 *Harvard Law Review* 963 (1998); see also Primus, "Canon, Anti-canon, and Judicial Dissent."

154 **merits of the opinion:** A search by Anita S. Krishnakumar found the *Lochner* dissent cited in 669 law review articles. "Evolution of the Canonical Dissent," 52 *Rutgers Law Review* at 782n7, 788 (2000).

154 **their own policy views:** William M. Wiecek, *The Lost World of Classical Legal Thought: Law and Ideology in America, 1886–1937* (1998).

154 **judicial heir of Holmes:** *Harris v. United States,* 331 U.S. 145, 147 (1947) (Frankfurter dissenting); *Winters v. New York,* 333 U.S. 507, 527 (1948) (Frankfurter dissenting).

154 **"New York walk again":** *Federal Housing Administration v. Darlington Inc.,* 358 U.S. 84, 92 (1958). The opinion was by Justice William O. Douglas.

154 **"particular economic theory":** For cases that cite Holmes's admonitions, see Krishnakumar, "Evolution of the Canonical Dissent," nn 37–42.

154 **"country and abroad":** Hand, *Bill of Rights,* 81.

155 **"way to correct it":** *Williamson v. Lee Optical Co.,* 348 U.S. 483, 488 (1955).

155 **every thirty-three cases:** ZoBell, "Division of Opinion," 202. Figures vary, but are fairly comparable, approximately 170 dissents in 5,930 cases.

156 **"at its command":** *Hammer v. Dagenhart,* 247 U.S. 251, 277, 281 (1918) (Holmes dissenting). See Walter I. Trattner, *Crusade for the Children* (1970), for the history of efforts to abolish child labor and the judicial response. It should be noted that earlier the Court had unanimously upheld state laws regulating child labor in *Sturges & Burns Mfg. Co. v. Beauchamp,* 231 U.S. 320 (1913). The justices drew a distinction between federal and state laws on this subject; the states clearly had police power authority to protect children, but questions existed whether the federal government had any police powers.

156 **thwart congressional proposals:** See Edward S. Corwin, "The Passing of Dual Federalism," 36 *Virginia Law Review* 1 (1950).

157 **individual liberties:** *United States v. Darby,* 312 U.S. 100 (1941). Even Justice McReynolds, the last of the conservative bloc known as the Four Horsemen, signed on to the opinion.

157 **opinion behind it:** *Tyson & Bro. v. Banton,* 273 U.S. 418, 446 (1927) (Holmes dissenting).

157 **overturned *Tyson:*** The majority reasoning that "private" transactions, such as ticket sales, could not be regulated was essentially rejected in *Nebbia v. New York,* 291 U.S. 502 (1934), but although the Court "distinguished" subsequent cases so as not to have to follow *Tyson,* the case was not fully overturned until 1965. *Gold v. DiCarlo,* 235 F. Supp. 817 (S.D.N.Y. 1964), aff'd, 380 U.S. 520 (1965).

157 **hostility to unions:** *Adair v. United States,* 208 U.S. 161 (1908). For judicial hostility to unions, see Christopher L. Tomlins, *The State and the Unions: Labor Relations, Law, and the Organized Labor Movement in America, 1880–1960* (1985).

158 **"the country at large":** *Adair,* 208 U.S. at 190 (Holmes dissenting).

158 **"to prevent it":** *Coppage v. Kansas,* 236 U.S. 1, 26 (1915) (Holmes dissenting).

158 **enforce labor rights:** *National Labor Relations Board v. Jones & Laughlin Steel Corporation,* 301 U.S. 1 (1937), and *National Labor Relations Board v. Friedman–Harry Marks Clothing Co.,* 301 U.S. 58 (1937).

158 **had any authority:** *Phelps Dodge Corp. v. National Labor Relations Board,* 313 U.S. 177 (1941).

158 **are worth noting:** Holmes dissented in a series of cases in the October 1929 term: *Safe Deposit and Trust Co. of Baltimore v. Virginia,* 280 U.S. 83 (1929), *Farmers Loan & Trust v. Minnesota,* 280 U.S. 204 (1930), and *Baldwin v. Missouri,* 281 U.S. 586 (1930), all of which denied states the power to levy

an inheritance tax on certain types of assets; the Court adopted Holmes's views and reversed all three of these cases in *State Tax Commission of Utah v. Aldrich,* 316 U.S. 174 (1942). He entered a vehement dissent against forum shopping in *Black & White Taxicab Co. v. Brown & Yellow Taxicab Co.,* 276 U.S. 518 (1928), in which he was joined by Brandeis and Stone. Ten years later, Brandeis, in his last major decision for the Court before retiring, wrote the landmark opinion in *Erie Railroad Co. v. Tompkins,* 304 U.S. 64 (1938), the only time in the Court's history that a prior decision was held unconstitutional. *Erie* did not put an end to forum shopping, but greatly reduced it, and significantly changed the leeway federal courts had in choice of law. Holmes also filed a dissent in *Evans v. Gore,* 253 U.S. 245 (1920), that held judges' salaries immune from the income tax, a decision reversed in *Helvering v. Gerhardt,* 304 U.S. 405 (1938).

159   **more than anarchists:** *United States v. Schwimmer,* 279 U.S. 644 (1929).

160   **"Sermon on the Mount":** *Id.* at 653 (Holmes dissenting).

160   **"thought that we hate":** *Girouard v. United States,* 328 U.S. 61 (1946).

160   **that took this view:** See in particular *Ozawa v. United States,* 260 U.S. 178 (1922), and *United States v. Bhagat Singh Thind,* 261 U.S. 204 (1923).

160   **"adopted and confirmed":** *Girouard,* 328 U.S. at 70 (Stone dissenting). Justices Reed and Frankfurter joined in the dissent.

161   **the Progressive Era:** For Brandeis, see Urofsky, *Brandeis;* Philippa Strum, *Louis D. Brandeis: Justice for the People* (1984); and Lewis J. Paper, *Brandeis* (1983). The older Alpheus Thomas Mason, *Brandeis: A Free Man's Life* (1946), is still valuable because Mason had the opportunity to interview the justice for his book.

161   **considered unacceptable:** The confirmation fight is explored in detail in Mason, *Brandeis,* chaps. 30 and 31, and Alden Todd, *Justice on Trial* (1964).

161   **policy should be allowed:** *Muller v. Oregon,* 208 U.S. 412 (1908).

163   **living Constitution:** Draft dissent in *United States v. Moreland,* 258 U.S. 433 (1922). Taft, who also disagreed with the majority, said he could not sign on to Brandeis's dissent because of this sentiment, which he feared would be used in ways he could not approve. Brandeis responded that while he strongly believed in the sentiment, the lines were not necessary in this context, and he would remove them. See Robert F. Post, "The Supreme Court Opinion as Institutional Practice: Dissent, Legal Scholarship, and Decisionmaking in the Taft Court," 85 *Minnesota Law Review* 1267, 1352–53 (2001).

163   **"great relief to the world":** Laski to Holmes, 13 January 1918, in Howe, *Holmes-Laski Letters,* 1:27.

164   **"make it more instructive":** See, for just one example, Paul A. Freund, "Justice Brandeis: A Law Clerk's Remembrance," 68 *American Jewish Archives* 11 (1977).

164   **"understand and believe":** Acheson's remarks are in 55 *Harvard Law Review* 191 (1941).

164   **"I write for that man":** Posted on *Legal History Blog,* 8 October 2013.

165   **article in an opinion:** *Adams v. Tanner,* 244 U.S. 590, 613n21 (1917) (Brandeis dissenting).

165   **"in the law journals":** Brandeis to Frankfurter, 10 October 1922, in *"Half Brother, Half Son": The Letters of Louis D. Brandeis to Felix Frankfurter,* ed. Melvin I. Urofsky and David W. Levy (1991), 121.

165   **"they are helping":** Brandeis to Frankfurter, 25 February 1924, in *id.,*

158. The case was *Washington v. Rolph,* 264 U.S. 213 (1925), which held workmen's compensation laws were inapplicable to longshoremen because they were covered by the interstate and foreign maritime laws. In his dissent at 228, Brandeis attacked the doctrine of *Southern Pacific v. Jensen,* 244 U.S. 205 (1916), upon which the Court relied. He argued that *Jensen* had been wrong to begin with, and he buttressed his dissent with copious citations of recent articles in law journals criticizing the *Jensen* doctrine.

165 **in all law schools:** Felix Frankfurter and J. Forrester Davison, *Cases and Materials on Administrative Law* (1932), became a standard text on the subject for many years.

165 **over to his side:** Melvin I. Urofsky, ed., "The Brandeis-Frankfurter Conversations," 1985 *Supreme Court Review* 299, 314, 328 (1985); Bickel gives several examples of suppressing dissents in *The Unpublished Opinions of Mr. Justice Brandeis.* At the time, all of the justices shared this opinion of not dissenting except when it could not be helped.

166 **"choosing my ground":** Jerome Frank, "Book Review," 10 *Journal of Legal Education* 401, 404 (1958); Ginsburg, "Dissent Is an 'Appeal' for the Future," 7.

166 **his classroom:** Strum, *Brandeis,* 347.

166 **the law schools:** Urofsky, *Brandeis,* chap.19.

166 **"scurrilous or abusive language":** Other laws that restricted speech included the Selective Service, Espionage, and Trading with the Enemy Acts of 1917 and the Immigration Act of 1918. Two good overviews are Harry N. Scheiber, *The Wilson Administration and Civil Liberties* (1960), and Paul L. Murphy, *World War I and the Origins of Civil Liberties in the United States* (1979).

167 **clung to this doctrine:** David M. Rabban, *Free Speech in Its Forgotten Years* (1997).

167 **"to be punished criminally":** *Patterson v. Colorado,* 205 U.S. 454 (1907). In 1915, Holmes again spoke for the Court in sustaining the constitutionality of a law punishing speech that had a tendency to encourage crime, even if there had been no criminal consequences of the speech. *Fox v. Washington,* 236 U.S. 273 (1915).

167 **"proximity and degree":** *Schenck v. United States,* 294 U.S. 47 (1919). One week later, the Court handed down two more speech tests in which Holmes wrote the majority opinion utilizing the clear and present danger test— *Frohwerk v. United States,* 249 U.S. 204 (1919), and *Debs v. United States,* 249 U.S. 211 (1919).

167 **"not through it":** Urofsky, "Brandeis-Frankfurter Conversations," 323–24. The same day as *Schenck,* Brandeis wrote for a unanimous Court in *Sugarman v. United States,* 249 U.S. 182 (1919), dismissing a challenge to the Espionage Act for lack of jurisdiction.

168 **speech and other rights:** Urofsky, *Brandeis,* 553–54; Zechariah Chafee, Jr., "Freedom of Speech in War Time," 32 *Harvard Law Review* 932 (1919), which became the basis for his classic book, *Freedom of Speech* (1920).

168 **listened carefully:** The story of how Holmes came to change his mind is well told in Thomas Healy, *The Great Dissent . . .* (2013).

168 **First Amendment:** Gerald Gunther, "Learned Hand and the Origins of Modern First Amendment Doctrine," 27 *Stanford Law Review* 719 (1975). In the appendix, Gunther provides the texts of all the letters between Hand and Holmes and between Hand and Chafee.

168 **present danger test:** *Abrams v. United States,* 250 U.S. 616 (1919). For the case, see Richard Polenberg, *Fighting Faiths: The Abrams Case, the Supreme Court, and Free Speech* (1987).

168 **"life is an experiment":** *Abrams,* 250 U.S. at 630 (Holmes dissenting); Polenberg, *Fighting Faiths,* 236. An interesting analysis by Vincent Blasi terms the Holmes dissent "the single most influential judicial opinion ever written on [free speech]." "Propter Honoris Respectum: Reading Holmes Through the Lens of Schauer: The Abrams Dissent," 72 *Notre Dame Law Review* 1343 (1997).

169 **Benjamin Gitlow:** *Gitlow v. New York,* 268 U.S. 652, 673 (1925) (Holmes dissenting).

169 **another restricted speech:** *Bridges v. California,* 314 U.S. 252, 262 (1941).

171 **"a strict and accurate sense":** *Hartzel v. United States,* 322 U.S. 680, 686 (1944). Interestingly, William O. Douglas, later to be a strong champion of free speech, dissented in *Hartzel.*

172 **would have found insulting:** *American Communications Association v. Douds,* 339 U.S. 382, 396 (1950).

172 **be a good thing:** *Dennis v. United States,* 341 U.S. 494 (1951). See Michal R. Belknap, *Cold War Political Justice: The Smith Act, the Communist Party, and American Civil Liberties* (1977).

172 **advocacies in *Gitlow*:** *Dennis,* 341 U.S. at 544, 550 (Frankfurter concurring); see Urofsky, *Frankfurter,* chap. 7.

173 **"free trade in ideas":** *Garner v. Louisiana,* 368 U.S. 157, 201 (1961) (Harlan concurring).

173 **several other cases:** *Bell v. Maryland,* 378 U.S. 226, 344 (1964) (Black dissenting); *New York Times v. Sullivan,* 376 U.S. 254, 276 (1964); and *Brown v. Louisiana,* 383 U.S. 131, 147 (1966) (Brennan concurring).

173 **one form or another:** *McConnell v. Federal Election Commission,* 540 U.S. 93, 265, 274 (2003) (Thomas concurring in part and dissenting in part); *Johanns v. Livestock Marketing Ass'n.,* 544 U.S. 550, 575 (2005) (Souter dissenting); *Morse v. Frederick,* 551 U.S. 393, 442 (2007) (Stevens dissenting in part); *Holder v. Humanitarian Law Project,* 130 S. Ct. 2705, 2733 (2010) (Breyer dissenting); and *Arizona Free Enterprise Club's Freedom Club PAC v. Bennett,* 131 S. Ct. 2806, 2837 (2011) (Kagan dissenting).

173 **intellectual challenge:** Vincent Blasi is one of the few scholars who believes that the *Abrams* opinion is about the practical consequences of dissent on the political system and is more than just an intellectual exercise. Blasi, "Propter Honoris Respectum."

174 **involvement in the war:** *Schaefer v. United States,* 251 U.S. 466 (1920).

174 **"The constitutional right":** *Id.* at 482, 495 (Brandeis dissenting). Justice Clarke dissented separately; he would have sent the case back to trial court for a new hearing.

175 **form of antiwar speech:** *Pierce v. United States,* 252 U.S. 239 (1920).

175 **been indicted as well:** *Id.* at 253 (Brandeis dissenting). The Christian Science case was *American School of Magnetic Healing v. McAnnuity,* 187 U.S. 94, 104 (1902).

175 **no heresy trials in the United States:** *United States v. Ballard,* 322 U.S. 78 (1944).

176 **regarding direct incitement:** *Masses Publishing Co. v. Patten,* 244 Fed. 535 (S.D.N.Y. 1917).

177 **speech in wartime:** *Gilbert v. Minnesota,* 254 U.S. 325 (1920).

177 **"not be repealed then":** Holmes to Felix Frankfurter, 22 December 1920, in *Holmes and Frankfurter: Their Correspondence, 1912–1934,* ed. Robert H. Mennel and Christine Compston (1996), 99.

177 **"I have difficulty":** *Gilbert,* 254 U.S. at 343 (Brandeis dissenting).

178 **a few years later:** *Meyer v. Nebraska,* 262 U.S. 390 (1923), and *Pierce v. Society of Sisters,* 268 U.S. 510 (1925). In *Meyer,* the Court struck down a state statute, passed during the anti-alien hysteria of 1919, that forbade the teaching of modern languages, other than English, to anyone in eighth grade and below. Meyer taught in a parochial school and used a German Bible history as a text. In *Pierce,* a unanimous Court invalidated an Oregon law requiring parents to send all children between the ages of eight and sixteen to public schools. The Klan-sponsored law had attempted to put all parochial schools out of business.

178 **not to the states:** *Barron v. Baltimore,* 32 U.S. 243 (1833).

178 **applied it to the states:** On this issue, see William E. Nelson, *The Fourteenth Amendment: From Political Principle to Judicial Doctrine* (1988), and Amar, *Bill of Rights.*

178 **"I think you go":** Holmes to Brandeis, n.d., on Gilbert return, Brandeis Court Papers, Harvard University Law Library; Howe, *Holmes-Pollack Letters,* 2:61.

178 **next important speech case:** In 1921, the Court heard a case where the postmaster general had condemned a Socialist Party newspaper for printing antiwar articles. He then said that future issues would also be dangerous and denied it second-class mailing privileges. Although, as Brandeis pointed out in dissent, this violated the doctrine of prior restraint, the Court majority, led by Clarke, held the government could impose such restraints in wartime. Holmes and Brandeis both dissented but separately. *United States ex rel. Milwaukee Socialist Democratic Publishing Co. v. Burleson,* 255 U.S. 407 (1921).

179 **"impairment by the States":** *Gitlow v. New York,* 268 U.S. 652, 666 (1925). A good examination of the case is Marc Lendler, *Gitlow v. New York: Every Idea an Incitement* (2012).

180 **justified the state's restriction:** See the analysis of Sanford's opinion in Harry Kalven Jr., *A Worthy Tradition: Freedom of Speech in America* (1988), chap. 11, where it is juxtaposed with Brandeis's *Whitney* opinion.

180 **"present conflagration":** *Gitlow,* 268 U.S. at 672 (Holmes dissenting).

180 **"proletarian dictatorship":** Holmes to Frankfurter, 14 June 1925, in Mennel and Compston, *Holmes and Frankfurter,* 184.

180 **her philanthropic work:** For Whitney, see Lisa Rubens, "The Patrician Radical: Charlotte Anita Whitney," 65 *California History* 158 (1986).

180 **found her guilty:** The circumstances of her trial, by modern standards, would certainly have led to a mistrial. The prosecution turned the trial into a denunciation of the Industrial Workers of the World, an organization with which Whitney had no direct ties, and the judge's instructions left the jury little choice but to find the defendant guilty. The verdict aroused nationwide condemnation, and even the sponsor of the California act expressed dismay that it should have been applied to Ms. Whitney, stating that "the law was never intended to halt free speech nor to punish persons for their thoughts."

181 **social and political order:** *Whitney v. California,* 274 U.S. 357 (1927). There has been a great deal written about the case, but by far the best article is

Vincent Blasi, "The First Amendment and the Ideal of Civic Courage: The Brandeis Opinion in *Whitney v. California*," 29 *William and Mary Law Review* 653 (1988).

181 **First Amendment grounds:** The fact that Brandeis concurred rather than dissented is the reason for the criticism found in Ronald K. L. Collins and David M. Skover, "Curious Concurrence: Justice Brandeis's Vote in *Whitney v. California*," 2005 *Supreme Court Review* 333 (2006). The two authors believe that Brandeis should have dissented and thus forced the First Amendment issue. There were, however, jurisdictional problems that, in his opinion, negated his ability to dissent on grounds that had not been raised earlier. Because he had on so many occasions criticized his colleagues for reaching out to take cases, it is highly unlikely that he would do that. The concurrence allowed him to note the jurisdictional issue and then address the First Amendment. And as anybody who has read the "concurrence" recognizes, it is a dissent, and one of the greatest in American constitutional history.

181 **"dissent can do":** Tushnet, *I Dissent,* 98–99. Collins and Skover have found an earlier version of this opinion that Brandeis had prepared as a dissent in *Ruthenberg v. Michigan,* a case similar to *Gitlow,* and Brandeis planned to go further than Holmes had. Then, on 2 March 1927, Ruthenberg died of acute peritonitis in a Chicago hospital. Brandeis filed the draft of the dissent and then brought it out when the Court heard *Whitney.*

181 **"civic courage":** Pnina Lahav, "Holmes and Brandeis: Libertarian and Republican Justifications for Free Speech," 4 *Journal of Law and Politics* 451, 458 (1988); Blasi, "Ideal of Civic Courage." The "re-fashioning of the Holmesian product" is examined in Wayne V. McIntosh and Cynthia L. Cates, *Judicial Entrepreneurship: The Role of the Judge in the Marketplace of Ideas* (1997), 32ff.

181 **"Those who won":** *Whitney,* 274 U.S. 357, 372, 375 (Brandeis concurring).

183 **Funeral Oration:** Lahav, "Holmes and Brandeis," 462.

183 **controversial policy matters:** *Bond v. Floyd,* 385 U.S. 116 (1966).

184 **First Amendment jurisprudence:** *Brandenburg v. Ohio,* 395 U.S. 444, 447 (1969). The concurrences are at 450.

184 **standard of judicial scrutiny:** *Grayned v. City of Rockford,* 408 U.S. 104 (1972).

184 **adopted by the Court:** *Central Hudson Gas & Electric Corp. v. Public Service Commission,* 447 U.S. 557, 577–79 (Blackmun and Stevens concurring), 594 (Rehnquist dissenting) (1980).

184 **more speech rather than less:** *Arizona Free Enterprise Club's Freedom Club PAC v. Bennett,* 131 S. Ct. 2806, 2835 (2011) (Kagan dissenting).

184 **lawyerly opinions:** See, among many others, Kalven, *Worthy Tradition,* chap. 11; Lillian A. BeVier, "The First Amendment and Political Speech . . . ," 30 *Stanford Law Review* 299 (1978); Ashutah A. Bhagwat, "The Story of Whitney v. California: The Power of Ideas," in *Constitutional Law Stories,* ed. Michael C. Dorf (New York, 2004), chap. 12; Helen Garfield, "Twentieth Century Jeffersonian: Brandeis, Freedom of Speech, and the Republican Revival," 69 *Oregon Law Review* 527 (1990). The only scholar I found who argued that Sanford's position is the better is Robert H. Bork, "Neutral Principles and Some First Amendment Problems," 47 *Indiana Law Journal* 1 (1971). The best analysis remains that of Blasi in "First Amendment and the Ideal of Civic Courage."

184 **runs a close second:** *Omstead v. United States,* 277 U.S. 438 (1928).

184 **"without understanding":** *Id.* at 478 (Brandeis dissenting).

185 ***New State Ice Company v. Liebmann:*** 285 U.S. 262 (1932).

186 **minds be bold:** *Id.* at 280, 302–3, 311 (Brandeis dissenting). Justice Stone joined the dissent. Justice Benjamin Cardozo, who had taken Holmes's seat, did not participate.

186 **great economic hardship:** Cited in Krishnakumar, "Canonical Dissent," 794.

186 **discourse on federalism:** See, for example, Stephen Breyer, *Making Our Democracy Work: A Judge's View* (2010). He opens chap. 10, "The States and Federalism," with a discussion of the Brandeis opinion.

187 **current economic distress:** *Liggett v. Lee,* 288 U.S. 517, 541, 547 (1933) (Brandeis dissenting).

187 **right to die:** *Cruzan v. Director, Missouri Department of Health,* 497 U.S. 261, 292 (1990) (O'Connor concurring); *Washington v. Glucksberg,* 521 U.S. 702, 737 (1997) (O'Connor concurring).

187 **"social experimentation":** *New York Times,* 8 November 1936.

187 **government was the solution:** This point is well made in G. Edward White, "Canonization of Holmes and Brandeis," 70 *NYU Law Review* at 602 (1995); see also Urofsky, *Brandeis,* chap. 28.

187 **"try to keep in line":** Cardozo to Brandeis, 17 October 1926, Brandeis Court Papers.

188 **illegal if reasonable:** *Standard Oil Co. v. United States,* 221 U.S. 1 (1911).

188 **violate the antitrust law:** *Chicago Board of Trade v. United States,* 246 U.S. 231 (1918).

188 **limited competition:** *American Column & Lumber Co. et al. v. United States,* 257 U.S. 377, 413 (1921). He told Frankfurter that he had been "waiting for a chance to say some of those things." Brandeis to Frankfurter, 31 December 1921, Felix Frankfurter Papers, Library of Congress, Washington, D.C.

188 **"all relevant facts":** *Chicago Board of Trade,* 246 U.S. at 238.

188 ***Cracking Oil* case:** *Standard Oil Co. (Indiana) v. United States,* 283 U.S. 163 (1931).

189 **patents could be licensed:** Charles D. Weller, "A 'New' Rule of Reason from Justice Brandeis's 'Concentric Circles' and Other Changes in Law," 44 *Antitrust Bulletin* 881, 919–25 (1999).

189 **"between courts and agencies":** G. Edward White, "Allocating Power Between Agencies and Courts: The Legacy of Justice Brandeis," 23 *Duke Law Journal* 195, 196–97 (1974).

189 **review of its findings:** See, for example, *Cincinnati, New Orleans, and Texas Pacific Railway v. ICC,* 162 U.S. 184 (1896); *ICC v. Cincinnati, New Orleans, and Texas Pacific Railway,* 167 U.S. 479 (1897); *ICC v. Alabama Midland Railway Co.,* 168 U.S. 144 (1897).

189 **state judicial scrutiny:** *Northern Pacific Railway Co. v. Solum,* 247 U.S. 477 (1918). The question was whether a Minnesota state court, in the absence of initial consideration by the ICC, could investigate the reasonableness of rate-setting practices of railroads operating in interstate commerce passing through Minnesota. Brandeis held that the railway's decision to follow the practices of the ICC trumped state claims.

190 **with interstate commerce:** *Pennsylvania v. West Virginia,* 262 U.S. 553 (1923).

190   **economic variables involved:** *Id.* at 605 (Brandeis dissenting).

190   **postwar America:** White, "Allocating Power," 214.

191   **what this phrase meant:** *Federal Trade Commission v. Gratz,* 253 U.S. 421 (1920).

191   **make its own determination:** *Federal Trade Commission v. Curtis Publishing Co.,* 260 U.S. 568 (1923).

191   **that the courts lacked:** See, for example, his dissents in *Ohio Water Co. v. Borough of Ben Avon,* 253 U.S. 287, 292 (1920), and *Crowell v. Benson,* 285 U.S. 22, 65 (1932).

191   **administrative in nature:** *United States ex rel. Milwaukee Socialist Democratic Publishing Co. v. Burleson,* 255 U.S. 407 (1921).

191   **denial of due process:** *Ng Fung Ho v. White,* 259 U.S. 276 (1922). The opinion substantially modified an earlier opinion by Holmes in *United States v. Ju Toy,* 198 U.S. 253 (1905).

191   **subject of federal jurisdiction:** Brandeis to Frankfurter, 6 March 1929 and 17 May 1931, Frankfurter Papers, Library of Congress. The books are Frankfurter and Wilbur G. Katz, *Cases and Other Authorities on Federal Jurisdiction and Procedure* (1931), and Frankfurter and J. Forrester Davison, *Cases and Other Materials on Administrative Law* (1931).

192   **fifteen years earlier:** *United States v. Morgan,* 307 U.S. 183, 191 (1939).

192   **in constitutional cases:** See, for example, William O. Douglas, "*Stare decisis* has . . . little place in American constitutional law." *We the Judges* (1956), 429.

192   **assumed canonical authority:** *Burnet v. Coronado Oil and Gas Co.,* 285 U.S. 393 (1932).

192   ***stare decisis* doctrine:** Colin P. Starger, "The Dialectic of Stare Decisis Doctrine," in *Precedent in the United States Supreme Court,* ed. Christopher J. Peters (2013), posted on H-LAW.

MISE-EN-SCÈNE 2

BRANDEIS IN *OLMSTEAD V. UNITED STATES* (1928)

196   **a low public profile:** See "The Case of the High-Tech Bootlegger," in Melvin Urofsky, *Supreme Decisions: Great Constitutional Cases and Their Impact* (2012), 225–40, and Philip Metcalfe, *Whispering Wires: The Tragic Tale of an American Bootlegger* (2007).

197   **against self-incrimination:** *Olmstead v. United States,* 277 U.S. 438 (1928). The main arguments for both sides are printed just before the opinion of the Court.

197   **illegality into evidence:** *Silverthorne Lumber Co. v. United States,* 251 U.S. 385 (1920); *Weeks v. United States,* 232 U.S. 383 (1914).

197   **in a federal court:** *Gambino v. United States,* 275 U.S. 310 (1927).

198   **"offices of the defendants":** *Olmstead,* 277 U.S. at 464.

198   **"meaning to the Fourth Amendment:"** *Id.* at 466.

198   **with Holmes and Brandeis:** The Butler dissent is at *id.* at 485 and that of Stone at 488.

199   **"play an ignoble part":** *Id.* at 469, 470 (Holmes dissenting).

200   **"Decency, security and liberty":** *Id.* at 277 U.S. at 471, 485 (Brandeis dissenting).

200   **press and commercial actors:** Samuel D. Warren and Louis D. Brandeis, "The Right to Privacy," 4 *Harvard Law Review* 193 (1890). A great deal

has been written about this article, which, until after World War II, was the most cited article in American law. For a good retrospective look, see Robert C. Post, "Rereading Warren and Brandeis: Privacy, Property, and Appropriation," 41 *Case Western Law Review* 647 (1991).

200 **on a constitutional basis:** The writing of the opinion is examined in Paul A. Freund, "The Evolution of a Brandeis Dissent," 10 *Manuscripts* 18 (1958).

201 **"The makers of our Constitution":** *Olmstead,* 277 U.S. at 478.

202 **"majority were right":** Mason, *William Howard Taft,* 227, 259; Henry F. Pringle, *The Life and Times of William Howard Taft: A Biography,* 2 vols. (1939), 991.

202 **"in favor of liberty, strictly":** Brandeis to Frankfurter, 15 June 1928, Frankfurter Papers, Library of Congress.

202 ***Olmstead* in 1937:** 48 Stat. 1103, 47 U.S.C. § 605; *Nardone v. United States,* 302 U.S. 379 (1937). The Court, with Brandeis in the 7–2 majority, held that the Communications Act applied to the federal government, that wiretapping in general was illegal, and that no wiretapping evidence secured without a warrant could be admitted into federal court.

202 **"Had a majority":** *Goldman v. United States,* 316 U.S. 129, 136 (1942) (Stone and Frankfurter dissenting); Murphy's dissent is also at 136. Jackson, who had been attorney general when the case had been brought, recused himself. Stone, it should be recalled, had been on the Court at the time of *Olmstead* and had joined Brandeis's dissent.

203 **"powerful dissent" in *Olmstead*:** *On Lee v. United States,* 343 U.S. 747, 758 (1952) (Frankfurter dissenting). The Douglas dissent is at 762 and that of Burton at 765. Justice Black also believed the evidence should not have been admitted but on different grounds.

203 **violation of the Fourth Amendment:** *Silverman v. United States,* 365 U.S. 505 (1961); Douglas's concurrence is at 512.

203 **"people, not places":** *Berger v. New York,* 388 U.S. 41 (1967); *Katz v. New York,* 389 U.S. 347, 351 (1967). Seven members of the Court joined the majority opinion. Douglas and Brennan used their concurrence (at 359) to reject the view expressed by White in his concurrence (362) that no warrant would be needed if the president or the attorney general decided a wiretap was needed for national security. Harlan also joined (360), but Black dissented (364), believing, as Taft did, that electronic eavesdropping did not constitute a search or seizure within the meaning of the Fourth Amendment. Thurgood Marshall did not take part.

204 **heart of the Brandeis opinion:** *Kyllo v. United States,* 533 U.S. 27 (2001); *Florida v. Jardines,* 133 S. Ct. 1409 (2013).

205 **"denotes not merely freedom":** *Meyer v. Nebraska,* 262 U.S. 390, 399 (1923). Interestingly, Holmes and Sutherland dissented. Two years later, McReynolds spoke for a unanimous Court in striking down a Ku Klux Klan–sponsored bill forbidding children in Oregon to attend parochial schools. *Pierce v. Society of Sisters,* 268 U.S. 510 (1925). See William G. Ross, *Forging New Freedoms: Nativism, Education, and the Constitution, 1917–1927* (1994).

206 **strict scrutiny by the courts:** *Skinner v. Oklahoma,* 316 U.S. 535, 541 (1942). Stone and Jackson concurred in the result but were unwilling to use equal protection analysis. For the case, see Victoria F. Nourse, *In Reckless Hands: Skinner v. Oklahoma and the Near Triumph of American Eugenics* (2008).

206 ***Griswold v. Connecticut*:** 381 U.S. 479 (1965). For the expansion of privacy

in cases beginning with *Griswold*, see David J. Garrow, *Liberty and Sexuality: The Right to Privacy and the Making of Roe v. Wade* (1994). The use of the word "privacy" in Court cases prior to *Griswold* dealt primarily with Fourth Amendment search and seizure issues. For example, Felix Frankfurter wrote that "the security of one's privacy against arbitrary intrusion by the police—which is at the core of the Fourth Amendment—is basic to a free society." *Wolf v. Colorado*, 338 U.S. 25, 27–28 (1949). However, Justice Douglas in his dissent in *Poe v. Ullman*, 367 U.S. 497, 510, 521n12 (1961), cites the Warren and Brandeis article as a source of the right of privacy.

206 **the marital chamber:** *Griswold*, 381 U.S. at 484, 486.

206 **history of the people:** *Id.* at 486 (Goldberg concurring).

206 **liberties such as privacy:** *Id.* at 499. Harlan had made this argument in his powerful dissent in *Poe*, 367 U.S. at 522. Justice White concurred and also wanted to rest the justification on the Fourteenth Amendment.

207 **terminate a pregnancy:** *Eisenstadt v. Baird*, 405 U.S. 438 (1972) (contraceptives for unmarried people); *Loving v. Virginia*, 388 U.S. 1 (1967) (antimiscegenation laws); *Boddie v. Connecticut*, 401 U.S. 371 (1971) (divorce); *Stanley v. Georgia*, 405 U.S. 557 (1969) (pornography); *Roe v. Wade*, 410 U.S. 113 (1973) (abortion).

207 **in the Constitution:** Bork, "Neutral Principles and Some First Amendment Problems." Some liberals also questioned whether Congress or the Court could create new rights. See John Hart Ely, *Democracy and Distrust* (1980), with its extensive analysis of the Ninth Amendment and its meaning.

207 **Griswold concurrence:** *Cruzan v. Director, Missouri Department of Health*, 497 U.S. 261 (1990). The case and the issue of right-to-die are explored in Melvin Urofsky, *Letting Go: Death, Dying, and the Law* (1993), and Peter G. Filene, *In the Arms of Others* (1998).

207 **changed that history:** *Bowers v. Hardwick*, 478 U.S. 186 (1986). After his retirement, Justice Lewis F. Powell, who had voted with the majority, admitted that he had probably been wrong. At the time, Powell said he knew no gay people, and he apparently did not know that one of his clerks that term was gay.

208 **"search for greater freedom":** *Lawrence v. Texas*, 539 U.S. 558, 578–79 (2003). The best single volume covering the issues and cases from *Hardwick* to *Lawrence* is Richards, *Sodomy Cases*.

CHAPTER 7: THE RETURN OF SERIATIM

209 **all nine justices:** This percentage excludes cases decided by *per curiam* opinions and does not count dissents and concurrences without opinions, or else the percentage of unanimity would have been even smaller. See Albert P. Blaustein and Roy M. Mersky, *The First Hundred Justices* (1978), table 9 at 137–41.

210 **nonconstitutional matters:** Robert Post, "Judicial Management and Judicial Disinterest: The Achievements and Perils of Chief Justice William Howard Taft," 1 *Supreme Court History* 50 (1998).

211 **statutory interpretation:** 43 Stat. 936 (1925). Taft's efforts are detailed in Mason, *William Howard Taft*, 107–14.

212 **their roles changed dramatically:** A number of contemporaries immediately recognized the far-reaching importance of the Judges' Bill. See Gregory Hankin, "U.S. Supreme Court Under New Act," 12 *Journal of the American*

Judicature Society 40 (1928); Felix Frankfurter and James M. Landis, *The Business of the Supreme Court* (1927), 260–61, 299.

212 **fell to 85.2 percent:** Stephen C. Halpern and Kenneth N. Vines, "Institutional Disunity, the Judges' Bill, and the Role of the U.S. Supreme Court," 30 *Western Political Quarterly* 472, 475 (1977).

212 **began to evaporate:** A related development that also gave the Court greater discretion over its docket came with Brandeis's opinion in *Erie Railroad Co. v. Tompkins,* 304 U.S. 64 (1938). Federal courts now had to use state decisional rules, cutting down on the number of appeals. The best source for the *Erie* decision is Edward A. Purcell Jr., *Brandeis and the Progressive Constitution* (2000).

212 **"one conclusion or another":** Cardozo, *Nature of the Judicial Process,* 164–65.

212 **"cases it decided":** Rehnquist, "The Supreme Court: Past and Present," 363.

213 **pressure against dissents collapsed:** David M. O'Brien, "Institutional Norms and Supreme Court Opinions: On Reconsidering the Rise of Individual Opinions," in *Supreme Court Decision-Making: New Institutionalist Approaches,* ed. Cornell W. Clayton and Howard Gillman (1999), 102.

214 **sake of the institution:** Jonathan Lurie, "Chief Justice Taft and Dissents: Down with the Brandeis Briefs!," 32 *Journal of Supreme Court History* 178, 181–82 (2007); Post, "Supreme Court Opinion," 1311.

214 **the Court's judgments:** Taft would no doubt have agreed with his predecessor, Edward Douglass White, who, although writing in dissent, conceded that "the only purpose which an elaborate dissent can accomplish, if any, is to weaken the effect of the [majority] opinion, and thus engender want of confidence in the conclusions of courts of last resort." Post, "Supreme Court Opinion," 1344, 1348.

215 **"statement of the law":** Quoted in Post, "Supreme Court Opinion," 1341.

215 **Brandeis and Holmes respected:** The best study of Taft's years on the Court remains Mason's *William Howard Taft,* although several scholars are currently working on the Court during the Taft years.

215 **voted *with* the majority:** By this, I do not mean that they blindly upheld property rights over legislative prerogatives; in those cases, they dissented. But the vast majority of the run-of-the-mill cases before the Court did not involve property rights.

215 **White House in 1916:** Regrettably, there is no good biography of Hughes, and the standard remains the "official" two-volume work of Merlo J. Pusey, *Charles Evans Hughes* (1952). Harlan Stone served on the Court throughout Hughes's tenure as chief, and Alpheus Thomas Mason's *Harlan Fiske Stone: Pillar of the Law* (1956) has a less-than-favorable view of Hughes. The most up-to-date study of the Hughes Court is William G. Ross, *The Chief Justiceship of Charles Evans Hughes, 1930–1941* (2007).

216 **running the conference:** Pusey, *Hughes,* 2:673. William O. Douglas, *The Court Years, 1939–1975* (1980), 215, 222.

217 **72 percent in 1940:** ZoBell, "Division of Opinion," 205.

217 **control of the brethren eroding:** Stacia L. Haynie, "Leadership and Consensus on the U.S. Supreme Court," 54 *Journal of Politics* 1158, 1167 (1992); Philip E. Urofsky, "The Douglas Diary, 1939–1940," 20 *Journal of Supreme Court History* 78 (1995).

217 **"discrete and insular minorities":** *United States v. Carolene Products Co.,* 304 U.S. 144, 152–53 (1938).

217 **stood at 58 percent:** ZoBell, "Division of Opinion," 205. For evaluations of Stone's tenure, see William M. Wiecek, *Birth of the Modern Constitution: The United States Supreme Court, 1941–1953* (2006), and Melvin I. Urofsky, *Division and Discord: The Supreme Court Under Stone and Vinson* (1997).

217 **"in which to work":** Douglas to Stone, 30 June 1941, and to Black, 22 June 1941, both in Douglas Papers, Library of Congress.

218 **before the Court:** Douglas, *Court Years,* 222.

218 **majorities were against him:** Prior to 1937, Stone had been on the losing end of a number of 5–4 decisions.

218 **"views of the minority":** Stone to McReynolds, 3 April 1930, Stone Papers, Library of Congress.

219 **dissent without anarchy:** Harlan Fiske Stone, "The Chief Justice," 27 *American Bar Association Journal* 407 (July 1941); for Stone's positive views on dissent, see his "Dissenting Opinions Are Not Without Value," 26 *Journal of the American Judicature Society* 78 (1942).

219 **the center chair:** He did not write 95 dissenting opinions, but voted in dissent that many times. Prior to Stone, no chief justice had ever dissented in more than 3 percent of cases, and John Marshall had dissented only 3 times in nearly 1,187 cases, a statistically insignificant number. After Stone, both Vinson and Earl Warren dissented in 12 percent of cases. Warren Burger voted against the majority in 7 percent of cases, and William Rehnquist in 9 percent. See Ulmer, "Exploring the Dissent Patterns of the Chief Justices," 50–67, and Haynie, "Leadership and Consensus on the U.S. Supreme Court."

219 **norm of consensus:** For these personalities, see Noah Feldman, *Scorpions: The Battles and Triumphs of FDR's Great Supreme Court Justices* (2010), and William Domnarski, *The Great Justices, 1941–1954: Black, Douglas, Frankfurter, and Jackson in Chambers* (2006). C. Hermann Pritchett, one of the leaders in exploring this era of the Court, also blames the breakdown in unanimity on both Stone's inability to lead and the presence of very strong-minded Roosevelt appointees. See *The Roosevelt Court: A Study in Judicial Politics and Values, 1937–1947* (1948). See also Thomas Walker, Lee Epstein, and William Dixon, "On the Mysterious Demise of Consensual Norms in the United States Supreme Court," 50 *Journal of Politics* 361 (1988), where Stone carries much of the blame.

220 **"firm-but-gentle way":** Fred Rodell, *Nine Men* (1955), 307. There is only one biography of Vinson, a relatively uncritical one by James E. St. Clair and Linda C. Gugin, *Chief Justice Fred M. Vinson of Kentucky: A Political Biography* (2002). See Wiecek, *Birth of the Modern Constitution,* and Urofsky, *Division and Discord.*

220 **reasoned discourse:** Douglas, "Dissent," 97, 104, 105; see also Stack, "Practice of Dissent in the Supreme Court," 2256–57.

221 **judging and legal reform:** O'Brien, *Storm Center,* 284. See also Laura Kalman, *The Strange Career of Legal Liberalism* (1996).

221 **"ambition and personal politics":** All cited in Ben W. Palmer, "Supreme Court of the United States: Analysis of Alleged and Real Causes of Dissents," 34 *American Bar Association Journal* 677, 678 (1948).

222 **Stone and Vinson years:** The various drafts and accompanying notes are in the Black Papers, Library of Congress.

222 **Truman to name Vinson:** The full story can be found in Urofsky, *Division and Discord,* 137 ff.

222 **in the 1930s:** One might expect that the dissent level for these four would be fairly low, because so often they were in the majority. But starting around 1935, they often found themselves in the minority. McReynolds, for example, only wrote sixty-five dissents in his twenty-six years on the bench. In his last terms, he rarely dissented and even voted to uphold the 1938 Fair Labor Standards Act, the provisions of which he had opposed all of his life. *United States v. Darby Lumber Co.,* 312 U.S. 100 (1941).

223 **the Roosevelt appointees:** Lee Epstein et al., eds., *The Supreme Court Compendium: Data, Decisions, and Developments,* 5th ed. (2012), 652–54.

223 **"the opinion here":** *Yates v. United States,* 356 U.S. 363, 367 (1958).

224 **1964 Civil Rights Act:** *Bell v. Maryland,* 378 U.S. 226, 261 (1964).

224 **"U.S.S.C.—venerated throughout":** Brandeis to Frankfurter, 6 February 1925, Frankfurter Papers, Harvard Law School Library.

225 **at the Court permanent:** Two good sources for the clerks are Todd C. Peppers and Artemus Ward, eds., *In Chambers: Stories of Supreme Court Law Clerks and Their Justices* (2012), and Edward Lazarus, *Closed Chambers: The Justices, Clerks, and Political Agendas That Control the Supreme Court* (1998).

225 **"to Gray's work":** Quoted in John Bilyeu Oakley and Robert S. Thomson, *Law Clerks and the Judicial Process: Perceptions of the Qualities and Functions of Law Clerks in American Courts* (1980), 14.

225 **and dissenting opinions:** See, for example, Bradley J. Best, *Law Clerks, Support Personnel, and the Decline of Consensual Norms on the United States Supreme Court* (New York, 2002), and Todd C. Peppers, *Courtiers of the Marble Palace: The Rise and Influence of the Supreme Court Law Clerk* (2006).

226 **"writing for the Justice":** John P. Frank, *Marble Palace: The Supreme Court in American Life* (1958), 117, 118.

226 **draft a minor decision:** Melvin I. Urofsky, "Getting the Job Done: William O. Douglas and Collegiality in the Supreme Court," in *"He Shall Not Pass This Way Again": The Legacy of Justice William O. Douglas,* ed. Stephen L. Wasby (1990), 39.

226 **"reorganization by the justice":** Rehnquist, *Supreme Court: How It Was, How It Is,* 299–300; Donahue, quoted in Best, *Law Clerks,* 42–43.

226 **"What are these able":** Richard A. Posner, *The Federal Courts: Crisis and Reform* (1985), 106.

CHAPTER 8: THE PRIMA DONNAS I

227 **called them prima donnas:** Feldman, *Scorpions.* A slightly more sympathetic view is Domnarski, *Great Justices.* Professor Brad Snyder suggested the term "prima donnas." In addition, three of the four men appointed by Harry S. Truman—Fred Vinson, Harold Burton, and Sherman Minton—have been deemed among the least influential justices in the Court's history and not only were intellectually overshadowed but often wound up as pawns in the scorpions' battles.

228 **low level of constitutional dialogue:** Statistics for unanimous and nonunanimous decisions, as well as for those with multiple dissents, can be found in Drew Noble Lanier, *Of Time and Judicial Behavior: United States Supreme Court Agenda-Setting and Decision-Making, 1888–1997* (2003), chap. 4.

228 **modern agenda of the Court:** Two useful surveys of this period are Wiecek, *Birth of the Modern Constitution,* and Urofsky, *Division and Discord.*

229 **rest of his life:** There is a great body of literature about Black. The most comprehensive work is Roger K. Newman, *Hugo Black: A Biography* (1994), but see also Tinsley E. Yarbrough, *Mr. Justice Black and His Critics* (1988), and Tony Freyer, ed., *Justice Hugo Black and Modern America* (1990).

230 **values of those absolutes:** One of the best discussions of Black's judicial philosophy is Mark Silverstein, *Constitutional Faiths: Felix Frankfurter, Hugo Black, and the Process of Judicial Decision Making* (1984), esp. chap. 4. See also Black's *Constitutional Faith* (1968).

230 **heed his teachings:** There are a number of books on Frankfurter, and the place to start is Michael E. Parrish, *Felix Frankfurter and His Times: The Reform Years* (1982), which deals with his career before going on the Court and is essential to understanding his judicial philosophy. Urofsky, *Frankfurter,* is highly critical. Perhaps the most revealing look is Joseph Lash, ed., *From the Diaries of Felix Frankfurter* (1975), which shows just how nasty he could be to the other justices.

231 **only for their futility:** In response to a query posted on H-LAW asking who taught Frankfurter opinions, and which ones, very few people answered, and their responses varied according to their teaching interests. In all but a few instances, they cited cases that had been overruled (*Wolf v. Colorado*) or dissents that were more laments of failure than arrows pointing to the future (*Barnette*).

231 **"Supreme Court window":** Frank, *Marble Palace,* 126.

232 **contentious in history:** On relations between the two, see James F. Simon, *The Antagonists: Hugo Black, Felix Frankfurter, and Civil Liberties in Modern America* (New York, 1989), and also Feldman, *Scorpions.*

232 **not once but thrice:** Sidney Fine, *Frank Murphy: The Washington Years* (1984), 159; Frankfurter to Charles Wyzanski, 10 March 1958, quoted in Bernard Schwartz, *Super Chief: Earl Warren and His Supreme Court* (1983), 39.

232 **would follow his lead:** See Melvin I. Urofsky, "Conflict Among the Brethren: Felix Frankfurter, William O. Douglas, and the Clash of Personalities on the United States Supreme Court," 37 *Duke Law Journal* 71, 71–76 (1988).

232 **"agreed on the end result":** Stone to Sterling Carr, 13 June 1943, quoted in Mason, *Stone,* 605; *Wall Street Journal,* 25 November 1941, 3.

232 **"I have ever met":** Urofsky, "Conflict Among the Brethren," 89–90.

233 **through legal argument:** G. Edward White, "The Anti-judge: William O. Douglas and the Ambiguities of Individuality," 74 *Virginia Law Review* 17, 18 (1988), which also appears as chap. 15 in his *American Judicial Tradition* (1988).

233 **chair of the SEC:** See Laura Kalman, *Legal Realism at Yale, 1927–1960* (1986), and for Douglas's stint at the SEC see Michael E. Parrish, *Securities Regulation and the New Deal* (1970).

234 **retire in late 1975:** Douglas wrote what amounted to a three-volume autobiography consisting of *Of Men and Mountains* (1950), *Go East, Young Man: The Early Years* (1974), and *The Court Years, 1939–1975* (1980). All three volumes are in many places unreliable. While Douglas's life and ideas have generated much literature, the best single volume remains James F. Simon, *Independent Journey* (1980). Commentary on his jurisprudence in several areas is in Wasby, *"He Shall Not Pass This Way Again."*

235 **two justices on the Court:** Pritchett, "Dissent on the Supreme Court," 47.

235 a constitutional protection: Melvin I. Urofsky, "William O. Douglas as a Common Law Judge," 41 *Duke Law Journal* 133 (1991).

236 adopted Douglas's view: Interview with Charles Miller, 2 March 1989. The first case is *Frank v. Maryland*, 359 U.S. 360, 374 (1959) (Douglas dissenting). *Frank* was overruled in the companion cases of *Camara v. Municipal Court of San Francisco*, 387 U.S. 523 (1967), and *See v. Seattle*, 387 U.S. 541 (1967).

236 "When I came into": Urofsky, "Conflict Among the Brethren," 80–81.

236 solicitor general for life: There is, unfortunately, no good biography of Jackson. Eugene Gerhart, *America's Advocate* (1958), is sympathetic and uncritical and relies heavily on the oral history memoir Jackson did with Columbia University. Glendon Schubert, *Dispassionate Justice: A Synthesis of the Judicial Opinions of Robert H. Jackson* (1969), focuses primarily on his written Court record. A highly perceptive analysis of Jackson is in White, *American Judicial Tradition*, chap. 11.

238 limits of executive authority: *Wickard v. Filburn*, 317 U.S. 111 (1942); *Youngstown Sheet & Tube Co. et al. v. Sawyer*, 343 U.S. 579, 634 (1952) (Jackson concurring).

238 "discrimination and persecution": There is a very good three-volume biography by Sidney Fine, of which the last, *Frank Murphy: The Washington Years*, covers his Court career. See also J. Woodford Howard Jr., *Mr. Justice Murphy: A Political Biography* (1968), which is more critical.

239 "pronouncements rest": *Thornhill v. Alabama*, 310 U.S. 88 (1940); the Brandeis suggestion is in *Senn v. Tile Layers Protective Union*, 301 U.S. 468, 478 (1937).

239 National Labor Relations Board cases: There is a fine biography by John M. Ferren, *Salt of the Earth, Conscience of the Court: The Story of Justice Wiley Rutledge* (2004).

240 "far in a master's work": Victor Brudney and Richard F. Wolfson, "Mr. Justice Rutledge: Law Clerks' Reflections," 25 *Indiana Law Journal* 455 (1950).

240 "in war or sports": Quoted in Pritchett, "Dissent on the Supreme Court," 42. This same article has a chart of agreement and disagreement among the justices for the October 1943 term. The highest rate of agreement was between Black and Douglas (86 percent), while Frankfurter and Black agreed in only half the cases. The chief dissenter this term was Owen Roberts, whose highest rate of agreement was with Frankfurter (62 percent); his agreement with everybody else was 50 percent or less, and only 24 percent with Douglas, 27 percent with Black. *Id.* at 47.

241 compulsory flag salutes: David Manwaring, *Render unto Caesar: The Flag Salute Controversy* (1962); the broader attack on the Witnesses, and their judicial campaign to secure religious freedom, is well told in Shawn Francis Peters, *Judging Jehovah's Witnesses: Religious Persecution and the Dawn of the Rights Revolution* (2000).

241 local school authorities: *Minersville School District v. Gobitis*, 310 U.S. 586 (1940); Fine, *Murphy*, 185.

241 "representatives themselves": Mason, *Stone*, 526–27.

242 "deeply cherished liberties": *Gobitis*, 310 U.S. at 597, 598, 600.

242 "searching judicial inquiry": *United States v. Carolene Products Co.*, 304 U.S. 144, 152–53 (1938).

242 "is unique in the history": *Gobitis*, 310 U.S. at 601, 604–5 (Stone dissenting).

243 "guarantees religious liberty": 51 *Harvard Law Review* 1418 (1938); *New Republic* 24 June 1940, 843. For other opinions, see Alan Barth, *Prophets with Honor: Great Dissents and Great Dissenters in the Supreme Court* (1974), 119–21.

243 "decision, nobly written": Mason, *Stone*, 532.

244 "reading the newspapers": Fine, *Murphy*, 187.

244 wrong in *Gobitis*: *Jones v. Opelika*, 316 U.S. 584, 623 (1942) (statement by Black, Douglas, and Murphy).

244 free exercise case: Wiecek, *Birth of the Modern Constitution*, 229. See also n104 there listing some of the leading casebooks that see *Barnette* as a speech case.

244 "their faith therein": *West Virginia State Board of Education v. Barnette*, 319 U.S. 624, 642 (1943).

245 "Catholic nor agnostic": *Id.* at 646, (Frankfurter dissenting).

245 "may disrupt society": Douglas, *Court Years*, 45; *Barnette*, 319 U.S. at 653.

245 review on state action: Frankfurter to Jackson, 4 June 1943, Frankfurter Papers, Harvard Law School Library; *Barnette*, 319 U.S. at 649, 653; Sanford Levinson, "Skepticism, Democracy, and Judicial Restraint: An Essay on the Thought of Oliver Wendell Holmes and Felix Frankfurter" (Ph.D. diss., Harvard University, 1969), 232.

246 "their use and misuse": Frankfurter to Hughes, 15 June 1943, Frankfurter Papers, Harvard Law School Library; Frankfurter to Roosevelt, 3 May 1943, in *Roosevelt and Frankfurter: Their Correspondence: 1928–1945,* ed. Max Freedman (1967), 699.

246 second flag salute case: See, for example, Fred Rodell, "Felix Frankfurter, Conservative," *Harper's* (October 1941), 449.

246 fifty years later: *Employment Division, Dept. of Human Resources of Oregon v. Smith*, 494 U.S. 872, 879 (1990).

246 *Reynolds v. United States:* 98 U.S. 145 (1879). The harshness evidenced in the *Smith* case toward divergent religious practices was tempered in the unanimous decision in *Church of the Lukumi Babalu Aye v. City of Hialeah,* 508 U.S. 520 (1993).

246 World War II: For internment and the resulting legal battles, see Peter Irons, *Justice at War* (1983). A less hostile approach that tries to put the internment into the larger context of a nation at war is Page Smith, *Democracy on Trial: The Japanese-American Evacuation and Relocation in World War II* (1995).

247 Frankfurter's language: *Hirabayashi v. United States,* 320 U.S. 81, 102 (1943).

248 "cannot lend my assent": Douglas to Stone, 31 May 1943, Douglas Papers, 7 June 1943, Stone Papers. See also the discussion of Douglas's conflicting views in Irons, *Justice at War,* 237–39.

248 "hands of the enemy": Frankfurter to Stone, 4 June 1943, two memos, Stone Papers; Frankfurter to Murphy, 10 June 1943, Frankfurter Papers, Harvard Law School Library.

248 reached the Court: The concurrences are at *Hirabayashi,* 320 U.S. at 105 (Douglas), 109 (Murphy), and 114 (Rutledge).

248 those in *Hirabayashi:* Jackson, conference notes, 16 October 1944, Jackson Papers, Library of Congress.

249 "I stop with *Hirabayashi*": Murphy, conference notes, 16 October 1944, in Irons, *Justice at War,* 322.

249 "**at will during wartime**": *Korematsu v. United States,* 323 U.S. 214 (1944). The comments are by Wiecek, *Birth of the Modern Constitution,* 356, and by Simon, *Antagonists,* 155. Commentators almost from the beginning have been highly critical of *Hirabayashi* and *Korematsu.* Two early and still powerful critiques are Eugene V. Rostow, "The Japanese-American Cases—a Disaster," 54 *Yale Law Journal* 489 (1945), and Nanette Dembitz, "Racial Discrimination and the Military Judgment: The Supreme Court's Korematsu and Endo Decisions," 45 *Columbia Law Review* 175 (1945).

249 **tore Black's opinion apart**: Douglas quashed his dissent when Black agreed to add a paragraph noting that the minority viewed the issues of evacuation and detention as inseparable. He later wrote in his memoirs that he always regretted not dissenting in the relocation cases, which were "ever on my conscience." *Court Years,* 279–80.

249 **the law's validity**: *Korematsu,* 323 U.S. at 225, 232–33 (Roberts dissenting).

250 **American security**: *Id.* at 233 (Murphy dissenting).

250 "**The principle then lies**": *Id.* at 242, 246 (Jackson dissenting). The development of Jackson's thinking in this case is examined in John Q. Barrett, "Judgments Judged and Wrongs Remembered . . . Justice Jackson's Korematsu Dissent," 68 *Law and Contemporary Problems* 57 (2005).

250 "**not ours,**" **he declared**: *Korematsu,* 323 U.S. at 225 (Frankfurter concurring).

250 **name of patriotism**: There have been no legal analyses of these cases that have approved the Court's decisions. For a scathing critique, see the "Leviticus" section by Jacobus ten Broek in Broek, Edward N. Barnhart, and Floyd W. Matsun, *Prejudice, War and the Constitution* (1954, 1968). Moreover, evidence has come out showing that the solicitor general knew that there was no military necessity and deliberately misled the Court as to the danger. Peter Irons, "Fancy Dancing in the Marble Palace," 3 *Constitutional Commentary* 35 (1986). Frankfurter, moreover, should have known better, because throughout the war he made it a point to meet with friends and former students to keep up on things. One of the people he met with was John J. McCloy, one of the officials responsible for the plan who certainly knew the truth of the allegations against the Japanese Americans.

251 **steel for defense needs**: The details of the strike, the government's response, and the journey through the courts, are well told in Marcus, *Truman and the Steel Seizure Case.*

252 **or in constitutional form**: *Id.* at 120–23; *Youngstown Sheet & Tube Co. et al. v. Sawyer,* 103 F. Supp. 569 (D.C. 1952).

253 **appeal to the Supreme Court**: 197 F.2d 582 (D.C. Cir. 1952).

253 **justify the seizure**: Howard Ball and Phillip J. Cooper, *Of Power and Right: Hugo Black, William O. Douglas, and America's Constitutional Revolution* (1992), 131; Robert J. Donovan, *Tumultuous Years* (1982), 386. David McCullough, *Truman* (1992), 897, reports that the chief justice was a regular visitor at the White House, and "out of friendship and loyalty" Vinson had offered advice on a subject he must have known would wind up facing a challenge in court.

253 "**most encouraging result**": Harold Burton Diary, entry for 16 May 1952, Burton Papers, Library of Congress.

253 **supported the government**: Conference notes, 16 May 1952, Douglas Papers.

253 **heard oral argument**: *Youngstown Sheet & Tube Co. v. Sawyer,* 343 U.S. 579 (1952).

254 "**Labor Management Relations Act**": *Id.* at 602 (Frankfurter concurring).

254 "the Constitution itself": *Id.* at 585; see the discussion of Black's position in Yarbrough, *Black and His Critics,* 39–42.

254 compensate the taking: *Youngstown Sheet & Tube,* 343 U.S. at 631 (Douglas concurring).

254 Framers had enumerated: *Id.* at 681 (Vinson dissenting).

255 "safeguard the nation": Harry S. Truman, *Memoirs,* 2 vols. (1955–1956), 2:478.

255 "relation to legislation": Louis Jaffe, "Mr. Justice Jackson," 68 *Harvard Law Review* 940, 989 (1955).

255 as to its intent: *Youngstown Sheet & Tube,* 343 U.S. at 637 (Jackson concurring).

256 in Black's opinion: *Id.* at 610–11 (Frankfurter concurring).

MISE-EN-SCÈNE 3
WILEY RUTLEDGE AND *IN RE YAMASHITA* (1946)

257 in early 1946: The literature on the case, nearly all critical of the majority ruling, is impressive given how few laypeople even know about it. Setting aside the many articles, one could look at A. Frank Reel, *The Case of General Yamashita* (1949), and Richard Lael, *The Yamashita Precedent* (1982). I have relied on two recent works, Ferren's *Salt of the Earth* and Allan A. Ryan, *Yamashita's Ghost: War Crimes, MacArthur's Justice, and Command Accountability* (2012).

258 early February 1942: Peter Thompson, *The Battle for Singapore* (2005).

259 would be acquitted: Fisher, *Constitution and 9/11,* 182.

259 "to commit sabotage": *Ex parte Quirin,* 317 U.S. 1 (1942); Presidential Proclamation No. 2561, 7 *Federal Register* 5101 (2 July 1942). For a full and critical view of the case, see Louis Fisher, *Nazi Saboteurs on Trial: A Military Tribunal and American Law* (2003).

259 *Ex parte Milligan:* 71 U.S. 2 (1866).

259 appeal to civilian courts: Jonathan Lurie, *Arming Military Justice,* vol. 1, *The Origins of the United States Court of Military Appeals, 1775–1950* (1992), 184n44.

260 "administrative agency": Black, memorandum on *Quirin,* 29 July 1942, Douglas Papers.

260 would be filed later: *Quirin,* 317 U.S. at 18.

260 he had succeeded: For Stone's composition of the case, see Mason, *Stone,* 658–64. For different views within the Court, see two memoranda by Stone dated 25 September 1942, Douglas Papers.

260 would be treated: See Fisher, *Constitution and 9/11,* and Pious, *War on Terrorism and the Rule of Law.*

261 authority to intervene: Jonathan Lurie, *The Supreme Court and Military Justice* (2013), chap. 1.

261 nation's highest court: Ryan, *Yamashita's Ghost,* 264.

261 "In essence, therefore": Brief in support of petition for habeas corpus, quoted in *id.* at 275.

262 "against foreign powers": *Foster v. Neilson,* 27 U.S. 253, 307 (1829).

263 requirements of the Constitution: Mason, *Stone,* 667–70; Ferren, *Salt of the Earth,* chap. 19. This summary is an abridgment of the give-and-take on the Court. After the dissenters raised the issue of due process, Black became troubled, and Stone tried to work some comments in, but this raised other difficulties. In the end the majority chose to ignore the due process claims.

263   "these proceedings": *In re Yamashita,* 327 U.S. 1, 19–23 (1946).

264   "in recent years": *Id.* at 25, 26, 39, 28 (Murphy dissenting).

265   "may be enforceable": *Id.* at 26, 31.

265   the majority's argument: Ferren, *Salt of the Earth,* 304.

265   "More is at stake": *Yamashita,* 327 U.S. at 41, 42–43 (Rutledge dissenting).

265   full due process of law: Here Rutledge disagreed with Murphy's conclusion
that the commission had been legally established. Rutledge also worried
about his colleague's tone—at one point, Murphy called the commission
proceedings "vengeance"—and so he did not join Murphy's dissent, although
Murphy joined his.

266   law-of-war violation: *Id.* at 53–55.

266   required for culpability: *Id.* at 51–53.

266   "It goes to the very": *Id.* at 45.

267   should be hanged: *Id.* at 51.

267   "I cannot accept": *Id.* at 81.

269   **Rutledge was striving:** Edward S. Corwin, *Total War and the Constitution*
(1947), 121; Charles Fairman, "The Supreme Court on Military Jurisdiction:
Martial Rule in Hawaii and the Yamashita Case," 59 *Harvard Law Review*
833, 872, 870 (1946). See also John T. Ganoe, "The Yamashita Case and the
Constitution," 25 *Oregon Law Review* 143, 155 (1946).

269   "they did not do it": Ryan, *Yamashita's Ghost,* 284–85.

269   "not too late": Ferren, *Salt of the Earth,* 321.

270   in American courts: *Johnson v. Eisentrager,* 339 U.S. 763 (1950).

270   habeas petition: *Id.* at 791 (Black dissenting).

270   "is a principal": The Uniform Code of Military Justice (UCMJ) can be
found at 10 U.S.C. 47, 64 Stat. 109. I am indebted to Jon Lurie for this
information. Under the UCMJ, a general court-martial can try belligerents
for war crimes, as well as local law crimes committed in occupied territory.
If the defendant is a lawful combatant, he may also be tried by an old-
style military commission, which is still provided in the UCMJ. In 2006
and 2009, in response to Supreme Court decisions regarding detainees at
Guantánamo, Congress created separate legal regimes for "underprivileged
belligerents," that is, those who did not fit into the normal definitions of who
could be tried under the UCMJ.

271   "arises directly when the acts": Quoted in Ryan, *Yamashita's Ghost,* 303–4.

274   about those events: Ryan, *Yamashita's Ghost,* 326–30. As of the present, the
United States has not adopted Protocol I, although it is a signatory to the
Geneva Convention.

274   insular possessions: *Rasul v. Bush,* 542 U.S. 466, 474–75 (2004). Until
July 4, 1946, the Philippines, the site of Yamashita's trial, was still a posses-
sion of the United States.

274   "far from satisfied here": *Hamdan v. Rumsfeld,* 548 U.S. 557, 618, 603
(2006).

274   in several decades: There were a few cases immediately following the war. In
Homma v. Patterson, 327 U.S. 759 (1946), and *Hiroto v. MacArthur,* 338 U.S.
197 (1948), the Court approved the legitimacy of other Japanese war trials.

CHAPTER 9: THE PRIMA DONNAS II

276   **discrimination against blacks:** *Nixon v. Herndon,* 273 U.S. 536 (1927), *Nixon
v. Condon,* 286 U.S. 73 (1932), and *Smith v. Allwright,* 321 U.S. 649 (1944).

276 **therefore nonjusticiable:** *Wood v. Broom,* 287 U.S. 1 (1932).

276 **the Illinois dispute:** *Luther v. Borden,* 48 U.S. (7 How.) 1 (1849). For the doctrine, see Philippa Strum, *The Supreme Court and "Political Questions": A Study in Judicial Evasion* (1974); *Colegrove* is covered at pp. 41–54.

276 **"The petitioners ask":** *Colegrove v. Green,* 328 U.S. 549, 552 (1946); Richard C. Cortner, *The Apportionment Cases* (1970), chap. 1.

277 **any workable remedy:** *Colegrove,* 328 U.S. at 565–66 (Rutledge concurring).

277 **"intended to prohibit":** *Id.* at 569 (Black dissenting). For his views on sovereignty, see Yarbrough, *Mr. Justice Black and His Critics,* 229–30.

278 **constitutional litigation:** *Gomillion v. Lightfoot,* 364 U.S. 339, 346–47 (1960).

279 **any particular remedy:** Seth Stern and Stephen Wermiel, *Justice Brennan: Liberal Champion* (2010), 184–86.

279 **6–2 majority:** Stewart, who had been unsure at the first conference, now joined the majority, while Whittaker, in Frankfurter's camp originally, had become ill and did not participate. He retired from the Court a few days later on 31 March.

279 **resolve the problem:** *Baker v. Carr,* 369 U.S. 186 (1962).

280 **by partisan politics:** *Id.* at 269 (Frankfurter dissenting). Harlan joined Frankfurter's dissent and dissented separately, at 330, saying that while the present system was far from perfect, he saw nothing in the Constitution compelling change, an opinion that Frankfurter joined.

280 **Alabama apportionment scheme:** *Reynolds v. Sims,* 377 U.S. 533 (1964).

281 **"ranked as fundamental":** *Palko v. Connecticut,* 302 U.S. 319, 327, 325 (1937).

281 **could or could not do:** Black to conference, 23 March 1945, Frankfurter Papers, Harvard Law School Library.

282 **"give a fair trial":** *Adamson v. California,* 332 U.S. 46, 50–51, 54 (1947); *Twining v. New Jersey,* 211 U.S. 78 (1908). For the development of the different arguments, and the personalities, see Wiecek, *Birth of the Modern Constitution,* 511–23.

282 **not be reaffirmed:** *Adamson,* 332 U.S. at 68, 70 (Black dissenting).

282 **"all doubtful evidence":** Newman, *Black,* 354. Black's essay started a scholarly cottage industry of its own. At Frankfurter's suggestion, Charles Fairman attacked Black's interpretation in "Does the Fourteenth Amendment Incorporate the Bill of Rights? The Original Understanding," 2 *Stanford Law Review* 5 (1949), which in turn triggered a response from William W. Crosskey in his *Politics and the Constitution in the History of the United States* (1953). Black also responded to Fairman more than twenty years later in his concurrence in *Duncan v. Louisiana,* 391 U.S. 145, 162 (1968). While Amar, *Bill of Rights,* argues that the framers of the Fourteenth did intend to incorporate the entire Bill of Rights, other scholars have found the evidence far from conclusive. See Michael Kent Curtis, *No State Shall Abridge: The Fourteenth Amendment and the Bill of Rights* (1986), and Nelson, *Fourteenth Amendment.*

283 **"is not whether an infraction":** *Adamson,* 332 U.S. 59, 67–68 (Frankfurter concurring).

284 **common set of principles:** *Rochin v. California,* 342 U.S. 165, 172 (1952); *Uveges v. Pennsylvania,* 335 U.S. 437, 449–50 (1948).

285 **was not that wrong:** *Adamson,* 332 U.S. at 123 (Murphy dissenting); Fine, *Murphy,* 503–4.

285 **unusual situations:** Both *Twining* and *Adamson* were eventually overruled, the former in *Malloy v. Hogan,* 378 U.S. 1 (1964), and the latter in *Griffin v. California,* 380 U.S. 609 (1965). See Richard C. Cortner, *The Supreme Court and the Second Bill of Rights* (1981), 228–29.

285 **"expected from the states":** *In re Oliver,* 333 U.S. 257, 286 (1948). Frankfurter and Jackson dissented on technical grounds.

285 *Weeks v. United States:* 232 U.S. 383 (1914).

286 **"constable has blundered":** *People v. Defore,* 242 N.Y. 13, 21 (1926).

286 **"search and seizure":** Murphy, conference notes, cited in Wiecek, *Birth of the Modern Constitution,* 525.

286 **test for due process:** *Wolf v. Colorado,* 338 U.S. 25 (1949).

286 **glosses to the text:** *Id.* at 39 (Black concurring).

287 **evidence—inadmissible:** *Id.* at 40 (Douglas dissenting).

287 **illegally obtained evidence:** *Id.* at 41 (Murphy dissenting).

287 **enforce the Fourth Amendment:** *Mapp v. Ohio,* 367 U.S. 643 (1961). For the case, see Carolyn N. Long, *Mapp v. Ohio: Guarding Against Unreasonable Searches and Seizures* (2006).

287 **other than the exclusionary rule:** *Mapp,* 367 U.S. at 661, 662 (Black concurring), at 666 (Douglas concurring).

288 **"sense of judicial restraint":** *Id.* at 672 (Harlan dissenting).

288 **"shocks the conscience":** *Adamson v. California,* 332 U.S. 46, 67–68 (1947) (Frankfurter concurring); *Rochin v. California,* 342 U.S. 165, 172, 173 (1952).

289 **"Anglo-American jurisdictions":** *Stein v. New York,* 346 U.S. 156, 199 (1953) (Frankfurter dissenting).

289 **"formulated anywhere":** *Malinski v. New York,* 324 U.S. 417 (1945) (Frankfurter concurring).

289 **death in Louisiana:** The trial had been perfunctory; court-appointed counsel had offered no defense and did not appeal the conviction, despite serious doubts as to whether Francis was guilty. His conviction rested on two confessions that might well have been coerced, if counsel had bothered to challenge them. The Court, however, was concerned not with the trial, which had not been appealed, but with the failure of the execution. The full story of the incident is told in Arthur S. Miller and Jeffrey H. Bowman, *Death by Installments: The Ordeal of Willie Francis* (1988).

289 **violate due process:** *Louisiana ex rel. Francis v. Resweber,* 329 U.S. 459 (1947).

289 **"I am prevented":** Frankfurter to Burton, 13 December 1946, Burton Papers. A year later, he learned that his good friend Learned Hand considered it personally shocking that Louisiana would insist on a "second go for a pound of flesh." Frankfurter said that while he personally found it "barbaric," he knew that the community, either in Louisiana or in the country at large, did not share his view, and "therefore I had no right to find a violation of the Due Process Clause." Frankfurter to Hand, 6 December 1947, Frankfurter Papers, Library of Congress. Frankfurter's role is analyzed in William M. Wiecek, "Felix Frankfurter, Incorporation, and the Willie Francis Case," 26 *Journal of Supreme Court History* 53 (2001).

290 **he had been proposing:** *Francis,* 329 U.S. at 472 (Burton dissenting).

290 **"enjoined by the Court":** *Id.* at 466, 471 (Frankfurter concurring).

290 **"would have felt":** C. Herman Pritchett, *Civil Liberties and the Vinson Court* (1954), 246.

290 **"confessions from them":** *Haley v. Ohio,* 332 U.S. 596, 601 (1947).

291 "Humility in this context": *Id.* at 602, 603 (Frankfurter concurring).

292 " 'clear and present danger' test": *Brandenburg v. Ohio,* 395 U.S. 444, 454 (1969) (Douglas concurring).

292 "justices of the Court": Black, *Constitutional Faith,* 50, 52.

292 "admonition for moderation": Douglas, *Court Years,* 47.

292 "Whether the Commonwealth": Frankfurter to Morison, 6 January 1942 [misdated 1941], Frankfurter Papers, Harvard Law School Library. Ellery Sedgwick was the editor of *The Atlantic Monthly,* which published Frankfurter's criticism of the judge and the trial in the Sacco and Vanzetti case.

293 offered by the First Amendment: See, for example, Black's concurring opinion, joined by Douglas, in the landmark case of *New York Times v. Sullivan,* 376 U.S. 254, 293 (1964), in which the Court held that the First Amendment protected the press from libel suits when they criticized public officials.

293 not penalizing speech: *Milk Wagon Drivers Union v. Meadowmoor Dairies,* 312 U.S. 287 (1941). The Black dissent is at 299 and that of Reed at 317. The Brandeis opinion is *Senn v. Tiles Layers Protective Union,* 301 U.S. 468 (1937).

293 the *Dennis* case: *Dennis v. United States,* 341 U.S. 494 (1951). For details about the case, see Belknap, *Cold War Political Justice.*

293 1940s and early 1950s: For this anticommunist hysteria, see Belknap, *Cold War Political Justice;* Stanley I. Kutler, *The American Inquisition* (1982); Richard Fried, *Nightmare in Red* (1990); and David Oshinsky, *A Conspiracy So Immense* (1983).

294 grounds for dismissal: Robert Justin Goldstein, *American Blacklist: The Attorney General's List of Subversive Organizations* (2008).

296 warnings from the bench: *Sacher v. United States,* 343 U.S. 1 (1952)

296 publicly attacked them: *Id.* at 14 (Black dissenting).

296 noble in the law: *Id.* at 23 (Frankfurter dissenting). Douglas joined both Black and Frankfurter, agreeing that "this is the classic case where the trial for contempt should be held before another judge. I also agree with Mr. Justice Black that petitioners were entitled by the Constitution to a trial by jury."

296 many other variables: See Kalven, *Worthy Tradition,* chaps. 9–16.

297 incited unlawful action: *Masses Publishing Co. v. Patten,* 244 Fed. 535 (S.D.N.Y. 1917). Hand, however, was overruled by the Second Circuit.

297 present danger test: *United States v. Dennis et al.,* 183 F.2d 201, 209 (2nd Cir. 1950); *Gitlow v. New York,* 268 U.S. 562 (1925).

298 "next crisis came along": Address to Law School of Hebrew University, Jerusalem, 22 December 1987, quoted in Robert M. Lichtman, "McCarthyism and the Court: The Need for an Uncommon Portion of Fortitude in the Judges," 39 *Journal of the Supreme Court Historical Society* 107 (2014).

298 "should be bold": Douglas, *Court Years,* 38.

298 communist leaders: A good overview is Arthur J. Sabin, *In Calmer Times: The Supreme Court and Red Monday* (1999).

298 *Bailey v. Richardson:* American *Communications Association v. Douds,* 339 U.S. 382 (1950); *Bailey v. Richardson,* 341 U.S. 918 (1951). *Bailey* relied heavily on the attorney general's list of suspected organizations, which had been upheld in *Joint Anti-Fascist Refugee Committee v. McGrath,* 341 U.S. 123 (1949).

298 never actually spoken: Kalven, *Worthy Tradition,* 193.

299   "avoid the danger": Dennis, 183 F.2d at 212.
299   "affirmance requires": Conference notes, 9 December 1950, Douglas Papers.
299   "signal is awaited": *Dennis,* 341 U.S. at 509.
299   action should occur: For an attack on this distortion of the original Holmes-Brandeis formulation, see Louis B. Boudin, " 'Seditious Doctrines' and the 'Clear and Present Danger' Rule," 38 *Virginia Law Review* 143 and 315 (1952). The decision is defended by Wallace Mendelson, "Clear and Present Danger—from Schenck to Dennis," 52 *Columbia Law Review* 313 (1952).
299   time for discussion: *Schaeffer v. United States,* 251 U.S. 466, 482, 483 (1920) (Brandeis dissenting). For a sharp critique (by a former Brandeis clerk) of the notion that application of the clear and present danger doctrine would leave the government powerless to protect itself, see Nathan Nathanson, "The Communist Trial and the Clear-and-Present-Danger Test," 63 *Harvard Law Review* 1167 (1950).
300   "found in a dictionary": *Dennis,* 341 U.S. at 517, 550, 521, 523 (Frankfurter concurring).
300   "Neither had Brandeis": Feldman, *Scorpions,* 347.
301   "Communist Party techniques": *Dennis,* 341 U.S. at 561, 562 (Jackson concurring).
301   "it seeks to accomplish": *Id.* at 573.
301   "The goblin'll get you": Ball and Cooper, *Of Power and Right,* 144.
301   "not destroy, the nation": Newman, *Black,* 402–3.
302   "are short ones": *Id.,* 404.
302   "To the Founders": *Dennis,* 341 U.S. at 579, 580 (Black dissenting).
303   "in a free society": *Id.* at 581.
303   "is not absolute": *Id.* (Douglas dissenting).
303   "Some nations less resilient": *Id.* at 588, 590.
303   "liberties of every citizen": *Id.* at 584, 583. For an examination of Douglas's speech jurisprudence, see L. A. Powe Jr., "Justice Douglas, the First Amendment, and the Protection of Rights," in Wasby, *"He Shall Not Pass This Way Again,"* 69–90.
303   gay marriage, civil rights: In the October 2012 term the justices heard cases on all of these issues: *Association for Molecular Pathology v. Myriad Genetics Inc.,* 133 S. Ct. 2107 (2013) (gene patent); *United States v. Windsor,* 133 S. Ct. 2884 (2013) (gay marriage); and *Shelby County v. Holder,* 133 S. Ct. 2612 (2013) (civil rights).

MISE-EN-SCÈNE 4: BLACK IN *BETTS V. BRADY* (1942)

307   "trained defense counsel": Quoted in Barth, *Prophets with Honor,* 81.
307   Sixth Amendment: *Johnson v. Zerbst,* 304 U.S. 458 (1938).
307   provide a lawyer: *Powell v. Alabama,* 287 U.S. 45 (1932).
307   applying to the high court: *Betts v. Brady,* 316 U.S. 455 (1942). Details of the Betts trial can be found in Barth, *Prophets with Honor,* 80–88, and Anthony Lewis, *Gideon's Trumpet* (1964), 109–10.
308   "by the Fourteenth Amendment": *Betts,* 316 U.S. at 464, 465.
308   "not represented by counsel": *Id.* at 473.
308   "The Sixth Amendment stands": *Zerbst,* 304 U.S. at 462–63.
309   counsel on request: *Betts,* 316 U.S. at 474 (Black dissenting). Black, it should be noted, had signed on to Cardozo's *Palko* opinion calling for selective incorporation. In *Betts,* he took the first step on what would become

one of the defining characteristics of his jurisprudence, the belief that the Fourteenth Amendment incorporated *all* of the protections of the first eight amendments and applied them to the states.

310 **"our own Bill of Rights"**: *New York Times,* 2 August 1942, quoted in Lewis, *Gideon's Trumpet,* 112.

310 **"often tenuous"**: Unsigned note, "Right to Counsel," 42 *Columbia Law Review* 1205, 1208 (1942).

310 **"enforce the Bill of Rights"**: *Foster v. Illinois,* 332 U.S. 134, 139 (1947). Black dissented at 139, Rutledge at 141, with all of the dissenters signing on to both opinions.

311 **"must have legal assistance"**: *Uveges v. Pennsylvania,* 355 U.S. 437, 441 (1948); see also *Bute v. Illinois,* 333 U.S. 640 (1948).

311 **"circumstances were 'special'"**: Yale Kamisar, "How Earl Warren's Twenty-Two Years in Law Enforcement Affected His Work as Chief Justice," 3 *Ohio State Journal of Criminal Law* 21 (2005).

311 **dissented in *Betts***: *Gryger v. Burke,* 334 U.S. 728 (1948); *Townsend v. Burke,* 334 U.S. 736 (1948).

311 **"cogency of their argument"**: Francis A. Allen, "The Supreme Court, Federalism, and State Systems of Criminal Justice," 8 *DePaul Law Review* 213, 230 (1959).

312 **reversed the conviction**: Lewis, *Gideon's Trumpet,* 114. The last case affirming conviction was *Quicksall v. Michigan,* 339 U.S. 660 (1950).

312 **"into that holding"**: *Hudson v. North Carolina,* 363 U.S. 697 (1960). Justice Clark's dissent is at 704; he was joined only by Justice Whittaker.

312 **noncapital case**: *Griffin v. Illinois,* 351 U.S. 12 (1956). Black spoke for himself, Chief Justice Warren, Douglas, and Brennan; Frankfurter concurred in the result but not the reasoning. Justices Burton, Minton, Reed, and Harlan dissented.

313 **"should be overruled"**: *McNeal v. Culver,* 365 U.S. 109, 116 (1961); the Douglas concurrence is at 117, 119.

313 **"equal protection of the laws"**: William J. Brennan Jr., "The Bill of Rights and the States," 36 *NYU Law Review* 761, 773 (1961).

313 **"overrule Betts and Brady"**: Newman, *Black,* 526. For relations between Black and Frankfurter, and their ultimate reconciliation, see Simon, *Antagonists.*

313 **applicable to the states**: *Carnley v. Cochran,* 369 U.S. 506, 517 (1962) (Black concurring). For details on choosing the "right" case, see Powe, *Warren Court and American Politics,* 381–85.

315 **"should be overruled"**: *Gideon v. Wainwright,* 372 U.S. 335, 339 (1963).

315 **"fair system of justice"**: *Id.* at 344–45, citing *Powell v. Alabama,* 287 U.S. 45, 68–69 (1932).

315 **to the states**: The Douglas opinion is at *Gideon,* 372 U.S. at 345, that of Clark at 347, and Harlan's is at 350.

316 **"Of course I would"**: Lewis, *Gideon's Trumpet,* 221–22.

316 **"and won 9–0"**: Powe, *Warren Court and American Politics,* 385. Powe also sees *Gideon* as a civil rights case. Although Gideon himself was white, the system he had been tried under had acted prejudicially to the poor and racial minorities for decades. The rest of the Warren Court's criminal procedure cases all came from the North.

316 **"to have a lawyer"**: Lewis, *Gideon's Trumpet,* 203.

317 **reached equilibrium:** See John Thomas Moran, *Gideon Undone: The Crisis in Indigent Defense Spending* (1983), a joint publication of the American Bar Association and the National Legal Aid and Defender Association.

317 **with lawyers' help:** Lewis, *Gideon's Trumpet,* 201.

317 **"happened in {Florida} soon":** Friedman, *Will of the People,* 273.

318 **"to see it overruled":** Newman, *Black,* 528.

CHAPTER 10: LOWER FEDERAL COURTS, THE STATES, AND FOREIGN TRIBUNALS

318 **"because we are final":** *Brown v. Allen,* 344 U.S. 443, 532, 540 (1953) (Jackson concurring).

319 **Foreign Intelligence Surveillance Court:** Information about the federal judiciary can be found at http://www.uscourts.gov, a site maintained by the Administrative Office of the U.S. Courts.

320 **cert in only 24:** Richard J. Richardson and Kenneth N. Vines, "Review, Dissent, and the Appellate Process: A Political Interpretation," 29 *Journal of Politics* 597, 600 (1967).

320 **decided correctly:** See, for example, *United States v. Windsor,* 133 S. Ct. 2675 (2013), constitutionally invalidating the Defense of Marriage Act (1996) and confirming the ruling of the Court of Appeals for the Second Circuit.

320 **"ambit of the lower courts":** Frankfurter and Landis, *Business of the Supreme Court,* 3–4.

321 **for white applicants:** *Hopwood v. Texas,* 78 F.3d 932 (5th Cir., 1996). When the law school requested a rehearing *en banc,* a majority of the judges voted no, but seven members of the circuit, none of whom had sat on the case, filed a dissent indicating that the motion to rehear should have been granted.

321 **several considerations:** *Grutter v. Bollinger,* 539 U.S. 306 (2003). In a companion case, *Gratz v. Bollinger,* 538 U.S. 244 (2003), the Court struck down the undergraduate admissions program where race was given, according to the majority, a determinative role. In response to these rulings, Michigan voters adopted a constitutional amendment that banned the use of race as a factor in admissions at state universities. The Court upheld the ban in *Schuette v. Coalition to Defend Affirmative Action,* 134 S. Ct. 1623 (2014).

321 **do not like to dissent:** Richard A. Posner, *How Judges Think* (2008), 32–34.

321 **considerable attention:** See, for example, Robert F. Blomquist, "Playing on Words: Judge Richard A. Posner's Appellate Opinions, 1981–82: Ruminations on Sexy Judicial Style During an Extraordinary Rookie Season," 68 *University of Cincinnati Law Review* 651 (2000), and by the same author, "Dissent, Posner Style: Judge Richard A. Posner's First Decade of Dissenting Opinions, 1981–1991—Toward an Aesthetics of Judicial Dissenting Style," 69 *Missouri Law Review* 73 (2004).

321 **"in which the issue":** Coffin, *Ways of a Judge,* 186. For the use of a dissent to signal the Supreme Court, see also Virginia A. Hettinger, Stefanie A. Lindquist, and Wendy L. Martinek, *Judging on a Collegial Court* (2005), 76–77.

322 **the majority opinion:** See, for example, Ginsburg, "Dissent Is an 'Appeal' for the Future"; Scalia, "Dissenting Opinion."

322 **"disputing a point":** Helen Wilson Nies, "Dissents at the Federal Circuit and Supreme Court Review," 45 *American University Law Review* 1519, 1520 (1996).

322 "a better argument": Alice Fleetwood Bartee, *Privacy Rights: Cases and Causes Won Before the Supreme Court* (2006), 23–24. She adds that it is also helpful if the attorney can show the case was lost on a closely divided vote.

322 "When a judge of one": Scalia, "Dissenting Opinion," 36–37.

322 "hopes were realized": Evan A. Evans, "The Dissenting Opinion—Its Use and Abuse," 3 *Missouri Law Review* 120, 131 (1938).

323 reliability and trustworthiness: *United States v. Ramirez-Lopez,* 315 F.3d 1143 (9th Cir., 2003).

323 "No kidding, man": *Id.* at 1159, 1160–61 (Kozinski dissenting). See also Gregory S. Fisher, "The Greatest Dissent?," 28 *Alaska Bar Rag* 30 (2004).

324 "a great country or what": Case dismissed by *United States v. Ramirez-Lopez,* 327 F.3d 829 (9th Cir., 2003).

324 writing dissentals: This section is based on Indraneel Sur, "How Far Do Voices Carry: Dissents from Denials of Rehearing En Banc," 2006 *Wisconsin Law Review* 1315, and Alex Kozinski and James Burnham, "I Say Dissental, You Say Concurral," 121 *Yale Law Journal Online* 601 (2012).

325 guarding the henhouse: *Crutchfield v. United States,* 142 F.2d 170, 177 (9th Cir., 1943) (Denman dissental).

325 not taking the case: *United States v. New York, New Haven & Hartford Railroad,* 276 F.2d 525, 549 (2nd Cir., 1960) (Clark dissental).

325 "did not participate in it": *Id.* at 553 (Friendly concurral).

325 "favorite local newspaper": *United States v. Stewart,* 597 F.3d 514, 519 (2nd Cir., 2010) (Pooler concurral).

326 good enough for the judges: *Isaacs v. Kemp,* 782 F.2d 896, 897 (11th Cir., 1986) (Hill dissental).

326 occur in state courts: There is a growing body of literature on state courts, but there is still relatively little on dissent in those courts. The little there is seems more concerned with how dissent fits into certain theoretical constructs. See, for example, Paul Brace and Melinda Gann Hall, "Neo-institutionalism and Dissent in State Supreme Courts," 52 *Journal of Politics* 54 (1990), and Dean Jaros and Bradley C. Canon, "Dissent on State Supreme Courts: The Differential Significance of Characteristics of Judges," 15 *Midwest Journal of Political Science* 322 (1971).

326 opposition to the death penalty: Patrick K. Brown, "The Rise and Fall of Rose Bird: A Career Killed by the Death Penalty," http://cschs.org/02 _history/images/CSCHS_2007-Brown.pdf. Very few cases have reached the Supreme Court regarding questions associated with elected judges. In *Caperton v. Massey Coal,* 556 U.S. 868 (2009), however, the Court held that the large donations made by a coal company tainted the judicial process, which required that the judge recuse himself from any case involving the company. Sandra Day O'Connor, herself a former state court judge, has spoken out against the practice of electing judges.

327 they may go further: See Lawrence Friedman, "Notable Dissents in State Constitutional Cases: The Virtue of Uncertainty," 68 *Albany Law Review* 373 (2005), which examines a case involving the Fourth Amendment's protection against unreasonable search and seizure, the Massachusetts Constitution's comparable provision, and the dissent by Justice Nolan. *Guiney v. Police Commissioner of Boston,* 582 N.E.2d 523 (Mass. 1991).

327 Constitution it is not: *San Antonio Independent School District v. Rodriguez,* 411 U.S. 1 (1973).

327 **"support the judgment"**: *Murdock v. Memphis,* 87 U.S. 590 (1875); *Fox Film Corp. v. Muller,* 296 U.S. 207, 210 (1935).

327 **majority opinion**: Unlike federal appeals courts, whose decisions are binding only within their circuit, a state intermediate appellate court's rulings govern the entire state unless reversed by the state supreme court.

327 **increased over the years**: A statistical sampling of Georgia Supreme Court opinions shows that it took thirty years (1846–1876) before the first hundred dissents were recorded. A second sample of a hundred covers 1910–1915, and the third sample took only two years (1950–1952) to generate a hundred. That same number occurred in fourteen months in 1980–1981, and twenty-two months in 1999–2001. R. Perry Sentell Jr., "Dissenting Opinions in the Georgia Supreme Court," 36 *Georgia Law Review* 539 (2002).

328 **"dissented from by them"**: Stanley H. Fuld, "The Voices of Dissent," 62 *Columbia Law Review* 923, 925 (1962).

328 **"A dissent can have"**: Leroy Rountree Hassell, "Appellate Dissent: A Worthwhile Endeavor or an Exercise in Futility?," 47 *Howard Law Journal* 383, 386 (2004). See also Sylvia H. Walbolt and Stephanie C. Zimmerman, " 'I Must Dissent.' Why?," 82 *Florida Bar Journal* 36 (2008), for other examples of the effects of dissents within a court.

328 **Supreme Court had seventeen**: Robert J. Sickels, "The Illusion of Judicial Consensus: Zoning Decisions in the Maryland Court of Appeals," 59 *American Political Science Review* 100 (1965).

328 **riled his colleagues**: Seymour Simon, "Giving Dissent Its Due," 18 *Chicago Bar Association Record* 34 (2004).

328 **in the latter group**: William E. Hirt, "In the Matter of Dissents Inter Judices de Jure," 31 *Pennsylvania Bar Association Quarterly* 256, 258n1 (1960).

328 **of dissenting opinions**: The state supreme court interpreted this as an economy measure, and dissenting opinions continued to be published in the *Southern Reporter,* a private publication. The prohibition was repealed in the 1921 constitution.

328 **and statutory law**: Brandon L. Bigelow and Dalman Garcia, "The Dissents of Justice Martha B. Sosman: Judicial Restraint and Intellectual Honesty," 42 *New England Law Review* 453 (2008); Jillian Kasow, "Judge Carmen Beauchamp Ciparick: A Glimpse into the Senior Associate Judge's Judicial Philosophy Through Her Dissents," 73 *Albany Law Review* 953 (2010); Peter A. Mancuso, "The Independent Jurist: An Analysis of Robert S. Smith's Dissenting Opinions," *id.* at 1019; David B. Oppenheimer and Allan Brotsky, eds., *The Great Dissents of the "Lone Dissenter": Justice Jesse W. Carter's Twenty Tumultuous Years on the California Supreme Court* (2010); and Katherine L. Brash, "Chief Justice O'Niell and the Louisiana Civil Code—the Influence of His Dissents," 19 *Tulane Law Review* 436 (1945).

329 **this type of education**: About this time, I attended the University of Virginia Law School, where dissents were important teaching tools in nearly all courses. One should add, of course, that in some cases professors believed the majority had been right, but the teaching device also proved applicable in those cases.

329 **recognized and applauded**: The following is based on Hassell, "Appellate Dissent," 386–87.

329 **colleagues on the bench**: Kermit V. Lipez, "Some Reflections on Dissenting," 57 *Maine Law Review* 313 (2005), has a section on "the audiences." Lipez was

then on the Court of Appeals for the First Circuit, but prior to that he had served on the Maine Supreme Judicial Court.

329 **just two years later:** *Stern v. Cincinnati Insurance Co.,* 477 S.E.2d 517 (Va. 1996), overruled in *Newman v. Erie Insurance Exchange,* 507 S.E.2d 348 (Va. 1998). Kimberly D. Richman has praised the role dissents have played as state judges have entered a whole new field of law—that of lesbians, gays, bisexuals, and transgender. See "Talking Back: The Discursive Role of the Dissent in LGBT Custody and Adoption Cases," 16 *Law and Sexuality* 77 (2007).

330 **"unjust and outmoded" law:** *Coleman v. Soccer Association of Columbia,* 2013 Md. LEXIS 460.

330 **"the crime and the defendant":** *Atkins v. Commonwealth,* 534 S.E.2d 312, 321 (Va. 2000) (Hassell dissenting).

331 **cruel and unusual punishment:** *Atkins v. Virginia,* 536 U.S. 304 (2002), overruling *Penry v. Lynaugh,* 492 U.S. 302 (1989).

331 **"The doctrine of *stare decisis*":** *Selected Risks Insurance Co. v. Dean,* 355 S.E.2d 579, 581 (Va. 1987).

331 **properly applicable:** See *Nunnally v. Artis,* 492 S.E.2d 126, 129 (Va. 1997), overruling *Scarpa v. Melzig,* 379 S.E.2d 307 (Va. 1989).

331 **"The Italian Constitutional High Court":** *New York Times,* 27 March 1957, 5, quoted in Fuld, "Voices of Dissent," 923.

332 **"understand and admire it":** Ruth Bader Ginsburg, "Remarks on Writing Separately," 65 *Washington Law Review* 133, 134 (1990). The quotation is from René David and John E. C. Brierley, *Major Legal Systems in the World Today,* 2nd ed. (1978), 129.

333 **divided in its reasoning:** Ginsburg, "Writing Separately," 136–37.

333 **to be kept secret:** Nadelmann, "Judicial Dissent," 420.

333 **does not have an opinion:** Dieter Grimm, "Judicial Dissent: General Principles," material prepared for a course in global constitutionalism at the Yale Law School and used with the kind permission of Dr. Grimm and Dean Robert Post, the two teachers of that course.

333 **still do not have dissents:** François Luchaire argues against the introduction of dissenting opinions in the French high court for pretty much all of the reasons familiar to those who have opposed dissents in the United States: dissents undermine the authority, the credibility, and the efficiency of the institution. "Is the Adoption of Dissenting Opinions in France Desirable?," trans. Hunter Smith. Mario Gorlani reaches a similar conclusion for Italian courts. Both in materials for the Global Constitutionalism course.

334 **a difficult case:** Ijaz Hussein, *Dissenting and Separate Opinions at the World Court* (1984), 2, 4.

334 **therefore be improper:** Nadelmann, "Judicial Dissent," 416–17.

335 **more than four centuries:** *Id.* at 421.

335 **violating the charter:** Allen Linden, "Flexible Federalism: The Canadian Way," in *Patterns of Regionalism and Federalism: Lessons for the U.K.,* ed. Jörg Fedtke and Basil S. Markesinis (2006), 42. In the United States, once a plaintiff has demonstrated reasonable evidence that a statute has violated a right, the burden falls on the government to show that the law has not done so. In Canada, there is more of a burden on the plaintiff to make the initial case that a right has been violated.

335 "concepts and solutions": Claire L'Heureux-Dubé, "The Dissenting Opinion: Voice of the Future?," 38 *Osgoode Hall Law Journal* 495, 496 (2000).

336 "constructive trust": The idea of the constructive trust is that a person may hold an equitable interest in property, even when that person does not have legal title, in cases where the denial of the equitable interest would result in the "unjust enrichment" of the legal owner.

336 by women for equality: The dissent is in *Murdoch v. Murdoch,* 1 S.C.R. 423 (1975); adopted as plurality opinion in *Rathwell v. Rathwell,* 2 S.C.R. 436 (1978), and then by majority in *Pettkus v. Becker,* 2 S.C.R. 834 (1980); L'Heureux-Dubé, "Dissenting Opinion," 505.

336 validated the new law: L'Heureux-Dubé, "Dissenting Opinion," 510–11. The validating opinion is in *Regina v. Mills,* 3 S.C.R. 668 (1999).

337 statute in question: Michael Hudson McHugh, "The High Court of Australia," 22 *Journal of Supreme Court History* 1, 2–3 (1997). McHugh served on the High Court from 1989 until 2005, when he reached the mandatory retirement age of seventy. The article gives a good overview of the history and operation of the High Court.

337 "decision is as it is": *Duncan v. Queensland,* 22 C.L.R. 556 (1916).

337 "hotly debated": Andrew Lynch, "Dissenting Judgments," in *The Oxford Companion to the High Court of Australia,* ed. Tony Blackshield, Michael Coper, and George Williams (2001), 217.

337 court's later development: Andrew Lynch, " 'The Intelligence of a Future Day': The Vindication of Constitutional Dissent in the High Court of Australia, 1981–2003," 29 *Sydney Law Review* 195, 209–10 (2007).

338 that very democracy: See, for example, L'Heureux-Dubé, "Dissenting Opinion," 503.

CHAPTER 11: CONTINUING THEMES,
FROM WARREN TO ROBERTS

339 "the story will turn out": Tushnet, *I Dissent,* 221.

340 First Amendment rights: In *Citizens United v. Federal Election Commission,* 558 U.S. 310 (2010), a 5–4 majority struck down key provisions of the McCain-Feingold Bipartisan Campaign Reform Act, overruling parts of *McConnell v. Federal Election Commission,* 540 U.S. 93 (2003), as well as overruling *Austin v. Michigan Chamber of Commerce,* 494 U.S. 652 (1990), which prohibited the spending of corporate money in federal elections. O'Connor had been in the majority in both of the earlier cases. The difference was not a change of attitudes—a majority of Americans favored the laws—but a change of personnel. Then the Court did away with overall contribution limits in *McCutcheon v. Federal Election Commission,* 134 S. Ct. 1434 (2014).

341 philosophy did occur: The two best survey volumes on the Warren Court are Powe, *Warren Court and American Politics,* and Michal R. Belknap, *The Supreme Court Under Earl Warren, 1953–1969* (2005). For interpretive essays on the justices, see Mark V. Tushnet, ed., *The Warren Court in Historical and Political Perspective* (1993).

341 far from unanimous: *Gideon v. Wainwright,* 372 U.S. 335 (1963), incorporated and applied the Sixth Amendment right to counsel. *New York Times v. Sullivan,* 376 U.S. 254 (1964), extended First Amendment protection to include criticism of public officials. In *Epperson v. Arkansas,* 393 U.S. 97

(1968), the Court found a state law prohibiting the teaching of evolution to violate the Establishment Clause, and in *Brandenburg v. Ohio*, 395 U.S. 444 (1969), the Court finally buried seditious libel.

341 **the 1957 term**: Lanier, *Of Time and Judicial Behavior*, 99–100.

341 **minority 202 times**: Epstein et al., *Supreme Court Compendium*, 652–53, 655.

341 **"ought to be expressed"**: O'Brien, *Storm Center*, 107–8.

341 **majority decisions**: Friedman, *Will of the People*, examines this process in regard to individual decisions.

341 **the basis of race**: Lacking any explicit statutory or constitutional basis to do so, the Court in the sit-in cases, starting with *Garner v. Louisiana*, 368 U.S. 157 (1961), managed to overturn the trespass decisions by resorting to technicalities. In *Bell v. Maryland*, 378 U.S. 226 (1964), Black, joined by Harlan II and White, dissented and argued that the owners of private property, such as restaurants and hotels, had a right to refuse service to anyone they chose. Douglas entered a concurrence arguing that businesses serving the public, under common law, could not discriminate. That view was adopted in the Civil Rights Act. Shortly afterward, in *Hamm v. Rock Hill*, 379 U.S. 306 (1964), the Court ruled that enactment of that law abated prosecutions against people who, if the act had been in force at the time of their arrest, would have been entitled to service.

341 **religious observance**: *Sherbert v. Verner*, 374 U.S. 398 (1963), essentially overruling *Braunfeld v. Brown*, 366 U.S. 599 (1961), and *Gallagher v. Crown Kosher Supermarket of Massachusetts*, 366 U.S. 617 (1971). Brennan, along with Douglas and Stewart, dissented in the latter cases. Chief Justice Warren wrote the majority opinions in those cases but joined the majority in *Sherbert*.

341 **accepted by the Court**: See Melvin I. Urofsky, *The Continuity of Change: The Supreme Court and Individual Liberties, 1953–1986* (1991), chaps. 7 and 8.

342 **forceful critics of the case**: Shortly after the Warren Court decided *Miranda*, Congress enacted a law, known as Section 3501, that provided a very broad and loose definition of what constituted a voluntary confession. No administration ever tried to use Section 3501 or defend it in court. But a conservative public advocacy group persuaded a Fourth Circuit panel to use it to override *Miranda*. In *Dickerson v. United States*, 530 U.S. 428 (2000), Rehnquist wrote for a 7–2 Court that *Miranda* was now "a constitutional rule" and therefore not subject to congressional override.

343 **"appeal to God for help"**: John D. Weaver, *Warren: The Man, the Court, the Era* (1967), 261; Schwartz, *Super Chief*, 441.

343 **Congress with prayer**: *Engel v. Vitale*, 370 U.S. 421, 444 (1962) (Stewart dissenting). Stewart was also the lone dissenter in the Bible-reading case, *School District of Abington Township v. Schempp*, 374 U.S. 203, 308 (1963) (Stewart dissenting).

343 **openly sectarian**: The response to *Schempp* proved a bit less hostile, but a Gallup poll showed that 70 percent of the people opposed it, and many southern districts basically ignored it.

344 **"for reform movements"**: There is only one biography, Tinsley E. Yarbrough, *John Marshall Harlan: Great Dissenter of the Warren Court* (1992). A good sampling of his opinions, speeches, and other writings is David L. Shapiro, ed., *Evolution of a Judicial Philosophy: Selected Opinions and Papers of Justice John M. Harlan* (1969).

345   **loyal opposition:** Joel B. Grossman, "Dissenting Blocs on the Warren Court: A Study in Judicial Role Behavior," 30 *Journal of Politics* 1068 (1968).

345   **with whom he had served:** Douglas, *Court Years,* 42. He also listed Frankfurter because, as he explained, whatever their philosophical differences Frankfurter had a good mind.

345   ***Poe v. Ullman:*** The full story of the case is in Garrow, *Liberty and Sexuality,* 168ff.

345   **the Court never issued:** *Poe v. Ullman,* 367 U.S. 497 (1961).

346   **Black and Harlan:** The Black sentence and Brennan's short concurrence are at *id.* 367 U.S. at 509, and Douglas's dissent begins there as well. Stewart's short dissent is at *id.* 367 U.S. at 555.

346   **"threat of prosecution":** *Id.* at 522 (Harlan dissenting).

347   **"be deemed constitutional":** Harlan to Joseph Omera, 19 September 1962, quoted in Belknap, *Supreme Court Under Earl Warren,* 202.

347   **"piece of judicial lawmaking":** White, *American Judicial Tradition,* 356.

348   **name of public health:** *Poe,* 367 U.S. at 539. For Fried's role, see Garrow, *Liberty and Sexuality,* 174. Although Professor Fried (now at the Harvard Law School) would not comment on his role in drafting the dissent, I am grateful to him for some suggestions on interpreting it.

349   **"valued by civilized men":** *Poe,* 367 U.S. at 550, citing *Olmstead v. United States,* 277 U.S. 438, 478 (1927) (Brandeis dissenting).

349   **Dr. C. Lee Buxton:** For Griswold's effort to get an arrest, see Garrow, *Liberty and Sexuality,* 196ff.

349   ***Griswold v. Connecticut:*** 381 U.S. 479 (1965).

350   **the years went on:** *Id.* at 486, 494 (Goldberg concurring).

350   **philosophy as any:** *Id.* at 499 (Harlan concurring).

351   **obscured by an inkblot:** Quoted in Tushnet, *I Dissent,* 188–89.

351   **Due Process Clause:** *Cruzan v. Director, Missouri Department of Health,* 497 U.S. 261 (1990).

351   ***Vacco v. Quill:*** *Washington v. Glucksberg,* 521 U.S. 702 (1997), and *Vacco v. Quill,* 521 U.S. 793 (1997). For the cases, see Melvin I. Urofsky, *Lethal Judgments: Assisted Suicide and American Law* (2000).

351   **equal protection ground:** *Compassion in Dying v. Washington,* 79 F.3d 790 (9th Cir. 1996), and *Quill v. Vacco,* 80 F.3d 716 (2nd Cir., 1996).

352   **unenumerated right of privacy:** Quoted in Tinsley E. Yarbrough, *David Hackett Souter: Traditional Republican on the Rehnquist Court* (2005), 130.

354   **hammer out differences:** O'Brien, *Storm Center,* 286–87, 108–9.

355   **little respect for Burger:** The newest and most balanced study is Earl M. Maltz, *The Chief Justiceship of Warren Burger, 1969–1986* (2000). A good example of the dysfunctional relations within the Court—and how early they appeared—can be found in Bob Woodward and Scott Armstrong, *The Brethren: Inside the Supreme Court* (1979), for which several members of the Court secretly spoke to the authors. For an appraisal showing how little his colleagues respected the chief justice, see the interview with William Brennan in *The New York Times Magazine,* 5 October 1986, just after Burger stepped down.

355   **shape the majority decision:** Maltzman, Spriggs, and Wahlbeck, *Crafting Law on the Supreme Court,* 64–65.

356   **have an abortion:** *Roe v. Wade,* 410 U.S. 113 (1973), decided along with *Doe*

    v. Bolton, 410 U.S. 179 (1973), which dealt with the more "modern" Georgia abortion statute. The literature on the case—not to mention on abortion in general—is enormous. See Garrow, *Liberty and Sexuality;* N. E. H. Hull and Peter Hoffer, *Roe v. Wade: The Abortion Rights Controversy* (2001); and Laurence H. Tribe, *Abortion: The Clash of Absolutes* (1990).

357 **"terminate her pregnancy":** *Roe,* 410 U.S. at 153. The drama surrounding Blackmun's travails in crafting the opinion can be found in Tinsley E. Yarbrough, *Harry A. Blackmun: The Outsider Justice* (2008), chap. 7; Greenhouse, *Becoming Justice Blackmun,* chap. 4; and Garrow, *Liberty and Sexuality,* 528ff.

357 **"society remains unchanged":** *Roe,* 410 U.S. at 168 (Stewart concurring), citing *National Mutual Insurance Co. v. Tidewater Transfer Co.,* 337 U.S. 582, 646 (1949) (Frankfurter dissenting).

357 **backs of the people:** *Doe,* 410 U.S. at 209 (Douglas concurring). In his short concurrence, Burger objected to the broad use of scientific and medical data, although he agreed that the woman's right resided within the Due Process Clause.

358 **"the *Lochner* era":** *Roe,* 410 U.S. at 171, 174 (Rehnquist dissenting); Yarbrough, *Blackmun,* 227.

358 **"life that she carries":** *Doe,* 410 U.S. at 221, 222 (White dissenting).

359 **"the side of change":** Justice Ginsburg made the comments at the University of Chicago Law School in May 2013, reported by Emily Bazelon on *Slate* on 14 May 2013.

359 **Court overruled *Roe:*** There are a number of cases involved; see Barbara Hinkson Craig and David O'Brien, *Abortion and American Politics* (1993).

360 **legislature thought reasonable:** *Planned Parenthood of Southeastern Pennsylvania et al. v. Casey,* 947 F.2d 682 (3rd Cir. 1991).

361 **a legitimate abortion:** *Planned Parenthood of Southeastern Pennsylvania et al. v. Casey,* 505 U.S. 833, 846 (1992).

361 **part reaffirming *Roe:*** *Id.* at 944 (Rehnquist concurring in the judgment and dissenting in part).

361 **equal opportunities:** A great deal of material, including key documents and cases, can be found in Gabriel Jack Chin, *Affirmative Action and the Constitution,* 3 vols. (1998).

362 **"they will not disappear":** *DeFunis v. Odegaard,* 416 U.S. 312, 348, 350 (1974) (Brennan dissenting).

363 **"the melting pot":** *Id.* at 320, 334, 336–37 (Douglas dissenting).

363 **"place on any lawyer":** *Id.* at 342, 343.

365 **ordering Bakke's admission:** *Regents of the University of California v. Bakke,* 438 U.S. 265 (1978). A good overview of the case is Howard Ball, *The Bakke Case: Race, Education, and Affirmative Action* (2000).

365 **"that's a good thing":** *New York Times,* 2 July 1978, sec. 6, p. 1; *Time,* 10 July 1978, 9.

366 **"evolving judicial doctrine":** *Bakke,* 438 U.S. at 353–56, 337, quoting from *Swann v. Charlotte-Mecklenburg Board of Education,* 402 U.S. 1, 46 (1971).

366 **Blackmun was getting there:** Stern and Wermiel, *Justice Brennan,* 451–55.

366 **"If you view the programs":** Marshall memorandum on *Bakke,* 13 April 1978, cited in Urofsky and Finkelman, *March of Liberty,* 2:987.

367 **violation of the law:** According to a biography of Stevens, the justice objected to the Davis plan, but over the course of his career Stevens became "more vocal in asserting the value of racial and ethnic diversity in certain settings."

Bill Barnhart and Gene Schlickman, *John Paul Stevens: An Independent Life* (2010), 269.

367 **been denied acceptance:** In addition to the two concurrence/dissents, Byron White, Thurgood Marshall, and Harry Blackmun wrote opinions, each emphasizing things that Brennan, in order to maintain his bloc of four, had omitted, such as the question (important to White) of whether Title VI allowed a private suit for enforcement.

368 **gender discrimination:** *United Steel Workers of America v. Weber,* 443 U.S. 193 (1979) (private sector); *Fullilove v. Klutznick,* 448 U.S. 448 (1980) (minority business); and *Johnson v. Transportation Agency, Santa Clara County,* 480 U.S. 616 (1987) (women).

368 **receive a preference:** *Johnson v. Transportation Agency* at 657 (Scalia dissenting).

368 **evidence of past discrimination:** *City of Richmond v. J. A. Croson Co.,* 488 U.S. 469 (1989). Brennan and Marshall were still on the Court at this time, and they joined Blackmun in dissent.

369 **the basis of race:** *Adarand Constructors Inc. v. Peña,* 515 U.S. 200 (1995). The 5–4 vote found Rehnquist, O'Connor, Scalia, Kennedy, and Thomas in the majority, and Stevens (who had opposed affirmative action in *Bakke*), Souter, Ginsburg, and Breyer in the minority, with Scalia and Thomas writing concurring opinions supporting the judgment, while Stevens, Souter, and Ginsburg filed dissents.

369 **in the Fifth Circuit:** *Hopwood v. Texas,* 78 F.3d 932 (5th Cir. 1996).

370 **students with lower scores:** There are many facets to this case that go beyond the purview of this book, including the nearly one hundred amicus briefs (seventy-eight in favor of affirmative action), many from the political, economic, and military leaders of the country favoring the plans. For more details, see Barbara A. Perry, *The Michigan Affirmative Action Cases* (2007).

370 **racial classification cases:** *Grutter v. Bollinger,* 539 U.S. 306 (2003); *Gratz v. Bollinger,* 539 U.S. 244 (2003).

371 **carefully tailored program:** *Fisher v. University of Texas at Austin,* 133 S. Ct. 2411 (2013).

371 **burdens on minorities:** *Schuette v. Coalition to Defend Affirmative Action,* 2014 U.S. Lexis 2932. Justice Elena Kagan recused.

371 **members of the same sex:** *Bowers v. Hardwick,* 478 U.S. 186 (1986). There is a growing literature on gay rights, but the best single volume is Richards, *Sodomy Cases.*

371 **no precedential value:** *Doe v. Commonwealth's Attorney,* 425 U.S. 901 (1976) (*per curiam*). Similarly, the statement in another case that sexual intimacy is "a key relationship of human existence, central to family life, community welfare, and the development of human personality" was clearly dictum, and thus nonbinding. *Paris Adult Theatre I v. Slayton,* 413 U.S. 49, 63 (1973).

372 **materials as obscene:** *Stanley v. Georgia,* 394 U.S. 557 (1969).

372 **Ninth and Fourteenth Amendments:** *Hardwick v. Bowers,* 760 F.2d 1202 (11th Cir. 1985).

373 **"activity on the other":** *Hardwick,* 478 U.S. at 190–91, 194.

373 **"This case is no more":** *Id.* at 199 (Blackmun dissenting).

374 **"associations with others":** *Id.* at 204, 205–6.

374 **such conduct "immoral":** Yarbrough, *Blackmun,* 285.

374 **"You was great":** *Hardwick,* 478 U.S. at 214, 211; Greenhouse, *Becoming Justice Blackmun,* 152.

374 **exclude whom they wanted:** *Hurley v. Irish-American Gay, Lesbian, and Bisexual Group of Boston,* 515 U.S. 557 (1995). Although the vote was unanimous, this is a strange case, because while the organization of the parade may be in private hands, there is an enormous amount of state action in terms of closing streets; police, fire, and EMT services; and cleanup afterward.

376 **"Colorado's Constitution":** *Romer v. Evans,* 517 U.S. 620, 623 (1996).

376 **cases in civil rights:** *Id.* at 630, 634, quoting from *Dept. of Agriculture v. Moreno,* 413 U.S. 528, 534 (1973).

377 **"homosexuals is evil":** *Romer,* 517 U.S. at 636 (Scalia dissenting).

377 **men as well as women:** *Oncale v. Sundowner Offshore Services Inc.,* 523 U.S. 75 (1998).

377 **leadership positions:** *Boy Scouts of America v. Dale,* 530 U.S. 640 (2000).

377 **Texas sodomy law:** Police had been called by a neighbor, Robert Royce Eubanks, who told officers that because of a domestic fight there was a man with a gun "going crazy." A deputy sheriff entered the Lawrence apartment with his gun drawn and found Lawrence and Garner engaging in sex, and because he witnessed the act, he arrested them. There was no gun, nor a man going crazy, but an investigation showed that Eubanks had earlier been accused of harassing Lawrence, who spurned his advances. Eubanks later admitted that he had lied about the disturbance, pleaded no contest to filing a false police report, and served fifteen days in jail.

378 **Whether the petitioners' criminal:** *Lawrence v. Texas,* 539 U.S. 558, 564 (2003).

379 **"Liberty protects the person":** *Id.* at 562.

379 **"sexual intercourse":** *Id.* at 566–67.

379 **"should control here":** *Id.* at 567, 578.

380 **"search for greater freedom":** *Id.* at 578–79.

380 **could change their laws:** *Id.* at 586, 599, 603–4 (Scalia dissenting).

381 **"marriage to homosexual couples":** *Id.* at 604–5. For a good analysis of Scalia's views on "text and tradition," see Ralph A. Rossum, *Antonin Scalia's Jurisprudence: Text and Tradition* (2006). A discussion of the *Lawrence* case is at pp. 161–63. Justice Thomas entered a brief dissent declaring that he thought the Texas law "uncommonly silly" and, were he a legislator, he would vote against it. As a judge, however, he had no business judging a legitimate exercise of the state's authority. *Lawrence,* 539 U.S. at 605 (Thomas dissenting).

381 **"people and their representatives":** Joan Biskupic, *American Original: The Life and Constitution of Supreme Court Justice Antonin Scalia* (2009), 228–29.

382 **support that institution:** White House Press release, 3 October 2003, http://www.georgewbush-whitehouse.archives.gov.

382 **the right to marry:** *Goodridge v. Dept. of Public Health,* 798 N.E.2d 941 (Mass. 2003).

382 **spring of 2013:** The best brief summary of the two cases is an e-book by Adam Liptak, the *New York Times* Supreme Court reporter, *To Have and Uphold.*

383 **defend section 3's constitutionality:** *United States v. Windsor,* 133 S. Ct. 2675 (2013).

383 **California Constitution's Equal Protection Clause:** *In re Marriage Cases,* 43 Cal. 4th 757 (2008). Following this decision, and before the passage of Proposition 8, a number of same-sex marriages took place, whose status was indeterminate during this litigation.

383 take that right away: *Perry v. Brown,* 671 F.3d 1052 (9th Cir. 2012).

383 standing under Article III: *Hollingsworth v. Perry,* 133 S. Ct. 2652 (2013).

384 "Constitution's Fifth Amendment": *Id.* at 2689–90, 2691, and 2693, citing H.R. Rep. No. 104–664 (1996), 16.

384 violation of equal protection: *Id.* at 2693–94, 2695.

384 "this institution in America": *Id.* at 2697–98 (Scalia dissenting).

385 "its traditional definition": *Id.* at 2710.

385 sky-is-falling approach: *Id.* at 2696, 2697 (Roberts dissenting).

385 believed it unconstitutional: See, for example, "ACLU of Virginia Says It Will File Federal Lawsuit Challenging State's Same-Sex Ban," *Washington Post,* 9 July 2013; "Couples Ask Illinois Judge for Quick Ruling in Lawsuit Seeking to Legalize Same-Sex Marriage," *Washington Post,* 10 July 2013; "PA Attorney General Won't Defend State's Gay Marriage Ban," *Washington Post,* 11 July 2013.

385 their rationale: *Washington Post,* 27 May 2014, A1.

386 "for the first time here": *Hollingsworth v. Perry,* 133 S. Ct. 2652, 2668 (2013).

387 "down an exit ramp": Liptak, *To Have and Uphold.*

387 voted on that question: 133 S. Ct. at 2668 (Kennedy dissenting).

MISE-EN-SCÈNE 5
MARSHALL, BRENNAN, AND CAPITAL PUNISHMENT

388 actually carried out: See V. A. C. Gatrell, *The Hanging Tree* (1994). The last execution in the United Kingdom took place in 1964, and capital punishment was abolished a few years later. In 2004, Protocol 13 of the European Convention on Human Rights became binding on the United Kingdom, prohibiting the restoration of the death penalty as long as Britain remained a party to the convention.

389 spying for Spain: For an overview of the death penalty in the United States, see Gordon M. Bakken, ed., *Invitation to an Execution: A History of the Death Penalty in the United States* (2010). According to the Espy file, 15,269 executions took place in the English colonies and then in the United States between 1608 and 2002. http://www.deathpenaltyinfo.org/executions-us -1608-2002-espy-file, accessed 23 August 2013.

389 Supreme Court's modern jurisprudence: Only two cases examining the Eighth Amendment in connection with the death penalty were decided in the nineteenth century. In *Wilkerson v. Utah,* 99 U.S. 130 (1878), the Court held that execution by firing squad did not constitute cruel or unusual punishment. Twelve years later, the Court upheld execution by electrocution against an Eighth Amendment challenge in *In re Kemmler,* 136 U.S. 436 (1890). For jurisprudence regarding the meaning of "cruel and unusual" prior to *Furman,* see Alan I. Bigel, *Justices William J. Brennan Jr. and Thurgood Marshall on Capital Punishment* (1997), 57–60.

389 were African American: Belknap, *Supreme Court Under Earl Warren,* 259. The memorandum was apparently triggered by a death penalty case, *Rudolph v. Alabama,* 375 U.S. 889 (1963). For an analysis of the document, see Robert S. Marsel, "Mr. Justice Arthur J. Goldberg and the Death Penalty: A Memorandum to the Conference," 27 *South Texas Law Review* 467 (1986).

390 Eighth and Fourteenth Amendments: *Furman v. Georgia,* decided along with *Jackson v. Georgia* and *Branch v. Texas,* 408 U.S. 238 (1972).

391 "that can be demonstrated": *Id.* at 405 (Blackmun dissenting).

391 "value of our American democracy": Stern and Wermiel, *Justice Brennan,* 418 ff. See also William J. Brennan Jr., "Constitutional Adjudication and the Death Penalty: The View from the Court," 100 *Harvard Law Review* 313 (1986).

391 improper police searches: *Korematsu v. United States,* 323 U.S. 214, 241 (1944) (Murphy dissenting); *Abbate v. United States,* 359 U.S. 187, 201 (1959) (Black dissenting); *Ullman v. United States,* 350 U.S. 422, 440, 449 (1956) (Douglas dissenting).

391 "violation of the Eighth Amendment": William J. Brennan Jr., "In Defense of Dissents," 37 *Hastings Law Journal* 427, 436–37 (1986).

392 contemporary standards, or excessive: *Furman,* 408 U.S. at 257 (Brennan concurring).

392 "the dignity of man": *Trop v. Dulles,* 356 U.S. 86, 100 (1958).

393 "activism runs amok": Robert H. Bork, *The Tempting of America* (1990), 219–21; Raoul Berger, "Brennan, 'Dignity,' and the Constitution," in *The Constitution of Rights,* ed. Michael J. Meyer and William A. Parent (1992), 134; Leonard W. Levy, *Original Intent and the Framers' Constitution* (1988), 372.

393 doing for years: Martha Minow, "Equality and the Bill of Rights," in Meyer and Parent, *Constitution of Rights,* 118.

393 "never cease to evolve": Stern and Wermiel, *Justice Brennan,* 423.

394 Court had to approve it: Bigel, *Brennan and Marshall,* 83–85.

394 "maturing society": *Trop,* 356 U.S. at 100–101.

394 "A few years back": Mello, *Against the Death Penalty,* 36. Mello's book has numerous stories of Marshall and the blatant injustice of southern law he fought against in the 1940s and 1950s. See also Howard Ball, "Thurgood Marshall's Forlorn Battle Against Racial Discrimination in the Administration of the Death Penalty . . . ," 27 *Mississippi College Law Review* 335 (2008).

394 "members of society": *Furman,* 408 U.S. 369 (Marshall concurring).

396 "purposeless vengeance": *Id.* at 314 (Marshall concurring).

396 "anything in the Constitution": *McGautha v. California,* 402 U.S. 183, 207 (1971).

396 understand it properly: Mark V. Tushnet, *Making Constitutional Law: Thurgood Marshall and the Supreme Court, 1961–1991* (1997), 152–53.

397 consistency in its use: *Furman,* 408 U.S. at 375 (Burger dissenting).

397 by appellate courts: For events following *Furman,* see Evan J. Mandery, *A Wild Justice: The Death and Resurrection of Capital Punishment in America* (2013).

397 *Gregg v. Georgia:* 428 U.S. 153 (1976). For the internal discussion of the various statutes, see John C. Jeffries Jr., *Justice Lewis F. Powell Jr.* (1994), 416–30, and Woodward and Armstrong, *Brethren,* 430–40.

397 "Eighth and Fourteenth Amendments": Stern and Wermiel, *Justice Brennan,* 408.

398 opposition to capital punishment: *Estelle v. Smith,* 451 U.S. 454, 474 (1981) (Marshall concurring). See also *Presnell v. Georgia,* 439 U.S. 14, 17 (1978) (Marshall concurring).

398 "With respect to cert.": Sheryll Cashin to Marshall, 21 February 1991, cited in Mello, *Against the Death Penalty,* 158–60.

398 **Stevens wrote the opinion:** *Id.* at 161; *Lankford v. Idaho,* 500 U.S. 110 (1991).

399 **in those circumstances:** Mark Kelman, "The Forked Path of Dissent," 1985 *Supreme Court Review* 227, 263. Kelman compares this one-sided acceptance with Justice Black's utilization of the "special circumstances" provision in *Betts v. Brady* to continue to push for the right to counsel.

399 **"Eighth and Fourteenth Amendments":** *Enmund v. Florida,* 458 U.S. 782 (1982). Blackmun and Stevens also joined the opinion. The Brennan sentence is at 801.

400 **clearly unconstitutional:** *Ford v. Wainwright,* 477 U.S. 399 (1986).

400 **" 'due process' proscribes it":** *Haley v. Ohio,* 332 U.S. 596, 602 (1948) (Frankfurter concurring). Blackmun's copy of this concurrence, which he apparently typed out himself, bears the date 16 April 1971.

400 **opposition to the death penalty:** See Greenhouse, *Becoming Justice Blackmun,* 162 ff., and Yarbrough, *Blackmun,* 315 ff.

401 **Marshall, and Stevens, dissented:** Greenhouse, *Becoming Justice Blackmun,* 165–74; *Darden v. Wainwright,* 477 U.S. 168, 188 (1986) (Blackmun dissenting).

401 **victim of this discrimination:** While on the Eighth Circuit, Blackmun had written an opinion rejecting statistical data. *Maxwell v. Bishop,* 398 F.2d 138 (8th Cir. 1968).

401 **"racially based discrimination":** *McCleskey v. Kemp,* 481 U.S. 279, 345 (1987) (Blackmun dissenting). For Brennan's dissent, see chap. 12.

401 **"I have voiced disappointment":** *Herrera v. Collins,* 506 U.S. 390, 430, 446 (1993) (Blackmun dissenting). When Herrera's attorney filed for a stay of execution, the Court turned him down, although Blackmun and Stevens dissented from that denial.

402 **"caprice, and mistake":** *Callins v. Collins,* 510 U.S. 1141, 1143–44 (1994) (Blackmun dissenting).

402 **"machinery of death":** *Id.* at 1145, 1159.

403 **below-average intelligence:** *Atkins v. Virginia,* 536 U.S. 304 (2002); *Penry v. Lynaugh,* 492 U.S. 302 (1989). In *Atkins,* Justice Scalia penned a strong dissent accusing the majority of reading its own views into the Constitution and deriding the reference to a growing consensus based on eighteen states. Twenty of the death penalty states, he pointed out, still executed those with below-average intelligence.

403 **to life imprisonment:** http://www.npr.org/2011/03/09/134394946/Illinois -abolishes-death-penalty, accessed 27 August 2013.

404 **"juvenile death penalty":** *Stanford v. Kentucky,* 492 U.S. 361 (1989), a case in which Brennan, Marshall, Blackmun, and Stevens dissented. *Roper v. Simmons,* 543 U.S. 551, 570 (2005).

404 **rather than death:** *Wiggins v. Smith,* 539 U.S. 510 (2003). One measure of how strong Wiggins's case was is that Chief Justice Rehnquist, a strong supporter of limiting post-conviction habeas appeals, voted to uphold his claim.

404 **factors in sentencing:** *Rompilla v. Beard,* 545 U.S. 374 (2005). The Court made it clear, however, that if the attorney acted responsibly, it would not second-guess the tactics.

405 **rape was excessive:** *Kennedy v. Louisiana,* 554 U.S. 407 (2008); *Coker v.*

Georgia, 433 U.S. 584 (1977). In a highly unusual aftermath, about a week after the decision the Justice Department said that government lawyers should have known that Congress in 2007 had made the rape of a child a capital offense in the military and should have informed the Supreme Court of that fact. Apparently, lawyers for neither side knew about this, and Kennedy in his opinion had relied on the fact that when Congress expanded the number of federal capital crimes in 1994, it did not include child rape.

405 **criminal justice system:** Four states in the modern era, Nebraska (2008), New York and Kansas (2004), and Massachusetts (1984), have had their death penalty statutes ruled unconstitutional by state courts. Following these decisions, the death rows in New York and Massachusetts disappeared, and attempts to reinstate capital punishment failed. Only Nebraska has performed executions since *Gregg,* the last one, however, in 1997. In February 2008, the state supreme court ruled electrocution unconstitutional. The Nebraska legislature enacted a bill providing for lethal injection, but there have been no recent executions. The only jurisdictions with current death penalty statutes that have not performed an execution since 1976 are New Hampshire and Kansas, although both have populated death rows. Also, New Jersey executed no one between 1976 and 2007, when it abolished the death penalty.

405 **41 percent said "unfairly":** http://www.gallup.com/poll/1606/death-penalty .aspx, accessed 26 August 2013; http://www.pewforum.org/2014/03/28/ shrinking-majority, accessed 21 April 2014.

CHAPTER 12: CODA

407 **"respectfully dissents":** Robert Barnes, "In Dissent, Judicial Restraint Flies out the Window," *Washington Post,* 22 July 2013, A15. What is somewhat surprising is that these highly emotional dissents came in a term when the Court decided 49 percent of the argued cases unanimously. For recent statistics, see SCOTUSblog.com.

407 **collecting his dissents:** Kevin A. Ring, ed., *Scalia Dissents: Writings of the Supreme Court's Wittiest, Most Outspoken Justice* (2004).

407 **considers faulty reasoning:** See, for example, Jay Michaelson's blog on the *Huffington Post,* 7 July 2013. The case is *United States v. Windsor,* 133 S. Ct. 2675, 2698, 2709 (2013) (Scalia dissenting). Scalia's comment sent many people running to their dictionaries looking for the meaning of the term. It is apparently British in origin, its first known use in 1872, meaning a disagreement.

407 **"my colleagues dissented":** The talk appeared as Ruth Bader Ginsburg, "The Role of Dissenting Opinions," 95 *Minnesota Law Review* 1, 4 (2010).

408 **"dissenting point anymore":** *Washington Post,* 22 July 2013, A15.

408 **223 of its own precedents:** O'Brien, *Storm Center,* 31.

408 **end of the discussion:** In only one instance has a Supreme Court constitutional opinion been overturned by an amendment. The Court ruling invalidating the income tax (*Pollock v. Farmers' Loan & Trust,* 157 U.S. 429 [1895]) was reversed by the Sixteenth Amendment.

408 **called into question:** *Northwest Austin Municipal Utility District v. Mukasey,* 557 U.S. 193 (2009). Only Justice Thomas thought section 5 unconstitutional.

409 **2013, not 1965:** *Shelby County v. Holder,* 133 S. Ct. 2612 (2013).

410 **do not require Senate confirmation:** See *Parson v. United States,* 167 U.S. 324 (1897), and *Shurtleff v. United States,* 189 U.S. 311 (1903).

411 **Congress could not limit:** *Myers v. United States,* 272 U.S. 52 (1926).

411 **limits on their removal:** *Id.* at 178 (McReynolds dissenting).

411 **fifty-five-page dissent:** *Id.* at 240. For the story of the case and how Brandeis developed his dissent, see Urofsky, *Brandeis,* 587–90. Holmes joined the dissenters and wrote a brief, two-paragraph dissent saying he agreed with them.

412 **separation of powers:** *Humphrey's Executor v. United States,* 295 U.S. 602 (1935). For the case, see William E. Leuchtenburg, "The Case of the Contentious Commissioner," in *The Supreme Court Reborn: The Constitutional Revolution in the Age of Roosevelt* (1995), 52–81. It should be noted that four of the members of Taft's majority—Van Devanter, Sutherland, Butler, and Stone—now voted to uphold Brandeis's contention that the regulatory agencies had to be protected.

412 **articles, and interviews:** For a list, see Collins, "Books by Supreme Court Justices."

413 ***Bush v. Gore:*** 531 U.S. 98 (2000). For a discussion of the politics involved, see Charles L. Zelden, *Bush v. Gore: Exposing the Hidden Crisis in American Democracy* (2008).

414 **"They think it's all politics":** Robert Barnes, "For Justices, Partisan Image Is Hard to Shake," *Washington Post,* 28 April 2014, A11. An even stronger charge of partisanship can be found in Adam Liptak, "The Polarized Court," *New York Times,* 11 May 2014, SR1.

414 **"hands of history":** Tushnet, *I Dissent,* 221.

416 **which is to be expected:** Two queries were posted on H-LAW in mid-April 2013, and responses came in over the next few weeks.

416 **so did the Supreme Court:** *McCleskey v. Kemp,* 481 U.S. 279 (1987). See David Baldus, Charles Pulaski, and George Woodworth, *Equal Justice and the Death Penalty* (1990).

416 **"criminal justice system":** *McClesky,* 481 U.S. at 312. After losing this case, McCleskey began another habeas action, arguing that he had been convicted because of statements made to prosecutors without benefit of counsel, and the Court, in *McCleskey v. Zant,* 499 U.S. 467 (1991), again sustained his conviction, and some years later he was executed.

416 **"Eighth and Fourteenth Amendments":** *McClesky,* 481 U.S. at 320 (Brennan dissenting). Brennan was joined by Marshall, Blackmun, and Stevens. In addition, Blackmun (joined by Brennan, Marshall, and Stevens) and Stevens (joined by Blackmun) dissented.

417 **"It is tempting to pretend":** *Id.* at 344–45.

418 **special prosecutors:** *Morrison v. Olson,* 487 U.S. 654 (1988). See Katy J. Harriger, *The Special Prosecutor in American Politics,* rev. ed. (2000).

419 **hard line and strident tone:** Biskupic, *American Original,* 136–37.

419 **"with absolute independence":** *Morrison,* 487 U.S. at 691–95.

419 **"separation of powers":** Rossum, *Antonin Scalia's Jurisprudence,* 55.

420 **"Where a private citizen":** *Morrison,* 487 U.S. at 704 (Scalia dissenting).

421 **Affordable Care Act (ACA):** *National Federation of Independent Business v. Sebelius,* 132 S. Ct. 2566 (2012).

422 **under the Spending Clause:** *Id.* at 2609 (Ginsburg concurring in part and with the judgment and dissenting in part).

423 **"In the early 20th century":** *Id.* at 2628–29. Ginsburg then went on to dissent from the Court's determination that Congress could not require the

expansion of the Medicaid program to include a greater proportion of people living near or under the poverty line.

425 **dissents and their importance:** Brennan, "In Defense of Dissents," 427.

425 **"worlds of literature and law":** *Id.* at 431, quoting *Trop v. Dulles,* 356 U.S. 86, 101 (1958).

426 **"doctrine seem correct":** Tushnet, *I Dissent,* 99. In his survey of "great" dissents, Professor Tushnet calls Brandeis's opinion in *Whitney v. California* the greatest, because it combines all of the elements needed for greatness and at a level no other dissenter has ever achieved.

426 **"toward a different path":** Brennan, "In Defense of Dissents," 437.

INDEX OF CASES CITED

INDEX

Page numbers in *italics* refer to illustrations.
Page numbers beginning with 429 refer to endnotes.

Austin decision of, 26
book published by, 412
Citizens United decision of, 26
and death penalty case, 404–5
dissents of, 27
on equal protection, 376, 377
on gay rights, 126, 376, 377, 378–9,
  381, 383–4, 386, 387
Guantánamo decision of, 31
in Pennsylvania abortion case, 361
public opinion and, 412
on right to privacy, 207–8
in same-sex marriage case, 383–4
and same-sex marriage cert petition,
  386, 387
Scalia's criticism of, 377, 381,
  384–5, 407
as sensitive to changing mores, 35
separate opinions by, 22
as swing vote, 26, 340
Texas sodomy opinion of, 378–9,
  381, 387
writings of, 35
Kent, James, 60
Kentucky, 59, 121*n*
Kenyon, Lord, 40
Killenbeck, Mark, 51
King's Court (King's Bench), 38–40,
  40, 43
Knox, Philander, 126, 134
Koontz, Lawrence L., Jr., 330
Korean conflict, 228, 238
Korean War, 30
Korematsu, Fred, 248
Kousser, J. Morgan, 443
Kozinski, Alex, 323–4
Ku Klux Klan, 106, 108, 457
Kyllo, Danny Lee, 203

labor law, 136, 137–49, 161
laissez-faire, 146, 221
Laski, Harold, 163, 168, 243, 447
Laskin, Bora, 335, 336
Latin America, 334–5
law, "instrumental" conception
  of, 61
Lawrence, John Geddes, 377–8,
  482
law review articles, 31–2, 35, 164–5

Law School Admission Test (LSAT),
  363, 370
Ledbetter, Lilly, 28–9, 29
legal arguments, 233
legal classicism, 192–3
Legal Defense Fund, 121, 389,
  394
legal formalism, 221
legal positivism, 337
legal realism, 152, 221
legal tender, 59
Lewis, Anthony, 312, 365
L'Heureux-Dubé, Claire, 335, 336
liberal legalism, 221
Liebmann, Ernest, 185–7
Lilly Ledbetter Fair Pay Law, 28–9, 29
Lincoln, Abraham, 56, 77, 80, 265,
  439
  assassination of, 82
  Cooper Union speech of, 78
  Dred Scott decision denounced by,
    76–8
  election of, 86
Linden, Allen, 335
liquor, 97
living Constitution, x, 163, 350, 390,
  425–6, 450
Llewellyn, Karl, 425
Lochner, Joseph, 140
Lochner's Home Bakery, 140
"Lost Cause, Worse Than Slavery, The"
  (cartoon), 108
Louisiana, 80, 84, 86–7, 89, 91–3, 94,
  96, 117–18, 289–91, 404–5
  Constitution of, 328
Louisiana Commission, 107
Louisville, Ky., 124
lower federal courts, xii, 4, 318–26,
  338
  concurring opinions in, 5
  dissent welcomed in, 18
Luchaire, Francois, 476
Lurie, Jonathan, 90, 467
Lynch, Andrew, 337

MacArthur, Douglas, 257, 258–9, 263,
  266, 268, 268, 269, 273, 274
Mack, Julian, Brandeis's influence on,
  187